Blue Book of
Airguns™
Fifth Edition

by Dr. Robert D. Beeman & John B. Allen
Edited by S.P. Fjestad

$24.95
Publisher's Softcover
Suggested List Price

Publisher's Limited
Edition Hardcover
Suggested List Price - $39.95

Blue Book of Airguns™
Fifth Edition

This book is the result of continual airgun research performed by attending shows and communicating with airgun dealers, collectors, company historians, contributing editors, and other knowledgeable industry professionals worldwide each year. This book represents an analysis of prices for which airguns have actually been selling during that period at an average retail level. Although every reasonable effort has been made to compile an accurate and reliable guide, airgun prices may vary significantly, depending on such factors as the locality of the sale, the number of sales we were able to consider, and economic conditions. Accordingly, no representation can be made that the airguns listed may be bought or sold at prices indicated, nor shall the author or publisher be responsible for any error made in compiling and recording such prices and related information.

All Rights Reserved
Copyright 2005
Blue Book Publications, Inc.
8009 34th Avenue South, Suite 175
Minneapolis, MN 55425 U.S.A.
Orders Only: 800-877-4867
Phone: 952-854-5229
Fax: 952-853-1486
Email: bluebook@bluebookinc.com
Website: http://www.bluebookinc.com

Published and printed in the United States of America
ISBN 1-886768-56-0

TABLE OF CONTENTS

ACKNOWLEDGEMENTS

André Wirth
Barry Abel
Bill Johnson
Bruce Stauff
Carolyn Gilman
Col. Keith Gibson
Colin Curry
Dani Navickas
Dave Nemanic
David Kosowski
Davis Schwesinger
Dean Fletcher
Dennis Baker
Dieter Anschütz
Don Howard
Dr. Bruno Brukner
Ed Niccum
Eduardo Poloni
Frank Tait
Frank Turner
Fred Ehrlich
Fred Liady
Gary Barnes
Geoffrey Baker

Gordon Bruce
Guillermo Sylianteng Jr.
Gurney Brown
Hans-Hermann Weihrauch
Hans Weller
Ingvar Alm
Jay Rasmussen
Jim & Ann Coplen
John Ford
John Groenewold
John Knibbs
John Walter
Jon Jenkins
Jon Oakleaf
Jörg Altenburger
Juan Manual
Kenth Friberg
Larry Hannusch
Lewis Reinhold
Mandy Cardoniga
Marv Adams
Matts Hammer
Michale Chao
Mike Driskill

Neal Punchard
Paul Kanieski
Peter DeRose
Phil Bulmer
Phillip Schreier
Ralph Heize Flamand
Randall Bimrose
Reiner Altenburger
Rick MacHale
Robert Spielvogel
Ron Sauls
Scott Pilkington
Steve Cary
Steve Loke
Susan Gardner
Ted Osborn
Tim Saunders
Tom & Edith Gaylord
Tony Hall
Toshiko Beeman
Trevor Adams
Ulrich Eichstädt
Wes Powers

ABOUT THE COVER & CREDITS

If "black guns" (i.e. Colt AR style firearms and other guns restricted by the Crime bill of 1994) have been a center of controversy in the firearms marketplace over the last decade, then the centerpiece on this Fifth Edition *Blue Book of Airguns* cover could lead the way over the next decade. This PCP .22 caliber Condor Model by AirForce Airguns of Fort Worth, Texas was released in 2004 and can push a pellet over 1250 feet per second, developing over 60 foot-pounds of muzzle energy, shoot 1/2-inch groups at 50 yards, run a pellet clean through a 2x4 at 100 yards, and all at a price that won't break the bank. If it's a toy you're looking for, this Condor is not it; this is serious equipment for the serious shooter.

Pictured below the Condor is a black pistol that can get the juices flowing. This Tim Jones of Hawley, Pennsylvania, custom single-shot PCP pistol is built on a Crosman Model 150 frame. The grip and forearm are carved from ebony and, when added to the .22 caliber precision Lothar Walther barrel, provide this tack driver with the look and feel of quality, easily confirming your suspicions that you can get what you pay for.

Featured on the back cover is a Crosman Corp. of East Bloomfield, NY Model 600 semi-automatic CO_2-powered pistol that, to the knowledgeable collector, just doesn't look quite right. If you said the finish and grips are wrong, you are right. This M-600 has a custom nickel finish and black grips that were put on in England. These changes may or may not add to this Crosman's desirability, but they surely make for a sharp looker. Next to this Model 600 is a holster made to fit the M-600 or its BB/.175 cal. brother, the M-677 Plink-O-Matic. In 1965 this pistol retailed in the $23 range and, for an additional $5, you could get the holster. One in 100% NIB condition with holster will retail in the $375 to $400 range today.

The little trinkets, pellet tins, targets, boxes, brochures, and advertising materials, which are also pictured from year to year on our covers, have grown into collectibles themselves - many times they will bring as much or more than the airguns themselves.

Cover design and layout - Clint H. Schmidt
Photography - Clint H. Schmidt
Airguns and accessories courtesy of Larry's Guns, Inc., S.P. Fjestad & Ingvar Alm

5th Edition credits:
Art Dept. - Clint H. Schmidt & Zachary R. Fjestad
Research & Contribution Coordinators - Dr. Robert Beeman & John Allen
Copyediting - Stacy M. Knutson
Cover & Text Printing - Bang Printing, located in Brainerd, MN

GENERAL INFORMATION

While many of you have probably dealt with our company for years, it may be helpful for you to know a little bit more about our operation, including information on how to contact us regarding our various titles, software programs, and other informational services.

Blue Book Publications, Inc.
8009 34th Avenue South, Suite 175
Minneapolis, MN 55425 USA
Phone: 952-854-5229 • Orders Only (domestic and Canada): 800-877-4867
Fax: 952-853-1486 (available 24 hours a day)
Website: http://www.bluebookinc.com
Email: bluebook@bluebookinc.com – we check our email at 9am, 12pm, and 3:30pm M - F (excluding major U.S. holidays). Please refer to individual email addresses listed below with phone extension numbers.

To find out the latest information on our products (including availability and pricing) and related consumer services, and up-to-date industry information (trade show recaps with photos/captions, upcoming events, feature articles, etc.), please check our website, as it is updated on a regular basis. Surf us – you'll have fun!

Since our phone system is equipped with voicemail, you may also wish to know extension numbers, which have been provided below:

Ext. 10 - Beth Marthaler (bethm@bluebookinc.com)
Ext. 11 - Katie Sandin (katies@bluebookinc.com)
Ext. 12 - John Andraschko (johnand@bluebookinc.com)
Ext. 13 - S.P. Fjestad (stevef@bluebookinc.com)
Ext. 15 - Clint Schmidt (clints@bluebookinc.com)
Ext. 16 - John Allen (johna@bluebookinc.com)
Ext. 17 - Zach Fjestad (zachf@bluebookinc.com)
Ext. 18 - Tom Stock (toms@bluebookinc.com)
Ext. 19 - Cassandra Faulkner (cassandraf@bluebookinc.com)
Ext. 22 - Stacy Knutson (stacyk@bluebookinc.com)

Office hours are: 8:30am - 5:00pm CST, Monday - Friday.

Additionally, an automated after-hours message service is available for ordering. All orders are processed within 24 hours of receiving them, assuming payment and order information is correct. Depending on the product, we typically ship either UPS, Media Mail, or Priority Mail. Expedited shipping services are also available domestically for an additional charge. Please contact us directly for an expedited shipping quotation.

All correspondence regarding technical information/values on airguns is answered in a FIFO (first in, first out) system. That means that letters, faxes, and email are answered in the order in which they are received.

Online subscriptions and individual downloading services for the *Blue Book of Gun Values*, *Blue Book of Modern Black Powder Arms*, *Blue Book of Airguns*, *Blue Book of Electric Guitars*, *Blue Book of Acoustic Guitars*, and the *Blue Book of Guitar Amplifiers* are available.

As this edition goes to press, the following titles/products are currently available, unless otherwise specified:

Blue Book of Gun Values, 26th Edition by S.P. Fjestad
Parker Gun Identification & Serialization, compiled by Charlie Price and edited by S.P. Fjestad
4th Edition *Blue Book of Modern Black Powder Arms* by John Allen & Dennis Adler
Blue Book 3-Pack CD-ROM - includes the databases from 26th Edition *Blue Book of Gun Values*, 4th Edition *Blue Book of Modern Black Powder Arms,* and 5th Edition *Blue Book of Airguns* (available August 2005)
Blue Book of Electric Guitars, 9th Edition, by Zachary R. Fjestad, edited by S.P. Fjestad
Blue Book of Acoustic Guitars, 9th Edition, by Zachary R. Fjestad, edited by S.P. Fjestad
Blue Book of Guitar Amplifiers, 2nd Edition, by Zachary R. Fjestad, edited by S.P. Fjestad
Blue Book of Guitars CD-ROM
Blue Book of Guitar Amplifiers CD-ROM
Blue Book of Guitars and Guitar Amplifiers Condensed, 1st Edition by Zachary Fjestad, edited by S.P. Fjestad
The Nethercutt Collection - The Cars of San Sylmar by Dennis Adler

If you would like to get more information about any of the above publications/products, simply check our website: www.bluebookinc.com.

We would like to thank all of you for your business in the past – you are the reason we are successful. Our goal remains the same – to give you the best products, the most accurate and up-to-date information for the money, and the highest level of customer service available in today's marketplace. If something's right, tell the world over time. If something's wrong, please tell us immediately – we'll make it right.

MEET THE STAFF

John B. Allen – Author &
Associate Editor Arms Division

Many of you may be familiar with
our names and/or have spoken with
us on the phone, but don't know
what we look like. Our pictures are
presented here so you can match our
faces with our names.

S.P. Fjestad with one millionth
Blue Book of Gun Values.

Cassandra Faulkner –
Executive Assistant Editor

Tom Stock – CFO

John Andraschko – Technology Director

Beth Marthaler – Operations Manager

Katie Sandin – Operations

Stacy Knutson – Proofreader/Operations

Clint Schmidt – Art Director

Zachary R. Fjestad – Author/Editor
Guitar & Amp Division

Bitey – Floor/wall/tight spaces Division
Manager (unseen by most employees)

HOW TO USE THIS BOOK

The prices listed in this edition of the *Blue Book of Airguns* are based on the national average retail prices a consumer can expect to pay. This is not an airguns wholesale pricing guide (there is no such thing). More importantly, do not expect to walk into a gun/pawn shop or airgun/gun show and think that the proprietor/dealer should pay you the retail price listed within this text for your gun. Resale offers on most models could be anywhere from near retail to 20%-50% less than the values listed, depending upon locality, desirability, dealer inventory, and profitability. In other words, if you want to receive 100% of the price (retail value), then you have to do 100% of the work (become the retailer, which also includes assuming 100% of the risk).

Percentages of original condition (with corresponding prices, if applicable) are typically listed between 20% and 100% for most recently manufactured airguns.

Please refer to "Anatomy of an Airgun" on pages 39-42 to learn more about the various airgun parts and terminology. Also, you may want to check the Glossary (pages 43-46) and the Abbreviations (page 47) for more detailed information about both nomenclature and airgun terminology.

A Trademark Index listing the current airgun manufacturers, importers, and distributors is provided on pages 427-430. This includes the most recent emails, websites, and other pertinent contact information for these individuals and organizations. The Index on pages 436-440 is a handy way to find the make/model you're looking for in a hurry.

To find an airgun in this text, first look under the name of the manufacturer, trademark, brand name, and in some cases, the importer (please consult the Index if necessary). Next, find the correct category name(s), typically Pistols, Rifles, and Shotguns.

Once you find the correct model or sub-model under its respective subheading, determine the specimen's percentage of original condition, and find the corresponding percentage column showing the price.

For the sake of simplicity, the following organizational framework has been adopted throughout this publication.

1. Trademark, manufacturer, brand name, importer, or organization is listed in bold face type alphabetically, i.e.,

AIRFORCE AIRGUNS, BSA GUNS (U.K.), LTD., DIANAWERK, MARKSMAN

2. Manufacturer information is listed directly beneath the trademark heading, i.e.,

Current manufacturer located in Austria. Currently imported by Pilkington Competition Equipment, LLC, located in Monteagle, TN. Previously imported and distributed by Nygord Precision Products, located in Prescott, AZ. Dealer or consumer direct sales.

3. Manufacturer notes may appear next under individual heading descriptions and can be differentiated by the following typeface:

Although often reported as starting with captive bolt cattle killers, the company made only three specimens of such guns. Initially concentrating on tranquilizer guns, Daystate generally is now recognized as the founder of modern PCP airguns, producing PCP air rifles by 1973. By 1987, high precision PCP rifles had become their main line. The publisher and authors of the *Blue Book of Airguns* wish to thank Tony Belas, Sales Manager at Daystate, for assistance with this section.

4. Next classification is the category name (normally, in alphabetical sequence) in upper case (inside a screened gray box), referring mostly to a firearm's configuration, i.e.,

PISTOLS, REVOLVERS, RIFLES, SHOTGUNS

5. Following a category name, a category note may follow to help explain the category, and/or provide limited information on models and values. They appear as follows:

Massive, heavily built airguns which could be considered as the ultimate development of the Gem line of airguns (see the "Gem" entry in the "G" section of this guide). Notable for a huge end plug on bottom end of the buttstock compression chamber.

6. Model names appear flush left, are bold faced, and capitalized either in chronological order (normally) or alphabetical order (sometimes, the previous model name and/or close subvariation will appear at the end in parentheses) and are listed under the individual category names. Examples include:

MODEL 55G, PLAINSMAN MODEL MA 22, FIREBIRD

7. Model descriptions are denoted by the following typeface and usually include information, i.e.,

- caliber(s), action type, cocking mechanism, operating system, feet per second (FPS), barrel lengths, finishes, weight, and other descriptive data are further categorized adjacent to model names in this typeface. This is where most of the information is listed for each specific model including identifiable features and possibly some production data (including quantity, approximate date of manufacture, discontinuance date, if known).

8. Variations within a model appear as sub-models, or sub-sub-models, they are differentiated from model names by an artistic icon (✳) prefix, or "less than" icon (>), are indented, and are in upper and lower case type. For example:

✳ *Model LG 300 Alutec*

and are usually followed by a short description of that sub-model. These sub-model descriptions have the same typeface as the model descriptions, i.e.,

-additional sub-model information that could include finishes, calibers, barrel lengths, special order features, and other production data specific for that sub-model.

9. Manufacturer and other notes/information appear in smaller type, and should be read since they contain both important and other critical, up-to-date information, i.e.,

    This is a Markham King design based upon the King No. 55.

10. Extra cost features/special value orders and other value added/subtracted features are placed directly under individual price lines or in some cases, category names. These individual lines appear bolder than other descriptive typeface, i.e.,

    Add $25 Nickel finish.
    Subtract 10% for left-hand model.

    On many guns less than 15 years old, these add/subtract items will be the last factory MSRs (manufacturer's suggested retail price) for that option.

11. On many discontinued models/variations, a line may appear under the price line, indicating the last manufacturer's suggested retail price (MSR) or vintage era retail price (RP) flush right on the page, i.e.,

    Last MSR was $855.

    1939 RP was $12.

12. Grading lines will normally appear at or near the top of each page. Price line format is as follows – when the price line shown below (with proper grading line) is encountered.

GRADING	100%	95%	90%	80%	60%	40%	20%
MSR $275	$225	$175	$125	$85	N/A	N/A	N/A

This 100% price on a currently manufactured airgun also assumes not previously sold at retail. In a many cases, N/As (Not Applicable) are listed and indicate that the condition is not frequently encountered so the value is not predictable. On a currently manufactured airgun, the lower condition specimens will bottom out at a value, and a lesser condition airguns value will approximate the lowest value listed. An MSR automatically indicates the airgun is currently manufactured, and the MSR (Manufacturer's Suggested Retail) is shown left of the 100% column. **This 100% price is the national average price a consumer will typically expect to pay for that model in 100% condition.** Recently manufactured 100% specimens without boxes, warranties, etc., that are currently manufactured must be discounted slightly (5%-20%, depending on the desirability of make and model).

GRADING	100%	95%	90%	80%	60%	40%	20%
	N/A	N/A	N/A	$995	$750	$645	$495

On vintage airguns, you may see N/As in the 100%-90% condition categories, as these original older guns are rarely encounted in 90%+ condition, and cannot be accurately priced. Higher condition factors may still exist, but if the only known sales have been of examples in 90% condition, a very desirable/collectible airgun may double or triple in value in the next higher condition range, so the value is not predictable.

A currently manufactured airgun without a retail price published by the manufacturer/importer will appear as follows:

GRADING	100%	95%	90%	80%	60%	40%	20%
No MSR	$375	$275	$200	$135	$85	N/A	N/A

Obviously, the 100% price is the national average price a consumer will pay for a gun in new condition. Again, this assumes NIB condition, and not previously sold at retail.

Since this publication consists of 440 pages, you may want to take advantage of our index (pages 436-440) as a speedy alternative to going through the pages, and our comprehensive Trademark Index (pages 427-430) for a complete listing of airgun manufacturers, importers, and distributors. Don't forget to read the editorial, including articles by Dr. Robert Beeman and Tom Gaylord.

CORRESPONDENCE/APPRAISALS/INFORMATION

AIRGUN QUESTIONS/APPRAISALS POLICY

Whether we wanted it or not, Blue Book Publications, Inc. has ended up in the driver's seat as the clearinghouse for information. To ensure that the research department can answer every question with an equal degree of thoroughness, a library, hundreds of both new and old factory brochures, price sheets, and dealer inventory listings are maintained and constantly updated. It's a huge job, and we answer every question like we could go to court on it. We have extended all of the following services to our website at www.bluebookinc.com.

POLICY FOR QUESTIONS

The charge is $10 per question, payable by a major credit card. All airgun questions are answered in a FIFO (first in, first out) system, guaranteeing that everyone will be treated equally. All pricing requests will be given within a value range only. Question telephone/fax hours are 9:00 a.m. to 4:00 p.m., M-F, CST, no exceptions please. You must provide us with all the necessary airgun information if you want an accurate answer. For email questions (airgun inquiries) please refer to www.bluebookinc.com. Letter questions (preferred, with photos) will also be answered in the order of arrival. Make sure you include the proper return address and phone number.

APPRAISAL INFORMATION

Written appraisals will be performed only if the following criteria are met:

We must have good quality photos with a complete description, including manufacturer's name, model, gauge/caliber, and barrel length. On some (depending on the trademark and model) a factory letter may be necessary. Our charge for a written appraisal is $20 per airgun, up to five airguns. At six airguns, the charge is normally $15 per airgun. Larger collections may be discounted somewhat, depending on the complexity and the size of the collection. Please allow two to three weeks response time per appraisal request.

ADDITIONAL SERVICES

Individuals requesting a photocopy of a particular page or section from any edition for insurance or reference purposes will be billed at $5 per page, up to five pages, and $3.50 per page thereafter.

TURNAROUND TIME

Our goal is to answer most telephone, mail, email, or faxed gun questions in no longer than three business days – unless we're away attending trade/gun shows. This also assumes that all information needed to process the question(s) is initially provided, otherwise delays may occur.

Please direct all gun questions and appraisals to the following address:

Blue Book Publications, Inc.

Attn: Research Dept.

8009 34th Ave. S., Suite 175

Minneapolis, MN 55425 USA

Phone: 800-877-4867 (Toll-free in U.S. & Canada)

Fax: 952-853-1486

www.bluebookinc.com

FOREWORD

Editor & Publisher S.P. Fjestad, with one millionth copy of the *Blue Book of Gun Values*. Hopefully, the *Blue Book of Airguns* will also reach this landmark someday!

From its humble beginning in 2001, the *Blue Book of Airguns* has come a long way in only four years. The first edition was the only publication in the airgun industry to provide information and pricing on both older and currently manufactured airguns. Even though it had only seventy pages for the A-Z sections, many airgun enthusiasts immediately realized its value. As a result, the first edition quickly sold out, and is now a collector's item.

The second edition followed in 2002. It maintained the 6 x 9 inch format, and the A-Z sections more than doubled in page count. For that edition, John Allen and Dr. Robert Beeman combined their skills and knowledge to make this publication *the* airgun reference guide.

Recognizing the need for images which would provide easier identification, the third edition was enlarged to an 8½ x 11 inch format, and hundreds of makes and models were now not only described and priced, but images also added immensely to the value of this publication. Page count was now at 312, and many people might remember the back cover, which featured a vintage advertisement, with a dad apparently taking aim at his wife as the kids looked on!

The fourth edition continued to grow—hundreds of additional images were included, and page count was now at 384. At $24.95 retail, there was no question that the *Blue Book of Airguns* was easily the best and most up-to-date reference work for the airgun industry. Many more vintage models had been added, and, for the first time, many collectors could finally identify what they had owned for many years. It is vital in any industry to provide the consumers as much information as possible. Without this reliable information and consumer education, an industry's growth will never reach its full potential.

The airgun industry now realizes and appreciates how much this publication has helped it out, even in its short time period. With timely articles by Tom Gaylord, the go-to guy in today's rapidly changing airgun marketplace, and Dr. Robert Beeman's fascinating editorial content based on his decades of experience, earning himself a well jus-tified "Godfather of the Airgun Industry" title, many readers finally understand how important the airgun industry has been for centuries.

This fifth edition—the newest—maintains its successful recipe: more information, more images, and up-to-date pricing. With page count now close to 450, and over 900 images imbedded in the A-Z text, it has never been easier to get the airgun information you are looking for.

This edition's eight-page color Photo Grading System™ ("PGS"— on pages 49-56) has been completely revised, and allows you to determine the various condition factors based on an airgun's remaining percentage of original condition. This is the third edition featuring this very important PGS, and it will help you gain a much better understanding of what to look for and how to grade airguns accurately. After all, the price is wrong if the condition isn't right.

Of course, the *Blue Book of Airguns* needs to keep readers up-to-date with the airgun industry's most recent offerings—no small feat, considering how far airgun technology has advanced over the past decade. Don't miss Tom Gaylord's "Gaylord Reports," an up-to-the-minute summary on what's new for 2005, his informative "A Look Inside the BB Gun Powerplant," and a feature on the airgun manufacturer AirForce.

Dr. Robert Beeman has provided a in-depth feature article on the history of "Beeman Airguns and the Adult Airgun Market of America" (pages 21-28). Additionally, in a follow-up to the Lewis and Clark airgun treatise in the fourth edition, some new evidence regarding the airgun Meriwether Lewis may have carried during the Lewis and Clark expedition is examined on pages 34-35.

Once again, the trademark index has been revised and greatly expanded. This is the most up-to-date listing available on both domestic and international airgun manufacturers, importers, distributors, and repair centers. The glossary, abbreviations, and grading criteria have also been revised and provide you with more listings for both airgun terminology and grading criteria.

As good as this new edition is, it is nevertheless a work in progress, and you have my word that future editions will continue to show significant improvements over this one. We are truly fortunate to be living in this golden age of airgunning, affording us an unprecedented amount of choices for caliber, types of powerplants, high performance, special features, and above all, an overall level of quality products at reasonable prices. Having been an airgun enthusiast for decades, the one thing I would like to ask of the airgun industry is that there be more standardization on how today's large crop of precharged pneumatic airguns get filled. After all, if you can't easily fill up the air reservoir of your airgun(s), you won't shoot it as much, and that's a mistake.

Thank you again for your help and support on this project, and we look forward to providing you with up-to-date and reliable airgun information for many editions to come.

Sincerely,

S.P. Fjestad
Editor & Publisher
Blue Book Publications, Inc.

This 5th Edition *Blue Book of Airguns* is landing in your hands with an attitude that is full of excitement, guaranteeing it a high place among the heavyweights of airgun titles. When you first picked this book up it was more than obvious that things have changed with the *Blue Book of Airguns*: there are fifty-six more pages, bringing the total now to four hundred forty. The A through Z sections have enjoyed a twenty percent increase, gaining over seventy-five new trademark (manufacturer) listings. If that isn't enough, we have added over one hundred new images, bringing this total to over nine hundred high resolution images to help in the identification of your airgun.

This edition's work started on Wednesday, December 29th, 2004 at 2:36 A.M. when Dr. Robert D. Beeman's first email hit my desktop's inbox, with almost one megabyte of information, about thirty-five pages of text (no images) covering forty-one new trademark listings. To add salt to this wound Robert had the nerve to mention in his note to me this should keep me out of trouble for a day or two! Robert, not one to spend much time sitting idle, followed that up on Thursday, December 30th, 2004 at 11:06 P.M. with a three hundred thirty-two kilobyte email—about fifteen pages (still no images) of information on fourteen new trademarks—with a note stating it looked like I might be running out of things to do. These two emails represented about six months of full-time work for Robert; and any of you who have tried to research an airgun know (because of the limited resource material available) that this is not easy.

So now the question is: "What's new this year?" If you are asking about the airgun industry, the easy answer is to check out "Gaylord Reports" on pages 14-18 for an overview of the 2005 hits at the SHOT Show (Shooting, Hunting, Outdoor Trade Show) which was held in Las Vegas, NV January 28th through the 31st. Four days were spent looking at every currently manufactured and new model airgun on the planet, picking up manufacturers' catalogs (a stack about four inches tall weighing eight pounds) and making contacts with existing/new manufacturers, importers, and distributors. Sound like fun? Try walking thirty miles making 327 (50 airgun, 277 firearms) stops at exhibitor booths to look at hardware and pick up catalogs and brochures in only four days. The feet hurt from walking, the back hurts from carrying paper, the mouth hurts from talking, the brains are fried by the mass of new information—and it's a blast (I love it)! While Tom writes in his "Gaylord Reports" that his enthusiasm may lead some people to think he is a little off center, I'm here to tell you we are all right on center and know how to enjoy our work. After all, if you can't enjoy it, you might as well find something else to do!

If you're wondering what is new in this 5th edition, the simple answer is "everything." Every model listing has been reviewed; all the currently/newly manufactured airguns that are represented at the major trade shows are included with values if available. New educational editorial has been added by experts in this industry to keep you up-to-date with current and old manufacturing techniques. "A Shot of Humor" on pages 29-30 is a must read bit that, if only we could have been a fly on the wall for, would have been well worth the price of admission. "Airgun Grading Criteria" and a new color section on pages 49-56 with new, expanded descriptions help you to better understand what to look for when evaluating the actual condition of an airgun. And be sure not to miss our electronic versions of the *Blue Book of Airguns* available either on CD-ROM or as an online annual subscription (updated quarterly, for the most current information available anywhere on the planet!).

This project is and will always be a "WIP" (Work In Progress), and I do and will always hate those three letters! That is not an excuse for missing a manufacturer or model that we should include; after all, that is part of this job. We do our best to cover as much as possible, and you can see by the increase in pages and information each year that things are improving. The one thing we ask from you is to let us know what you want or are looking for. If your favorite airgun model or manufacturer is not listed let us know and we will get to work on it. I'm available Monday through Friday, 8:30-5:00 and 24-7 with voicemail and email, and page five has all the contact information you should need.

In closing I would like to thank everyone that has had a hand in this book. Most of you are listed in "Acknowledgements" or "Meet the Staff" but, if you were missed, thanks.

By the way, Thanks For Holding!!!

John B. Allen

WELCOME TO THE FIFTH EDITION!

By Dr. Robert D. Beeman

A gain, welcome to the fifth edition of the *Blue Book of Airguns*. Even I am astonished at how each edition of this work seems to be a quantum leap up from the last one! I submitted new or greatly enlarged sections on no less than seventy-five airgun brands and makes for this edition and over one hundred new photographs. We have even greater in-depth coverage of virtually every major brand of airguns on the planet. Some of this material was provided from airgun makers and enthusiasts from every corner of the globe. As always, the help of these wonderful contributors is tremendously appreciated and will be of value to virtually every airgun collector and trader in the world. Also important is the assistance provided by many notes about single points or small bits of information. The cumulative effect of these inputs is what makes these guides better and better.

1. This will always be a WORK IN PROGRESS. Each edition is a call for more information. We will take the blame for any error or omission the first time it appears, but if you find an error or have additional information it is UP TO YOU to let us know for the good of all future readers! We cannot guarantee that your inputs will be included, but we do promise to always consider them very seriously. (Please send your inputs by fax or snail mail to the Blue Book offices, or, best, directly email them to BlueBookedit@Beemans.net.)

2. This is NOT JUST A PRICE GUIDE. I consider values to be of third priority in the *Blue Book of Airguns*. First and second are the identification of airguns and establishing basic information about them and their makers. Further, we have established a policy of making each *Blue Book of Airguns* of lasting value. Thus, although the prices may

become of historical interest, the articles should have continuing interest and value. The first edition had articles on "Selecting an Airgun," "Collection Protection," and "The Most Collectible Airguns of the 20th Century." The feature of the second edition was the most through study ever presented of the Lukens airguns produced about 1800 in Philadelphia – America's first precision pneumatic arms (one has been suspected of being the airgun carried by Lewis and Clark), plus the first of a series on airgun powerplants by Tom Gaylord, and a definitive article on collecting Crosman airguns. The powerplant series continues right into the present edition. Those issues with a "Review of Airgun Literature" should be of basic need to all airgunners. The present edition features a presentation which should be interesting and, hopefully, of basic historical value about the role of Beeman Precision Airguns and the development of the adult airgun market in America.

This is not a profit-oriented matter for me, so, I can recommend, without conflict, that the wise airgunner, or student or collector of airguns, strive to develop a complete collection of the *Blue Book of Airguns*. The hardbound editions are the most durable, and because they are produced in extremely small quantities, mainly for VIPS, they are the best value and investment.

3. This is a developing set of STANDARDIZED NAMES. Just as such standardization of names has been important to groups as diverse as stamp collectors and bird watchers, such standardization of names should have real value to airgun collectors and students. We are starting to see ads and auction listings for things such as "Daisy, 3rd Model, Variation 2" or "Hubertus Air Pistol, small frame version"—instead of a listing that did not communicate the full identity, and thus the value, of the gun. Some adjustments will be necessary as more information appears, but the goal is clarity of expression.

AIRGUNS AS A PUBLIC HAZARD???

Recently there has been a good deal of notice in America's news media about the "terrible threat" of powerful new airguns. An abstract of the paper which has stirred much of this interest is at this website: http://pediatrics.aappublications.org/cgi/content/full/114/5/1357. It stated that:

"Between 1990 and 2000, the US Consumer Product Safety Commission reported 39 non-powder gun/related deaths, of which 32 were children younger than 15 years. The introduction of high-powered air rifles in the 1970s has been associated with approximately 4 deaths per year."

There has been quite a bit of excited talk about this summary of old information in the U.S. media – especially by the anti-gun crowd. Four deaths per year actually does not seem very high for devices, owned by tens of millions of people, which must be dangerous to carry out the function for which they were designed: shooting outdoors where one is exposed to side winds and where the flattest possible trajectory is desirable because it is almost impossible to guess the exact distance of the target and to compensate for the highly arched path of low velocity projectiles. During the stated period, U.S. shooters were using tens, perhaps hundreds, of millions of such airguns and firing billions of airgun projectiles per year (almost eight billion annually just from Daisy)—so actually the injury record is astonishingly LOW! During the same time, firearms, skateboards, and bicycles, to mention only a few items that also must be dangerous to carry out their intended functions, have accounted for many, many fold this number of injuries! A previous study by the U.S. Consumer Product Safety Commission itself is interesting. They established a Hazard Index based on the number of injuries per 100,000 persons. These ratings are much higher for products which are used by youth, such as airguns, because they multiply the basic index by 2.5 for such products. Nevertheless, gas, air and spring guns had an index of only 1.9 as compared with 2.8 for paper money and coins, 3.0 for fishing equipment, 4.9 for skates and skateboards, 5.8 for floors, 8.7 for beds, 25.4 for stairs, and 35.7 for bicycles. These figures suggest that bicycles are 1,736% more hazardous than airguns, and that beds and fishing equipment are respectively 357% and 58% more hazardous! Firearms are not under the jurisdiction of the CPSC, but the number of unintentional firearm related deaths per YEAR declined from 526 deaths in 1993 to 213 deaths in 1999. (Quite a contrast to the 3.9 per year average for airgun deaths!).

The alarmists mainly are pushing the idea that the pump pneumatics (the main models involved are Daisy and Crosman pump pneumatics of only moderate 160 to 700 FPS velocity) are something new, different, and alarmingly dangerous. However, Benjamin has been selling huge numbers of multi-stroke pump pneumatics for over a century; Crosman introduced such models eighty-one years ago and Daisy has had such models for over thirty-two years!! Certainly long enough for many generations of the public to get used to the idea that all youth-oriented, multiple-stroke, pump pneumatic airguns are not just like the very different, single-stroke "Red Ryder" BB gun! The misdirected anti-gun folks want to see airguns outlawed or all reduced to muzzle velocities under 350 FPS! (It is interesting to note that injuries by really high power airguns, 800 to 1200+ FPS, are so low as to be almost off the radar screen! But the agitators could cause "the baby to be thrown out with the bathwater" when attacking the mass of youth-oriented airguns. The legislators certainly do not know the difference—or care!). As the agitators "discover" adult airguns, they will be after them—never mind that these guns are almost free of public problems: the fact that there had never been a crime or public problem with .50 caliber centerfire rifles did not deter the "let's make a law" folks from going after them!

What also is NOT noted is that almost all of these 39 injuries were the result of intentional shootings or reckless handling of guns, especially when the young people were allowed to use these guns with little or no adult supervision! Many of the injuries were related to youth violence with airguns and firearms. Actually, this whole matter speaks of misdirected concern. After a very recent long and very intense investigation (see other notes about this on the following website: www.beemans.net) by the U.S. Consumer Product Safety Commission, the CPSC chairman Hal Stratton reported in 2004 that:

1. "The Commission (CPSC) has never found that air rifles, or any model of air rifle, constitute a substantial product hazard."
2. "All of the injuries that can be attributed to the guns at issue in this case (CPSC vs. Daisy) were preventable. They all involved either someone pointing the gun at someone and pulling the trigger or playing with the gun in an inappropriate manner - all in violation of widely known and accepted safety rules for the use of guns."

The anti-gun hysterics would lead us to believe that something new has arrived and there is a growing, spreading problem! Wrong on both counts. What these anti-gun articles and even the CPSC are NOT mentioning is the trend in airgun injuries. DESPITE the FACT that airgun makers have not adopted the doom-sayers' unreasonable demands to reduce velocity below that capable of perforating human skin, adding the very undesirable automatic safeties (see www.Beemans.net), etc., the trend of injuries is sharply down. This is thoroughly documented in another very recent paper: "Trends in BB/pellet gun injuries in children and teenagers in the United States, 1985-99" by M.H. Nguyen et. al. in Injury Prevention, August 2002: pages 185-191. There it is shown that "BB/pellet gun related and firearm related injury rates show similar declines since the early 1990s. These declines coincide with a growing number of prevention efforts aimed at reducing injuries to children from unsupervised access to guns and from youth violence."

What is also not noted is that American airgun makers have spent tens of millions of dollars on programs to teach safe airgun handling to many millions of young people. The huge programs of Daisy alone probably have prevented thousands of airgun injuries. The NRA also has big airgun safety programs which address the REALITY of promoting safe handling, storage, and parental supervision of the millions of airguns already out there, instead of worrying about making inappropriate changes on the much fewer new ones being sold! The problem is the shooter, not the gun.

DO NOT BE DECEIVED—an attack on "youth-oriented airguns" is the starting point—the camel's nose in the tent: adult airgunners must not overlook these battles or they, like the Brits and Aussies (as announced in my greeting to the Fourth Edition of the *Blue Book of Airguns*), may suddenly find themselves with outlawed airguns and wonder what hit them!! ∎

Gaylord Reports

What's New for 2005

By Tom Gaylord
Freelance airgun writer

I wish I could tell you personally my impressions of the airgun market in 2005. That, of course, is the principal intent of this column, but if you and I were face to face, my animated behavior would either convince you I was going off the deep end or else this year will be one of the historic watershed years in which major events unfold in our hobby. My close friends will tell you that I stepped off the deep end long ago, so I think they would tell you to listen to what I have to say.

Our story began at the National Rifle Association airgun breakfast, which is held on opening day of every SHOT Show. Everyone attending SHOT with an interest in airguns is invited by the NRA to attend the breakfast and hear what exciting new things are happening. For the past several years, I've been asked to give my own impressions on the state of airguns in the U.S., but this time the program was far more significant.

This year, Executive Vice President of the NRA Wayne LaPierre addressed the group. His brief talk was a listing of many of the things the organization does to protect the shooting sports, with airguns being the principal thrust of his speech. If you are aware of their stand on the Second Amendment, you can well imagine what he said, so I will not elaborate. Of greater significance was that he addressed the airgun breakfast!

For decades, interest in airguns has been growing within the ranks of the NRA, but not at the official level. The association was founded in 1873 for the promotion of formal rifle target shooting to remedy the unbelievably poor marksmanship demonstrated by most soldiers during the American Civil War. The American military was concerned that if American men did not receive some good training prior to military emergencies, the defense of this nation would be at high risk, so they influenced the founding of the National Rifle Association to promote such training.

History lesson aside, the NRA has a longstanding tradition of firearms marksmanship. Airguns have never been seen as an avenue of interest for anything but youth training. And, until very recently, the corporate level of the NRA has not kept pace with the rapid advancements in airgun technology that started in the 1960s.

That said, there are individual NRA staff members like Rosemary Herr, H.Q. Moody, John Venskoske, Matt Szrasmoski, Dave Baskin and others who have quietly championed airguns as useful tools for training all ages, genders, and physical capabilities. These people know what all of you know—that airguns are great for improving shooting skills, plus they have some safety advantages over firearms that make them especially desirable. Airguns have therefore grown in the past ten years as a grassroots movement inside the NRA but have not really been acknowledged by the old guard. That has now changed.

Once the organization began taking official notice of what airguns are doing today, it quickly learned about the tens of thousands of seniors who quietly supplement their shooting with airguns costing several times the price of a nice sporting firearm. They have seen field target demonstration matches at Camp Perry, where the U.S. National Matches are held every year, and they have seen a level of marksmanship that would make a sniper school proud. And, this year, they officially awoke to the growing future of airguns in American shooting.

Whenever Wayne LaPierre addresses a group, that group is assured of official recognition by the organization. This year marked the confirmation of airguns as an official part of the National Rifle Association. We learned from H.Q. Moody, another NRA speaker, that there are now 12,000 clubs using airguns for training and competition and are actively affiliated with the association. The dream of millions of airgunners is about to be realized through America's premiere shooting organization!

Dieter Anschütz was honored by the organization for donating some of the proceeds from the sale of his new Anschütz target air pistol to the NRA Airgun Endowment. Joshua Ungier, owner of Pyramyd Air, was also recognized for donating over $7,000 to the NRA Airgun Endowment.

NRA Executive Vice President Wayne LaPierre at the airgun breakfast.

When the breakfast ended, the SHOT Show began. As you'd expect, most American manufacturers showed up in force with impressive booths and elaborate displays. However, many smaller European makers simply walked the show or just didn't bother to come. One impressive exception was Air Arms.

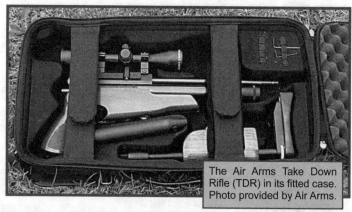

The Air Arms Take Down Rifle (TDR) in its fitted case. Photo provided by Air Arms.

AIR ARMS

This British manufacturer brought several brand new air rifles to the show. One of them is the Take Down Rifle, or TDR. It comes in a form-fitted semi-soft case and assembles into a nifty precharged carbine. Beeman sold cased takedown sets like this in the early 1990s, but there wasn't as much interest in PCP guns back then. Today there is a whole new crop of airgunners to enjoy the compact portability offered by compressed air.

Air Arms also listened to last year's NRA presentations, where they asked manufacturers to develop target air rifles for their programs. There weren't 12,000 clubs in the program then, but we were told there soon would be. Bill Saunders of Air Arms took the message to heart and held a year-long dialog with NRA staffers about exactly what was needed. The outcome of his effort is what I believe will be a world-beater target air rifle.

This new air rifle is truly astounding. Look at the photo, and you'll see the

Ready to go. Photo provided by Air Arms.

same gun with different features. For example, the buttstock separates from the rest of the air rifle, meaning clubs can have an air rifle for both left- and right-handed shooters without buying an entire second air rifle! Simply swap out the butt for either preference. But, there is MUCH more!

Because both butts are target butts with fully adjustable buttplates and sporter butts, this air rifle may qualify for both the NRA Sporter and Precision class competitions. If that comes to pass, you have a very affordable precision-class air rifle with a pedigreed trigger that carries over into the sporter class.

The price of this air rifle was not finalized when we went to press, and many of the final competition details, such as its legality for both class-

es, has yet to be finalized; but, all serious target shooters should watch this one closely. When Olympic target air rifles are selling for more than $2,000, this might be one that you can buy for a lot less. This was the single most important airgun product at the 2005 SHOT Show.

BEEMAN

Beeman brought out a new sporter and two new target air rifles. The sporter is a synthetic-stock version of their venerable Spanish springer. The stock material is grippy and very ergonomic. The action is a traditional breakbarrel, capable of 1,000 FPS in .177 caliber with light pellets. This comes in .177 and .22 calibers.

The Beeman FWB P70 target rifle has been replaced with the Model 700. It has the same anti-recoil feature that made the P70 one of the

Air Arms builds the same air rifle with interchangeable butts, making it possible to fit right- or left-handed shooters and to change from sporter to precision class. At press time, the jury was still out on whether or not the latter will be permitted in competition. A great rifle at a great price.

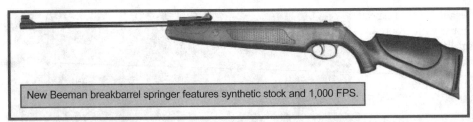

New Beeman breakbarrel springer features synthetic stock and 1,000 FPS.

The new P40 adds adjustable weights to an already superb target pistol. More grip adjustability is the chief improvement this year. Photo provided by Beeman.

Beeman Feinwerkbau 700 Universal carries on the tradition of world dominance in 10-meter target shooting. Photo provided by Beeman.

best world-class air rifles. The new airgun is available in both an ergonomic Alu (aluminum) model with every adjustment known to man, including adjustable sight radius, and a more affordable wood-stocked Universal version.

The venerable Beeman P34 target pistol has advanced to the P40. The Morini grips are now even more adjustable, plus the adjustable weights add more balancing options in this model. The anti-recoil feature continues to let this air pistol dominate competition with only a few rivals.

CROSMAN

Crosman always has several surprises for us, and this year they are big ones! First, they've created a true semiautomatic pellet-firing carbine with realistic blowback action. Called the Nightstalker, the new air rifle borrows the twelve-shot magazine from the tried-and-true 1077 for a basic load of fun that should prove exciting to everyone.

The power source is Crosman's 88-gram AirSource disposable cartridge, which not only provides gas for lots of shots (up to 400 in some airguns), it also contains the power for the blowback mechanism. The new air rifle harkens back to the golden days of the 600 pistol, which younger shooters only know from stories and articles. In those days, airgunners knew how to spray and pray and weren't shy about doing it! I can't wait to get my hands on a new Nightstalker to test! They should be available this summer.

More news at Crosman is the same word that reverberated throughout the SHOT Show this year. That word is "airsoft," or to use

Crosman's term, "soft air."

Last year I reported that Crosman brought lots of airsoft guns to market, and they kept up the pace for 2005. The new guns are both springers and auto-electrics. Many are clear-bodied versions of models already in the Crosman line, but a few are completely new.

The Pulse R70 is an automatic electric gun (AEG) that comes with rechargeable batteries and a Picatinny rail for mounting accessories. Besides looking way cool, it retails for well under $100.

DAISY

The boys and girls from Rogers, Ark., brought out a new multi-pump pneumatic this year. The Powerline 901 shoots either steel BBs or lead pellets at speeds up to 750 FPS. Veterans will recognize a passing resemblance to Daisy's 800-series multi-pumps, but the 901 allows the use of steel BBs as well as lead pellets through a rifled barrel. TruGlo open adjustable sights complement the air rifle.

For those with active imaginations, there's the new Daisy 008 air pistol. A CO_2 gun with an eight-shot rotary magazine, it allows mixing steel BBs and lead pellets. Each pull of the trigger sends a shot downrange at up to 485 FPS, so play extra-safe with this one, especially when shooting BBs.

Why 008? Because it's one up from 007—and mostly because the magazine holds eight shots. The air pistol looks ultra-modern, though it doesn't copy any specific model.

LOGUN

The Logun boys walked the aisles like pros, despite the youthful age of the company. In England they are associated with several more mature brands of airgun accessories, so their marketing cadre has been around the block a time or two.

The biggest surprise from Logun this year was the hushed

Crosman's Nightstalker is a revolutionary semiautomatic pellet air rifle that uses the huge 88-gram AirSource cartridge. With twelve shots in a magazine, this will be the next great fun pellet gun. Photo provided by Crosman.

Crosman enters the airsoft AEG market with the Pulse R70, an electric full-auto for under $100! Photo provided by Crosman.

Daisy's new 901 multi-pump shoots both BBs and pellets from a rifled barrel. TruGlo sporter sights front and rear are adjustable. Photo provided by Daisy.

"Shaken, not stirred," is the catchword for the one-better 008 CO_2 pistol from Daisy. Actually, the model number refers to the number of BBs and pellets held in the rotary magazine. Photo provided by Daisy.

announcement of a budget-priced air rifle. The hush wasn't embarrassment, but rather the final machinations of a sales strategy designed to penetrate the U.S. market with a product on which they can still make money. The strong Euro and weak dollar has made manufactured goods from Europe expensive in the American market at the very moment in time when our demand for airguns is exploding. Germany, England and other traditional airgun manufacturing countries are scrambling to find ways to sell us what we now seem to want very much.

Logun took a precharged rifle action and dropped it into a synthetic stock. The Eagle, as it is called, will retail here for—well, that was the issue at the SHOT Show. Logun reps didn't exactly know what it would sell for, but a number whispered to me was below $700. When you compare that to their standard stickers that quickly rise above $1,000, you see how serious they must be about competing here in the States. I wonder if the first ad will read, "The Eagle has landed"?

The new air rifle is ambidextrous, with a bolt handle that takes just minutes to switch. The trigger is fully adjustable and Logun reps say it challenges the finest match-grade units, which says a lot. The synthetic thumbhole stock fits all shooters, and the adjustable buttpad hides a cavity for a battery to power Logun's Lamp, which is a low-light hunting accessory that has yet to catch on here in the U.S. That's a lot of features in a budget-priced PCP!

Another air rifle in Logun's bag got a serious upgrade this year. The S-16 repeater has not exactly flown off dealers' shelves in this country, so for 2005 Logun shrouded the barrel. A shroud around the barrel allows a decent level of silencing without running afoul of ATF silencer restrictions, because there is nothing that can be removed and put on a firearm.

The new S-16 looks much more finished and complete with the contoured fat shroud sticking out of the receiver. Logun says the new air rifle will be available in a 32 foot-pound American version, as well as the traditional British 12 foot-pound air gun. Will it be enough to rejuvenate interest in the air rifle? Time will tell.

LEAPERS

Leapers' booth was filled with new scopes for airgunners, including their very popular tactical series that allow the installation of optional sidewheels for parallax adjustment. These models and their "Bug Buster" dual-illuminated mil-dot that focuses down to *nine feet* caused a big stir among airgunners in 2004.

This year, the big deal at Leapers was that new magic word—airsoft. While they have been importing value-priced Chinese spring guns and mini AEGs for several years, this year they had an "Oh-Oh!" on display. In fact, they had several.

What's an Oh-Oh? It's when a manufacturer or importer figures out something fundamental that poises them for a light-year jump ahead of their competition.

What would you think of a full metal-body paramilitary design with wood stock and all the nice features (like Hop Up) you expect to see on the top Japanese brands? What if the company that displayed it was a proven go-getter like Leapers?

"Look upon my works, ye Mighty, and despair!" That might sum up the feelings of the onlookers as Leapers prepares to enter the airsoft arena in a big way.

The naysayers will tell you that the Chinese knock off everyone's look and feel indiscriminately, which is why I found the business thrust of Leapers owner, David Ding, particularly interesting. He is now into the fifth iteration of an airgun scope line which copies no other scope on the market. Leapers scopes are leading airgun technology and causing others to play catch-up. He said the market is saturated with low-priced airguns and accessories and his vision is to add a lot of value to the products he sells, and that business will be done "according to Hoyle."

So, when I saw the metal and wood Kalashnikov and the metal and synthetic M4 airsoft guns sitting on his shelves, both bristling with Leapers mounts and optics, I knew they didn't come from Japan. I pressed him for a release date on these airguns, but he would not commit. He said the show response had been overwhelming (I bet!), and many folks had attempted to buy the display airguns from him, but there was more development work to be done. I know both the company and the man well enough to know these airguns are under devel-

The S16 was improved with a shrouded barrel this year. Photo provided by Logun.

Batteries in the butt, adjustable buttpad and trigger, and synthetic thumbhole stock make the new Logun Eagle a worthy entry-level PCP. Photo provided by Logun.

Leapers' metal body AK has a real wood stock and Picatinny tri-rail for mounting anything tactical. When they finally reach the market, these realistic airsoft guns should be impressive!

opment right now and we should watch the Leapers website for an announcement—this year, I hope.

I now also know Leapers intends playing the airsoft super-realistic replica gun game by the book, with licensing agreements where required. If they do, they'll separate the wheat from the chaff, just like they have in the airgun scope market over the past five years!

Looking good enough to eat, these 6mm airsoft paintballs from Airsoft Solutions, Inc. are actually edible, though the nutritional value is low. Several companies are racing to perfect the technology of balls that won't break inside the airgun but will break reliably on impact. When that happens, airsoft paintballs will probably supplant traditional .68-caliber markers as the ammunition (and guns!) of choice for gamers.

AIRSOFT

Now for the biggest news from SHOT. To appreciate what's happening with airsoft, you must first consider paintball. For many years, paintball products were not shown at the SHOT Show, ostensibly because the sport has people shooting at one another.

This year, though, paintball was allocated space at the show; and they came in with a splash, to make a poor pun. The entire show was plastered with huge banners proclaiming the profits to be had with paintball products, and National Paintball Supply paid a reported $75,000 to park their tractor-trailer in front of the entrance, where an adjoining tent had live demonstrations.

Now, what has paintball got to do with airsoft? Well, the same crowd is interested in both technologies, and airsoft guns are increasingly being substituted for paintball in traditional skirmish games. They hurt far less and the risk of injury is much lower with the decreased energy of the 6mm plastic balls. There are even 6mm paintballs, though that technology still has a way to go before it will be as reliable as the .68-caliber paintball.

So, paintball took the 2005 SHOT Show by storm, which put airsoft on everyone's mind. Can they be far behind? They have quietly been represented in many booths over the past few years, but this year the talk was out in the open and laced with a dash of awe.

This year, there were several meetings within the airsoft community held at the SHOT Show. The one I attended was hosted by Specialized Distribution and had over eighty people listening to recent changes in the law and marketing opportunities for airsoft. Some were folks just getting started and didn't know what they didn't know. Specialized Distribution put their large new catalog and a DVD movie about airsoft into their hands while business cards flew like snowflakes at a late season Packers' game.

Down on the exhibit floor, guys were coming up to me and asking, "Did you see that M1A a couple of rows over? It's an airsoft!" Folks, when the BAR was produced in limited quantity as an airsoft gun a few years ago, it sold for thousands of dollars! Know why? Because you could buy a real wood and steel BAR and take it home that same day! If somebody ever figures out that Americans are willing to pay for such things, the airsoft market is going to break wide open. From what I saw in Las Vegas, the cracks are already forming.

QUACKENBUSH

He didn't make it to SHOT, but Dennis Quackenbush is a legitimate airgun maker and he does have a new product this year. For several years, he has been lamenting the success of his big bore Outlaw-series air rifles that people won't let him stop making. He originally thought he might make a total of a hundred or so air rifles, but the path has been beaten to his door and he now finds it necessary to crank out a hundred at a time just to keep the whiners at bay.

This year, he added an air pistol, and what a pistol it is! The Outlaw air pistol is a single-shot precharged pistol that comes in .25, .308, 9mm and .45 calibers. There have also been some .50-caliber Outlaw air pistols made, and Dennis may well make a few more if there's a demand.

Barrels range from ten inches to sixteen inches and power tops 100 foot-pounds in .45 caliber. There are three shots in the larger calibers, but he has tuned the .25 to get more.

If the gun looks familiar, that's because it is assembled on a Crosman 2240 frame. Quackenbush keeps manufacturing costs low by using some commercial parts. He makes the barrels and actions. The calibers are selected to use commercial cast-lead bullets available through the mail or in any good gun store.

Outlaw pistols start at $500. Compare that to a 50 foot-pound Korean pistol at the same price or a boutique one-off large bore air pistol selling for thousands.

SUMMARY

This year marks a watershed for airguns. The NRA counts 12,000 affiliated clubs shooting targets with them—and those are just the paper-punchers! Airsoft is rising like a rocket within the airgun ranks and may soon be the chief profit center of all airgunning sports. Some manufacturers have been caught off guard while others are leading the charge. Expect to see many more new models as 2005 unfolds. ∎

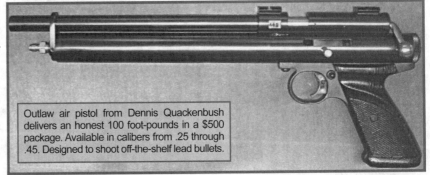

Outlaw air pistol from Dennis Quackenbush delivers an honest 100 foot-pounds in a $500 package. Available in calibers from .25 through .45. Designed to shoot off-the-shelf lead bullets.

A LOOK INSIDE THE BB GUN POWERPLANT

Blue Book looks inside the century-old American BB gun

By Tom Gaylord

Show an airgun of almost any type to someone who doesn't know airguns, and they'll call it a BB gun. Many will call it a Red Ryder. Veteran airgunners are used to this reaction from the public, but when they get with other enthusiasts, the conversation sometimes becomes deeper and more precise. However, not always! Very few airgunners are aware of just how a BB gun powerplant really works, so let's take a look.

Daisy helped me with this project by donating the shot tube and spring mechanism for one of their modern lever-action airguns. We'll call it a Red Ryder, and it may well be, but this mechanism is common to more than just a single model. Because I have a modern mechanism to examine, I'll concentrate on that, but if you take the time to look at the older models, you'll see that a lot of their design has been carried forward.

The BB gun powerplant is a hybrid of both the spring-piston and the catapult designs. We looked at spring-piston guns in the *Blue Book of Airguns*, 3rd Edition, but we haven't looked at catapult guns yet. The mechanism we will examine uses gravity to feed the BBs, though other types, such as the spring-powered, forced-feed magazine found in a Daisy model 25 pump BB gun, also use this powerplant. For the rest of this discussion, please refer to the illustration.

1. Prepare to fire: The gun is cocked and ready to fire, with the hollow air tube retracted just behind the next BB. The BB is held in place by a small magnet, so even if you point the gun straight down, it should stay in place until fired. The "magazine" is nothing more than the

hollow cavity formed between the inner shot tube (the true barrel) and the outer sheetmetal "barrel" of the gun. When the muzzle is elevated to cock the lever, gravity pulls the BBs down against a sloped surface that has a funnel-like channel at its lowest end. The BBs organize into a single column in this channel, and they drop down

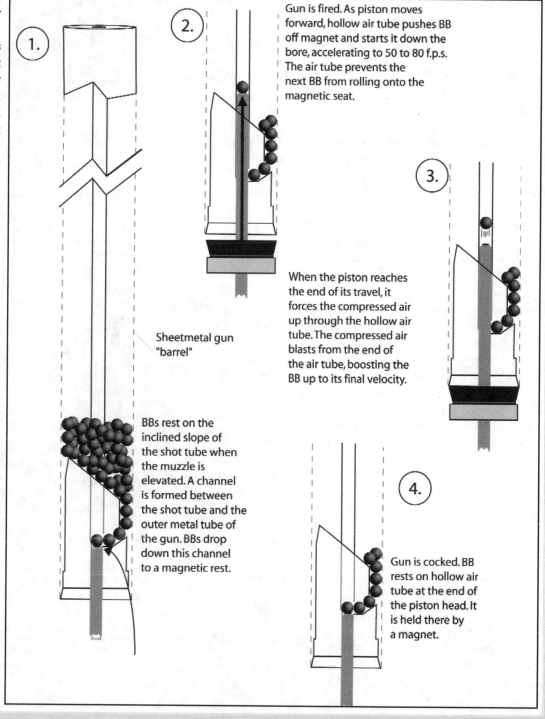

2. Gun is fired. As piston moves forward, hollow air tube pushes BB off magnet and starts it down the bore, accelerating to 50 to 80 f.p.s. The air tube prevents the next BB from rolling onto the magnetic seat.

1.

Sheetmetal gun "barrel"

BBs rest on the inclined slope of the shot tube when the muzzle is elevated. A channel is formed between the shot tube and the outer metal tube of the gun. BBs drop down this channel to a magnetic rest.

3. When the piston reaches the end of its travel, it forces the compressed air up through the hollow air tube. The compressed air blasts from the end of the air tube, boosting the BB up to its final velocity.

4. Gun is cocked. BB rests on hollow air tube at the end of the piston head. It is held there by a magnet.

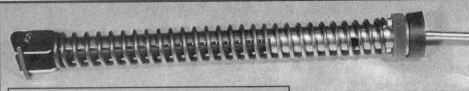

The mainspring is held captive by the piston assembly. A spring anchor in the gun holds the back of the spring steady when the cocking lever withdraws the piston and compresses the spring. Notice the long air tube that projects from the front of the black piston seal on the right. It fits inside the shot tube assembly, where it aligns with the barrel.

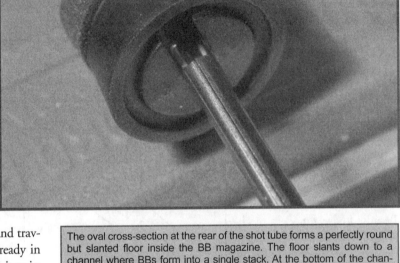

This close-up of the end of the piston seal shows the hole in the base of the air tube. This hole conducts the compressed air up the hollow tube, where it exits behind the BB. The air tube also pushes the BB off its magnetic seat and accelerates it to low velocity before the air blast hits it.

toward the BB seat where the magnet is located. All of this action depends on the muzzle being elevated, and nothing but gravity holds those BBs in place; so, they realign this way every time the gun is cocked.

2. Gun is fired: The sear has released the piston so the mainspring drives it forward. At the same time, the air tube that projects from the center of the piston has pushed the BB off its magnetic seat and started it down the barrel. A low initial velocity is imparted by this mechanical catapulting action. This is the catapult part of the powerplant.

3. The compressed-air blast: The piston has slammed to a stop against the back of the shot tube, squeezing all the air from the compression chamber and through the hole at the back of the air tube. The air is now highly compressed and travels up the air tube, where it exits behind the BB that is already in motion. It imparts a boost of velocity to the BB, accelerating it to its terminal velocity. This is the spring piston part of the powerplant.

At this point the gun is uncocked.

4. Gun is cocked: Cocking withdraws the piston and air tube assembly, making room for a BB to roll down and be captured by the magnetic seat. The gun is now ready to fire again.

That's the cycle of the BB gun powerplant. As you now can see, it relies on both a catapult action and a spring piston to do its job. The combination of these two forces works like the booster rockets in a space vehicle; only in this instance, the boost means that the mainspring can be made light enough for younger folks to cock, yet still supply adequate power to launch a BB.

There are other types of BB gun powerplants; however, the one we looked at in this issue is by far the most common and most important type of BB gun powerplant there is. In the next edition, we will look at the catapult powerplant, which is an airgun that uses no air! ■

The oval cross-section at the rear of the shot tube forms a perfectly round but slanted floor inside the BB magazine. The floor slants down to a channel where BBs form into a single stack. At the bottom of the channel, a hole in the shot tube allows one BB to fall onto a magnetic seat when the air tube is withdrawn during cocking. This organization of BBs occurs every time the muzzle is elevated during cocking. The white synthetic seal at the back of the shot tube mates with the piston seal to cushion it when it comes forward. Though this is a modern version of the mechanism, it has worked essentially the same way for about a century.

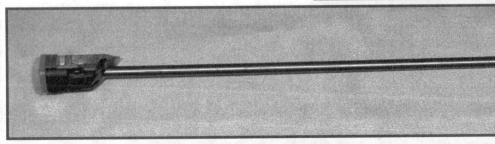

The shot tube is the real barrel. The outside sheet metal "barrel" is for looks as well as forming the outside wall of the BB magazine. The slanted plastic at the breech of the shot tube is what organizes BBs and sends them down to the magnetic seat one at a time to be shot from the gun.

BEEMAN AND THE ADULT AIRGUN MARKET IN AMERICA
(THOSE THRILLING DAYS OF YESTERYEAR?)

By Dr. Robert D. Beeman

"Return with us now to those thrilling days of yesteryear!"

While that may have been a great theme to introduce the Lone Ranger program on old time radio, yesteryear really wasn't very thrilling for the adult airgun market in America. Even if we only return to about 1970, we find a startling contrast with today.

Even in England, there was no *Airgun World* or *Airgunner* magazine. Daystate had not even been founded and thus had not yet developed the first modern PCP airguns. In America also, there were no airgun periodicals, no airgun forums, and no airgun shows. Airgun Field Target shooting was unknown and the NRA didn't even have an Airgun Committee. Not only were there no national airgun standards, there wasn't even a Non-Powder Gun Products Association to develop them. One of the only serious collectors of airguns was the late Charter Harrison, who, as may be the fate of serious airgun collectors, ended up dying in a mental institution. AirSoft guns had not yet been invented and paintballing was restricted to a few forest rangers who may have splatted the backside of a fellow tree-marker. Even among the tiny handful of European airguns sold here, the top velocity was about 700 FPS. To be sure, Crosman, Benjamin, and a few others, had been producing some fairly potent airguns, and had been trying for decades to develop interest among adults, but the reality was that the overwhelming majority of those "fairly powerful" airguns were used by youths and virtually all Americans thought that "airguns were for kids"! Adult airgunning just was not any sort of significant market.

Something happened during those three decades to give rise to a thriving adult airgun market in America. Steve Fjestad, head honcho at Blue Book Publications, was somehow convinced that Robert and Toshiko Beeman had a major hand in this development and asked me to record something about this matter. I feel rather diffident about writing about ourselves, and an outside viewer may have a clearer view, so I am just going to update and edit the well done, but now very rare, paper by the late Bill Bridgewater, then president of the National Alliance of Stocking Gun Dealers. This article, "Dr. Robert Beeman Selected to Receive Lifetime Achievement Award[1] for Extraordinary Contributions to the Shooting Sports Industry" appeared January 1993: pp. 5-14 in the *Alliance Voice*.

The Press Democrat *newspaper in Santa Rosa, California announced on March 4, 1993 that "Robert Beeman, founder of Beeman Precision Airguns in Santa Rosa, was presented the 1992 Lifetime Achievement Award by the National Alliance of Stocking Gun Dealers. Beeman was hailed as the 'Father of the Adult Airgun Market of the United States.' Beeman, and his wife, Toshiko, founded this company in 1972 in their home in San Anselmo. After building it into a multi-million dollar operation that sells airguns in 50 countries, they moved the firm to Santa Rosa in 1986."*

Robert's interest in airguns started over one-half century ago when, as an eight-year-old, he received a Daisy Model 25 BB gun as a birthday gift. Many BB guns and pellet guns followed. He delighted not only in the shooting of these guns, but in taking them apart again and again to see how they worked and what he could do to modify them.

Robert's first chance to actually design an airgun came years later while working on a Master of Science thesis on the migration of elk in the Selway/Bitterroot wilderness of Idaho. He selected a 200 square mile study area. One of the prime problems was to determine which elk moved from one point to another, and when, within their areas. He had different areas on his study map marked in different colors, and it occurred to him that if he could mark the elk with such colors, he could visually determine their movements. So, in the fall of 1954, he set about building some compressed airguns to mark elk with various colors of aniline dyes. Perhaps these were the first paint marker guns. Some of these guns were rigged along trails to fire as "trap guns." They were fixed and hidden in the bushes and tripped by the passage of a large animal along the trail. Perhaps not all of the marked animals were elk; there were rumors of some brightly colored hunters and forest rangers coming out of Beeman's study area!

While teaching college in Southern California, Robert was selected by the National Science Foundation from a group of 100 U.S science teachers nominated as "most outstanding teachers" to receive full support for study towards doctorate degrees of science. He elected to go to Stanford University. He remembers this as a particularly fascinating part of his life because it ranged from a sailing ship scientific expedition in the South Pacific to radioactive cell marking to electron microscopy. After receiving his Ph.D. in 1966, he took a position as a professor at San Francisco State University where he helped organize, and became the first chairman of, that University's Department of Marine Biology. His scientific career included the publication of many technical articles and books, published all over the world. His specialty was the Aplysid mollusks. Less than a dozen other scientists, including Emperor Hirohito of Japan, were authorities on this group. Robert's Japanese in-laws were duly impressed to think that someone in their family actually corresponded with the Emperor (through the Grand Chamberlain, of course!).

Beeman's interest in airguns was unabated. Responding to a small classified ad in a gun magazine, Robert obtained several fine European spring piston airguns from Bob Law, an airgun hobbyist in West Virginia who had started a small business called Air Rifle Headquarters. These guns renewed his interest in airguns.

The Beemans soon discovered that virtually all of the true adult airguns of this century had been made in Europe. Therefore, in 1972, Dr. and Mrs. Beeman visited the four leading European airgun makers: Weihrauch, Feinwerkbau, and Dianawerk in West Germany, and Webley and Scott in England. The European airgun factory owners all lamented that they felt that there had never been a truly successful introduction of true adult airguns into the United States. They simply could not understand why. Some ship-

---

[1]*Less than ten such Lifetime Achievement Awards have been made. Among other persons selected by members of the Alliance of Stocking Gun Dealers were: Roy Weatherby, John Browning, Horace Smith & Daniel Wesson, Bill Ruger, etc.*

ments had been brought in by a few U.S. gun companies, and more recently, very limited numbers had been imported by Air Rifle Headquarters. However, none of these attempts had been followed by a substantial flow of orders. Although "adult airguns" had been known in the United States even before the advent of the large bore airgun carried by the Lewis and Clark Expedition in 1802-06, and although there was a small surge of "gallery" airguns after the Civil War, there really wasn't a significant adult airgun market in the United States prior to 1972. Little did the Beemans realize that rather soon their firm would be importing adult airguns into the U.S. at over one hundred times the peak volume of Air Rifle Headquarters and would end up selling over 100 million dollars worth of adult airgun products.

In 1974, the Beemans had determined that over 99% of American shooters had never even heard of such guns. Almost all gun dealers told them that the only airguns that they knew of were domestic BB and pellet guns and that there "wasn't any demand for anything else." The basic problem seemed to be that the only significant attempts to introduce these guns had been through major American gun companies who introduced them at the distributor/jobber level. It was clear to the Beemans that the problem had several facets and was going to need several new approaches. It wasn't just that the U.S. market was almost completely unaware of these guns and their makers. If that had been all there was to the problem, the Beemans' job would have been far simpler. What overshadowed that lack of knowl-

Cover of Lifetime Award Issue, Jan. 1993

edge was that most U.S. shooters and dealers already had a very clear image of airguns, and that image was of domestic BB and pellet guns. Use of such guns then was almost completely restricted to youth. Shooters couldn't conceive of paying as much, even more, for an airgun as for a firearm. Dealers didn't want to stock them because "nobody would buy a 'BB gun' that costs that much, and besides, I don't want kids hanging around my shop." So, the sale of airguns largely was restricted to youth-oriented domestic airguns sold by chain stores and discount houses.

All of the right ingredients came together for the development of the American adult airgun market about 1975. Products had reached a good level of development in Europe, the U.S. market evidently was ready, and Robert and Toshiko Beeman seem to have been just the right people, with the right background and the right approach, to finally make "adult airgunning" emerge in the United States as a significant, commercial success. What the market was ready for was Beeman's information-intense approach about excellent and intriguing products, direct to consumers, rather than through the conventional chain of distribution. The

Beemans' background of academic communication on one hand and marketing experience on the other seems to have been the ideal catalyst. Robert Beeman "wrote the book" on the subject for that period and circumvented their original lack of promotion funds by a blitz of ready-to-publish material for gun magazine editors and others involved in public information—even those as "far out" as the *Whole Earth Manual*, *Mother Earth News*, *Soldier of Fortune*, and *Survival* magazine.

It was natural for Dr. Beeman to draw on his decades of experience as a technical writer and science professor to start what amounted to an educational writing campaign. Editors always need articles and illustrations, so he started writing articles about adult airguns, providing ready-made color photographs for gun magazine covers, preparing the first *Airgun Digest* book, stimulating gun writers to write about adult airguns, and producing Beeman's own national airgun newsletters and a catalog. And that certainly wasn't "just a catalog"! The Beeman "catalog" intentionally was big and technical; really an educational introduction and guide. At that time, a simple catalog of these special airguns would

Beeman Airgun Scopes - the Beeman company shunned the idea of cheap telescopic sights for airguns and specified the design of the first top-quality scopes for adult airguns. Upper: Beeman 66R scope—first scope designed for hunting and field use with high power field airguns, 2-7X, objective lens focused, parallax-free, from 7 yards to infinity. Lower: Beeman SS-1. Beeman designed "Short Scope" for use on compact adult sporting air rifles. (This specimen is an extremely rare "camo" version.)

not have meant much. Most of the readers literally would not have understood the products.

Very early, the Beemans decided on a strategy of applying a single, "American" name, Beeman, to several products whose names were not only unfamiliar, but hard for Americans to pronounce. This gave coherent identity to the products. Beeman created a snowballing support by means of a deliberate program to develop the Beeman name as synonymous with quality and uniqueness in adult airguns. The simultaneous development of high quality, new Beeman products was always linked with a program to make these matters news and of interest throughout the industry and gun-oriented organizations. Between 1975 and 1993, Beeman products appeared on more gun magazine covers than products of any other airgun company; even more than those of most firearm companies. This continuing drive led to a continuing growth of sales.

The strategy of developing deep market penetration of the Beeman brand as synonymous with quality was extremely successful. An extensive dealer survey revealed that 95% of dealers felt that Beeman's adult airguns were the best in the market; 99% said that the Beeman Precision Airgun Catalog/Guide was excellent, the best of its kind. Ninety percent expressed satisfaction with doing business with the company. Quite a development for an "escaped professor" who claims that he "didn't know anything about business"!

Although Beeman started as retail mail order, they quickly realized that the only way to volume and real growth was through wholesale sales. To that end and to break the "Catch 22" logjam of dealers not buying such products because they were convinced that there was no demand for them, they started a program to turn their thousands of mail order customers into salesmen to the dealers! That is, even though Beeman then had virtually no dealers, the Beeman newsletter started to direct consumers to ask for special sale prices on Beeman guns "at their local Beeman dealer." They also set up a nationwide network of about 40 sales representatives to call on dealers in all 50 states.

Most of the dealers probably didn't pay much attention to it when they got their first inquiry. However, when several real live customers, virtually with money in hand, had asked for Beeman products, their interest was up! About the same time, the Beemans saw to it that the mail brought each dealer a Beeman Dealer Newsletter and their big catalog/guide. The arrival of the Beeman Sales Rep, with Beeman guns in hand, sale priced and sold on a guaranteed sale basis (they only ever received three guns back as unsold!) coincided with this. They followed this with large displays of Beeman products at the national trade shows. At that time, Beeman was the only one displaying such products, thus they were very newsworthy for the media and drew the curiosity of many dealers, particularly those who had already been hit with that one-two-three punch. After two or three years of dealer development, Beeman used almost the same approach to develop the jobbers. That is, they announced specials to the dealers which were "available through your local jobber." Jobbers who had never heard of these products suddenly started to receive calls from dealers who wished to purchase Beeman products. Then the newly-created Beeman Jobber Newsletter started arriving, followed by the Beeman Sales Representative in person, backed up by a newly-expanded Beeman telemarketing program direct from Beeman's headquarters in California.

Of course, well before this had gone very far, Robert had to retire from his position at the university and ask Mrs. Beeman to leave her position as a buyer in a major department store to come and work with him and the small Beeman staff. At first, she was not convinced there was enough for her to do. When Beeman's staff hit 50 persons and the sales were several million dollars per year, this complaint was not heard again! As Beeman grew, the U.S. firms that had not been able to get imported airguns into the mainstream of the American gun market withdrew or dropped away. Beeman bought out the final airgun inventories of Winchester, Harrington and Richardson, HyScore, and Air Rifle Headquarters.[2] Over 95% of the airguns above the toy level from Germany and England were being imported by Beeman. Webley & Scott, Weihrauch, Westinger and Altenburger (FWB), Norica, and the makers of H&N and Silver Jet/Jet pellets all assigned exclusive American distribution contracts to the Beeman company. Westinger and Altenburger even assigned Beeman the American ownership of the Feinwerkbau trademark and name.

The Beemans knew that if they were successful in creating a large scale interest in adult airguns among American shooters and gun dealers that eventually they would create competition.

---

[2]*Air Rifle Headquarters was forced to close by severe health problems of Bob Law. Beeman's helped him stay afloat for a couple more years by supplying him airguns at their landed costs, even though his orders had become far too small to directly qualify for such quantity import prices. Their final help was to buy some of his equipment and literature, but, of course, since they were supplying his last guns only as he needed them, they never did buy any guns from him at closeout prices.*

The Weihrauchs and Beeman worked closely to produce the Beeman R1. The late Hans Weihrauch and Christel Weihrauch, co-owners of the Weihrauch company, rushed half-way across Germany to confer with Robert Beeman at a Bavarian Autobahn rest stop to settle final details of the then radically new R1 stock. Such was the partnership of the two companies for decades.

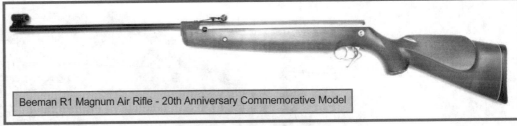

Beeman R1 Magnum Air Rifle - 20th Anniversary Commemorative Model

interactively designed by Robert Beeman and Gary Goudy, one of America's top custom stock makers. An automatic safety, to protect the gun from "bear trap" damage also was incorporated. The sum result was the Beeman R1 "magnum" adult air rifle. Introduced in 1981, it broke all previous American sales records for adult airguns. (A plainer version, generally of lower power, spun off in Europe as the HW80, was not as successful because of European power restrictions.)

Even in 2005, a quarter century after its birth, adult airgun experts are still writing[3] that the Beeman R1 is the standard by which all other spring-piston air rifles are judged. Incredibly accurate, tough, handsome, uncomplicated, easy to shoot, and self-contained—needing only pellets—the Beeman R1, in calibers from .177 to .25, became all the air rifle that most hunters would ever need. Tom Gaylord, one of America's leading airgun writers [see articles in this book], enthused that "the Beeman R1 is the rifle that brought America fully into the world of adult airguns."[4]

Previously, airguns traditionally had been produced in .177 and .22 calibers. One of Beeman's main accomplishments was to produce the first full line of precision .20 and .25 caliber airguns and pellets and actually create the first commercial success of these calibers in adult airguns. The .20 caliber served as a perfect compromise between the .177 and .22 calibers and soon became Beeman's biggest seller for sporting use. The .25 caliber proved to be the only bore that could efficiently handle the air flow of their most powerful air rifles.

The most thoroughly Beeman gun of all is the Beeman P1 magnum air pistol. Beeman produced the first design drawings of this gun in 1981, and produced their own detailed model of the P1 in their plant in 1983. The first production appeared in early 1985. Beeman had designed the P1 to fit a market gap for a high power, spring piston sporting air pistol. It was an immediate success, and went on to set adult air pistol standards and records. One of the first prototypes of the P1 was a single stroke pneumatic. This version was later developed as the Beeman P2 Match Pistol.

Fine pellets were always one of the mainstays of the Beeman business. The Beeman Silver Jet, a unique pointed pellet with multiple sealing rings, which they introduced in 1973, and sold in especially handsome silver-foil, Beeman-designed boxes, color-coded for caliber, was the leading precision field pellet for many years.

At first, Beeman labeled established designs of pellets, specifying only certain quality control and specification levels. (Makers privately admitted that they resold pellet lots, which Beeman

Beeman's strategy was to take the position of leadership in the production of regular production adult airguns, to obtain deep and high quality penetration of the market with the Beeman name, and to continue to grow as the market grew. By the time they retired in 1993, although they then had attracted several competitors, Beeman's imports of adult English and German airguns was still greater than any other U.S. company. The Beeman name had became synonymous with quality, even a generic term to many, meaning "high quality, adult airgun." Certainly not as generic as Kleenex or Scotch Tape, but a real factor! "Just like a Beeman" was rarely true, but it was one of the key lines of salesmen selling competing products and an unintended acknowledgment of Beeman's position.

While the size of Beeman's early orders only justified the production of regular models with special specifications, Robert was soon developing specifications and design ideas for new adult airguns that would be uniquely suited to the demanding American market. He was surprised to find that apparently all of the spring piston airguns previously on the market had been developed empirically. That is, the guns were designed and built with very limited theoretical considerations and then tested to determine their performance. Early in 1979, Beeman jumped forward by utilizing the field's first computer simulations. These simulations, varying one factor of the gun after another, and then in various permutations of each other, quickly did what it might have taken scores of experimental prototypes to accomplish. In effect, the Beemans could see, via these simulations, what various design permutations should cause in the way of performance. The result was the first imported airgun actually designed for the American adult market, performing at what was then an entirely new power level (up to 1000 FPS). Development of this gun included the production of the first American-styled adult air rifle stock. This was

[3]Elliott, Jock. 2005. A Perennial Favorite- The Beeman R1. The Accurate Rifle, Jan.pp.53-57.
[4]Gaylord, Tom. 1995. The Beeman R1. GAPP Inc. 174 pp.

Beeman P1 Prototypes I and II: When Beeman Precision Airguns was designing the Beeman P1 air pistols, the Weihrauch Factory in Mellrichstadt, Germany sent prototype I (upper item). This functioning prototype followed the Beeman specifications but not the styling. So the Beemans made this exact scale plaster model (Prototype II, lower item). Look carefully; it is an extremely fragile item, hand-carved from a block of Plaster of Paris and finished with black shoe polish. Only the grips and rear sight are real! The production Beeman P1 and later, the HW 45 (its overseas copy), followed this model exactly. Courtesy of Beeman Collection.

mechanism. Although the Beeman SS scopes were very well received for that purpose, they were also very successful on semi-automatic and full automatic assault rifles and sub-machine guns. When such guns were equipped with Beeman SS scopes, they could go from high firepower to almost sniper level accuracy just by switching the gun to semi-automatic. When the Beemans first produced these scopes, they didn't dream that they would be so popular with SWAT and anti-terrorist teams and military and police groups around the world!

Robert's extreme attention to detail extended to an unusually wide range of accessories which helped build the company's special market position. Most of these were his own design, or at least considerable improvement. Old time Beeman customers remember the special Beeman lubricants and gun care items, Pell-Seat, Pell-Size, Adjustable Muzzle Brake cocking aid, special cases and holsters, adjustable base aperture sights, scope stops, pellet pouches, "Professional" carved leather slings, targets, special cleaning rods, custom stocks and grips, and a wide range of promotional items, even including a musical teddy bear version of the company bear cub mascot, "Boswell."

The Beemans promoted their products not only by trade shows, shooting event displays, and hundreds of display ads in virtually all of America's sporting publications, but also in their own publications: mail and dealer counter versions of the *Beeman Shooter News, Beeman Dealer News, Beeman Jobber News, Dollar Notes to Beeman Reps*, scores of *Beeman Technical Bulletins*, owner and shop manuals, the world-famous Beeman *Used Gun Lists*, and the star item, the *Beeman Precision Airgun Guide*. These were produced by their own in-house ad agency, DavKan Associates. (A name derived from Robert's and Tosh's middle names: David and Kanzaki.) DavKan's fully professional staff, and their illustration and typesetting equipment, would have been the envy of many outside advertising agencies.

wouldn't accept, to other markets.) Again, it shortly became apparent that Beeman's sales volume and the special needs of this growing market justified the production of special Beeman pellet designs. Their first airgun pellet design, the world's first hollow point pellet, was the Beeman Silver Bear. While still selling well, the Silver Bear hollow point was increasingly upstaged by another Beeman development, a heavy, "big mouth" hollow point pellet amusingly trademarked the "Crow Magnum"!

Beeman also developed several scopes especially suited for adult airguns. Originally, gun makers thought of airgun scopes as cheap, small tube devices. Beeman moved way up to top grade one-inch tube scopes with reticles resistant to the two-way snap of spring-piston airguns, quick adjustment elevation and windage knobs, and introduced the concept of using objective focus rings, with settings as close as five meters (sixteen feet), on lower power scopes specifically built for their American airgun customers. These generally are credited with being the first true adult airgun scopes.

A rather surprising product story resulted from Beeman's development of their famous Short Scopes: the Beeman SS-1, SS-2 and SS-3. The short, incredibly precise optical column of these scopes had been computer-designed at great cost for another, unrelated optical purpose. Beeman had this optical arrangement built into a super tough scope form by one of Japan's leading optical companies. These scopes combined the concept of using lenses of camera quality, rather than binocular quality, in a short, rugged optical column. It was originally planned that these would be ideal for adult airguns, compact and proof against the unusual, sharp two-way snap of the spring piston

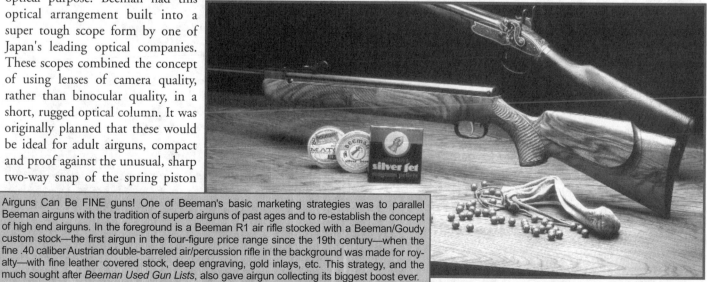

Airguns Can Be FINE guns! One of Beeman's basic marketing strategies was to parallel Beeman airguns with the tradition of superb airguns of past ages and to re-establish the concept of high end airguns. In the foreground is a Beeman R1 air rifle stocked with a Beeman/Goudy custom stock—the first airgun in the four-figure price range since the 19th century—when the fine .40 caliber Austrian double-barreled air/percussion rifle in the background was made for royalty—with fine leather covered stock, deep engraving, gold inlays, etc. This strategy, and the much sought after *Beeman Used Gun Lists*, also gave airgun collecting its biggest boost ever.

The Weihrauchs and Beemans meet in the Weihrauch home. Left to right: Egon Wilsker (president of Wischo Co.), Hans Hermann Weihrauch (director-to-be of Weihrauch), Christel Weihrauch (wife of Hans Sr. and co-director of Weihrauch), Robert Beeman (President of Beemans), Toshiko Beeman (VP and General Manager of Beemans), and the late Hans Weihrauch Sr. (then co-director of Weihrauch).

market until it had grown many fold and were content with a majority of the much greater total market—when they sold the company! The route of raising prices was completely unexpected by the DN folks, and one of their top men later quipped that it was "unfair"!

Robert's role in the establishment of airgun standards is a key part of the Beeman legacy. Early in the 1970s, the main American airgun makers formed the Non-Powder Gun Products Committee to work with ASTM and the Consumer Products Safety Commission to develop safety standards for airguns in America. This was an excellent move to pre-empt legislators and governmental clerks from establishing inappropriate standards. While the standards were to be voluntary, they would have the force of law because they would become industry and government approved guidelines for all airgun legislation and liability lawsuits. Robert was one of the first members and stayed almost two decades to become their vice president and longest term member. While he thoroughly approved of the group's basic objectives, he saw the potential for major problems if standards aimed at American-made, youth-oriented airguns conflicted with the needs and guns of adult airgunners. In addition to decades of helping the committee, Robert created a lasting benefit to the adult airgun market by creating special categories and exemptions for adult airguns, match and training airguns, custom made airguns, tranquilizer and scientific purpose airguns, paintball guns, etc. He literally left his marks by adding the word "death" to required warnings and by establishing international marks, to be stamped on the gun instead of English words, to indicate whether it was designed for pellets, darts, lead shot, and/or steel shot.

Robert Beeman has written and produced over 200 airgun publications, manuals, etc. It may well be that the depth of this coverage is unmatched throughout the world's gun market. The impact of the Beeman newsletters and other publications, reaching hundreds of thousands of the world's airgunners, was astonishingly impressive. Some market experts credit this writing output as being the key factor in developing the American adult airgun market from almost zero to its present position.

Sometimes progress came in a sudden unexpected jolt. At one of the big IWA gun trade shows in Nürnberg, Germany in the early 1980s, the Dynamit Nobel/Diana/RWS folks invited the Beemans into their booth's backroom, thanked them for developing the "impossible USA market" and announced that they would now "shoot Beeman out of the water" with prices which Beeman could not afford to meet. The Beemans were pretty worried when they returned home and wondered what to do. Robert felt that there was only one answer—and it was based on the fact that the guns which he had designed and Weihrauch was producing to their very tight design and spec controls really were better than the other airguns. So, instead of an answering volley in a futile price cutting war, they announced a significant increase in prices and launched a new quality awareness program—based on a "Tap the Cap" theme—referring to tapping the solid, beautifully-machined, steel rear receiver block of the Beeman rifles (see a Beeman R1) vs. the thin sheet metal receiver cap on the competitors' sporters. The Beeman sales soared and they kept the majority of the

Biographical Sketch of Robert and Toshiko Beeman

Robert and his wife, Toshiko, form a very close partnership, both from a personal and business standpoint. Many people are

Toshiko Beeman is honored by the Webley Company. The late Keith Faulkner, President of Webley and Scott, presents Mrs. Beeman, in Robert's office, with the last of a Webley & Scott .410 shotgun, made and decorated just for her. We later hired Keith away to become Vice President and Chief Engineer of Beeman Precision Airguns.

amazed to find a husband and wife who worked in close harmony in the same hard-driving business. Robert served as the President with the role of directing the business, writing copy for the Beeman catalog and a constant flow of technical bulletins and articles, plus directing marketing and financing, while Tosh served as Senior Vice President and General Manager, running the operation on a day-to-day basis. While Robert also directed research and development, Mrs. Beeman also was a key member of the Beeman overseas factory design teams which have been responsible for the development of so many advanced airgun products. Together they served as a very strong product development and negotiation team in their travels throughout the world. Robert's background in German, French, Spanish and Italian was helpful, and Tosh's fluency in Japanese was invaluable. Both are avid shooters and gun collectors, and their hands-on experience with both airguns and firearms in the shop and field has been crucial to the development of airguns and other gun products.

Robert and Tosh have enjoyed many hours together in other activities such as backpacking, fishing, photography, world travel, etc. One of their special shared joys is the Beeman vintage and antique airgun collection, the largest such collection in the world, covering thousands of airguns from all over the world from the early 1700s to the present time.

Robert and Tosh's interests and ability to work together also extended to some other large projects. Together, with their own hands, they built their own home in the beautiful wooded hills of Marin County, California, and then did much of the construction work when they moved the Beeman Precision Airgun business from their home to a commercial area near the shores of San Francisco Bay. After expanding into five adjacent warehouses

there, they realized they should have their own facility. Robert's building experience and study qualified him to pass the examination for a California General Builders Contracting License. So, in addition to running the rather large Beeman gun business, he was the general contractor for the construction of their new home on a ranch in the California wine country and the 25,000 square foot Beeman Building in Santa Rosa, California.

Well before the move to Santa Rosa, the Beemans hired Keith Faulkner, then President of the world famous, venerable gun firm of Webley & Scott in England, a mechanical engineer and expert in spring piston airguns, to be a Vice President of the Beeman Company. The combination of Dr. Beeman, with his scientific, airgun, and marketing background, and Keith Faulkner's engineering was very productive. However, Mr. Faulkner was to enjoy the beautiful view from his new office in Santa Rosa only for a short time. He passed away, in his 40s, due to an incredibly rare bone marrow disease in December of 1986. This stimulated Robert to begin serious plans for retirement.

Dr. and Mrs. Beeman developed very close relationships with the top staff and family owners of key European airgun and pellet factories and Japanese optic and pellet factories. Although these relationships grew from the amazement of these companies as to the growth and volume of Beeman sales, they became not only lasting friendships but smoothly working teams to mutually develop new products.

The Future of Adult Airgunning in the USA

Robert Beeman firmly believes that not only are adult airguns one of the few growing and healthy profit centers in the shooting market, but that airguns may well be the salvation of the shooting sports! Most potential and inactive shooters are now urban or suburban. Their opportunities for shooting firearms have been greatly curtailed due to urbanization, legislation, social changes, and fewer places to shoot lethal

Meeting in the Black Forest: "Feinwerkbau" is really Westinger and Altenburger, a very sophisticated arms maker in the Black Forest at the headwaters of the Neckar River in Germany. Here, in a historical meeting at the factory, are (left to right) the late Ernst Altenburger (co-founder of FWB), his wife Frau Altenburger, their son Jörg Altenburger (director/chief engineer of FWB), and Robert Beeman.

Robert and Toshiko Beeman relax on a favorite rock outcropping on their California ranch.

weapons. However, these very factors work to the advantage of airgunners; airguns may be shot in suburban, and even indoor, locations without heroic measures to contain bullets and with no air pollution problem. And, airguns continue to be far freer from oppressive legislation. One of the few ways remaining for persons to become introduced, or re-introduced, to the pleasure of shooting is via airguns. It has been shown again and again that such new, or renewed, interest in shooting leads to purchases, not only of airguns but to purchases and greater recreational use of firearms. Without an influx of new shooters into the market, ownership of sporting guns will dwindle and the Second Amendment eventually will become of academic interest only!

More and more gun and sporting goods dealers are seeing the "handwriting on the wall" concerning the future of firearm sales.

This future has already happened in Europe where most recreational shooting by adults is now done with airguns like Beeman's models. Thousands of dealers who would not have considered airguns, especially adult airguns, as part of their product mix just a few years ago now consider adult airguns an essential part of their inventory. Some of Beeman's best dealers report that they have made a major section of "adult airguns" in their stores, even going so far as to make these guns a feature area at the expense of their sluggishly selling long firearms or hunting clothing.

Robert Beeman feels that adult airguns are now in a "win-win" position. If the shooting sports increase, adult airgunning will increase as a now accepted part of those sports. If firearms are subject to greater restrictions of purchase and use, people will turn (as they did in Europe) to airgunning for the pleasures of shooting. He is emphatic that the long-term trend for the adult airgun market can only lead up for the very long foreseeable future, and that most gun dealers who survive the next decade will indeed develop adult airgun centers. Robert and Toshiko should be proud of their key role in the development of what is now a key part of the U.S. shooting market.

Post-script: The Beemans sold Beeman Precision Airguns to S/R Industries of Maryland on April 1, 1993. S/R moved the business, including many of the former employees, to Huntington Beach, California to be close to Marksman Products, another of their companies. Robert and Toshiko retired to their cattle ranch in California and have become so immersed in world travel, art, airgun research, over a thousand hours a year on the *Blue Book of Airguns*, and maintaining the world's largest airgun website (www.Beemans.net) that they wonder how they ever had time for running a business. As the Beemans entered their well-earned retirement, promoting the concept of adult airguns no longer seemed to be a matter of pushing that mythical big rock up the hill! ■

Additional information on the Beeman story and a wealth of airgun information may be found at www.beemans.net. (The Beemans, and this website, no longer have any connection with the new Beeman Precision Airgun Company.)

Hans Hermann Weihrauch and Robert Beeman hiking on the Beeman Ranch. Hans Hermann came to live in the Beeman's home and work in the Beeman Company to learn more about the American market—and to prepare for becoming the director of the Weihrauch Company in Germany. To this day, the Weihrauchs and Beemans consider each other almost as family.

A SHOT OF HUMOR

By Dr. Robert D. Beeman

Our adventures in the international airgun market over the decades were by no means all serious. There were many amazing and humorous moments. We would like to share a couple of these true stories below, and we hope that you will share our enjoyment of them.*

OKAY!

The Yewha airguns were an especially strange chapter in the history of Beeman Precision Airguns. In the early 1970s, when our business was still based in our home, we had a fellow, who claimed to be a representative of the Unification Church (AKA "Moonies" - after their leader, the Rev. Moon, of Korea), come to our home and show us the Yewha BBB air rifle (which I later renamed as the "Dynamite" in such places as our *Gun Digest* copy) and give us an interesting set of sample Yewha air rifles. (Dynamite, Volcanic, two variations of a double-action revolving rifle, an FWB 300 copy, and a bolt action match rifle with a spitting image FWB match sight.) All these designs were multi-stroke pump pneumatics featuring a pump-rod-at-the-muzzle action—the better ones had special locking foot pedals. He explained that the BBB (Dynamite) was a .25 caliber air shotgun/rifle that was very popular in Korea where civilians are forbidden to have firearms. He showed us color photos of obscenely huge piles of Chinese ringnecked pheasants killed by Korean shooting club members with this model and said that it also could be used with a .25 caliber lead ball to kill deer. We agreed to buy fifty of the Dynamites at $35 each, complete with Yewha-marked case, ammo belt, and packages of shot cases and wads. He commented that he had three hundred more of the Dynamites in a local warehouse, but as our operation was still very small at that stage, we felt well supplied with fifty. As a parting joke, I said, "well, if you ever want to sell the rest of your guns for $10 each, let us know!" At that time, I didn't know about the vast differences that can exist between the Oriental and Occidental perceptions of humor.

About eight months later, at night in a driving rainstorm, we answered our doorbell to find a different, completely soaked, young Korean man, standing humbly on our doormat—looking for all the world like a drowned rat. We stared at him, wondering who and what he was—and he said "OKAY." We, of course, wanted to know "okay, what?" After a bit of language barrier delay, we learned that he had the three hundred remaining Yewha airguns in a truck outside and wanted the "promised" $10 cash for each of them right now! Needless to say, we did some hard and fast running around to come up with $3000 cash! After the cash transfer, more disciples promptly unloaded all of the hardwood cases of the

rifles into our living room and then disappeared into the night!

We, of course, had some super sales of Yewhas in our newsletters for awhile, but we never did have the chance to buy inventory of the other Yewha rifle models. They did not even bill us for the samples nor ask us for their return!

The final strange twist came about a year later. A reporter from the *San Francisco Chronicle* appeared at our doorstep and wanted to know if we had anything to say before his newspaper exposed us as a front for Reverend Moon's Unification Church! We were stunned and invited him in to tell us what the hell he was talking about! He claimed that his sister had been taken in and "brainwashed" by that church and that he was trying to break this "cult's" local organization and to "free" his sister. He said that he knew that we were members of this evil conspiracy because we were selling airguns made by the church and that he had discovered copies of our catalogs on the floor of a San Francisco printing press which had just been raided for using "slave labor" from the church. Seems that, quite unknown to us, our catalog printer had sub-contracted our catalog printing job out to an underground printer with incredibly low rates—reportedly using unpaid subjects of the church as labor. We wouldn't let the reporter out of our house until we convinced him that these were coincidences that did not prove that we had anything to do with the weird doings of any cult!

A SALESMAN'S ULTIMATE NIGHTMARE

Early in the 1980s, noticing that an adult airgun market, based largely on European spring piston airguns, finally was beginning to be important in the USA, some Chinese factories developed the idea of selling airguns to that potentially huge market. After some asking around, their sales leaders were told that Beeman Precision Airguns was the largest American importer of airguns. So, they decided to send a representative to see us, hopefully to come back with a large order.

Indirectly preparing for this moment, the selected industry representative almost certainly had been studying English and overseas business procedures for many years. Now that he had been anointed with this special responsibility, he surely went into some weeks of intense preparation—honing his English skills and practicing his sales presentation over and over. This was to be his big moment and perhaps a turning point for his industry.

At the arranged time, he arrived at my office with a sample of

Yewha B3 Dynamite

an underlever, spring piston air rifle, looking as calm as he possibly could—but obviously under great pressure from within. Joining me for the evaluation of the airgun was our new Vice President, the now late Keith Faulkner. We had just hired Keith away from his former position as President of Webley and Scott Guns in England. Keith was an engineer by training and experience, and a very critical observer, even a bit cynical, by nature.

The Chinese sales representative showed us his gun. We were not very enthusiastic—its tolerances and detailing seemed far below the level of our German and English imports. Still, the representative, surely more than a bit concerned by our cool reaction, continued his demonstration. He assured us that we could import such rifles for about seven dollars each. We knew that a few minor importers were selling such guns in the USA for about $39.95— less dollars per gun than we were used to, but representing a profit percentage that was worlds above our other imports. However, we had dedicated ourselves to the concept that the Beeman label would represent "Quality First."

The idea was presented that perhaps we could sell such airguns under another name, just as Sears sells their best tools under the Craftsman name, but uses the Dunlap brand for those customers who are more concerned with price. So, the sales presentation continued, but with more perspiration showing on the visitor's forehead.

We asked if we could specify changes in design and features. No problem, he eagerly replied. We asked what minimum order would be required to make the stocks to our design instead of the rather crude pattern of this specimen. We knew that gearing up stock-making machinery usually required a minimum run of one thousand to ten thousand stocks. He really surprised us by saying that the minimum order would be one. He explained that his factory did not yet have automatic stock shaping machines—each stock was handmade—but this was cheaper than machine made because even the shop foreman earned less than $35 per month! So, if we wanted, every stock could be different!

Then Keith began to look at technical details. He wanted to know if the rifles had an "anti-beartrap" mechanism—a system which would prevent the cocking arm from flying up and injuring the gun, and possibly the shooter, if the trigger were accidentally released when the lever was down. He asked the representative if he understood what an anti-beartrap mechanism was. Now, quite animated, the agent assured us in rising volume and increasingly accented English: "Oh, yes, yes, I understand; we have very fine anti-beartrap mechanism." The strain on his English ability was beginning to show and he clearly was ever more tense. He was reaching hard to find the right English words and sentence structures to express himself.

Keith, ever the doubting engineer, wanted a demonstration of the anti-beartrap mechanism. So he asked the representative to cock the gun, but to leave the lever hanging down after the piston had fully compressed the mainspring and engaged the sear. The agent quickly cocked the gun and he stood there holding the rifle with its cocking lever loosely hanging down. Keith asked him to now pull the trigger to show us that the lever would not slam upward. Slowly, with his eyes very, very wide, the sole representative of his industry, many thousands of miles from home, the fellow squeezed the trigger. Suddenly, there was a loud metallic sound. The lever flew up, snapped off, arched across the room and clattered to the floor, and the sudden impact of the bear trap action caused the stock to split into two pieces in the representative's hands.

He looked down at the lever on the floor near the president's desk and the pieces of the stock in his hands and very calmly uttered a perfect English language response:

"Oh, shit!"

OKAY, WE CAN TAKE A HINT!

Mrs. Beeman and I have a special feeling for the American-made HyScore Air Pistols, not just because of the wonderful design (can you believe that "bumper car" repeating mechanism?) but because of our special relationship with the late Steve Laszlo (founder and president of HyScore). For some reason, he gravitated to us and we became fine friends. The standing joke every time that we would meet would be him asking us "Well, do you want to buy all the HyScore pistol machinery today?" I'd always say: "When you add a politically correct safety to the design and cut the price 90%." (After all the good reamers, etc. were cherry-picked over and removed, the "interesting" Richard Marriott-Smith of England purchased the whole pile for next to nothing and proceeded to put out the ill-fated British HyScore pistol—still without a safety and, almost as a bid to kill potential sales to the USA, with a silencer!). As noted in the HyScore introduction in *Blue Book of Airguns*, Steve sent us the NIB specimens of the delightful Acvoke and Abas Major air pistols that his brother Andrew Lawrence (nee Laszlo) had used, but never acknowledged, in designing the concentric piston HyScore air pistols. He also sent us a huge box of "junk" that they had cleaned out of the "loft"—just a wonderful array of well preserved specimens of all the prototypes of the HyScore pistols, as well as prototypes of air pistols which they had never put into production—a compact pneumatic, a never produced, self-scoring metal target, etc. Later in 1980, Mrs. Beeman and I had the last dinner anyone ever had with Steve and his really delightful, very intelligent wife (staff member at NY Metropolitan Museum of Art) in San Francisco. They were on the way to Hawaii for a vacation and he died of a heart attack there. We unknowingly called his New York office to find out when he was supposed to be back, and asked if he was still in Hawaii. The office staff of one said "Well, I guess that you could say that!" but she would say nothing more. We learned of his death through friends and, after a couple of months to allow things to settle down, we called and asked to pay up our account (we owed in the low four figures). We were referred to his lawyer who told us, in no uncertain terms, that the Laszlo children wanted no contact with his old "gun trade" and that they wanted "our kind" to please go away and not bother them again! He said that as far as they were concerned, the accounts no longer existed. Okay, we can take a hint. ■

*Please be assured that we relate these reports in a positive spirit and that we do not intend to nor desire to offend anyone by them.

AIRFORCE AIRGUNS
THIS TEXAS COMPANY BUILDS THE AMERICAN DREAM

by Tom Gaylord, Technical Director of AirForce Airguns

The Condor joined the Talon and Talon SS as the latest release from AirForce in 2004. It is the world's most powerful smallbore air rifle, producing the same power as a .22 short rimfire cartridge—yet, with all that power. It retains the tack-driving accuracy of the other AirForce rifles.

Talons, Talon SSs and Condors ready to ship. All models and calibers are stocked for U.S. sales. Other markets place larger orders that are typically assembled to specification as they arrive.

Ask any American about the great icons of youth, and the Daisy BB gun will be among those things most mentioned. BB guns are one of this nation's unique gifts to the world. However, to obtain true adult airguns, you've had to look to England and Germany. That came to an end in 1997, when the company that was to become AirForce first offered its own version of a modern black air rifle to the world. Since then, sales of American-made precision precharged air rifles have caught up to and, in many cases, exceeded, those of the famous old European makers.

A rifle from AirForce is different in many ways from conventional sporting precharged airguns, and it is these unique characteristics that have vaulted the brand to the top of its field. Let's look at some of the differences and, along with them, the company that makes these unique rifles.

DESIGNED FOR MANUFACTURE

Foremost among the design features is that all AirForce airguns are designed to be manufactured. That may sound obvious, but it's actually the biggest thing setting these airguns apart from all others.

Most air rifles are designed first, produced as prototypes for testing, and then finally redesigned for production. They follow the production model invented by Samuel Colt in the 1850s. That model was a marvel for its time, as it defined the rest of the production process for most operations. It lasted well into World War II and has become embedded in the mind of the public. Think of any documentary you've seen of high-rate production, and it comes into focus. Envision rows of machines doing specific jobs that come together as a product at the end and you'll have the right picture.

Henry Ford perfected this model in 1908 and gave us the modern production facility of the early twentieth century. He actually taught the world how to efficiently produce consumer goods. In his plant, the work moved from one machine to another, and each station performed only one operation. The product grew by accretion.

Ford's method lasted for almost a full century, but has now been replaced by the machines, processes, and materials of modern technol-

ogy. The push to get human labor out of the production equation that panicked the labor unions in the 1960s has become a blessing for mankind.

Because the Ford model was so well understood and because machine tools were built to support it, a lot of manufacturing is still done the old way—especially in smaller industries such as those that make adult airguns. Go into any British airgun production facility today and you'll find modern CNC machines being employed by the management styles of Ford's Rouge River plant. One British maker of high-end adult air rifles actually brags that each rifle they produce has almost four hours of human labor invested in it. No wonder most of their models cost over a thousand dollars!

In sharp contrast, AirForce decided to make their rifles a new way. Their airguns are designed to support the most efficient and modern manufacturing methods. If a machine can do the job, the gun is designed to accommodate it. The sleek "black rifle" look that attracts so much attention is actually the foundation of a gun designed to be made by machines to the greatest extent possible. Lots of turned parts nestle concentrically inside a powerplant unlike anything on the mar-

A pair of Bridgeport mills support manufacturing and R&D. One has been upgraded with a CNC controller. A wire EDM machine works around the clock to keep up with precision trigger and safety parts.

Guns are assembled in batches of 100, 200, and 300. Custom racks roll batches to where the work is done and out to packing when everything is complete.

A typical five-shot group from a .22 Talon SS shot at 25 yards. Usually, the tester will shoot off-center to preserve the aim point, but this time he blew the X-ring away on the first shot. At the new AirForce production facility there will be room for a 100-yard range.

ket. The frame is an extrusion of aircraft aluminum that contains these parts in their proper relationship and tolerances, along with an ingenious trigger and automatic safety mechanism.

Look at any European trigger, and you'll see a boxy arrangement of pins, springs, and levers that resembles a conventional firearms unit. In sharp contrast, the AirForce trigger is a tandem arrangement of parts, some of which actually relocate themselves during cocking. It's so unlike any conventional design that it requires study and often explanation before it can be understood—even by gunsmiths!

When you buy a European precharged airgun, you get just one gun. Pick your caliber and features carefully, because they are locked into the product. An AirForce air rifle lets you change the caliber or barrel length in five minutes, using just two Allen wrenches. No other adult air rifle has this capability and none of them come with a video. The skimpy pamphlet that comes with most British adult air rifles assumes you understand precharged airguns quite well to begin with. The Germans have much better manuals, but no company other than AirForce gives you a video.

ACCURACY

"Only accurate rifles are interesting," states the famous quote from Townsend Whelen. Adult air rifles, especially precharged models, are all very accurate. AirForce guns have barrels made by Lothar Walther, so they fit right in with the other brands and are capable of shooting a one-inch five-shot group at fifty yards. This kind of accuracy assumes a perfect day and a good shooter shooting off a rigid benchrest. But under ideal conditions, even better groups have been recorded.

The sniper school of the 82nd Airborn Division has grouped as small as 0.54 inches at fifty yards with the Talon SS shooting off a bipod. Instructors at the U.S. Army Sniper School at Fort Benning have used the Talon SS for unofficial marksmanship training. The U.S. Military Academy at West Point incorporates several score of Talons in a formal marksmanship program. But that's just the tip of the iceberg.

The U.S. Department of Agriculture has embraced the Talon and Talon SS wholeheartedly for pest elimination all over the United States. There is a story of several thousand pigeons being taken by just one shooter in a short time frame. It puts us in mind of the legendary buffalo stands that decimated the herds of the 1870s, though we are hardly in the same jeopardy with the "flying rats."

Commercial pest control companies have been just as quick to recognize the benefits of a quiet air rifle with adjustable power for eliminating birds in shopping malls and huge warehouse-type discount stores. When the target is a sparrow perched next to a light fixture on the ceiling, it helps if the rifle has controlled power to kill the bird but not shoot through the roof or the fixtures. And, the quiet report of the SS model is favored for this covert indoor work that's typically done at 3:00 a.m.

At the other end of the scale, raccoons, woodchucks, and other medium-sized mammals are being taken by exterminators with the powerful new Condor. Adjustable power from 19 to 60+ foot-pounds

All AirForce airgun models are based on an aircraft aluminum frame that's machined from an extrusion. Current CNC machines can handle only one frame-sized piece of extrusion at a time, but the CNC lathe recently added has a bar feeder altered to handle long extrusions for continuous operation. The extrusion goes in one end and a finished frame, like the one shown here, rolls out the other side. After machining, the frame is deburred, tumbled, bead-blasted, hard-anodized and lasered with graphics before being assembled into a complete gun.

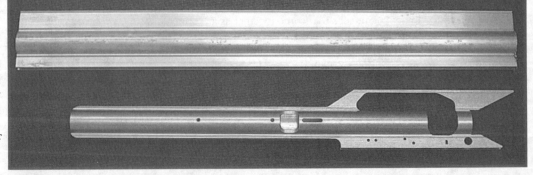

AirForce's ultramodern CNC lathe can perform all operations without human intervention. Custom tooling was created to handle the frame with precision at all times. A bar feeder allows continuous operation of this machine-intensive job.

and the same fine accuracy as the Talon and Talon SS make the Condor the perfect hunting air rifle. No other smallbore air rifle in the world can match its 20+ shots at greater than 50 foot-pounds on a single charge of air.

The best feature of the AirForce guns is the interchangeable barrel option. A Talon SS owner can shoot quietly in a suburban setting with plenty of power and accuracy for squirrels at forty yards, then switch to a 24-inch barrel that almost doubles the gun's power. Accuracy remains the same for all barrels and calibers, but the longer barrels really extract all the power that compressed air has to offer.

MANUFACTURING AND SALES

Another trend in manufacturing today is outsourcing—getting others to make parts for you. AirForce turns this around using the most modern production machinery to bring the bulk of its manufacture under its own roof. That sounds a lot like the Ford model, except for one thing—the capability of modern computer-controlled production machines. People are not needed to tend the modern production machines, if the product is planned right. Fully automated CNC and EDM machines quietly churn out perfectly dimensioned parts that require a minimum of finishing before assembly, thus keeping a control on costs. Because these machines are also super-accurate, they keep the quality of the end product as high as possible at the same time. The goal is to require as little hand-fitting as possible.

GROWING THEIR FUTURE

Sales have pushed the company out of leased industrial space into a new building of their own construction. The floor plan was laid out to support the entire manufacturing operation, from the intake of raw materials to the shipment of guns and accessories to distributors and dealers. The building is also modular to support future expansion plans both upward and out.

On the drawing board are several accessories plus entirely new guns that will make even greater use of the new production machinery and improved workflow. The black rifle styling that now extends to a complete line of accessories, training literature, promotional pieces and sales support material will continue to define AirForce products for the foreseeable future.

Dealers are impressed that they get a fully integrated product line similar to what the large firearms manufacturers offer, instead of the

piecemeal models and skimpy support so common in the adult airgun community. With a product as technical as a precharged air rifle, you need strong dealer support, training materials, and a technical hotline to back it all up. The European manufacturers simply cannot compete on that level in this country.

The company also supports dealers by extensive advertising, the appearance of editorial pieces in key magazines, and sales support literature like catalogs. The marketing program at AirForce goes well beyond just a presence on the Internet, though they have recently revised their website with a new one that's matched to the rest of their marketing materials.

WHAT DOES IT ALL MEAN?

Despite their integrated manufacturing/marketing approach and the use of modern production technology, AirForce does not have the airgun world in the palm of its hand. For starters, the radical styling of their guns turns off those who want more traditional-looking airguns. Thus, a large segment of the adult market goes unpenetrated. If the company were to make a wood-and-steel gun, however, you can be certain that it would be designed for production first, much the same as every Ruger.

The training materials they produce have caused the spread of adult air rifles to conventional gun stores, broadening their sales potential enormously. This will benefit other brands, as gun dealers become increasingly comfortable with the technology of precharged airguns in general. It should also increase public demand for more information when the guns are used by those without a high level of technical expertise. Gun publications may find more demand for airgun articles and more airgun dealers who are willing to advertise.

The cost of a precision adult air rifle will remain in the affordable column despite what happens to the Euro/dollar relationship. As long as Lothar Walther barrels remain affordable, AirForce will continue to use them to achieve the same fine accuracy as rifles costing two and three times as much. That will keep the door open for the average shooter who wants to investigate the fascinating world of precision airgunning.

So this upstart company that builds non-traditional airguns may turn out to have a major impact on the future of the hobby, both at home and abroad. Love 'em or hate 'em—it's no longer possible to ignore the black air rifles from Texas! ∎

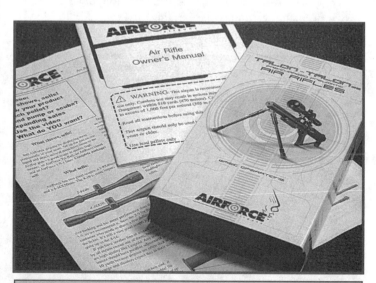

AirForce sends not only a sixteen-page owner's manual but also a free one-hour VHS video of instruction with every new gun. For their dealers there are several publications tailored to support retail sales and after-sales service. They have set the standard for adult airgun publications.

THE LEWIS AND CLARK AIR RIFLE

A PRELIMINARY NOTE ON NEW EVIDENCE

by Dr. Robert D. Beeman

The search for the air rifle carried on the Lewis and Clark Expedition, during the years 1803 to 1806, has taken an amazing turn. This study has now reached a point where solid new information impacts the considerations of the Lewis Air Rifle like solid new information on "weapons of mass destruction" in Iraq would impact considerations of the present war in Iraq. Detailed new studies of an actual Girandoni military repeating air rifle and continuing study, both here and overseas, of the Girandoni system, and his-

Left to right: two reporters, R. Beeman, Rick Keller, and Ernie Cowan.

torical documents, apparently have removed all of the objections, such as those presented in the Fourth Edition of the *Blue Book of Airguns*, to such a rifle being carried by Captain Meriwether Lewis on the U.S. Army Corps of Discovery expedition to the Pacific Northwest. This new information has led the author, and several arms curators and Lewis and Clark experts, to conclude that we not only have learned much new information about the Girandoni airguns, but that we evidently have indeed located the actual air rifle carried by Meriwether Lewis: a 22 shot, .463 (11.75 mm) caliber, Girandoni repeating air rifle.

Details of this new study are presented on the website www.Beemans.net under the heading of Lewis Air Rifle - New Evidence. (Updates will be made as appropriate - this is

Col. Craig C. Madden, Deputy Commandant of the US Army War College (left), ordered the Lewis airgun program. Also pictured is Col. Robert Dalessandro, Director of the US Army Heritage and Education Center.

not a final presentation.) The U.S. Army War College, at Carlisle, Pennsylvania, requested the loan of this gun until at least November 15, 2005. Readers are encouraged to contact the War College as to information on the times that it will be on public view. Additional material is being prepared for publication in appropriate publications, such as *We Proceeded On* (the journal of the Lewis and Clark Trail Heritage Society), the Sixth Edition of the *Blue Book of Airguns*, *American Rifleman*, *Addictive Airgunning*, etc. Notice of these publications will be made in the "What's New" section of the www.Beemans.net website.

The Lewis and Clark expedition ranks as one of the most significant events and turning points in American history. If this expedition had not successfully occurred, just when it did,

Chris Semancik (Arms and Ordnance Curator, War College) with the Girandoni copy.

the United States of America might not now have the incredible wealth and power which was added to the new nation by the development of the unknown areas of the Louisiana Purchase, the addition of the Western states, the control of our western areas and coast, and even the completion of Columbus' dream of a Western access to the Orient. Lewis' airgun may have had a pivotal role in this matter.

General Hal Nelson, retired Director of the Center of Military History, fires the Girandoni.

Rick Keller with Model 1800/1803 (a museum copy of one of the 15 flintlocks made for Lewis) standing in for Bill Clark.

Ernie Cowan, rest arms, maker of the museum copy Girandoni, standing in for Meriwether Lewis.

John Giblin, Chief Curator of War College, with the Girandoni copy.

DEFENDING **YOUR** SECOND AMENDMENT RIGHT TO OWN GUNS, HUNT, SHOOT, PROTECT YOURSELF AND SO MUCH MORE...

For nearly 130 years the National Rifle Association has been the leader in defending our Second Amendment right to keep and bear arms as well as protecting our hunting rights and traditions. We're fighting the gun banners and animal rights fanatics on all fronts. By joining the NRA, or renewing your existing membership, you will help to keep our unique American traditions alive.

When you join NRA you will receive these great benefits:

- NRA Black and Gold Shooters Cap
- A no-annual-fee NRA Visa card (for qualified individuals)
- Your choice of NRA monthly publications, *America's 1st Freedom, American Hunter* or *American Rifleman*

- $10,000 Personal Accident Insurance
- $1,000 in ArmsCare Firearm Insurance
- Hotel, Car Rental and Interstate Moving Discounts
- Discounts at local Gun Stores and other Retail Outlets

And much, much, more...

- -

NATIONAL RIFLE ASSOCIATION

☐ 1 Year Regular.........$35 ☐ 3 Year Regular.........$85

☐ 5 Year Regular.........$125 Date_____

NRA Recruiter #X012415

If renewal, give ID# ☐☐☐☐☐☐☐☐

Payment Information:

Mr./Mrs./Ms._____

☐ Check/Money Order

Street:_____ Apt.#:_____

Charge to: ☐ MC ☐ VISA ☐ Amex

City:_____ State:_____ Zip_____

☐ Discover Expiration Date ☐☐☐☐

Daytime Phone: (____)_____

Credit Card#

Choose ONE Magazine: ☐ America's 1st Freedom

☐☐☐☐☐☐☐☐☐☐☐☐☐☐☐☐

☐ American Rifleman ☐ American Hunter

Member Signature_____

Contributions gifts or membership dues made or paid to the National Rifle Association of America are not refundable or transferable and are not deductible as charitable contributions for Federal Income Tax purposes.
Mail with payment to: NRA, 11250 Waples Mill Rd., Fairfax, VA 22030

THE NRA FOUNDATION AIR GUN ENDOWMENT

An Enduring Legacy

The National Rifle Association of America has long recognized the importance of air gun sports in America. Through safety training, marksmanship development, and competitive opportunities the NRA reaches thousands of youths and adults with air gun shooting programs.

In an effort to ensure these programs continue well into the future, The NRA Foundation has established the *Air Gun Endowment*, a permanent fund that will provide funding support in perpetuity. The Air Gun Endowment is the cornerstone of NRA's commitment to the future of air gun sports. A portion of the interest generated by the fund will be used for qualified air gun programs with the balance reinvested to provide an ongoing source of income for air gun programs for generations to come.

The NRA Foundation's Air Gun Endowment will be used to support air gun programs nationwide, such as firearm safety training and program development for shooting sports clubs, schools, and youth-serving organizations like the Boy Scouts of America and 4-H.

You can provide an enduring legacy for air gun sports by contributing to The NRA Foundation's Air Gun Endowment. Donations made to this endowment are tax-deductible to the fullest extent of the law.

WHAT IS AN AIRGUN?

Where Should the Line Be?

by Dr. Robert D. Beeman

Isn't an airgun simply a gun that fires a projectile by means of air? Shall we draw some lines about what should be included in the *Blue Book of Airguns*? When several of us in the airgun industry tried to produce voluntary standards for the industry we immediately realized that we had to stretch and include CO_2 gas, Freon, etc.—even spring power. We finally described our subject as "non-powder guns" as contrasted to "powder guns." So, strictly speaking we are talking about "non-powder guns," but the common, albeit inexact, term will always be "airgun."

Like so many lines, the lines around collectible "airguns" can be fuzzy. I think that the *Blue Book of Airguns* basically should be restricted to airguns which fire penetrating projectiles for hunting or target use, and not include paint markers or firearm look-alikes that shoot toy plastic balls—but this must not be a sharp line. Most airgun collectors would include those historical airguns which gave rise to the main paintball business or are paintball versions of typical airguns, like the Crosman 3357 revolvers or the simple Benjamin paintball guns. And we proudly and delightfully include the Nelson paintball markers, produced by Daisy and Crosman, which gave rise to the whole paintball gun market. Sophisticated paintball and firearm-replica AirSoft guns now form huge areas of their own, and should be covered in special guides.

Surely limited coverage should be given to catapult guns which use a spring or band to drive the projectile. However, too tight a line would exclude the Daisy 179 Peacemaker, the Bullseye/Sharpshooter parlor pistols, and the Johnson indoor target rifle—long-time favorites at airgun shows. And this would even exclude the rare Lightning—the basic model of the antique Quackenbush line—for which keen airgun collectors will pay $4,000 and more!

Certain guns probably should be included. There is no other good place to put them and many actually are variations of "regular" airguns. These would include conduit guns (firing a CO_2 cylinder as the projectile?!), some tranquilizer guns, military trainers, water squirters of the airgun kind (Daisy DeMoulin Initiation Series and Radcliffe—among the most interesting of all airguns!), airguns firing actual arrows, etc. Most of these "odd fellows" are listed in other airgun guides, regularly sold at airgun shows, and have been reviewed as airguns by top airgun writers. Others should be included just because they are fun, and that is what airgunning is all about. An outstanding example is the Shin Sung "Celebration"—a confetti-blasting airgun, an anomaly in the line of a major airgun maker, which looks for all the world like a fine brass trumpet—and is worth ten century notes! A few gas/air spearguns, especially ones in the main lines of airgun makers, also add spice.

Common sense would guide us to excluding true toys which fire suction cup darts, ping pong balls, etc and "spud guns"—they will fit nicely into toy guides. Tradition and practical matters would exclude super specialized airguns which fire pigeons against airplane test windows, drive DNA particles into research trees, etc.

Tranquilizer guns are another gray area. Again, I think that we certainly should include those that are derived from "regular" airguns and must include those that live multiple lives, like the LD "Rancher" rifle, a delightful design that fires pellets, arrows, frog and fish spears, and tranquilizer darts.

Our "odd fellows" don't belong in a firearm guide or a toy guide. They do give flavor and seasoning to our mixture; we must not throw them out into nothingness and invite generations of collectors to badger us include them! Some of them are among the most prized holdings of many airgun collectors (Daisy water squirters, military trainers, first Nelson paintball guns, QB Lightning, Airrow guns, etc.). Let's ride with the current norm, an interesting mix. It is so easy and so tempting to be rigid and make up rules. We really should list and value those early, historically valuable items that circulate in the airgun shows, ads, and web auctions. To not list values of the less regular airguns, especially the older ones, some very interesting and very desirable, is really to condemn them to not having value! We should go with the tradition that has been selling these items as airguns; in most cases they are gaining value faster than more conventional models—simply because they are more interesting and increasingly hard to find!

Tradition is more important than pigeonholes. Like art, music, or even pornography, we cannot clearly define the lines and, in any case, there can never be agreement as to what should be in and what should be out! Sure, there should be lines, but they must be "warm, fuzzy lines." ∎

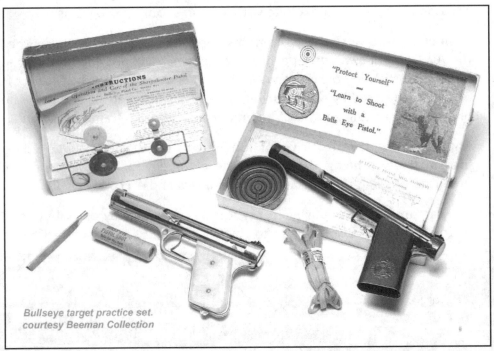

Bullseye target practice set. courtesy Beeman Collection

ANATOMY OF AN AIRGUN

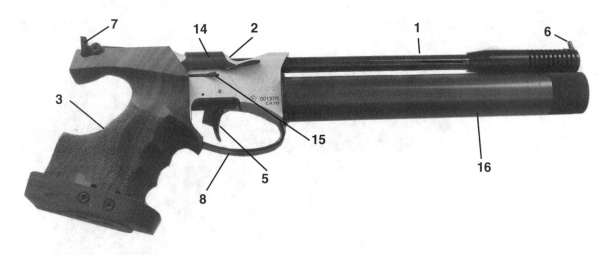

CO₂ & PCP

1. Barrel	7. Adjustable Rear Sight	13. CO₂ Cylinder Retaining Screw
2. Breech Area	8. Trigger Guard	14. Bolt Control Lever
3. Grip	9. Barrel Housing	15. Firing Pin Stop Lever
4. Safety	10. Hammer	16. Compressed Air Cylinder
5. Trigger	11. Cylinder	
6. Front Sight	12. Cylinder Catch	

ANATOMY OF AN AIRGUN

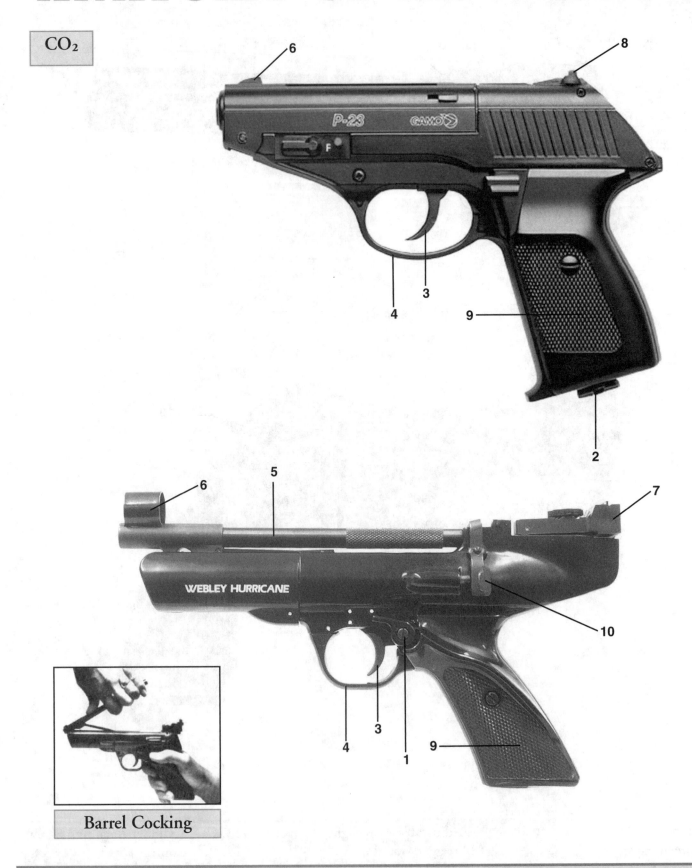

CO₂

P-23 GAMO

WEBLEY HURRICANE

Barrel Cocking

1. Safety
2. CO₂ Cylinder Retaining Screw
3. Trigger
4. Trigger Guard
5. Barrel
6. Front Sight
7. Adjustable Rear Sight
8. Rear Sight
9. Grip
10. Barrel Release Thumb Latch

ANATOMY OF AN AIRGUN

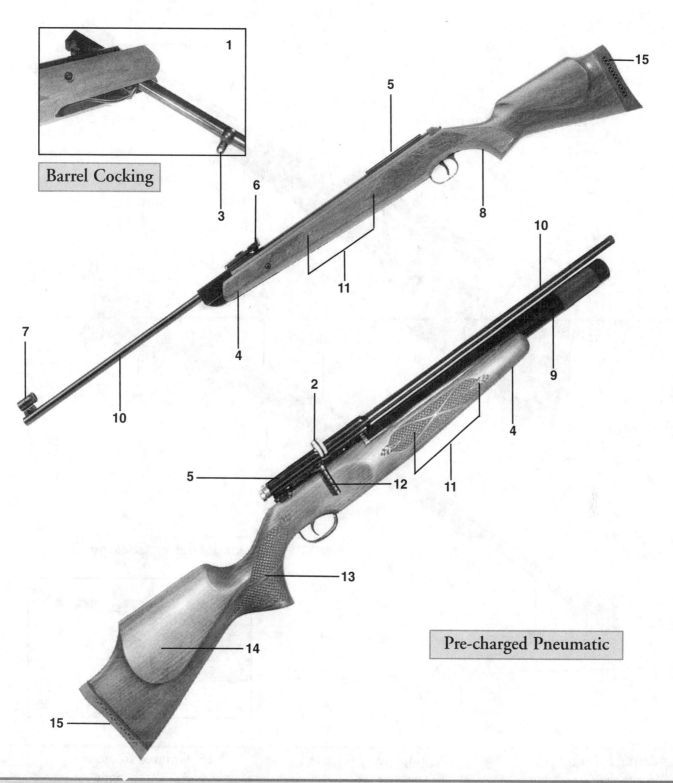

Barrel Cocking

Pre-charged Pneumatic

1. Barrel Cocking (barrel is pulled downward)
2. Rotary Mag
3. Sling Swivel Studs
4. Forend
5. Grooved Receiver
6. Adjustable Rear Sight
7. Globe Front Sight
8. Semi-Pistol Grip
9. Tube Air Reservoirs
10. Barrel
11. Checkered Forearm
12. Bolt Handle
13. Full Pistol Grip
14. Monti Carlo Check Piece
15. Ventilated Recoil Pad

ANATOMY OF AN AIRGUN

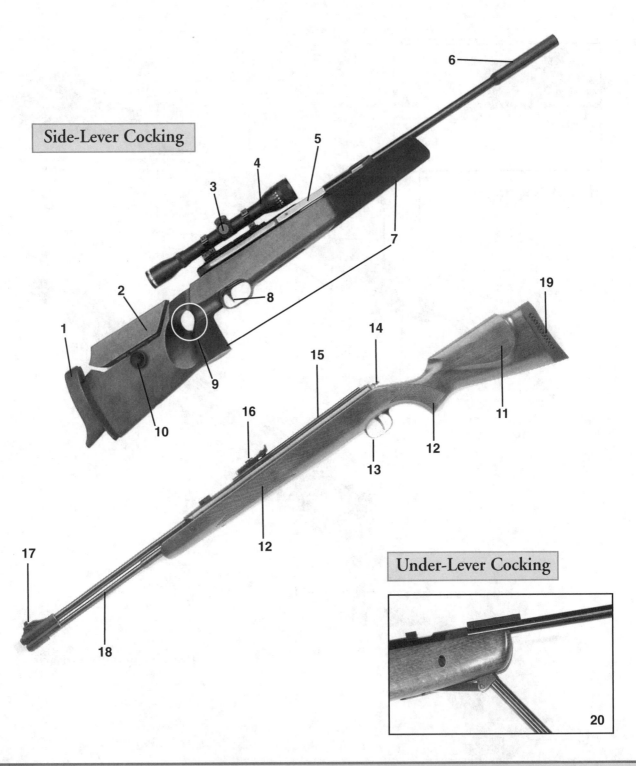

Side-Lever Cocking

Under-Lever Cocking

1. Adjustable Buttplate
2. Adjustable Cheekpiece
3. Vertical/Horizontal Scope Adjustments
4. Scope
5. Side-Lever For Cocking (lever is pulled out to the side)
6. Muzzle Weight
7. Stippling
8. Trigger
9. Thumbhole Stock Design
10. Knob for Adjusting Cheekpiece
11. Monte Carlo Cheekpiece
12. Stock Checkering
13. Trigger Guard
14. Safety
15. Grooved Receiver
16. Adj. Rear Sight
17. Front Sight
18. Under-Lever (for cocking)
19. Vent. Recoil Pad.
20. Under-Lever Cocking (under-lever pivots downward)

GLOSSARY

ACTION
The working heart of an airgun; generally all of the working parts other than the stock, barrel, and sights (may or may not include the air compression or gas/air storage system).

AIRGUN
A gun that utilizes compressed air or gas to launch the projectile.

APERTURE SIGHT
A rear sight assembly consisting of a hole or aperture located in an adjustable rear sight through which the front sight and target are aligned.

BB
"Air Rifle Shot" balls of lead or steel, which are used as projectiles in airguns. Restricted to 0.173 in. to 0.180 in. diameter.

BACK STRAP
The part of the revolver or pistol frame which is exposed at the rear of the grip.

BARREL
The steel tube which a projectile travels through.

BARREL BAND
A metal band, either fixed or adjustable, around the forend of a gun that holds the barrel to the stock.

BARREL COCKING
Also known as "break barrel." The action of pivoting the barrel downward or upward compresses the mainspring of a spring-piston action into firing position.

BARREL SHROUD
An outer metal tube that encloses the true barrel within it. Often used to conceal and protect the tiny tube that is the real barrel in BB guns—the real barrel in such guns may be more correctly known as the "shot tube." The barrel shroud is sometimes incorrectly referred to as the barrel.

BEAVERTAIL FOREND
A wider than average forend.

BLUING
The chemical process of artificial oxidation (rusting) applied to gun parts so that the metal attains a dark blue or nearly black appearance.

BORE
Internal dimensions of a barrel (smooth or rifled) which can be measured using the metric system (ie. millimeters), English system (i.e. inches), or by the gauge system (see gauge). On a rifled barrel, the bore is measured across the lands. Also, the traditional English term is used when referring to the diameter of a shotgun muzzle ("gauge" in U.S. measure).

BOTTLE-FED
A pre-charged pneumatic airgun with a removable gas/air tank.

BREAK-OPEN
A type of gun action which is cocked by "breaking open" the gun in the mid-line, generally just about over the trigger. In break-open BB guns, this causes internal rods to be pulled back and cock the piston.

BREECH
The opening to the rear chamber portion of the barrel.

BREECH SEAL
A seal which is designed to prevent propulsive gases from leaking out from behind the projectile. Usually an o-ring, circle of leather, or synthetic material. (Called a "barrel washer" in England.)

BULK FILL
CO_2 guns filled from large tanks.

BULL BARREL
A heavier than normal barrel with little or no taper.

BUTTPLATE
A protective plate attached to the butt of the buttstock. May be metal, plastic, or rubber. Sometimes airgun makers use a rubber recoil pad although the recoil dampening effect may not be needed.

BUTTSTOCK
Usually refers to the portion of a long gun that comes in contact with the shooter's shoulder.

CALIBER
The diameter of the bore (measured from land to land). It does not designate bullet diameter.

CHECKERING
A functional decoration consisting of pointed pyramids cut into the wood. Generally applied to the pistol grip and forend/forearm areas affording better handling and control.

COCKING INDICATOR
Any device which the act of cocking moves into a position where it may be seen or felt in order to notify the shooter that the gun is cocked.

COLOR CASE HARDENING
A method of hardening steel and iron while imparting colorful swirls as well as surface figure. Normally, the desired metal parts are put in a crucible packed with a mixture of charcoal and finely ground animal bone to temperatures in the 800° C to 900° C range, after which they are slowly cooled, and then submerged into cold water.

COMB
The portion of the stock on which the shooter's cheek rests.

COMPENSATOR
A recoil-reducing device that mounts on the muzzle of a gun to deflect part of the propelling gases up and rearward. Also called a "muzzle brake."

COMPRESSED AIR

Air at greater than atmospheric pressure. Guns which use compressed air include hose-fed airguns, spring-piston airguns, pump pneumatics, and pre-charged pneumatics.

CONCENTRIC PISTON

An arrangement in spring piston airguns where the barrel serves as a piston guide for a compression piston which encircles and rides on the barrel.

CROWNING

The rounding or chambering normally done to a barrel muzzle to insure that the mouth of the bore is square with the bore axis and that the edge is countersunk below the surface to protect it from impact damage. Traditionally, crowning was accomplished by spinning an abrasive-coated brass ball against the muzzle while moving it in a figure-eight pattern, until the abrasive had cut away any irregularities and produced a uniform and square mouth.

CYLINDER

In airguns, especially spring piston airguns, it is the cylinder-shaped main body or reciever. In such guns it is also known as the body tube or reciever.

DETENT

A spring-loaded cam which aids in holding an airgun mechanism, especially the barrel, in the closed position.

DIABOLO

A term used when referring to the style of pellets with a constricted waist.

DIOPTER

European term for aperture or peep sight. Usually refers to a target grade sight.

DOUBLE ACTION

The principle in a revolver or auto-loading pistol wherein the hammer can be cocked and dropped by a single pull of the trigger. Most of these actions also provide capability for single-action fire. In auto-loading pistols, double action normally applies only to the first shot of any series, with the hammer being cocked by the slide for subsequent shots.

DOUBLE ACTION ONLY

Hammer no longer cocks in single action stage.

DOUBLE-BARRELED

A gun consisting of two barrels joined either side by side or one over the other.

DOUBLE-SET TRIGGER

A device that consists of two triggers, one to cock the mechanism that spring-assists the other trigger, substantially lightening trigger pull.

DOVETAIL

A flaring machined or hand-cut slot that is also slightly tapered toward one end. Cut into the upper surface of barrels and sometimes actions, the dovetail accepts a corresponding part on which a sight is mounted. Dovetail slot blanks are used to cover the dovetail when the original sight has been removed

or lost; this gives the barrel a more pleasing appearance and configuration.

ENGLISH STOCK

A straight, slender-gripped stock.

ENGRAVING

The art of carving metal in decorative patterns. Scroll engraving is the most common type of hand engraving encountered. Much of today's factory engraving is rolled on, which is done mechanically. Hand engraving requires artistry and knowledge of metals and related materials.

ETCHING

A method of decorating metal gun parts, usually done by acid etching or photo engraving.

FOREARM (=FOREND)

Usually a separate piece of wood in front of the receiver and under the barrel used for hand placement when shooting.

FOREND (=FOREARM)

Usually the forward portion of a one-piece rifle or shotgun stock, but can also refer to a separate piece of wood.

FRONT STRAP

That part of the pistol grip frame that faces forward and often joins with the trigger guard.

GAS-SPRING SYSTEM

The type of operating system in which the main spring is replaced by (and uses) a gas-filled cylinder with a piston to generate the energy to move a projectile through the barrel (inappropriately sometimes called "gasram" or "gas strut").

GRAVITY FEED MECHANISM

A magazine which feeds projectiles, generally round balls or BBs, to the projectile feeding area by the simple, dependable action of gravity.

GRIP

The handle used to hold a handgun, or the area of a stock directly behind and attached to the frame/receiver of a long gun.

GRIPS

Can be part of the frame or components attached to the frame used to assist in accuracy, handling, control, and safety of a handgun. Some currently manufactured handguns have grips that are molded with checkering as part of the synthetic frame.

GROOVE

The spiral cuts in the bore of a rifle or handgun barrel that give the bullet its spin or rotation as it moves down the barrel.

GROOVED RECEIVER

The straight cuts in the upper portion of the receiver used when attaching a scope.

HEEL

Back end of the upper edge of the buttstock at the upper edge of the buttplate or recoil pad.

LAMINATED STOCK

A gunstock made of many layers of wood glued together under pressure. Together, the laminations become very strong, preventing damage from moisture, heat, and warping.

LANDS

Portions of the bore left between the grooves of the rifling in the bore of a firearm. In rifling, the grooves are usually twice the width of the land. Land diameter is measured across the bore, from land to land.

LOADING GATE

The area on an airgun which, when opened, allows for the insertion of the projectile.

LOADING TAP

An airgun mechanism into which single projectiles may be loaded and then moved into firing position. Varieties include: pop-up, turning (faucet), and swinging.

MAGAZINE (mag.)

The container within or attached to an airgun which holds projectiles to be fed into the gun's chamber.

MAINSPRING

The spring which, when compressed and then released, generates the energy to move a projectile through the barrel.

MANNLICHER STOCK

A full-length slender stock with slender forend extending to the muzzle (full stock) affording better barrel protection.

MICROMETER SIGHT

A finely adjustable sight.

MONTE CARLO STOCK

A stock with an elevated comb, used primarily for scoped rifles.

MUZZLE

The forward end of the barrel where the projectile exits.

MUZZLE BRAKE

A recoil-reducing device attached to the muzzle. Some "muzzle brakes" do not actually reduce recoil, but rather mainly are used as cocking aids.

MUZZLE WEIGHT

A weight (usually adjustable) equalizing device attached at muzzle end of the barrel used to balance and stabilize the barrel.

PARALLAX

Occurs in telescopic sights when the primary image of the objective lens does not coincide with the reticle. In practice, parallax is detected in the scope when, as the viewing eye is moved laterally, the image and the reticle appear to move in relation to each other.

PARKERIZING

Matted rust-resistant oxide finish, usually matte or dull gray, or black in color, usually found on military guns.

PEEP SIGHT

Rear sight consisting of a hole or aperture through which the front sight and target are aligned.

PELLET

An airgun projectile that is not a ball. Available in many styles, including wadcutter (target and high impact), pointed (high penetration), round nose (general use), and hollow point (expands on impact).

PNEUMATIC

A term referring to the use of air/gas pressure as an energy source. In airguns it propels the BB or pellet out of the barrel.

PRE-CHARGED PNEUMATIC SYSTEM

The type of operating system that uses an externally charged chamber (either integral or removable) of compressed air or gas to generate the energy to move a projectile through the barrel.

PULL

The distance from the forward center of the trigger curve to the rear surface of the buttplate. A pull of 14.3 inches is a typical adult size.

RECEIVER

The central area of an airgun's mechanism which serves to house or connect some or all of these parts: trigger mechanism, power mechanism, barrel, stock. A round airgun receiver generally is referred to as the body tube, cylinder, compression tube, or reciever. In air pistols, it generally is referred to as the frame.

RECOILLESS

A mechanical design that allows an airgun to be shot with little or no felt recoil.

REPEATER/REPEATING

A term used when referring to an airgun being capable of firing more than one shot without having to manually reload.

RESERVOIR

Storage area for airgun projectiles. Generally not connected to the projectile feeding area or magazine.

RIB

A raised sighting plane affixed to the top of a barrel.

RIFLING

The spirally cut grooves in the bore of a rifle or handgun. The rifling stabilizes the bullet in flight. Rifling may rotate to the left or the right, the higher parts of the bore being called lands, the cuts or lower parts being called the grooves. Most U.S.-made barrels have a right-hand twist, while British gun makers prefer a left-hand twist. In practice, there seems to be little difference in accuracy or barrel longevity.

SCHNABEL FOREND

The curved/carved flared end of the forend that resembles the beak of a bird (Schnabel in German). This type of forend is common on Austrian and German guns, and was popular in the U.S., but the popularity of the Schnabel forend/forearm comes and goes with the seasons.

SIDE LEVER

The lever located on the side of an airgun used for cocking the mainspring into firing position.

SIDE-LEVER COCKING
The action of pivoting the side lever compresses the mainspring of a spring-piston action into firing position.

SINGLE ACTION
A design which requires the hammer to be manually cocked for each shot. Also, an auto loading pistol design which requires manual cocking of the hammer for the first shot only.

SKIRT
The flaring, thin area of diabolo-style pellets that engages the rifling in a barrel and acts as an air seal.

SLING SWIVELS
Metal loops affixed to the gun on which a carrying strap is attached.

SOUND MODERATOR ("Silencer")
Device which reduces the discharge sound by one decibel or more. All versions, including built-in models, probably are illegal in the United States, unless accompanied by a $200 federal permit and, if required, a state permit. (See www.Beemans.net.)

SPRING-FED MAGAZINE
A projectile storage area which is designed to feed the projectiles to the firing or loading area by means of a spring-loaded projectile follower.

SPRING-PISTON SYSTEM
Airgun operating system that uses a metal or gas mainspring to push a piston, which in turn uses a cushion of air to push the projectile through the barrel.

STIPPLING
The roughening of a surface (with the use of a special punch or tool) to provide the shooter with a better grip.

STOCKS
See grip.

TAKEDOWN
A gun which can be easily taken apart in two sections for carrying or shipping.

TANG(S)
The extension straps of the receiver to which the stock is attached.

TOP LEVER
The lever located on the top of an airgun used for cocking the mainspring into firing position.

TOP-LEVER COCKING
The action of pivoting the top lever (generally found on air pistols) upward compresses the mainspring of a spring-piston action into firing position.

UNDER LEVER
The lever located under an airgun used for cocking the mainspring into firing position.

UNDER-LEVER COCKING
The action of pivoting the under lever downward compresses the mainspring of a spring-piston action into firing position.

YOUTH DIMENSIONS
Usually refers to shorter stock dimensions and/or lighter weight enabling youth/women to shoot and carry a lighter, shorter airgun.

WUNDHAMMER SWELL
A swelling of the pistol grip area of a rifle stock, intended to give support to the palm of the firing hand.

English/American Translations of Airgun Terms

English	American
Horizontal Sight Adjustment	Windage
Vertical Sight Adjustment	Elevation
Joint Washer, Barrel Washer	Breech Seal
Loading Lever	Cocking Arm
Fixing Screw	Lock Screw
Kit	Equipment
Barrel Fixing Plunger, Barrel Latch	Detent
Cranked Spring	Spring w/Straight Leg(s)
Back Block	Receiver End Cap
Bead	Front Sight
Receiver Sight	Peep Sight
Mains Line Tension	House Current
Fore-end	Forearm
Cylinder, Body	Receiver, Body Tube
Grub Screw	Headless Screw
Calibre	Caliber
Arrestor Projections	Scope Stop
Anti-Clockwise	Counter Clockwise
Nought	Zero (the number)
Strip	Disassemble
Fix (a design)	Finalize a Design
Sort Out	Fix, figure out, Organize
Knackered	Needs Repair
One Off (on orders)	One On (on orders)
Brilliant	Excellent
Spot On	Absolutely Appropriate
One Off	Unique

ABBREVIATIONS

AA	*Addictive Airgunning*		MC	Monte Carlo
AAG	*American Air Gunner*		ME	Muzzle Energy
adj.	Adjustable		MFC	Muzzle Flip Compensator
AG	*Airgunnner*		MFG/mfg.	Manufactured/Manufacture
AGNR	*Air Gun News & Report* Magazine		MK	Mark
AL	*Airgun Letter*		MSR	Manufacturer's Suggested Retail
AR	*Airgun Revue* Magazine		MV	Muzzle Velocity
AW	*Airgun World* Magazine		N	Nickel
B	Blue		N/A	Not Applicable or Not Available
BA	Bolt Action		NIB	New in Box
BACS	Brocock Air Cartridge System		No.	Number
BB	Air Rifle Shot		OA	Overall
BBC	Break Barrel Cocking		OAL	Overall Length
BBL	Barrel		OB	Octagon Barrel
BC	Barrel Cocking		OCT	Octagon
BF	Bulk Fill or Bottle Fed		OD	Outside Diameter
BO	Break Open		PCP	Pre-Charged Pneumatic
BP	Buttplate		PG	Pistol Grip
BT	Beavertail		POR/P.O.R.	Price on Request
ca.	Circa		PSI	Pounds per Square Inch
cal.	Caliber		PTFE	Power Intesification Piston System
CB	Crescent Buttplate		QD	Quick Detachable
CC	Case Colors		RB	Round Barrel
CH	Cross Hair		RH	Right Hand
CO₂	Carbon Dioxide		REC	Receiver
COMP	Compensated/Competition		RPM	Rounds Per Minute
CP	Concentric Piston		S/N	Serial Number
CYL	Cylinder		SA	Single Action
DA	Double Action		ser.	Serial
DB	Double Barrel		SG	Straight Grip
DISC	Discontinued		SL	Side Lever
DST	Double Set Triggers		SP	Spring Piston
DT	Double Triggers		SPEC	Special
DWJ	*Deutsches Waffen Journal*		SPG	Semi-Pistol Grip
EXC	Excellent		Spl.	Special
FA	Forearm		SS	Single Shot or Stainless Steel
FE	Fore End		SSP	Single Stroke Pneumatic
FPS	Feet Per Second		ST	Single Trigger
g./gm.	Gram		TBD	To Be Determined
ga.	Gauge		TD	Takedown
GD	*Gun Digest*		TGT	Target
GOVT	Government		TL	Top Lever
gr.	Grain		TT	Target Trigger
GR	*Guns Review*		UIT	Union Internationale de Tir
GS	Gas Spring		UL	Under Lever
HB	Heavy Barrel		USA	United States of America or *U.S. Airguns*
HC	Hard Case		VG	Very Good
intro.	Introduced		V/Visier	*VISIER* magazine
LA	Lever Action		w/	With
LH	Left Hand		w/o	Without
LOP	Length of Pull		WD	Wood
LPI	Lines Per Inch		WFF	Watch for Fakes
LT	Light		WO	White Outline
Mag.	Extra Powerful; Magnum		WW	World War
mag.	Magazine or Clip			

AIRGUN GRADING CRITERIA

The following descriptions are provided to help evaluate condition factors for both vintage and currently/recently manufactured airguns. **Please refer to the eight-page color Photo Grading System (PGS) to determine the correct grade for your airgun(s).** Once the percentage of original condition has been determined, getting the correct value is as simple as finding the listing and selecting the correct condition factor. Also included are both the NRA Modern and Antique Condition Standards for firearms as a comparison, including a conversion chart for converting percentages to NRA Modern Standards. "N/As" throughout this book are used to indicate that values can't be accurately established because of rarity, lack of recorded sales, or other factors that may preclude realistic pricing within a condition factor. **All digital photos in the following Photo Grading System are courtesy of Dr. Robert D. Beeman.**

100% - all original parts, 100% original finish, perfect condition in every respect, inside and out. On currently manufactured airguns, the 100% value assumes not previously sold at retail.

95% - all original parts, near new condition, very little use; minor scratches or handling dings on wood, metal bluing near perfect, except at muzzle or sharp edges.

90% - all original parts, perfect working condition, some minor wear on working surfaces, no corrosion or pitting, minor surface dents or scratches, sharp lettering, numerals and design on metal and wood; unmarred wood, fine bore.

80% - good working condition, minor wear on working surfaces, no broken or replacement parts, sharp lettering, numerals and design on metal and wood, some surface freckling/light rust (especially on vintage airguns).

60% - safe working condition, sharp lettering, numerals and design on metal and wood, some scratches, dings, and chips in wood, good bore, may have some corrosion and pitting.

40% - well-worn, perhaps requiring replacement of minor parts or adjustments, sharp lettering; numerals and design on metal and wood, on older airguns, major surface rust and pitting may be present, but do not render the airgun unsafe or inoperable.

20% - most of original finish is gone, metal may be seriously rusted or pitted, cleaned or reblued, principal lettering, numerals and design on metal still legible, wood may have serious scratches, dings, and may be refinished and/or cracked, both minor and major repairs may be present.

NRA MODERN CONDITION DESCRIPTIONS

New - not previously sold at retail, in same condition as current factory production.

Perfect - in new condition in every respect.

Excellent - new condition, used but little, no noticeable marring of wood or metal, bluing near perfect (except at muzzle or sharp edges).

Very Good - in perfect working condition, no appreciable wear on working surfaces, no corrosion or pitting, only minor surface dents or scratches.

Good - in safe working condition, minor wear on working surfaces, no broken parts, no corrosion or pitting that will interfere with proper functioning.

Fair - in safe working condition, but well-worn, perhaps requiring replacement of minor parts or adjustments which should be indicated in advertisement, no rust, but may have corrosion pits which do not render article unsafe or inoperable.

CONVERTING TO NRA MODERN STANDARDS

When converting from NRA Modern Standards, the following rules generally apply:

New/Perfect - 100% with or without box. Not mint - new (i.e., no excuses). 100% on currently manufactured firearms assumes NIB condition and not sold previously at retail.

Excellent - 95%+ - 99% (typically).

Very Good - 80% - 95% (should be all original).

Good - 60% - 80% (should be all original).

Fair - 20% - 60% (may or may not be original, but must function properly and shoot).

Poor - under 20% (shooting not a factor).

NRA ANTIQUE CONDITION DESCRIPTIONS

Factory New - all original parts; 100% original finish; in perfect condition in every respect, inside and out.

Excellent - all original parts; over 80% original finish; sharp lettering, numerals and design on metal and wood; unmarred wood; fine bore.

Fine - all original parts; over 30% original finish; sharp lettering, numerals and design on metal and wood; minor marks in wood; good bore.

Very Good - all original parts; none to 30% original finish; original metal surfaces smooth with all edges sharp; clear lettering, numerals and design on metal; wood slightly scratched or bruised; bore disregarded for collectors firearms.

Good - some minor replacement parts; metal smoothly rusted or lightly pitted in places, cleaned or reblued; principal lettering, numerals and design on metal legible; wood refinished, scratched, bruised or minor cracks repaired; in good working order.

Fair - some major parts replaced; minor replacement parts may be required; metal rusted, may be lightly pitted all over, vigorously cleaned or reblued; rounded edges of metal and wood; principal lettering, numerals and design on metal partly obliterated; wood scratched, bruised, cracked or repaired where broken; in fair working order or can be easily repaired and placed in working order.

Poor - major and minor parts replaced; major replacement parts required and extensive restoration needed; metal deeply pitted; principal lettering, numerals and design obliterated, wood badly scratched, bruised, cracked, or broken; mechanically inoperative, generally undesirable as a collector's firearm.

AIR PISTOLS

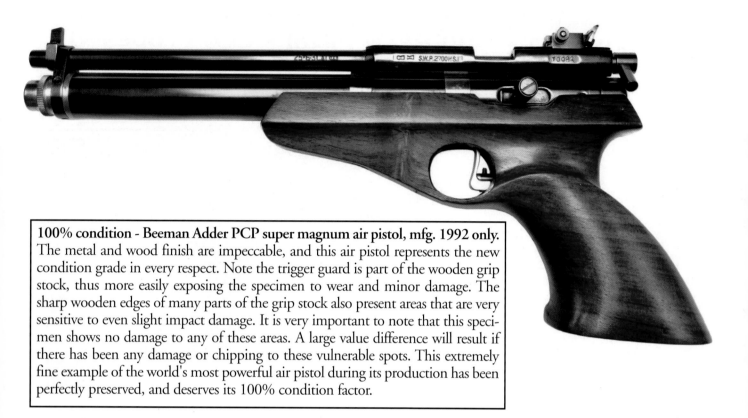

100% condition - **Beeman Adder PCP super magnum air pistol, mfg. 1992 only.** The metal and wood finish are impeccable, and this air pistol represents the new condition grade in every respect. Note the trigger guard is part of the wooden grip stock, thus more easily exposing the specimen to wear and minor damage. The sharp wooden edges of many parts of the grip stock also present areas that are very sensitive to even slight impact damage. It is very important to note that this specimen shows no damage to any of these areas. A large value difference will result if there has been any damage or chipping to these vulnerable spots. This extremely fine example of the world's most powerful air pistol during its production has been perfectly preserved, and deserves its 100% condition factor.

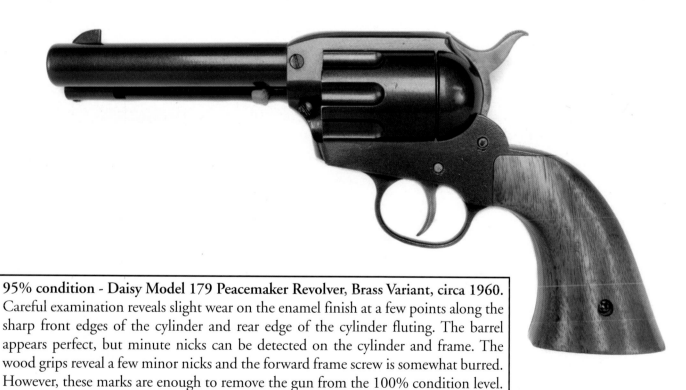

95% condition - **Daisy Model 179 Peacemaker Revolver, Brass Variant, circa 1960.** Careful examination reveals slight wear on the enamel finish at a few points along the sharp front edges of the cylinder and rear edge of the cylinder fluting. The barrel appears perfect, but minute nicks can be detected on the cylinder and frame. The wood grips reveal a few minor nicks and the forward frame screw is somewhat burred. However, these marks are enough to remove the gun from the 100% condition level. Note that Daisy guns, if painted, usually have a slightly patterned, very characteristic paint finish. Unlike many airgun paint finishes, the special color and texture of the Daisy finish is difficult to fake. The 2.7 lb. weight identifies this variant.

AIR PISTOLS

NEW "JET POWERED" Pistol - CO₂ Propelled

Winsel

This set includes Pistol with Propellent Tube and an extra Tube - both filled with CO₂ Pro-

Easy to

POWERFUL
Shoots .22 Cal. Pellets

JUST PUSH
← THIS LEVER TO COCK AND LOAD

90% condition - Winsel Jet CO_2 Pistol, Winsel Corporation of Rochester, New York, circa 1948. This interesting CO_2 pistol is virtually like new, with the original factory purple box, complete with the usually missing "Mailing carton for return of empty tube". A slight roughness on the rear edge of the forward body ring, slight discoloration on the upper rear tube of the receiver, and a slightly nicked grip screw give this air pistol a 90% condition factor. Most of these pistols are found without the big CO_2 tube under the barrel, because the tubes had to be returned to the factory for recharging; the factory closed and most of the tubes were lost.

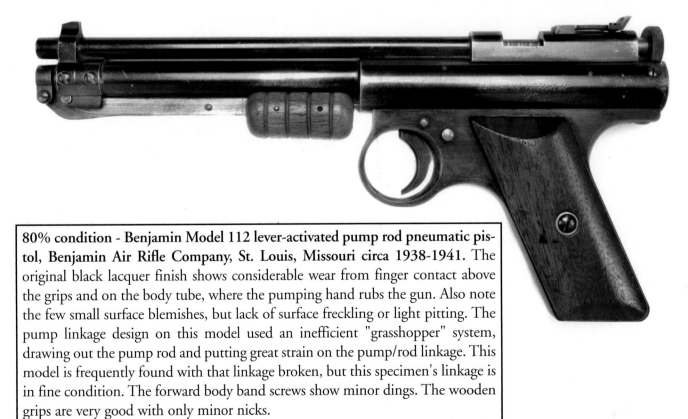

80% condition - Benjamin Model 112 lever-activated pump rod pneumatic pistol, Benjamin Air Rifle Company, St. Louis, Missouri circa 1938-1941. The original black lacquer finish shows considerable wear from finger contact above the grips and on the body tube, where the pumping hand rubs the gun. Also note the few small surface blemishes, but lack of surface freckling or light pitting. The pump linkage design on this model used an inefficient "grasshopper" system, drawing out the pump rod and putting great strain on the pump/rod linkage. This model is frequently found with that linkage broken, but this specimen's linkage is in fine condition. The forward body band screws show minor dings. The wooden grips are very good with only minor nicks.

AIR PISTOLS

60% condition - Milbro Model 2 Push Barrel Cocking Air Pistol, Millard Brothers, Motherwell, Lanarkshire, Scotland, circa late 1950s. These common and simple early air pistols ("British Dianas") are becoming of increased interest to collectors. This specimen is typical of these generally well used airguns. The push tube barrel shows considerable discoloration from handling with sweaty hands, and the outer barrel cover, and especially the receiver, show considerable freckling and some small pitting. The lower edge of the trigger is worn bare, indicating a very large number of discharges. The wooden grip is sound and without major flaws but is almost covered with small nicks and scratches. The wooden grip indicates early production, and adds considerably to this air pistol's desirability and value.

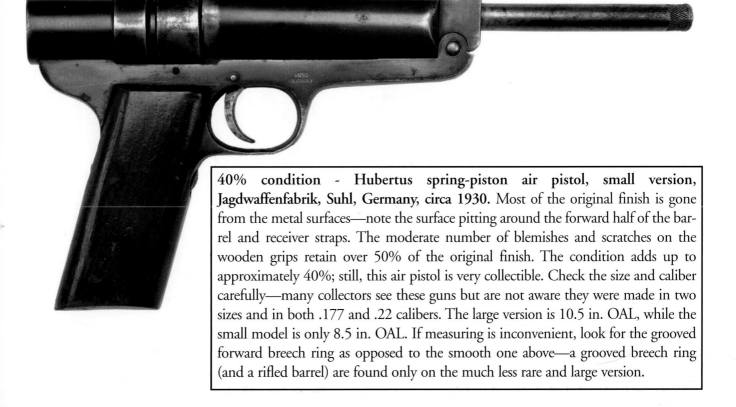

40% condition - Hubertus spring-piston air pistol, small version, Jagdwaffenfabrik, Suhl, Germany, circa 1930. Most of the original finish is gone from the metal surfaces—note the surface pitting around the forward half of the barrel and receiver straps. The moderate number of blemishes and scratches on the wooden grips retain over 50% of the original finish. The condition adds up to approximately 40%; still, this air pistol is very collectible. Check the size and caliber carefully—many collectors see these guns but are not aware they were made in two sizes and in both .177 and .22 calibers. The large version is 10.5 in. OAL, while the small model is only 8.5 in. OAL. If measuring is inconvenient, look for the grooved forward breech ring as opposed to the smooth one above—a grooved breech ring (and a rifled barrel) are found only on the much less rare and large version.

AIR PISTOLS

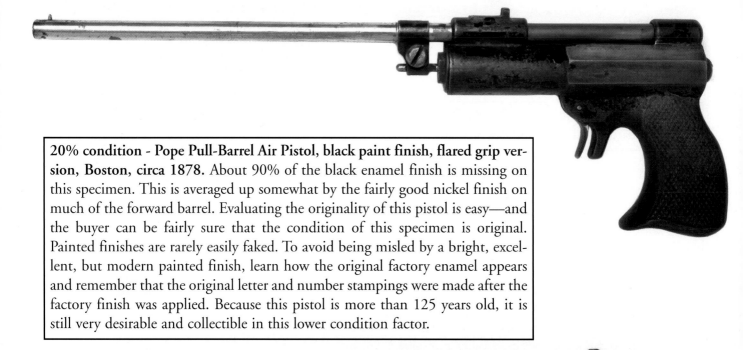

20% condition - Pope Pull-Barrel Air Pistol, black paint finish, flared grip version, Boston, circa 1878. About 90% of the black enamel finish is missing on this specimen. This is averaged up somewhat by the fairly good nickel finish on much of the forward barrel. Evaluating the originality of this pistol is easy—and the buyer can be fairly sure that the condition of this specimen is original. Painted finishes are rarely easily faked. To avoid being misled by a bright, excellent, but modern painted finish, learn how the original factory enamel appears and remember that the original letter and number stampings were made after the factory finish was applied. Because this pistol is more than 125 years old, it is still very desirable and collectible in this lower condition factor.

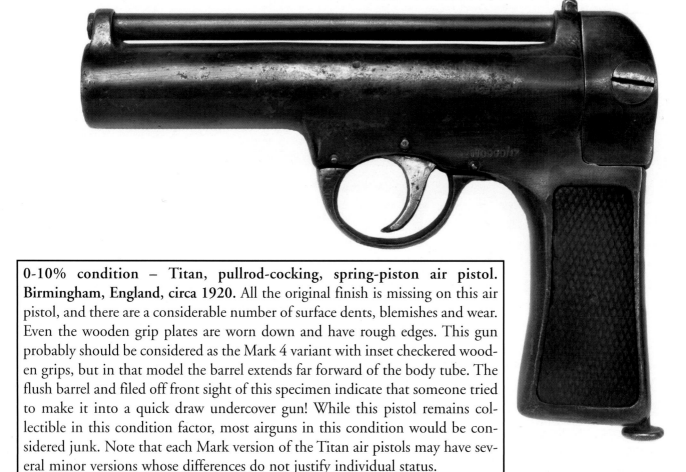

0-10% condition – Titan, pullrod-cocking, spring-piston air pistol. Birmingham, England, circa 1920. All the original finish is missing on this air pistol, and there are a considerable number of surface dents, blemishes and wear. Even the wooden grip plates are worn down and have rough edges. This gun probably should be considered as the Mark 4 variant with inset checkered wooden grips, but in that model the barrel extends far forward of the body tube. The flush barrel and filed off front sight of this specimen indicate that someone tried to make it into a quick draw undercover gun! While this pistol remains collectible in this condition factor, most airguns in this condition would be considered junk. Note that each Mark version of the Titan air pistols may have several minor versions whose differences do not justify individual status.

AIR RIFLES & SHOTGUNS

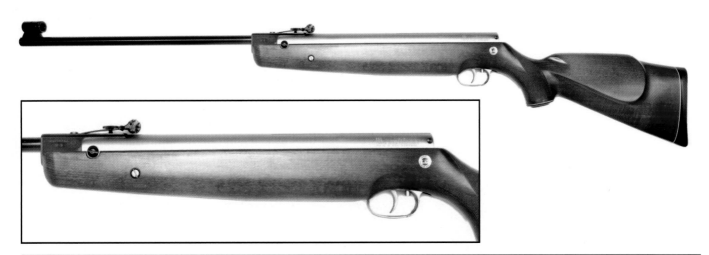

100% condition - Beeman R1 Commemorative, spring piston, barrel cocking rifle; regular model mfg. 1981 to date, this variant mfg. only 1992. 100% condition means perfect in every respect—inside and out. There is no wear or even thinning of the finish on any surface or edge. Unlike many makes/models made into commemoratives, the Beeman R1 was issued in a commemorative version only once—to celebrate the 20th anniversary of the Beeman Precision Airgun Company. The barrel is blued, the receiver has a stainless steel color, and a cloisonné commemorative disk is inletted into the left side of the stock. The R1 was the predecessor of the Weihrauch HW80 and is considered to be the first successful model released in the American adult airgun marketplace.

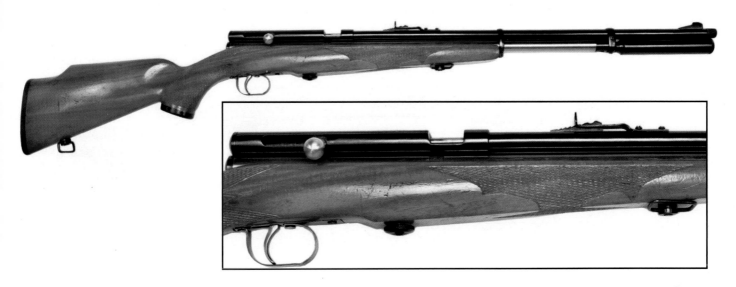

95% condition - Pampanga Bulk Fill CO_2 .22 rifle, Pampanga gun-making area of the Philippines, circa 1980s. Philippine airguns are becoming more popular with American and other collectors than they were less than a decade ago. Knowing what to look for is essential with these guns, which frequently are not marked. This specimen's aircraft aluminum and stainless steel is perfect at all points—the stock has only minor marks, which can be a characteristic of new Philippine airguns. The workmanship and features on this air rifle are a major step above those of standard Philippine airgun production. Pampanga airguns generally do not have any prominent maker's marks. Information critical to identifying them is given in the Philippine Airgun section under "P" in this text.

AIR RIFLES & SHOTGUNS

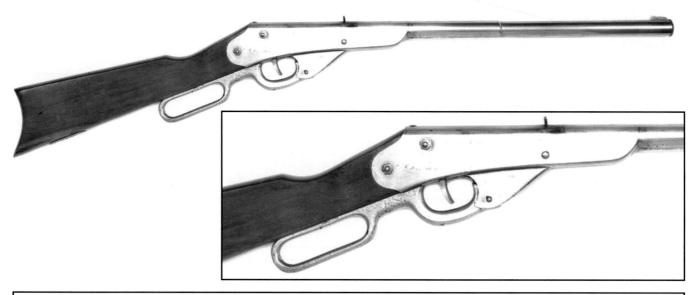

90% condition - Daisy Model H, BB Rifle, circa 1913-20. Upon initial observation, this air rifle looks worn on the lever arm, but closer inspection reveals that it's a porous casting from the factory. Note light stock scratching and small dents—normal for this condition factor. The nickel metal finish, an option at the time, and now more desirable than blue, also shows little wear. Minor metal discolorations (in front of the rear sight, the back of the receiver, and the bottom of the barrel in front of the receiver) may disappear with proper cleaning. A metal tag firmly tacked to the lower edge of the buttstock and letters engraved on the receiver, instead of detracting from the value, add a great deal—and explain the condition. The marking "W.R.A. Co." reflects the fact that this gun came out of the Winchester Repeating Arms Company collection.

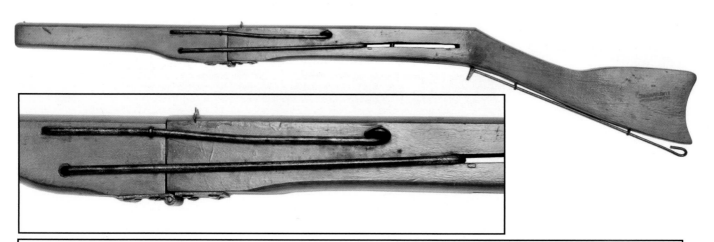

80% condition - Markham/King Chicago wooden BB gun, circa 1888. It is astonishing to find a boy's BB gun over 115 years old in such outstanding condition. Only the expected moderate rust on the metal rods and hinges and a couple of blemishes and nicks in the original wood finish bring this gun down from 100% condition. Some of the wood roughness may have been original. Note that the usually absent cleaning/BB clearing rod under the stock is present. The cleaning rod and clearly stamped original factory markings on the side of the buttstock add to this air rifle's desirability factor and originality. This specimen has avoided the drying and handling splits which are often found in examples of this model.

AIR RIFLES & SHOTGUNS

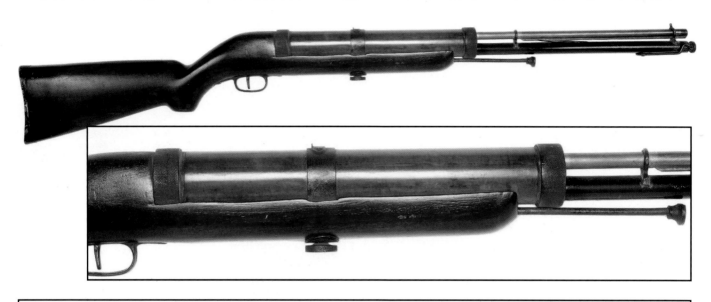

60% condition - Paul Air Shotgun, .410 bore, early version, Beecher, Ilinois, circa 1924. This air shotgun shows considerable aging, as would be expected in a gun over 80 years old. The brass has a heavy patina and some steel parts, such as the large knurled rings, are exhibiting serious surface rust. The barrel and pump tube solder joints are still strong and show no sign of re-soldering. The varnish on the edge of the buttplate is chipping. The stock finish seems original but shows considerable, but not abusive, use. All things considered, a 60% rating for this old veteran is appropriate and its early version status and desirability make it very collectible, while a 60% modern airgun would be marginal as a collector's item.

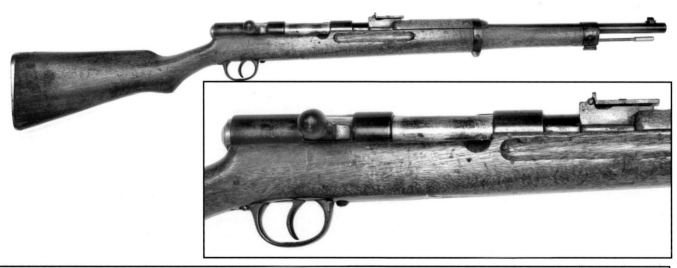

40% condition - Japanese Military Training Air Rifle, bolt action, single shot, spring piston action, circa 1940. Remember, this air rifle was used by the Japanese military for training, and helps explain its overall condition factor. The stock shows the usual brutal dents, gouges, and scratches of a used military long arm. Virtually all metal surfaces are showing signs of patina and some areas exhibit slight pitting. Note the bolt discoloring. This rough condition is normal and expected in such specimens. A 40% condition factor is appropriate for this basically sound, interesting and historically significant airgun which may be sought after by both airgun and military arms collectors. Production reportedly stopped after very limited production as the Japanese war machine needed real firearms instead of air powered trainers.

AIR RIFLES & SHOTGUNS

20% condition - Oskar Will Bugelspanner air rifle, trigger guard underlever cocking action, double-volute spring piston action, manufactured by Venuswaffenwerk in Zella-Mehlis, Germany, circa 1880-1910. This condition factor is typical for a well used air rifle of this age with steel/iron parts. Metal surfaces show a dark, grayish heavy patina and some parts are slightly loose. Brass parts show a deep, old patina, indicating that this air rifle has not been recently polished. The curved stock shows scars and dents that indicate heavy use and abuse. Despite its appearance, this German air rifle still fires well. While American airgun collectors may find Bugelspanner rifles, only a tiny portion of them are represented by these older original versions. In spite of its condition, this 20% specimen is more desirable in a collection than a recent production version with a bright new nickel finish and a shiny stock.

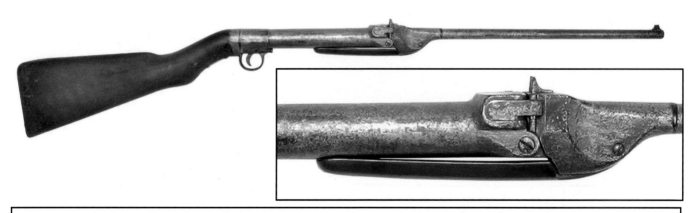

0-10% condition – Kynoch Swift barrel-cocking, spring piston air rifle, mfg. in Witton, Brimingham, Warwickshire, England, circa 1908. Not only is all the original finish gone from both the metal and wood, but the heavily pitted metal has been painted with ordinary gray paint. The stock has worm holes and patching. This specimen still retains the Kynoch name stamped into the wood of the buttstock, but the huge, claw-like, spring loaded detent hooks, one on each side of the breech, identify this model even at a distance. Most airguns in this condition belong in the trash bucket, but this one, manufactured by a world-famous gunmaker almost a century ago, is still very desirable and interesting, making extensive restoration, while expensive, a definite possibility.

A SECTION

ABT

Previous manufacturer located at 715-727 North Kedzie St., Chicago, Illinois circa 1925-1958. The company name is an acronym of the founders' names: Gus Adler, Jack Bechtol, and Walter Tratsch. Producers of carnival and shooting gallery BB pistols, BB rifles, and supplies. Developed Air-O-Matic airgun design, patented April 19, 1932, pat. no. 1854605 and Oct. 6, 1942, pat. no. 2297947. Other patents to 1949.

Most of the known ABT guns are pistols which were captive mounted in highly decorated wooden boxes serving as miniature, coin-operated firing ranges. These were used for entertainment and as covert/rigged games of chance. These game guns were manufactured from 1925 to about 1958. There are no production records from about 1941 to 1946 due to WWII. The shooting box part of the company's history is detailed at www.crowriver.com/abt.htm.

It is not clear when hose-fed compressed air ABT airguns were made, but the patents run from 1932 through 1949. ABT apparently applied for Arrow-Matic as a trademark, and so marked at least some guns, but were granted the Air-O-Matic trademark for semi-automatic airguns that are fed from a patented, pre-loaded fiber tube of BBs that was inserted into a unique rear- or top-feeding loading chute when the gun was opened by pulling back the top of the receiver or a side bolt. At least three versions of shoulder-fired, hose pneumatic rifles and one similar pistol are known. Also known is a sliding pump action rifle, unmarked, but with exactly the same unusual, complex, loading chute.

Virtually all ABT specimens are well worn from hard shooting gallery use, but are very durable due to rugged, excellent construction. Carnival airguns are now becoming more popular with airgun collectors, and values can be expected to rise accordingly.

GRADING	100%	95%	90%	80%	60%	40%	20%

PISTOLS

CAPTIVE SHOOTING BOX PISTOL - .40 cal., spring action, tube-fed repeater, 2.6 in. smoothbore blue barrel, 8.7 in. OAL, 2.9 lbs., no safety. Mfg. 1925-1958.

courtesy Beeman Collection

	N/A	N/A	$180	$150	$100	$75	$50

AIR-O-MATIC GALLERY PISTOL - .173 cal., hose pneumatic, semi-automatic repeater, patented pop-up loading chute loaded by insertion of patented, fiber, pre-loaded tube of BBs, 7.1 in. smoothbore barrel, 12.7 in. OAL, 2.6 lbs., no safety. Probably mfg. 1930s to 1940s.

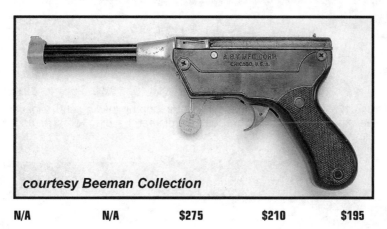

courtesy Beeman Collection

	N/A	N/A	$275	$210	$195	$175	$150

RIFLES

AIR-O-MATIC REAR LOADER - .173 cal., hose pneumatic, semi-auto repeater, loading chute pops out of rear of receiver for insertion of patented, fiber, pre-loaded tube of BBs, approx. 16 in. smoothbore barrel within longer barrel shroud, stamped with 1932 patent date, model name cast in plastic buttplate. No safety, approx. 42 in. OAL, approx. 5 lbs.

GRADING	100%	95%	90%	80%	60%	40%	20%

✳ *Air-O-Matic Variant I* - large sheet metal receiver extends almost to bottom edge of the middle of the stock.

courtesy Beeman Collection

	N/A	N/A	N/A	$350	$325	$300	$275

✳ *Air-O-Matic Variant II* - small receiver in line with barrel above one piece stock.

courtesy Beeman Collection

	N/A	N/A	N/A	$325	$300	$275	$250

AIR-O-MATIC TOP LOADER - .173 cal. semi-auto repeater, hose pneumatic, loading chute pops out of top of receiver for insertion of patented, fiber, pre-loaded tube of BBs, approx. 23 in. smoothbore barrel within larger barrel shroud which is topped by a small full-length tube, Metal box-like receiver divides stock into two pieces, stamped with 1942 and 1949 patent dates, model name cast in plastic buttplate, no safety, approx. 42 in. overall, approx. 5.6 lbs.

✳ *Knob Variant* - short, straight-pull knob. Early.

courtesy Beeman Collection

	N/A	N/A	N/A	$300	$250	$200	$150

✳ *Bolt Variant* - long, lifting bolt. Later.

courtesy Beeman Collection

	N/A	N/A	N/A	$300	$250	$200	$150

AIR-O-MATIC SLIDE ACTION - .173 cal., hose pneumatic, repeater, pop up loading chute loaded by insertion of patented, fiber, pre-loaded tube of BBs, 23 in. smoothbore barrel, unusual two diameter sliding forearm, no safety, no markings, 42.5 in. OAL, 7.1 lbs. Probable mfg. 1940s.

courtesy Beeman Collection

	N/A	N/A	N/A	$275	$225	$175	$125

GRADING	100%	95%	90%	80%	60%	40%	20%

ARS (AIR RIFLE SPECIALISTS)

Current importer located in Pine City, NY. Dealer or consumer direct sales.

ARS currently imports airguns from Shin Sung, located in Korea, and previously imported Farco airguns from the Philippines. For information on Farco airguns, see the "F" section.

RIFLES

ADVENTURE DB - .22 cal., PCP, removable mag., pistol gip stock, 41.3 in. QAL, 8.2 lbs. Mfg. 1990s.

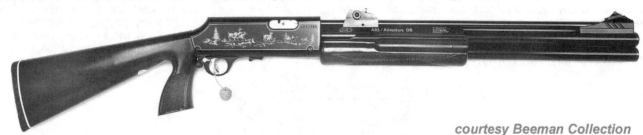

courtesy Beeman Collection

	$550	$475	$395	$325	$250	N/A	N/A

HUNTING MASTER AR6 - .177, .20, .22, or .25 (disc.) cal., PCP, exposed cocking hammer, six-shot rotary mag., 25.5 in. blue finish barrel, 1000+- FPS (.22), adj. rear peep sight, grooved receiver, checkered Monte Carlo walnut stock, rubber butt pad, 6.75 lbs., 41.25 OAL. Mfg. in Korea.

MSR	$580	$450	$365	$285	$235	$175	N/A	N/A

Add $20 for extra six-shot cylinder.

Add $50 for charging unit.

Add 10% for .20 cal.

HUNTING MASTER AR6 MAGNUM - .22 cal., PCP, six-shot rotary mag., 22.75 in. blue finish barrel, alloy receiver with gold burnish finish, 1000 FPS, adj. rear sight, checkered walnut stock and forearm, 6.75 lbs. Mfg. in Korea, disc.

	$425	$350	$275	$195	$150	N/A	N/A

Last MSR was $580.

Add $20 for extra six-shot cylinder.

Add $50 for charging unit.

CAREER II (CAREER 707) - .22 cal., PCP, six-shot (or side-loading SS) lever action, 22.75 in. blue barrel, 1000 FPS, adj. diopter rear sight, hooded front sight, checkered walnut stock and forearm, 7.75 lbs. Mfg. in Korea; new 1995.

MSR	$580	$450	$365	$285	$235	$175	N/A	N/A

KING HUNTING MASTER - .22 cal., PCP, five-shot rotary mag. Mfg. in Korea, disc.

	$425	$350	$275	$195	$150	N/A	N/A

Last MSR was $580.

MAGNUM 6 - .22 cal., CO_2 or PCP, six-shot, similar to the King Hunting Master. Mfg. in Korea, disc.

courtesy Howard Collection

	$425	$350	$275	$195	$150	N/A	N/A

Last MSR was $500.

HUNTING MASTER 900 - 9mm cal., PCP, side lever (for inserting pellets), 26.75 in. barrel, 900 FPS, wood stock. Mfg. in Korea, disc.

	$900	$700	$550	$400	$300	N/A	N/A

Last MSR was $1,000.

FIRE 201 - 9mm cal., PCP, SL, smooth bore or rifled barrel, 900 FPS, beech stock. Mfg. in Korea, 2000.

	$450	$365	$285	$235	$175	N/A	N/A

Last MSR was $595.

QB 77 - .177 or .22 cal., CO_2, SS, 21.5 in. barrel, hardwood stock, 5.5 lbs. Mfg. in China, disc. 2001.

	$150	$115	$80	$65	$50	N/A	N/A

Last MSR was $149.

GRADING	100%	95%	90%	80%	60%	40%	20%

ABAS MAJOR

Previously manufactured by A.A. Brown & Sons located at 1 Snake Lane, Alvechurch Birmingham, England, circa 1945-1946.

Albert Arthur Brown and his sons, Albert Henry Brown and Sydney Charles Brown were co-patentees and partners in developing and producing the Abas Major air pistol. (ABAS = initials of A. Brown and Sons.)

PISTOLS

ABAS MAJOR - .177 cal., concentric piston SP action, tap loading, trigger guard and forward edge of grip frame swings forward under the 7.6 in. barrel to cock the mainspring, counterclockwise rifling, blue, black crinkled paint, or aluminum finish, no safety. Walnut Grip Variant: smooth walnut grips, blued, some with black crackle paint, earliest production with lever release button on bottom of grip. Smooth Plastic Grip Variant: smooth brown composition grips, blued, most common variant. Checkered Plastic Grip Variant: checkered brown plastic grips, 8.1 in. OAL, 2.7 lbs. Less than 1870 known of all variants, mfg. early 1945 to late 1946. Ref: AW: 1978, Apr. 1982.

courtesy Beeman Collection

$800	$725	$650	$575	$500	$450	$400

Add 10% for release button on bottom of grip.

Add 10% for black enamel.

Add 15% for Walnut Grip Variant.

Add 20% for original factory box with Abas Major pellets.

ABBEY ALERT

For information on Abbey Alert airguns, see Produsit in the "P" section.

ACCLES & SHELVOKE LTD.

Previous manufacturer located at Talford Street Engineering Works, Birmingham, Warwickshire, England. Founded by James Accles and George Shelvoke in 1913.

Accles & Shelvoke originally produced humane cattle killers patented by James Accles and Charles Cash. Before WWII, the firm manufactured the Warrior, an air pistol developed and patented by association of Frank Clarke and Edwin Anson. They may have also produced the prototypes of the Titan air pistols for Frank Clarke. After WWII, the company produced the Acvoke air pistol, designed by John Arrowsmith. They were still recorded as making humane cattle killers in 1960. Air pistols were produced from 1931 to 1956. The authors and publisher wish to thank John Atkins for his valuable assistance with the following information in this edition of the *Blue Book of Airguns*.

PISTOLS

ACVOKE - .177 cal., SP, SS, concentric piston, cocked by pivoting grip forward with the aid of a lever which folds down from grip backstrap, 8 in. rifled BBL, blue finish, vertically ribbed plastic grips marked "ACVOKE" in an oval logo, 8.6 in. OAL, 2.0 lbs. Mfg. c. 1946-1956. Ref: GR Oct. '80.

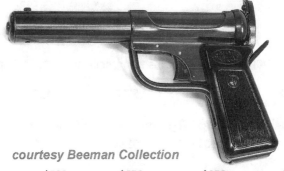

courtesy Beeman Collection

$550	$500	$450	$350	$300	$250	$175

Add 20% for original factory box.

Add 10% for cork adapter.

GRADING	100%	95%	90%	80%	60%	40%	20%

WARRIOR - .177 or .22 cal. SL, SP, SS, 8 in. rifled barrel, blue or nickel finish. Chamfered Lever Variant: Outer front corner of cocking lever very noticeably angled (chamfered), circular trigger guard, early production without serial numbers. Square Cocking Lever Variant: curved outer front corner of cocking lever is squarish, recurved trigger guard, serial numbered, 8.6 in. OAL, 2.2 lbs. Mfg. 1931-39. Ref. GR Apr. 80 and AW Sept 81.

courtesy Beeman Collection

	100%	95%	90%	80%	60%	40%	20%
	$900	$850	$800	$750	$700	$550	$450

Add 25% for Chamfered Lever Variant.
Add 40% for nickel finish.
Add 30% for .22 cal.
Add 25% for Abercrombie and Fitch markings (MONOGRAM label stamped on LHS).
Add 20% for factory box.

ACVOKE

For information on Acvoke, see Accles & Shelvoke Ltd. above.

AERON CZ s.r.o.

Current manufacturer located in Brno, Czech Republic. Currently imported and/or distributed by Top Gun Air Guns Inc., located in Scottsdale, AZ, Airguns of Arizona located in Gilbert, AZ, Pyramyd Air, Inc. located in Bedford Heights, OH. Previously imported by Euro-Imports, located in Pahrump, NV, Century International Arms, Inc., located in St. Albans, VT, and Bohemia Arms, located in Fountain Valley, CA.

For information on Tau model pistols and rifles previously manufactured by Aeron, see Tau BRNO in the "T" section.

PISTOLS

MODEL B95 - .177 cal., CO_2 refillable from tank or 12-gram capsule, SS, 8.3 in. Lothar Walther barrel, 425 FPS, adj. rear sight, adj. trigger, adj. barrel weight, adj. pistol grip, 2.4 lbs. Disc. 2004.

	100%	95%	90%	80%	60%	40%	20%
	$350	$250	$200	$145	$100	N/A	N/A

Add 5% for left-hand grip.

MODEL B96 - .177 cal., CO_2 bulk fill or 12-gram cylinder, five shot, 8.3-10 in. Lothar Walther barrel, 443 FPS, adj. rear sight, adj. trigger, adj. barrel weight, adj. pistol grip, 2.4 lbs.

	100%	95%	90%	80%	60%	40%	20%
No MSR	$575	$450	$350	$250	$150	N/A	N/A

Add 10% for left-hand model.

B97 CHAMELEON - .177 cal., CO_2, similar to Model B96 except SS.

	100%	95%	90%	80%	60%	40%	20%
	$375	$295	$235	$195	$150	N/A	N/A

MODEL B98 - .177 cal., PCP, five shot, 8.3 in. Lothar Walther barrel, 443 FPS, adj. sights, adj. trigger, adj. barrel weight, adj. pistol grip, 2.4 lbs.

courtesy Aeron

	100%	95%	90%	80%	60%	40%	20%
No MSR	$849	$650	$500	$350	$275	N/A	N/A

Add 5% for left-hand grip.

GRADING	100%	95%	90%	80%	60%	40%	20%

MODEL B99 - .177 cal., PCP, SS, 8.3 in. Lothar Walther barrel, 425 FPS, adj. rear sight, adj. trigger, adj. barrel weight, adj. pistol grip, 2.4 lbs.

No MSR	$695	$550	$450	$300	$245	N/A	N/A

Add 5% for left-hand grip.

MODEL B100 - .177 cal., PCP, SS, competition target pistol.

	$735	$600	$495	$400	$325	N/A	N/A

Add 5% for left-hand grip.

MODEL ACZ101 SPIDER .177 cal., PCP, SS, 8.3 in. Lothar Walther barrel, 443 FPS, adj. sights, adj. trigger, adj. barrel weight, adj. pistol grip, 2.4 lbs.

courtesy Aeron

No MSR	$735	$600	$495	$400	$325	N/A	N/A

Add 5% for left-hand grip.

RIFLES

MODEL B40/B41/B41-5 - .177 (Model B40 and B41) or .22 (Model B41-5) cal., CO_2, SS (Model B41 and B41-5) or five shot (Model B40), 15.75 in. barrel, 476-410 FPS, UIT target model, adj. sight, adj. trigger, adj. cheek piece, adj. buttplate, wood stock, 9.5 lbs. Disc. 2005.

	$210	$185	$150	$115	$85	N/A	N/A

MODEL B40J/B41J/B41J-5 - .177 (Model B40J and B41J) or .22 (Model B41J-5) cal., CO_2, SS (Model B41J and B41J-5) or five shot (Model B40J), 15.75 in. barrel, 476-410 FPS, UIT target model, adj. sight, adj. trigger, adj. cheek piece, adj. buttplate, wood stock, 9.5 lbs. Disc. 2005.

	$210	$185	$150	$115	$85	N/A	N/A

AIR ARMS

Current manufacturer located in East Sussex, England. Currently imported Pyramyd Air, Inc. located in Bedford Heights, OH, Pomona Air Guns located in Victorville, CA, and Top Gun Air Guns, Inc., located in Scottsdale, AZ, Previously imported by Dynamit Nobel-RWS, Inc. Dealer or consumer direct sales.

Air Arms is a division of the parent company NSP Engineering Ltd. and has been manufacturing airguns since the mid-1980s. The latest Air Arms models, S300, S310, S400, S410, and the Pro-Target (designed by three-time world champion Nick Jenkinson and gunsmith Ken Turner), are pre-charged pneumatics that can be filled from a SCUBA tank, allowing many shots to be fired from one charge. The remaining models, Pro-Sport, TX200 Mk III, TX200 HX, and Pro-Elite are spring piston rifles. All Air Arms models feature Walther barrels.

RIFLES

BORA/BORA AL - .177 or .22 (Bora AL) cal., SL, SP, SS, with (Bora AL) or w/o 35 shot mag. over barrel, 11 in. rifled steel barrel, blue finish, 625 FPS, two-stage adj. trigger, sling swivels, beech Monte Carlo stock with checkered PG and vent. recoil pad, 35.5 in. OAL, 7.7 lbs.

	$275	$225	$175	$125	$75	N/A	N/A

Add 20-40% for Bora AL.

CAMARGUE/CAMARGUE AL - .177 or .22 (Camargue AL) cal., SL, SP, SS, with (Camargue AL) or w/o 35 shot mag. over barrel, tap-loading, 15 in. rifled steel barrel, blue finish, 625 FPS, two-stage adj. trigger, sling swivels, walnut Tyrolean-style stock with checkered PG and vent. recoil pad, 39.8 in. OAL, 7.94 lbs.

	$450	$375	$325	$275	$225	N/A	N/A

Add 20-40% for Camargue AL.

EV2 - .177, PCP, SS, side lever loading, 16.15 in. rotary swaged barrel, black finish, quick release charging connector, adj. trigger, silver color multi-adj. cheekpiece, forearm, and butt plate, competition stock, spirit level, wind indicator, approx. 40.5 in OAL, 9.12 lbs. New 2004.

No MSR	$1,800	$1,550	$1,250	N/A	N/A	N/A	N/A

Last MSR was $1,150.

Add 15% for MK III Model or for optional laminate stock.

GRADING	100%	95%	90%	80%	60%	40%	20%

KHANSIN/KHANSIN AL - .177 or .22 (Khansin AL) cal., SL, SP, SS, with (Khansin AL) or w/o 35 shot mag. over barrel, tap-loading, 15 in. rifled steel barrel, specially polished blue finish, 625 FPS, two-stage adj. trigger, sling swivels, walnut thumbhole stock with checkered PG and vent. recoil pad, 39.8 in. OAL, 7.94 lbs.

	$400	$325	$275	$225	$175	N/A	N/A

Add 20-40% for Camargue AL.

MISTRAL/MISTRAL AL - .177 or .22 (Mistral AL) cal., SL, SP, SS, with (Mistral AL) or w/o 35 shot mag. over barrel, 15 in. rifled steel barrel, blue finish, 625 FPS, two-stage adj. trigger, sling swivels, beech Monte Carlo stock with checkered PG and vent. recoil pad, 39.8 in. OAL, 7.94 lbs.

courtesy Beeman Collection

	$350	$275	$225	$175	$125	N/A	N/A

Add 20-40% for Mistral AL.

NJR100 - similar to the TX200, except has hand-picked barrel for accuracy, adj. cheekpiece, forearm, and shoulder pad, 10.75 lbs.

	$1,425	$1,200	$1,000	$750	$500	N/A	N/A

Last MSR was $2600.

Add 5% for left-hand.

PRO-ELITE - .177 or .22 cal., BBC, SP, 18 ft/lbs. (.177), 22 ft/lbs. (.22), 14 in. Walther barrel, beech Monte Carlo stock with cheekpiece, 9.3 lbs.

	$469	$350	$280	$225	$180	N/A	N/A

PRO-SPORT - .177 or .22 cal., SP, 9.7 in., 12-groove Walther barrel, multi-adj. two-stage trigger, sound moderator, ergonomically designed high comb beech or walnut sporter stock, 9 lbs.

No MSR	$600	$475	$380	$300	$245	N/A	N/A

Add 20% for walnut stock.

PRO-TARGET/PT MK III/ HUNTER - .177 or .22 cal. (Hunter), PCP, sliding bolt action, 12-groove 16 in. Walther barrel, multi-adj. trigger system, quick release charging connector, free-floating barrel (MK III), competition adj. cheekpiece, wood grain laminate, or optional red or blue laminate stock with multi-adj. butt pad, 6.6 lbs. Disc. 2001.

	$850	$675	$550	$450	$350	N/A	N/A

Last MSR was $1,150.

Add 15% for MK III Model or for optional laminate stock.

SM100 - .177 or .22 cal., PCP, 22 in. barrel, adj. two-stage trigger, beech stock, 8.5 lbs. Disc. 1994.

	$700	$600	$480	$365	$275	N/A	N/A

Last MSR was $975.

Add 10% for left-hand variation.

S200/S200T - .177 or .22 cal., PCP, BA, SS, built-in pressure gauge, 18.9 in. rotary swaged barrel, black finish, two-stage adj. trigger, beech wwith vent. recoil pad (S200) or adj. cheekpiece, butt pad (S200T), stock, and forearm, 34.3-36.5 in. OAL, 6.17-6.61 lbs. New 2004.

No MSR	$430	$345	$275	$225	N/A	N/A	N/A

Add 15% for S200T.

S300 - .177 cal. or .22 cal., PCP, bolt action, 12-groove 19.7 in. Walther barrel, multi-adj. two-stage trigger, quick release charging connector, beech or walnut stock with Monte Carlo-style cheekpiece, 6.6 lbs. Disc. 2001.

	$350	$275	$225	$175	$125	N/A	N/A

Last MSR was $469.

Add 30% for optional deluxe thumbhole version and gold-plated trigger.

S310 - .177 cal. or .22 cal., similar to S300, except has ten-shot magazine. Disc. 2001.

	$450	$375	$325	$275	$225	N/A	N/A

Last MSR was $569.

Add 30% for optional deluxe thumbhole version and gold-plated trigger.

S400 (CARBINE/CLASSIC/XTRA HI-POWER) - .177 or .22 cal., PCP, bolt action, single shot, built-in pressure gauge, 12-groove 15.4 (Carbine) or 19.7 in. Walther barrel, multi-adj. two-stage trigger, quick-release charging connector, beech or walnut stock with Monte Carlo-style cheekpiece, hand checkered forearm and pistol grip, approx. 6.6 lbs. New 2001.

No MSR	$535	$475	$375	$275	$225	N/A	N/A

Add 10% for Classic or Xtra Hi-Power.
Add 25% walnut stock.
Add 30% for optional deluxe thumbhole walnut stock.

GRADING	100%	95%	90%	80%	60%	40%	20%

S410 (CARBINE/CLASSIC/XTRA HI-POWER) - .177 or .22 cal., PCP, bolt action, ten-shot mag., built-in pressure gauge, 12-groove 15.4 (Carbine) or 19.7 in. Walther barrel, multi-adj. two-stage trigger, quick-release charging connector, beech or walnut stock with Monte Carlo-style cheekpiece, hand checkered forearm and pistol grip, approx. 6.6 lbs. New 2001.

	No MSR	$675	$550	$450	$350	N/A	N/A	N/A

Add 10% for Classic or Xtra Hi-Power.

Add 25% walnut stock.

Add 30% for optional deluxe thumbhole walnut stock.

S410 ERB - .177 or .22 cal., PCP, bolt action, ten-shot mag., similar to S410 except has adj. power. New 2005.

	No MSR	$745	$650	$550	$450	N/A	N/A	N/A

Add 25% for walnut stock.

Add 30% for optional deluxe thumbhole walnut stock.

S410TDR (TAKE DOWN RIFLE) - .22 cal., PCP, bolt action, ten-shot mag., modular format with 14 in. barrel, takedown buttstock (no tools needed), two-stage adj. trigger, adj. butt pad, pressure gauge, trigger safty, and carrying case, 34.25 OAL, 5.5 lbs. New 2005.

	No MSR	$775	$675	$575	$475	N/A	N/A	N/A

TM100 - similar to XM100, except with adj. cheekpiece and shoulder pad, target-style stock, 8.75 lbs.

	$1,000	$850	$680	$475	$350	N/A	N/A

Last MSR was $1,650.

Add 5% for left-hand model.

TX200/TX200SR - .177 or .22 cal., UL, SP, 15.75 in. barrel, 913/800 FPS, 9.2 lbs.

	$460	$400	$310	$250	$175	N/A	N/A

Last MSR was $560.

Add 15% for walnut stock.

Add 10% for left-hand variation.

Add 10% for recoilless S.R. model.

✱ **TX200 MK III** - .177 or .22 cal., UL, SP, 14.1 in. Walther barrel, sound moderator, beech or walnut stock with Monte Carlo-style cheek piece, latest version of the TX200 Series, 9.25 lbs.

	No MSR	$480	$375	$275	$195	N/A	N/A	N/A

✱ **TX200 HC** - .177 or .22 cal., UL, SP, 7 in. Walther barrel, beech or walnut stock with Monte Carlo-style cheekpiece, carbine version of TX200 MK III. 8.5 lbs.

	No MSR	$480	$375	$275	$195	N/A	N/A	N/A

XM100 - similar to the SM100, except has quick-release tank connector and walnut stock, 8 lbs. Disc. 1994.

	$800	$680	$540	$400	$300	N/A	N/A

Last MSR was $1,260.

Add 10% for left-hand variation.

AIRBOW

Previous trademark used by Robin Parks for a pneumatic rifle which fires special hollow arrows.

Research is ongoing with this trademark, and more information may be included both in future editions and online.

RIFLES

AIRBOW - .38 cal. arrows inserted into barrel shroud over the barrel, PCP, SS, black composition body, detachable buddy bottle, red plastic safety, Daisy spot sight, extendable stock of M16 carbine style, 35 in. OAL with stock extended, 5.0 lbs.

courtesy Beeman Collection

	$375	$325	$275	$200	$125	N/A	N/A

GRADING	100%	95%	90%	80%	60%	40%	20%

AIR CANES

As the name suggests, these are canes containing an airgun mechanism.

Air canes are a whole collecting field in themselves, but they form a delightful and key part of most quality airgun collections. Wolff´s book (1958) has one of the few fairly good discussions regarding these intriguing guns. He points out that while cane firearms were novelty weapons of no great practical value, air canes were one of the pinnacles of airgun effectiveness and utility – and certainly stand as some of the finest examples of wonderfully intricate and beautifully made airgun mechanisms. In most specimens, the gun function was concealed, but some bear trigger guards, shoulder stocks, or other obvious evidence as to their nature. Most, apparently, were designed for self-defense or as a method of carrying a hunting arm while out walking – in those days, the transition between town and country could come rather quickly.

The mechanism almost always was pneumatic, usually being charged by numerous strokes from a separate pump. A few have a self-contained pump and a few use pre-charged air cartridges, and extremely rare variants featured a spring-piston mechanism. The typical pattern was two parts: the rear half of the gun was the tubular air reservoir and valve mechanism; the forward half contained the barrel and lock mechanism. These lock mechanisms were often jewel-like in their detail and operation.

Rather commonly, there were two barrels, a smooth bore in which a rifled barrel was nestled, or vice versa. The rifled barrels usually were brass, bearing an elegantly scalloped rifling of twenty-two or more shallow, low-friction grooves. A ramrod was housed within the nest of barrels, with its handle forming the screw-off base tip of the cane. The trigger, typically, is simply a button which protrudes only when the gun is ready to be put up to your cheek, aimed, and fired. Sights and even a trigger guard may be present externally.

The Golden Age of air canes was in the 1800s when English air canes dominated the field. Key makers of London and Birmingham included John Blanch, Edward Reilly, and James Townsend. An airgun was part of the attire of many a well-dressed English gentleman of the late 1800s. Most specimens were sold in fitted cases with their pump and accessories. These accessories often included a rifle-style, buttstock-shaped air reservoir or skeleton wooden buttstock which could be carried in the huge pockets of a gentleman´s "great coat" until extra air volume and/or steadiness of fire were needed from the air cane. Weight varied from 1.5 to over 8 pounds; calibers generally were in the .30 to .36 area, but ranged from .177 to .75!

The projectiles of air canes generally were lead balls, cast from the molds included in cased outfits. However, imagination seemed to be the only limit as to what could be fired from these amazing guns. Shot, darts, arrows, bullets, and even harpoons and multi-pronged fish and frog spears have been utilized!

There recently has been a small renaissance in air canes. In the 1980s, Harper produced some wonderful modern air canes in England. As these utilized the Brocock air cartridges instead of a built-in air reservoir, they could be made very slim and truly elegant. The handles sometimes were wonderfully carved dogs' heads or other figures. Fold-out triggers were virtually undetectable in the fine engraving. In the United States, also in the 1980s, the famed airgun maker Gary Barnes produced an amazingly intricate and functionally astonishing full automatic air cane!

Cue Ball CO$_2$ Air Canes are a configuration of air canes made to resemble a black metal cane with a billiard ball for its knob. The authors and publisher wish to thank Mr. John Caruth for the following information in this edition of the *Blue Book of Airguns*.

These air canes fire a CO$_2$ cylinder as the projectile, with astonishing force and range. Firing causes the seal on the CO$_2$ cylinder to be pierced. Pressure builds until the cylinder itself is propelled from the muzzle. The cylinder, as a projectile, gathers additional velocity from jetting action. The inventor apparently wishes to remain anonymous because of the mistaken idea that these air canes would be considered as "destructive devices" by the BATF because they are over .50 caliber. Actually, BATF has no jurisdiction over these air canes because they are not firearms! John Caruth obtained six of these aircanes and had twenty-five of them reproduced by Tom Allison in the 1990s. The original maker also made a few specimens which retain the CO$_2$ cylinder but fire a conventional .45 caliber lead ball. The original price for these Cue Ball CO$_2$ Air Canes was $350. Values now run from about $400 to $500 for the cylinder-shooting Cue Ball CO$_2$ air canes and about $450 to $550 for the ball-firing Cue Ball CO$_2$ air canes.

Values of air canes vary greatly, but a typical British air cane in good condition generally will sell from $1,000 to $2,000. A case, accessories, and fine condition will add greatly to the value.

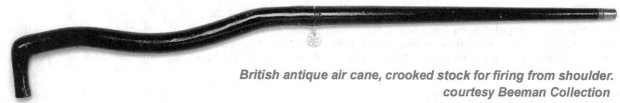

British antique air cane, crooked stock for firing from shoulder.
courtesy Beeman Collection

AIRFORCE AIRGUNS

Current manufacturer and distributor located in Fort Worth, TX. Dealer and consumer direct sales.

The project to design and produce the AirForce Talon began in 1994. Shipping began in the U.S. during 1999. The Talon Series has pre-charged single shots with variable power. They were first marketed in England under the name Gun Power Stealth, and they are manufactured in Fort Worth, TX, by designer John McCaslin.

RIFLES

CONDOR - .177 or .22 cal., single shot, PCP (490cc compressed air bottle doubles as shoulder stock), external thumb-pressure-operated adj. power system allows 600-1,300 FPS (depending on cal. and pellet weight), 24 in. Lothar Walther barrel (interchangeable for cal.), aircraft-grade aluminum alloy and polymer construction with three integrated dovetail rails for accessories, two-stage adj. trigger, black anodized finish, 6.5 lbs. (gun and bottle), 38.75 in., OAL. New 2004.

MSR	$570	$550	$475	$395	N/A	N/A	N/A	N/A

GRADING	100%	95%	90%	80%	60%	40%	20%

Add 10% for fiberoptic open sights or refill clamp.

AirForce Airguns offers accessories for all models (too many to list). Contact AirForce Airguns (see Trademark Index) for price and availability.

TALON - .177 or .22 cal., single shot, PCP (compressed air bottle doubles as shoulder stock), external thumb-pressure-operated adj. power system allows 400-1000 FPS (depending on cal. and pellet weight), 18 in. Lothar Walther barrel (interchangeable for cal.), aircraft-grade aluminum alloy and polymer construction with three integrated dovetail rails for accessories, two-stage adj. trigger, black anodized finish, 5.5 lbs. (gun and bottle), 32.6 in., OAL. New 1998.

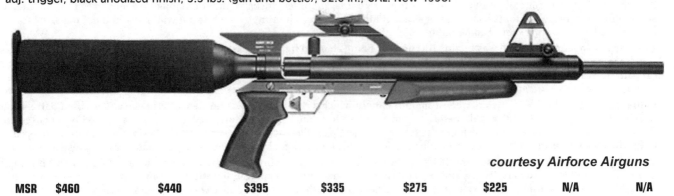

courtesy Airforce Airguns

MSR	$460	$440	$395	$335	$275	$225	N/A	N/A

Add 10% for fiberoptic open sights or refill clamp.

AirForce Airguns offers accessories for all models (too many to list). Contact AirForce Airguns (see Trademark Index) for price and availability.

TALON SS - .177 or .22 cal., similar to Talon, except has 12 in. Lothar Walther barrel in an extended shroud with muzzle cap sound moderator system, 5.25 lbs. (gun and bottle), 32.75 in., OAL. New 2000.

courtesy Airforce Airguns

MSR	$480	$460	$415	$350	$295	$245	N/A	N/A

Add 10% for fiberoptic open sights or refill clamp.

AirForce Airguns offers accessories for all models (too many to list). Contact AirForce Airguns (see Trademark Index) for price and availability.

AIRGUNAID

Previous manufacturer located in Chelmsford, Essex, Great Britain circa 1980-82.

Research is ongoing with this trademark, and more information will be included both in future editions and online. Basically these are Scottish Diana rifles fitted with a .20 cal. barrel. It took the Brits a while to pick up on this caliber, which was introduced to precision spring piston airguns by the Beeman company in the 1970s. Average original condition specimens are typically priced in the $100 to $200 range.

AIRGUN EXPRESS, INC.

Current importer with retail catalog sales located in Montezuma, IA.

Mail order and catalog sales of many major brand airguns including Beeman, Crosman, Daisy, Gamo, Mendoza (importer), RWS, and others. Please contact the company directly for more information and prices of their products (see Trademark Index listing).

AIR GUN INC.

Current importer and distributor located in Houston, TX.

Air Gun Inc. currently imports Industry Brand airguns. Please refer to the "I" section section of this book for information on these airguns.

AIR LOGIC

Previous manufacturer and distributor located in Forest Row, Sussex, England. Air Logic had limited importation into the U.S.

GRADING	100%	95%	90%	80%	60%	40%	20%

RIFLES

GENESIS - .22 cal., SL, single-stroke pneumatic, 630 FPS, bolt-action sliding barrel by Lothar Walther, recoilless, adj. trigger, 9.50 lbs. Mfg. began in 1988. Disc.

	100%	95%	90%	80%	60%	40%	20%
	$575	$450	$360	$295	$225	N/A	N/A

Last MSR was $750.

AIR MATCH

Previous trademark manufactured in Italy circa 1980s. Previously imported by Kendall International located in Paris, KY.

PISTOLS

AIR MATCH MODEL 400 - .177 cal., SL, single-stroke pneumatic, adj. trigger, UIT target model, 2 lbs.

	100%	95%	90%	80%	60%	40%	20%
	$320	$260	$180	$105	$60	N/A	N/A

AIR MATCH MODEL 600 - .177 cal., SL, single-stroke pneumatic, adj. sights, adj. trigger, UIT target model, 2 lbs.

	100%	95%	90%	80%	60%	40%	20%
	$350	$280	$200	$125	$80	N/A	N/A

ALROS

Current manufacturer of CO_2 and PCP rifles located in Staffs, United Kingdom. 1993 - present.

The authors and publisher wish to thank Mr. Tim Saunders for assistance with this information.

RIFLES

SHADOW - .177, .20, or .22 cal., PCP, SS or eight-shot mag., BA (RH or LH), blue finish, beech or walnut stock, with or without thumbhole. Sporting rifles in four variants (three with built-in air reservoir): M60 Hunter, M100 Carbine, M140 Standard, and the Shadow 400 variant with removable 400 cc buddy bottle, 39/40 in. OAL, 7-7.5 lbs. Mfg. beginning in 1997.

	100%	95%	90%	80%	60%	40%	20%
	$650	$575	$500	$400	$300	$250	$200

Add 10% for Shadow 400.
Add 20% for eight-shot magazine.
Add 10% for walnut stock.
Add 25% for thumbhole walnut stock.

STARFIRE - similar to Shadow, except has two 12 gm. CO_2 cylinders, power level set at UK 12 ft. lb. limit, approx forty shots per charge.

Current values not yet determined.

TRAILSMAN - .177, .20, or .22 cal., PCP, SS, BA (RH or LH), 16mm Lothar Walther barrel, blue finish, adj. tubular stock, composition grips, takedown construction. Two variants: Trailsman Standard with built-in reservoir under barrel, 5 lbs. Trailsman 400 with removable 400 cc buddy bottle reservoir, 6 lbs. New late 1990s.

	100%	95%	90%	80%	60%	40%	20%
	$530	$450	$375	$300	$225	$175	$125

Add 10% for Trailsman 400.

AIRROW

Current trademark manufactured by Swivel Machine Works located in Milford, CT.

Swivel Machine Works started manufacturing powerful, arrow-firing rifles and pistols beginning in 1990, and has recently started manufacturing pellet-firing air rifles. Contact the manufacturer directly for information and prices on their arrow-firing models.

PISTOLS

AIRROW PISTOL ABS 013 - arrow firing, PCP, SS, takes down to watertight case (provided), 24.8 in. OAL, 5 lbs. Mfg. 1990-date.

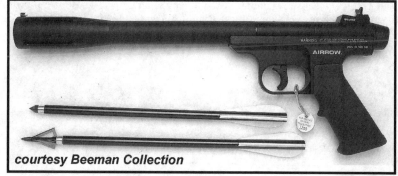

courtesy Beeman Collection

	100%	95%	90%	80%	60%	40%	20%
	$1,500	$1,250	$1,000	$750	$500	N/A	N/A

GRADING	100%	95%	90%	80%	60%	40%	20%

RIFLES

AIRROW MODEL A-8SRB STEALTH - 177, .22, or .38 cal., CO_2 or PCP, SS or nine-shot mag., 20 in. rifled BBL, 1100 FPS, scope rings included, 35 in. OAL, 7.5 lbs.

	MSR	$2,299	$2,299	$1,995	$1,650	$1,250	$995	N/A	N/A

Many options available.

AIRROW CARBINE - arrow firing, PCP, SS, takes down to watertight case (provided). Mfg. 1990-date.

courtesy Beeman Collection

	$3,000	$2,500	$2,000	$1,500	$1,000	N/A	N/A

AIR SOFT

Term currently used to identify a configuration of gun copies primarily manufactured in the Orient.

In the last two decades a new type of gun has appeared. The so-called "Air Soft" guns originally were designed to be a type of "non-gun" for customers whose local laws highly restricted or forbade the ownership of actual firearms. Generally, they are made in the styling (sometimes very exact styling) of well-known firearms. Models ranged from copies of famous handguns to heavy machine guns. They soon became popular with customers who wanted to collect, and even have the sensation of firing, guns which were too expensive, too highly regulated, or too dangerous for general ownership. Most fire relatively harmless 6 mm diameter light plastic balls at muzzle velocities below 300 FPS. Even those which fire at somewhat higher power generally are not capable of inflicting serious injury to humans or property. Balls filled with paint or made of aluminum sometimes are available but have not been very popular and may be difficult to buy locally. Many of the Air Soft guns are not designed to fire paintballs or metal balls and may be damaged or ruined by their use.

The classification of Air Soft guns has led to some interesting legal questions. Without a doubt, they are not firearms and are not dangerous or lethal weapons. In fact, they are not weapons in any sense unless one might use them as a club. They may use carbon dioxide, compressed air, or mechanical means, including electrical micro-motors to propel their projectiles – so some are not even truly airguns. Federal law requires the versions firing plastic balls to have at least their muzzle areas conspicuously marked with blaze orange color, but illegal unmarked imports often appear.

From a safety standpoint, by far the largest caution is to not brandish them where they might be mistaken for dangerous weapons. There have been cases were individuals used such guns in holdups or pointed them at police officers in dark alleys or where several teenagers wearing ski masks appeared with exact lookalikes of AK 47s, Thompson sub-machine guns, M16 rifles, etc. at their schools – distinctly unwise moves. But certainly over 99.9% are used and enjoyed harmlessly – often as enjoyable substitutes for potentially harmful real guns.

Production of Air Soft guns, mainly in the Orient, has become a huge market. They range from toy-like, almost insulting imitations to very sophisticated, expensive copies of heavy machine guns which may use well-made metal or even original parts from deactivated real automatic weapons. This is now a collecting field in itself and will not be covered in this guide unless a specimen has special historical significance. Values run from a couple of dollars for plastic specimens which only suggest their design origin to hundreds of dollars for those sophisticated specimens with well-made, or even original, metal parts. There is a great deal of information on Air Soft guns available on the Web.

Two examples are illustrated: Left (very realistic example): A Daisy copy of an Uzi sub-machine gun, with replica cartridges and magazine (produced before the requirement for blaze orange markings). Right (caricature, toy-like example): representation of AK-47 rifle. Note that the package of the projectiles is labeled: "BB BULLETS" – but the contents are neither BBs nor bullets! Ref. *Blue Book of Airguns*, edition 4.

courtesy Beeman Collection

GRADING	100%	95%	90%	80%	60%	40%	20%

AMERICAN ARMS, INC.

Previous manufacturer and importer located in North Kansas City, MO until 2000.

Even though American Arms, Inc. imported Norica airguns, they are listed in this section because of their private label status. Importation began in late 1988 and was discontinued in 1989. For more information and current pricing on imported American Arms, Inc. firearms, please refer to the *Blue Book of Gun Values* by S.P. Fjestad (also available online).

PISTOLS

IDEAL - .177 cal., BBC, SP, 400 FPS, adj. sights, 3 lbs.

	$75	$60	$45	$30	$20	N/A	N/A

Last MSR was $105.

RIFLES

JET RIFLE - .177 cal., BBC, SP, 855 FPS, adj. double-set triggers, hardwood stock, 7 lbs.

	$100	$85	$70	$55	$40	N/A	N/A

Last MSR was $160.

Subtract $35 for Junior Model.

COMMANDO - .177 cal., BBC, SP, 540 FPS, adj. sights, 5 lbs.

	$80	$65	$50	$40	$25	N/A	N/A

Last MSR was $115.

AMERICAN GALLERY AIRGUNS

This is a group of fairly well-defined airguns which were produced by American gunsmiths just before and after the U.S. Civil War (1861-65).

Travel to the country was difficult for city folks at the time these guns were made. These airguns, typically provided by concessionaires in indoor ranges, provided a means of satisfying the desire to shoot. Again, Wolff (1958) has one of the few good discussions of these interesting airguns which had been unappreciated for a long time. Now they are becoming increasingly hard to acquire as demand and understanding has soared.

These airguns are highly stylized from European patterns, such as those made by Josef Rutte of Bohemia around 1830. All have a huge central spring cylinder ahead of the trigger guard, containing a double volute mainspring system. All have leather piston seals and smoothbore barrels. The two main cranking methods are by a crank handle ("Kurblespanner") or by a lever pivoted at the buttplate and typically shaped into the trigger guard in the forward end ("Bügelspanner"). And while virtually all are breech loaders, the particular methods of loading and cocking are classified into six groups.

1. Primary New York: Apparently among the earliest of American gallery airguns, these seem to have developed from European forms which use a detachable crank handle to cock the mainspring. The European forms have a tip-up breech; the American forms developed an unusual breech which opened by twisting the receiver. Famous makers include David and Joseph Lurch, G. Fisher, and August Mock.

2. Secondary New York: A small group featuring the twist-breech loading of the Primary forms, but cocked by a cocking lever formed by a rearward extension of the trigger guard. A gun of this type by John Zuendorff has been credited as being used in the draft riots of the American Civil War.

3. Upstate New York: A small, special group. The main feature is a hand-operated revolving cylinder with the barrel attaching to the receiver with a pin, wedge, and bottom strap in a manner and styling very similar to an open-top Colt revolver. 12- or 13-shot cylinders are known. The only makers listed by Wolff are Charles Bunge and C. Werner.

4. St. Louis: The key characteristic is a long cocking lever of which the forward end is formed by the trigger guard and the remainder concealed in a groove in the under edge of the buttstock. The barrel tips up for breech loading. The stocks have separate buttstock and forearm sections. A large group; famous makers include Bandle, Blickensdoerfer, and Stein.

5. New England: The buttstock and forearm are one piece. A fixed, two-piece cocking lever along the forward side of the receiver swings up and back for cocking. The barrel tips up or twists to a loose open position for loading. This type is rare. Two known makers are Eggers and Tonks.

6. Top Lever Gallery Air Rifle: Cocks by pulling back on heavy lever inserted into comb of rifle. Illustration shows the lever partially up for clarity. Very rare.

About 1870 the gallery gun design, so well-developed in America, migrated to Europe and was continued as the European "Bügelspanner" for almost a century by several makers, most notably Oscar Will of Zella-Mehlis, Germany. Will frequently marked his guns as "Original Will" to distinguish them from the many copies -- some of these copies, amusingly, were then marked as "Original". Unmarked copies are rather common.

Values of American Gallery Airguns have escalated from a few hundred dollars only a decade ago, to $1,000 or $2,000 more recently, and especially rare forms, such as Upstate New York models, bear asking prices of up to five thousand dollars. The later European "Bügelspanner" generally sells for $200 to $300, with the "Original Will" marking and better condition adding to the price.

Primary New York

Secondary New York

Upstate New York

St. Louis

New England

Top Lever

courtesy Beeman Collection

AMERICAN LUGER

For information on American Luger airguns, see Schimel in the "S" section.

AMERICAN TOOL WORKS

Previous manufacturer of BB guns in Chicago, IL. This company purchased other BB gun makers and produced BB guns under American, Sterling, Upton, and Wyandotte trademarks.

The authors and publisher wish to thank Dennis Baker and John Groenewold for their valuable assistance with the following information in this edition of the *Blue Book of Airguns*. Most guns by American Tool Works were typical SP, LA, BB rifles of rather plain appearance, except for the big 1000-shot repeaters with an octagonal barrel tube, walnut stock, and bright nickel

GRADING	100%	95%	90%	80%	60%	40%	20%

plating. The factory tools went from buyer to buyer and finally ended up with Markham-King in 1929. King dumped the tools in the Detroit River and Daisy finally consumed King and the designs and patents. Guns were made circa 1891-1928 (see Dunathan, 1971). Additional research is underway on this complex group. Information given here must be considered as tentative. Information and illustrations from other collectors is solicited at BBA6info@Beemans.net.

RIFLES

AMERICAN DART RIFLE - BB/.174 cal., SP, LA, SS, loaded with feathered darts through a cover plate under the barrel, all sheet metal, barrel marked "American Dart Rifle, Upton Machine Company, St. Joseph, Michigan. Ca. 1912-20".

	100%	95%	90%	80%	60%	40%	20%
	$900	$800	$750	$700	$650	$550	$450

STERLING SINGLE SHOT

There appear to be three variations. This model is under research, and more information will be made available in future editions of this guide.

STERLING MODEL D - BB/.174 cal., SP, LA, 1000 shot, octagon barrel tube, nickel or blue finish, 32.2 in. OAL, 2.4 lbs.

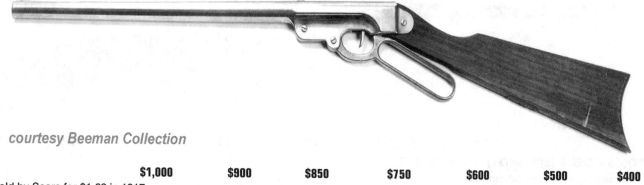

courtesy Beeman Collection

	100%	95%	90%	80%	60%	40%	20%
	$1,000	$900	$850	$750	$600	$500	$400

Sold by Sears for $1.68 in 1917.

STERLING MODEL G - BB/.174 cal., 1000 shot, SP, LA, octagon barrel tube, nickel or blue finish, barrel marked "American Tool Works". 36 in OAL, 2.4 lbs.

courtesy Beeman Collection

	100%	95%	90%	80%	60%	40%	20%
	$1,000	$900	$850	$750	$600	$500	$400

UPTON SPECIAL - BB/.174 cal., similar to Sterling Model G, except marked "Upton", 500-shot repeater.

	100%	95%	90%	80%	60%	40%	20%
	$500	$450	$400	$375	$325	$300	$225

Offered by Sears.

UPTON SINGLE SHOT - BB/.174 cal., similar to Sterling Single Shot, except marked "Upton".

	100%	95%	90%	80%	60%	40%	20%
	$300	$250	$200	$175	$150	$125	$85

Offered by Sears in 1922 for $1.15.

UPTON MODEL 20 - BB/.174 cal., SP, LA, SS, round barrel cover with distinctive humped ridge under barrel cover ahead of trigger guard, straight grip, slab sided stock, marked as made by Upton Machine Co. in St. Joseph, Michigan, patent dates of 1914 and 1923, 32.3 in., OAL.

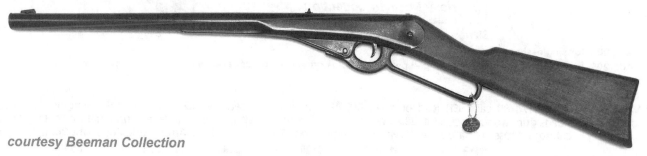

courtesy Beeman Collection

	100%	95%	90%	80%	60%	40%	20%
	$450	$350	$300	$275	$250	$225	$175

GRADING	100%	95%	90%	80%	60%	40%	20%

UPTON MODEL 30 (350 SHOT) - SP, LA, SS, round barrel cover with humped ridge under barrel cover ahead of trigger guard, straight grip, slab side stock, marked as made by Upton Machine Co. in St. Joseph, Michigan. Patent dates of June 13, 1914 Others Pending. 32.3 in. OAL.

    Current values not yet determined.

UPTON MODEL 40 - BB/.174 cal., similar to Upton Model 20, except 1000 shot.

	$500	$450	$400	$375	$325	$300	$225

    Sold by Sears in 1922 for $1.48.

UPTON MODEL 50 (500 SHOT) - SP, LA, SS, round barrel cover with humped ridge under barrel cover ahead of trigger guard, straight grip, slab side stock, marked as made by Upton Machine Co.in St. Joesph, Michigan. Patent dates of 1914 and 1923, 32.3 in. OAL.

    Current values not yet determined.

UPTON MODEL C - BB/.174 cal., SP, LA, very Daisy-like styling with pistol grip stock.

courtesy Beeman Collection

	$300	$250	$200	$175	$150	$125	$85

UPTON MODEL F (500 SHOT) - SP, LA, SS, 32.3 in. OAL.

    Current values not yet determined.

WYANDOTTE - BB/.174 cal., similar to Upton Model 40, except marked "All Metal Products, Wyandotte, Michigan".

	$500	$450	$400	$375	$325	$300	$225

    Also made under the Sears name as the Ranger Repeating Air Rifle.

AMPELL

    Previous trade name of air and gas guns manufactured by Playtime Products located at 48 E. Main Street, Honeoye, NY, circa 1968-1975. Some production in Canada.

PISTOLS

ACRO 1/S-177/S-220 - .175/BB or .22 cal., CO_2, SS pellet or lead ball (S-177 or S-220) or 80-shot gravity feed mag., cocking gun also loads gun for each shot, all exposed parts cast metal with matte black finish, combination cocking knob/manual safety -- cannot be reset to safe after moving to fire position, 350 FPS, 11.5 in. OAL, 2.6 lbs.

courtesy Beeman Collection

	$85	$65	$55	$45	$40	$35	$25

    Add 20% for single-shot pellet pistols.

    Add 20% for original factory kit with Ampell pellets and CO_2 cylinders and papers.

RIFLES

BB MAGNUM M44 - .174/BB cal., SSP, lead or steel BB, 48-shot gravity feed magazine, 350+ FPS, swinging forearm cocks, charges, and loads gun, wood stock, styled like Winchester M-1894 but without cocking lever, combination cocking knob/manual safety -- cannot be reset to safe after moving to fire position, 38 in. OAL, 4.5 lbs. AmpellRifleModelAmpBBMagB0882.tif

	$175	$150	$125	$100	$75	$50	$40

    Add 15% for original factory box and papers.

GRADING	100%	95%	90%	80%	60%	40%	20%

ANICS GROUP

Current manufacturer established in 1990, and located in Moscow, Russia. Currently imported by Compasseco located in Bardstown, KY and European American Armory Corp. located in Sharpes, FL. Previously imported by Air Rifle Specialists located in Pine City, NY. Anics Group was originally an importer of Western-made airguns and firearms. In 1996, they began manufacturing their own line of CO_2 guns, semi-autos, and revolvers.

PISTOLS

MODEL A-10 - BB/.175 cal., CO_2, semi-auto, fifteen-shot mag., 450 FPS, checkered plastic grips, blue or silver finish, wooden checkered grips on silver models, adj. rear sight.

No MSR	$100	$75	$50	$35	$20	N/A	N/A

MODEL A-101M (MAGNUM) - BB/.175 cal., CO_2, semi-auto, fifteen-shot, 490 FPS, compensator, checkered plastic grips, blue or silver finish, wooden checkered grips on silver models, adj. rear sight.

No MSR	$100	$75	$50	$35	$20	N/A	N/A

MODEL A-111 - BB/.175 cal., CO_2, semi-auto, fifteen-shot, 450 FPS, contoured plastic grips, blue or silver finish, adj. rear sight.

No MSR	$100	$75	$50	$35	$20	N/A	N/A

MODEL A-112/A-112L (LASER) - BB/.175 cal., CO_2, semi-auto, fifteen-shot, 490 FPS, adj. rear sight, or with built-in laser housed in barrel lug automatically activated with slight pull of the trigger, contoured plastic grips, blue or silver finish.

No MSR	$100	$75	$50	$35	$20	N/A	N/A

Add $50 for Model A-112L (Laser).

MODEL A-3000 SKIF - BB/.175 or .177 cal., CO_2, SA or DA, 28-shot rotary mag., 500 FPS, thumb-release safety, grooved trigger guard, ambidextrous mag. release, three-dot adj. target sights, fiberglass-reinforced polyamide frame and grip, matte black or matte black with silver finish slide, hard plastic carrying case, loading tool, and spare rotary magazine, 1 lb. 9 oz. New 2001.

courtesy Howard Collection

No MSR	$125	$110	$80	$50	$35	N/A	N/A

Add 10% for silver slide (Model A-3000 Silver).
Add 20% for long barrel (Model A-3000 LB).

REVOLVERS

MODEL A-20 - BB/.175 cal., CO_2, SA or DA, thirty-shot, 410 FPS, loaded through cylinder (five BBs in each chamber), adj. rear sight, contoured plastic grips, CO_2 cartridge loads through base of grip, cylinder rotates when gun is fired, blue or silver finish. Disc.

	$120	$95	$80	$65	$40	N/A	N/A

MODEL A-201 MAGNUM - BB/.175 cal., CO_2, SA or DA, thirty-shot, 460 FPS, loaded through cylinder (five BBs in each chamber), adj. rear sight, contoured plastic grips, CO_2 cartridge loads through base of grip, cylinder rotates when gun is fired, blue or silver finish.

	$125	$105	$80	$65	$40	N/A	N/A

ANSCHÜTZ

Current manufacturer established in 1856, and located in Ulm, Germany. Currently imported and distributed by Champion's Choice, located in LaVergne, TN, Champion's Shooter's Supply, located in New Albany, OH, Gunsmithing, Inc., located in Colorado Springs, CO, and International Shooters Service, located in Fort Worth, TX. Currently distributed by Pilkington Competion Equipment LLC located in Monteagle, TN.

Models 2001 and 2002 were previously imported by Precision Sales Intl., Inc. Models 333, 335, and 380 were previously imported by Crosman from 1986 to 1988. Model 380 was also previously imported by Marksman. Research is ongoing with this trademark, and more information will be included both online and in future editions. For more information and current pricing on both new and used Anschütz firearms, please refer to the *Blue Book of Gun Values* by S.P. Fjestad (also available online).

GRADING	100%	95%	90%	80%	60%	40%	20%

PISTOLS

DOLLA MARK II - .177 cal., SP, SS, push-barrel cocking, may or may not be stamped "KEENFIRE" on wooden grips, no barrel shroud, mainspring visible around barrel when not cocked, nickel-plated finish, load by unscrewing plug at back end of barrel, 8.1 in. OAL (uncocked), 0.6 lbs. Mfg. pre-WWII.

courtesy Beeman Collection

	N/A	N/A	$195	$150	$125	$95	$75

Add 30% for "KEENFIRE" marking (for American market only).
More primitive, but better materials, than JGA - sometimes with Dolla medallions.

JGA (MODEL 100) - .177 cal. darts, pellets, or shot, SP, SS, push-barrel cocking, mainspring covered by barrel shroud, black plastic body with JGA molded into brown plastic checkered grips, nickel plating on barrel shroud, trigger guard, and trigger, load by unscrewing plug at back end of barrel. 8.3 in. OAL uncocked, 0.5 lbs. Mfg. post-WWII.

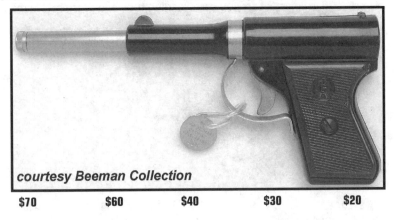

courtesy Beeman Collection

	$70	$60	$40	$30	$20	N/A	N/A

Also known as IGA.

MODEL M5 JUNIOR - .177 cal., PCP, similar to Model M10, except shorter and lighter.

	$600	$500	$400	$300	$200	N/A	N/A

MODEL LP@ ANSCHÜTZ - .177 cal., PCP, UIT match pistol, 8.93 in. barrel with compensator, internal stabilizer, adj. trigger, adj. sights, adj. Morini grip, 2.47 lbs. 16.54 OAL. New 2001.

No MSR	$1,150	$995	$875	$695	$595	N/A	N/A

　❋ **Model LP@ ANSCHÜTZ Junior** - .177 cal., PCP, UIT match pistol, 7.5 in. barrel with compensator, internal stabilizer, adj. trigger, adj. sights, adj. Morini grip, 1.92 lbs. 13.98 OAL. New 2004.

No MSR	$1,150	$995	$875	$695	$595	N/A	N/A

　❋ **Model LP@ ANSCHÜTZ Light** - .177 cal., PCP, UIT match pistol, similar to Model LP@ ANSCHÜTZ except has extra small (XS) grip, 2.05 lbs. 16.54 OAL. New 2005.

　As this edition went to press, U.S. availability had yet to be established on this model.

MODEL M10 - .177 cal., PCP, 492 FPS, 9.50 in. barrel with compensator, adj. trigger, sights and pistol grip, special dry firing mechanism, walnut grips. Mfg. by SAM in Switzerland 1997-98.

	$700	$550	$475	$400	$300	N/A	N/A

Last MSR was $1,395.

RIFLES

MODEL 220 - .177 cal., SL, SP, SS, suppressed recoil system, twin metal piston rings, 18.5 in. barrel, no safety, precision match stock, aperture sight, 44.3 in. OAL, 10.4 lbs. Approx. 11,000 mfg.1959-1967.

	$475	$385	$325	$250	$175	N/A	N/A

MODEL 250 - .177 cal., SL, SP, SS, suppressed recoil system using unique oil pot designed by Hermann Wild, precision match stock, aperture sight. 18.5 in. BBL. 44.7 in. OAL, 10.9 lbs. Mfg. 1968 to the early 1980s.

	$450	$365	$315	$235	$150	N/A	N/A

GRADING	100%	95%	90%	80%	60%	40%	20%

MODEL 275 - .173 (4.4 mm) lead balls cal., Schmeisser system BA, six or twelve round removable box magazine, 17.3 in. barrel, Mauser-style swinging manual safety, 41.7 in. OAL, 5.9 lbs. Intro. mid-1950s.

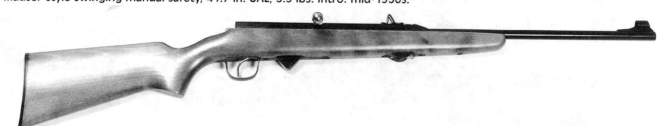

courtesy Beeman Collection

No MSR	$425	$350	$250	$200	$145	N/A	N/A

MODEL 330 - .177 cal., BBC, SP, SS, Junior version of Model 335 sporter, 16.5 in. BBL, 40.6 in. OAL, 6.3 lbs.

	$150	$125	$100	$75	$50	N/A	N/A

MODEL 333 - .177 or .22 cal., BBC, SP, 700 FPS, adj. trigger, 18 in. barrel, 6.75 lbs.

	$180	$125	$90	$75	$60	N/A	N/A

Last MSR was $175.

MODEL 335 - .177 or .22 cal., BBC, SP, 700 FPS, adj. trigger, 18.50 in. barrel, 7.50 lbs. Disc. 2003.

	$275	$225	$190	$140	$100	N/A	N/A

Last MSR was $200.

Add $10 for Model 335 Mag. .22 cal.

MODEL 380 - .177 cal., UL, SP, 600-640 FPS, match model, removable cheekpiece, adj. trigger, stippled walnut grips. Disc. 1994.

	$750	$595	$475	$375	$295	N/A	N/A

Last MSR was $1,250.

Subtract 10% for left-hand variation.
Add 10% for Moving Target Model.

MODEL 2001 - .177 cal., SL, single stroke pneumatic, 10 lbs. 8 oz.

	$1,250	$920	$815	$625	$500	N/A	N/A

Last MSR was $1,800.

Subtract 10% for left-hand variation.
Add $80 for Running Target Model.

MODEL 2002 - .177 cal., PCP, 26 in. barrel, adj. buttplate and cheekpiece, 10.50 lbs. New 1997.

No MSR	$1,150	$995	$850	$700	$550	N/A	N/A

✳ *Model 2002 ALU* - .177 cal., PCP, single shot, easy-exchange 350-shot air cylinder with manometer, 25.2 in. barrel, aluminum alloy stock features adj. laminate pistol grip and laminate forearm, adj. alloy cheekpiece, shoulder stock and buttplate attach to alloy frame, 42.5 in. OAL, 10.8 lbs. New 2000.

No MSR	$1,350	$1,200	$1,00	$825	$625	N/A	N/A

✳ *Model 2002 Club* - .177 cal., PCP, SS, 25.2 in. barrel, Walnut stock with adj. cheekpiece and buttplate, 42.5 in. OAL, 10.8 lbs. Mfg. 2000-05.

	$915	$800	$675	$550	$450	N/A	N/A

Last MSR was $1,065.

✳ *Model 2002 D-RT* - .177 cal., PCP, SS, Running Target Model, 33.8 in. BBL, 51.5 in. OAL, 9.2 lbs.

No MSR	$1,295	$1,150	$935	$775	$595	N/A	N/A

✳ *Model 2002 Junior* - .177 cal., PCP, SS, 20.8 in. barrel, similar to Model 2002, except 35 in. OAL, 7.9 lbs. Disc. 2005.

	$915	$800	$675	$550	$450	N/A	N/A

Last MSR was $1,065.

MODEL 2002 SUPERAIR - .177 cal., SL, SSP, SS, 25.2 in. BBL, aluminum alloy or color laminated wood stock with adj. buttplate and cheekpiece, 42.5 in. OAL, 10.50 or 11 (aluminum) lbs. New 1992.

No MSR	$1,150	$995	$850	$700	$550	N/A	N/A

Add $200 for ALU stock.

MODEL 2020 FIELD - .177 cal., PCP, SS, similar to Model 2002 CA ALU, 25.2 in. barrel, 690 FPS, 10.36 lbs.

No MSR	$1,350	$995	$850	$700	$550	N/A	N/A

MODEL 2025 FIELD - .177 cal., PCP, SS, 25.2 in. barrel, similar to Model 2020 Field, 803 FPS. 10.36 lbs.

No MSR	$1,395	$1,075	$850	$700	$550	N/A	N/A

MODEL 2027 BIATHLON - .177 cal., PCP, straight pull action, five-shot mag., 24 in. barrel, fully adj. sights, adj. match trigger, walnut stock with adj. cheek/butt plate and four mag. holder, 803 FPS. 9 lbs. Mfg. 2003-2005.

	$1,295	$1,115	$875	$725	$575	N/A	N/A

Last MSR was $1,400.

GRADING	100%	95%	90%	80%	60%	40%	20%

MODEL 8002 - .177 cal., PCP, single shot, easy-exchange 350-shot air cylinder with manometer, 25.2 in. barrel, color laminate wood stock features adj. laminate pistol grip and laminate forearm, adj. alloy cheekpiece, 42.5 in. OAL, 9.2 lbs. New 2005.

courtesy Anschütz

No MSR	$1,645	$1,350	$1,050	$850	N/A	N/A	N/A

✳ *Model 8002 ALU* - .177 cal., PCP, single shot, easy-exchange 350-shot air cylinder with manometer, 25.2 in. barrel, aluminum alloy stock features adj. laminate pistol grip and laminate forearm, adj. alloy cheekpiece, shoulder stock and buttplate attach to alloy frame, 42.5 in. OAL, 9.24 lbs. New 2005.

No MSR	$1,740	$1,450	$1,250	$950	N/A	N/A	N/A

✳ *Model 8002 Cub* - .177 cal., PCP, single shot, similar to Model 8002 except has walnut stock, 42.5 in. OAL, 8.8lbs. New 2005.

No MSR	$995	$775	$600	$450	N/A	N/A	N/A

✳ *Model 8002 Junior* As this edition went to press, U.S. availability had yet to be established on this model.

MODEL 9003 PREMIUM BENCHREST - .177 cal., PCP, similar to Model 9003 Premium Benchrest except includes seven stock decoration stickers and box with accessories, 9.9 lbs. New 2005.

courtesy Anschütz

No MSR	$1,895	$1,495	$1,150	$950	$800	N/A	N/A

✳ *Model 9003 Premium* - .177 cal., PCP, tension-free connection and vibration dampening of the barreled action in aluminum stock with soft link shock absorber, adj. buttplate, adj. cheekpiece, adj. forend, 9.9 lbs. New 2004.

No MSR	$1,895	$1,495	$1,150	$950	$800	N/A	N/A

HAKIM MILITARY TRAINING RIFLE - .22 cal., UL, SP, SS, rifled, tap-loading, full military style stock and sights, receiver ring marked with skull and Arabic markings for National Union Youth Movement, other Arabic markings for: "Training Airgun, Anschütz, Germany 1955", Caliber 5.5mm, 10.5 lbs. Approx. 2800 mfg. 1954. Ref: AR2 :27-29.

courtesy Beeman Collection

	N/A	N/A	$450	$375	$300	$225	$150

Built 1955 for Egyptian Government; based on Anschütz Model 1954 air rifle.

ANSON, E. & CO.

Previous manufacturer located in Birmingham, England circa 1890-1945.

Edward Anson and Company was a gunsmithing business, previously active from about 1890 to 1945. Models produced were

GRADING	100%	95%	90%	80%	60%	40%	20%

the Ansonia air rifle (apparently a copy of the MGR rifle of Mayer & Grammelspacher), Star air pistols, and small numbers of the Firefly air pistol. They designed, with Frank Clarke, but did not produce, the Westley Richards Highest Possible air pistols and the Accles & Shelvoke Warrior air pistol. Ref: AW-May 1984.

PISTOLS

STAR - underlever, mfg. 1922-1940. Rare, no other information at this time.

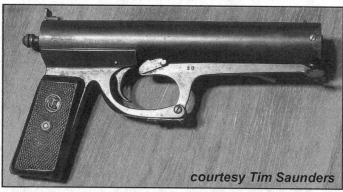

courtesy Tim Saunders

FIREFLY - .177 cal., push-barrel cocking, SP, smoothbore, concentric mainsprings, wooden barrel cover, frame and grip are heavy cast iron, marked "O.K." on left side of trigger, "ANSON" on the right side, and "FIREFLY" on frame above trigger. Mfg. 1932-1933.

courtesy Beeman Collection

$375	$325	$275	$225	$175	$150	$125

Add 40% for factory box.

Distributed by the Midland Gun Company (later absorbed by Parker and Hale), Birmingham, England.

RIFLES

ANSONIA - .177 cal., BBC, SP, 17 in. octagonal barrel with nine-groove RH rifling, adj. sights, barrel screwed into barrel block, lever detent like MGR but two-piece barrel marked "The Ansonia", 41.5 in. OAL, 7.5 lbs. Mfg.1905-10.

courtesy Beeman Collection

$900	$825	$750	$675	$600	$500	$400

ANSONIA Mk.2 - similar to Ansonia, except simpler, fixed sight, and the barrel and barrel block are one piece.
Values TBD

APACHE (aka FIRE-BALL)

Previous trademark manufactured by Burhans and Associates of CA, or one of their subsidiaries, in 1948-1949.

The authors and publisher wish to thank Jon Jenkins and John Groenewold for their valuable assistance with the following information in this edition of the *Blue Book of Airguns*.

The Apache rifle evidently is California's first publicly marketed airgun and is one of the shortest lived of all American airgun designs, apparently having been produced only in 1948 and 1949.

Apache guns are marked on the forward pump tube plug (if at all) with "Burhans and Associates" or "National Cart Corporation", or just the word "Fire-ball", or "Apache". Some markings included an address with the word "Fire-ball" or "Apache" but not the company name. Charles Burhans operated the National Cart Corporation, so these various markings imply the same

GRADING	100%	95%	90%	80%	60%	40%	20%

origin. Although not precision airguns, the genius of the Apache rifle lay in using the larger .25 caliber barrel and the ability to quickly change calibers.

Apache airguns were available in various design configurations, but there is some interesting confusion about which variations were actually produced. What was advertised does not always match what is actually seen in known specimens. The original rifle was advertised as always having a .175 caliber insert barrel, but there are a number of specimens which do not have any threads at the muzzle. Such a lack makes it impossible to fix a sub-caliber barrel. They were also advertised as having a hollow space in the buttstock for a tube of ammunition, but apparently none were made with this feature. Eight-shot .175 caliber Fireball rifles were advertised in 1948, but none have been reported. A version called the SIMCO Texan was specified in 1949 dealer literature as taking regular .22 caliber pellets, but only .25 caliber specimens are known. And the pistols were promoted as coming in real wooden boxes, but rather fragile cardboard factory cartons seem to have been the reality. If you have clear evidence of the existence of presently unknown features or models, please contact Blue Book Publications or email: BBAupdates@Beemans.net.

Early production Apache rifles used a plastic stock and forearm. Plastic technology was only beginning at the time, and these plastic stocks were prone to frequent breakage. Production was switched to hardwood stocks as early as March 1948. Since both were available at the same time, it is possible to find mismatched guns. Two buttstock attachment techniques were used with no clear definition between production runs. Attaching the buttstock with a bolt through the pistol grip is the least common variation. The standard, most common arrangement is a long bolt, hidden by the buttplate, running through the length of the buttstock. Both the steel and brass parts were chemically blued. On both the rifles and pistols only the brass .25 caliber barrel was rifled. Apache rifles are known with all possible combinations and variations of parts. Apparently, any parts handy at assembly time were used. Guns with various screws in the receiver, a plastic buttstock and a wooden forearm, completely unmarked, and/or with poor finishing of the metalwork were produced and should not be considered prototype efforts or mistakes.

It is clear that the first versions of the rifle were single shot. The second form of the rifle had a receiver which allowed the addition of a ten-shot magazine assembly. These rifles omit the .25 caliber loading port on the top of the frame and can only be fired with .25 caliber balls using the magazine. Some rifles were sold as .25 caliber repeaters only and some included the .175 barrel. These seem to require muzzle loading in the early versions, but later versions could be loaded through a small hole in the top of the receiver. All non-repeater guns equipped with the .175 barrel liner had to be muzzle-loaded when the liner was being used. Bolt handles on the non-repeater guns were fragile and specimens often have this item broken or missing.

In the spring of 1948, a pistol was added to the Apache line. Available first as a single shot in .25 caliber, the pistol was soon offered as a six-shot repeater with the same interchangeable caliber feature and spring-fed magazine as the rifles. The first production models of the pistols had heavy die-cast frames, similar to the rifles; later production featured an aluminum frame. These frames generally were polished to give the appearance of chrome plating, but some were painted black. Grips on the pistols were either wood (common), black, or ivory plastic (scarce). The .175 insert for the pistol attached using the same type of threaded muzzle arrangement as the rifle. There are rare examples of the pistols with a friction fit, rather than a threaded arrangement, for the insert. The pump tube is thin-wall brass tubing prone to failure at the pivot points. The performance of the pistols was rather moderate in both calibers.

In 1949, the Apache tooling was acquired by Standard Interstate Machine Company (SIMCO) in Glendale, CA. By June of 1949, SIMCO had begun manufacturing an Apache-type model air rifle marked on the buttplate as the Texan. Apparently, the Apache tooling and parts were also used to produce the SIMCO rifles. These generally were marked "SIMCO" in an oval on the front left side of the receiver. Guns are known with both the SIMCO marking on the receiver and an Apache marking on the pump tube plug. Some SIMCO guns are not marked at all. Apparently, Apache parts were simply utilized until exhausted, but SIMCO guns generally are identifiable by their careful finishing. The final preparation of the metalwork is better and the finishing itself is of a greater consistency than the former Apache production. The stock lacquer is darker and more opaque than on Apache rifles and is more carefully applied. Some SIMCO rifles are marked with the word "Texan" in script on the buttplate. This buttplate marking appears to be the exception. Manufacturing of the Apache/Simco line seems to have ceased in 1949.

There are no known examples of SIMCO pistols. The last address for SIMCO was on Hollywood Way in Burbank, CA. Ref: AGNR – Apr. 1986.

PISTOLS

APACHE - FIRE-BALL PISTOL - BB/.175 and .25 cal. dual cal., or .25 cal. only, UL multi-pump pneumatic, smooth or rifled (.25 cal.), walnut or plastic grips, die-cast zinc or aluminum frame, polished or all blue paint finish. Mfg. 1948-1949.

courtesy Beeman Collection

✳ *First Variation* - heavy cast zinc receiver (similar to rifle), usually .25 cal. SS only, 8.25 in. rifled barrel.1.9 lbs, 11.9 in. OAL.

	100%	95%	90%	80%	60%	40%	20%
	$450	$395	$350	$295	$195	$145	$85

Add 25% for factory box and literature.

GRADING	100%	95%	90%	80%	60%	40%	20%

Add 10% for painted receiver.

Add 10% for ivory-colored grips.

Add 50% for press-fit inner barrel.

Subtract 10% for missing name.

Subtract 15% for missing .175 barrel insert on guns with threaded muzzle rings.

✹ **Second Variation** - .25 cal., SS or repeater with six-round spring fed mag., aluminum receiver, polished or painted blue, 8.25 in. rifled barrel with removable smoothbore .175 cal. liner (may attach via screw threads in end of barrel or press-fit), wooden or plastic (ivory or black) grips. 1.3 lbs without barrel liner.

	100%	95%	90%	80%	60%	40%	20%
	$350	$295	$250	$195	$150	$95	$65

Add 25% for factory box and literature.

Add 10% for painted receiver.

Add 10% for ivory-colored grips.

Add 50% for press-fit inner barrel.

Subtract 10% for missing name.

Subtract 15% for missing .175 barrel insert on guns with threaded muzzle rings.

RIFLES

APACHE/FIRE-BALL/TEXAN - BB/.175 and .25 cal. dual cal., or .25 cal. only, UL multi-pump pneumatic, smooth or rifled (.25 cal.), 940 FPS, plastic and/or hardwood stock and forearm, black finish, die-cast zinc or aluminum frame, 36.3 in. OAL, 5.5-6.5 lbs. Mfg. 1948-1949.

courtesy Beeman Collection

✹ **First Variation** - .25 cal., with round loading port in top of receiver, may include .175 threaded barrel insert, SS, plastic buttstock and forearm.

	100%	95%	90%	80%	60%	40%	20%
	$315	$270	$240	$180	$160	$120	$90

Add 25% for factory box and literature.

Add 15% for "Texan"-marked buttplate, MSR was $14.95.

Add 10% for .25 cal. only.

Add 25% for SIMCO-marked guns.

Add 100% for chrome plating on all metalwork.

Subtract 15% for missing name.

Subtract 25% for missing .175 barrel insert on guns with threaded muzzle rings.

Subtract 25% for broken bolt (40% if missing).

✹ **Second Variation** - .175 or .25 cal., SS with .175 cal. threaded barrel insert loaded from the muzzle, later versions have a small round loading port in the top, or side of receiver or six-shot repeater, hardwood buttstock attached via a bolt through bottom of pistol grip.

courtesy Beeman Collection

	100%	95%	90%	80%	60%	40%	20%
	$275	$270	$235	$205	$125	$90	$65

Add 25% for factory box and literature.

Add 15% for "Texan"-marked buttplate, MSR was $14.95.

Add 10% for .25 cal. only.

Add 25% for SIMCO-marked guns.

Add 100% for chrome plating on all metalwork.

Subtract 15% for missing name.

Subtract 25% for missing .175 barrel insert on guns with threaded muzzle rings.

Subtract 25% for broken bolt (40% if missing).

Transitional guns -- either buttstock or forearm of contrasting material (hardwood or plastic) priced as Variation Two or Three depending on method of buttstock attachment.

GRADING	100%	95%	90%	80%	60%	40%	20%

✷ ***Third Variation*** - similar to Second variation, except has hardwood buttstock attached by long bolt running from under butt-plate.

	$260	$225	$195	$160	$120	$85	$60

Add 25% for factory box and literature.
Add 15% for "Texan"-marked buttplate, MSR was $14.95.
Add 10% for .25 cal. only.
Add 25% for SIMCO-marked guns.
Add 100% for chrome plating on all metalwork.
Subtract 15% for missing name.
Subtract 25% for missing .175 barrel insert on guns with threaded muzzle rings.
Subtract 25% for broken bolt (40% if missing).

ARMIGAS (ARMIGAS-COMEGA)

Previous manufacturer located at Via Valle Inzino, Brescia, Italy.

Associated with Atillio Zanoletti. Maker of gas-powered rifles, circa 1961 to early 1980s.

RIFLES

OLIMPIC - .177 cal., CO_2, repeater, feeds from spring-fed magazine along length of RHS of barrel, magazine removes for loading, tends to jam during operation, bulk feed CO_2 valve at muzzle end, 22 in. barrel, no safety, marked with Armigas brand, Olimpic name, and "BREV. INTERN" ("International Patent"), 4.5 mm, 38 in. OAL, 5.5 lbs.

courtesy Beeman Collection

	N/A	$750	$600	$500	$400	$300	N/A

ARMSCOR

Current trademark manufactured by Arms Corporation of the Philippines, located in Manila, Philippines. No current importation, previously imported by Armscor Precision International, located in Las Vegas, NV. For more information and current pricing on both new and used Arms Corporation of the Philippines firearms, please refer to the *Blue Book of Gun Values* by S.P. Fjestad (also available online).

PISTOLS

ARMSCOR PISTOL - .22 cal., CO_2, SL, 7.50 in. barrel, 500 FPS, fixed sights, 2.2 lbs. Disc. 2002.

	$165	$125	$85	$60	$45	N/A	N/A

Last MSR was $112.

RIFLES

ARMSCOR EXECUTIVE - .22 cal., CO2, bolt action, 22 in. barrel, 700 FPS, leaf-type rear sight, hooded front sight, beech stock with checkered grip and forearm, manual safety, 5.75 lbs. Disc. 2002.

courtesy Howard Collection

	$145	$115	$90	$70	$50	N/A	N/A

Last MSR was $120.

ARMSCOR STANDARD - .22 cal., CO_2, bolt action, 22 in. barrel, 700 FPS, leaf-type rear sight, hooded front sight, beech stock, manual safety, 5.75 lbs. Disc. 2002.

	$135	$95	$80	$65	$50	N/A	N/A

Last MSR was $112.

GRADING	100%	95%	90%	80%	60%	40%	20%

ARMSCOR RETRACTABLE - .22 cal., CO_2, bolt action, 22 in. barrel, 700 FPS, leaf-type rear sight, hooded front sight, retractable composite shoulder stock with pistol grip, 6 lbs. Disc. 2002.

courtesy Howard Collection

| $165 | $125 | $85 | $70 | $55 | N/A | N/A |

Last MSR was $112.

ARROW

Previous trademark used by a few different manufacturers including Friedrich Langenham located in Zella - St. Blasii, Thüringen, Germany, the State Industry Factory located in Shanghai, China, and William Heilprin located in Philadelphia, PA.

These are completely unrelated makers. Please see the individual makers' names in this guide.

ARTES de ARCOS

Previous manufacturer located in Madrid and Barcelona, Spain.

ASAHI

Previous trademark manufactured by Kawaguchiya located in Japan circa 1948-1955.

Research is ongoing with this trademark, and more information will be included both online and in future editions. Copy of pre-WWII Jeffries pattern BSA underlever. Average original condition specimens are typically priced in the $100 range. The most recent specimens with a modern-looking half stock are rare and typically command an extra $50.

courtesy Beeman Collection

ATLAS AIR GUN MANUFACTURING CO.

Previous manufacturer located in Ilion, NY circa 1889.

See Atlas Gun Co.

ATLAS AIR RIFLE MANUFACTURING CO.

Previous manufacturer located in Ilion, NY circa 1953-56.

Manufacturer of a pump-up pneumatic rifle. Research is ongoing with this trademark, and more information will be included both online and in future editions.

ATLAS GUN CO.

Previous manufacturer located in Ilion, NY circa 1886-1906.

The Atlas Gun Company of Ilion, New York is another of the links between key parts of the world airgun developmental picture. It was founded around 1886 by George P. Gunn of the Haviland & Gunn Company whose designs were the foundation of most modern production airguns. The Atlas company was then consumed by Daisy in 1906 as part of their aggressive program to eliminate competition.

The first Atlas gun was the 1886 model, a break-open BB gun using an unusual gravity repeater mechanism incorporating three iron rods as a BB raceway. Gunn was granted a patent for the design in 1895. The last of the Atlas BB guns have peculiar ring lever cocking arms which extend forward instead of back from the trigger and have a finger ring instead of the traditional loop. These guns typically have the name "ATLAS" cast into the frame, which also has a special shape. The combinations of these features are so distinctive that these models may be identified from quite far away. The Dandy BB gun that appeared in the 1897 Sears mail order catalog had these beacon features, but is without the Atlas marking. It almost surely was produced by Atlas.

GRADING	100%	95%	90%	80%	60%	40%	20%

RIFLES

1886 ATLAS BREAK-OPEN REPEATER - .180 cal., BB, BC, SP, brass smoothbore barrel, break-open action, gravity-fed magazine, sheet metal frame and grip frame, wire trigger guard, nickel finish. Walnut stock with deep crescent butt, stamped in a circle: "Atlas Gun Company, Pat. Mar. 9, 1886. USE B.B. SHOT. Ilion, New York, Patent applied for". No safety. Circa 1886-1890.

	N/A	N/A	$1,500	$1,200	$1,000	$900	$750

1899 VICTOR BREAK-OPEN REPEATER - .180 cal., BB, BC, SP, brass smoothbore barrel, break-open action, gravity-fed magazine, sheet metal frame and grip frame, wire trigger guard, nickel finish. Walnut stock with deep crescent butt, stamped "VICTOR". No safety. Circa 1899-1906.

	N/A	N/A	$1,200	$1,000	$900	$800	$600

1900 ATLAS LEVER ACTION REPEATER - .180 cal., BB, BC, SP, brass smoothbore barrel, distinctive lever action with ring lever ahead of trigger, gravity-fed magazine, sheet metal barrel sheath, cast iron cocking lever, receiver frame and grip frame. Walnut stock with crescent butt. Lettering cast into grip frame: "ATLAS". No safety. First version circa 1900-03.

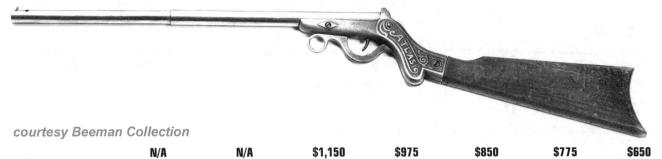

courtesy Beeman Collection

	N/A	N/A	$1,150	$975	$850	$775	$650

Add 20% for brass frame.

Subtract 20% for last version – simpler frame with Atlas name in script. Circa 1903-06.

DANDY LEVER ACTION REPEATER - .180 cal. BB, BC, SP, brass smoothbore barrel, distinctive lever action with ring lever ahead of trigger, gravity-fed magazine, sheet metal barrel sheath, cast iron cocking lever, receiver frame and grip frame. Walnut stock with crescent butt. No lettering on frame. No safety. Sears mail order version (Dandy evidently was a trade name for Sears and other sellers). Circa 1892.

	N/A	N/A	$1,050	$875	$750	$675	$575

NEW DANDY - gravity-fed repeater similar to Dandy, same cast iron parts, cocking lever, and action, nickel finish. The only marking is on the RHS of slab sided stock: "NEW DANDY MODEL 94". 32.2 in. OAL, 2.5 lbs. Mfg. circa 1894.

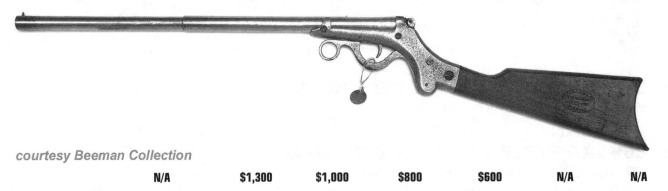

courtesy Beeman Collection

	N/A	$1,300	$1,000	$800	$600	N/A	N/A

B SECTION

BAM (BEST AIRGUN MANUFACTURER IN CHINA)

Current trademark manufactured by Jiang Su Xin Su Machinery Manufacturing Co. Ltd. located in WuXi, JiangSu Province, China. Currently imported and distributed by Xisico USA, Inc. located in Houston, TX.

GRADING	100%	95%	90%	80%	60%	40%	20%

RIFLES

MODEL XS-B3-1 - .177 or .22 cal., SL, SP, 15 in. barrel, 540/410 FPS, black finish, metal collapsible buttstock, grooved pistol grip and forearm, hooded front and adj. rear sights, trigger safety, 7.15 lbs.

	100%	95%	90%	80%	60%	40%	20%
MSR $80	$60	$50	$40	$30	N/A	N/A	N/A

MODEL XS-B4-2 - .177 or .22 cal., UL, SP, 17.5 in. barrel, 630/480 FPS, black finish, semi-pistol grip wood stock with buttplate, hooded front and adj. rear sights, sling swivels, trigger safety, 7 lbs.

	100%	95%	90%	80%	60%	40%	20%
MSR $50	$35	$30	$25	$20	N/A	N/A	N/A

MODEL XS-B7 - .177 or .22 cal., SL, SP, 15 in. barrel, 540/410 FPS, black finish, semi-pistol grip wood stock with buttplate, hooded front and adj. rear sights, scope rail, trigger safety, 7 lbs.

	100%	95%	90%	80%	60%	40%	20%
MSR $70	$60	$50	$40	$30	N/A	N/A	N/A

MODEL XS-B12 - .177 cal., BBC, SP, 16.38 in. barrel, 950 FPS, black finish, semi-pistol grip Monte-Carlo wood stock with buttplate, hooded front and adj. rear sights, trigger safety, 6.6 lbs.

	100%	95%	90%	80%	60%	40%	20%
MSR $90	$80	$70	$60	$50	N/A	N/A	N/A

MODEL XS-B15 - .177 cal., BBC, SP, 14.4 in. barrel, 480 FPS, black finish, semi-pistol grip wood stock with buttplate, hooded front and adj. rear sights, trigger safety, 5.5 lbs.

	100%	95%	90%	80%	60%	40%	20%
MSR $50	$40	$30	$20	$15	N/A	N/A	N/A

MODEL XS-B18 - .177 or .22 cal., BBC, SP, 16.38 in. barrel, 850/650 FPS, black parkerized finish, semi-pistol grip Monte Carlo wood stock with buttplate, hooded front and adj. rear sights, trigger safety, 6.9 lbs.

	100%	95%	90%	80%	60%	40%	20%
MSR $100	$90	$75	$50	$40	N/A	N/A	N/A

MODEL XS-B20 - .177 cal., BBC, SP, 16 in. barrel, 930 FPS, blue finish, semi-pistol grip Monte Carlo wood stock with recoil pad, hooded front and adj. rear sights, Rekord trigger and auto-safety, 7.26 lbs.

	100%	95%	90%	80%	60%	40%	20%
MSR $160	$135	$105	$90	$75	N/A	N/A	N/A

MODEL XS-B21 - .177 or .22 cal., SL, SP, 19.5 in. barrel, 950/715 FPS, blue finish, semi-pistol grip Monte Carlo wood stock with recoil pad, adj. hooded front and adj. rear sights, double automatic trigger safety, 9.68 lbs.

	100%	95%	90%	80%	60%	40%	20%
MSR $180	$150	$115	$95	$85	N/A	N/A	N/A

MODEL XS-B30 - .177 or .22 cal., SL, SP, 17.3 in. barrel, 1100/900 FPS, blue finish, semi-pistol grip Monte Carlo wood stock with recoil pad, adj. trigger, adj. hooded front and adj. rear sights, double automatic trigger safety, 44.5m OAL, 9.4 lbs. New 2005.

	100%	95%	90%	80%	60%	40%	20%
MSR $199	$175	$140	$110	$95	N/A	N/A	N/A

MODEL XS-B40 - .177 or .22 cal., UL, SP, 14.1 in. barrel, 1050/850 FPS, black finish, adj. trigger, Monte Carlo semi-pistol grip wood stock with recoil pad, hooded front and adj. rear sights, sling swivels, trigger safety, 41.3 OAL, 9.3 lbs. New 2005.

	100%	95%	90%	80%	60%	40%	20%
MSR $295	$250	$195	$150	$95	N/A	N/A	N/A

MODEL XS-B50/MODEL XS-B51 - .177 or .22 cal., PCP, 18.5 in. barrel, 1000 FPS, blue finish, semi-pistol grip or thumbhole (Model XS-B51, new 2005) Monte Carlo wood stock with recoil pad, manual safety. New 2003.

	100%	95%	90%	80%	60%	40%	20%
MSR $400	$375	$325	$250	$200	N/A	N/A	N/A

Add $50 for Model XS-B51 (thumbhole stock).

BBM

For information on BBM air pistols, see Steiner in the "S" section.

BRNO

See Aeron CZ s.r.o. listing in the "A" section.

BSA GUNS (U.K.), LTD.

Current manufacturer, BSA Guns (UK), Ltd., previously known as "The Birmingham Small Arms Co. Ltd." and "BSA GUNS Ltd.," founded in 1861 and always located in Birmingham, England. Presently owned by Gamo of Spain. Currently imported into USA by Precision Airgun Distribution located in Gilbert, AZ. Previously imported by Compasseco, Inc. located in Bardstown, KY, Precision Sales, Westfield, MA (1995-2002), Dynamit-Nobel/RWS, Ithaca Gun Co. (1975-1979), Marksman, Savage Arms, and others.

The history of BSA air rifles is based on the patents of, and the early marketing of, airguns by Lincoln Jeffries. Therefore, the introduction to the Lincoln section of this book is prerequisite to this section. The serious study of BSA airguns absolutely requires reference to the BSA books by John Knibbs. The authors and publisher wish to thank John Groenewold and John Knibbs for their assistance with the following information in this edition of the *Blue Book of Airguns*.

The Lincoln Jeffries underlever air rifle made by BSA proved so successful that by 1906 BSA had begun marketing them under their own name and in several different models. The air rifles commonly referred to as "Lincoln Jeffries," "Lincoln patent," "Lincoln," "H," and "Light" models are actually stamped "H The Lincoln Air Rifle" or "L The Lincoln Air Rifle" and should be easy to identify. See Lincoln in the "L" section of this guide.

The bayonet type underlever cocking handle was the original Lincoln Jeffries design. The front end of this lever bears a small handle, or "bayonet" dropping down from, but parallel to, the barrel. Original bayonet underlevers just had a bend where they engaged the latch mechanism. Later ones were strengthened by additional metal bracing ("fillets or fences") on the sides of the bend area. The bayonet underlever was replaced by the much more reliable and less obtrusive side button underlever in 1911. Beginning in 1919, BSA started to replace side button underlevers with front button underlevers. Old-style underlevers were sometimes replaced with newer versions during repairs and modifications, and this may confuse present identification.

Although well-designed and well-built, the early BSA air guns can be difficult to identify. Early practice at the factory was to use up existing old parts wherever possible on new models. Hence numerous variations exist. Several duplicate names for different models of different sizes and configurations also exist.

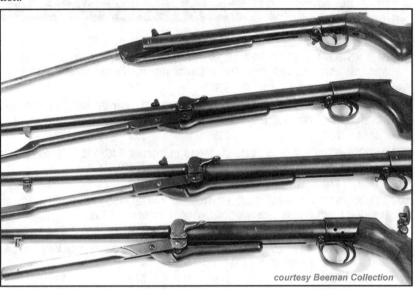

courtesy Beeman Collection

The designations of Improved Model B and Improved Model D bring up the question: "Where are the Models A through D?" A great deal of study seems to rather conclusively show that there never were any such models, except perhaps as developmental steps in the minds and long-lost notes of BSA airgun designers. The existing models certainly represent improvements over developmental steps that never came into production. Furthermore, the BSA designers made additional improvements in their "Improved Models" B and D, without changing the public designations. They probably did this with the idea that they were avoiding confusion, but the result was that vendors, customers, and repair shops could not be sure of what parts they were ordering or what would be shipped to them. This type of confusion was not well controlled until new models were produced after WWII.

Serial numbers and their prefixes are very important as they designate the model variation of the gun, date of manufacture, sear mechanism, and/or the caliber. In mid-1914 BSA started to mark new air cylinders by photo etching. However, some air rifles were assembled from parts with stamped lettering long after that date. The photoetching process was not perfected then. Many guns which originally had photoetched markings now appear unmarked because the etching has been worn off or buffed off during refinishing. Additionally, many different models were assembled using old parts from stock; thus there are considerable variations, even within a single model. The serial number and its prefix generally will allow cross-referencing to factory records and published lists, but often caliber and physical measurements must also considered. Specimens may be up to almost 100 years old; many have been repaired or modified with parts that may not even resemble the original parts. Using the information given here and some ingenuity, it should be possible to fairly well identify most BSA airguns. For serial number lists, production information, and a great deal of additional detail, one must consult the BSA references by John Knibbs. (His book sales partner in the USA is John Groenewold Airguns.)

BSA airguns made prior to 1939 were marked with a single-digit "bore" size. These are not to be confused with model numbers. The bore size usually is marked on top of the gun near the piled arms symbol and loading port. Number 1 bore is .177 in. (4.5 mm). Number 2 is referred to as .22 in. (5.5 mm) but is actually 5.6 mm. Conventional 5.5 mm German and American .22 inch caliber pellets generally would not give optimal performance in Number 2 bore airguns. In the 1980s, Beeman Precision Airguns, then Webley's exclusive agent in the large USA market, insisted that Webley standardize their ".22 or No. 2 bores" to fit the German .22 in./5.5 mm precision pellets. Webley complied and BSA quietly followed suit soon after. Number 3 bore is .25 in. cal. (6.35 mm).

For information and current pricing on both new and used BSA firearms, please refer to the *Blue Book of Gun Values* by S.P. Fjestad (also available online).

For additional information on the origin of Lincoln Jeffries and BSA underlever air rifles, see "Lincoln" in the "L" section of this text.

BSA also manufactured firearms: military, sporting, and target rifles and shotguns. These are discussed in *The Golden Century* by John Knibbs.

PISTOLS

240 MAGNUM - .177 or .22 cal., TL, SP, SS, 510/420 FPS, 6 in. barrel, two-stage adj. trigger, adj. rear sight, sights separate from barrel on up-swinging top receiver unit, integral scope rail, one-piece walnut grip, automatic safety, 9 in. OAL, 2 lbs. Mfg. 1994-2000.

courtesy Tim Saunders

$260	$220	$190	$150	$115	$75	N/A

Last MSR was $259.

GRADING	100%	95%	90%	80%	60%	40%	20%

SCORPION - 177 or .22 cal., BBC, SP, SS, 7.9 in barrel, 510/380 FPS, automatic safety, 3.4 lbs., 15.3 in. OAL. Mfg. 1973-1993.

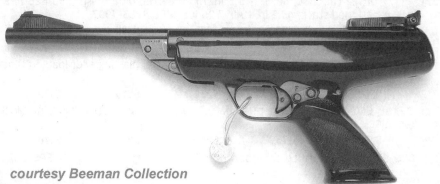

courtesy Beeman Collection

✳ **Scorpion MK I** - KEMATEL sights. Mfg. 1973-1985.

	100%	95%	90%	80%	60%	40%	20%
	$225	$200	$175	$150	$125	$100	$75

Add 25% for boxed with all accessories.
Subtract 10% for missing cocking aid.

✳ **Scorpion MK II** - integral scope groove, steel and plastic sights. Mfg. 1985-1993.

	100%	95%	90%	80%	60%	40%	20%
	$250	$225	$200	$175	$150	$125	$100

Last MSR was $190.

Add 25% for boxed with all accessories. Subtract 10% for missing cocking aid.

RIFLES: BARREL COCKING

Subtract 20% for specimens equipped with gas-spring unit (sometimes inappropriately called "gas ram" or "gas strut"). Such modification makes the gun non-original, voids the manufacturer's warranty, and may cause cumulative injury to gun. Length measurements may vary by about 0.25 in. or so within models.

BREAKDOWN PATTERN - .177 cal., BBC, SP, SS, 18.5 in. barrel, marked "Breakdown Pattern", no serial number prefix from 1933 to 1936, "B" prefix after 1936, 41.5 in. OAL. Mfg. 1933-1939.

	100%	95%	90%	80%	60%	40%	20%
	$500	$450	$400	$325	$275	$200	$100

BSA's first barrel cocking air rifle.

BUCCANEER - .177 or .22 cal., BBC, SP, SS, similar to Scorpion MK II pistol, except black, brown, or camouflage composite thumbhole stock, 18.5 in. rifled barrel, marked "BUCCANEER" on top of compression tube, 35.5 in. OAL. Mfg. 1977-1983.

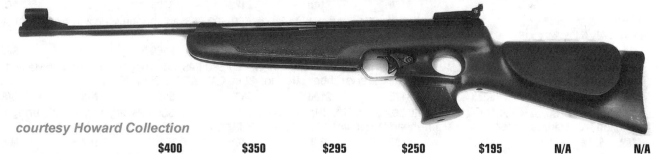

courtesy Howard Collection

	100%	95%	90%	80%	60%	40%	20%
	$400	$350	$295	$250	$195	N/A	N/A

Add 25% for boxed with all accessories.

CADET - .177 cal., BBC, SP, SS, rifled barrel, blue finish, 37.5 in. OAL, 4.75 lbs. Mfg. 1946-1959.

	100%	95%	90%	80%	60%	40%	20%
	$200	$180	$160	$140	$120	$100	$60

✳ **Cadet Major** - .177 cal., BBC, SP, SS, rifled barrel, blue finish, 42 in. OAL, 5.5 lbs. Mfg. 1947-1959.

	100%	95%	90%	80%	60%	40%	20%
	$200	$180	$160	$140	$120	$100	$60

LIGHTNING - .177 or .22 cal., BBC, SP, SS, 10 (British version) or 15 in. rifled barrel, blue finish, variation of the Supersport, 39.5 in. with Volumetric sound moderator or 33 in. w/o Volumetric sound moderator OAL, 6.1 lbs. New 1997.

MSR $414	100%	95%	90%	80%	60%	40%	20%
	$359	$300	$225	$175	$125	N/A	N/A

British version with 10 in. barrel and BSA Volumetric sound moderator (requires $200 federal transfer tax in USA).

✳ **Lightning XL** - .177 or .22 cal., BBC, SP, SS, 10 (British version) or 15 in. rifled barrel, blue finish, similar to Lightning exsept, redesigned stock and adj. two-stage trigger. New 2005.

As this edition went to press, U.S. availability had yet to be established on this model.

MERCURY - .177 or .22 cal., BBC, SP, SS, 18.5 in. rifled barrel, blue finish, 700/550 FPS, serial number prefixes "W" and "Z," adj. rear and globe front sights, 43.5 in. OAL, 7.25 lbs. Mfg. 1972-1980.

	100%	95%	90%	80%	60%	40%	20%
	$300	$260	$230	$200	$175	$135	$95

✳ **Mercury S** - .177 or .22 cal., BBC, SP, SS, 18.5 in. rifled barrel, blue finish, 825-600 FPS, adj. rear and globe front sights, oil finished and checkered walnut stock, thicker barrel, 44.5 in. OAL. 7.25 lbs. New 1980-disc.

	100%	95%	90%	80%	60%	40%	20%
	$350	$305	$265	$230	$200	$155	$110

GRADING	100%	95%	90%	80%	60%	40%	20%

MERCURY CHALLENGER - .177 or .22 cal., BBC, SP, SS, 18.5 in. rifled barrel, blue finish, 850-625 FPS, adj. rear and globe front sights, Maxi-Grip scope rail, redesigned stock, 43.5 in. OAL, 7.25 lbs. Mfg. 1983-1997.

	$300	$260	$230	$200	$175	$135	$95

Last MSR was $205.

MERLIN MK I - .177 or .22 cal., BBC, SP, SS, 14.25 in. rifled barrel, blue finish, plastic pellet loading block, 36 in. OAL, 3.5 lbs. Mfg. 1962-64.

	$300	$275	$250	$210	$170	$140	$100

✼ *Merlin MK II* - .177 or .22 cal., BBC, SP, SS, 14.25 in. rifled barrel, blue finish, metal pellet loading block, anti-bear-trap device, 36 in. OAL, 3.5 lbs. Mfg. 1964-1968.

	$300	$275	$250	$210	$170	$140	$100

METEOR - .177 or .22 cal., BBC, SP, SS, 18.5 in. rifled or smoothbore barrel, blue finish, 650-500 FPS, adj. rear and fixed front sights, 6 lbs. New 1959.

✼ *Meteor MK I* - .177 or .22 cal., BBC, SP, SS, 18 in. rifled or smoothbore barrel, blue finish, 650-500 FPS, adj. rear and fixed front sights, 41 in. OAL, 5.25 lbs. Mfg. 1959-1962.

	$180	$160	$140	$120	$100	$80	$60

✼ *Meteor MK II* - .177 or .22 cal., BBC, SP, SS, 18 in. rifled or smoothbore barrel, blue finish, 650-500 FPS, more streamlined appearance, improved adj. rear and fixed front sights, first use of plastic rear body tube cap, 41 in. OAL, 5.25 lbs. Mfg. 1962-68.

	$180	$160	$140	$120	$100	$80	$60

✼ *Meteor MK III* - .177 or .22 cal., BBC, SP, SS, 18 in. rifled or smoothbore barrel, blue finish, 650-500 FPS, more robust stock with squared-off forearm, adj. rear and fixed front sights, 41 in. OAL, 6 lbs. Mfg. 1969-1973.

courtesy Beeman Collection

	$180	$160	$140	$120	$100	$80	$60

✼ *Meteor MK IV* - .177 or .22 cal., BBC, SP, SS, 18.5 in. rifled barrel, blue finish, 650-500 FPS, adj. bridge style and fixed front sights, 41 in. OAL, 6 lbs. Mfg. 1973-93.

	$180	$160	$140	$120	$100	$80	$60

✼ *Meteor MK V* - .177 or .22 cal., BBC, SP, SS, 18.5 in. rifled barrel, blue finish, 650-500 FPS, adj. bridge style and fixed front sights, 41 in. OAL, 6 lbs. Mfg. 1977-93.

	$180	$160	$140	$120	$100	$80	$60

✼ *Meteor MK 6* - .177 or .22 cal., BBC, SP, SS, 17.5 in. rifled barrel, blue finish, 760-580 FPS, adj. trigger, adj. bridge style and fixed front sights, scope grooves, anti-beartrap, manual safety, rubber buttpad, 42 in. OAL, 7.5 lbs. New 1993.

MSR $252	$223	$175	$125	$85	$55	N/A	N/A

✦ *Meteor MK 6 Carbine* - .177 or .22 cal., BBC, SP, SS, 15 in. rifled barrel, blue finish, 760-580 FPS, adj. trigger, adj. bridge style and fixed front sights, scope grooves, anti-beartrap, manual safety, rubber buttpad, 39 in. OAL, 5.7 lbs. New 1993.

MSR $280	$250	$195	$145	$105	$75	N/A	N/A

✼ *Meteor Super* - .177 or .22 cal., BBC, SP, SS, 19 in. rifled or smoothbore barrel, blue finish, 650-500 FPS, Monte Carlo stock, adj. rear and fixed front sights, vent. recoil buttpad, 41 in. OAL, 6 lbs. Mfg. began in 1967. Disc.

	$210	$185	$160	$140	$115	$90	$70

SHADOW - .177 or .22 cal., BBC, SP, SS, rifled barrel, blue finish, same action as Scorpion MK II pistol with black, brown, or camouflage (Trooper) thumbhole composite stock, marked "SHADOW" on compression tube, cocking aid, 27 in. OAL. Mfg. 1985-86.

	$450	$425	$400	$375	$350	$325	$300

Add 25% for boxed with all accessories.
Add 25% for Trooper model.

SUPERSPORT - .177, .22, or .25 cal., BBC, SP, SS, 850/625/530 FPS, 18 in. rifled barrel, blue finish, Monte Carlo stock with vent. recoil pad, anti-beartrap, manual safety, 41 in. OAL, 6.6 lbs. New 1986.

✼ *Supersport America* - .177, .22, or .25 cal., BBC, SP, black finish, 850/625/530 FPS, black Monte Carlo composite stock with vent. recoil pad.

	$250	$225	$200	$185	$160	N/A	N/A

✼ *Supersport MK I* - .177, .22, or .25 cal., BBC, SP, rifled barrel, blue finish, 850/625/530 FPS. Mfg. 1986-87.

	$230	$200	$170	$150	$125	N/A	N/A

Last MSR was $279.

✼ *Supersport MK I Carbine* - .177, .22, or .25 cal., BBC, SP, rifled barrel, blue finish, 850/625/530 FPS, 14 in. barrel. Mfg. 1986-87.

	$255	$225	$185	$160	$145	N/A	N/A

Last MSR was $279.

GRADING	100%	95%	90%	80%	60%	40%	20%

✱ **Supersport MK2 E/E (Magnum)** - .177, .22, or .25 (disc.) cal., BBC, SP, 18.50 in. rifled barrel, blue finish, 950/750/600 FPS, 42 in. OAL, approx. 6.6 lbs. New 1987.

	MSR $340	$295	$235	$185	$135	$100	N/A	N/A

✱ **Supersport MK2 SS Carbine E/E** - .177, .22 or .25 cal., BBC, SP, SS, 950/750/650 FPS, 15.5 in. barrel, 39 in. OAL, 6.2 lbs. New 1987.

	MSR $283	$265	$215	$165	$115	$80	N/A	N/A

MODEL 635 MAGNUM - .177, .22 or .25 cal., BBC, SP, SS, rifled barrel, blue finish, 850-625 FPS, 7.25 lbs.

	$300	$260	$230	$200	$175	$135	$95

RIFLES: MODIFIED REAR/UNDER LEVER COCKING

See also Lincoln in the "L" section of this book for the Lincoln underlever rifles from which BSA underlever air rifles were developed.

Subtract 20% for specimens equipped with gas-spring unit (sometimes inappropriately called "gas ram" or "gas strut"). Such modification makes the gun non-original, voids the manufacturer's warranty and may cause cumulative injury to gun. Length measurements may vary by about 0.25 in. or so within models.

AIRSPORTER - .177, .22, or .25 cal., UL, SP, SS, 1020/800/550 FPS, tap loader, tapered breech plug, blued finish, 8 lbs.

courtesy Beeman Collection

First underlever to have cocking lever hidden in forearm. Carbine versions with 14 in. barrels do not bring a premium.

✱ **Airsporter Club** - .177 cal. only, 7.5 lbs. Mfg. 1948-1959.

	$300	$270	$225	$190	$140	$100	$65

✱ **Airsporter MK I** - mfg. 1948-1959.

	$300	$270	$225	$190	$140	$100	$65

✱ **Airsporter MK II** - mfg. 1959-1965.

	$300	$270	$225	$190	$140	$100	$65

✱ **Airsporter MK III** - serial number prefixes "EF," "EG," and "GE." Mfg. began in 1965. Disc.

	$300	$270	$225	$190	$140	$100	$65

✱ **Airsporter MK VII** - disc. 2001.

	$300	$270	$225	$190	$140	$100	$65

Last MSR was $375.

✱ **Airsporter RB2 Magnum** - rotary breech replaced tap loading breech, 18 in. rifled barrel, 8.50 lbs. Mfg. 1991-2000.

	$300	$270	$225	$190	$140	$100	$65

Last MSR was $450.

Add 25% for Crown Grade RB2 with laminated wood stock.

✦ **Airsporter RB2 Magnum Carbine** - similar to Airsporter RB2 Magnum, except has 14 in. barrel.

	$300	$270	$225	$190	$140	$100	$65

Last MSR was $474.

✱ **Airsporter RB2 Stutzen** - mfg. began in 1992. Disc.

	$360	$325	$275	$225	$165	$120	$80

✱ **Airsporter S** - oil finish, checkered walnut stock; heavier barrel, 0.5 inch longer. Mfg. began in 1979. Disc.

	$345	$310	$260	$215	$160	$115	$75

✱ **Airsporter Stutzen** - full length stock. Mfg. 1985-1992.

	$360	$325	$275	$225	$165	$120	$80

Last MSR was $540.

✱ **Airsporter RB2 Magnum Carbine** - rotary breech replaced tap loading breech, 18 in. rifled barrel, 8.50 lbs. Mfg. 1991-2000.

	$300	$270	$225	$190	$140	$100	$65

Last MSR was $450.

Add 25% for Crown Grade RB2 with laminated wood stock.

AIRSPORTER S CENTENARY (COMMEMORATIVE) - .177 or .22 cal., SP, UL, SS, tap marked "BSA Piled Arms Centenary 1982 - One of One Thousand" on top of air chamber, blue finish, three-quarter length Stutzen-style checkered walnut stock with Schnabel forend (cocking lever contained in forend) and PG cap with trademark, Mk. X 4x40mm scope, QD sling swivels and leather sling, shooting kit, BSA patch, BSA gun case, and certificate numbered to rifle. Mfg. 1982 only.

	$1,000	$950	$800	N/A	N/A	N/A	N/A

Last MSR was $650.

Add 10% for gun case, accessories and all literature.

Mfg. in 1982 to commemorate 100 years of BSA "Piled Arms" symbol, three Martini Henry .577 SS rifles piled in military fashion.

GRADING	100%	95%	90%	80%	60%	40%	20%

BSA AIR RIFLE - .177 cal., UL (bayonet style), SP, SS, faucet tap loading, Marked: "THE BSA AIR RIFLE" (1905) or "THE BSA AIR RIFLE (Lincoln Jeffries Patent)" (1906-1907), 43.5 in. OAL. Mfg. 1905-07.

	100%	95%	90%	80%	60%	40%	20%
	$500	$450	$400	$325	$275	$200	$100

BSA IMPROVED PATTERN - .177 cal., UL (bayonet style), SP, SS, tap loading, new patented breech plug retaining plate and larger chamber in the breech plug, breech plates marked "P. Par.," 43.5 in. OAL. Mfg. 1906-1907.

	100%	95%	90%	80%	60%	40%	20%
	$500	$450	$400	$325	$275	$200	$100

This model may have been what would have been called the Model C or D.

GOLDSTAR - .177 or .22 cal., UL, SP, 18.50 in. barrel, two-stage adj. trigger, hardwood stock, ten-shot rotary magazine, 950/750 FPS, 8.50 lbs. Mfg. 1991-2001.

	100%	95%	90%	80%	60%	40%	20%
	$500	$450	$400	$300	$200	N/A	N/A

Last MSR was $847.

Magazine was developed from VS2000.

* ***Goldstar E/E (Magnum)*** - .177 or .22 cal., UL, SP, 1020/625 FPS, 17.50 in. barrel, two-stage adj. trigger, hardwood stock, ten-shot rotary magazine, 8.50 lbs. Disc. 2001.

	100%	95%	90%	80%	60%	40%	20%
	$450	$400	$350	$300	$200	N/A	N/A

Last MSR was $700.

E/E = "Export Extra"- power above 12 ft. lb., the British legal limit.

GUN LAYING TEACHER - .177 cal., UL (modified to rear), SP, SS, very special variation of Improved Model D underlever air rifle. Cocked by lever behind breech. Instead of a stock it had a system of heavy rails to allow function as a miniature artillery piece for teaching military artillery crews. Known as the Admiralty Pattern guns, these all had a solenoid-operated trigger mechanism. Second unmarked ("Improved Model" or "Inside Barrel Model") variation made late 1930s-early 1940s; used into the 1950s. Fits inside a tank's cannon barrel for training tank gunners.

courtesy Beeman Collection

	100%	95%	90%	80%	60%	40%	20%
	N/A	N/A	$3,200	$2,500	$1,750	$1,250	$850

This gun was designed in 1911, was first delivered in June of 1915, and the last of the only 212 produced were delivered in January of 1916. The entire period of production was seven months.

IMPROVED MODEL B - .177 cal., UL (bayonet style), SP, SS, tap loading, marked with "Improved Model B", Standard version: 43.3 in. OAL, Light version: 39 in. OAL. Mfg. 1907-1908.

	100%	95%	90%	80%	60%	40%	20%
	$800	$700	$600	$400	$300	$200	$150

IMPROVED MODEL D - .177, .22, or .25 (1908-1918 only) cal., SP, SS, UL (bayonet, side button, end button styles), 1.125 (Juvenile) or 1.25 in. dia air cylinder.

Approximately 600 total 25 cal. mfg. in Ordinary and Light versions. Most .25 cal. were sent to India where they saw rough use; very few exist today. There are five size variations (not marked as such) plus the Military models. Size may vary by about 0.25 in.

* ***Junior*** - .177 or .22 cal., 1.25 in. OD, 34.25 in. OAL. Approx. 1097 mfg. 1912-14.

	100%	95%	90%	80%	60%	40%	20%
	$800	$700	$600	$500	$400	$300	$200

* ***Juvenile*** - .177 or .22 cal., air cylinder 1.125 in. OD, folding leaf rear sight, 34.25 in. OAL. Approx. 600 mfg. 1913-14.

	100%	95%	90%	80%	60%	40%	20%
	$1,000	$900	$800	$700	$600	$400	$300

* ***Light*** - .177, .22, or .25 (1908-1918 only) cal., 39 in. OAL.

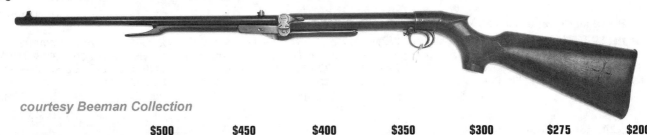

courtesy Beeman Collection

	100%	95%	90%	80%	60%	40%	20%
	$500	$450	$400	$350	$300	$275	$200

Add 500% for original .25 cal. barrels.

GRADING	100%	95%	90%	80%	60%	40%	20%

✳ **Military Model** - .177 or .22 cal., UL, SP, SS, very special variation of Improved Model D for military training; duplicated size, balance, and sights of Lee-Enfield military rifles. Variation one: .177 in. cal. only, simple bayonet cocking lever. Variation two: .177 or .22 cal., bayonet underlever cocking lever with side reinforcements ("fillets or fences") at bend point. Variation three: .22 (No. 2 bore) cal. only, side button cocking lever. Approx. 430 total of all variations mfg. 1907-1914.

courtesy Beeman Collection

	N/A	N/A	$3,200	$2,500	$1,500	$995	NA

✳ **Ordinary** - .177, .22, or .25 (1908-1918) cal., 43.5 in. OAL.

	$500	$450	$400	$350	$300	$275	$200

Add 500% for original .25 cal. barrels.

✳ **Sporting** - .22 (No. 2 bore) cal., 45.5 in. OAL. Mfg.1909-1917.

	$500	$450	$400	$350	$300	$275	$200

STANDARD - .177 or .22 (No. 2) cal., UL, SP, SS, marked "STANDARD". Mfg. 1919-39.

All air rifles made between WWI and WWII were marked "STANDARD".

✳ **Standard Variant 1** - Giant or "Long Tom" (common nicknames, not marked as such), S or T serial number prefixes, 45.5 in. OAL.

courtesy Beeman Collection

	$500	$450	$400	$325	$275	$200	$100

Add 25% for T serial number prefix.

✳ **Standard Variant 2** - Light (not marked as such) - L or A serial number prefixes.

courtesy Beeman Collection

	$500	$450	$400	$325	$275	$200	$100

Add 25% for A serial number prefix.

✳ **Standard Variant 3** - .177 cal. only, comes in two verisons. Club No. 1 version: "CLUB" markings. 45.5 in. OAL. Mfg. 1922-30. Club No. 4 version: "CLUB NO. 4" markings, C or CS serial number prefixes, 45.5 or 45.25 in .OAL. Mfg. 1930-39.

courtesy Beeman Collection

	$500	$450	$400	$325	$275	$200	$100

Add 25% for C serial number prefix.

CLUB model designations and world wide patent details photoetched on top of the compression tube.

STUTZEN MK 2 - .177, .22 cal., or .25 cal., concealed UL, SP, rifled barrel, blue finish, 1020/800/675 FPS, 14 in. barrel, rotating breech, Monte Carlo stock with cheek piece and rosewood Schnabel fore cap, Maxi Grip scope rail, 6.25 lbs. Mfg. 1997-2000.

	$560	$485	$380	$335	$285	N/A	N/A

Last MSR was $700.

GRADING	100%	95%	90%	80%	60%	40%	20%

SUPERSPORT - .177 or .22 cal. , UL, SP, SS, 990/665 FPS, 18.5 in. rifled barrel, blue finish, rotating breech for loading pellets, large diameter air cylinder, nylon parachute piston seal, plain ambidextrous beech stock, rubber buttplate, adj. trigger, 43.8 in., OAL, 7.2 lbs. Mfg. 1987-1992.

	$250	$225	$175	$125	$75	N/A	N/A

✳ *Supersport Custom* - .177 or .22 cal. , UL, SP, SS, 990/665 FPS, 18.5 in. rifled barrel, blue finish, rotating breech for loading pellets, large diameter air cylinder, nylon parachute piston seal, checkered walnut stock w/ cheekpiece and ventilated recoil pad, Maxi-grip sight rail, heavy barrel, adj. metal two stage trigger, manual safety on RHS, 43.8 in. OAL, 7.8 lbs. Mfg. 1987-1992.

courtesy Beeman Collection

	$350	$300	$250	$200	$150	N/A	N/A

SUPERSTAR - .177, .22, or .25 cal., UL, SP, SS, 1020/800/675 FPS, 18.50 in. rifled barrel, blue finish, rotating breech for loading pellets, checkered beech stock, Maxi Grip scope rail, two-stage trigger, 43 OAL, approx. 7.75 lbs. Mfg. 1992-94.

	$420	$375	$315	$260	$185	$125	N/A

Last MSR was $470.

✳ *Superstar Carbine* - .177, .22, or .25 cal., UL, SP, SS, 850/625/530 FPS, 14 in. rifled barrel, blue finish, rotating breech for loading pellets, checkered beech stock, Maxi Grip scope rail, two-stage trigger, 39.5 OAL. Mfg. 1992-94.

	$420	$375	$315	$260	$185	$125	N/A

Last MSR was $470.

SUPERSTAR MK2 E/E - .177, .22, or .25 cal., UL, SP, 18.5 in. rifled barrel, blue finish, 950/750/600 FPS, rotating breech for loading pellets, Monte Carlo stock, Maxi Grip scope rail, adj. two-stage trigger, 43 in. OAL, 8.50 lbs. Mfg. 1994-2001.

	$480	$450	$350	$275	$215	N/A	N/A

Last MSR was $350.

E/E = "Export Extra"- power above 12 ft. lb., the British legal limit.

✳ *Superstar MK2 Carbine E/E* - .177, .22, or .25 cal., UL, SP, SS, 950/750/600 FPS, 14 in. rifled barrel, blue finish, rotating breech for loading pellets, Monte Carlo stock, Maxi Grip scope rail, adj. two-stage trigger, approx. 8. lbs. Mfg. 1994-2001.

	$480	$410	$350	$275	$215	N/A	N/A

Last MSR was $350.

E/E = "Export Extra"- power above 12 ft. lb., the British legal limit.

✳ *Superstar MK2 Magnum* - .177, .22, or .25 cal., UL, SP, 18.5 in. rifled barrel, blue finish, 1020/800/675 FPS, rotating breech for loading pellets, Monte Carlo stock, Maxi Grip scope rail, adj. two-stage trigger, 43 in. OAL, 8.50 lbs. Mfg. 2001-2003.

	$480	$450	$350	$275	$215	N/A	N/A

Last MSR was $540.

RIFLES: PRECHARGED PNEUMATICS

FIREBIRD - .177 or .22 cal., PCP, UL rotating breech action, SS, 1100/800 FPS, 17.5 in. barrel, adj. trigger and power level, beech Monte Carlo stock with vent. recoil pad, 42 in. OAL, 7.25 lbs. Mfg. 2001-03.

	$300	$250	$200	$150	$100	N/A	N/A

$350.

✳ *Firebird Carbine* - .177 or .22 cal., PCP, UL rotating breech action, SS, 1100/800 FPS, 13 in. barrel, adj. trigger and power level, beech Monte Carlo stock with vent. recoil pad, 39 in. OAL, 7.5 lbs. Mfg. 2001-03.

	$350	$300	$225	$175	$125	N/A	N/A

Last MSR was $395.

HORNET/HORNET MULTI SHOT - .22 cal., PCP, SS or ten-shot mag. (new 2004), micro-movement cocking mechanism, SLC pressure regulator, 18.5 in. match grade free-floating barrel, 850 FPS, blue finish, adj. two-stage trigger, checkered beech Monte Carlo stock with vent. recoil pad, 37.5 in. OAL, 7.9 lbs. New 2003.

MSR	$778	$750	$650	$550	$450	$350	N/A	N/A

Add $75 for Hornet Multi-Shot.

✳ *Hornet Carbine* - .22 cal., PCP, SS or ten-shot mag. (new 2004), micro-movement cocking mechanism, pressure regulator, 15.75 in. match grade free-floating barrel, 850 FPS, blue finish, adj. two-stage trigger, checkered beech Monte Carlo stock with vent. recoil pad, 34 in. OAL, 7.5 lbs. New 2003.

MSR	$778	$750	$650	$550	$450	$350	N/A	N/A

SPITFIRE - .177 or .22 cal., PCP, BBC, SS, 1100/800 FPS, 17.5 in. barrel, beech Monte Carlo stock with vent. recoil pad, 40.5 in. OAL, 7.2 lbs. New 1999.

MSR	$465	$450	$350	$285	$225	$185	N/A	N/A

GRADING	100%	95%	90%	80%	60%	40%	20%

✳ *Spitfire Carbine* - .177 or .22 cal., PCP, BBC, SS, 1100/800 FPS, 14.5 in. barrel, beech Monte Carlo stock with vent. recoil pad, 39 in. OAL, 7.25 lbs. New 1999.

	MSR $526	$495	$395	$325	$265	$215	N/A	N/A

✳ *Bisley Spitfire* - .177 or .22 cal., PCP, BBC, SS, similar to Spitfire except lower power designed for 10-Meter Match use with rear match aperature sight with an interchangeable front sight. New 2005.

	MSR $641	$625	$550	$450	$350	$250	N/A	N/A

SUPERTEN - .177 or .22 cal., PCP, BA, 200cc bottle, ten-shot rotary mag., 1000/800 FPS, 17.25 in. rifled barrel, match grade trigger, beech or walnut Monte Carlo stock with adj. pad, 37.5 in. OAL, approx. 7.75 lbs. New 1996.

✳ *SuperTEN MK1* - .177 or .22 cal., PCP, BA, ten-shot rotary mag., 1000/800 FPS, 17.25 in. rifled barrel, match grade trigger, beech or walnut Monte Carlo stock with adj. pad, 37.5 in. OAL, approx. 7.75 lbs. Mfg. 1996-2001.

	$750	$600	$525	$475	$425	N/A	N/A

Last MSR was $880.

✳ *SuperTEN MK2* - .177 or .22 cal., PCP, BA, ten-shot rotary mag., 1250/1050 FPS, 17.25 in. rifled standard or Bull (new 2004) free-floating match grade barrel, adj. match grade trigger, checkered beech or walnut Monte Carlo stock with adj. pad, 37.5 in. OAL, Approx. 7.9 lbs. New 2001.

	MSR $1,049	$995	$850	$700	$625	$575	N/A	N/A

Add 30% for walnut stock.
Add 20% for Bull barrel.

✳ *SuperTEN MK2 Carbine* - .177 or .22 cal., PCP, BA, ten-shot rotary mag., 1050/850 FPS, 13.25 in. standard or Bull (new 2004) rifled free-floating match grade barrel, adj. match grade trigger, checkered beech or walnut Monte Carlo stock with adj. pad, 33.5 in. OAL, Approx. 6.6 lbs. New 2001.

	MSR $1,161	$1,050	$900	$750	$625	$550	N/A	N/A

Add 30% for walnut stock.
Add 20% for Bull barrel.

TECH STAR - .22 cal., PCP, SS, 100cc reservoir, micro-movement cocking mechanism, pressure regulator, 18.5 in. barrel, 1000 FPS, blue finish, adj. rear fixed front sights, adj. two-stage trigger, checkered beech Monte Carlo stock with vent. recoil pad, 37 in. OAL, 6.6 lbs. New 2004.

	MSR $546	$435	$350	$275	$225	$175	N/A	N/A

RIFLES: SIDE LEVER COCKING

VS 2000 - .177 or .22 cal., SL, SP, nine-shot repeater, rifled barrel, blue finish, 850-625 FPS, 9 lbs. Approx. ten were mfg. Disc. 1986.

	$3,000	$2,800	N/A	N/A	N/A	N/A	N/A

Last MSR was $330.

B.S.F. "BAYERISCHE SPORTWAFFENFABRIK"

Previous manufacturer located in Erlangen, Germany. Previously imported by Kendell International located in Paris, KY, and by Beeman Precision Arms under the Wischo label.

B.S.F. (Bayerische Sportwaffenfabrik) is the base brand for airguns marked B.S.F., Bavaria, and Wischo. B.S.F. was founded in 1935 and produced a few airguns before the pressures of WWII took over. Production began again in 1948 and put an emphasis on solid, simple construction. The Model S54 remains as a classic of solid, elegant construction for a sporter air rifle. B.S.F.'s own production was generally sold under the Bavaria label. The Wischo Company of Erlangen, one of Europe's leading gun distributors, distributed large numbers, especially to Beeman Precision Airguns in the USA, under the Wischo label. The collapse of their British agent, Norman May & Co, in 1980 resulted in the dismissal of most of the 130 workers. The Schütt family sold the business to Herbert Gayer, who refined the production considerably . However, this was not enough to prevent further decline of the company. It was then purchased by the Hermann Weihrauch Company in nearby Mellrichstadt in the late 1980s. By incorporating some HW design and cosmetic features and parts, a surprisingly good line of upper economy level airguns was developed to supplement the top-of-the-line, regular HW models. Weihrauch manufactures versions of B.S.F. models for Marksman (Marksman Models 28, 40, 55, 56, 58, 59, 70, 71, 72, and 75).

PISTOLS

B.S.F. (WISCHO) MODEL S-20 - .177 cal., BBC, 450 FPS, 2.5 lbs. Disc. 1988.

courtesy Beeman Collection

	$125	$110	$75	$65	$55	N/A	N/A

Last MSR was $130.

GRADING	100%	95%	90%	80%	60%	40%	20%

B.S.F. (WISCHO) MODEL CM - similar to Model S-20 except is target style. Disc. in 1988.

courtesy Beeman Collection

	$150	$125	$90	$75	$65	N/A	N/A

RIFLES

BAVARIA MODEL 35 - .177 cal., BBC, SP, 500 FPS, 4.50 lbs.

	$150	$120	$100	$75	$50	N/A	N/A

Last MSR was $125.

BAVARIA MODEL 45 - .177 cal., BBC, SP, 700 FPS, 6 lbs.

	$165	$125	$105	$85	$60	N/A	N/A

Last MSR was $125.

BAVARIA MODEL 50 - .177 cal., BBC, SP, 700 FPS, 6 lbs.

	$175	$130	$110	$85	$60	N/A	N/A

BAVARIA MODEL S 54 - .177 or .22 cal., UL, SP, 685/500 FPS, 8 lbs.

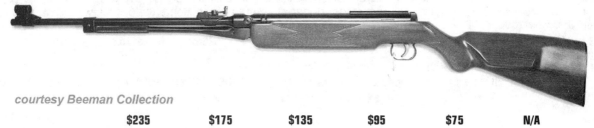

courtesy Beeman Collection

	$235	$175	$135	$95	$75	N/A	N/A

Add 10% for Sport Model, plain stock, disc. 1986.
Add 20% for M Model—angular cheekpiece, aperture sight, disc. 1986.
Ref: ARG: 37-44.

❋ **Model S 54 Deluxe** - .177 or .22 cal., UL, SP, 19.1 in. rifled barrel (12 grooves RH), tap-loader, hand checkered walnut stock, cast aluminum buttplate. 46.8 in. OAL, 8.6 lbs., no safety.

courtesy Beeman Collection

	$395	$335	$285	$245	$195	N/A	N/A

Add 20% for pre-1980 stock, forearm round in cross section, hand checkering.

BAVARIA MODEL S 55/55 N - .177 or .22 cal., BBC, SP, 16.1 in. rifled barrel (12 grooves, RH), 870/635 FPS, no safety, 40.6 in. OAL, 6.4 lbs. Disc. 1986.

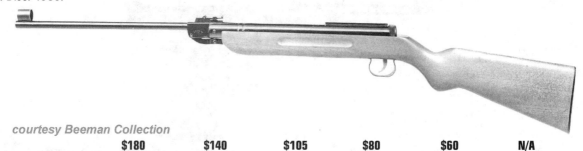

courtesy Beeman Collection

	$180	$140	$105	$80	$60	N/A	N/A

Add 10% for Deluxe Model (checkered grip).
Add $30 for Special Model 55 N (N = "Nussbaum," German for walnut).

GRADING	100%	95%	90%	80%	60%	40%	20%

BAVARIA MODEL S 60 - .177 or .22 cal., BBC, SP, 800/570 FPS, 6.50 lbs.

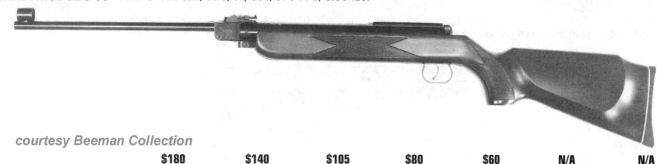

courtesy Beeman Collection

	$180	$140	$105	$80	$60	N/A	N/A

BAVARIA MODEL S 70 - .177 or .22 cal., BBC, SP, 19.1 in. barrel, 855/610 FPS, checkered Monte Carlo stock, ventilated rubber buttplate, 7 lbs.

	$265	$225	$185	$145	$105	N/A	N/A

BAVARIA MODEL S 80 - .177 or .22 cal., BBC, SP, 800/570 FPS, 8.25 lbs.

	$210	$180	$140	$105	$80	N/A	N/A

Last MSR was $185.

BAHCO

Previous manufacturer, Aktiebolaget Bahco (AB Bahco), has roots dating back to 1862 as a metal working business in Stockholm and Enköping, Sweden. No longer produces airguns.

BAHCO, which, due to a strange font used in the stamping of the name, appears to read as "BAMCO" and is so listed in many places, is a brand name of Aktiebolaget Bahco (AB Bahco).

This Swedish firm has roots dating back to the founding of a steel works in 1862 by Göran Fredrik Göransson, which developed exceptional quality saws under the same "Fish & Hook" brand that their tools bear today. Their most famous products, based on 118 patents granted to Johan Johansson from 1888 to 1943, are the adjustable spanner wrench ("Crescent wrench") and adjustable pipe wrench ("monkey wrench"). They have produced over 100 million examples of those world famous tools. According to Walter (2001) they also formerly specialized in bayonets and military equipment and produced gas-powered rifles under the Excellent brand from 1906 to 1915 with the patents of Ewerlöf and Blómen. Today the Bahco name can be found on garden and other tools in almost any large hardware or warehouse store, but no longer on airguns.

The Bahco Model 1S air rifle is very similar to the Excellent C2 air rifle and is sometimes listed with it. The Bahco Model 1S clearly is the older design. The full relationship of the Bahco and Excellent brand airguns has yet to be determined. (See Excellent in the "E" section of this guide.)

RIFLES

MODEL 1S - .177 cal., SS, trombone-style slide action pump pneumatic, smoothbore octagonal BBL, breech block swings to side to load, no safety. Mfg. circa 1900.

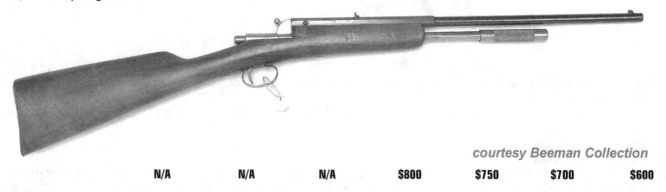

courtesy Beeman Collection

	N/A	N/A	N/A	$800	$750	$700	$600

BAIKAL

Current trademark of products manufactured by the Russian State Unitary Plant "Izhevsky Mechanichesky Zavod" (SUP IMZ), located in Russia. Currently imported by European American Armory, located in Sharpes, FL; Compasseco, located in Bardstown, KY; and Pyramyd Air, Inc., located in Pepper Pike, OH. Dealer sales. For more information and current pricing on both new and used Baikal firearms, please refer to the *Blue Book of Gun Values* by S.P. Fjestad (also available online).

First known to American airgunners after WWII by the Baikal IZh 22, a typical Russian simple, but fairly sturdy, break barrel .22 cal. air rifle. Baikal also manufactures many models that are not currently available in the American marketplace.

GRADING	100%	95%	90%	80%	60%	40%	20%

PISTOLS

IZh 46/46M - .177 cal., UL, single-stroke pneumatic, single shot, 460 (IZH 46M) or 410 (IZH46) FPS, micrometer fully adj. rear target sight, adj. international target grip, five-way adj. trigger, hammer-forged rifled 10 in. barrel, 2.4 lbs.

courtesy Baikal

	MSR	$349	$270	$245	$200	$155	$100	N/A	N/A

Subtract 25% for IZh 46.

IZh 53M - .177 cal., BBC, SP, SS, 360 FPS, adj. rear sight, adj. trigger, rifled 8.8 in. barrel, black plastic target grip, 16.3 in OAL, 2.4 lbs.

courtesy Baikal

	MSR	$50	$50	$45	$35	$25	$20	N/A	N/A

IZh 153M - .177 cal., BBC, SP, SS pistol, black plastic stock with thumb rest and finger grooves.

courtesy Beeman Collection

$75	$65	$55	$50	$40	$30	$20

IZh MP654K (MAKAROV SEMI-AUTO) - .177 cal, CO_2 (capsule loads in magazine), single or double action, thirteen-shot, 3.8 in. barrel, 380 FPS, 1.6 lbs. Disc. 2003.

$100	$85	$70	$55	$40	N/A	N/A

Last MSR was $120.

RIFLES

IJ 22 - .177 cal., BBC, SP, SS, 17.90 in. rifled barrel, 410-498 FPS, vertical lever breech-lock on LHS of barrel, brass lined, rifled barrel, blued finish, trigger guard, grip cap and buttplate of dark red plastic hardwood stock with unique shoulder up behind end cap, plastic inset marked "IJ 22", typically sold new with extra mainspring and seals, 40.8 OAL, 5.2 lbs. Mfg. in USSR circa 1970s.

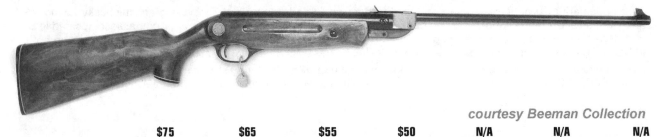

courtesy Beeman Collection

$75	$65	$55	$50	N/A	N/A	N/A

Also sold internationally as Vostok, in Britain as Milbro G530, and in USA as HyScore 870 Mark 3.

GRADING	100%	95%	90%	80%	60%	40%	20%

IZh 60 - .177 cal., SL, SP, 460 FPS, 16.50 in. barrel, telescoping stock, 5 lbs. 6 oz. Disc.

	100%	95%	90%	80%	60%	40%	20%
	$90	$80	$65	$50	$40	N/A	N/A

Last MSR was $140.

IZh 61 - .177 cal., SL, SP, five-shot mag., 490 FPS, 17.80 in. barrel, polymer telescoping stock, 6.4 lbs.

MSR $100	$90	$80	$70	$60	$50	N/A	N/A

IZh 32BK - .177 cal., SL, SP, 541 FPS, integral rail for scope mount, adj. buttplate, adj. cheek piece, adj. trigger, walnut stock, 11.68 in. barrel, 12.13 lbs. Mfg. 1999-2002.

	$750	$650	$525	$425	$275	N/A	N/A

Last MSR was $1,100.

This model is designed for ten-meter running target competition.

IZh 38 - .177 cal., BBC, SP, SS, 410-498 FPS MV, very short pull, 40.8 in OAL, 5.2 lbs.
Current values not yet determined.

IZh DROZD - .177 lead balls cal., CO_2, 330 FPS, 10 in. barrel. New 2003.

MSR $219	$200	$160	$120	$80	$60	N/A	N/A

IZh MP512 - .177 cal., BBC, SP, SS, 490 FPS, integral rail for scope mount, adj. sights, polymer stock, 17.70 in. barrel, 6.20 lbs. New 1999.

MSR $50	$50	$40	$30	$20	$15	N/A	N/A

IZh MP512M2 - .22 cal., similar to IZH MP512, except .22 cal., 590 FPS.

MSR $65	$60	$50	$40	$30	$20	N/A	N/A

IZh MP513 - .177 cal., BBC, SP, SS, 1000 FPS, integral rail for scope mount, adj. sights, European wood stock, 17.70 in. barrel, 6.20 lbs. New 2003.

courtesy Baikal

MSR $160	$140	$110	$85	$60	$50	N/A	N/A

IZh MP532 - .177 cal., SL, SP, 460 FPS, IZH-46 action, fully adj. rear sight, hooded front sight, adj. butt pad, adj. trigger, 15.75 in. barrel, 9.26 lbs. New 1999.

MSR $599	$495	$400	$325	$265	$165	N/A	N/A

BALCO-SUB

Manufacturer of CO_2 spear pistols at 6 Menexelon Street, Kato Kifisia, Greece.

PISTOL

BALCO PRO - CO_2, SS, heavy plastic, aluminum, and stainless steel. 22.9 in. OAL, 2.3 lbs.

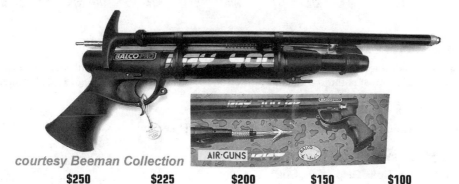

courtesy Beeman Collection

AIR-GUNS

	$250	$225	$200	$150	$100	N/A	N/A

Add 10% for factory plastic sheath.

BARNES, GARY

Current custom manufacturer located in New Windsor, MD.

Drawing on twelve years' experience as a knife maker, Barnes applies very unique artistic skill and design as well as mechanical creativity to his airguns. All parts, including the barrels, are of his design and making. He specializes in large bore, high power, high accuracy airguns, often with exotic, unique styling and decoration.

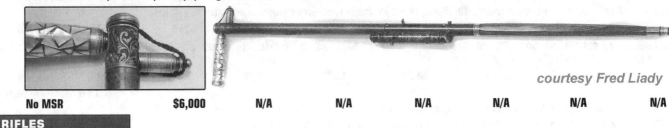

GRADING	100%	95%	90%	80%	60%	40%	20%

AIRCANES

AUTOCANE - .27 cal., PCP, full auto/500 RPM, Brazilian rosewood handle with mother-of-pearl mosaic and metallic grout, acid etched steel body with top deeply engraved. 39.8 in. OAL, 4.7 lbs.

courtesy Fred Liady

No MSR	$6,000	N/A	N/A	N/A	N/A	N/A	N/A

RIFLES

FIRST MODEL - .45 cal., PCP (2600 PSI), cross bolt repeater, 48 in. OAL, 10 lbs. Mfg. circa 2000.

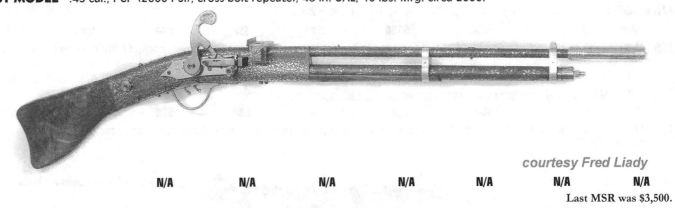

courtesy Fred Liady

N/A	N/A	N/A	N/A	N/A	N/A	N/A

Last MSR was $3,500.

HIGH PLAINS CARBINE - .375 cal. 500 FPS, SS, PCP, BA, 36 in. OAL, 6.2 lbs. New 2001.

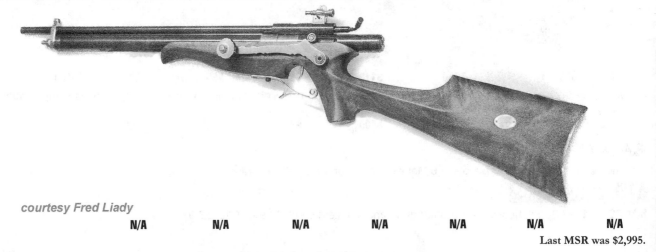

courtesy Fred Liady

N/A	N/A	N/A	N/A	N/A	N/A	N/A

Last MSR was $2,995.

BARNETT INTERNATIONAL

Research is ongoing with this trademark, and more information will be included both online and in future editions. Average original condition specimens on most common Barnett models are typically priced in the $150-200 range.

BARTHELMS, FRITZ (FB RECORD)

For information on Fritz Barthelms, please refer to FB Record in the "F" section.

BASCARAN, C. y T. SRC

Previous manufacturer located in Eibar, Guipuzcoa, Spain.

Bascaran, C. y T. SRC manufactured airguns under the Cometa tradename. Research is ongoing with this trademark, and more information will be included both in future editions and online. Average original condition specimens on most common Bascaran, C. y T. SRC models are typically priced in the $75-$125 range.

BAVARIA

For information on Bavaria airguns, see B.S.F. "Bayerische Sportwaffenfabrik" in this "B" section.

GRADING	100%	95%	90%	80%	60%	40%	20%

BAYARD

Previously manufactured by Anciens Éstablissements Pieper in Herstal Liége, Belgium.

This company is best known for their semi-auto pistol manufacture. They produced a .177 cal., SP, BBC, SS air rifle for HyScore of New York, post-WWII. A mounted knight logo and "Bayard" may be stamped on the side of the body tube. Has a buttplate with cast letters "BELGIUM" in a vertical row. There are two known versions. One has a spring-loaded J-shaped pellet seating device on the side of the breech. Very well made with hand checkered hardwood stock. Very good condition specimens are valued at about $275. Add $50 for pellet seating model.

BEC EUROLUX AIRGUNS

Current trademark distributed by BEC Inc., located in Alhambra, CA.

RIFLES

MODEL BEC 15AG - .177 cal., BBC, SP, SS, 14.5 in. barrel, 500 FPS, black finish, walnut-tone hardwood stock, 5.5 lbs.

	100%	95%	90%	80%	60%	40%	20%
MSR $69	$60	$50	$40	$30	$20	N/A	N/A

MODEL BEC 18AG - .177 or .22 cal., BBC, SP, SS, 16.5 in. barrel, 850/700 FPS, black finish, walnut-tone hardwood stock, 6.9 lbs.

	100%	95%	90%	80%	60%	40%	20%
MSR $99	$85	$60	$50	$40	$30	N/A	N/A

MODEL BEC 21AG - .177 or .22 cal., BBC, SP, SS, 20 in. barrel, 1000/800 FPS, black finish, walnut-tone hardwood stock, 9.9 lbs.

	100%	95%	90%	80%	60%	40%	20%
MSR $189	$160	$115	$85	$60	$50	N/A	N/A

BEDFORD & WALKER

Previous manufacturer located in Boston, MA circa 1880s.

Former gunmaking partnership of Augustus Bedford and George A. Walker in Boston, MA, USA. Manufactured the Eureka air pistol based on the Quackenbush push-barrel design with a loading bolt patented by Walker in 1876. Production started in the Pope Brothers & Company plant, then went to the Bedford and Walker plant, and finally transferred to the H.M. Quackenbush plant from the 1880s until 1893. Quackenbush featured the pistol in his catalogs and listed a sale of seventy-four Eureka air pistols in 1886. (Bedford worked in the Quackenbush factory for several years and he, Pope, Walker, and Quackenbush were close associates – so there is a good deal of overlap and confusion about the origin, production, and sales of their designs).

PISTOLS

EUREKA STANDARD - .21 cal., SP, SS push-plunger, Japan black or nickel finish.

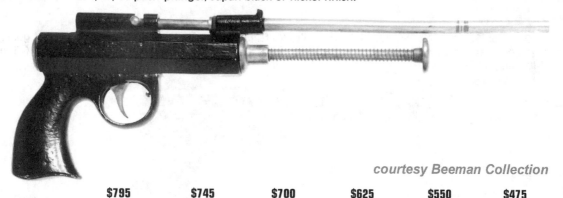

courtesy Beeman Collection

100%	95%	90%	80%	60%	40%	20%
$795	$745	$700	$625	$550	$475	N/A

Add 10% for nickel finish.
Add 20% for wire shoulder stock.

EUREKA DELUXE - .21 cal, SP, SS push-plunger, nickel finish, rosewood inserts on flared grip, hardwood case with locking lid, wire shoulder stock, wrench, and box of slugs or darts.

courtesy Beeman Collection

100%	95%	90%	80%	60%	40%	20%
N/A	$2,000	$1,500	$1,000	$750	$650	$500

GRADING	100%	95%	90%	80%	60%	40%	20%

BEEMAN PRECISION AIRGUNS

Current manufacturer and importer located in Huntington Beach, CA. Dealer and consumer direct sales.

The Beeman company was founded by Robert and Toshiko Beeman in 1972 in San Anselmo, CA. Originally named Beeman´s Precision Airguns, the company began by importing airgun models and pellets from Weihrauch, Feinwerkbau, Webley, Dianawerk, Handler and Natermann, Hasuike, and other overseas companies. After moving to San Rafael, CA, the name of the company was changed to Beeman Precision Airguns, Inc. They began to design their own models of airguns and airgun pellets to be produced by Weihrauch, Webley, Norica, Handler and Natermann, and Hasuike. Among the many airgun items introduced by the Beemans were the first telescopic sights built especially for high power sporting air rifles and the first hollow point airgun pellets. By the late 1970s, the Beeman company was importing over 90% of the adult airguns brought into the USA.

Although several other companies, notably Winchester and Hy-Score, had previously attempted to introduce adult airguns to the American shooting market, Beeman is credited with the first successful, commercial development of the adult airgun market in the United States. Tom Gaylord, founder and former editor of *Airgun Letter, Airgun Revue,* and *Airgun Illustrated Magazine,* recorded in his book *The Beeman R1* that "the Beeman R1 is the rifle that brought America fully into the world of adult airguns." (Versions of the Beeman R1, generally lower in power or less deluxe, are marketed in other parts of the world as the Weihrauch HW 80.) Other models were produced for Beeman by Norica, Erma, FAS, Record, Sharp, Air Arms, Titan, Gamekeeper, and others. In 1983 Beeman added certain precision firearms to its line and changed its name to Beeman Precision Arms, Inc. On April 3, 1993, Robert and Toshiko sold most of the assets of their company to S/R Industries of Maryland. S/R moved the company to Huntington Beach, CA to be near one of its other holdings, Marksman Industries, and restored the name of Beeman Precision Airguns. The company has continued to feature the very high quality airguns which had become synonymous with the Beeman name and added an economy line for mass marketers.

Beeman has exclusive rights to any airguns officially marketed in the U.S. under the names Beeman, Feinwerkbau, and Beeman designed models manufactured by Weihrauch and others. Some models, marketed by Beeman in the late 1970s and early 1980s, were manufactured in Germany by Mayer & Grammelspacher (Dianawerk). Early production of those airguns used Diana model numbers under the "Beeman's Original" brand, but later shipments were marked with the Beeman name and model numbers. Very small stampings on the Dianawerk receivers indicate the month and year of manufacture.

Beeman imported Feinwerkbau and Weihrauch Airguns, which appear under their respective headings in this section. Beeman/Webley airguns are incorporated into this section, as are economy airguns that are only promoted through chain stores under the Beeman name.

Additional material on the history of the Beeman company, the Beemans, the history of airguns, the development of the airgun market in the USA, and a wide range of other airgun information is available at www.Beemans.net.

For more information and current values on used Beeman firearms, please refer to the *Blue Book of Gun Values* by S.P. Fjestad (also available online).

PISTOLS

ADDER - .177, .20, .22 or .25 cal., 940/850/775/630 FPS (14 to 20 ft. lbs. ME), PCP, SS, bolt action, grip, trigger guard, and forearm from one piece of select hardwood, smooth grips, scope grooves, blue receiver end cap, 10.5 in. barrel, 16.5 in. OAL, manual safety, 2.75 lbs. Mfg. in England 1992.

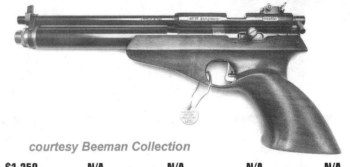

courtesy Beeman Collection

$1,250	N/A	N/A	N/A	N/A	N/A	N/A

Last MSR was $530.

Add 10% for .20 cal.
Ten guns were manufactured.

FAS 604 - .177 cal., TL, SP, SS, 380 FPS, 2.2 lbs. Mfg. in Italy. Disc. 1988.

$295	$250	$195	$150	$100	N/A	N/A

Last MSR was $495.

Add 10% for left-hand variation.

HW 70/HW70A/HW70S - .177 cal., BBC, SP, 440 FPS, two-stage adj. trigger, 6 in. rifled steel barrel, blue/black epoxy or silver (HW 70S, mfg. 1992 only) finish, hooded front and adj. rear (scope grooves added to rear sight base HW 70A 1992) sights, one-piece composition grip and forearm. 2.4 lbs. Mfg. in Germany with importation beginning in 1972.

MSR	$215	$175	$135	$105	$90	$75	N/A	N/A

Add 20% for HW70S with silver finish.
Subtract 20% for safety.
Add 10% for Santa Rosa address.

Early versions did not have a retainer screw in the side of the rear body plug. The plug may come loose and fly out (recalled).

GRADING	100%	95%	90%	80%	60%	40%	20%

HURRICANE - .177 or .22 (disc.) cal., TL, SP, SS, 500 FPS, plastic grips with RH thumbrest, adj. rear sight supplied with adapter which replaced rear sight with scope mounting dovetail, hooded front sight, aluminum grip frame cast around steel body tube, RH manual safety, black epoxy finish, 8 in. button rifled barrel, 11.2 in. OAL, 2.4 lbs. Mfg. in England with importation beginning in 1990.

	100%	95%	90%	80%	60%	40%	20%
MSR $275	$235	$195	$150	$115	$95	N/A	N/A

Add 10% for wood grips.

Add 15% for finger groove Beeman "combat" wood grips.

Add 20% for Beeman factory markings with San Rafael address.

Add 10% for Beeman factory markings with Santa Rosa address.

Add 20% for large deluxe factory box with form-fitting depressions, including depression for mounted scope, in hard plastic shell with red flocked surface.

Add 10% for factory box with molded white foam support block.

Add 20% for Model 20 scope combo.

MODEL 700 - .177 cal., BBC, SP, 460 FPS, 7 in. barrel, 3.1 lbs. Disc. 1981.

	100%	95%	90%	80%	60%	40%	20%
	$125	$100	$75	$50	$40	N/A	N/A

Last MSR was $122.

Add 20% for left-hand grip.

Add 20% for Beeman walnut stock.

Add 50% for Beeman folding metal shoulder stock.

Mfg. for Beeman in Germany by Mayer & Grammelspacher. First imports marked "Beeman's Original Model 5".

MODEL 800 - .177 cal., BBC, SP, SS, 460 FPS, 7 in. barrel, Giss patent double opposing piston recoilless mechanism, 3.2 lbs. Disc. 1982.

courtesy BeemanCollection

	100%	95%	90%	80%	60%	40%	20%
	$225	$175	$150	$125	$100	N/A	N/A

Last MSR was $191.

Add 10% if stamped "Beeman's Original".

Add 20% for left-hand grip.

Add 20% for Beeman walnut stock.

Add 50% for Beeman folding metal shoulder stock.

Mfg. for Beeman in Germany by Mayer & Grammelspacher. First imports marked "Beeman's Original Model 6".

MODEL 850 - similar to Model 800 with same rotating barrel shroud as the Model 900. Disc. 1982.

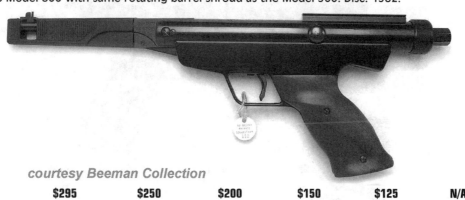

courtesy Beeman Collection

	100%	95%	90%	80%	60%	40%	20%
	$295	$250	$200	$150	$125	N/A	N/A

Last MSR was $225.

Add 20% for left-hand grip or scope mount (shown in picture).

Add 20% for Beeman walnut grip (shown in picture).

Add 50% for Beeman metal wire shoulder stock (fitting shown in picture).

Mfg. in Germany for Beeman by Mayer & Grammelspacher.

GRADING	100%	95%	90%	80%	60%	40%	20%

MODEL 900 - .177 cal., BBC, SP, 490 FPS, 7.1 in. barrel, double opposing piston recoilless mechanism, rotating barrel shroud, target model with adj. walnut match grips, match micrometer sights, 3.3 lbs. Disc. 1981.

	$375	$295	$250	$195	$145	N/A	N/A

Last MSR was $445.

Add 10% if stamped "Beeman's Original".

Add 10% for left-hand grip.

Add 20% for fitted factory case.

Mfg. in Germany for Beeman by Mayer & Grammelspacher. First imports marked "Beeman's Original Model 10".

NEMESIS - .177 or .22 cal., TL, SS, single-stroke pneumatic, 385/300 FPS, two-stage adj. trigger, black or brushed chrome finish, manual safety, adj. open sights, integral scope rail, 2.2 lbs. Mfg. in England. 1995-disc.

	$150	$125	$110	$90	$75	N/A	N/A

Last MSR was $200.

Add 10% for brushed chrome finish.

P1 MAGNUM - .177, .20, .22 (disc.1995) cal., TL, SP, SS, single (.22) or dual power action, 600/480 FPS in .177, 500/420 FPS in .20, two-stage trigger, scope groove, barrel and sights in same unit, walnut grips, Colt 1911A1 styling, accepts any custom grips designed for the 1911A1. Mfg. in Germany with importation beginning in 1985.

courtesy Beeman Collection

MSR	$475	$385	$325	$265	$225	$175	N/A	N/A

Add 10% for .22 cal.

Add 10% for Santa Rosa address.

Add 15% for grooved Combat grips (shown in picture).

Add 30% for Beeman shoulder stock (walnut) - designed by R. Beeman.

Add 100% for gold plating.

Add 30% for stainless steel style or blue/stainless dual finish.

Add 100% for Commemorative Model, enameled 20th year logo inletted into deluxe rosewood grip (25 mfg. 1992 only).

Designed by Robert Beeman; engineered by H.W. Weihrauch Company. The P1 was the predecessor of the Weihrauch HW 45.

P2 - .177 or .20 (mfg. 1990-93) cal., TL, SSP, SS, similar to Beeman P1 except single-stroke pneumatic, not dual power, 435/365 FPS, two-stage adj. trigger, walnut grips. Mfg. in Germany with importation 1990-2001.

courtesy Beeman Collection

	$275	$235	$190	$165	$125	N/A	N/A

Last MSR was $385.

Add 20% for match grips. Add 30% for .20 cal.

Add 10% for Santa Rosa address.

GRADING	100%	95%	90%	80%	60%	40%	20%

P3 - .177 cal., TL, SSP, 410 FPS, cocking the hammer allows the top frame to swing up as a charging lever, automatic safety and beartrap prevention, adj. rear sight, rifled steel barrel, built-in muzzle brake, two-stage trigger, anatomical polymer composite grip, 1.7 lbs. Mfg. in Germany with importation beginning in 1999.

courtesy S.P. Fjestad

MSR $225	$175	$145	$115	$90	$75	N/A	N/A

Add 20% for Millennium Model with gold trigger, hammer, and safety.

Add 50% for P3 Combo with 5021 scope and accessories.

TEMPEST - .177 or .22 (disc.) cal., TL, SP, SS, 500/400 FPS, plastic grips with RH thumb rest, adj. rear sight, aluminum grip frame cast around steel body tube, compact version of Hurricane (Tempest bodies produced by grinding off rear section of Hurricane castings), RH manual safety, 6.87 in. button rifled barrel, black epoxy finish, 9.2 in. OAL, 2.0 lbs. Mfg. in England 1981 to date.

MSR $235	$195	$155	$125	$95	$80	N/A	N/A

Add 10% for Beeman wood grips.

Add 15% for finger groove Beeman "combat" wood grips.

Add 20% for Beeman factory markings with San Rafael address.

Add 10% for Beeman factory markings with Santa Rosa address.

Add 20% for large factory box 11.6 x 8.6 inches, black with logo.

Add 10% for medium factory box 10.2 x 6.6 inches, black with logo.

WOLVERINE - .177 or .25 cal., PCP, SS, BA, 10.5 in. barrel, 940/630 FPS (14 to 20 ft. lbs. ME), similar to Adder except has stippled grip select walnut, solid brass rear receiver cap, match trigger, scope grooves, 16.5 in. OAL, manual safety, 3.0 lbs. Mfg. in England 1992.

courtesy Beeman Collection

$1,795	N/A	N/A	N/A	N/A	N/A	N/A

Last MSR was $700.

One of the world's most powerful air pistols. Ten guns were manufactured.

RIFLES

MODEL 100 - .177 cal., BBC, SP, 660 FPS, 18.7 in. barrel, 6.0 lbs. Disc. 1980.

$125	$95	$80	$65	$55	N/A	N/A

Last MSR was $155.

Add 10% if stamped "Beeman's Original".

Mfg. in Germany by Mayer & Grammelspacher. First imports marked "Beeman's Original Model 27".

MODEL 200 - .177 cal., BBC, SP, 700 FPS, 19 in. barrel, 7.1 lbs. Disc. 1979.

$125	$95	$80	$65	$55	N/A	N/A

Last MSR was $197.

Add 10% if stamped "Beeman's Original".

Less than 100 mfg. in Germany by Mayer & Grammelspacher. First imports marked "Beeman's Original Model 35".

GRADING	100%	95%	90%	80%	60%	40%	20%

MODEL 250 - .177, .20, or .22 cal., BBC, SP, 830/750/650 FPS, 20.5 in. barrel, 7.8 lbs. Disc. 1981.

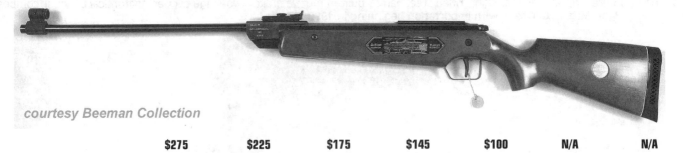

courtesy Beeman Collection

	$275	$225	$175	$145	$100	N/A	N/A

Last MSR was $217.

Add 50% for Commemorative model (shown), Diana emblem in stock (approx. 20 Beeman 250s were so marked).

Add 30% for Long Safety version - safety bolt projects 1.225 in. (29 mm) from rear end of receiver and is not stamped "N". Such guns were recalled as a hazard and a shorter safety, stamped "N", installed.

Add 60% for .20 cal. version (approx. 40 were produced).

Manufactured in Germany by Mayer & Grammelspacher.

MODEL 400 - .177 cal., SL, SP, 650 FPS, 19 in. barrel, target model with match micrometer aperture sight, 10.9 lbs. Disc. 1981.

	$800	$700	$600	$450	$300	N/A	N/A

Last MSR was $615.

Add 10% if stamped "Beeman's Original".

Add 15% for left-hand stock and lever.

Add 15% for Universal model (adj. cheekpiece).

Mfg. in Germany by Mayer & Grammelspacher. First imports marked "Beeman Original Model 75".

MODEL GH500 COMBO - .177 cal., BBC, SP, SS, Belgium Matte finish, ported muzzle brake, 525 FPS, Monte Carlo sporter style composite stock, automatic safety, adj. 3-7x20 Beeman scope, 38.5 in. OAL, 5 lbs. Mfg. in USA. New 2004.

MSR	$90	$75	$60	$50	$40	N/A	N/A	N/A

MODEL GH650 - .177 cal., BBC, SP, 650 FPS, sporter trigger, automatic safety, walnut stained beech Monte Carlo stock with recoil pad, ported muzzle brake, 4x32mm Beeman scope, 41.5 in. OAL, 5.9 lbs. New 2003.

MSR	$190	$165	$135	$105	$80	$50	N/A	N/A

Last MSR was $149.

MODEL GH1050/GH1050 COMBO - .177 or .22 cal., BBC, SP, 812/1000 FPS, rifled steel barrel, fiberoptic sights with fully adj. rear, or 3-9x32 scope with muzzle brake (GH1050 Combo), two-stage adj. trigger, ambidextrous black synthetic stock with recoil pad, automatic safety, 45.67 in. OAL, 6.4 lbs. New 2005.

MSR	$220	$185	$150	$115	$85	$65	N/A	N/A

Add 25% for GH1050 Combo Model.

MODEL GS700 - .177 cal., BBC, SP, 700 FPS, two-stage trigger, automatic safety, walnut stained beech stock, 6.9 lbs. Mfg. in Spain, disc. 2001.

	$100	$90	$80	$70	$55	N/A	N/A

Last MSR was $149.

MODEL GS950 - .177 or .22 cal., BBC, SP, 950/750 FPS, blue finish, adj. rear and fixed front fiberoptic sights, two-stage trigger, automatic safety, walnut stained Monte Carlo stock, 46.25 in. OAL, 7.25 lbs. Mfg. in Spain, new 2001.

MSR	$250	$210	$175	$145	$110	$90	N/A	N/A

✳ *Model GH950 Combo* - .177 or .22 cal., BBC, SP, 950/750 FPS, includes Model GS950 with ported muzzle brake, either 4x32mm or 3-9x32mm Beeman scope with adj. objective and target turrets with caps, and 250-count tin of hollow point pellets. New 2003.

MSR	$320	$265	$215	$175	$125	$95	N/A	N/A

Add 10% for GH950 Combo with 3-9x32mm Beeman scope.

MODEL GS1000 - .177 or .22 cal., BBC, SP, 1000/765 FPS, micrometer adj. rear and blade front sights, two-stage adj. trigger, automatic safety, checkered European sporter style walnut stained stock with PG and recoil pad, 46.75 OAL, 7.5 lbs. Mfg. in Spain, new 2001.

courtesy Beeman Collection

MSR	$280	$235	$190	$135	$105	$85	N/A	N/A

GRADING	100%	95%	90%	80%	60%	40%	20%

✳ *Model GH1000 Combo* - .177 or .22 cal., BBC, SP, 1000/765 FPS, includes Model GS1000 with ported muzzle brake, either 3-9x32mm or 3-12x40mm Beeman scope with adj. objective and target turrets with caps, and 250-count tin of hollow point pellets. New 2003.

MSR $420	$335	$275	$215	$175	$145	N/A	N/A

Add 5% for 3-12x40mm Beeman scope.

MODEL GT600 - .177 cal., BBC, SP, 600 FPS, sporter trigger, automatic safety, walnut stained beech stock, 5.9 lbs. Mfg. in Spain, disc. 2001.

	$80	$70	$60	$50	$40	N/A	N/A

Last MSR was $119.

MODEL GT650 - .177 cal., similar to Model GT600. Mfg. in Spain 2001-2002.

	$90	$85	$80	$70	$50	N/A	N/A

Last MSR was $135.

MODEL HW30 - .177 or .20 (disc.) cal., BBC, SP, SS, 675/600 FPS, two-stage non-adj. trigger, plain beech stock with or w/o butt-plate, automatic safety, 40.0 in. OAL, adj. rear sight (early versions all metal), 5.5 lbs. 40.0 in. OAL. Mfg. in Germany new 1972.

MSR $295	$245	$195	$155	$115	$80	N/A	N/A

Add 10% for no safety.
Add 20% for .20 caliber.
Add 10% for San Rafael or Santa Rosa address.
Add 20% for early M versions - stock with cheekpiece, deep forearm, and rubber buttplate.

MODEL HW50 - .177 cal., BBC, SP, SS, 700 FPS, non-adj. trigger, plain beech stock w/o cheekpiece or buttplate, automatic safety, heavy machined receiver cap, front sight with interchangeable posts, 43.1 in. OAL, 6.9 lbs. Mfg. in Germany 1972-95.

courtesy Beeman Collection

	$250	$200	$190	$165	$140	N/A	N/A

Subtract 25% for sheet metal receiver cap (post 1994 mfg.).
Add 10% for no safety.
Add 20% for early M versions - stock w/cheekpiece, deep forearm, and rubber buttplate.

HW55SM/HW55MM/HW55T - .177 cal., BBC, SP, 660-700 FPS, match aperture sight, with beech stock checkered pistol grip (HW55SM), walnut stock with checkered grip, forearm and cheekpiece (HW55MM), or deluxe Tyrolean walnut stock with deep dish cheekpiece (HW55T), 43.7 in OAL, 7.8 lbs.

	$495	$425	$325	$250	N/A	N/A	N/A

Add 20% for HW55MM.
Add 50% for HW55T, 25 Beeman specimens made and imported.

MODEL HW 77 - .177, .20, or .22 cal., UL, SP, SS, 830/770 FPS, blue finish, automatic safety, two-stage adj. trigger, beech high comb Monte Carlo hand cut checkered PG sporter stock, white-lined grip cap and rubber recoil pad, factory stamped with Santa Rosa address, automatic safety, 43.7 in OAL (carbine version 39.7 in. OAL), 8.7 lbs. Mfg. in Germany 1983-1998.

	$395	$375	$350	$295	$225	$150	$125

Last MSR was $600.

Add 10% for left-hand variation.
Add 15% for .20 cal.
Add 50% for Tyrolean stock (deep cup cheekpiece, RH only).
Beginning in 1995, the Model HW 77 can be upgraded to the power of the Model HW 77 Mk II.

✳ *Model HW 77 MKII Carbine* - .177 cal., SP, UL, SS, 930 FPS, similar to Model HW 77, except 11.5 in. barrel, Huntington Beach address, 39.7 in. OAL, 8.7 lbs. Mfg. in Germany new 1999.

MSR $675	$575	$450	$350	$295	$245	$180	$115

MODEL HW97 - .177 or .20 cal., UL, SP, 800/750 FPS, automatic safety, two-stage adj. trigger, beech stained Monte Carlo stock with high cheekpiece, 44.1 in. OAL, 9.2 lbs. Mfg. in Germany new 1995.

✳ *Model HW97 MKI* - .177 or .20 cal., UL, SP. Mfg. 1995-1998.

	$475	$395	$325	$250	$175	N/A	N/A

Add 5% for .20 cal.
Add 15% for .177 cal. Centennial Model with blue/gray laminate stock.

✳ *Model HW97 MKII* - .177 or .20 cal., UL, SP, similar to Model HW97 MKI except velocity increased to 930 FPS for .177 and 820 FPS for .20 cal. Mfg. 1999-2001.

	$475	$395	$325	$250	$175	N/A	N/A

Add 20% for .20 cal. Millennium Model with blue/gray laminate stock.

GRADING	100%	95%	90%	80%	60%	40%	20%

✻ *Model HW97 MKIII* - .177 or .20 cal., UL, SP, similar to Model HW97 MKII, except shortened barrel to improve appearance, balance, and lock time, 40.25 in. OAL, 9.2 lbs., Mfg. in Germany new 2002.

	100%	95%	90%	80%	60%	40%	20%
MSR $675	$575	$475	$395	$305	$225	N/A	N/A

MODEL R1/R1-AW/R1 CARBINE - .177, .20, .22, or .25 (disc.) cal., BBC, SP, SS, 19.3 in. barrel, blue or nickel plated (R1-AW) finish, 1000/610 FPS, new design using some Weihrauch Model HW 35 parts with designed changes to greatly increase power, speed, cocking ease and efficiency, beech Monte Carlo stock, hand cut checkered pistol grip with palm swell and white lined grip cap, forearm extends to front end of barrel block, white lined rubber buttplate with molded BEEMAN lettering, solid steel receiver cap, 14.3 in. LOP, 45.2 in. OAL, 8.5 lbs. Mfg. in Germany 1981 to date.

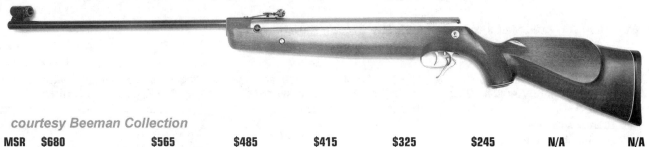

courtesy Beeman Collection

	100%	95%	90%	80%	60%	40%	20%
MSR $680	$565	$485	$415	$325	$245	N/A	N/A

Add 20% for Santa Rosa address.

Add 90% for custom grade.

Add 25% for Field Target Model.

Add 400% for Goudy/Beeman custom stock.

Add 105% for X fancy stock.

Add 10% for left-hand variation.

Add 25% for blue/silver finish.

Add 50% for Tyrolean stock (less than 25 mfg.).

Add 60% for commemorative model (50 mfg. 1992 only - 20th year commemorative medallion inlaid into stock, silver/blue metal finish, deluxe).

Add 20% for AW Model with electroless nickel finish and black Kevlar/graphite/fiberglass stock, available in .20 cal. carbine only, 9.7 lbs.

Deduct 20% for gas spring retrofit (inappropriately called gas ram or strut).

Chrome and gold-plated variations of the R1 with RDB prefix serialization may exceed retail values by 150%-300%. This is the first spring piston airgun to reach 1000 FPS MV. Designed by Robert Beeman, stock design by Robert Beeman and Gary Goudy; engineered by H.W. Weihrauch. Predecessor of Weihrauch HW 80 and considered as first successful start of adult airgun market in USA. Ref: Gaylord, 1995, *The Beeman R1*.

MODEL R1 LASER® - .177, 20, .22, or 25 cal., similar to Model R1, except Laser® spring piston unit for up to an additional 200 FPS, laminated sporter stock inlaid with baked enamel Beeman Laser® logo. Mfg. 1988-2001.

✻ *Model R1 Laser® MK I* - metal pistol grip gap replaced by rosewood in 1994. Mfg. 1988-1995.

		100%	95%	90%	80%	60%	40%	20%
		$1,200	$1,000	$900	N/A	N/A	N/A	N/A

Add 25% for Mark 1 with Santa Rosa address.

Add 10% for metal grip cap.

✻ *Model R1 Laser® MK II* - similar to Model R1 Laser® MK I, except no pistol grip cap. .25 cal. disc. Mfg. 1995-99.

		100%	95%	90%	80%	60%	40%	20%
		$1,000	$950	$850	N/A	N/A	N/A	N/A

✻ *Model R1 Laser® MK III* - similar to Model R1 Laser® MK II, except gas spring version. Mfg. 1999-2001.

		100%	95%	90%	80%	60%	40%	20%
		$900	$850	$800	N/A	N/A	N/A	N/A

MODEL R5 - .20 cal., BBC, SP, SS, similar to Feinwerkbau Model 124, except upgraded deluxe stock, receiver incorrectly factory stamped "Model 125, 5.mm/.22 cal." Four mfg. in Germany 1981.

courtesy Beeman Collection

	100%	95%	90%	80%	60%	40%	20%
	$2,500	$2,000	N/A	N/A	N/A	N/A	N/A

Ref: Beeman (1998) AR3:61-62.

GRADING	100%	95%	90%	80%	60%	40%	20%

MODEL R6 - .177 cal., BBC, SP, SS, 815 FPS, two stage trigger, automatic safety, plain beech stock, rubber buttplate, automatic safety, 41.8 in OAL, 7.1 lbs. Mfg. in Germany. 1995-2001.

	100%	95%	90%	80%	60%	40%	20%
	$225	$195	$150	$125	$95	N/A	N/A

Last MSR was $285.

Add 150% for custom grade.

MODEL R7 - .177 or .20 cal., BBC, SP, SS, 700/620 FPS, two-stage adj. trigger, beech stock with Monte Carlo comb, forearm extending to front end of barrel block, 14.3 in. LOP, scope grooves, hand checkered pistol grip, rubber buttplate with molded "BEE-MAN", all metal sights, automatic safety, 40.2 in. OAL, 6.1 lbs. Mfg. in Germany 1983 to date. Ref: AA, (March 2003).

MSR	$375	$325	$265	$210	$165	$110	N/A

Add 15% for .20 cal.

Add 20% for San Rafael or Santa Rosa address.

Add 10% for no safety (new 1986).

Add 20% for RDB versions, early production, soft rubber buttplate with Beeman name, cheekpieces with sharp edges and sweeping outline, greater detailing.

MODEL R8 - .177 cal., BBC, SP, SS, 720 FPS, two-stage adj. trigger, beech stock similar to Model R7, except sharply defined cheekpiece, 14.3 in. LOP, solid steel receiver cap, metal sights, scope grooves, automatic safety, 43.0 in. OAL, 7.1 lbs. Mfg. in Germany 1983-1997.

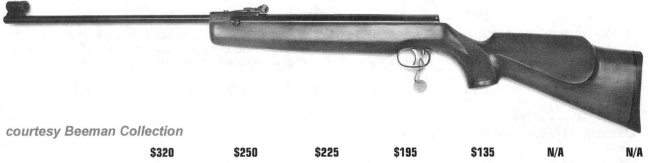

courtesy Beeman Collection

	100%	95%	90%	80%	60%	40%	20%
	$320	$250	$225	$195	$135	N/A	N/A

Last MSR was $380.

Add 20% for Santa Rosa address.

Add 20% for RDB versions, early production, soft rubber buttplate with Beeman name, cheekpieces with sharp edges and sweeping outline, greater detailing.

MODEL R9/R9 COMBO - .177 or .20 cal., BBC, SP, SS, 1000/800 FPS, adj. trigger, automatic safety, beech stock, with or without (Model R9 Goldfinger) adj. rear and globe front sights, receiver cut for scope mounts, 4x32mm or 3-9x32mm (Model R9 Combo new 2003) Beeman scope, muzzle brake (Model R9 Goldfinger Combo new 2003), 43.0 in. OAL, 7.3 lbs. Mfg. in Germany new 1995.

courtesy Beeman Collection

MSR	$425	$365	$295	$235	$185	$135	$95	N/A

Add $80 for Model R9-Deluxe with hand checkered grip, white lined grip cap and buttplate.

Add 25% for laminate stock.

Add 5% for "Goldfinger" version with gold-plated trigger.

Add $70 for Model R9 Combo with 4x32mm Beeman adj. objective scope with target turrets with caps and tin of pellets.

Add $100 for Model R9 Combo with 3-9x32mm Beeman adj. objective scope with target turrets with caps and tin of pellets.

Add $100 for Model R9 Goldfinger Combo with 4-12x40mm Beeman adj. objective scope with target turrets and caps.

MODEL R10 - .177, .20, or .22 cal., BBC, SP, SS, 1000/750 FPS, smooth walnut finished beech stock, forearm ends at barrel pivot, solid steel machined receiver cap, automatic safety, 45.8 in. OAL, 7.5 lbs. Mfg. in Germany 1986-1995.

	100%	95%	90%	80%	60%	40%	20%
	$395	$350	$300	$195	$150	N/A	N/A

Last MSR was $400.

Add 25% for Model R10 Deluxe, hand checkered grip, white lined grip cap and buttplate, forearm extends to forward end of barrel block.

Add 15% for .20 cal.

Add 100% for Laser Model (laminated stock).

Add 95% for custom grade walnut stock.

Add 100% for custom fancy walnut stock.

GRADING	100%	95%	90%	80%	60%	40%	20%

Add 110% for extra fancy walnut stock.

Subtract 5% for left-hand variation.

Add 20% for RDB versions, early production, soft rubber buttplate with Beeman name,cheekpieces with sharp edges and sweeping outline, greater detailing.

MODEL R11 - .177 cal., BBC, SP, SS, 925 FPS, 19.6 in. barrel with sleeve, adj. cheekpiece and buttplate, adj. trigger, scope ramp on receiver, no sights, 43.5 in. OAL, 8.75 lbs. Mfg. in Germany 1994-95.

	$425	$400	$350	$300	$250	N/A	N/A

* *Model R11 MK II* - .177 cal., BBC, SP, SS, 925 FPS, similar to Model R11, except has dovetailed receiver for scope mounting, improved trigger and end cap. Mfg. in Germany with importation beginning in 1995.

courtesy Beeman Collection

MSR $675	$555	$445	$375	$285	$230	N/A	N/A

MODEL RX - .177, .20, .22, or .25 cal., BBC, Theoben GS, SS, 1125/960/810/650 FPS, adj. velocity, deluxe Monte Carlo beech stock with cheekpiece, forearm extends to forward end of barrel block, hand checkering and white-lined PG cap, white-lined rubber buttplate with molded BEEMAN letters, all metal sights, scope grooves, automatic safety, 45.7 in. OAL, 8.7 lbs. Mfg. in Germany 1990-1992.

	$350	$300	$250	$200	$150	N/A	N/A

Last MSR was $470.

Add 15% for .20 and .25 cal.

Add 50% for Field Target version with adj. cheekpiece.

Add 10% for left-hand variation.

Add 25% for Power Adjustment Pump.

This models' GAS-SPRING piston system sometimes is inappropriately referred to as a "gas-ram" or "gas strut" system.

MODEL RX-1 - similar to Model RX, except adj. two-stage trigger and stamped with small "1" on rear of receiver. Mfg. in Germany 1992-2001.

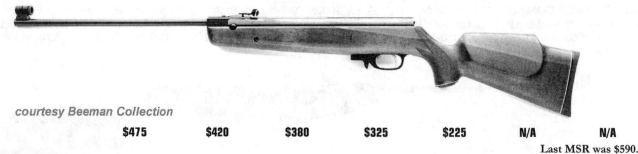

courtesy Beeman Collection

	$475	$420	$380	$325	$225	N/A	N/A

Last MSR was $590.

Add 10% for left-hand variation

Add 15% for Santa Rosa address.

Add 30% for hand checkered walnut "Luxury" stock.

Add 50% for Commemorative model with 20th Anniversary disc inlaid into stock.

Add 25% for Power Adjustment Pump.

MODEL RX-2 - .177, .20, or .22, cal., similar to Model RX-1, except laminated stock and improved non-adj. trigger,. 9.8 lbs., Mfg. in Germany new 2001.

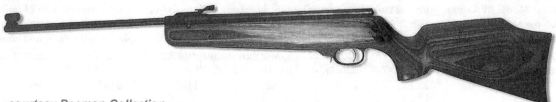

courtesy Beeman Collection

MSR $750	$645	$555	$450	$365	$275	N/A	N/A

MODEL S-1 - .177 cal., BBC, SP, SS, 900 FPS, two-stage adj. trigger, automatic safety, beech stock, 45.5 in OAL, 7.1 lbs. Mfg. in Spain 1995-1999.

	$150	$100	$75	$60	$40	N/A	N/A

Last MSR was $210.

GRADING	100%	95%	90%	80%	60%	40%	20%

MODEL SLR-98 - .22 cal., GS, UL, similar to Model UL-7, blue finish, 780 FPS, seven-shot removable mag., automatic safety, 39 in. OAL, 7.9 lbs. Mfg. in Germany 2001-04.

courtesy Beeman Collection

	$1,195	$950	$750	$600	$485	N/A	N/A

Last MSR was $1,385.

MODEL SS550 TARGET/SS550 HUNTER COMBO - .177 cal., BBC, SP, SS, Belgium Matte finish, 550 FPS, ambidextrous Monte Carlo sporter style composite stock with pad, sporter grade trigger, automatic safety, diopter rear and hooded front sights or 4x20 scope with ported muzzel brake (SS550 Hunter Combo), 36.5-38.5 in. OAL, 5 lbs. New 2005.

MSR	$70	$55	$40	$30	$20	N/A	N/A

Add 30% for SS550 Hunter Combo.

MODEL SS650/SH650 HUNTER COMBO - .177 cal., BBC, SP, 700 FPS, sporter trigger, automatic safety, walnut stained beech stock with recoil pad, fiberoptic sights or ported muzzle brake and 4x32mm Beeman scope (SH650 Hunter Combo), 39.5-41 in. OAL, 5.9-8.7 lbs. New 2005.

MSR	$100	$85	$65	$55	$45	$35	N/A	N/A

Add 20% for SH650 Hunter Combo.

MODEL SS1000/SH1000 HUNTER COMBO - .177 or .22 cal., BBC, SP, 1000/800FPS, adj. fiberoptic sights or 3-9x32 AO/TT scope (SH1000 Combo), two-stage adj. trigger, automatic safety, sporter style walnut stained stock with PG and recoil pad, 44.5 OAL, 9-10 lbs. New 2005.

MSR	$170	$145	$115	$85	$65	$45	N/A	N/A

Add 20% for SH1000 Combo Model.

AIR WOLF - .20, .22, or .25 cal., 940/822/660 FPS, PCP, SS, BA, light high comb walnut stock, hand checkered PG, white-lined rubber recoil pad, 20.8 in. barrel, blue finish, no sights, scope grooves, manual safety, 37 in. OAL, 5.6 lbs. Mfg. in England 1992 only.

	$950	$850	$750	$650	$550	N/A	N/A

Last MSR was $680.

Add 5% for .20 cal.

Add 10% for charging adapter with gauge.

Approx. 10-20 mfg.

BEARCUB - for information on this model, see Webley & Scott, LTD. in the "W" section.

CARBINE C1 - field carbine with shotgun butt and straight grip.

For information on this model, see Webley & Scott, LTD. in the "W" section.

CLASSIC MAGNUM - .20 or .25 cal., 910/680 FPS, BBC, GS, SS, 15 in. barrel, automatic lever safety, checkered walnut stock with angular forearm extending just forward of barrel base block, 44.5 in. OAL, 8.3 lbs. Mfg. in England 1992 only.

	$890	$750	$590	$475	$350	N/A	N/A

Last MSR was $895.

Add 5% for .20 cal.

Add 15% for power adjustment pump.

CROW MAGNUM I - .20 or .25 cal., 1060/815 FPS, BBC, GS, SS, 16 in. barrel, automatic safety (thin metal piece), smoothly curved trigger, built-in scope base, no sights, polished steel muzzle weight, 46 in. OAL, 8.6 lbs. Mfg. in England 1992-1993.

	$850	$750	$625	$500	$350	N/A	N/A

Add 5% for .20 cal.

Add 15% for power adjustment pump.

CROW MAGNUM II - .20 or .25 cal., 1060/815 FPS, BBC, GS, SS, 16 in. barrel, automatic safety (rugged metal strip), "beak shaped" trigger centered in guard, Dampa Mount scope rings provided for built-in scope rail, no sights, polished steel muzzle weight, 46.0 in. OAL, 8.6 lbs. Mfg. in England 1993-1995.

	$950	$750	$600	$450	$300	N/A	N/A

Last MSR was $1,220.

Add 15% for power adjustment pump.

GRADING	100%	95%	90%	80%	60%	40%	20%

CROW MAGNUM III - .20, .22, or .25 cal., BBC, GS, 1060/1035/815 FPS, 16 in. barrel, similar to Crow Magnum II, except two stage adj. trigger, redesigned piston with steel face and O-rings, extended compression cylinder, deluxe hand checkered Hyedua ambidextrous stock, 46.0 in. OAL, 8.6 lbs. Mfg. in England. 1995-2001.

	100%	95%	90%	80%	60%	40%	20%
	$1,000	$800	$650	$500	$350	N/A	N/A

Last MSR was $1,220.

Add 15% for power adjustment pump.

CROW MAGNUM IV - .20, .22, or .25 cal., BBC, GS, 1060/1035/815 FPS, 16 in. barrel, similar to Crow Magnum III, except automatic safety with protective "bump" inside forward curve of trigger guard, straighter trigger profile and moved back in guard, 46.0 in. OAL, 8.6 lbs. Mfg. in England, 2001-04.

courtesy Beeman Collection

	100%	95%	90%	80%	60%	40%	20%
	$1,150	$950	$750	$550	$400	N/A	N/A

Last MSR was $1,355.

ECLIPSE - for information on this model, see Webley & Scott, LTD. in the "W" section.

FALCON 1 - .177 cal., BBC, SP, SS, 640 FPS, 43 in. OAL, 6.7 lbs. Mfg. in Spain 1981-1984.

courtesy Beeman Collection

	100%	95%	90%	80%	60%	40%	20%
	$150	$125	$115	$95	$75	N/A	N/A

FALCON 2 - .177 cal., BBC, SP, SS, 580 FPS, 41 in. OAL, 5.9 lbs. Mfg. in Spain 1981-1984.

courtesy Beeman Collection

	100%	95%	90%	80%	60%	40%	20%
	$120	$85	$65	$55	$45	N/A	N/A

Last MSR was $110.

FWB 124 - see the Feinwerkbau entry in the "F" section of this guide for FWB Model 124 designed for the USA market, plus special Beeman versions such as Custom, and Custom Deluxe.

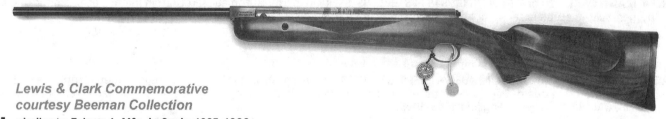

Lewis & Clark Commemorative
courtesy Beeman Collection

FX 1 - similar to Falcon 1. Mfg. in Spain 1985-1992.

	100%	95%	90%	80%	60%	40%	20%
	$155	$125	$105	$75	$45	N/A	N/A

Last MSR was $140.

FX 2 - similar to Falcon 2. Mfg. in Spain 1985-1992.

	100%	95%	90%	80%	60%	40%	20%
	$125	$100	$85	$65	$45	N/A	N/A

GRADING	100%	95%	90%	80%	60%	40%	20%

GAMEKEEPER - .25 cal., PCP, SS, quick-change air cylinder, 15 in. barrel, 680 FPS, steel receiver, composition detachable buttstock, stock, barrel, and air cylinder remove to pack gun into briefcase, steel barrel weight, no sights, scope grooves, manual lever safety, 36.3 in. OAL, 8.2 lbs. Mfg. in England 1992-93.

courtesy Beeman Collection

Last MSR was $990.

Total of five imported, values start in the $2,000 range.

KODIAK - .22 or .25 cal., BBC, SP, 17.50 in. barrel, 865/775 FPS, deluxe Monte Carlo stock with cheekpiece, grip cap and rubber buttplates with white line spacers, PTFE, muzzle threaded for Beeman Air Tamer or Webley Silencer, automatic safety, 45.6 in. OAL, 8.9 lbs. Mfg. in England, new 1993.

courtesy Beeman Collection

	100%	95%	90%	80%	60%	40%	20%
MSR $725	$600	$525	$415	$315	$220	N/A	N/A

Add 10% for Air Tamer (muzzle unit without baffles).

Add 10% for Webley Silencer.

Muzzle threaded for silencer on this model (if silencer is present). Transfer to qualified buyer requires $200 federal tax in USA.

MAKO - .177 cal., PCP, SS, BA, 930 FPS, hand cut checkered beech stock, adj. trigger, manual safety, 38.5 in. OAL, 7.3 lbs. Mfg. in England 1995-2002.

		$750	$650	$795	$400	$295	N/A	N/A

Last MSR was $1,000.

Add 50% for FT Model with checkered thumbhole stock.

MAKO MKII - .177 or .22 cal., PCP, SS, BA, 1000/860 FPS, checkered walnut stock, two stage adj. trigger, scope grooves, no sights, manual safety, 37 in. OAL, 5.5 lbs. Mfg. in England, new 2003.

MSR $999	$825	$700	$550	$450	$325	N/A	N/A

MANITOU FT - .177 cal. PCP, SS, 21 in. barrel, angular stock with adj. cheekpiece, 36.3 in. OAL, 8.75 lbs. Mfg. in England 1992 only.

	$895	$750	$565	$495	$350	N/A	N/A

Last MSR was $995.

Add 20% for left-hand variation.

Add 10% for charge adapter with gauge.

Total of ten guns were imported into the U.S.

OMEGA - for information on this model, see Webley & Scott, LTD. in the "W" section.

SILVER BEAR COMBO (SB500) - .177 cal., BBC, SP, SS, Belgium Matte finish, ported muzzle brake, 500 FPS, Monte Carlo sporter style composite stock, vented recoil pad, automatic safety, adj. 4x20 Beeman scope, 37 in. OAL, 5 lbs. Mfg. in USA, new 2002.

MSR $72	$65	$55	$45	$35	N/A	N/A	N/A

SUPER 7 - .22 or .25 (1994 only) cal., PCP, seven-shot mag., quick-change 280 cc air cylinder (bottle), 19 in. barrel, 990 FPS (.22 cal.), checkered walnut stock, manual safety, 41 in. OAL, 7.25 lbs. Mfg. in England 1992-94.

	$1,100	$950	$800	$650	$500	N/A	N/A

Last MSR was $1,575.

Add 5% for .25 cal.

GRADING	100%	95%	90%	80%	60%	40%	20%

SUPER 12 - .20, .22 or .25 cal., PCP, twelve-shot mag., 850 FPS (.25 cal.), quick-change air cylinder (bottle), checkered walnut stock, manual safety, 41.7 in. OAL, 7.8 lbs. Mfg. in England 1994-2001.

courtesy Beeman Collection

$1,400	$1,195	$975	$795	$595	N/A	N/A

Last MSR was $1,675.

Add 5% for .20 cal. or .25 cal.

SUPER 12 MKII - .20, .22 or .25 cal., similar to Super 12, except match trigger assembly and new style stock. Mfg. 2001-04.

$995	$900	$750	$600	$450	N/A	N/A

Last MSR was $2,015.

SUPER 17/17FT - .177 cal., PCP, seventeen-shot rotary mag., 1090 FPS, quick-change air cylinder (bottle), laminated target stock, adj. match trigger, adj. buttplate, optional adj. cheekpiece. Mfg. in England 1998-2002.

$1,400	$1,225	$995	$875	$595	N/A	N/A

Last MSR was $1,675.

Add 40% for Field Target model.

UL-7 - .22 cal., UL, GS, 12 in. barrel, 780 FPS, manual safety, seven-shot rotary mag., checkered walnut stock, 39 in. OAL, 8.1 lbs. Mfg. in England 1992-93.

$1,195	$995	$775	$650	$495	N/A	N/A

Last MSR was $1,560.

Add 10% for power adjustment pump.

Approx. eight were imported to the U.S. 1992-93.

VULCAN I - for information on this model, see Webley & Scott, LTD. in the "W" section.

VULCAN II - for information on this model, see Webley & Scott, LTD. in the "W" section.

VULCAN III - for information on this model, see Webley & Scott, LTD. in the "W" section.

WOLF PUP - .20, .22, or .25 cal., PCP, SS, BA, 13.5 in. barrel, 910/800/645 FPS, light high comb walnut stock, hand checkered grip, white-lined rubber recoil pad, no sights, scope grooves, manual safety, 31.5 in. OAL, 5.0 lbs. Mfg. in England, 1992 only.

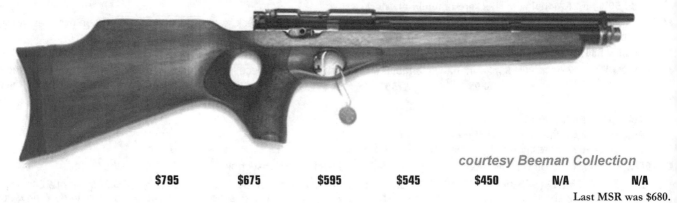

courtesy Beeman Collection

$795	$675	$595	$545	$450	N/A	N/A

Last MSR was $680.

Add 5% for .20 cal.
Add 10% for charging adapter with gauge.
Add 25% for Deluxe Model with thumbhole stock and match trigger.
Approx. 10-20 mfg.

BENELLI

Current manufacturer located in Urbino, Italy. Benelli USA, located in Accokeek, MD, was formed during late 1997 and is currently importing all Benelli shotguns. Benelli air pistols are currently imported by Larry's Guns, located in Portland, ME.

For more information and current pricing on both new and used Benelli firearms, please refer to the *Blue Book of Gun Values* by S.P. Fjestad (also available online).

GRADING	100%	95%	90%	80%	60%	40%	20%

PISTOLS

KITE - .177 cal., PCP, match pistol, 9.45 in. barrel, 475 FPS, adj. trigger, adj. sights, adj. wood grip, 16.89 in. OAL, 2.36 lbs. New 2003.

	MSR N/A	$869	$750	$595	$465	$395	N/A	N/A

Because of no current importation, contact the manufacturer directly (see Trademark Index) for price and availability.

KITE YOUNG - .177 cal., PCP, match pistol, 7.48 in. barrel, 475 FPS, adj. sights, adj. wood grip 14.82 OAL, 2.13 lbs. New 2003.

	MSR N/A	$799	$650	$550	$425	$350	N/A	N/A

BENJAMIN AIR RIFLE COMPANY

Current trademark manufactured by Crosman Corp. located in East Bloomfield, NY. Previously located in Racine, WI. Benjamin was purchased in January 1992 by Crosman Air Guns, located in East Bloomfield, NY. Dealer and consumer direct sales.

The Benjamin Air Rifle Company has its roots in the St. Louis Air Rifle Company, founded by Walter Benjamin in 1899. The St. Louis Air Rifle Company produced several unique, but unreliable, air rifles until 1901. Because of low production, and the propensity of these guns to break and become unrepairable, very few specimens of St. Louis air rifles exist today. Sales of these air rifles are too infrequent to establish price levels. Some replicas were produced in the 1990s.

The Benjamin Air Rifle Company was formed in 1902 when Walter Benjamin purchased the patent rights from the defunct St. Louis Air Rifle Company. Production from 1902 to 1904 and from 1906 to 1986 was in St. Louis, MO (extremely limited production of the Single Valve Model "B" by the W.R. Benjamin Company from 1904 to 1906 was in Granite City, IL). Regular production facilities were not established until 1908 when the Benjamin Air Rifle and Manufacturing Company became a wholly owned subsidiary of the Wissler Instrument Co. In 1977, the Benjamin Air Rifle Company purchased Sheridan Products in Racine, WI, and moved production there from 1986 to 1994. In 1991, they started to merge the Benjamin and Sheridan pistol designs, as the pistol models shifted to a Sheridan-type design and were marketed as Benjamin/Sheridan. Crosman Airguns purchased the combined companies in February 1992, and marketed the Benjamin CO_2 rifles as Benjamin/Sheridan 1993-1998, in addition to the Benjamin pump-up rifles 1994-98. During 1998-2000, the Crosman company began to again catalog and promote the .177 and .22 caliber guns under the Benjamin brand and the .20 caliber guns under the Sheridan name.

The only name to appear on some of the guns made during the interesting decade of the 1990s is in the required warning that cautions users to contact the "Benjamin Sheridan" offices in New York for an owner's manual. Many gun authorities would not consider such an address in a warning as a brand designation, any more than they would consider these guns to be Crosmans, because the Crosman Company is now using the Crosman name in the contact address.

Thus there is a period of about seven years, which to some degree continues to be unclear, where there is some confusion as to the names under which these various airguns were known. It is clear that the shooting public, and most dealers, continued their perception of these guns as Sheridans or Benjamins and never really accepted the Benjamin/Sheridan brand. As noted, Crosman recognized this brand perception and wisely began to again market the guns under the well-known separate Sheridan and Benjamin names. Now this guide is forced to consider all of the current models of these two lines under the poorly accepted name of Benjamin/Sheridan, even including such models as the Sheridan Blue and Silver Streak .20 caliber rifles, or to allow current shooters and dealers to find a particular model and learn its probable value by following each model series under their best known names. Since the concept of the Benjamin/Sheridan designation was a Benjamin idea, most models will be considered in the Benjamin section. Thus, this guide is following the designations used by the manufacturer's marketing department, the current catalogs, and virtually all shooters and dealers by considering the .177 and .22 caliber guns as Benjamins, and the .20 caliber guns as Sheridans. At this time, this really is only of academic interest because the guns produced since 1991 generally are purchased only as shooters; buyers of current models usually are not concerned with the nuances of name designations. There surely will come a time in the future, especially for the Sheridan PB and HB20 models, and the HB17 and HB22 pistols made in WI, where the manufacturing address and markings will be of importance in determining values. The marking of "Benjamin Franklin" on some older models evidently has no significance, except as a marketing ploy.

From about 1935 until recently, Benjamin used a model numbering system for both its air rifles and pistols. Model numbers ending in 0 are smooth bore for lead or steel BBs and .177 caliber pellets or darts; model numbers ending in 7 are rifled for .177 caliber pellets or darts; model numbers ending in 2 are rifled for .22 caliber pellets or darts. To keep things interesting, it is apparent that the ever-frugal A.P. Spack and his son, who ran the company during most of its early history, might not have bothered to change stamping dies when they changed model numbers in their advertisements and bulletins. So a gun advertised and sold as a Model 107 might have come out of the factory stamped as Model 177, etc. Such situations evidently were confined to guns which actually were the same, but were under different model numbers, i.e. apparently no guns were stamped with incorrect numbers. Ref: AAG - July 1991.

Values on Benjamin models are based on guns in good working order with no missing parts. Guns that have had their finish removed and the brass polished have their value reduced to one half or less of the 90% value.

PISTOLS

Although the Benjamin Air Rifle Company is best known for its pneumatic rifles, pneumatic pistols had been added to the line by 1935. There is mention of air pistols on Benjamin letterheads as early as 1908, but actual pistols probably were not introduced until about 1935 when *Popular Science Monthly* illustrated a Series 100 air pistol as a new high-power air "pistol." Evidently, Walter Benjamin did not invent the Benjamin air pistols. He certainly would have patented them, but no patents for the Benjamin air pistols have been uncovered. The air pistols may have come out of the efforts of Milhalyi and Spack to fill time during the Depression.

The Benjamin air pistols began with the simple pump rod-at-the-muzzle design. By 1938, an intriguing but mechanically weak hand lever mechanism had been added to some of the pistol models to operate the muzzle-based pump rod. Both of these rod-at-the-muzzle designs disappeared with the entry of the USA into WWII in 1941. Benjamin pneumatic air pistols reappeared in 1945 with the now familiar swinging arm pump handle mechanism. All single-shot pistols are bolt action and breech-loading.

GRADING	100%	95%	90%	80%	60%	40%	20%

MODEL 100 SERIES (MODELS 100, 122, AND 177) - BB/.175, .177 or .22 cal., pump-up pneumatic, SS, rifled or smoothbore barrel, rod-at-the-muzzle, black finish, wood grips. Mfg. 1935-41.

courtesy Beeman Collection

	100%	95%	90%	80%	60%	40%	20%
	$155	$125	$105	$90	$55	N/A	N/A

Add 30% for black nickel finish.

Add 25% for box and instruction sheet.

When the Models 110, 117, and 122 were introduced, the catalog designation of the Model 177 was changed to 107, and the catalog designation of the Model 122 was changed to 102. However, apparently no guns were ever marked as 102 or 107.

MODEL 110 SERIES (MODELS 110, 112, AND 117) - BB/.175, .177 or .22 cal., pump-up pneumatic, SS, rifled or smoothbore barrel, combination rod-at-the-muzzle/lever hand ("grass-hopper") pump, black nickel finish, wood grips. Mfg. 1938-41.

courtesy Beeman Collection

	100%	95%	90%	80%	60%	40%	20%
	$175	$150	$120	$110	$65	N/A	N/A

Subtract 25%-75% for broken or incomplete pump/rod linkages.

Add 25% for box and instruction sheet.

MODEL 122 - see Model 100.

MODEL 130 SERIES (MODELS 130, 132, AND 137) - BB/.175, .177 or .22 cal., pump-up pneumatic, SS, rifled or smoothbore barrel, with swinging lever hand pump, black nickel or matte finish, wood or plastic grips. Mfg. 1946-85.

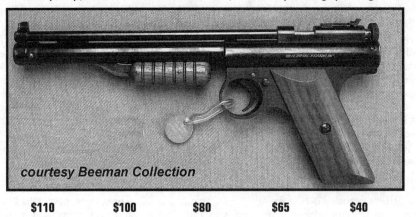

courtesy Beeman Collection

	100%	95%	90%	80%	60%	40%	20%
	$110	$100	$80	$65	$40	N/A	N/A

Last MSR was $85.

Add 10% for wood grips.

Add 30% for black nickel.

Add 15% for box and instruction sheet of plastic grip versions.

Add 35% for box and instruction sheet of wood grip versions.

GRADING	100%	95%	90%	80%	60%	40%	20%

MODEL 150 - BB/.175 cal., pump-up pneumatic, smoothbore, repeating eight-shot, combination rod-at-the-muzzle/lever hand pump, black nickel finish, wood grips. Mfg. 1938-41.

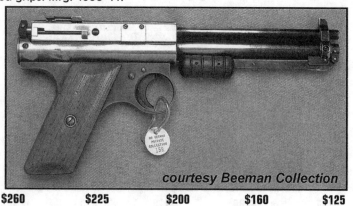

courtesy Beeman Collection

	$260	$225	$200	$160	$125	N/A	N/A

Subtract 25%-75% for broken or incomplete pump/rod linkages.

Add 25% for box and instruction sheet.

MODEL 160 - BB/.175 cal., pump-up pneumatic, smoothbore, repeating, eight-shot, swinging lever hand pump, black nickel finish, wood grips. Mfg. 1947-60.

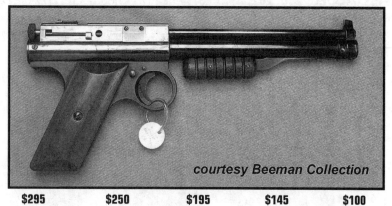

courtesy Beeman Collection

	$295	$250	$195	$145	$100	N/A	N/A

Add 25% for box and instruction sheet.

MODEL 177 - see Model 100.

MODEL 232 SERIES (MODELS 232 AND 237) - .177 or .22 cal., pump-up pneumatics, SS, BA, swinging lever hand pump, rifled barrel, black matte finish, plastic or wood grips. Mfg. 1985 only.

	$115	$105	$85	$75	$45	N/A	N/A

Add 10% for wood grips.

Add 15% for box and instruction sheet.

MODEL 242 SERIES (MODELS 242 AND 247) - .177 or .22 cal., pump-up pneumatics, SS, BA, swinging lever hand pump, rifled barrel, black matte finish, wood or plastic grips. Mfg. 1986-92.

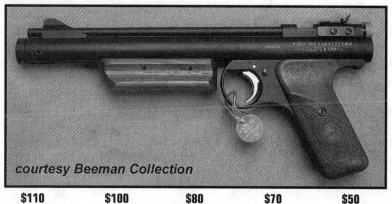

courtesy Beeman Collection

	$110	$100	$80	$70	$50	N/A	N/A

Last MSR was $95.

Add 10% for wood grips

Add 5% for box and instruction sheet.

GRADING	100%	95%	90%	80%	60%	40%	20%

MODEL 250 SERIES (MODEL 250, 252, AND 257) - BB/.175 smoothbore, .177 or .22 cal., 8-gram CO_2 cylinder, single-shot, rifled barrel, compact model, black nickel finish, wood grips. Mfg. 1952-56 (Model 250), and 1953-56 (Models 252 and 257).

courtesy Beeman Collection

	$150	$130	$110	$95	$65	N/A	N/A

Add 10% for no serial number.
Add 20% for Models 252 or 257.
Add 35% for box and instruction sheet.

MODEL 260 "ROCKET" SERIES (MODELS 260, 262, AND 267) - BB/.175 smoothbore, .177 or .22 cal., 8-gram CO_2 cylinder, single-shot, rifled barrel, blue finish, plastic grips. Mfg. 1957-64 (Model 260), 1956-64 (Model 267), and 1956-73 (Model 262).

	$125	$110	$100	$90	$45	N/A	N/A

Add 25% for box and instruction sheet.
Add 50% for Benjamin Target Practice Outfit and bell target.

MODEL 422 - .22 cal., semi-auto, ten-shot, 8-gram CO_2 cylinder, black finish, plastic grips. Mfg. 1969-73.

courtesy Beeman Collection

	$115	$100	$95	$80	$55	N/A	N/A

Add 25% for box and instruction sheet.

MODEL 1300 SERIES (MODELS 1300 AND 1320) - BB/.175 smoothbore or 22 cal., rifled barrel, pump-up pneumatic with swinging lever, fifty-shot (Model 1300) BB/.175 smoothbore, or thirty-five-shot (Model 1320, .22 cal.), black finish, plastic grips. Mfg. 1959-64.

	$220	$200	$180	$160	$120	$100	$75

Add 25% for Model 1320.
Add 30% for box and instruction sheet.

MODEL 2600 SERIES (MODELS 2600 AND 2620) - BB/.175 smoothbore, .22 cal., 8-gram CO_2 cylinder, thirty-five-shot, blue finish, plastic grips. Mfg. 1959-64.

	$250	$220	$200	$180	$140	$110	$90

Add 25% for Model 2620.
Add 25% for box and instruction sheet.

MODEL H17 SERIES (MODELS H17, HB17, HB20, AND HB22) - .177, .20 (Model HB20 disc. 1998), or .22 cal., single shot pump-up pneumatics, BA, 9.38 in. rifled brass barrel, 525/460 FPS, bright nickel (H17 Model, disc. 1999) or matte black (HB Models), walnut grips, 2.5 lbs. New 1991.

MSR	$147	$115	$95	$75	$65	$40	N/A	N/A

Add 10% for Wisconsin address.
Add 15% for bright nickel finish, Model H17.
Add 5% for box and instruction literature.

This Series replaced the Benjamin 242 Series, marketed under the Benjamin/Sheridan name from 1991 to 1998. All versions are now discontinued, except for the HB17 and HB22, which now are marketed under the Benjamin name, and the HB20, which is marketed under the Sheridan name.

GRADING	100%	95%	90%	80%	60%	40%	20%

MODEL E17 SERIES (MODELS EB17, E17, EB20, E20, EB22, AND E22)

MODEL E17 SERIES (MODELS EB17, E17, EB20, E20, EB22, AND E22) - .177, .20, or .22 cal., CO_2, BA, single-shot, 6.38 in. rifled brass barrel, 500/425 FPS, matte black (EB) or bright nickel (E) finish, walnut grips, 1.75 lbs. New 1992.

	MSR $131	$110	$90	$75	$60	$40	N/A	N/A

Add 15% for bright nickel finish.

Add 25% for nickel finish and walnut grips.

Add 5% for box and instruction literature.

Add $20-$30 for factory holster in 95%+ condition.

This Series was marketed under the Benjamin/Sheridan name from 1991 to 1998. In 1998, all versions were discontinued except for the EB17, which now is marketed under the Benjamin name, and the EB20, which now is marketed under the Sheridan name. (See Introduction to Benjamin section for information on guns produced during the 1990s).

See also: SHERIDAN

RIFLES

The designation of early Benjamin models is confusing, partly because Walter Benjamin tended to categorize his airguns by patents, rather than external features or appearance. Evidently, no guns are marked as models A, B, C, or D. The first appearance of any Benjamin letter model, in original Benjamin literature, was the model C.

Benjamin Models 300, 310, 312, 317, 360, 367, 700, 710, 720, 3030, 3100, 3120, 3600, and 3620 were recalled by Crosman in 1998.

ST. LOUIS 1899 - one of the predecessors to the Benjamin air rifles, made by the Walter Benjamin´s St. Louis Air Rifle Company. Single-shot pneumatic, bicycle-type air pump under the barrel, muzzle loading. Octagonal barrel is blackened wood over a brass tube, smoothbore brass barrel liner. Simple trigger pinches shut a rubber tube serving as air reservoir. 35.8 in. OAL, 1.5 lbs. Extreme rarity precludes accurate pricing on this model.

Rarity precludes accurate pricing.

ST. LOUIS 1899 REPLICA - for information and image of this model, see Russ Snyder in the "S" section.

ST. LOUIS 1900 - single-shot pneumatic. The big evolutionary step forward in this model is the incorporation of the hand pump into the body tube of the gun. A wooden rod, bearing a washer, has been inserted into the body tube over the barrel. Multiple in and out strokes of this rod charge the gun. This gun uses the same curved barrel found in the 1899 model and the same simple rubber air supply hose pinched shut by the trigger action. This gun is marked on the slab sided buttstock with the logo of the St. Louis Air Rifle Company. Extreme rarity precludes accurate pricing on this gun.

Made by Walter Benjamin's St. Louis Air Rifle Company, also known as Improved St. Louis or St. Louis No. 2.

ST. LOUIS 1900 REPLICA - for information and an image of this model, see Russ Snyder in the "S" section.

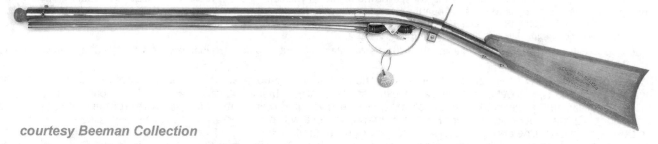

courtesy Beeman Collection

MODEL "A" (MODEL 1902) - BB/.175 cal. (smoothbore), barrel under the body tube, wooden pumping rod with operation instructions pasted onto it, receiver with a flat, vertical rear face; trigger guard cast as part of receiver, stock stamped: "Benjamin Air Rifle Company". Extremely rare.

courtesy Beeman Collection

This is the first Benjamin – referred to as "The Benjamin Air Rifle" by Walter Benjamin.

Evidently, there were at least three other very different appearing, unsuccessful variations of the Model "A" patent in the 1903-06 period. These were designated by Walter Benjamin as the Models 9 and 10, numbers which refer to design levels beginning in the St. Louis Air Rifle Company, and the "Benjamin Repeating Air Rifle." These variations use the same valve arrangement, and also have the barrel underneath the body tube, but have a gently sloping top surface behind the body tube. These variations presently are known only from Walter Benjamin´s scrapbook.

Extreme rarity precludes accurate pricing on this model.

GRADING	100%	95%	90%	80%	60%	40%	20%

MODEL "B" SINGLE VALVE MODEL - BB/.175 cal. (smoothbore), barrel above body tube, large conspicuous external figure-seven-shaped trigger lever. Extremely rare. Mfg. 1904-08.

courtesy Beeman Collection

Caution: the breech cap may fail explosively if these guns are charged.

The 1904-06 variation, identifiable by a solid cast metal breech cap was produced by the W.R. Benjamin Co. The 1908 variation, mfg. by the reorganized Benjamin Air Rifle & Manufacturing Company, has a sheet metal breech cap.

Extreme rarity precludes accurate pricing on this model.

MODEL C (1908) - BB/.175 cal. (smoothbore), same valve arrangement as the Model "B" but with a patented safety trigger to prevent dangerous bursting, gun can fire without the trigger being pulled, smaller trigger lever visible on top, but enclosed by receiver at back, breech cap stamped with "Benjamin Air Rifle & Manufacturing Co.", and 1899 to 1906 patents, not stamped with any model designation, sides of upper rear receiver unit without projections to side, barrel stops about .75 in. short of front end of body tube. Very rare.

courtesy Beeman Collection

The above early Benjamins are single-shot (except for the unknown Repeater model), rod-at-the-muzzle, smoothbore, muzzle-loading, pump-up pneumatic air rifles with walnut quarter stocks. The reader is referred to *The St. Louis and Benjamin Air Rifle Companies*, D.T. Fletcher – Publisher, 1999, ISBN-1-929813-04-X. These guns are quite rare and values are therefore difficult to establish. Prices are on a wide-ranging, individual "willing seller and willing buyer" basis.

There apparently is no "Model D" Benjamin. An unsuccessful attempt to put a conical exhaust valve in a "Model C" may have represented the "Model D."

MODELS E AND F - BB/.175 cal. (smoothbore), rod-at-the-muzzle, pump-up pneumatics, muzzle-loading, walnut quarter stock, nearly identical to the Model C, but with a flat exhaust valve rather than a ball valve, Model E is the patent pending version, round turret-like unit projects to each side of upper rear receiver unit, rear sight about even with front end of one-piece stock, front sight is a triangular blade soldered to top of barrel, Model F was produced after the patent was issued, round turret-like unit projects to each side of upper receiver unit, rear sight about 1 in. back from front end of stock, front sight is a thin metal blade straddling each side of the barrel, Model E guns are the first Benjamins marked with a model letter; they use the Model C flat breech cap overstamped around the edge: "MODEL E PAT. PENDING", Model F breech cap is stamped as such and bears 1906-17 patent dates.

courtesy Beeman Collection

$235	$195	$165	$135	$110	N/A	N/A

Add 40% for box and instruction sheet.

The Models E and F are the first really successful and reasonably safe production pneumatic air rifle models (by any manufacturer) and were extremely popular for 25 years, from 1910 to 1935.

Extreme rarity precludes accurate pricing on this model.

GRADING	100%	95%	90%	80%	60%	40%	20%

MODEL G (MODEL 200) - similar to Models E and F, BB/.175 cal. smoothbore, muzzle loading, rod-at-the-muzzle, rear sight is a peep sight hole in a metal flange at rear end of receiver, walnut half stock, black nickel finish.

courtesy Howard Collection

	100%	95%	90%	80%	60%	40%	20%
	$225	$190	$160	$125	$100	N/A	N/A

Add 40% for box and instruction sheet.

The single-shot Model 200 and the Benjamin Automatic (Model 600) repeater introduced the very different 1928 Mihalyi in-line valve design which is the basis for all later Benjamin valve systems. This is the first model to correct the accidental discharge problems of the Models C through F.

MODEL AUTOMATIC (MODEL 600) - BB/.175 cal., semi-auto, twenty-five-shot, magazine-fed smoothbore for lead air rifle shot, rod-at-the-muzzle, similar valves as the single-shot Model 200, walnut half stock with pistol grip, black nickel finish, early versions are marked "Automatic" on the side plate.

courtesy Beeman Collection

	100%	95%	90%	80%	60%	40%	20%
	$400	$350	$300	$250	$175	$150	$125

Add 15% for "Automatic" marking.
Add 35% for box and instruction sheet.

MODEL 300 SERIES (MODELS 300, 317/307, AND 322/302) - BB/.175 smoothbore, .177 or .22 cal., single-shot, bolt action, pump-up pneumatics with rod-at-the-muzzle, rifled barrel, black finish, walnut stock. Mfg. 1934-1940.

courtesy Howard Collection

	100%	95%	90%	80%	60%	40%	20%
	$225	$195	$170	$145	$100	N/A	N/A

Add 100% for "one-piece bolt" variation, marked as "Model 300" on the side of the body tube (approx. 12 mfg.).
Add 30% for black nickel.
Add 25% for box and instruction sheet.

This Series was the first Benjamin to use spring action triggers. The Model 317, with its muzzle pump rod, was later marketed, but not marked, as the Model 307, after a new Model 317, here known as the "317 PH" version, with a swinging pump handle. To be "consistent," the Model 322 was then marketed as the 302. The "Models" 302 and 307 almost surely exist only as catalog, and owner´s manual, designation variations of guns actually marked as Models 322 and 317.

MODEL 310 SERIES (MODEL 310, 312 AND 317) - BB/.175 smoothbore, .177 or .22 cal., single-shot, bolt-action, breech-loading, pump-up pneumatic with swinging pump handle, rifled barrel, black finish, walnut stock. Mfg. 1940-1969.

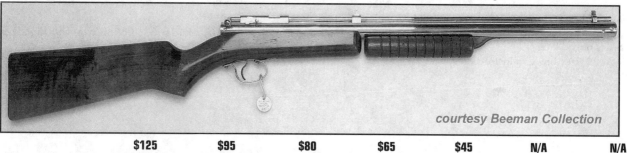

courtesy Beeman Collection

	100%	95%	90%	80%	60%	40%	20%
	$125	$95	$80	$65	$45	N/A	N/A

Add 20% for CS versions with custom deluxe walnut stock.

GRADING	100%	95%	90%	80%	60%	40%	20%

Add 20% for two-piece cocking bolt.

Add 25% for black nickel.

Add 25% for box and instruction sheet.

Note: this version of the Model 317, with its swinging pump handle, is known as the "317PH"; a different Model 317, with a pump rod at the muzzle, was marketed, but not marked, as the 307, after this new version was introduced.

MODEL 340 SERIES (MODELS 340, 342, AND 347) - BB/.175 smoothbore, .177 or .22 cal., SS, rifled barrel, similar to Model 310 series but has centrally positioned tang safety, traditional grooved "corn-cob," checkered, or smooth walnut pump handle. Mfg. 1969-86 (Model 340), and Mfg. 1969-92 (Models 342 and 347).

courtesy Beeman Collection

$145	$125	$115	$95	$70	N/A	N/A

Last MSR was $110.

Add 15% for traditional grooved, "corn-cob" pump handle.

Add 10% for Williams peep sight.

Add 10% for 4x15 scope.

Add 10% for box and instruction sheet.

Add 20% for two-piece cocking bolt.

MODEL 352 - .22 cal., single shot, 8-gram CO_2 cylinder, bolt-action carbine, rifled barrel, rotating ring safety, black finish, walnut stock.

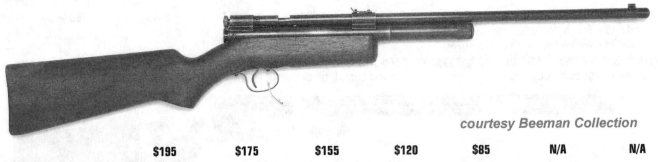

courtesy Beeman Collection

$195	$175	$155	$120	$85	N/A	N/A

Add 35% for box and instruction sheet.

MODEL 360 SERIES (MODELS 360, 362, AND 367) - BB/.175 smoothbore, .177 or .22 cal., 8-gram CO_2 cylinder, SS, BA, rifled barrel, breech-loading, black finish, 21 in. walnut half stock, manual safety latch. New 1956-57.

courtesy Beeman Collection

$195	$165	$130	$100	$75	N/A	N/A

Add 20% for CS versions with 24.5 in. deluxe walnut custom stock.

Add 20% for rounded outer edge of muzzle, with recessed end of barrel liner (typical form is flat muzzle with slightly protruding brass barrel liner).

Add 25% for box and instruction sheet.

GRADING	100%	95%	90%	80%	60%	40%	20%

MODEL 392 SERIES (MODELS 392, S392, 397, S397, AND 397C)

.177 (Model 397) or .22 cal. (Model 392), multi-pump pneumatic, bolt-action, single-shot, 19.38 in. rifled brass barrel, 700-750 FPS, black matte (Model 392 and Model 397 Disc.1994) or nickel (Model S397) finish, adj. rear sight, American hardwood stock and forearm, 5.5 lbs. New 1992.

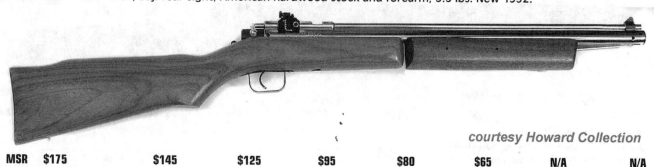

courtesy Howard Collection

MSR $175	$145	$125	$95	$80	$65	N/A	N/A

Add 10% for nickel finish.
Add 20% for Model 397C disc.
Add 10% for Williams peep sight.
Add 15% for 4x15 scope.
Add 5% for box and instruction sheet.

The S versions have a silver color finish. The Model 397C is a carbine version, 3 in. shorter and over a pound lighter. Marketed under the Benjamin/Sheridan name 1994-1998. All models are discontinued except the 392, 397, and S397, which now are marketed under the Benjamin name. (See Benjamin introduction section.)

MODEL G392 SERIES (MODELS G392, GS392, G397, AND GS397)

.177 (Model G397) or .22 (Model G392 Disc.) cal., CO_2, bolt-action, single-shot, 19.38 in. brass rifled barrel, 500-600 FPS, black (Model G392 & Model G397) or nickel (Model GS392 and Model GS397 Disc.) finish, American hardwood stock, adj. rear sight, 5 lbs.

MSR $160	$140	$115	$90	$80	$65	N/A	N/A

Add 10% for nickel finish (S versions).
Add 10% for Williams peep sight.
Add 15% for 4x15 scope.
Add 5% for box and instruction sheet.

Models G392 and G397 were marketed under the Benjamin/Sheridan name 1993-1998. The S prefix indicates silver finish. A .20 cal. version, the Model F9, was marketed under the Sheridan/Benjamin name 1993-1998. As of 1998, the Model G392 had been discontinued, and the G397 was again marketed under the Benjamin name (see Benjamin introduction and Sheridan Model F section).

MODEL 600 - see Model Automatic.

courtesy Howard Collection

MODEL 700 - BB/.175 cal. smoothbore, pump-up pneumatic with rod-at-the-muzzle pump, twenty-five-shot magazine, black nickel finish, walnut stock. Disc. 1939.

courtesy Howard Collection

$225	$200	$180	$170	$150	$125	$100

Add 10% for early versions marked 700 on left side (later versions marked 700 on end cap).
Add 35% for box and instruction sheet.

GRADING	100%	95%	90%	80%	60%	40%	20%

MODELS 710 AND 720 - BB/.175 cal. smoothbore, pump-up pneumatic with swinging pump handle, twenty-five-shot magazine, black nickel finish, walnut stock. Model 720 Mfg. 1947-1964, and Model 710 was disc. 1941.

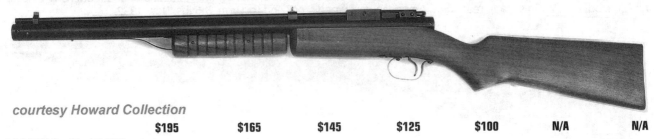

courtesy Howard Collection

	$195	$165	$145	$125	$100	N/A	N/A

Add 30% for Model 710.
Add 25% for box and instruction sheet.
The Model 710 is pre-WWII, the Model 720 is post-WWII.

MODEL 3030 - BB/.175 cal. smoothbore, 8-gram CO_2 cylinder, breech-loading, bolt action, thirty-shot, black finish, walnut half stock. Mfg. circa 1962-1976.

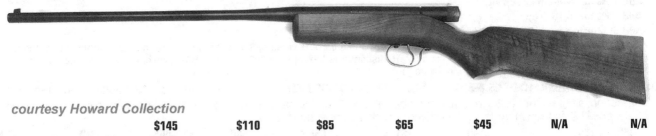

courtesy Howard Collection

	$145	$110	$85	$65	$45	N/A	N/A

Add 25% for box and instruction sheet.

MODEL 3100 SERIES (MODELS 3100 AND 3120) - BB smoothbore 100-shot (Model 3100) or .22 cal. lead ball, rifled 85-shot (Model 3120), pneumatic with swinging pump handles. The 3100 was first produced in 1958 followed by the 3120 in 1959. These dates seem to apply to all four of this type: 2600; 2620, 1300; 1320, 3100; 3120, and 3600; 3620. Benjamin offered .22 cal. lead balls, but the BB guns were much more popular, because BBs were more widely available. Mfg. 1959-1985.

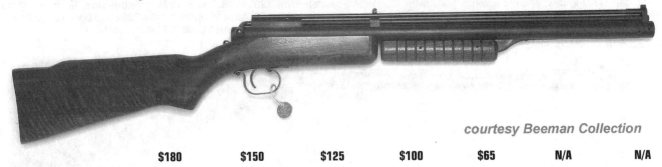

courtesy Beeman Collection

	$180	$150	$125	$100	$65	N/A	N/A

Add 20% for box and instructions.
Add 30% for .22 cal (Model 3120).

MODEL 3600 SERIES (MODELS 3600 AND 3620) - BB smoothbore 100-shot or .22 cal. lead ball, rifled 85-shot, CO_2, 8-gram cylinders. Mfg. 1959-64.

courtesy Beeman Collection

	$250	$200	$180	$170	$135	$120	$100

Add 25% for box and instructions.
Add 50% for .22 cal. (Model 3620).
Add 30% for custom grade stock (24.5 in.).

MODEL RM622 - .22 cal., BBC, SP, SS, rifled steel barrel, blue finish, 825 FPS, checkered Monte Carlo hardwood stock, swivel sling mounts, rubber butt pad, hooded front and adj. rear peep sights, 7.5 lbs. Mfg. 2002-04.

	$200	$185	$165	$145	$120	N/A	N/A

GRADING	100%	95%	90%	80%	60%	40%	20%

MODEL RM777 - .177 cal., BBC, SP, SS, rifled steel barrel, blue finish, 1100 FPS, checkered Monte Carlo hardwood stock, swivel sling mounts, rubber butt pad, hooded front and adj. rear peep sights, 8.4 lbs. Mfg. 2002-04.

	100%	95%	90%	80%	60%	40%	20%
	$200	$185	$165	$145	$120	N/A	N/A

LEGACY MODEL B1K77X/B1K77XRT - .177 cal., BBC, SP, SS, rifled steel barrel, blue finish, 1000/700 FPS, checkered Monte Carlo hardwood or Realtree Hardwoods (B1K77XRT New 2005) stock, vented rubber butt pad, fiberoptic front and adj. rear peep sights, 43 in. OAL, 6.5 lbs. New 2004.

MSR $225	$200	$185	$165	$145	$120	N/A	N/A

Add $28 for Legacy Model B1K77X with scope.

LEGACY MODEL B5M77X - .177 cal., BBC, SP, SS, rifled steel barrel, blue finish, 495 FPS, checkered Monte Carlo hardwood stock, vented rubber butt pad, fiberoptic front and adj. rear peep sights, 43 in. OAL, 6.5 lbs. New 2004.

MSR $140	$125	$100	$85	$25	N/A	N/A	N/A

LEGACY MODEL B8M22 - .22 cal., BBC, SP, SS, rifled steel barrel, blue finish, 800 FPS, checkered Monte Carlo hardwood stock, vented rubber butt pad, fiberoptic front and adj. rear peep sights, 43 in. OAL, 6.5 lbs. New 2004.

MSR $112	$95	$85	$65	$45	N/A	N/A	N/A

MODEL N8M22 (LEGACY 822) - .22 cal., BBC, SP, SS, rifled steel barrel, blue finish, 700 FPS, checkered Monte Carlo hardwood stock, vented rubber butt pad, fiberoptic front and adj. rear peep sights, 43 in. OAL, 6.5 lbs. New 2004.

	$200	$185	$165	$145	$120	N/A	N/A

Last MSR was $225.

AS392T - .22 cal., CO_2, 88g AirSource cylinder, SS, rifled steel barrel, 610 FPS, black finish, American hardwood stock, ramp front and adj. rear sights, 36.5 in. OAL, 5.25 lbs. New 2004.

MSR $195	$195	$160	$135	$115	$85	$60	$40

COMMEMORATIVE EDITION RIFLE

MODEL 87 (CENTENNIAL MODEL) - .177 or .22 cal., pump-up pneumatic, single-shot, breech loading, rifled barrel, polished brass finish, full-length walnut stock with inset bronze medallion, approx. 400 mfg. Mfg. 1987 only.

	$395	$325	$310	$250	$175	$125	$100

Last MSR was $250.

Add 20% for .177 cal.

Subtract 25% for missing factory soft side case marked "Benjamin" and manual.

Beware of "seconds" that have standard serial numbers instead of the special 00XXXX sequence. Offered during 1987 as a limited edition "Centennial" issue, the real Centennial for Benjamin was in 2002.

BENJAMIN/SHERIDAN

Previous marketing name used by the Benjamin Company and Crosman Airguns from 1991 to about 1998.

See the introduction to the "Benjamin" section.

BENYAMIN

Unknown maker, possibly of the Philippines or the U.S., mid-20th century.

Not a copy of Benjamin features. Multiple stroke pump pneumatic with swing metal pump lever. SS, faucet-style breech. Marked "Benyamin Super" with horse head figures. Full width receiver with slab sides bearing figure of rearing horse. Adult scale buttstock with Monte Carlo comb, cheekpiece, and checkering. Sling swivels on left side of gun. Extreme rarity precludes accurate pricing on this model.

courtesy Beeman Collection

BERETTA, PIETRO

Current manufacturer located in Brescia, Italy. Currently imported by Beretta USA Corp., located in Accokeek, MD. Currently distributed by Crosman Corp. located in East Bloomfield, NY since 2003. Previously distributed by Beretta USA Corp., located in Accokeek, MD 2000-2003. Dealer sales.

Beretta USA Corp. was formed in 1977, and has been the exclusive importer of Beretta firearms since 1980. Beretta introduced a complete line of air pistols in 2000, which are identical in size, appearance, and model designation to the 9mm Model 92FS. Although the Model 92FS air pistol is identical in appearance to the Beretta 9mm semi-auto, it is not a semi-auto air pistol, but rather utilizes the traditional eight-shot rotary clip loaded at the breech and functions in the same way as a single or double action revolver. The barrel is recessed within a 9mm size muzzle, making this the most authentic-looking air pistol in production today. The slide is marked "Pietro Beretta Gardone V.T." on the left

GRADING	100%	95%	90%	80%	60%	40%	20%

along with the PB logo, and marked "Carl Walther Alexandria/VA." on the right side. The guns are manufactured for Beretta by Umarex Sportwaffen GmbH, the present owner of Walther. For more information and current pricing on both new and used Beretta firearms, please refer to the *Blue Book of Gun Values* by S.P. Fjestad (also available online).

PISTOLS

MODEL 92FS - .177 cal., CO_2, SA or DA, eight-shot cylinder mag., 4.5 in. rifled steel barrel, 425 FPS, fixed front, interchangeable rear sight, ambidextrous safety, plastic grips or optional checkered wood grips, available in blue or nickel finish, standard, match, and trophy (disc. 2003) versions, includes carrying case and two rotary mags., 2.78 lbs. to 3.0 lbs. New 2000.

MSR	$260	$210	$165	$125	$105	$85	N/A	N/A

Add $20 for nickel finish.
Add $56 for wood grips.
Add $20 for Model 92FS Match with compensator.
Add $243 ($265 in nickel) for Model 92FS Trophy with compensator, scope, and mount (disc. 2003).

BIG CHIEF

Previous tradename used by unknown British maker for a folded metal BB gun believed to be pre-WWII. For information on Big Chief airguns, see Produsit in the "P" section.

BIJOU

For information on Bijou airguns, see Decker in the "D" section.

BISLEY

For information on Bisley airguns, see Lincoln Jefferies in the "L" section.

BLACK MAJOR

For information on Black Major airguns, see Milbro in the "M" section.

BOBCAT

For information on Bobcat airguns, see Milbro in the "M" section.

BONEHILL, C.G.

See Britannia listing.

BOONE

Previous trademark manufactured by Target Products Corp. located in Jackson, MI.

The Boone Air Pistol is a .173 cal., has a gravity-fed magazine, and a rearward-moving spring piston. Research is ongoing with this trademark, and more information will be included both online and in future editions. Average original condition specimens on most common Boone models are typically priced in the $40-$90 range. Add 20% for original box.

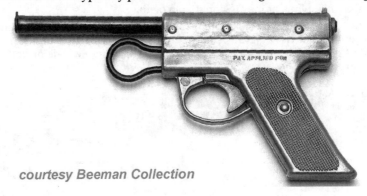

courtesy Beeman Collection

BOWKETT, JOHN

Current airgunsmith and designer, located in England.

From about the 1970s to date, John Bowkett has been one of Europe's leading airgun designers. He is famous for individual production of advanced design air pistols and rifles. Designs usually start as a pistol and evolve into a rifle if successful. He designed airguns for Titan in the 1900s.

RIFLES

BOLT ACTION 25 - .25 cal, 650 FPS, SS, PCP, bolt action, 44 in. OAL, 8 lbs. Mfg. early 1980s.
Values TBD.

GRADING	100%	95%	90%	80%	60%	40%	20%

BOLT ACTION 32 - .32 cal., 600 FPS, SS, PCP, bolt action, 42 in. OAL, 8.3 lbs. Mfg. early 1980s.

courtesy Tim Saunders

Values TBD.

BRITANNIA

Previous trademark manufactured by C.G. Bonehill located in Birmingham, England circa 1903-08.

The Britannia name has also been used for a small British push-barrel air pistol of unknown origin, probably made in the 1930s, having a value in the $75 range for gun only or, in the $150 range with original box.

RIFLES

Massive, heavily built airguns which could be considered as the ultimate development of the Gem line of airguns (See the "Gem" entry in the "G" section of this guide). Notable for a huge end plug on bottom end of the buttstock compression chamber.

BRITANNIA ANGLO-SURE SHOT MK I - .177, .22, or .25 cal., BBC, SP, SS air rifles with the SP located in the buttstock, 21 in. rifled BBL, dual power by moving the sear stop screw allows different levels of mainspring compression, first small production in Germany with variations in sights, breech latch, and power adjustments but total production probably less than 3500, 35.5 in. OAL, 6.5 lbs. Mfg. circa 1905-1908.

courtesy Beeman Collection

$1,200	$1,000	$800	$600	$550	$500	$450

Add 20% for .22 caliber.

IMPROVED BRITTANIA - .25 cal., BBC, SP, 13 in. barrel, clumsy arrangement of pulling the entire barrel/receiver unit upwards from the frame for cocking, pellet loading via inefficient curved chute with rotating cover, 44.5 in. OAL. Mfg. 1908-09.

courtesy Beeman Collection

$2,000	$1,800	$1,600	$1,500	$1,400	$1,250	$1,100

BRITISH CHIEF

For information on British Chief airguns, see "Big Chief" in this section.

courtesy Beeman Collection

BRITISH CUB

For information on British Cub, see Dolla in the "D" section.

GRADING	100%	95%	90%	80%	60%	40%	20%

BRITON

Previous trademark ascribed to the T.J. Harrington Company of Walton, Surrey, England, or Edwin Anson or Frank Clark, both of Birmingham, England.

A brand of telescoping barrel, spring-piston air pistol. Research is ongoing with this trademark, and more information will be available both online and in future editions. Average original condition specimens on most common models are typically priced in the $295 range.

courtesy Beeman Collection

BROCOCK

Current manufacturer located in Birmingham, England. Due to the legal issues in the UK with Brocock selling the Air Cartridge Rifles and Pistols, there is no current importation. Previously imported and distributed exclusively by Airguns of Arizona. Brocock was formed in 1989. Some of Brocock's airguns are manufactured (under contract to specifications) by other manufacturers including Cuno Melcher (ME Sportwaffen), Weihrauch Sport, A. Uberti & C., and Pietta. Dealer and consumer direct sales.

All current production Brocock air pistols and rifles use the dedicated BACS (Brocock Air Cartridge System). This unique system based on the .38 BAC uses a compressed air cartridge which contains a sophisticated valve system which when filled with air and loaded with a pellet, enables these airguns to feel, function, and look like real breech loading firearms.

Brocock was formed by the Silcock brothers (hence the name) to buy the liquidated Saxby and Palmer company in 1989. Brocock manufactured an air cartridge system whose roots go back to a British patent of 1872 used in a Giffard gas gun. The modern form, initially known as a 'TAC' (Tandem Air Cartridge, so called because of the twin sealing arrangement either end of the valve stem) later became 'BACS' (Brocock Air Cartridge System). An air cartridge is a manganese bronze, cartridge-like case that holds air pressure at around 2,700 psi. A spring loaded exhaust valve is opened by the gun's firing pin striking a button located where a primer would be found in a firearm cartridge. The valve opens and the escaping air propels a pellet from a screw-on nosecone.

Air cartridges can be individually charged with a 'Slim Jim' scissor pump. This rather strenuous step, requiring up to six or eight pumps per cartridge, can be avoided by using various devices to charge cartridges quickly and in bulk from SCUBA tanks.

Brocock manufactured the Safari, Predator and Fox rifles in Birmingham but also imported guns especially designed for air cartridges only from Cuno Melcher (ME Sportwaffen), Weihrauch Sport, Aldo Uberti, Pietta and Armi San Marco. The latter three converted some of their replica antique firearm designs into air cartridge airguns.

All air cartridge guns were built so as to make conversion into a firearm very difficult. On early Saxby and Palmer revolvers this included pinning the barrel to prevent its exchange and deleting a portion of the forward end of the cylinder. Pinning the barrels became standard but, during the mid 1990s, the unattractive deletion of the forward end of the cylinders was replaced with machining the spaces between the individual chambers.

Despite the safeguards against conversion, there were a very limited number of cases where criminals using sophisticated machining equipment managed to turn some of these airguns into firearms. Such conversions often were dangerous and these criminals reportedly sometimes lost body parts or their lives when converted guns exploded.

American airgunners take warning!: As of January 2004 the manufacture, importation, sale or transfer of all air cartridge guns was banned by the United Kingdom government. Existing UK owners were given three months in which to apply for a highly restricted Section 1 firearms certificate should they wish continue owning their guns, or to hand them to a police station for destruction without compensation. These guns can't be traded in the UK, or even exported, and thus have no commercial value in the UK.

Brocock is still selling their CO_2 and blank firing guns which were unaffected by the 2004 ban. Attempts are being made to have air cartridge guns manufactured outside of the UK and to import them directly into the USA, but development or continued success of such a program seems unlikely.

The authors and publisher wish to thank Mr. Tim Saunders for his assistance with this section of the *Blue Book of Airguns*.

PISTOLS

MODEL PARA PPK 380 - .22 cal., BACS, 3 in. barrel, 300 FPS, seven-shot, blue or nickel finish, black composite or walnut grips, fixed sights, 1.45 lbs., Mfg. by ME Sportwaffen.

MSR	$175		$160	$135	$105	$75	$55	N/A	N/A

Add $30 for nickel finish and walnut grips.

GRADING	100%	95%	90%	80%	60%	40%	20%

REVOLVERS

MODEL 1851 NAVY - .22 cal., BACS, SA, 5 or 7.5 in. barrel, 410 FPS, six-shot, blue with case color frame and brass grip strap frame or nickel finish, walnut grips, fixed sights, 2.4 lbs. Mfg. by Pietta.

courtesy Tim Saunders

MSR	$343	$300	$255	$200	$155	$105	N/A	N/A

Subtract $40 for all-brass frame (Model 1851 Navy Sheriff).

MODEL 1858 REMINGTON ARMY - .22 cal., BACS, SA, 5.5 or 8 in. barrel, 410 FPS, six-shot, blue with brass frame finish, walnut grips, fixed sights, 2.4 lbs. Mfg. by Pietta.

courtesy Tim Saunders

MSR	$286	$260	$215	$155	$105	$85	N/A	N/A

Add $55 for steel frame.

MODEL 1860 NM ARMY - .22 cal., BACS, SA, 6.5 or 8 in. barrel, 410 FPS, six-shot, blue with brass frame finish, walnut grips, fixed sights, 2.75 lbs. Mfg. by Pietta.

MSR	$286	$260	$215	$155	$105	$85	N/A	N/A

Add $55 for steel frame.

MODEL 1862 REB CONFEDERATE - .22 cal., BACS, SA, 5 in. barrel, 410 FPS, six-shot, blue with case color frame finish, brass and walnut grips, fixed sights, 2.4 lbs. Mfg. by Pietta.

MSR	$286	$260	$215	$155	$105	$85	N/A	N/A

MODEL 1873 CATTLEMAN SA - .22 cal., BACS, SA, 4.75, 5.5, or 7.5 in. barrel, 410 FPS, six-shot, blue with color case hardened frame or nickel finish, walnut, polymer pearlite, or polymer ivory grips, brass or steel grip frame, fixed sights, 2.6 lbs. Mfg. by Uberti.

MSR	$569	N/A	$550	$495	N/A	N/A	N/A	N/A

Add $100 for polymer pearlite or ivory grips.

Because of limited availability, call the importer for pricing and availability.

MODEL 1875 REMINGTON SA - .22 cal., BACS, SA, 5.5, or 7.5 in. barrel, 410 FPS, six-shot, blue with color case hardened frame finish, walnut grips, fixed sights, 2.6 lbs. Mfg. by Uberti.

Because of limited availability, call the importer for pricing and availability.

MODEL 1877 THUNDERER SA - .22 cal., BACS, SA, 3, 3.5, 4, or 4.75 in. barrel, 410 FPS, six-shot, blue with color case hardened frame or nickel finish, walnut grips, fixed sights, 2.6 lbs. Mfg. by Uberti.

Because of limited availability, call the importer for pricing and availability.

MODEL BISLEY SA REVOLVER - .22 cal., BACS, SA, 4.75, 5.5, or 7.5 in. barrel, 410 FPS, six-shot, blue with color case hardened frame, walnut grips, fixed sights, 2.6 lbs. Mfg. by Uberti.

Because of limited availability, call the importer for pricing and availability.

MODEL BISLEY TARGET FLATTOP - .22 cal., BACS, SA, 4.75, 5.5, or 7.5 in. barrel, 410 FPS, six-shot, blue with color case hardened frame, walnut grips, adj. rear sight, 2.6 lbs. Mfg. by Uberti.

MODEL COMBAT - .22 cal., BACS, SA/DA, 2.5 in. barrel, 380 FPS, six-shot, blue finish, molded grips, fixed sights, 2 lbs. Mfg. by Weihrauch.

MSR	$319	$290	$245	$195	$145	$95	N/A	N/A

GRADING	100%	95%	90%	80%	60%	40%	20%

MODEL COMPACT - .22 cal., BACS, SA/DA, 2.25 in. barrel, 325 FPS, five-shot, blue or nickel finish, molded or walnut grips, fixed sights, 2.24 lbs. Mfg. by ME Sportwaffen.

MSR $175	$160	$135	$105	$75	$55	N/A	N/A

Add $30 for nickel finish and walnut grips.

MODEL MAGNUM - .22 cal., BACS, SA/DA, 3 in. barrel, 350 FPS, five-shot, blue or nickel finish, molded or walnut grips, adj. rear sight, 1.38 lbs. Mfg. by ME Sportwaffen.

MSR $143	$135	$105	$75	$55	$35	N/A	N/A

Add $40 for nickel finish and walnut grips.

MODEL ORION 3 - .22 cal., BACS, SA/DA, 3 in. barrel, 410 FPS, six-shot, blue finish, molded grips, adj. rear sight, 2 lbs. Mfg. by Weihrauch.

MSR $319	$290	$245	$195	$145	$95	N/A	N/A

MODEL ORION 6 - .177 or .22 cal., BACS, SA/DA, 6 in. barrel, 550/410 FPS, six-shot, blue finish, molded grips, adj. rear sight, 2.3 lbs. Mfg. by Weihrauch.

MSR $319	$290	$245	$195	$145	$95	N/A	N/A

Add 25% for Model Orion 66, chrome plated.

MODEL POCKET - .177 or .22 cal., BACS, SA/DA, 1.5 in. barrel, 300 FPS, five-shot, blue finish, molded grips, adj. rear sight, 1.2 lbs

MSR $143	$135	$105	$75	$55	$35	N/A	N/A

MODEL SPECIALIST - .22 cal., BACS, SA/DA, 4 in. barrel, 410 FPS, six-shot, blue finish, molded grips, adj. rear sight, 2.24 lbs. Mfg. by Weihrauch.

courtesy Beeman Collection

MSR $319	$290	$245	$195	$145	$95	N/A	N/A

MODEL TEXAN - .177 or .22 cal., BACS, SA, 5.5 in. barrel, 550/410 FPS, six-shot, all blue or blue with case color frame and gold-plated trigger guard/grip straps finish, walnut grips, fixed sights, 2.86 lbs. Mfg. by Weihrauch.

MSR $328	$300	$255	$200	$155	$105	N/A	N/A

Add $25 for case color frame and gold plating.

Because of limited availability, call the importer for pricing and availability.

RIFLES

MODEL 1866 YELLOWBOY CARBINE - .22 cal., BACS, six-shot, lever action, 19 in. barrel, 598 FPS, blue finish with brass receiver, walnut stock and forearm, blue forearm barrel band, adj. rear sight, 7.4 lbs. Mfg. by Uberti.

Because of limited availability, call the importer for pricing and availability.

MODEL 1866 SPORTING RIFLE - .22 cal., BACS, twelve-shot, lever action, 24 in. barrel, 598 FPS, blue finish with brass receiver, walnut stock and forearm, brass forearm cap, adj. rear sight, 8.1 lbs. Mfg. by Uberti.

MODEL 1871 ROLLING BLOCK RIFLE - .22 cal., BACS, SS, rolling block action, 17.7 barrel, 598 FPS, blue finish, walnut stock, adj. rear sight, 5.7 lbs. Mfg. by Uberti.

MSR $895	N/A	$850	$795	N/A	N/A	N/A	N/A

MODEL 1873 CARBINE - .22 cal., BACS, six-shot, lever action, 19 in. barrel, 598 FPS, blue finish with color case hardened receiver, walnut stock and forearm, blue forearm barrel band adj. rear sight, 7.4 lbs. Mfg. by Uberti.

MSR $895	N/A	$850	$795	N/A	N/A	N/A	N/A

Because of limited availability, call the importer for pricing and availability.

MODEL 1873 PISTOL GRIP SPORTING RIFLE - .22 cal., BACS, twelve-shot, lever action, 24 in. barrel, 598 FPS, blue finish with color case hardened or nickel receiver, checkered walnut pistol grip stock and forearm, blue forearm cap, adj. rear sight, 8.1 lbs. Mfg. by Uberti.

MODEL FOX RIFLE - .22 cal., BACS, SS, 14.7 barrel, 598 FPS, blue finish, wire stock, folding trigger, 4X32 scope included, 2.65 lbs. Mfg. by Brocock.

MSR $303	$275	$225	$185	$145	$95	N/A	N/A

Because of limited availability, call the importer for pricing and availability.

MODEL REVOLVER CARBINE - .22 cal., BACS, six-shot, SA revolver action, 18 in. barrel, 520 FPS, blue finish, walnut stock, fixed sights, 4.4 lbs. Mfg. by Uberti.

GRADING	100%	95%	90%	80%	60%	40%	20%

MODEL HERALD RIFLE - .22 cal., BACS, bolt action. Mfg. by Brocock. Disc.

	N/A	$800	$600	$400	$200	N/A	N/A

MODEL PREDATOR RIFLE - .22 cal., BACS, six-shot, bolt action, 17.7 in. barrel, 598 FPS, blue finish, checkered beech stock, two-stage adj. trigger, 5.7 lbs. Mfg. by Brocock.

MSR $515	$470	$400	$325	$255	$165	N/A	N/A

MODEL SAFARI RIFLE - .22 cal., BACS, SS, bolt action, 17.7 in. barrel, 598 FPS, blue finish, checkered beech stock, two-stage adj. trigger, 6.5 lbs. Mfg. by Brocock.

MSR $431	$392	$325	$255	$165	$130	N/A	N/A

BROLIN ARMS, INC.

Previous importer located in Pomona, CA 1997-99, and previously located in La Verne, CA 1995-97. For more information and current values on used Brolin Arms, Inc. firearms, please refer to the *Blue Book of Gun Values* by S.P. Fjestad (also available online).

RIFLES

SM 1000 - .177 or .22 cal., SL, SP, SS, 1100/900 FPS. adj. front and rear sights, match barrel, automatic safety, Monte Carlo beech stock, 9.125 lbs.

	$155	$130	$115	$85	$55	N/A	N/A

Last MSR was $200.

Add 10% for checkered stock.
Add 30% for adj. buttplate.

BROWN, A.A. & SONS

See Abas Major listing in the "A" section.

BROWN

Previously manufactured by O.H. Brown located in Davenport, IA.

PISTOLS

STANDARD MODEL BROWN PISTOL - .22 cal., multi-pump pneumatic, 7.5 in. rifled barrel, 17 in. overall, unique pump system behind the barrel compressed air on both push and pull strokes providing very high power, steel parts deep blue finished, select walnut grips, adj. rear sight, exceptionally well made, rare, featured only in 1939 Stoeger catalog, original instructions are an actual engineer´s blueprint, 2.4 lb.

courtesy Beeman Collection

$2,200	$1,900	$1,800	$1,650	$1,500	$1,350	$1,200

1939 retail price was $12.

Add 25% for original box and blueprint instructions.
Approximate retail for Colt Woodsman Sport Model in 1930 was $32.50.

DELUXE MODEL BROWN PISTOL - .22 cal., similar to Standard Model, except 10 in. barrel and checkered select walnut grips, very rare, 2.5 lb.

courtesy Beeman Collection

$2,750	$2,350	$2,250	$2,050	$1,500	$1,850	$1,500

1939 retail price was $20.

Add 25% for original box and blueprint instructions.

GRADING	100%	95%	90%	80%	60%	40%	20%

BROWNING

Current manufacturer with headquarters located in Morgan, UT.

The Browning Airstar was mfg. by Rutten Airguns SA, located in Herstal-Liege, Belgium. It is the first air rifle with a battery-powered electronic cocking system. Less than 400 examples were available for the U.S. market. For more information and current pricing on both new and used Browning firearms, please refer to the *Blue Book of Gun Values* by S.P. Fjestad (also available online).

RIFLES

BROWNING AIRSTAR - .177 cal., electronic cocking mechanism powered by rechargeable Ni-Cad battery (250 shots per charge), 780 FPS, flip-up loading port, warning light indicates when spring is compressed, electronic safety with warning light, 17.5 in. fixed barrel, hooded front sight with interchangeable sight inserts, adj. rear sight, frame grooved for scope mount, beech wood stock, came in Browning box, 9.3 lbs.

	100%	95%	90%	80%	60%	40%	20%
	$595	$500	$450	$350	$250	N/A	N/A

Last MSR was $1,000.

Originally marketed in Europe through Browning dealers for $1,000. Was available in the U.S., and marked with both the Browning and Rutten names, and Browning Trademark.

BULLS EYE & SHARPSHOOTER

Previous trademark manufactured by Bull´s Eye Pistol Co. located in Rawlins, WY circa 1928-1960s.

The Bulls Eye catapult air pistol was powered by elastic bands. The Shapshooter was introduced as a smaller version of the Bulls Eye circa 1938. The production of these models was moved to La Jolla, CA circa 1948, and the company name was changed to Bull´s Eye Mfg. Co. Research is ongoing with this trademark, and more information will be included both online and in future editions. Average original condition specimens on most common Bulls Eye and Sharpshooter models are typically priced in the $60 range for unboxed models with short body, grip plates, and conventional-looking trigger guard to over $250 for early versions with a long body, sheet metal grip, and very thin trigger guard in original box. Ref: AR 1 : 52-54, AR 2 : 54-57, AR4 : 31-39.

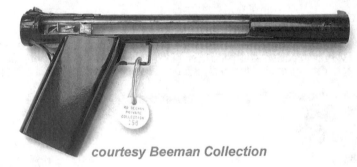 

courtesy Beeman Collection

BURGO

For information on Burgo, see Weihrauch Sport in the "W" section.

BUSSEY

Previous trademark of airguns previously manufactured by G.G. Bussey and Company located in London, England from 1870 to about 1914.

Based on a 1876 patent awarded to George Gibson Bussey for a simple airgun. The appearance is suggestive of a Quackenbush Model 1 air rifle, but there is almost no similarity in construction. Unusual spring piston action required removal of the barrel for cocking. An accessory plunger was inserted in the open action and used to push the piston backward until engaged by the sear. A pellet or dart was then placed in the breech and the barrel reinserted for firing. Extremely few specimens are known; one measured 29 in. long with a .21 caliber 9.5 in. smoothbore barrel. Research is ongoing with this trademark, and more information may be included both online and in future editions. Rarity precludes accurate pricing at this time.

BULLS EYE

Previous trademark of Bulls Eye Air Rifle Company, former producer of sheet metal BB guns in Chicago from 1907 to an unknown date.

Produced a lever, gravity feed BB repeater and a single shot break-open BB gun. Both were well built; the lever cocking action used a lever system similar to that of a Colt Model 1860 revolver. The stocks are unusual in being fitted over the grip frames rather than into them. Ref. Dunathan (1957). Research is ongoing with this trademark, and more information will be included both in future editions and online.

C SECTION

C Z (CESKA ZBROJOVKA)

Current manufacturer located in Uhersky Brod, Czech Republic, since 1936. No current importation, previously imported by CZ-USA located in Kansas City, KS.

Research is ongoing with this trademark, and more information will be included both online and in future editions. For more information and current pricing on both new and used CZ firearms, please refer to the *Blue Book of Gun Values* by S.P. Fjestad (also available online).

GRADING	100%	95%	90%	80%	60%	40%	20%

PISTOLS

TEX MODEL 3 (CZ-3) - .177 cal., BBC, SP, 400 FPS, 7.50 in. barrel, adj. sights, plastic stock.

MSR	N/A	$80	$70	$60	$50	$40	N/A	N/A

SLAVIA APP661 - .177 cal., CO_2, Luger-style, semi-auto repeater, vertical removable mag., 7.8 in OAL, 1.4 lbs.

courtesy Beeman Collection

	$125	$100	$75	$60	$45	N/A	N/A

SLAVIA ZVP (Vzduchová Pistole) - .177 in. cal., BBC, SP, SS, very solidly built, blued steel, hand checkered hardwood grips, 13.4 in. OAL, 2.4 lbs. Mfg. 1960-72.

courtesy Beeman Collection

	$95	$80	$65	$50	$35	N/A	N/A

RIFLES

CZ MODEL Vz-35 - 4.35 mm lead ball, SP, rear bolt cocks action, gravity-fed magazine with trap lid, almost exact copy of Czech military rifle, with actual bayonet, 54.1 in. OAL (with bayonet), 9.7 lbs (with bayonet). Dates TBD.

courtesy Beeman Collection

	N/A	$750	$650	$550	$495	$395	$295

Add 10% for bayonet.

CZ MODEL Vz-36 - 4.4 mm, SP, TL, cocks by swinging lever attached to right side of action up and back, military style stock w/ hand-guards, gravity fed repeater.

Military trainer, reportedly 4 known. Values TBD.

GRADING	100%	95%	90%	80%	60%	40%	20%

MILITARY AIRGUN Vz-47 (CZ-BB) - BB/.175, .177 cal., BA, military training gun, mfg. for Czech Army, U.S. supply sold out in 2000, still available in Czechoslovakia. Mfg. began circa 1947.

	N/A	$350	$295	$200	$150	$100	N/A

CZ 200 - .177 or .22 cal., PCP, BA, SS, 18.92 in. rifled barrel, black finish, beech stock and forearm, adj. trigger, mounting blocks for sight system of choice. New 2001.

> While advertised starting in 2001, this model has yet to be manufactured.

CZ 200 S - .177 or .22 cal., similar to CZ 200, except sport stock with recoil pad. New 2001.

> While advertised starting in 2001, this model has yet to be manufactured.

CZ 200 T - .177 cal., similar to CZ 200, except competition stock with adj. cheek piece and buttplate. New 2001.

SLAVIA 236 - .177 in. cal., BBC, SP, SS, hardwood stock with fluted forearm.

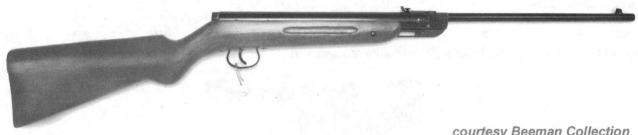

courtesy Beeman Collection

	$80	$65	$50	$35	$25	N/A	N/A

SLAVIA 612 - .177 in. cal., BBC, SP, SS, all metal except for buttstock, similar to Dianawerk Model 15, 32 in. OAL, Mfg. 1955-1965.

courtesy Beeman Collection

	$65	$40	$30	$25	$20	N/A	N/A

SLAVIA 625 - .177 cal., BBC, SP, 450 FPS, 15.75 in. barrel, adj. sights, wood stock, 4 lbs. Disc. 2003.

	$50	$40	$30	$20	$10	N/A	N/A

Last MSR was $60.

SLAVIA 630 (CZ 77) - .177 cal., BBC, SP, 700 FPS, 21 in. barrel, adj. sights, wood stock, 6.6 lbs.

courtesy C Z

MSR	N/A	$75	$70	$60	$50	$40	N/A	N/A

SLAVIA 631 (CZ 77 LUX) - .177 cal., BBC, SP, 700 FPS, 21 in. barrel, adj. sights, checkered wood or synthetic stock, 6.6 lbs.

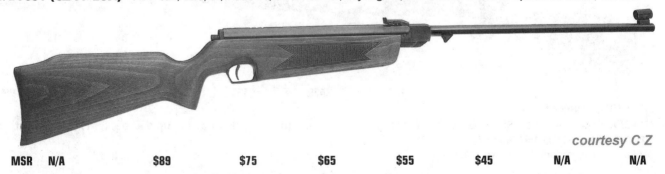

courtesy C Z

MSR	N/A	$89	$75	$65	$55	$45	N/A	N/A

GRADING	100%	95%	90%	80%	60%	40%	20%

CAP-CHUR EQUIPMENT

For information on CAP-CHUR Equipment tranquilizer guns, see Palmer Chemical & Equipment Co. in the "P" section.

CARBO-JET

For information on Carbo-Jet airguns, see Schimel in the "S" section.

CAROLUS

Previous trademark manufactured by Hellstedt, located in Eskilstuna, Sweden.

PISTOL

CAROLUS - .177 cal. UL, SP, SS, one-piece wood stock, marked LHS with script CAROLUS, blue finish, stamped with a shield design with a contained S. Mfg. 1941-1943.

courtesy Beeman Collection

$395	$325	$275	$225	$175	N/A	N/A

Add 20% for factory box.

Box is blue with white label and red and black printing, marked Hellsteds Eskilstuna Svensk kvalitéprodukt Refflad pipa, kaliber 4,5 Skottställd på 6 meter Utmärkt övningsvapen LUFTPISTOLEN Carolus ESKILSTUNAFABRIKAT PRIS KR. 19.

CASELMAN

Previous trademark manufactured by Jeff Caselman, located in Cameron, MO circa 1990 to 1994.

Only one or two .32 cal. and one .45 cal. were made. Five or six specimens of the 9mm variety are known. The Caselman airguns are fully automatic and are fed from a 3000 PSI bottle which serves as the buttstock. It is perhaps the first successful self-contained, fully automatic airgun. The 9mm guns have a .356 in. bore, firing from a twenty-six-round vertical spring-fed magazine. Bullets are 122 grain flat point, soft lead, fired dry at about 750 FPS, MV, about 150 ft./lb. ME. Rate of fire about 600 RPM. The .45 cal. gun fires twenty rounds of 225 grain flat soft lead bullets at a somewhat higher rate of fire. Ad claims: "Will saw off a 2x4 at 25 yards!" The maker also sold plans and a video for a .30 in. cal. version. Caution: some units may have been built from plans by workers less skilled than this designer/maker. The authors and publisher wish to thank John Caruth for his valuable assistance with the following information in this edition of the *Blue Book of Airguns*.

RIFLES: FULL AUTOMATIC

CASELMAN RIFLE - .32, 9mm, or .45 cal., extremely fine construction, 26 in. bench rest grade barrels and firing from a closed bolt allow great accuracy, 48 in. OAL, 16.5 lbs. Values established only for 9mm guns. Mfg. circa 1990-94.

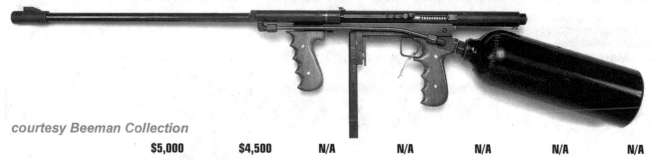

courtesy Beeman Collection

$5,000	$4,500	N/A	N/A	N/A	N/A	N/A

CENTERPOINT

For information on Centerpoint airguns, see Philippines Airguns in the "P" section.

CERTUS

Previous trademark manufactured by Cogswell & Harrison (Gunmakers) Ltd., located in London, England. Manufactured in Feltham, Middlesex, England.

Cogswell & Harrison is still one of England's most prestigious old gunmaking firms. Founded in 1770 by Benjamin Cogswell, the firm was very highly regarded for dueling pistols and military sidearms for officers. For the last century or so, they have been best known for extremely fine double barrel shotguns and double barrel rifles. Prices begin at about $20,000 and involve about a two-year wait for delivery. Edgar Harrison was granted British patent 330105 for an airgun in June 1930. Pistols relating to this patent were produced only in late 1929 and into 1930.

The Certus is a solid, barrel cocking, spring-piston air pistol with just a superficial resemblance to a Webley air pistol with its barrel running the length of the gun above the compression tube. The Certus has a quite complex mechanism with the barrel pivoting at the rear for cocking, opposite to the Webley front pivot. A 1929 factory catalog indicated that it was offered both as an air pistol and with a long barrel and removable stock as a very compact air rifle. The barrel was rifled and only available in .177 cal. It was all beautifully blued steel except for select walnut grips. Only three specimens were reported as known in an August 2002 *Airgun World* article by Tim Saunders, but a very few more do exist. Current retail value will run in the $2,500-$3,500 range depending on condition and whether original box or case is included.

courtesy Beeman Collection

CHALLENGER ARMS CORPORATION

Previous distributor of airguns under the Challenger, and later the Plainsman, brands located in Eagle Rock (annexed to City of Los Angeles), CA.

These guns probably were made by Goodenow Manufacturing Company of Eric, PA about 1953-58. They included a pump pneumatic shotgun, a pump pneumatic and CO_2 rifle, a very solidly built pump pneumatic pistol and, finally, an equally well built CO_2 pistol. Construction and design was too good to be competitive at the time. Self-contained valve units, seals, and pump washers were designed for owner replacement.

There is considerable confusion about the Plainsman name. It was first applied to the solidly built guns distributed by Challenger Arms Corporation and later used by Healthways for these same guns and then by Healthways for an entirely different, more economical series of CO_2 rifles and pistols. (Healthways probably did not actually manufacture any of the Plainsman airguns listed below, but rather only sold acquired inventory and packaged, perhaps made, shot shells with the Plainsman name combined with the Healthways brand.) Even later, the brand of Plainsmaster was used by Marksman for their Model 1049 CO_2 pistol. Marksman also used the name "Plainsman" for a slide action BB rifle.

Dunathan's American BB Gun (1971) first reported two airgun models with the Challenger name. However, the gun he listed as an 1886 Challenger actually represents only a single patent model made by Markham and is marked "Challenge". The second gun, listed as an 1887 Challenger, actually was made in small numbers, but its maker is not known (probably not Markham) and there seems to be no justification for referring to it under the Challenger name. The first verified use of the Challenger name for airguns seems to have been by the Challenger Arms Corporation. The Challenger name was again used in 1982-89 by Crosman for their versions of barrel cocking, spring-piston adult air rifles made by Dianawerk and Anschütz and, in 2000, on their own Model 2000 Challenger CO_2 bolt action rifle. Ref: AGNR - Jan. 1986.

For additional information on Plainsman Model airguns, see Healthways, Inc. in the "H" section.

PISTOLS

PLAINSMAN PNEUMATIC PISTOL - .177 or .22 cal., swinging arm pump pneumatic, SS, blue finish.

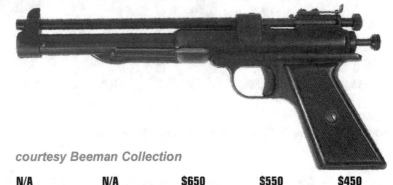

courtesy Beeman Collection

	N/A	N/A	$650	$550	$450	$350	$295

Add 10% for Challenger name instead of Plainsman.
Add 20% for .177 cal.

GRADING	100%	95%	90%	80%	60%	40%	20%

PLAINSMAN GAS PISTOL - .177 or .22 caliber, CO$_2$, SS, blue finish.

courtesy Beeman Collection

	N/A	N/A	$750	$650	$550	$350	$250

Add 10% for Challenger name instead of Plainsman.
Add 20% for .177 cal.

RIFLES

PLAINSMAN PNEUMATIC RIFLE - .177 or .22 cal., swinging forearm multiple pump pneumatic, bolt or knurled knob action, SS, hardwood pump handle/forearm and buttstock.

courtesy Beeman Collection

✳ **Bolt Handle Variant** - .177 or .22 cal., cocking rod with bolt handle.

	$600	$525	$375	$325	$275	$225	$175

Add 10% for .177 cal.

✳ **Knurled Knob Variant** - .177 or .22 cal., cocking rod with knurled knob handle.

	$625	$550	$400	$350	$300	$250	$200

Add 10% for .177 cal.

PLAINSMAN GAS RIFLE - .22 cal., CO$_2$, SS, similar to Plainsman Pneumatic Rifle except, one piece hardwood stock.

✳ **Bolt Handle Variant** - .22 cal., CO$_2$, SS, cocking rod with bolt handle.

courtesy Beeman Collection

	$750	700	$650	$600	$550	$450	$400

Add 10% for bulk fill version.

✳ **Knurled Knob Variant** - .22 cal., CO$_2$, SS, cocking rod with knurled knob handle.

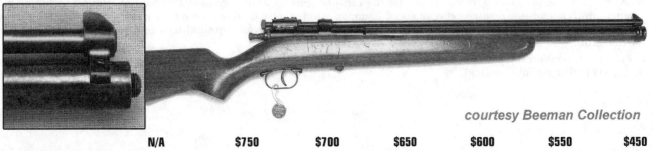

courtesy Beeman Collection

	N/A	$750	$700	$650	$600	$550	$450

Add 10% for bulk fill version.

GRADING	100%	95%	90%	80%	60%	40%	20%

SHOTGUNS

PLAINSMAN AIR SHOTGUN - .28 cal., swinging arm pump pneumatic, similar to Plainsman Pneumatic Rifle, except .28 cal. and marked "S" on RHS, forward side of receiver, uses special pre-packed cardboard shot tubes, hardwood pump handle/forearm and buttstock, five to ten pumps produced enough power to drive a small pattern of shot into a pine board at ten meters.

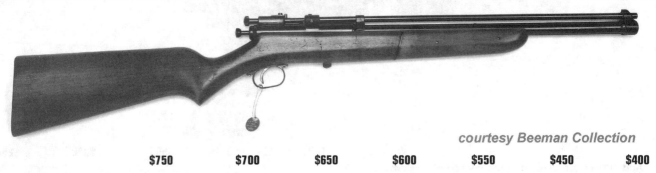

courtesy Beeman Collection

$750	$700	$650	$600	$550	$450	$400

CHINESE STATE FACTORIES

In 1987, John Walter wrote in the Fourth Edition of *The Airgun Book*: "The Chinese products are usually crudely if reasonably sturdily made, and offer lower power and inferior accuracy than most of their Western European rivals." Some of these products are unauthorized copies of European designs such as the Chinese GLOBE, an imitation Feinwerkbau Model 65 air pistol, illustrated here. The value of this gun would be under $150 in 100% condition, but many of the new specimens are so roughly finished as to appear somewhat worn. While many of the airgun products from the Chinese State Factories have improved since then, the collector and shooter should carefully balance quality, backing, durability, ownership pride, and price.

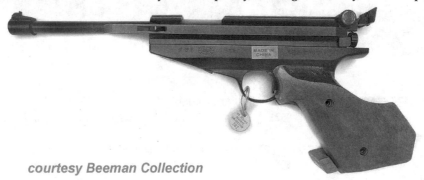

courtesy Beeman Collection

CLASSIC

For information on Classic airguns, see Gun Toys SRL in the "G" section.

COGSWELL & HARRISON

For information on Cogswell & Harrison airguns, see Certus in this section.

For more information and current pricing on both new and used Cogswell & Harrison firearms, please refer to the *Blue Book of Gun Values* by S.P. Fjestad (also available online).

COLT´S MANUFACTURING COMPANY, INC.

Current manufacturer located in Hartford, CT. Colt airguns are currently imported and serviced exclusively by Crosman Corp. located in East Bloomfield, NY since 2003. Previously imported and serviced exclusively by Daisy Manufacturing Company located in Rogers, AR.

Colt airguns are manufactured by Umarex, the current owner of Walther. Colt airguns are faithful copies of the famous Model 1911 A1. With the size and weight of a real Colt, five versions are available, including a special 160th Anniversary model. Many of the same precision options offered for the cartridge pistols have been available for the airguns, including a barrel compensator, competition (tuning set with speed hammer, rapid release double thumb safety, beavertail grip safety, grip with thumb guard, backstrap, sights) features, and Colt Top Point (Red Dot) heads-up sighting scope. All models are pre-drilled for the Serendipity SL optical sight.

For more information and current pricing on both new and used Colt firearms, please refer to the *Blue Book of Gun Values* by S.P. Fjestad (also available online).

GRADING	100%	95%	90%	80%	60%	40%	20%

PISTOLS

GOVERNMENT MODEL 1911 A1 - .177 cal., CO_2, semi-auto, SA and DA, eight-shot cylinder magazine, 395 FPS, post front/adj. rear sight, trigger safety, grip safety, 5 in. rifled steel barrel, polished blue or nickel finish, checkered black plastic or smooth wood grips, 2.38 lbs.

MSR $220	$195	$165	$135	$100	$80	N/A	N/A

Add $26 for nickel finish.

Add $30-$50 for compensator.

Add $40-$60 for wood grips.

160TH ANNIVERSARY MODEL 1911 A1 - .177 cal., CO_2, semi-auto, SA and DA, eight-shot cylinder magazine, 393 FPS, post front/adj. rear sight, trigger safety, grip safety, 5 in. rifled barrel, polished black finish with checkered white grips, slide marked with Colt 160th Anniversary banner, Colt logo, and floral scrollwork, 2.38 lbs. Disc. 2003.

	$195	$150	$115	$90	$65	N/A	N/A

Last MSR was $249.

MODEL 1911 A1 GOLD CUP - .177 cal., CO_2, semi-auto, SA and DA, eight-shot cylinder magazine, 393 FPS, post front/adj. rear sight, trigger safety, grip safety, 5 in. rifled barrel, standard black finish with checkered black plastic grips, 2.38 lbs. Disc. 2003.

	$225	$165	$125	$100	$75	N/A	N/A

Last MSR was $279.

Add $20 for nickel plated finish.

MODEL 1911 A1 TROPHY MATCH - .177 cal., CO_2, semi-auto, SA and DA, eight-shot cylinder magazine, 393 FPS, post front/adj. rear sight, trigger safety, grip safety, includes bridge mount, Top Point (red dot) sight, all competition accessories, carrying case and two rotary magazines. Disc. 2003.

	$555	$475	$395	$295	$195	N/A	N/A

Last MSR was $699.

Add $100 for nickel plated finish.

COLUMBIA

Probably made by the Adams & Westlake Company, Chicago, IL about 1905 to 1915.

One model, a simple push-barrel, single shot, sheet metal BB gun. Marked "COLUMBIA" with Adams & Westlake name and address in a circular logo.

Research is ongoing with this trademark, and more information will be included both online and in future editions.

RIFLES

COLUMBIA - .180 cal. BB, SS, SP. Only one model known, an unusual push-barrel cocking system, sheet metal BB gun. To cock, entire upper body of gun is moved back to cocked position. Unusual tap-loading mechanism looks like an oil lamp part (Adams and Westlake were a large oil lamp manufacturer). Marked "COLUMBIA" in one-inch letters on the side of the buttstock. Stock also with circular logo: "MADE BY ADAMS & WESTLAKE CO. CHICAGO. PAT. APPLD." Nickel-plated metal; slab sided stock. 2.5 lbs., 8.5 in. smoothbore barrel, 33.3 in. OAL. Value in good condition at least $2500.

courtesy Beeman Collection

Extremely rare, perhaps less than two or three specimens known (much more rare than 1st or 2nd model Daisy!).

COLUMBIAN

Previous manufacturer located in Philadelphia, PA. Often formerly known as Heilprin.

Included here are the BB guns designed by Elmer Bailey, more properly known as Bailey airguns, and Columbian airguns, designed by William Heilprin. They are "large, impressive, and expensive BB guns," made from 1893 to about 1920. The original models, designed by Bailey, had the frame, receiver, and cocking lever made of cast iron and were heavy, extremely sturdy airguns, though difficult to repair. The figures of various animals were part of ornate cast iron surface designs. Columbian air rifles were less heavy; the final model, the Model M, was entirely sheet metal – but still very impressively built. They were unusual in providing an automatic safety, a feature of dubious safety value, which proved very unpopular in BB guns produced by other makers throughout the 20th century.

The current prices of the Buffalo and the Fox repeater versions have been about $900 to $1100.

COMATIC

For information on Comatic airguns, see Venturini in the "V" section.

GRADING	100%	95%	90%	80%	60%	40%	20%

COMENTO

For information on Comento, see Bascaran in the "B" section.

COMET

For information on Comet airguns, see Milbro in the "M" section.

COMPASSECO, INC.

Current importer located in Bardstown, KY.

Compasseco has been importing airguns from China since the mid-1980s, and most were priced well under $100. During the past several years, the Compasseco line has been considerably improved and expanded.

PISTOLS

TECH FORCE SS2 - .177 cal., SL, SP, 520 FPS, recoilless action, includes carrying case, match adj. trigger, 2.75 lbs.

	MSR $295	$236	$195	$155	$115	$75	N/A	N/A

TECH FORCE S2-1 - .177 cal., BBC, SP, 2.6 lbs.

	MSR $30	$25	$20	$20	$15	$10	N/A	N/A

TECH FORCE 8 - .177 cal., BBC, SP, 400 FPS, adj. rear sight, ambidextrous polymer grip, 7.25 in. barrel, 2.6 lbs. Disc. 2004.

		$45	$35	$30	$20	$15	N/A	N/A

Last MSR was $60.

TECH FORCE 35 - .177 cal., UL, SP, 400 FPS., adj. rear sight, 2.8 lbs.

	MSR $50	$35	$25	$20	$15	$10	N/A	N/A

RIFLES

BS-4 OLYMPIC - .177 cal., 640 FPS, SL, SP, recoilless, adj. trigger, micro adj. diopter sight, stippled stock, adj. buttplate, case, 43.3 in. OAL, 10.8 lbs.

	MSR $495	$435	$355	$265	$175	$85	N/A	N/A

TECH FORCE 6 - .177 cal., SL, SP, 800/750 FPS, all metal, tactical configuration, folding stock, adj. rear sight, 35.5 in. OAL, 6 lbs.

	MSR $70	$55	$45	$35	$25	$15	N/A	N/A

TECH FORCE 11 - .177 cal., BBC, SP, 600 FPS, trigger safety, Monte Carlo stock, 38.5 in. OAL, 5.5 lbs.

	MSR $35	$30	$20	$15	$10	$5	N/A	N/A

TECH FORCE 12 - .177 cal., BBC, SP, 750 FPS, trigger safety, Monte Carlo stock, 40 in. OAL, 5.7 lbs. New 2003.

	MSR $70	$55	$45	$40	$35	$30	N/A	N/A

TECH FORCE 20 - .177 or .22 cal., BBC, SP, 1000/750 FPS, dovetail receiver, adj. sights, adj. trigger, trigger safety, Monte Carlo stock, recoil pad, 43 in. OAL, 7.3 lbs. Mfg. 2003-05.

		$120	$90	$70	$55	$35	N/A	N/A

Last MSR was $150.

TECH FORCE 21 - .177 or .22 cal., SL, SP, 1000/750 FPS, dovetail receiver, adj. sights, adj. trigger, trigger safety, Monte Carlo stock, recoil pad, 46 in. OAL, 9.3 lbs. New 2003.

	MSR $140	$120	$100	$75	$60	$50	N/A	N/A

TECH FORCE 22 - .177 or .22 cal., BBC, SP, 700/600 FPS, adj. sights, trigger safety, Monte Carlo stock, 43 inb. OAL, 6.4 lbs.

	MSR $36	$30	$25	$20	$15	$10	N/A	N/A

TECH FORCE 22A - similar to Tech Force 22, except has ramp front sight. Disc. 2004.

		$40	$30	$25	$20	$15	N/A	N/A

Last MSR was $46.

TECH FORCE 25 - .177 or .22 cal., BBC, SP, 1000/800 FPS, adj. trigger with safety, Monte Carlo stock, adj. buttplate, 46.2 in. OAL, 7.5 lbs.

	MSR $125	$100	$80	$60	$40	$30	N/A	N/A

TECH FORCE 31 - .177 cal., SL, SP, 750/550 FPS, adj. rear sight, folding stock, 36 in. OAL, 7 lbs.

	MSR $75	$65	$55	$45	$35	$25	N/A	N/A

TECH FORCE 34 - .177 or .22 cal., UL, SP, 850/650 FPS, trigger safety, Monte Carlo hardwood stock, 41 in. OAL, 7.7 lbs. New 2004.

	MSR $53	$45	$35	$30	$25	$20	N/A	N/A

TECH FORCE 36 - .177 cal., UL, SP, 900 FPS, trigger safety, Monte Carlo stock, 7.4 lbs. Disc. 2004.

		$85	$75	$60	$45	$30	N/A	N/A

Last MSR was $95.

TECH FORCE 38 - .177 or .22 cal., UL, SP, 850/650 FPS, trigger safety, hardwood stock, 7 lbs.

	MSR $53	$45	$40	$35	$30	$20	N/A	N/A

GRADING	100%	95%	90%	80%	60%	40%	20%

TECH FORCE 38D - .177 cal., similar to Tech Force 38, except includes 4x20 scope. Disc. 2004.

	100%	95%	90%	80%	60%	40%	20%
	$65	$50	$40	$30	$20	N/A	N/A

Last MSR was $74.

TECH FORCE 38GD - .177 or .22 cal., similar to Tech Force 38, except has Monte Carlo stock and lengthened under-lever. Disc. 2002.

	100%	95%	90%	80%	60%	40%	20%
	$45	$35	$30	$20	$15	N/A	N/A

Last MSR was $60.

TECH FORCE 40 - .177 or .22 cal. SL, SP, Monte Carlo hardwood stock with recoil pad, adj. trigger with safety, 41 in. OAL, 9.2 LBS. New 2005.

	100%	95%	90%	80%	60%	40%	20%
MSR $260	$225	$195	$150	$125	N/A	N/A	N/A

TECH FORCE 40D - .177 or .22 cal., BBC, SP, 700/600 FPS, hardwood stock, trigger safety, 43.5 in. OAL, 6.5 lbs.

	100%	95%	90%	80%	60%	40%	20%
MSR $40	$32	$25	$20	$15	$10	N/A	N/A

TECH FORCE 41 - .177 cal., SL, SP, 800 FPS, hardwood Monte Carlo stock, trigger safety, 40.5 in. OAL, 7.2 lbs. Disc. 2004.

	100%	95%	90%	80%	60%	40%	20%
	$40	$35	$30	$20	$10	N/A	N/A

Last MSR was $50.

TECH FORCE 50/51 - .177 or .22 cal., PCP, semi-pistol grig or thumbhole (Tech Force 51) Monte Carlo wood stock with recoil pad, muzzle brake, manual safety. New 2005.

	100%	95%	90%	80%	60%	40%	20%
MSR $340	$300	$265	$235	$195	N/A	N/A	N/A

Add $25 for .22 cal.
Add $20 for thumbhole stock.

TECH FORCE 51 - .177 cal., BBC, SP, 500 FPS, hardwood/folding stock with pistol grip, automatic safety, adj. sights, 14 in. barrel, 6 lbs. Disc. 2001.

	100%	95%	90%	80%	60%	40%	20%
	$60	$50	$40	$30	$20	N/A	N/A

Last MSR was $70.

TECH FORCE 66 - .177 cal., SL, SP, ten-shot mag., 750 FPS, 18 in. barrel, tactical configuration, includes briefcase and 4x32 scope. Disc. 2002, reintroduced 2005.

	100%	95%	90%	80%	60%	40%	20%
MRS $100	$80	$60	$50	$50	$40	N/A	N/A

TECH FORCE 67 - .177 cal., similar to TF 66, except SS, includes briefcase and 4x32 scope. Mfg. 2001-04.

	100%	95%	90%	80%	60%	40%	20%
	$65	$50	$40	$30	$20	N/A	N/A

Last MSR was $74.

TECH FORCE 78/78T - .177 or .22 cal., two CO_2 cartridges or built in bulk fill adaptor (Tech Force 78T new 2005) 20.50 in. barrel, 600 FPS, bolt action, wood stock, adj. trigger, 40 in. OAL, 6.6 lbs.

	100%	95%	90%	80%	60%	40%	20%
MSR $90.	$75	$60	$40	$30	$20	N/A	N/A

Add 15% for Tech Force 78T (new 2005).

TECH FORCE 79 - .177 or .22 cal., CO_2, 700/520 FPS, bolt action, 20.50 in. barrel, grooved receiver, competition or ambidextrous thumbhole wood stock, adj. trigger, diopter peep sight, 40 in. OAL, 6.6 lbs. New 2001.

	100%	95%	90%	80%	60%	40%	20%
MSR $180	$145	$125	$85	$65	$45	N/A	N/A

TECH FORCE 79T - .177 or .22 cal., CO_2, built in bulk fill adaptor, 700/550 FPS, bolt action, 20.50 in. barrel, grooved receiver, competition or ambidextrous thumbhole wood stock, adj. trigger, diopter peep sight, 40 in. OAL, 7.4 lbs. New 2005.

	100%	95%	90%	80%	60%	40%	20%
MSR $199	$165	$145	$95	$75	$50	N/A	N/A

TECH FORCE 88 - .177 cal., SL, SP, 850 FPS, 19.50 in. barrel, adj. sights, safety, 7.50 lbs.

	100%	95%	90%	80%	60%	40%	20%
MSR $95	$85	$65	$45	$35	$25	N/A	N/A

TECH FORCE 89 - .177 cal., SL, SP, bullpup configuration, extending buttplate, 600 FPS, 25 in. overall length. Mfg. 1999-2001.

	100%	95%	90%	80%	60%	40%	20%
	$80	$70	$50	$35	$25	N/A	N/A

Last MSR was $110.

TECH FORCE 97 - .177 or .22 cal., UL, SP, 900/700 FPS, 19.50 in. barrel, adj. sights, grooved receiver for scope mounting, automatic safety, oil finished Monte Carlo stock with recoil pad, 43 in. OAL, 7.40 lbs. New 1999.

	100%	95%	90%	80%	60%	40%	20%
MSR $100	$85	$70	$45	$30	$20	N/A	N/A

Add $15 for an installed MacCari spring.

TECH FORCE 99 - .177 or .22 cal., UL, SP, 1000/800 FPS, 19.50 in. barrel, MacCari spring, adj. sights, grooved receiver for scope mounting, automatic safety, oil finished Monte Carlo stock with recoil pad, 7.50 lbs. New 2000.

	100%	95%	90%	80%	60%	40%	20%
MSR $169	$135	$115	$80	$55	$40	N/A	N/A

TECH FORCE 510 - .177 cal., UL, multi-stroke pneumatic, 300-750 FPS, ten-shot mag., adj. sights, adj. wire stock, 15 in. BBL, 4.50 lbs.

	100%	95%	90%	80%	60%	40%	20%
MSR $85	$75	$60	$40	$30	$20	N/A	N/A

COUGAR

For information on Cougar airguns, see Milbro in the "M" section.

CROSMAN CORP.

Current manufacturer located in East Bloomfield, NY.

The Crosman airgun line began with the production of the "First Model" Crosman pneumatic rifle by the Crosman Brothers Co. in June 1923. That rifle was based on a patent by William A. MacLean. In addition to being chauffeur to wealthy heavy construction contractor P.H. Murray, MacLean had developed a tiny business producing "Universal Pellets," .22 caliber diabolo-style pellets. These probably were for American owners of BSA air rifles whose supply of British pellets had been cut off by World War I. MacLean was intrigued by an airgun brought back from Europe by Murray, probably one of those BSA air rifles, and wished to "improve" upon its power source. Apparently he devised the idea of combining a highly accurate rifled barrel firing .22 caliber lead pellets with the then current American airgun pump rod system of the smoothbore Benjamin BB airguns. This pumping system had been well-known in America since the models of Bouron, Hawley (Kalamazoo), and Johnson and Bye in the late 1800s.

The oft-told tale that Murray´s unidentified air rifle, which so impressed MacLean, was a French Giffard pneumatic rifle is contro-verted by the facts that MacLean was already involved with .22 caliber waisted pellets and that such Giffard guns had not been made for almost a half century. Murray, a pacifist and not at all interested in guns, almost surely would not have purchased a vintage Gif-fard. It is very probable that he would have brought back a BSA air rifle, then popular all over Europe but not common in America, because he knew that his chauffeur was interested in airguns and had a part-time business making pellets for such guns.

The Crosman Brothers Co., which made those first Crosman air rifles, was an offshoot of the then famous Crosman Brothers Seed Company located in Fairport, NY. Crosman Brothers became the Crosman Rifle Company in August 1923 and then the Crosman Arms Co. in 1925. The Crosman Arms Company later became Crosman Air Guns. The Crosman history has been traced, and its air-guns discussed and illustrated, by Dean Fletcher in his excellent books, *The Crosman Rifle, 1923-1950* (1996), *The Crosman Arms Handbooks* (1996), and *75 Years of Crosman Airguns* (1998).

Crosman expended heroic efforts to develop adult interest in airguns, but ended up a co-leader of the youth market instead. Ironi-cally, it probably was the development of the Crosman pump rifle, and especially the development of mass production, low-cost ver-sions of it, that pre-empted the significant introduction of adult-level spring-piston airguns into the United States. Crosman airguns became a product primarily of interest to, and eventually designed for, youthful shooters. Despite the past efforts of Crosman and others, the development of a significant American adult airgun market was delayed until the 1970s. Crosman´s primary concern over the last few decades has been competition with the other leader of the American youth airgun market, Daisy.

Crosman acquired the combined Benjamin/Sheridan companies in February 1992. Collectors and traders may encounter some confu-sion due to the Crosman name appearing, sometimes alone, on airguns made in the 1990s, which generally are known as Benjamin and Sheridan models. (See the introduction to the Benjamin section in this book.)

Crosman produced some airguns under the name of their president, P.Y. Hahn, and under several private labels, such as J.C. Higgins for Sears and Ted Williams for Wards. While guns sold to the general public might come back to the factory one by one, private label models had the potential to come back en mass. Thus, the models sold to Sears and Wards usually represented the very best efforts and quality control that Crosman could muster. Collectors generally covet these, and other special production guns, and should expect to pay a 10% to 20% or greater premium. Guns produced for the Canadian and Mexican markets also command premium prices, especially when accompanied by appropriate original boxes. It is not possible to list all Crosman variations, and surely there are variations, even models, out there that even the factory does not know about.

As with many airguns, originality of parts may be hard to determine. The parts were not serial numbered. Newer parts were often placed, sometimes under company mandate, in older guns during repairs. In older Crosman airguns, the .177 caliber versions gener-ally are much less common, while in the most recent models the .l77 caliber is the most common.

As noted, during most of the last three-quarters of a century, Crosman generally was known for pellet guns primarily used by older youth. Crosman carried an adult precision airgun line, consisting of the Models 6100-6500, from 1982-89. During 2000, the company introduced the Challenger 2000 Series, a single shot, bolt action, CO_2 three position target rifle.

Caution: Do not depend on Crosman ads or catalogs to see detailed features. Their ad departments and agencies frequently used illustrations from previous periods.

For information on Crosman airguns manufactured for other trademarks, see the Store Brand Cross-Over List at the back of this text.

HANDGUNS

MODEL 36 FRONTIER - BB/.175 cal., CO_2, one Powerlet, SA, chambers hold 6 BBs; spring-fed tubular magazine holds 12 more. Full size, full weight replica of Colt Single Action revolver. Basically a continuation of the Hahn/Crosman Model 45, Series I - Mfg. 1970-1971, Series II - Mfg. 1972-1975.

courtesy Robert Lutter

$105	$85	$70	$55	$45	N/A	N/A

Add 20% for original factory box.
Add 25% for original Western-style holster.

GRADING	100%	95%	90%	80%	60%	40%	20%

MODEL 38C COMBAT - .177 or .22 cal., CO_2, one Powerlet, SA or DA, six-shot revolving cylinder, 3.5 in. barrel, full size cast alloy metal replica of .38 cal. Smith & Wesson revolver, 350-400 FPS, .177 cal., 2.4 lbs. First Variant: metal rear sight and cylinder, mfg. 1964-1973. Second Variant: plastic rear sight and cylinder, Mfg. 1973-1976. Third Variant: .177 cal., mfg. 1976-1981.

courtesy Robert Lutter

$90	$75	$65	$50	$40	N/A	N/A

Add 20% for original factory box.

Add 400% for chrome finish salesman sample.

MODEL 38T TARGET - .177 or .22 cal., similar to Model 38C Combat, except 6 in. barrel. First Variant: metal rear sight and cylinder, mfg. 1964-1973. Second Variant: plastic rear sight and cylinder, mfg. 1973-1976. Third Variant: .177 cal., mfg. 1976-1985.

courtesy Beeman Collection

$90	$75	$65	$50	$40	N/A	N/A

Add 20% for original factory box.

Add 400% for chrome finish salesman sample.

MODEL 44 PEACEMAKER - .177 or .22 cal., CO_2, one Powerlet, single action six-shot revolving pellet, wood grips, full size replica of Colt Peacemaker. Series I - mfg. 1970-1971, Series II - mfg. 1972-1975, Series III - mfg. 1976-1981.

courtesy Robert Lutter

$100	$95	$90	$80	$60	N/A	N/A

Add 20% for original factory box.

Add 20% for original factory Western low slung holster.

MODEL 45 (HAHN "45") - BB/.175 cal., CO_2, one Powerlet, SA, chambers hold 6 BBs, spring-fed tubular magazine holds 12 more. Full size, full weight replica of Colt Single Action Army revolver. Hahn 45 became Crosman Model 45, but casting dies were not changed, so Crosman Model 45 specimens are marked with the P.Y. Hahn Co. name. Became the Model "Frontier 36" in 1970. Mfg. 1958-1970. Variation: Sears (J.C. Higgins).

courtesy Robert Lutter

100%	95%	90%	80%	60%	40%	20%
$80	$70	$60	$50	$40	N/A	N/A

Add 20% for "Fast Draw" holster.
Add 20% for JC Higgins/Sears version.
Add 20% for original factory box.

MODEL 88 SKANAKER PISTOL - .177 cal., CO_2, 550 FPS, bulk fill tank, SS, target model. Mfg. 1987-1991.

courtesy Beeman Collection

100%	95%	90%	80%	60%	40%	20%
$450	$350	$300	$250	$200	N/A	N/A

Last MSR was $795.

Add $65 for carrying case.
As of Dec. 31, 1991, Crosman liquidated its supply of Skanaker pistols due to expiration of Skanaker name use contract.

MODEL 105 (BULLSEYE) - .177 cal., pneumatic pump, pump lever with one or two open loops, SS, 8.4 in rifled barrel, adj. rear sight, blue finish, checkered tenite grips. 31 oz. Mfg. 1947-1953.

courtesy Robert Lutter

100%	95%	90%	80%	60%	40%	20%
$100	$90	$80	$75	$70	$50	$30

Add 30% for original factory-marked box.

GRADING	100%	95%	90%	80%	60%	40%	20%

MODEL 106 (BULLSEYE) - .22 cal., similar to Model 105. Mfg. 1948-1953.

courtesy Robert Lutter

	$100	$90	$80	$75	$70	$50	$30

Add 30% for original factory-marked box.

MODEL 111 - .177 cal., CO_2, 10 oz. separate gas cylinder, SS, 8 1/8 in. rifled barrel, adj. rear sight, blue finish, molded tenite grips. 5.50 lbs. Mfg. 1950-1954.

courtesy Robert Lutter

	$200	$170	$150	$130	$110	$80	$50

Add 30% for original CO_2 tank. (Readers are advised not to charge original Crosman CO_2 Models 111 and 112 pistols. Models 113 and 114 rifles are first CO_2 tanks.)

Add 20% for original box.

Add 30% for "introduction year" box with gold-colored paper lining and insert cut to hold gun. (Models 111 and 112.)

Add 75% for gun with Model A306 dealer display case, tank, bell target, pellets. (Typical premium for such displays in other models.)

These are guns without hose or attached gas tank.

MODEL 112 - .22 cal., similar to Model 111. Mfg. 1950-1954.

courtesy Robert Lutter

	$200	$170	$150	$130	$110	$80	$50

Add 30% for original CO_2 tank. (Readers are advised not to charge original Crosman CO_2 Models 111 and 112 pistols. Models 113 and 114 rifles are first CO_2 tanks.)

Add 20% for original box.

Add 30% for "introduction year" box with gold-colored paper lining and insert cut to hold gun. (Models 111 and 112.)

Add 75% for gun with Model A306 dealer display case, tank, bell target, pellets. (Typical premium for such displays in other models).

These are guns without hose or attached gas tank.

GRADING	100%	95%	90%	80%	60%	40%	20%

MODEL 115 - .177 cal., similar to Model 111, except 6 in. barrel. Mfg. 1951-1954.

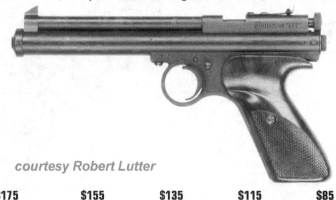

courtesy Robert Lutter

	$175	$155	$135	$115	$85	$65	$40

Add 30% for original CO_2 tank. (Readers are advised not to charge original Crosman CO_2 tanks.)

Add 20% for original box.

Add 75% for gun with Model A306 dealer display case, tank, bell target, pellets. (Typical premium for such displays in other models.)

MODEL 116 - .22 cal., similar to Model 112, except 6 in. barrel. Mfg. 1951-1954.

courtesy Robert Lutter

	$175	$155	$135	$115	$85	$65	$40

Add 30% for original CO_2 tank. (Readers are advised not to charge original Crosman CO_2 tanks.)

Add 20% for original box.

Add 75% for gun with Model A306 dealer display case, tank, bell target, pellets. (Typical premium for such displays in other models.)

MODEL 130 - .22 cal., pneumatic pump, SS. First Variant: with walnut grips and pump handle. Mfg. 1953-1954. Second Variant: with formed metal pump handle. Mfg. 1955-1970.

courtesy Robert Lutter

	$85	$65	$55	$45	$35	N/A	N/A

Add 20% for wood cocking handle.

Add 40% for original factory-marked box.

GRADING	100%	95%	90%	80%	60%	40%	20%

MODEL 137 - .177 cal., similar to Model 130. First Variant: with spoon handle breech cover, aluminum breech, and fingertip recocking. Mfg. 1954. Second Variant: .177 cal., with formed metal pump handle. Mfg. 1956-1962.

courtesy Robert Lutter

	$120	$90	$75	$65	$55	N/A	N/A

Add 20% for wood cocking handle.
Add 40% for original factory-marked box.

MODEL 150 - .22 cal., 12.5 gm. CO_2 cylinder (Powerlet), SS, Type 1 - with two-piece barrel and breech assembly. First type 1 variation: rotating adj. power cocking knob. Second type 1 variation: non-adjustable power. Mfg. 1954-1956. Type 2 - with one-piece breech/barrel. Mfg. 1956-1967.

courtesy Robert Lutter

	$110	$90	$75	$65	$55	N/A	N/A

Add 20% for Type 1 (except for special versions).
Add 150% for Type 1 Sears/J.C. Higgins Model 150 with grey-crinkle finish on frame and loading port.
Add 40% for SK (Shooting Kit) version.
Add 30% for Sears/Ted Williams version.
Add 30% for Wards Model 150.
Add 75% for Mexican version.
Add 100% for Canadian version.
Add 20-40% for standard factory-marked box (five variations).
More than 20 variations are known, plus there are an unknown number of foreign models.

✳ *Model 150C Medalist* - .22 cal., similar to Model 150, except chrome plated and wood presentation box. Mfg. 1957-1961.

	$250	$200	$145	$120	$100	N/A	N/A

✳ *Model 150PK* - .22 cal., similar to Model 150, except has portable metal target backstop. Mfg. 1959-1960.

	$145	$120	$100	$85	$70	N/A	N/A

MODEL 157 - .177 cal., similar to Model 150. Type 1 - with two-piece barrel and breech assembly. First type 1 variation: rotating adj. power cocking knob. Second type 1 variation: non-adjustable power. Mfg. 1954-1956. Type 2 - with one-piece breech/barrel. Mfg. 1956-1967.

courtesy Robert Lutter

	$110	$90	$75	$65	$55	N/A	N/A

Add 75% for Type 1.
Add 40% for SK (Shooting Kit) version.

GRADING	100%	95%	90%	80%	60%	40%	20%

Add 30% for Sears/Ted Williams version.
Add 75% for Mexican version.
Add 100% for Canadian version.
Add 20-40% for standard factory marked box (5 variations).
More than 20 variations are known, plus there are an unknown number of foreign models.

MODEL 338 - BB/.175 cal., CO_2, one Powerlet, semi-auto replica of Walther P38 military pistol, twenty-shot magazine, cast metal. Mfg. 1986-1991.

courtesy Robert Lutter

	$45	$40	$35	$30	$20	N/A	N/A

Add 10% for original box.

MODEL 357 FOUR - .177 cal. pellets, CO_2, one Powerlet, SA/DA revolver, replica of Colt Python firearm, ten-shot rotary clip, 4 in. rifled barrel, 350 FPS, black finish, adj. rear sight, 27 oz. Mfg. 1983-1997.

courtesy Robert Lutter

	$60	$50	$45	$40	$35	N/A	N/A

Add 10% for factory box.
Add 60% for silver finish.

✳ *Model 357 4GT* - .177 cal., similar to Model 357 Four, except gold color accents and black grips. Mfg. 1997. Disc.

	$60	$50	$45	$40	$35	N/A	N/A

Add 10% for factory box.
Add 60% for silver finish.

MODEL 3574W - .177 cal. pellets, CO_2, one Powerlet, SA/DA revolver, ten-shot rotary clip, 4 in. rifled barrel, 435 FPS, black finished, adj. rear sight, 32 oz. Disc. 2004.

	$45	$35	$25	$20	$15	N/A	N/A

Last MSR was $61.

✳ **MODEL 357GW** - .177 cal. pellets, similar to Model 3574W, except also includes extra 8 in. barrel, three ten-shot rotary clips, five paper targets, red dot sight and mounts, and hard case. Disc. 2004.

	$85	$75	$65	$55	$45	N/A	N/A

Last MSR was $100.

GRADING	100%	95%	90%	80%	60%	40%	20%

MODEL 357 SIX - .177 cal., similar to Model 357 Four, except has 6 in. barrel. Mfg. 1983-97.

courtesy Robert Lutter

	$60	$50	$45	$40	$35	N/A	N/A

Add 10% for factory box.
Add 60% for silver finish.

* **Model 357 6GT** - .177 cal., similar to Model 357 Six, except had gold accents and black grips. Mfg. 1997. Disc.

	$60	$50	$45	$40	$35	N/A	N/A

Add 10% for factory box.
Add 60% for silver finish.

MODEL 3576W - .177 cal. pellets, CO_2, one Powerlet, SA/DA revolver, ten-shot rotary clip, 6 in. rifled barrel, 435 FPS, black finished, adj. rear sight, 32 oz.

MSR $61	$45	$35	$25	$20	$15	N/A	N/A

* **Model 357GW** - .177 cal. pellets, CO_2, one Powerlet, SA/DA revolver, ten-shot rotary clip, 6 and 8 in. rifled barrel, 435 FPS, black finished, adj. rear and red dot sights, padded case, 32 oz. New 2005.

MSR $100	$85	$75	$65	$50	N/A	N/A	N/A

MODEL 357 EIGHT - .177 cal., similar to Model 357 Four, except 8 in. barrel. Mfg. 1984-96.

courtesy Robert Lutter

	$80	$65	$50	$40	$30	N/A	N/A

Add 10% for factory box.
Add 60% for scope or silver finish.

MODEL 380 ROCKET - CO_2, one Powerlet, underwater speargun, one- or two- (early mfg.) piece grips. Mfg. 1959-60.

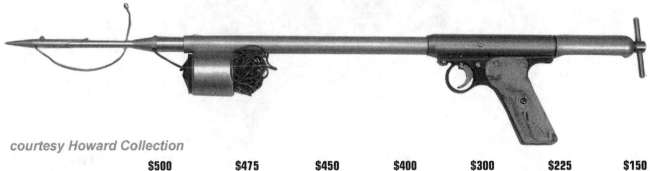

courtesy Howard Collection

	$500	$475	$450	$400	$300	$225	$150

Add 10% for two-piece grips.

GRADING	100%	95%	90%	80%	60%	40%	20%

MODEL 451 - CO_2, one Powerlet, semi-auto, six-shot, styled after Colt 45 Automatic. 4.75 in. barrel. Mfg. 1969-70.

courtesy Beeman Collection

	$400	$350	$325	$300	$275	$200	$150

Add 20% for original factory box.

MODEL 454 - BB/.175 cal., CO_2, one Powerlet, semi-auto, styled after Colt Woodsman. sixteen-shot spring-fed magazine, adj. sights, brown Croswood grips. First variant: has coin slot piercing screw. Mfg. 1972-1977. Second variant (BB-Matic): has ring piercing screw lever. Mfg. 1978-1982.

courtesy Robert Lutter

	$50	$45	$40	$35	$25	N/A	N/A

Add 10% for first variant.

Add 20% for original factory box.

MODEL 455 - .177 cal., CO_2, SS, pellet (Crosman/Blaser 45 conversion unit) converts Colt 45 Automatic firearm (series 70 or earlier) or clones to .177 cal. pellet use, CO_2, single shot. Mfg. in Germany. Mfg.1987-1988.

	$150	$125	$100	$75	$60	N/A	N/A

Add 10% for original factory box.

MODEL 600 - .22 cal., CO_2, one Powerlet, semi-auto, sophisticated trigger design, ten-round spring-fed magazine, considered by many as the pinnacle of Crosman airgun development, often converted into custom airguns, original specimens are becoming scarce. Variations: three distinct variations based on CO_2 piercing caps. First variant: non-piercing cap. Second variant: piercing cap like Model 160 Standard. Third variant: push button piercing. Sears variant: Sears markings. Mfg. 1960-1970.

courtesy Robert Lutter

	$295	$250	$195	$170	$145	$125	$100

Add 75% for Sears variant.

Add 20% for original factory-marked box.

Add 20% for original holster.

GRADING	100%	95%	90%	80%	60%	40%	20%

MODEL 677 PLINK-O-MATIC - BB/.175 cal., CO_2, one Powerlet, semi-auto, rare BB version of the Model 600. Mfg. 1961-1964.

	N/A	$375	$325	$275	$225	$175	N/A

Add 35% for original factory box.

MODEL 971BF (BLACK FANG) - BB/.175, .177 cal., spring piston, seventeen-shot mag. (BB), smooth steel barrel, 250 FPS (BB), black finish, synthetic grip/frame, fixed sights, 10 oz. Mfg. 1996-2002.

	$15	$10	$5	N/A	N/A	N/A	N/A

MODEL 972BV (BLACK VENOM) - BB/.175 cal., spring piston, .177 cal., seventeen-shot mag. (BB), SS pellet/dart, smooth steel barrel, 270 FPS (BB), 245 FPS (.177 pellet), black finish, synthetic grip/frame, adj. sights, 15 oz. Mfg. 1996-present.

MSR $25	$22	$15	$10	N/A	N/A	N/A	N/A

MODEL 1008 (REPEATAIR) - .177 cal. pellet, CO_2, one Powerlet, semi-auto, eight-shot mag. SA/DA action, 4.25 in. rifled barrel, 430 FPS, adj. rear sight, replica of Smith & Wesson pistol, 17 oz. Mfg. 1992-1997.

	$60	$55	$50	$45	$40	N/A	N/A

MODEL 1008B (REPEATAIR) - .177 cal., pellet, CO_2, one Powerlet, eight-shot clip, M-1008B with black frame, 4.25 in. rifled barrel, 430 FPS, adj. rear sight, 17 oz. Mfg. 1997-present.

MSR $66	$55	$45	$30	$20	$15	N/A	N/A

✳ *Model 1008SB (Repeatair)* - .177 cal., similar to Model 1008B, except has silver frame. Mfg. 1997-present.

MSR $67	$55	$45	$35	$30	$20	N/A	N/A

✳ *Model 1008BRD (Repeatair)* - .177 cal., similar to Model 1008B, except has red dot sight. Mfg. 1997-present.

MSR $76	$65	$55	$45	$35	$25	N/A	N/A

✳ *Model 1008AK/1008SBAK (Repeatair Air Pistol Kit)* - .177 cal., kit includes Model 1008B or 1008SB pistol, red dot sight, shooting glasses, two Powerlet CO_2, 250-ct. package of pellets, and clamshell case.

MSR $77	$65	$55	$45	$35	$25	N/A	N/A

Add $2 for Model 1008SBAK kit with Model 1008SB pistol.

✳ *Model 1078BG/1078SBG (Repeatair Shooters Kit)* - .177 cal., kit includes Model 1008B or 1008SB pistol, three eight-shot clips, three paper targets, three Powerlet CO_2, 250-ct. package of pellets, and clamshell case.

MSR $77	$65	$55	$45	$35	$25	N/A	N/A

Add $2 for Model 1078SBG kit with Model 1008SB pistol.

MODEL 1300 MEDALIST II - .22 cal., UL (forearm) pneumatic, SS, self-cocking, sliding breech cover, cocking lever flared at forward end, 460 FPS, 11.75 in. OAL. Mfg. 1970-1976.

courtesy Robert Lutter

	$80	$70	$65	$60	$50	N/A	N/A

Add 20% for factory box.

MODEL 1322 MEDALIST - .22 cal., UL (forearm) pneumatic, SS, three-ring cocking knob, sliding breech cover, cocking lever straight along bottom edge, 13.6 in. overall. First variant: manual cocking, has steel breech cover. Mfg. 1977-1981. Second variant: has plastic breech cover. Mfg. 1981-1996. Third variant: brass bolt action. Mfg. 1998-2000.

courtesy Robert Lutter

	$65	$55	$45	$40	$30	N/A	N/A

Add 25% for first variant.

GRADING	100%	95%	90%	80%	60%	40%	20%

MODEL 1357 "SIX" - BB/.175 cal., CO_2, break-open, clip loading (six-shot), one Powerlet, SA/DA, replica of .357 police revolver, 465 FPS, limited distribution may be Michigan only. Mfg. 1988-1996.

	$55	$50	$48	$45	$40	N/A	N/A

MODEL 1377 AMERICAN CLASSIC - .177 cal., similar to Model 1322, pellet only, single shot, brass bolt action, 10.25 in. rifled barrel, 560 FPS, adj. rear sight, 32 oz. First variant: has manual cocking and steel breech. Mfg. 1977-1981. Second variant: has plastic breech. Mfg. 1981-1996. Also sold as Model 1388 "rifle" with shoulder stock. Mfg. 1982-1988.

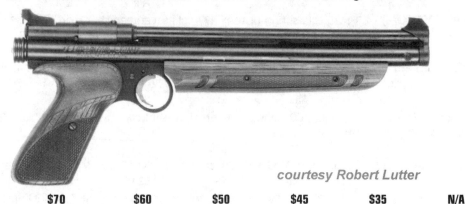

courtesy Robert Lutter

	$70	$60	$50	$45	$35	N/A	N/A

Add 20% with shoulder stock (Model 1388 "rifle").

✳ *Model 1377C* - .177 cal. pellet only, single shot, brass bolt action, 10.25 in. rifled barrel, 600 FPS, adj. rear sight, 32 oz. Mfg. 1998-present.

MSR	$64	$55	$48	$40	$30	$20	N/A	N/A

MODEL 1600 POWERMATIC - BB/.175 cal., CO_2, one Powerlet, semi-auto replica of Colt Woodsman, seventeen-shot spring-fed magazine, fixed sights, (economy version of Model 454). First variant: flathead gas filler cap screw. Second variant: barrel-shaped filler cap screw. Mfg. 1979-1990.

courtesy Robert Lutter

	$60	$50	$40	$30	$20	N/A	N/A

MODEL 1861 SHILOH - BB/.175, .177 pellet cal., CO_2, one Powerlet, SA revolver, patterned after US Civil War Remington cap and ball revolver, 370 FPS, 1.9 lbs. Mfg. 1981-1983.

courtesy Robert Lutter

	$75	$70	$65	$60	$50	N/A	N/A

Add 20% for factory box.

MODEL 2210SB - .22 cal. pellet, CO_2, one Powerlet, SS, 7.24 in. rifled barrel, 435 FPS, silver-colored finish, adj. rear sight, fiberoptic front sight, 20 oz. Mfg. 1999-2003.

	$50	$42	$35	$25	$20	N/A	N/A

GRADING	100%	95%	90%	80%	60%	40%	20%

MODEL 2240 - .22 cal. pellet, CO_2, one Powerlet, SS, 7.25 in. rifled barrel, 460 FPS, black finish, adj. rear sight, 29 oz. Mfg. 1999-present.

	100%	95%	90%	80%	60%	40%	20%
MSR $64	$55	$45	$35	$25	$20	N/A	N/A

MODEL 3357 - .50 cal. version of the Model 357 CO_2 revolver, designed for firing paintballs.

courtesy Robert Lutter

	100%	95%	90%	80%	60%	40%	20%
	$80	$65	$50	$40	$30	N/A	N/A

MODEL AAII (Auto Air II) - BB/.175 cal. repeater, .177 pellet cal. SS, CO_2, one Powerlet, 480FPS (BB), 430 FPS (pellet), black finish, adj. rear sight. Mfg. 1991-1996.

	100%	95%	90%	80%	60%	40%	20%
	$25	$20	$15	$10	$8	N/A	N/A

Add 5% for factory box.

✹ *Model AAIIB (Auto Air II)* - BB/.175 cal. repeater, .177 pellet cal. SS, CO_2, one Powerlet, smooth barrel, 480 FPS-BB, 430 FPS-pellet, black finish, adj. rear sight, 13 oz. Mfg. 1997-present.

	100%	95%	90%	80%	60%	40%	20%
MSR $45	$35	$28	$20	$15	$10	N/A	N/A

✹ *Model AAIIB/AAIIBRD (Auto Air II)* - BB/.175 cal. repeater, .177 pellet cal. SS, CO_2, one Powerlet, smooth barrel, 480 FPS (BB), 430 FPS (pellet), black finish, adj. rear sight, red dot sight, 13 oz. Mfg. 1997-present.

	100%	95%	90%	80%	60%	40%	20%
MSR $59	$50	$40	$30	$20	$15	N/A	N/A

MODEL C40 (CROSMAN 75TH ANNIVERSARY COMMEMORATIVE) - .177 cal., CO_2, eight-shot clip, 4.25 in. rifled barrel, 430 FPS, Zinc alloy frame, silver finish, adj. rear sight, optional laser sight (C40 LS), new 1999, 40 oz. New 1998.

	100%	95%	90%	80%	60%	40%	20%
MSR $138	$125	$100	$75	$60	$50	N/A	N/A

Add $45 for Model C40LS Kit with three clips, laser sight, and foam-padded case.

MODEL CB40 (CROSMAN 75TH ANNIVERSARY COMMEMORATIVE) - .177 cal., CO_2, eight-shot clip, 4.25 in. rifled barrel, 430 FPS, zinc alloy frame, black finish, adj. rear sight, optional laser sight CB40LS new 1999, 40 oz. Mfg.1998-2003.

	100%	95%	90%	80%	60%	40%	20%
	$95	$75	$60	$50	$40	N/A	N/A

Add $30 for CB40LS.

MODEL CK92 - .177 cal., CO_2, eight-shot, 435 FPS, rifled steel barrel, solid die-cast zinc (frame, slide action release, safety), adj. rear sight, black or silver finish. Mfg. 2000-03.

	100%	95%	90%	80%	60%	40%	20%
	$105	$95	$80	$60	$50	N/A	N/A

Add $20 for silver finish.

MODEL MARK I - .22 cal., CO_2, one Powerlet, SS, styled like Ruger .22 semi-auto firearm, rifled 7.25 in. barrel, 43 oz. First variant: adj. power. Mfg. 1966-1980. Second variant: non-adj. power. Mfg. 1981-1983.

courtesy Robert Lutter

	100%	95%	90%	80%	60%	40%	20%
	$150	$125	$100	$75	$55	N/A	N/A

Subtract 20% for second variant.
Add 10% for factory box.

GRADING	100%	95%	90%	80%	60%	40%	20%

MODEL MARK II - BB/.175 cal., .177 cal. pellet, similar to Model Mark I. First variant: SS Mfg. 1966-1980. Second variant: without adjustable power. Mfg. 1981-1986.

courtesy Robert Lutter

	$135	$105	$85	$70	$50	N/A	N/A

Subtract 20% for second variant.
Add 10% for factory box.

MODEL SA 6 - .22 cal., CO_2, one Powerlet, SA six-shot, replica of Colt Peacemaker Single Action revolver. Mfg. 1959-1969.

courtesy Robert Lutter

	$120	$105	$85	$70	$55	N/A	N/A

Add 20% for factory box.
Add 20% for factory quick draw holster.

MODEL SSP 250 SILHOUETTE PISTOL - .177 cal., CO_2, one Powerlet, SS, dual power settings, interchangeable .20 and .22 cal rifled steel barrels available. Mfg. 1989-1995.

courtesy Beeman Collection

	$110	$100	$90	$80	$70	$45	$30

Add 25% for each additional caliber barrel.
Add 20% for factory box.

MODEL SSP-250 (ZZZ TRANQUILIZER DART GUN) - .50 cal., pump pneumatic, single-shot dart gun, modified from Crosman SSP-250 by outside fabricator.

	$250	$200	$150	$100	$75	N/A	N/A

GRADING	100%	95%	90%	80%	60%	40%	20%

MODEL V300 - BB/.175 cal., rear grip strap lever cocking, SP, SA, twenty-three-shot spring-fed magazine. Mfg. 1963-1964.

courtesy Robert Lutter

	$175	$150	$125	$100	$75	N/A	N/A

Add 20% for factory box.

MODEL Z-77 UZI REPLICA - BB/.175 cal., CO_2, one Powerlet, semi-auto, gravity-fed twenty-shot magazine, with folding stock (but classed as pistol by Crosman). Mfg. 1987-1989.

	$175	$150	$125	$100	$75	N/A	N/A

Subtract 20% for missing sling.
Clamshell packaging on new gun.

JET LINE MODEL 101 (CONDUIT GUN) - CO_2 pistol which fires 12 gram Powerlet carrying wire-pulling fish line through large conduits for electric work (i.e. Powerlet is the projectile!). Produced by Crosman Fabricators with Crosman parts, 10.5 in. OAL (gun only), 1.4 lbs.

courtesy Beeman Collection

	$350	$295	$245	$200	$170	$150	$100

Add 20% for factory box.

✳ *Jet Line Compact Model 101(Conduit Gun)* - compact version of Model 101 Jet Line pistol. Only marking is a large "C" on each of the orange plastic grip plates. Light gray alloy body. 1.1 lbs. 7.1 in. OAL , gun only.

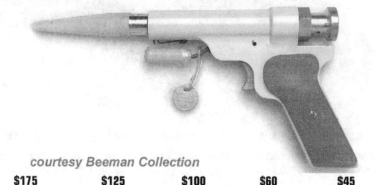

courtesy Beeman Collection

	$175	$125	$100	$60	$45	N/A	N/A

Add 50-100% for original accessories, holster, special spools of line, plastic projectile guides, funnels, box, etc.

RIFLES

FIRST MODEL RIFLE ("1923 MODEL," HI-POWER, OR PLUNGER MODEL) - .22 cal., rifled, bicycle-style plunger rod pump under the barrel, pneumatic, SS. First variant: peep sight mounted in dovetail slot forward of the pellet loading port of receiver; no elevation adjustment, machined steel receiver, steel compression tube. Second variant: peep sight, adjustable for elevation

GRADING	100%	95%	90%	80%	60%	40%	20%

and windage, mounted on bridge-type bracket behind the pellet loading port, steel barrel and compression tube. Third variant: nickel-plated brass compression tube, die-cast receiver with logo: "Crosman Rochester, N.Y. Pat. April 23-23". Mfg. 1923-24.

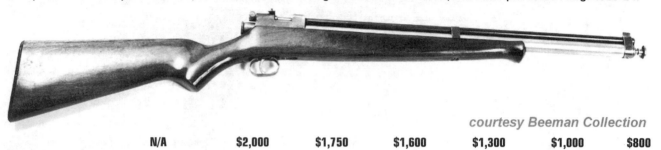

courtesy Beeman Collection

	N/A	$2,000	$1,750	$1,600	$1,300	$1,000	$800

Add 50% for first variation.

Add 20% for third variation.

Subtract 60-70% for "made-up specimens" recently assembled from parts, usually combined with non-Crosman, recently made receivers – often with sharp edges and somewhat different shape and material.

Subtract 30% for refinished metalwork. Be especially cautious with refinished specimens,(compare with specimen known to be authentic).

Subtract 50% for any cocking knob other than short knurled type on First, Second, or Third Model Crosman rifles.

SECOND MODEL RIFLE (FIRST LEVER MODEL – "1924 MODEL") - .22 cal., rifled barrel, the first lever-action pump pneumatic, conspicuous "beer barrel" pump-lever handle protrudes under front of gun, single shot, no variations reported, extremely rare. Mfg. 1923-24.

courtesy Beeman Collection

	N/A	$2,900	$2,750	$2,400	$1,800	$1,450	$1,250

Sometimes refered to as the "1924 Model" but that can be confusing because production began in 1923 and many, much later, models carry the 1924 patent date – which leads collectors to refer them as 1924 Models.

THIRD MODEL RIFLE (SECOND LEVER MODEL) - .22 cal., rifled, first swinging forearm pump pneumatic, SS, produced by both Crosman Rifle Co. (3-4 employees) and Crosman Arms Co. Rarest of the first three Crosman air rifle models. Mfg. 1924-25.

courtesy Beeman Collection

	N/A	N/A	$2,400	$2,000	$1,750	$1,500	$1,000

MODEL 1 - .22 cal., swinging forearm pump pneumatic, SS, adj. Williams rear sight, wood stock/forearm, 10 pumps = 635 FPS. First variant: tapered steel barrel housing, mfg. 1981-82. Second variant: straight steel barrel housing, plastic sight sleeve, 5.1 lbs. Mfg.1982-85.

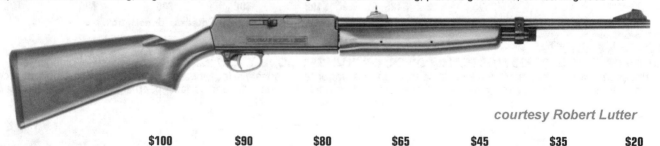

courtesy Robert Lutter

	$100	$90	$80	$65	$45	$35	$20

Subtract 20% for second variant.

Add 20% for factory box.

GRADING	100%	95%	90%	80%	60%	40%	20%

MODEL 66 POWERMASTER - BB/.175 cal., eighteen-shot mag. (plus 200 round reservoir) or .177 cal. pellet single shot, swinging forearm pump pneumatic. First variant: with zinc receiver. Mfg. 1983-88. Second variant: with plastic receiver, 3.9 lbs. Mfg. began in 1988. Disc.

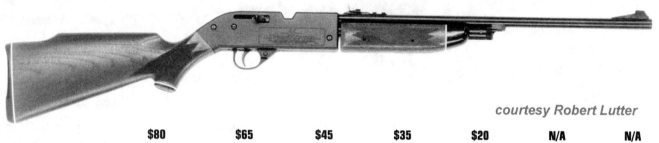

courtesy Robert Lutter

	$80	$65	$45	$35	$20	N/A	N/A

Add 20% for first variant.
Add 20% for factory box.

* **Model 66RT Powermaster** - similar to Model 66 Powermaster, except has camo stock and forearm. Mfg. 1993-94.

	$100	$80	$65	$45	$35	N/A	N/A

* **Model 66BX Powermaster** - BB/.175 cal. eighteen-shot mag. (plus 200 round reservoir), or .177 cal. five-shot mag. pellet SS, swinging forearm pump pneumatic, bolt action, 680 FPS (BB), 645 FPS (pellet), 20.5 in. rifled steel barrel, black finish, brown checkered synthetic stock and forearm, fiberoptic front and adj. rear sights, 2.9 lbs.

MSR $63	$55	$45	$35	$25	$20	N/A	N/A

MODEL 70 - .177 cal., pellet, CO_2, BA, copy of Winchester Model 70, 650 FPS, full wood stock and forearm, 41 in. OAL, 5.8 lbs. Mfg. 1973-80.

courtesy Howard Collection

	$120	$95	$75	$55	$35	N/A	N/A

Last MSR was $49.

MODEL 73 SADDLE PAL - .175/BB cal., sixteen-shot repeater or .177 cal. pellet SS; CO_2, one Powerlet, plastic stock, Winchester style lever, 3.2 lbs. First variant: Mfg. 1976-77. Second variant: Mfg. 1977-83.

courtesy Robert Lutter

	$50	$45	$40	$35	$25	$20	$20

Add 10% for factory box.

MODEL 84 CHALLENGER - .177 cal., CO_2, match rifle, 720 FPS, fully adj. sights, walnut stock, adj. cheekpiece and buttplate, every Model 84 was "individually hand produced by Crosman model shop," not a "real production gun," 11 lbs. Mfg. 1985-1992.

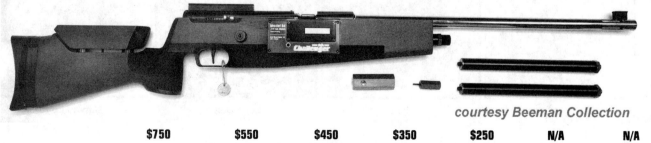

courtesy Beeman Collection

	$750	$550	$450	$350	$250	N/A	N/A

Last MSR was $1,295.

The Crosman Model 84 was the first U.S.-made air rifle designed to compete with established European models. Unlike its competitors, it is CO_2, with a digital gauge mounted on the forearm to show remaining pressure.

GRADING	100%	95%	90%	80%	60%	40%	20%

MODEL 99 - .22 cal., CO$_2$, one Powerlet, dual power selection, lever action, resembles Savage lever action big game rifle, 5.8 lbs. Mfg. 1965-1970.

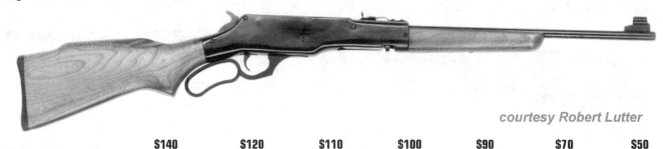

courtesy Robert Lutter

	$140	$120	$110	$100	$90	$70	$50

Add 20% for factory box.

MODEL 100 - .177 cal. version of Model 101 (see Model 101). Mfg. 1940-50.

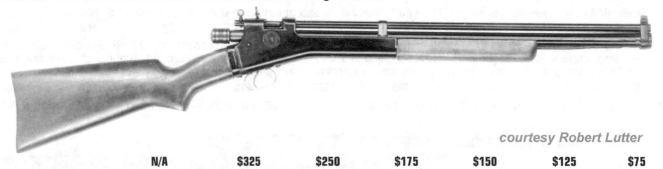

courtesy Robert Lutter

	N/A	$325	$250	$175	$150	$125	$75

The Barrel Problem: Some variations have brass barrels and brass body tubes, some have steel barrels with brass tubes, and in others both are steel. Dean Fletcher reports that from about 1925 to early 1927, barrels were rifled steel, probably made by nearby Remington Arms. From about 1927 to 1946, barrels were all bronze. From 1946 to 1947, barrels were either bronze or steel and in 1948 they were all bronze. Crosman preferred bronze for ease of tooling and because condensation which resulted from adiabatic cooling of discharge did not so easily corrode bronze.

MODEL 100 "CG" - .177 cal. version of Model 101 "CG" (see Model 101 "CG").

MODEL 101 ("1926 MODEL", SILENT .22 RIFLE) - .22 cal., pneumatic pump, SS, die-cast receiver with logo, pat. Oct. 28, 1924 Crosman Arms Co. Rochester, N.Y. This has been the standard Crosman air rifle for over 25 years. No model number markings, but may show serial numbers, numerous part variations are known: curved vs. straight bolt handles, short vs. medium knurled edge cocking knobs, round stamped aperture discs vs. hexagonal machined discs, various valve details, etc. For identifying post-WWII models see Fletcher`s *The Crosman Arms Library*, Vol. 2 - Crosman Arms Model 101 & 121-GC Engineering Parts Drawings. Mfg. 1925-1950+.

courtesy Robert Lutter

Straight Logo	Premier Logo	Logo Disc	Curved Logo

GRADING	100%	95%	90%	80%	60%	40%	20%

Short Knurled Knob	**Long Knurled Knob**	**5 Groove Knob**	**Diabolo Knob**

The Barrel Problem: Some variations have brass barrels and brass body tubes, some have steel barrels with brass tubes, and in others both are steel. Dean Fletcher reports that from about 1925 to early 1927, barrels were rifled steel, probably made by nearby Remington Arms. From about 1927 to 1946 barrels were all bronze. From 1946 to 1947 barrels were either bronze or steel and in 1948 they were all bronze. Crosman preferred bronze for ease of tooling and because condensation which resulted from adiabatic cooling of discharge did not so easily corrode bronze.

✳ *Period One Model 101 "Crosman Pneumatic Rifle"* - .22 cal. All variations: receiver area where barrel enters is octagonal, walnut stock and forearm, knurled cocking knob, rare in excellent condition. Mfg. late 1925-29.

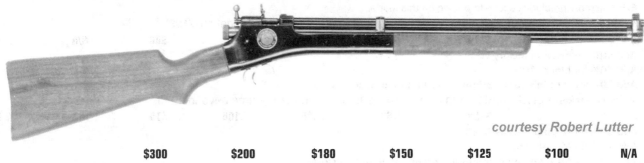

courtesy Robert Lutter

	$300	$200	$180	$150	$125	$100	N/A

Add 50% for original factory box.

Add 10% for high-comb stock or original checkering.

Add 20% for Model 100.

1925-1926 - production models have un-flared trigger and "Famous American manufactured" (Remington?) steel barrel. Circular logo cast into right side of receiver: "PAT. OCT. 28 1924, CROSMAN ARMS CO. ROCHESTER N.Y."

1927-1929 - production models have flared trigger, Crosman manufactured bronze barrel, long (1/2 inch) knurled cocking knobs. Disc logo version: on a stamped metal plate impressed into side of receiver - "CROSMAN ARMS COMPANY MADE IN U.S.A. TRADE (PELLET) MARK PATENTED ROCHESTER N.Y."

Note: the presence of a "diabolo pellet" cocking knob is an anomaly. "Diabolo pellet" cocking knobs are for the 121 "CG" series gas rifles (p/n. 121-15) only. However, the presence of this improved cocking knob enhances the look and functionality and, therefore, does not detract from value.

✳ *Premier Brand Version* - logo cast on receiver reads: "PREMIER 22 RIFLE PATENTED OCT 28. 1924". Also known from specimens bearing a lettered disc (probably 1927-29). Not marked Crosman anywhere. Rare.

	$300	$200	$180	$150	$125	N/A	N/A

Add 50% for original factory box.

Add 20% for Model 100.

Add 10% for high-comb stock or original checkering.

✳ *Period Two Model 101 "Crosman Silent Rifle"* - .22 cal. All variations: Receiver area is round where barrel enters, walnut stock, long knurled cocking knob, hexagonal rear sight disc., decal applied to forearm. Mfg. 1930-1940.

	$225	$175	$150	$125	$100	N/A	N/A

Add 50% for original factory box.

Add 20% for Model 100.

Add 10% for high-comb stock or original checkering.

Note: the presence of a "diabolo pellet" cocking knob is an anomaly. "Diabolo pellet" cocking knobs are for the 121 "CG" series gas rifles (p/n. 121-15) only. However, the presence of this improved cocking knob enhances the look and functionality and, therefore, does not detract from value.

✦ *Clickless Variant* - "clickless" (hard rubber) forearm. Mfg. 1938-1939.

	$190	$160	$130	$100	$75	N/A	N/A

Add 50% for original factory box.

Add 20% for Model 100.

Add 10% for high-comb stock or original checkering.

GRADING	100%	95%	90%	80%	60%	40%	20%

❊ ***Period Three Model 101*** - .22 cal., all models: five-ring cocking knob, hardwood stock and forearm. Mfg. post- WWII (1946-50+).

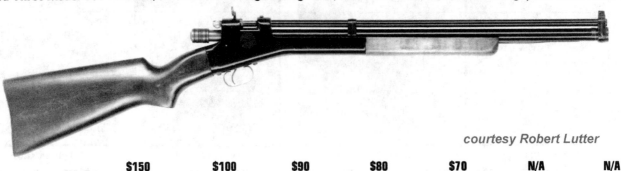

courtesy Robert Lutter

	$150	$100	$90	$80	$70	N/A	N/A

Add 50% for original factory box.

Add 20% for Model 100.

Add 10-15% for high-comb, original checkering, or walnut stock.

Note: the presence of a "diabolo pellet" cocking knob is an anomaly. "Diabolo pellet" cocking knobs are for the 121 "CG" series gas rifles (p/n. 121-15) only. However, the presence of this improved cocking knob enhances the look and functionality and, therefore, does not detract from value.

Extreme rarity precludes accurate pricing on this model.

✦ ***1949 Variant*** - knurled rear sight, large adjustment knob (same as on Model 107/108).

	$175	$130	$100	$90	$80	N/A	N/A

Add 50% for original factory box.

Add 20% for Model 100.

Add 10-15% for high-comb, original checkering, or walnut stock.

✦ ***Sears Variant*** - black crinkle finish paint, mfg. 1949-50 and for some time beyond 1950.

	$180	$160	$130	$100	$75	N/A	N/A

Add 50% for original factory box.

Add 20% for Model 100.

Add 10-15% for high-comb, original checkering, or walnut stock.

❊ ***Model 101 "Camp Perry" Variant*** - first American CO_2 guns, introduced at 1931 Camp Perry matches. Commonly referred to as "hose guns," since CO_2 is supplied via a hose connected to a central tank. Sold only as part of shooting gallery.

courtesy Beeman Collection

❊ ***Model 101 "CG" Variation*** - .22 cal., CO_2, 4.5 oz. cylinder vertically attached to gun, same rear sight assembly as found on standard model 101, sold to public, circa 1948-1949, but only through Crosman authorized (ASA) shooting clubs. Typical value $175-$225. Subtract $75 for no CO_2 tank.

MODEL 102 - .22 cal., pump-lever pneumatic, ten-round mag., no model number markings, some specimens have pellet logo, others are plain, side of receiver may or may not be marked with "Crosman 22/Patented Oct. 28, 1924/Other patents pending", early versions sometimes have simple checkering on forearm (mfg. 1929-1950) 1929-1940 models are distinguished by knurled cocking knob and walnut stocks, 1945-1950 models have a five-ring cocking knob. Clickless variant: "clickless" hard rubber forearm, mfg. only 1938-39. Mfg. 1929-1950.

courtesy Robert Lutter

	N/A	$250	$200	$175	$150	$120	$80

Add 20% for clickless variant.

Add 60% for original factory box.

Subtract 25% for 1945-1950 mfg.

GRADING	100%	95%	90%	80%	60%	40%	20%

✴ *Model 102 "OSS" Variant* - .22 cal., fifteen-shot pump pneumatic repeater for lead balls, round hole loading port, produced during WWII for the U.S. Office of Special Services.

Crosman claims that 2000 were delivered. An invoice for 1000 is known from contract #623. 957 specimens were inventoried in a U.S. government warehouse in Calcutta in January of 1945. Only one specimen is known to exist.

✴ *Model 102 "CG" Variant* - .22 cal., CO_2, ten-round magazine repeater, 4.5 oz. cylinder vertically attached to gun.

MODEL 104 - .177 cal., pump-lever pneumatic, ten-shot mag., similar to Model 102, except for caliber. Mfg. 1949 only.

courtesy Robert Lutter

	N/A	$250	$225	$200	$175	$150	$125

Add 60% for original factory box.

MODEL 107 (TOWN & COUNTRY) - .177 cal., pump-lever pneumatic, SS, micro-precision rifling, heavy all wood stock/forearm, instant selection of front sights, 37.8 in. OAL, massive, extremely well built. 6.1 lbs. Mfg. 1949.

courtesy Robert Lutter

	N/A	$1,000	$850	$750	$650	$500	$350

Add 50% for original factory box.

MODEL 108 (TOWN & COUNTRY) - .22 cal., similar to Model 107. Mfg. 1949.

	N/A	$500	$425	$375	$325	$250	$175

Add 50% for original factory box.

MODEL 109 (TOWN & COUNTRY JR.) - .177 cal., pneumatic pump, SS. Mfg. 1949-1951.

courtesy Robert Lutter

	N/A	$195	$165	$120	$95	$60	$45

Add 40% for original factory box.

MODEL 110 (TOWN & COUNTRY JR.) - .22 cal., similar to Model 109. Mfg. 1949-1951.

	N/A	$160	$140	$100	$80	$50	$35

Add 40% for original factory box.

GRADING	100%	95%	90%	80%	60%	40%	20%

MODEL 113 - .177 cal., CO_2, 10 oz. charged from separate cylinder, SS, early Models 113 and 114 with fat, straight-line stock, later models with tapered, thin stock. Mfg. 1950-1955.

courtesy Robert Lutter

	$200	$180	$160	$150	$125	$90	$65

Subtract 25% for missing CO_2 tank.

Add 20% for straight-line stock.

Add 60% for original factory box.

MODEL 114 - .22 cal., CO_2, 10 oz. separate cylinder, SS. Mfg. 1950-1955.

	$175	$155	$135	$125	$100	$75	$35

Add 15% for brass barrel.

Add 20% for straight-line stock.

Add 75% for "salesman sample" with Crosman Arms logo buttplate as on Models 107-108.

Subtract $50 for no CO_2 tank.

Add 60% for original factory box.

MODEL 117 (SHOOT-A-SCORE) - .21 cal., CO_2, hose for use with large central gas tank, magazine repeater. Extremely rare. One specimen known. Mfg. 1947-1955.

MODEL 118 - .22 cal., CO_2, 10 oz. separate cylinder, magazine repeater. Mfg. 1952-54.

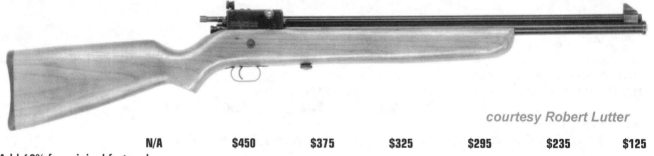

courtesy Robert Lutter

	N/A	$450	$375	$325	$295	$235	$125

Add 60% for original factory box.

Subtract $50 for no CO_2 tank.

MODEL 120 - .22 cal., pneumatic pump, SS. Variant one: brass early. Variant two: steel. Mfg. 1952-1954.

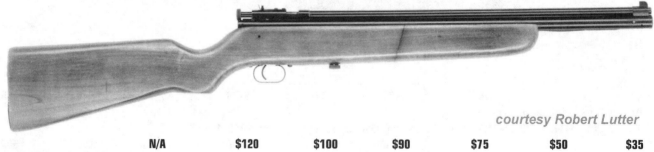

courtesy Robert Lutter

	N/A	$120	$100	$90	$75	$50	$35

Add 20% for variant one.

Add 10% for original white bead sight.

Add 30% for original factory box.

GRADING	100%	95%	90%	80%	60%	40%	20%

MODEL 121 "CG" - .210 cal., CO_2, SS, 4.5 oz. cylinder, vertically attached to gun, adj. peep sight. Mfg. 1946-49.

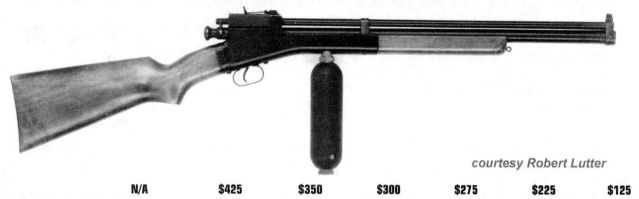

courtesy Robert Lutter

	N/A	$425	$350	$300	$275	$225	$125

Subtract $75 for no CO_2 tank.

Add $50-$75 for Slant-Tank variant, a small fitting added (circa 1949) to "CG" models to improve position of CO_2 tank.

Sold to commercial shooting galleries, shooting clubs, hospitals, and industrial companies for employee recreation. Ergonomic variations: various factory-added modifications intended to ease pellet loading, bolt operation, and cocking. Presumably intended for use by VA hospitals and others for rehabilitation.

Note: .21 caliber intended to restrict supply of pellets to Crosman brand only. Original Crosman .210 pellet container, and some other sources, refer to this model as the Crosman Gas Carbine, Model 200 (caution: do not charge original CO_2 cylinders unless professionally hydro-tested).

MODEL 122 "CG" - .22 cal., CO_2, SS, 4.5 oz. cylinder vertically attached to gun, adj. peep sights (see Model 121 "CG").

MODEL 123 (100 CG, SHOOT-A-SCORE) - .177 cal., CO_2, 4.5 oz. cylinder with 47.5 degree angle from stock, SS. Mfg. 1946-50.

courtesy Beeman Collection

	N/A	$500	$425	$375	$325	$275	$175

Subtract $75 for no CO_2 tank.

MODEL 125 RAWHIDE - BB/.175 cal., single stroke swinging forearm pump pneumatic, repeater with thirty-five-shot magazine, 300 FPS, Crosman's first BB rifle and first single stroke pump pneumatic, 5 lbs. Mfg. 1973-1974. Recalled by factory.

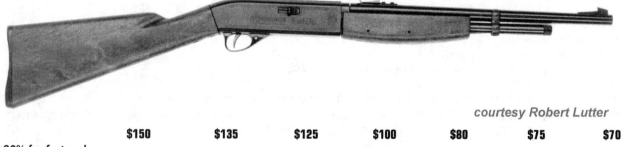

courtesy Robert Lutter

$150	$135	$125	$100	$80	$75	$70

Add 20% for factory box.

MODEL 140 - .22 cal., pneumatic pump, swinging forearm, single shot, 4.8 lbs. First variant: spoon handle breech cover, aluminum breech, fingertip recocking, mfg. 1954. Second variant: spoon handle breech cover, aluminum breech, auto recocking, mfg. 1955-57. Third variant: without spoon handle breech cover, steel breech. Mfg. 1956-62. Fourth variant: die-cast trigger housing, mfg. 1961-68.

courtesy Robert Lutter

$135	$105	$90	$75	$55	N/A	N/A

Add 10% for first variant. Add 40% for third variant. Add 20% for factory box.

GRADING	100%	95%	90%	80%	60%	40%	20%

MODEL 147 - .177 cal., similar to Model 140. First variant: with spoon handle breech cover and aluminum breech, and auto recocking, mfg. 1955-56. Second variant: with steel breech and without spoon handle breech cover, mfg. 1956-62.

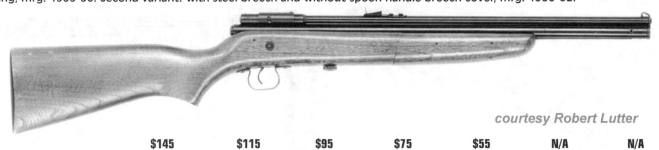

courtesy Robert Lutter

	100%	95%	90%	80%	60%	40%	20%
	$145	$115	$95	$75	$55	N/A	N/A

Add 10% for first variant.
Add 20% for factory box.

MODEL 147 BP - BB/.175 cal. or .177 cal. pellet version of Model 147, has magnetic bolt tip for steel BBs, rifled barrel. Mfg. 1964-1966.

courtesy Robert Lutter

	100%	95%	90%	80%	60%	40%	20%
	$195	$165	$135	$100	$75	N/A	N/A

Add 20% for factory box.

MODEL 160 - .22 cal., CO_2, two Powerlets, bolt action, SS, full wood stock. First variant: automatic safety, without barrel band, mfg. 1955-56. Second variant: barrel band, Model 360 peep sight, mfg. 1956-59. Third variant: die cast trigger housing, Model S331 peep sight, mfg. 1960-71.

courtesy Robert Lutter

	100%	95%	90%	80%	60%	40%	20%
	$200	$160	$130	$100	$80	N/A	N/A

Subtract 25% for first and second variants.
Add 15% for peep sight.
Add 50% for Ted Williams version.
Add 25% for "Military" version with sling and swivels (Model 160SP).
Add 20% for factory box.
Dean Fletcher´s 1998 book, *The Crosman Arms Model '160' Pellgun*, is a must-have reference.

MODEL 166 (HAHN SUPER BB REPEATER) - BB/.175 cal., CO_2, one Powerlet, Winchester-style lever action repeater, spring-fed thirty-shot magazine. First product of P.Y. Hahn Mfg. Co., Fairport, NY. Mfg.1958-71.

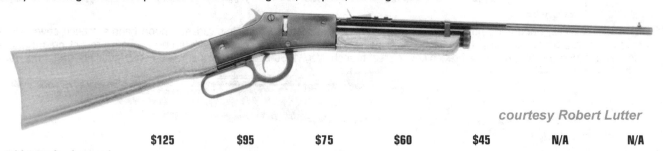

courtesy Robert Lutter

	100%	95%	90%	80%	60%	40%	20%
	$125	$95	$75	$60	$45	N/A	N/A

Add 20% for factory box.

GRADING	100%	95%	90%	80%	60%	40%	20%

MODEL 167 - .177 cal., similar to Model 160. First variant: with automatic safety and without barrel band, mfg. 1956. Second variant: with barrel band and Model 360 peep sight, mfg. 1956-59. Third variant: with die-cast trigger housing and Model S331 peep sight, mfg. 1960-66.

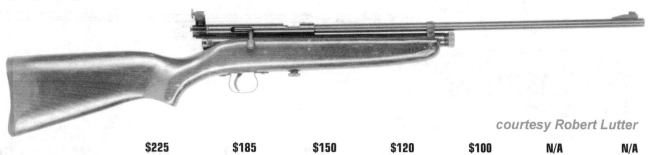

courtesy Robert Lutter

	100%	95%	90%	80%	60%	40%	20%
	$225	$185	$150	$120	$100	N/A	N/A

Add 15% for peep sight.
Subtract 25% for first and second variants.
Add 20% for factory box.

MODEL 180 - .22 cal., CO_2, one Powerlet, bolt action, SS, full wood stock, 4 lbs. First variant: cross bolt safety, mfg. 1956-59. Second variant: die-cast trigger housing. Mfg. 1962-67.

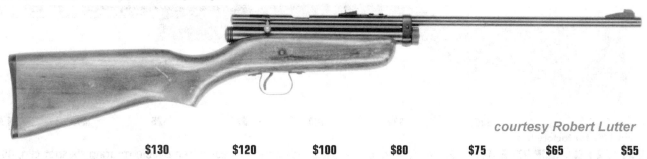

courtesy Robert Lutter

	100%	95%	90%	80%	60%	40%	20%
	$130	$120	$100	$80	$75	$65	$55

Subtract 20% for first variant.
Add 20% for factory box.

MODEL 187 - .177 cal., similar to Model 180. First variant: has cross bolt safety. Mfg. 1956-62. Second variant: with die-cast trigger housing. Mfg. 1962-66.

courtesy Robert Lutter

	100%	95%	90%	80%	60%	40%	20%
	$145	$135	$110	$90	$80	$70	$60

Subtract 20% for first variant.
Add 20% for factory box.

MODEL 197 - 10 oz., CO_2 cylinder (not a gun). Excellent condition = $50 (caution: do not charge original cylinders, for firing use modern stainless steel cylinders only). Mfg. 1950-1970.

MODEL 200 - see Model 121 "CG."

MODEL 262 - .177 cal., CO_2, one Powerlet, bolt action, SS, 38.25 in. OAL, 625 FPS, 4.8 lbs. Mfg. 1991-93.

	100%	95%	90%	80%	60%	40%	20%
	$90	$80	$75	$70	$65	N/A	N/A

Add 10% for factory box.

* *Model 262Y* - youth version of Model 262, 33.75 in. OAL, 610 FPS, 4.7 lbs. Mfg. 1991-93.

	100%	95%	90%	80%	60%	40%	20%
	$90	$80	$75	$70	$65	N/A	N/A

Add 10% for factory box.

GRADING	100%	95%	90%	80%	60%	40%	20%

MODEL 400 - .22 cal., CO_2, two Powerlets, spring-fed, "swing feed" ten-round mag., full wood stock. First variant: cross bolt safety. Mfg. 1957-62. Second variant: die-cast trigger housing. Mfg. 1962-64.

courtesy Robert Lutter

	100%	95%	90%	80%	60%	40%	20%
	$150	$140	$135	$125	$115	$90	$70

Subtract 20% for first variant.
Subtract 25% for missing magazine.
Add 20% for factory box.

MODEL 500 POWERMATIC - BB/.175 cal., CO_2, one Powerlet, semi-auto fifty-shot, 350 FPS. Mfg. 1970-79.

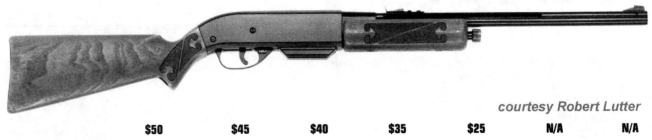

courtesy Robert Lutter

	100%	95%	90%	80%	60%	40%	20%
	$50	$45	$40	$35	$25	N/A	N/A

Add 10% for factory box.

MODEL 622 PELL-CLIP REPEATER - .22 cal., CO_2, one Powerlet, slide action forearm, removable rotating six-shot clip, 450 FPS. Mfg. 1971-78.

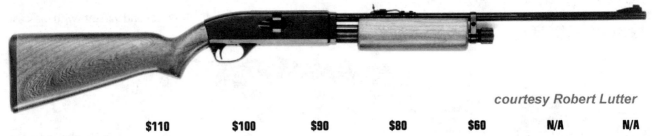

courtesy Robert Lutter

	100%	95%	90%	80%	60%	40%	20%
	$110	$100	$90	$80	$60	N/A	N/A

Add 20% for factory box.
Add 100% for gas tube extending well forward of muzzle.

MODEL 664X - BB/.175 cal. eighteen-shot mag. (plus 200 round reservoir) or .177 cal. five-shot mag. pellet single shot, swinging forearm pump pneumatic, bolt action, 680 FPS (BB), 645 FPS (pellet), 20.5 in. rifled steel barrel, black finish, brown checkered synthetic stock and forearm, fiberoptic front and adj. rear sights, four-power scope (M-0410) included, 2.9 lbs. Disc. 2004.

	100%	95%	90%	80%	60%	40%	20%
	$50	$40	$30	$20	$15	N/A	N/A

Last MSR was $60.

✳ *Model 664GT* - similar to Model 664X, except has black stock and forearm and gold accents. Mfg. 1997-2003.

	100%	95%	90%	80%	60%	40%	20%
	$65	$50	$40	$30	$25	N/A	N/A

✳ *Model 664SB* - similar to Model 664X, except has silver barrel and silver scope. Mfg. 1994-present.

MSR	$75	95%	90%	80%	60%	40%	20%
	$65	$45	$35	$25	$20	N/A	N/A

MODEL RM650 BB SCOUT - .177 cal., LA, SP, SS, smooth bore steel barrel, 300 FPS, black finish, checkered hardwood stock and forearm, 2.8 lbs. Mfg. 2002-03.

	100%	95%	90%	80%	60%	40%	20%
	$38	$30	$25	$20	$15	N/A	N/A

GRADING	100%	95%	90%	80%	60%	40%	20%

MODEL 700 - .22 cal., CO_2, one Powerlet, SS, rotary tap loading. Mfg. 1967-71.

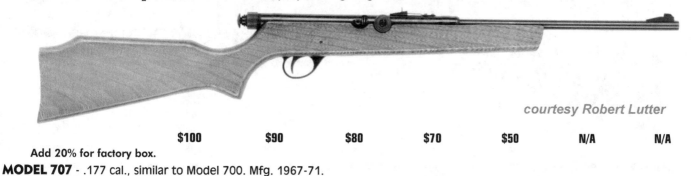

courtesy Robert Lutter

| | $100 | $90 | $80 | $70 | $50 | N/A | N/A |

Add 20% for factory box.

MODEL 707 - .177 cal., similar to Model 700. Mfg. 1967-71.

| | $100 | $90 | $80 | $70 | $50 | N/A | N/A |

Add 20% for factory box.

MODEL 760 POWERMASTER - combination BB/.175 cal. repeater (180-shot gravity-fed magazine) and .177 cal. pellet SS, 10 pumps = 595 FPS (BB), BA. The first short-stroke pump pneumatic, developed in Canada as "Canadian Boy" from Model 130 pistol. Large number of variations; key variations listed. Canadian Boy: original 1964 version, continuous wood stock and forearm, mfg. 1964. First variant: wooden stock and forearm. Mfg. 1966-70. Second variant: styrene stock/forearm, scope mount grooves. Mfg. 1971-74. Third variant: self-cocking, styrene stock, wood forearm. Mfg. 1974-75. Fourth variant: ABS stock and forearm. Mfg. 1975-77. Fifth variant: manual cocking. Mfg. 1977-80. Sixth variant: plastic bolt. Mfg. 1980-83. Seventh variant: plastic receiver, welded sights. Mfg. 1983-91. Eighth variant: shortened barrel, pressed on sights. Mfg. began in 1991. Disc.

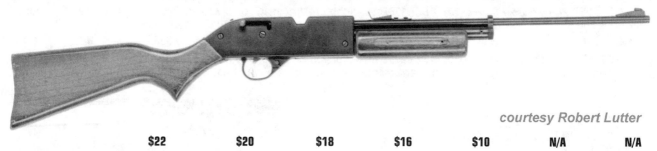

courtesy Robert Lutter

| | $22 | $20 | $18 | $16 | $10 | N/A | N/A |

Subtract 10% for smoothbore (prior to 1981).
Add $500+ for Canadian Boy.
Add 400% for first variant.
Add 25% for factory scope.
Add 25% for wood stock (except Canadian Boy and first variant).
Add 5% for factory box.

* **Model 760/20 (Model 760 20th Year Commemorative)** - BB/.175 cal. repeater or .177 cal. pellet single-shot pneumatic, similar to Model 760. Mfg. 1985.

courtesy Robert Lutter

| | $65 | $50 | $35 | N/A | N/A | N/A | N/A |

Variation: Model 760/20-999. Special presentation commemoratives; individually engraved name plates and wall plaques. Special order by Crosman sales rep for key buyers and senior staff. Designed as a wall-mounted item, generally not used. Will bring a premium.

GRADING	100%	95%	90%	80%	60%	40%	20%

✳ *Model 760 XL Powermaster* - BB/.175 cal. repeater or .177 cal., deluxe version of Model 760, brass-plated receiver, hooded front sight. Mfg. 1978-80.

courtesy Robert Lutter

	$25	$20	$16	N/A	N/A	N/A	N/A

✳ *Model 760AB Pumpmaster* - BB/.175 cal. repeater or .177 cal. SS pellet, pneumatic, similar to Model 760 with black stock and forearm. Mfg. began in 1997. Disc.

	$25	$20	$16	N/A	N/A	N/A	N/A

✳ *Model 760B Pumpmaster* - BB/.175 cal. eighteen-shot mag. or .177 cal. five-shot mag. pellet, multi-pump pneumatic, 17 in. smooth bore steel barrel, 600 FPS (BB), black finish, brown synthetic stock and forearm, fiberoptic front and adj. rear sights, 2.75 lbs. Mfg. 1997-present.

MSR $46	$41	$35	$30	$25	$20	N/A	N/A

✳ *Model 760BRD Pumpmaster* - BB/.175 cal. eighteen-shot mag. or .177 cal. five-shot mag. pellet, similar to Model 760B, except red dot sight included.

MSR $62	$55	$48	$40	$35	$25	N/A	N/A

✳ *Model 760SK Pumpmaster Starter Kit* - BB/.175 cal. eighteen-shot mag. or .177 cal. five-shot mag. pellet, Model 760SK kit includes 600 BBs, 250 .177 cal. pellets, red dot sight, shooting glasses and five NRA targets.

MSR $67	$60	$55	$48	$40	$35	N/A	N/A

MODEL 761 XL - BB/.175 cal. repeater or .177 cal., deluxe version of Model 760, brass-plated receiver, hooded front sight, wood stock. First variant: mfg. 1972-78. Second variant: manual cocking. Mfg. 1978-81.

courtesy Robert Lutter

	$30	$25	$20	N/A	N/A	N/A	N/A

MODEL 764SB - BB/.175 cal. repeater or .177 cal. SS pellet, pneumatic, similar to Model 760B with silver BBL, black stock and forearm, and scope. Mfg. 1994-present.

MSR $61	$55	$45	$35	$25	$20	N/A	N/A

MODEL 766 AMERICAN CLASSIC - BB/.175 cal. repeater or .177 cal. pellet SS, multi-stroke pump pneumatic, 10 pumps = 710 FPS (BB), modeled after Remington autoloader firearm. First variant: tapered plastic BBL housing. Mfg. 1975-81. Second variant: tapered steel barrel housing. Mfg. 1977-83. Third variant: straight steel barrel housing. Mfg. 1981-82.

courtesy Robert Lutter

	$60	$50	$45	$40	$30	N/A	N/A

Add 10% for first variant.
Add 15% for second variant.
Add 10% for original box.
Add 50% for wood stock (pre-1983).

MODEL 781 - BB/.175 cal. repeater or .177 cal. pellet SS, single pump pneumatic, smoothbore, 450 FPS (BB), four-shot clip, 195 round reservoir, 2.9 lbs. Mfg. 1983-95.

	$40	$35	$32	$30	$20	N/A	N/A

GRADING	100%	95%	90%	80%	60%	40%	20%

✳ *Model 781AK Action Kit* - kit includes Model 7781 rifle, adj. 4 x 15 mm scope, 250-count .177 cal. pellets, 350 BBs, five NRA targets, and shooting glasses. New 2002.

MSR	$67	$60	$50	$40	$30	$20	N/A	N/A

✳ *Model 7781* - similar to Model 781, except has black stock and forearm. New 2002.

MSR	$51	$45	$40	$30	$25	$20	N/A	N/A

MODEL 782 BLACK DIAMOND - BB/.175 cal. repeater or .177 cal. pellet SS, CO_2, one Powerlet, five-shot clip. Mfg. began in 1990. Disc.

	$25	$20	$15	$10	$5	N/A	N/A

✳ *Model 782B* - .177 cal., CO_2, similar to Model 782 Black Diamond. Disc. 2002.

	$55	$45	$35	$25	$20	N/A	N/A

MODEL 788 BB SCOUT - BB/.175 cal., multi-pump pneumatic, gravity-fed twenty-shot mag., 2.5 lbs., 500 FPS (BB). First variant: short pump stroke. Mfg. 1978-79. Second variant: long pump stroke. Mfg. 1979-90.

courtesyRobert Lutter

	$45	$40	$35	$30	$20	N/A	N/A

Add 20% for short stroke variant.
Add 10% for factory box.

✳ *Model Black Fire* - variation of Model 788, black stock/forearm. Mfg. 1996-97.

	$50	$45	$40	$35	$30	N/A	N/A

Add 20% for short stroke variant.
Add 10% for factory box.

MODEL 790 OUTBACKER - BB/.175 cal. repeater or .177 cal. pellet, single pump pneumatic, five-shot pellet clip, plastic stock with hidden canteen, 450 FPS (BB), 2.8 lbs. Mfg. 1990-91.

	$60	$55	$50	$45	$30	N/A	N/A

Subtract 25% for missing canteen.

MODEL 795 SPRINGMASTER - .177 cal., BBC, SP, SS, 500 FPS, rifled steel barrel, hooded front adj. rear sights, black finish, checkered synthetic stock. Mfg. 1995-1997.

	$75	$65	$55	$45	$35	N/A	N/A

✳ *Model 795 Springmaster* - .177 cal., similar to Model 795 Springmaster, except 600 FPS. New 1997.

MSR	$73	$65	$57	$50	$43	$35	N/A	N/A

MODEL 1077 REPEATAIR - .177 cal., CO_2, one Powerlet, twelve-shot mag. repeater, 20.4 in. rifled steel barrel, 625 FPS, black finish, checkered black synthetic stock, fiberoptic front and adj. rear sights, 3.7 lbs. New 1994.

MSR	$79	$70	$60	$55	$50	$45	N/A	N/A

✳ *Model 1077CA Constant Air* - similar to Model 1077 RepeatAir, except bulk fill tank kit. Mfg. 1995.

	$180	$155	$130	$105	$75	N/A	N/A

✳ *Model 1077LB RepeatAir* - similar to Model 1077 RepeatAir, except black laminated hardwood stock. Mfg. 2002-03.

	$85	$75	$65	$55	$45	N/A	N/A

✳ *Model 1077LG RepeatAir* - similar to Model 1077 RepeatAir, except green laminated hardwood stock. Mfg. 2002-03.

	$85	$75	$65	$55	$45	N/A	N/A

✳ *Model 1077RD RepeatAir* - similar to Model 1077 RepeatAir, except red dot sight included. Disc. 2004.

	$85	$75	$65	$55	$45	N/A	N/A

Last MSR was $91.

✳ *Model 1077SB RepeatAir* - similar to Model 1077 RepeatAir, except has silver barrel. Mfg. 1995.

	$75	$65	$55	$45	$35	N/A	N/A

✳ *Model 1077W RepeatAir* - similar to Model 1077 RepeatAir, except has walnut stock. Mfg. 1997-present.

MSR	$123	$110	$95	$85	$75	$65	N/A	N/A

✳ *Model 1077KT RepeatAir Action Kit* - .177 cal., CO_2, kit includes Model 1077 rifle, large-lens red dot sight, extra removable mag., three twelve-shot rotary clips, 250-count .177 cal. pellets, three Powerlet CO_2 cartridges, five NRA targets, and shooting glasses.

MSR	$97	$90	$80	$70	$60	$50	N/A	N/A

✳ *Model AS1077T AirSource* - .177 cal., CO_2, 88g AirSource cylinder, twelve-shot rotary mag. repeater, 20.4 in. rifled steel barrel, 625 FPS, black finish, checkered black synthetic stock, fiberoptic front and adj. rear sights, 3.7 lbs. New 2004.

MSR	$113	$100	$90	$80	$70	$60	N/A	N/A

Upgrade kit (Model AS1077AD approx. $40) available for Model 1077 RepeatAir rifles manufactured since May 1999.

GRADING	100%	95%	90%	80%	60%	40%	20%

MODEL 1200 NIGHTSTALKER - .177 cal., CO_2, semi-auto blowback action, twelve-shot mag., 88 gram AirSource cylinder, 16.7 in. rifled steel BBL, 525 FPS, ergonomic Bullpup configuration with PG, black polymer construction, 30.5 in. OAL, 4.1 lbs. New 2005.

As this edition went to press, retail pricing had yet to be established.

Model NS1204A comes with red dot sight, flashlight, bipod and two weaver rail mounts for the Model NS1200.

MODEL 1388 - BB/.175 cal. or .177 cal. pellet, pneumatic, SS, BA, 10.25 in. rifled barrel, 560 FPS, adj. rear sight, plastic breech, Model 1377 pistol with shoulder stock. Mfg. 1982-88.

	$85	$70	$60	$50	$45	N/A	N/A

MODEL 1389 BACKPACKER - .177 cal., multi-pump pneumatic, SS, detachable stock, green, 10 pumps = 560 FPS, 3.3 lbs. Mfg. 1989-98.

	$65	$60	$50	$45	$30	N/A	N/A

MODEL 1400 PUMPMASTER - .22 cal., multi-pump pneumatic, SS, 10 pumps = 580 FPS, 5.5 lbs., wood stock/forearm. Highly desired by shooters who have them upgraded and converted for current field use. As with certain other Crosman models sought by shooters, values are determined more by desirability of certain versions for shooting and conversion than rarity. It is increasingly difficult for collectors to locate completely original specimens. First variant: has breech cover. Mfg. 1968-72. Second variant: has bolt handle. Mfg. 1972-73. Third variant: has bolt handle, slim-line stock. Mfg. 1973-78.

courtesy Robert Lutter

	$100	$90	$80	$60	$50	N/A	N/A

Add 30% for second and third variants.

Add 10% for factory box.

MODEL 1760 - .177 cal., CO_2, one Powerlet, BA, SA, one-piece walnut stock, 24 in. rifled steel barrel, black finish, hardwood stock, adj. rear sight, 600 FPS, 4.8 lbs. Mfg. 1999-present.

MSR $92	$80	$65	$50	$40	$35	N/A	N/A

MODEL 1894 - .177 cal., CO_2, LA, two 12 gram Powerlets located in the buttstock, eight-shot rotary mag., 15 (carbine) or 18.9 (rifle) in. barrel, 610 FPS, blue finish, hardwood stock with plastic butt plate and forearm, hooded front and adj. rear sights, crossbolt safety, 7.5 lbs (rifle). Disc. 2002.

	$250	$215	$175	$145	$100	N/A	N/A

MODEL 1924 - See Second Model and notes about the designation of 1924 Model.

MODEL 2000 CHALLENGER - .177 cal., CO_2, BA, SS, 485 FPS, adj. rear target sight, hooded front sight with removable aperture, matte or gloss black, blue, dark blue, red, silver, or grey composite stock with adj. cheekpiece and buttplate, 36.25 in. OAL, 7 lbs. Mfg. 2000-01.

	$300	$225	$190	$155	$100	N/A	N/A

Add $50 for gloss black, blue, dark blue, red, silver, or grey stock.

✳ *Model CH2000 Challenger* - .177 cal., CO_2, BA, SS, 485 FPS, rifled barrel, adj. rear target sight, hooded front sight with removable aperture, matte black finish, black composite stock with adj. cheekpiece and buttplate, 36.25 in. OAL, 6.95 lbs. New 2001.

MSR $430	$275	$235	$190	$155	$100	N/A	N/A

MODEL 2100 CLASSIC - BB/.175 cal. repeater or .177 cal. pellet SS, swinging forearm multi-stroke pump pneumatic, 10 pumps = 795 FPS (BB), 4.8 lbs. Similar to Model 766. Mfg. began in 1983. Disc.

courtesy Robert Lutter

	$65	$60	$50	$45	$30	N/A	N/A

✳ *Model 2100SB* - similar to Model 2100 Classic, except has zinc plated barrel. Mfg. 1995-96.

	$70	$65	$60	$50	$45	N/A	N/A

✳ *Model 2100W* - similar to Model 2100 Classic, except has walnut stock and forearm. Mfg. 1997-2003.

	$110	$90	$70	$65	$60	N/A	N/A

GRADING	100%	95%	90%	80%	60%	40%	20%

✳ **Model 2100B** - similar to Model 2100 Classic, except has fiberoptic front sight. Mfg. 1997-present.

	100%	95%	90%	80%	60%	40%	20%
MSR $76	$65	$55	$45	$35	$25	N/A	N/A

MODEL 2104GT - similar to Model 2100, except has gold accents and scope. Mfg. 1997-2003.

	$75	$60	$50	$40	$30	N/A	N/A

MODEL 2104X - similar to Model 2100, except with 4 x 15 mm scope. New 2002.

MSR $85	$75	$65	$55	$45	$35	N/A	N/A

MODEL 2175W 75TH ANNIVERSARY COMMEMORATIVE - .177 cal., handcrafted American walnut stock and forearm with limited edition antique brass 75th anniversary medallion inlaid. Mfg 1998 only.

	$125	$110	$90	N/A	N/A	N/A	N/A

MODEL 2200 MAGNUM - .22 cal., pneumatic, SS, similar to Model 2100, adj. rear sight 4.8 lbs. First variant: with chrome-plated receiver. Mfg. 1978-82. Second variant: with black receiver with silkscreen and straight steel barrel housing with plastic sight sleeve. Mfg. 1982-83. Third variant: with brown stock and forearm. Mfg.1983-89.

courtesy Robert Lutter

	$65	$55	$45	$35	$30	N/A	N/A

Add 25% for first variant.
Add 10% for second variant.

✳ **Model 2200B** - .22 cal., similar to Model 2200 Magnum, except straight barrel housing. Mfg. 1989-present.

MSR $84	$70	$60	$50	$45	$30	N/A	N/A

✳ **Model 2200W** - similar to Model 2200 Magnum, except has walnut stock and forearm. Mfg. 1997-2003.

	$105	$85	$65	$60	$50	N/A	N/A

MODEL 2250B - .22 cal., CO_2, one Powerlet, BA, SS, synthetic detachable skeleton stock, black finish, 14.6 in. rifled steel barrel, fiberoptic front and adj. rear sights, 4X scope, 550 FPS, 3.3 lbs. Mfg. 1998-present.

MSR $93	$80	$70	$60	$50	$40	N/A	N/A

✳ **Model AS2250XT AirSource** - .22 cal., CO_2, 88g AirSource cylinder, BA, SS, synthetic detachable skeleton stock, black finish, 14.6 in. rifled steel barrel, fiber optic front and adj. rear sights, 4X32 mm scope, 550 FPS, 5.12 lbs. New 2004.

MSR $158	$145	$125	$100	$80	$65	N/A	N/A

MODEL 2260 - .22 cal., CO_2, one Powerlet, BA, SS, one-piece walnut stock, 24 in. rifled steel barrel, black finish, hardwood stock, adj. rear sight, 600 FPS, 4.8 lbs. New 1999.

MSR $92	$80	$70	$60	$50	$40	N/A	N/A

MODEL 2264X - .22 cal., similar to Model 2260, except 4x32mm scope (M-4032) included. Mfg. 1999-2002.

	$125	$100	$85	$70	$50	N/A	N/A

MODEL 2275W 75TH ANNIVERSARY COMMEMORATIVE - .22 cal., pneumatic pump-up, 595 FPS, handcrafted American walnut stock and forearm. Mfg 1998 only.

	$125	$110	$90	N/A	N/A	N/A	N/A

MODEL 2289G BACKPACKER - .22 cal., swinging forearm pump pneumatic, BA, SS, detachable synthetic skeleton stock and forearm, 14.6 in. rifled steel barrel, black finish, fiberoptic front and adj. rear sights, 525 FPS, 2.9 lbs Mfg. 1998-2002.

	$60	$50	$40	$30	$20	N/A	N/A

MODEL 2576 (MODEL 760 25th YEAR COMMEMORATIVE) - BB/.175 cal., repeater or .177 cal. limited edition, similar to Model 760 original styling, except "Tootsie Roll" pump handle, etc. Mfg. 1991.

	$45	$40	$30	$20	$15	N/A	N/A

MODEL 3100 - .177 cal., BBC, SP, SS, 600 FPS, one-piece hardwood stock, 6 lbs. (imported, Bascaran, Spain), mfg. 1987-90.

	$80	$75	$70	$65	$45	N/A	N/A

MODEL 3500 SLIDEMASTER - BB/.175 cal., push-barrel cocking, SP, twenty-two shot repeater, one-piece hardwood stock, updated version of Model V350. Mfg. 1970-73.

	$120	$110	$100	$95	$75	N/A	N/A

Add 30% for factory box.

GRADING	100%	95%	90%	80%	60%	40%	20%

MODEL 6100 (DIANAWERK MODEL 45) - .177 cal., BBC, SP, 830 FPS, 20.50 in. barrel, 8.4 lbs. Mfg. 1982-88.

courtesy Robert Lutter

	$195	$160	$130	$95	$75	N/A	N/A

Last MSR was $235.

Basically, a Diana Model 45 with a modified Diana Model 35 stock.

MODEL 6300 (ANSCHÜTZ MODEL 333) - .177 cal., BBC, SP, 700 FPS, 18.50 in. barrel, 6.8 lbs. Mfg. 1986-89.

courtesy Robert Lutter

	$125	$110	$95	$80	$60	N/A	N/A

Last MSR was $175.

MODEL 6500 (ANSCHÜTZ MODEL 335) - .177 cal., BBC, SP, 700 FPS, 18.50 in. barrel, 7.7 lbs. Mfg. 1986-88.

courtesy Robert Lutter

	$180	$160	$140	$100	$75	N/A	N/A

Last MSR was $200.

The three German air rifles (M-6100, M-6300, and M6500) represented Crosman's 1980s "Challenger Line" excursion into adult precision air rifles. Fletcher's 1998 book notes that this line "caught between RWS on the low end and Beeman on the high end, never really had a chance."

MODEL 760/20-999 - see Model 760.

MODEL AIR-17 - BB/.175 cal. repeater or .177 cal., swinging forearm pump pneumatic, five-shot pellet clip, twenty-one-round BB magazine, 195 round BB reservoir, replica of Colt AR-15 sporting high-power rifle. Mfg. 1985-90.

courtesy Robert Lutter

	$150	$125	$100	$85	$65	N/A	N/A

MODEL BLACK FIRE - similar to Model 788, except has black stock and forearm. Mfg. 1996-97.

	$50	$40	$30	$25	$20	N/A	N/A

MODEL BLACK LIGHTNING - BB/.175 cal., single stroke pump pneumatic, twenty-shot magazine, 300 round reservoir, replica of Remington Model 1187 shotgun, 350 FPS, 150 round BB container shaped like shotgun shell. Mfg. began in 1997. Disc.

	$25	$20	$18	$15	$12	N/A	N/A

Subtract 10% for missing shotgun style BB container.

MODEL BLACK SERPENT - similar to Model 781, except has black stock and forearm. Mfg. 1996-2002.

	$45	$40	$30	$25	$20	N/A	N/A

GRADING	100%	95%	90%	80%	60%	40%	20%

MODEL C1K77 QUEST 1000 - .177 cal., BBC, SP, SS, rifled steel (scope stop) barrel, blue finish, 1000 FPS, hardwood Monte Carlo style stock, rubber butt pad, hooded front and adj. rear fiberoptic sights, OAL 45 in., 6 lbs. New. 2004.

	100%	95%	90%	80%	60%	40%	20%
MSR $113	$90	$75	$60	$50	N/A	N/A	N/A

✳ **Model C1K77X Quest 1000** - .177 cal., similar to Model C1K77, except with 4x32 mm fully adj. scope. New 2004.

	100%	95%	90%	80%	60%	40%	20%
MSR $141	$115	$95	$80	$65	N/A	N/A	N/A

MODEL C5M77 QUEST - .177 cal., BBC, SP, SS, rifled steel (scope stop) barrel, blue finish, 495 FPS, hardwood Monte Carlo style stock, rubber butt pad, hooded front and adj. rear fiberoptic sights, OAL 41.5 in., 5.5 lbs. New. 2005.

	100%	95%	90%	80%	60%	40%	20%
MSR $113	$90	$75	$60	$50	N/A	N/A	N/A

MODEL M-1 CARBINE - BB/.175 cal., push-barrel, SP, smoothbore, twenty-two-shot gravity-fed magazine, 180 round reservoir, basically a Model 3500 styled as replica of US M1 .30 cal. carbine. First variant: wood stock, mfg. 1966-67. Second variant: plastic stock. Mfg. 1968-76.

courtesy Robert Lutter

	100%	95%	90%	80%	60%	40%	20%
	$150	$125	$100	$85	$65	N/A	N/A

Add 60% for wood stock.

MODEL RM177 - .177 cal., BBC, SP, SS, rifled steel barrel, blue finish, 825 FPS, checkered hardwood English style stock, rubber butt pad, sling mounts, hooded front and adj. peep rear sights, 7.1 lbs. Mfg. 2002.

	100%	95%	90%	80%	60%	40%	20%
	$110	$90	$75	$60	$45	N/A	N/A

✳ **Model RM177** - .177 cal., similar to Model RM177, except 4x32 (M-4032) scope included. Mfg. 2002.

	100%	95%	90%	80%	60%	40%	20%
	$125	$95	$80	$65	$50	N/A	N/A

MODEL RM277 - .177 cal., BBC, SP, SS, rifled steel barrel, blue finish, 825 FPS, hardwood Monte carlo style stock, rubber butt pad, hooded front and adj. rear sights, 7.1 lbs. Mfg. 2002-03.

	100%	95%	90%	80%	60%	40%	20%
	$110	$90	$75	$60	$45	N/A	N/A

✳ **Model RM277X** - .177 cal., similar to Model RM177, except 4x32 (M-4032) scope included. New 2002-03.

	100%	95%	90%	80%	60%	40%	20%
	$125	$95	$80	$65	$50	N/A	N/A

MODEL RM422 - .22 cal., BBC, SP, SS, rifled steel barrel, blue finish, 825 FPS, hardwood Monte Carlo style stock, rubber butt pad, hooded front and adj. rear sights, 7.1 lbs. Mfg. 2003-04.

	100%	95%	90%	80%	60%	40%	20%
MSR $140	$115	$95	$75	$60	$45	N/A	N/A

MODEL RM522 - .22 cal., BBC, SP, SS, rifled steel barrel, blue finish, 825 FPS, hardwood Monte Carlo style stock, rubber butt pad, hooded front and adj. rear sights, 7.9 lbs. Mfg. 2002-03.

	100%	95%	90%	80%	60%	40%	20%
	$150	$120	$90	$75	$60	N/A	N/A

MODEL RM577 - .177 cal., BBC, SP, SS, rifled steel barrel, blue finish, 1000 FPS, hardwood Monte Carlo style stock, rubber butt pad, hooded front and adj. rear sights, 7.9 lbs. Mfg. 2002-03.

	100%	95%	90%	80%	60%	40%	20%
	$150	$120	$90	$75	$60	N/A	N/A

✳ **Model RM577X** - .177 cal., similar to Model RM177, except 4x32 (M-4032) scope included. Mfg. 2002-03.

	100%	95%	90%	80%	60%	40%	20%
	$175	$150	$120	$90	$75	N/A	N/A

MODEL RM677 - .177 cal., BBC, SP, SS, rifled steel barrel, blue finish, 1000 FPS, checkered hardwood thumbhole stock, rubber butt pad, hooded front and adj. rear peep sights, 7.5 lbs. Mfg. 2002.

	100%	95%	90%	80%	60%	40%	20%
	$185	$165	$145	$120	$90	N/A	N/A

MODEL RM877 - .177 cal., BBC, SP, SS, rifled steel barrel, blue finish, 1100 FPS, checkered hardwood Monte Carlo style stock, rubber butt pad, hooded front and adj. rear peep sights, 7.5 lbs. Mfg. 2002.

	100%	95%	90%	80%	60%	40%	20%
	$225	$185	$165	$145	$120	N/A	N/A

MODEL V350 - BB/.175 cal., push-barrel, SP, hardwood stock, variation of Quackenbush Model 7. Mfg. 1961-69.

courtesy Robert Lutter

	100%	95%	90%	80%	60%	40%	20%
	$65	$60	$50	$45	$30	N/A	N/A

Add 20% for factory box.
Add 200% for factory gold-plated version.

GRADING	100%	95%	90%	80%	60%	40%	20%

SHOTGUN

MODEL 1100 TRAPMASTER - .380 bore, CO_2, two Powerlets, SS. Mfg.1968-1971.

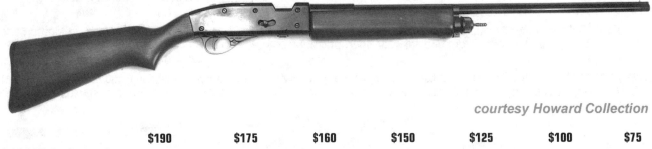

courtesy Howard Collection

$190	$175	$160	$150	$125	$100	$75

Add 20% for factory box.
Add 75% for complete trap set (trap, loading outfit, cases, etc.).
Add 200% for factory gold-plated version.
Add 75%-200% for high quality conversion to slug firing rifles.

CUB

For information on Cub airguns, see Milbro in the "M" section and Langenhan in the "L" section.

CYCLOID/RAPID

Previous trade names previously manufactured by Cycloid Cycle Co. and Rapid Rifle Co., Grand Rapids, MI circa 1889-1900.

The Cycloid and Rapid BB guns are all metal and completely nickel plated. Any boy discovering one of these spectacular and most unusual air rifles under the Christmas tree surely would not be able resist immediately running out with it to show the entire neighborhood! There has been considerable confusion about the maker. Dunathan, in the classic *American BB Gun* book, indicates that A.K. Wheeler founded the Rapid Rifle Company in Grand Rapids, MI in 1898 to produce some version of these air rifles. He reports that they were known under the names Cycloid, Cyclone, and New Rapid. However, at least two versions are known. One version, almost surely the earliest, has a cast iron receiver with cast script letters reading "Cycloid" on the left side and "Cycloid Cycle Co., Grand Rapids, Michigan" on the right. A more streamlined, simplified form, all sheet metal, is stamped, in simple block capitals, as the RAPID made by the RAPID RIFLE CO., GRAND RAPIDS, MICH. USA. It would appear that manufacture began under the name Cycloid as made by the Cycloid Cycle Co. and soon terminated under the name RAPID as made by the Rapid Rifle Co. Perhaps no specimens of the gun are known to be marked Cyclone and there doesn't seem to be any justification for the name "New" Rapid. Dunathan reports that the strange design was invented by Frank Simonds, Chauncey Fisher, and Hugh Ross, and that the company failed before the patent was issued in December 1901.

Aside from the all-metal construction, the most conspicuously strange aspect of the gun's design is an extremely long cocking lever, terminating in a Winchester-style cocking loop *behind* the base of the metal pistol grip. Internally, instead of the mainspring being coiled around or within the piston unit there is a rather long metal piston completely ahead of the forward end of the coiled mainspring. Two long, chain-like links attached to the hooked forward end of the exceptionally long cocking lever pull back the cocking assembly in a manner similar to a break action BB gun. The poor efficiency and high cost of such a design, in the face of considerable emerging competition, probably fated the design to a life of only a year or two, making these guns among the rarest, and most interesting, of American production airguns.

RIFLES

CYCLOID - .180/BB shot cal., muzzle-loading SS, SP, cast iron receiver and cocking lever, balance of parts sheet metal, nickel plated finish, cocking lever pivoted behind the trigger, with a Winchester-style hand loop behind the base of the pistol grip, "Cycloid" is cast in script on LHS of receiver, and "Cycloid Cycle Co, GRAND RAPIDS, MICH. PATD." is cast on RHS of receiver. 31.7 in. OAL, 2.7 lbs. Mfg. circa 1898.

courtesy Beeman Collection

N/A	N/A	$1,800	$1,500	$1,250	$1,000	$900

GRADING	100%	95%	90%	80%	60%	40%	20%

RAPID - .180/BB shot cal., muzzle-loading SS, SP, cast iron receiver and cocking lever, balance of parts sheet metal, nickel plated finish, cocking lever, pivoted behind the trigger, with a Winchester-style hand loop behind the base of the pistol grip, stamped in a circular logo on side of receiver "RAPID RIFLE CO. LTD. RAPID. PAT. APP. FOR, GRAND RAPIDS, MICH. USA", 31.5 in. OAL, 2.2 lbs. Mfg. circa 1900.

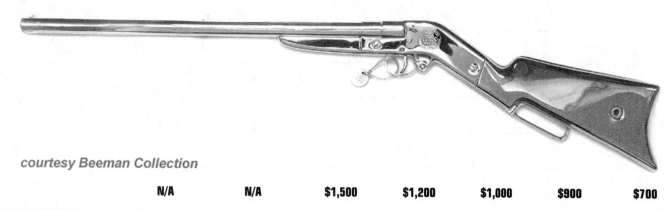

courtesy Beeman Collection

		N/A	N/A	$1,500	$1,200	$1,000	$900	$700

CYCLONE

For information on Cyclone, refer to the Cycloid/Rapid section above.

NOTES

D SECTION

DAISY MANUFACTURING CO., INC.

Current manufacturer and distributor located in Rogers, AR established circa 1895. Previously located in Plymouth, MI 1895-1958. Dealer and consumer direct sales.

Daisy is one of the oldest and largest airgun manufacturers in the world, and for more than a century has produced some of the most coveted air rifles of all time. Vintage Daisy air rifles from the late 1880s can command prices up to $10,000. Daisy is also the maker of the famous Daisy Model 25 and Red Ryder lines. For vast numbers of young boys in the rural America from the 1910s to the 1950s, and then in the developing suburbs of 1950 to about 1979, having an adult show you how to use a Daisy Model 25 slide action BB gun or a Red Ryder lever action BB gun was an integral part of growing up.

Clarence Hamilton, known to firearm collectors as the manufacturer of Hamilton .22 caliber boys' firearms, invented the First Model all-metal Daisy air rifle while working at the Plymouth Iron Windmill Company in Plymouth, MI. The Plymouth Iron Windmill Company (founded 1882) became the Daisy company in 1895 and continued operations in Plymouth until their move to their present location in Rogers, AR in 1958. The company has made a variety of products, but most of its production has been oriented towards BB guns and pellet rifles. The Model 25 slide action BB gun is often considered to be Daisy's most successful model, the model which was mainly responsible for Daisy's outstanding reputation. Made from 1914 to 1979, an amazing span of sixty-five years, the Model 25 is Daisy's longest running model. With approx. fifty-eight variants, total production of the Model 25 was over twenty million by 1979, more than all Ford Model T and Volkswagen "Bug" automobiles combined. The Model 25 probably also was the gun which gave Daisy the reputation of having the hardest hitting BB guns. With a bit of normal dieseling, many specimens could drive a steel BB out at speeds up to 450 FPS. Even that power was well exceeded by several lines of barrel cocking and side-lever air rifles, capable of velocities of 600 to 1000 FPS, which the company sold from the early 1960s to the present. And in the 1980s Daisy introduced a line of Daisy firearms – economical rifles using the potent (about thirty times the energy of a Daisy 880), but inexpensive, .22 long rifle ammunition.

Well over three decades ago, in 1972, Daisy started its own production of medium-powered pellet guns with the introduction of the "Powerline" Model 880. Contrasting quite completely with the one-cocking-stroke, lever and slide action BB guns, the Model 880 was their first swinging-arm, multiple-pump pneumatic pellet rifle. When fully pumped, these rifles can reach velocities of 680+ FPS. Although basically designed as accurate pellet rifles for field use, even sporting a scope sight or scope base, Daisy made it possible for users to shoot these new pellet rifles economically with BBs by providing them with amazing new rifling – dodecahedral flats in a helical pattern. This special rifling gave a stabilizing spin to even a steel projectile without cutting into the projectile or being injured by a hard steel projectile. The higher velocity of the Powerline guns gave the guns greater utility and greater effective accuracy in outdoor field shooting. The very name "Powerline" is a clear reference to high power, although these guns are by no means as strong as many other airguns now on the market.

While Daisy Powerline airguns were designed for use by shooters at least sixteen years old, Daisy has designated some of its BB guns, designed especially for youth over ten years old with adult supervision, as Youthline models. Mindful of the fact that about 350 FPS is generally accepted as the minimum impact velocity at which a steel BB can perforate the human skin, the Youthline models are all designed to fire below that velocity at the muzzle. In addition to general public sales, these guns have been featured for well over a half-century in Daisy's huge shooting safety and education programs and events (see the Daisy "Take Aim at Safety" program at www.daisy.com).

Daisy made limited excursions into the field of high level competition airguns with their introductions of the German Feinwerkbau match airguns in the early 1970s and the Spanish El Gamo match airguns in the early 1990s. Because they were designed as match guns, they produced muzzle speeds in the 550-700 FPS range. Neither line was very strongly marketed and both were dropped rather soon. Much greater success was achieved with match-type guns of their own manufacture: the Model 753 and 853 rifles and the Model 747 and 777 pistols. Daisy now is presenting further expansion of their "Olympic-level" models. They also are marketing the Winchester QP "Quick Power" break-barrel air rifles (made in Turkey), which have the high power produced by the single stroke of barrel cocking airguns, and a popular new lever action Winchester Model 1894 replica.

There simply is no "master" guide to Daisy airguns at the time of this book's printing. The pioneering work, Dunathan's 1971 book, *The American BB Gun*, has long been somewhat of a "bible" to American BB gun collectors, but it was only moderately accurate even when it came out. Jim Thomas made a bit of an update of Dunathan's book in 1989, but we still don't have a definitive guide. In 2001, Neal Punchard, a long-time Daisy collector, published "*Daisy Air Rifles & BB Guns* – The First 100 Years," a wonderfully illustrated general presentation of Daisy products over their first century of production (refer to review of Airgun Literature in the 2nd edition *Blue Book of Airguns* and the www.Beemans.net website).

Daisy airguns are a large and complicated collecting group; this preliminary attempt at a model and value listing cannot be complete. Continual input from collectors and researchers will be necessary for greater and greater completeness and accuracy in future editions. Please direct your inputs, no matter how small or large, to BlueBookEdit@Beemans.net or Blue Book Publications.

Unless otherwise noted, all Daisy airguns are spring piston designs in BB/.173 cal. The values quoted generally assume working condition. Many buyers will insist on a significant discount for lack of operation.

Commemorative Model Warning: Surplus parts remaining after production of various post-1952 commemorative model airguns have found their way into the market. These parts have sometimes been used to construct or "enhance" regular production models. Sometimes the only way to detect such fraudulent specimens is to ask the Daisy company to compare the stamped registration number against their production records.

For information on Daisy airguns manufactured for other trademarks, see the Store Brand Cross-Over List at the back of this text.

For more information and current pricing on both new and used Daisy firearms, please refer to the *Blue Book of Gun Values* by S.P. Fjestad (also available online).

GRADING	100%	95%	90%	80%	60%	40%	20%

CATEGORY INDEX

This Category Index is provided to help speed the process of locating a Daisy airgun in this text. The categories are in alphabetical order based on the configuration of the Daisy in question (i.e. pistol or rifle, type of action, cocking mechanism, or operating system).

PISTOLS: CO_2 POWERED
PISTOLS: PNEUMATIC POWERED
PISTOLS: SPRING POWERED
RIFLES: BREAK ACTION, PRE-1900 (CAST METAL FRAME)
RIFLES: BREAK ACTION, POST-1900
RIFLES: BREAK BARREL COCKING
RIFLES: LEVER ACTION
RIFLES: LEVER ACTION, BUZZ BARTON SERIES
RIFLES: LEVER ACTION, DEFENDER SERIES
RIFLES: LEVER ACTION, DEMOULIN INITIATION SERIES
RIFLES: LEVER ACTION, RED RYDER SERIES
RIFLES: PNEUMATIC & CO_2 POWERED
RIFLES: PUMP/SLIDE ACTION
RIFLES: VL SERIES

PISTOLS: CO POWERED

MODEL 008 - BB/.175 or .177 cal., CO_2, semi-auto pistol, eight-shot rotary mag., rifled steel barrel, fixed sights, black finish, molded black checkered grips, rotary hammer block safety, 480 FPS, 7.1 in. OAL, 1 lb. New 2005.

MSR	$79	$75	$65	$55	$45	N/A	N/A	N/A

MODEL 15XT - BB/.175 or .177 cal., CO_2, semi-auto pistol, fifteen-shot built-in mag., smoothbore steel barrel, fixed sights, black finish, molded black checkered grips, manual trigger block safety, 425 FPS, 1 lb. New 2002.

MSR	$48	$43	$34	$28	$22	$16	N/A	N/A

MODEL 15XTP - BB/.175 or 177 cal., similar to Model 15XT, except has Max Speed electronic point sight. New 2002.

MSR	$70	$60	$55	$45	$35	$25	N/A	N/A

MODEL 15XK - BB/.175 or .177 cal., CO_2, semi-auto pistol, Model 15XT pistol kit including shooting glasses, NRA competition targets, 350 BBs, 12-gram CO_2 cylinders. New 2002.

MSR	$54	$50	$45	$40	$30	$20	N/A	N/A

MODEL 41 - .22 cal., BA, replica of S&W Model 41, CO_2, single shot, chrome plated. Mfg. circa 1984.

	$150	$125	$90	$70	$50	N/A	N/A

MODEL 44 (970) - .177 cal., CO_2, replica of S&W 44 Magnum revolver, six-shot swing-out cylinder. Mfg. 1984-2001.

	$75	$60	$50	$40	$35	N/A	N/A

MODEL 45 - .177 cal., CO_2, semi-auto pistol, thirteen-shot drop-in mag., rifled steel barrel, fiberoptic fixed sights, black finish, molded black checkered grips, manual lever type trigger block safety, 400 FPS, 1.25 lb. Disc. 2002.

	$65	$55	$48	$40	$30	N/A	N/A

Last MSR was $70.

MODEL 45 GI - .177 cal., CO_2, thirteen-shot semi-auto. Colt 45 variant: replica of Colt 1911 .45 auto firearm. Smith & Wesson 45 variant: replica of Smith & Wesson .45 auto firearm. Mfg. 1992-97.

	$60	$50	$35	$30	$25	N/A	N/A

MODEL 45XT - .177 cal., CO_2, semi-auto pistol, thirteen-shot drop-in mag., rifled steel barrel, fiberoptic fixed sights, black finish, molded black checkered grips, manual lever-type trigger block safety, 400 FPS, 1.25 lb.

	$45	$40	$30	$25	$20	N/A	N/A

MODEL 91 - .177 cal., CO_2, SL, SS, wood grips, 10.25 in. barrel, 425 FPS, 2.4 lbs. Imported from Hungary 1991-97.

	$415	$360	$280	$225	$150	N/A	N/A

This was imported by Daisy as an entry level match target pistol.

MODEL 92 - .177 cal., semi-auto, styled like Beretta firearm pistol, ten-shot pellet feed. Mfg. in Japan, 1986-94.

	$75	$60	$50	$40	$30	N/A	N/A

MODEL 93 - BB/.175 or .177 cal., CO_2, semi-auto pistol, fifteen-shot drop-in mag., smooth bore steel barrel, fixed sights, black finish, molded brown checkered grips, manual trigger block safety, 400 FPS, 1.1 lb. Disc. 2004.

	$50	$40	$30	$25	$20	N/A	N/A

Last MSR was $60.

MODEL 100 - BB/.175 cal., CO_2, semi-auto pistol, 200-shot. Mfg. 1962.

	$80	$65	$50	$35	$20	N/A	N/A

GRADING	100%	95%	90%	80%	60%	40%	20%

MODEL 200 - BB/.175 cal., CO_2, semi-auto, 200-shot. Mfg. 1963-76.

courtesy Beeman Collection

	$45	$40	$35	$30	$25	N/A	N/A

MODEL 400GX (DESERT EAGLE) - BB/.175 or .177 cal., CO_2, semi-auto pistol, twenty-shot drop-in mag., smooth bore steel barrel, fixed sights, black (1994-97) or gold frame and black slide finish, molded black textured grips, manual lever safety, 420 FPS, 1.4 lb. Disc. 2002.

	$69	$55	$40	$30	$20	N/A	N/A

MODEL 454 - BB/.175 cal., CO_2, semi-auto, twenty-shot. Mfg. 1994-99.

	$45	$35	$30	$30	$25	N/A	N/A

MODEL 500 RAVEN - .177 cal. CO_2, SS, 500 FPS. Mfg. 1994-98.

	$80	$65	$55	$45	$35	N/A	N/A

MODEL 617X - .177 cal. pellet or .177 (4.5mm) BB , CO_2, semi-auto pistol, six-shot rotary magazine holds pellets and BBs simultaneously, rifled steel barrel, fiberoptic fixed sights, black finish, molded black checkered grips, rotary hammer block safety, 485 FPS (BB) 425 FPS (Pellet), 1.3 lb. New 2004.

MSR $74	$65	$50	$40	$30	$20	N/A	N/A

MODEL 622X - .22 cal., CO_2, semi-auto pistol, six-shot rotary mag., rifled steel barrel, fiberoptic fixed sights, black finish, molded black checkered grips, rotary hammer block safety, 400 FPS, 1.3 lb. Disc. 2004.

	$75	$65	$50	$40	$30	N/A	N/A

Last MSR was $80.

MODEL 645 - .177 cal., CO_2, semi-auto pistol, thirteen-shot drop-in mag., rifled steel barrel, fiberoptic fixed sights, black and nickel finish, molded black checkered grips, manual trigger block safety. Colt 45 variant: styled like a Colt 1911 (1992-97). S&W 45 variant: styled like a S&W .45 auto, 400 FPS, 1.25 lb. Disc. 2004.

	$75	$65	$50	$40	$30	N/A	N/A

Last MSR was $80.

MODEL 693 - BB/.175 or .177 cal., CO_2, semi-auto pistol, fifteen-shot drop-in mag., smooth bore steel barrel, fixed sights, black and nickel finish, molded black checkered grips, manual trigger block safety, 400 FPS, 1.1 lb.

MSR $53	$50	$45	$40	$30	$20	N/A	N/A

MODEL 5693 - BB/.175 or .177 cal., CO_2, semi-auto pistol, kit including Model 693 pistol, shooting glasses, NRA competition targets, 350 BBs, 12-gram CO_2 cylinders, 1.1 lb.

MSR $70	$65	$60	$55	$40	$30	N/A	N/A

MODEL 780 - .22 cal., CO_2, BA, SS, replica of S&W Model 41 firearm, blue paint finish, Daisy´s continuation of S&W Model 78G CO_2 pistol. Mfg.1982-83.

	$125	$90	$60	$40	N/A	N/A	N/A

MODEL 790 - .177 cal., CO_2, BA, SS, replica of S&W Model 41 firearm, blue paint finish, Daisy´s continuation of S&W Model 79G CO_2 pistol. Mfg. 1982-88.

	$125	$90	$60	$40	N/A	N/A	N/A

GRADING	100%	95%	90%	80%	60%	40%	20%

MODEL 807 "CRITTER GITTER" - .38 cal., CO_2, BA, SS, 250 FPS, designed to shoot lead shot or patched ball with open ended cylinder as a cartridge (made in Germany by Umarex for Daisy, but Daisy decided not to continue production), very few went into the U.S. market, and some were sold in Germany. No box produced for U.S. market, 12.2 in. OAL, 2.2 lbs. Mfg. 1988 only.

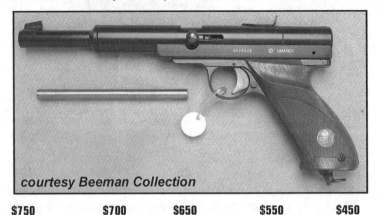

courtesy Beeman Collection

	$750	$700	$650	$550	$450	$350	$325

Add 20% for German box.

MODEL 1200 - BB/.175 cal., CO_2, sixty-shot, plastic grips. Mfg. 1977-1989.

	$50	$35	$25	N/A	N/A	N/A	N/A

MODEL 1270 - .177 cal., CO_2, sixty-shot pump action repeater, molded polymer forend doubles as pump handle, molded black polymer grip, custom plated finish, 420 FPS, smooth bore steel barrel, adj. rear sight, cross bolt trigger block safety, 1.1 lbs. Disc. 2002.

	$40	$30	$20	$15	$10	N/A	N/A

MODEL 1500 - BB/.175 cal., CO_2, similar to Model 1200, except chrome plated. Mfg. 1988 only.

	$35	$30	$25	N/A	N/A	N/A	N/A

MODEL 1700 - .177 cal, CO_2, replica of Glock semi-auto firearm, uses Model 1200 valving. Mfg. 1991-96.

courtesy Beeman Collection

	$35	$30	$25	N/A	N/A	N/A	N/A

MODEL 2003 - .177 cal., CO_2, thirty-five-shot, helical clip, semi-automatic, plastic grips. Mfg. 1995-2001. Can be converted to full auto, and therefore dropped by Daisy.

	$120	$100	$80	$60	N/A	N/A	N/A

PISTOLS: PNEUMATIC POWERED

MODEL 717 - .177 cal., side-lever cocking, single-stroke pneumatic, single shot, 360 FPS, rifled steel barrel, adj. rear sight, molded brown checkered grips with right-hand thumb rest, crossbolt trigger block safety, 2.25 lbs.

MSR $153	$140	$115	$95	$75	$55	N/A	N/A

MODEL 722 - .22 cal., similar to Model 717. Mfg. 1981-96.

	$100	$80	$60	N/A	N/A	N/A	N/A

MODEL 747 TARGET PISTOL - .177 cal., SL, SSP, SS, 360 FPS, Lothar Walther rifled barrel, adj. trigger, left- or right-hand grips available, 3.1 lbs. New 1987.

MSR $204	$175	$125	$95	$75	$65	N/A	N/A

MODEL 777 TARGET PISTOL - .177 cal., SL, SSP, SS, Lothar Walther rifled barrel, 360 FPS, wood target-style grips, 3.2 lbs. Mfg. 1990-97.

	$215	$175	$155	$130	$100	N/A	N/A

MODEL 1140 - .177 cal. pellet, SSP, SS. Mfg. 1995-2000.

	$60	$55	$50	$45	$40	N/A	N/A

GRADING	100%	95%	90%	80%	60%	40%	20%

PISTOLS: SPRING POWERED

MODEL 62 TARGET PISTOL - .177 cal., UL, SP, SS. Mfg. by Gamo in Spain 1975-78.

	$90	$75	$50	$35	$25	N/A	N/A

MODEL 118 DAISY TARGETEER - .118 cal., #6 lead or steel shot (Daisy #6 in two sizes of metal tube), SL, SP, indoor shooting gallery air pistol, all-metal construction, fixed rear sight 1937-41, adj. rear sight 1949-52, chrome-plated (1949-52), blue (1937-51) or painted (1937-52) finish. Mfg. 1937-52.

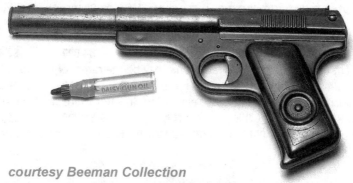

courtesy Beeman Collection

	$150	$125	$90	$70	$50	N/A	N/A

Add 35% for chrome plating on Targeteer pistols separate from shooting gallery sets.

Add 10% for non-adjustable rear sight.

✴ ***Number 320*** - variation: Targeteer shooting gallery set with spinning targets and molded plastic trap, nickel finish gun. Vintage shooting gallery set in good condition is uncommon. Mfg. 1949-52.

	$400	$250	$200	$150	$100	N/A	N/A

MODEL 177 BULLSEYE TARGET PISTOL - BB/.175 cal., target pistol, 150-shot, blue or painted finish, Plymouth or Rogers. Mfg. 1957-78.

	$75	$65	$50	$40	$35	N/A	N/A

Add 30% for Rogers factory box.

Add 50% for Plymouth factory box.

Add 50% for Family Fun Set with extra tube for shooting corks.

MODEL 179 PEACEMAKER REVOLVER - BB/.175 cal., SP, twelve-shot. Mfg. 1960-81.

	$110	$80	$65	$50	$35	N/A	N/A

✴ ***Model 179 Peacemaker (Solid Brass Variant)*** - BB/.175 cal., variation mfg. of solid cast brass, very heavy, painted gray. Serial numbers to 22 are known, 10.5 in. OAL, 2.7 lbs.

courtesy Beeman Collection

	$750	$650	$500	N/A	N/A	N/A	N/A

MODEL 180 PEACEMAKER REVOLVER - BB/.175 cal., similar to Model 179, except boxed set with revolver with holster. Mfg. 1960-81.

	$250	$200	$175	$150	$125	N/A	N/A

MODEL 188 - BB/.175 cal., UL, SP, twenty-four-shot. Mfg. 1979-89.

	$50	$40	$35	$30	$20	N/A	N/A

MODEL 288 - BB/.175 cal., UL, SP, twenty-four-shot. Mfg. 1991-2001.

	$25	$20	$15	N/A	N/A	N/A	N/A

MODEL 579 TEXAS RANGER - BB/.175 cal., Texas Rangers set of two matching guns similar to Model 197, each with grips imbedded with miniature Texas Rangers badges, barrels stamped "1823 - Texas Rangers - 1973", special box, booklet on Texas Ranger history. Mfg. 1973-74.

	$500	$400	$300	N/A	N/A	N/A	N/A

GRADING	100%	95%	90%	80%	60%	40%	20%

MODEL 5179 NRA COMMEMORATIVE - Mfg. 1971-72.

	100%	95%	90%	80%	60%	40%	20%
	$150	$125	$100	N/A	N/A	N/A	N/A

RIFLES: BREAK ACTION, PRE-1900 (CAST METAL FRAME)

This grouping includes the early Daisy cast metal lever and break action BB guns, mfg. 1888-1900.

1ST MODEL - large BB/.180 cal., single-shot, muzzle-loading brass tubing barrel and air chamber, cast iron or brass frame, wire skeleton stock without wood, nickel plated, post front sight, V-notch rear sight integral with top cocking lever. Production quantities were very low, but unknown (despite previous claims). Mfg. by Plymouth Iron Windmill Co. 1889-95. Dates on variants unknown.

❊ *Variant One* - cocking lever marked "Pat. Appl. For PIW", cast iron frame.

	100%	95%	90%	80%	60%	40%	20%
	N/A	N/A	N/A	$4,000	$2,800	$2,500	$2,000

❊ *Variant Two* - similar to variant one, but with brass frame. This may be the rarest of the Daisy First Models.

	N/A	N/A	N/A	$7,000	$6,000	$4,500	$4,000

❊ *Variant Three* - similar to variant two, brass frame with reinforcing rib where wire stock enters frame.

	N/A	N/A	N/A	$4,000	$2,800	$2500	$2,000

❊ *Variant Four* - cocking lever marked "DAISY PAT. AUG. 1889 PLYMOUTH, MICH.", cast brass frame, no verifiable information on production quantities or mfg. dates.

courtesy Beeman Collection

	N/A	N/A	N/A	$2,800	$2,500	$2,000	$1,800

❊ *Variant Five* - similar to variant four, but with much more prominent, more highly raised cast lettering.

	N/A	N/A	N/A	$2,800	$2,500	$2,000	$1,800

Warning on Daisy First Models: reportedly there are fake specimens of some of the rarest versions of early cast metal Daisy airguns. Sometimes this takes the form of fake cocking levers on legitimate specimens of more common models. Careful measurements may be necessary to detect such fraudulent arrangements. It may be best to consult with a trusted Daisy expert before purchasing some of the most valuable specimens.

Replicas: For collectors who cannot locate some of the rarest models or are not willing to spend the large amounts necessary to obtain them, there are some legitimate replicas available.

2ND MODEL - large BB/.180 cal., break-open design, SS, brass tubing barrel and air chamber, cast iron frame, wire skeleton stock, nickel-plated post front sight, V-notch rear sight integral with breech, left frame marked "Daisy Imp´d Pat´ May 6, 90", right frame marked "MFG. BY P.I.W. & CO. PLYMOUTH MICH." Quantities unknown, but far less than 1st Model. 31.5 in. OAL, 2.6 lbs. Mfg. by Plymouth Iron Windmill Co, 1890-91. Extremely rare.

courtesy Beeman Collection

	N/A	N/A	N/A	$4,500	$3,500	$3,000	$2,500

3RD MODEL - large BB/.180 cal., break open design, SS, brass tubing barrel and air chamber, cast iron frame, wire skeleton stock with or without wood insert, nickel plated, post front sight, V-notch rear sight, frame marked "Daisy Pat. May 6, 90, July 14, 91", 31.5 in. OAL, 2.3 lbs. Mfg. 1893-94. Rare.

❊ *Variant 1* - checkered frame, wire stock without wood insert, grip frame marked "NEW DAISY".

	N/A	N/A	N/A	$2,500	$2,000	$1,800	$1,500

❊ *Variant 2* - wire stock with wood insert, frame marked "NEW DAISY".

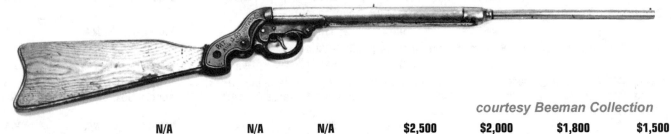

courtesy Beeman Collection

	N/A	N/A	N/A	$2,500	$2,000	$1,800	$1,500

GRADING	100%	95%	90%	80%	60%	40%	20%

❋ *Variant 3* - wire stock without wood insert, patent dates on left side of grip frame

	N/A	N/A	N/A	$2,500	$2,000	$1,800	$1,500

❋ *Variant 4* - wire stock with wood insert, patent dates on left side of grip frame.

	N/A	N/A	N/A	$2,500	$2,000	$1,800	$1,500

❋ *Variant 5 ("Model 96")* - marked "MODEL 96". Mfg. 1896.

	N/A	N/A	N/A	$2,000	$1,750	$1,500	$1,250

❋ *Variant 6* - marked "MODEL" only on right side of frame, marked "DAISY" on left side (possibly from modified Model 96 mold). Mfg. 1897.

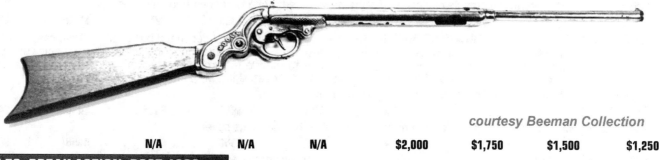

courtesy Beeman Collection

	N/A	N/A	N/A	$2,000	$1,750	$1,500	$1,250

RIFLES: BREAK ACTION, POST-1900

This grouping starts with the 20th Century models mfg. beginning circa 1898.

20TH CENTURY CAST IRON FRAME SINGLE SHOT
- BB/.180 cal., break action, SS, sheet metal barrel. Removable shot tube. Cast iron trigger, trigger guard, and frame (except as noted below), nickel finish, fixed sights, marked on the right side "20th CENTURY", on the left side marked "DAISY" between bullseyes. Slab-sided stocks. Stocks impressed on left side, "Daisy Mfg. Co., May 6, 90 July 14, 91". Mfg. 1898-1902.

❋ *First Variant* - wire stock without wood, checkered cast brass below barrel.

	N/A	N/A	$1,500	$1,000	$750	$500	$400

❋ *Second Variant* - wood stock, checkered cast brass below barrel.

	N/A	N/A	$500	$350	$250	$200	$150

❋ *Third Variant* - wire stock without wood, sheet metal wrap around base of barrel.

	N/A	N/A	$1,500	$1,000	$750	$500	$400

❋ *Fourth Variant* - wood stock, sheet metal wrap around base of barrel.

	N/A	N/A	$500	$350	$250	$200	$150

20TH CENTURY CAST IRON FRAME REPEATER
- BB/.180 cal., break action, forty-shot, marked on right side "REPEATER", left side marked "DAISY". Mfg. 1898-1902.

❋ *First Variant* - wood stock, checkered cast brass below barrel.

	N/A	N/A	$2,000	$1,700	$1,500	$1,200	$1,000

❋ *Second Variant* - wood stock, sheet metal wrap around base of barrel.

	N/A	N/A	$900	$700	$600	$500	$400

Note: 20th Century models with checkered cast brass below the barrel sometimes are referred to as "Fourth Model" Daisys.

20TH CENTURY SHEET METAL FRAME SINGLE SHOT
- BB/.180 cal., break action, sheet metal barrel and frame, cast iron trigger guard and trigger, removable shot tube, nickel finish, peep sight. Mfg.1903-10.

courtesy Beeman Collection

❋ *First Variant* - two-step body tube (forward end of body tube steps down to barrel diameter in two steps), right side of frame with letters "PATENTED" plus patent numbers in indented rectangle, left side of frame is marked "DAISY" in indented rectangle, cast iron spring anchor (plate inside lower edge of body tube - open action to view). Slab-sided stock.

	N/A	N/A	$300	$250	$200	$150	$125

❋ *Second Variant* - similar to First Variant, except printing on right side of frame changed to just patent dates, slab-sided stock, most common of Sheet Metal 20th Century air rifles.

	N/A	N/A	$225	$175	$150	$125	$110

GRADING	100%	95%	90%	80%	60%	40%	20%

✱ *Third Variant* - similar to second variant, except stock is oval in profile, two-step barrel.

	N/A	N/A	$300	$250	$200	$150	$125

✱ *Fourth Variant* - one-step body tube, cast iron spring anchor, long body tube (10.7 in.), 7 in. barrel.

	N/A	N/A	$300	$250	$200	$150	$125

✱ *Fifth Variant* - similar to fourth variant, except shorter body tube (10 in.), 7.4 in. barrel.

	N/A	N/A	$300	$250	$200	$150	$125

✱ *Sixth Variant* - similar to fourth variant (10.7 in. body tube, 7 in. barrel), except has sheet metal spring anchor.

	N/A	N/A	$300	$250	$200	$150	$125

✱ *Seventh Variant* - indented rectangle on both side of frame stamped "DAISY" between two bullseyes.

	N/A	N/A	$500	$350	$250	$200	$150

20TH CENTURY SHEET METAL FRAME REPEATER - BB/.180 cal., break action, sheet metal barrel and frame, cast iron trigger guard and trigger, shot tube and magazine tube remove together as a unit, magazine visible as small removable tube parallel under barrel housing from forward end of one-step body tube to muzzle (not really a repeater; unique forty-shot magazine must be moved to release each BB into firing position), nickel finish, peep sight. Mfg.1903-1910.

✱ *First Variant* - shot tube release is tiny latch behind front sight.

	N/A	N/A	$700	$600	$500	$450	$400

✱ *Second Variant* - shot tube release is a latch under the barrel with a magazine cover.

	N/A	N/A	$700	$600	$500	$450	$400

✱ *Third Variant* - shot tube release is a spring-loaded front sight which moves in an L-shaped slot to allow shot tube removal (Hough-style shot tube system).

courtesy Beeman Collection

	N/A	N/A	$750	$650	$550	$500	$450

✱ *Fourth Variant* - indented rectangle on both sides of the frame, stamped "DAISY" between two bullseyes.

	N/A	N/A	$800	$700	$600	$550	$500

MODEL A REPEATER - BB/.180 cal., break action, 350-shot loading port behind blade front sight, repeater, nickel. Frame is marked "DAISY" between bullseyes, address and patents are on barrel top. Mfg. 1908-14.

	N/A	N/A	$3,500	$3,000	$2,000	$1,500	$1,250

MODEL A SINGLE SHOT - BB/.180 cal., break action, SS, marked on barrel: "DAISY SINGLE SHOT MODEL A". Mfg. 1908-14.

	N/A	N/A	$3,500	$3,000	$2,000	$1,500	$1,250

MODEL C REPEATER - BB/.175 cal., break action, 350-shot. Mfg. 1910-14.

courtesy Beeman Collection

	N/A	N/A	$500	$300	$250	$200	$150

MODEL C SINGLE SHOT - BB/.175 cal., break action, SS, nickel finish. Mfg.1911-14.

	N/A	N/A	$500	$300	$250	$200	$150

MODEL 20 "LITTLE DAISY" - BB/.175 cal., break action, Daisy´s smallest BB rifle.

✱ *Variant 1 (Frameless Model)* - nickel finish, no metal around grip. Mfg. 1908-11.

	N/A	N/A	$1,500	$1,000	$750	$500	$400

✱ *Variant 2 (Grip Frame Model)* - nickel finish, metal around grip (full grip frame), regular style cast iron trigger in trigger guard. Mfg. 1912-15.

	N/A	N/A	$700	$500	$350	$300	$200

GRADING	100%	95%	90%	80%	60%	40%	20%

✳ *Variant 3 (Ring Trigger Model)* - nickel or blue finish, cast iron ring trigger without guard, full grip frame. Mfg. 1915-37.

courtesy Beeman Collection

| | N/A | N/A | $300 | $250 | $200 | $150 | $125 |

MODEL 21 SIDE BY SIDE - BB/.175 cal., break action, ribbed barrel divider, dark and light brown plastic stock. Mfg. 1968-72.

| | $1,000 | $750 | $600 | $450 | $350 | $300 | $250 |

Last MSR was approximately $25.

✳ *Sears Model 21 Sears Side by Side* - BB/.175 cal., break action, checkered barrel divider, wooden stock. Mfg. 1968 only.

| | $1,500 | $1,100 | $900 | $750 | $600 | $400 | $350 |

Approximately 48 walnut stock sets were mfg. by Reinhart Fajen, Inc.

MODEL 104 SIDE BY SIDE - BB/.175 cal., break action, 96-shot spring-fed repeater, sheet metal, side-by-side barrel tubes with Model 25-type shot tubes, left and right shot tubes marked L and R, dummy sidelocks, blue, walnut stock, stamped designs of game birds, dogs, and scrolls. Approx. 45,000 mfg. 1938-40.

courtesy Beeman Collection

| | $1,500 | $1,100 | $900 | $750 | $600 | $400 | $350 |

MODEL 106 - BB/.175 cal., break action, 500-shot, painted finish, Plymouth or Rogers address. Mfg. 1957-58.

| | $150 | $110 | $65 | $45 | N/A | N/A | N/A |

Add 20% for Plymouth address.

MODEL 181 - BB/.177 cal., break action, boxed set, special target with gun. Mfg. 1949 only.

| | $1,500 | $1,200 | $1,000 | $700 | $400 | N/A | N/A |

SENTINEL REPEATER - large BB/.180 cal., break action, 303-shot magazine. Sentinel models are not marked Daisy, but are shown in Daisy ads of the time. Mfg. 1900-02. Ref: AR4.

✳ *Variant 1* - 20th Century model frame ,marked "SENTINEL" on grip frame. Made for A.F. Chaffee.

| | N/A | N/A | $1,200 | $950 | $700 | $500 | $350 |

✳ *Variant 2* - marked "SENTINEL" on stock.

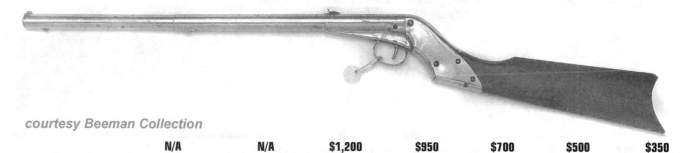

courtesy Beeman Collection

| | N/A | N/A | $1,200 | $950 | $700 | $500 | $350 |

SENTINEL SINGLE SHOT - large BB/.180 cal., break action. Mfg. circa 1908.

✳ *Variant 1* - marked "SENTINEL" on grip frame.

| | N/A | N/A | $900 | $700 | $600 | $400 | $250 |

✳ *Variant 2* - marked "SENTINEL" on stock.

| | N/A | N/A | $900 | $700 | $600 | $400 | $250 |

GRADING	100%	95%	90%	80%	60%	40%	20%

RIFLES: BREAK BARREL COCKING

MODEL 91 - .177 cal., BBC, SS, economy model made in Hungary by FEG.

	$50	$45	$40	$30	$20	N/A	N/A

MODEL 120 - .177 cal. pellet, BBC. Mfg. by El Gamo in Spain, 1984-85.

courtesy Howard Collection

	$75	$50	$40	$30	N/A	N/A	N/A

MODEL 130 - .177 cal. pellet, BBC. Mfg. by Milbro in Scotland, 1983-85.

	$75	$50	$40	$30	N/A	N/A	N/A

MODEL 130 (EL GAMO) - .177 cal. pellet, BBC, auto pellet feed, 800 FPS, adj. micrometer sight, 5.75 lbs. Mfg. by El Gamo in Spain 1986-93.

	$100	$85	$70	N/A	N/A	N/A	N/A

Last MSR was $150.

MODEL 131 - .177 cal. pellet, BBC, 630 FPS, adj. micrometer sight, 5.4 lbs. Mfg. by El Gamo in Spain.

	$75	$60	$50	N/A	N/A	N/A	N/A

Last MSR was $120.

MODEL 160 - BB/.175, .177 cal. pellet or dart, blue finish. Mfg. by Milbro in Scotland, 1965-74.

courtesy Beeman Collection

	$75	$50	$30	N/A	N/A	N/A	N/A

Note: This was a Diana brand airgun made by Milbro in Scotland, not to be confused with Diana brand airguns from Dianawerk in Rastatt, Germany. At the end of WWII, England was given the Diana brand and Dianawerk´s (Mayer and Grammelspacher) factory machinery as war reparations. The defeated Germans had to install all new machinery and temporarily use "Original" as a brand. Milbro, with the old German equipment, went out of business, and the Diana brand was restored to Dianawerk in Germany.

MODEL 220 - .177 cal. pellet, BBC, SP, blue finish. Mfg. by Milbro in Scotland (see note about Diana brand in Model 160 listing), 1965-70.

courtesy Beeman Collection

	$85	$60	$40	N/A	N/A	N/A	N/A

MODEL 225 - .177 cal. pellet, BBC, SP, blue finish. Mfg. by Milbro in Scotland, 1971-74.

	$110	$90	$45	N/A	N/A	N/A	N/A

MODEL 230 - .22 cal., BBC, SP, blue finish. Mfg. by Milbro in Scotland, 1965-74.

	$80	$55	$35	N/A	N/A	N/A	N/A

MODEL 250 - .22 cal., BBC, SP, blue finish. Mfg. by Milbro in Scotland, 1965-74.

	$130	$100	$65	$50	N/A	N/A	N/A

GRADING	100%	95%	90%	80%	60%	40%	20%

MODEL 1000 - .177 cal., BBC, 1000 FPS, adj. rear with hooded front sight, hardwood Monte Carlo stock, 6.125 lbs. New 1997. Disc.

	100%	95%	90%	80%	60%	40%	20%
	$135	$115	$90	N/A	N/A	N/A	N/A

Last MSR was $175.

MODEL 1170 - .177 cal., BBC, 800 FPS, adj. micrometer sight, 5 1/2 lbs. Disc.

	100%	95%	90%	80%	60%	40%	20%
	$85	$70	$55	N/A	N/A	N/A	N/A

NO. 100 MODEL 38 - BB/.175 cal., BBC, SS, blue finish. Mfg. 1938-41, and 1948-52.

	100%	95%	90%	80%	60%	40%	20%
	$175	$120	$70	$50	N/A	N/A	N/A

Last MSR was $110.

RIFLES: LEVER ACTION

This grouping includes models with a Winchester-style lever under the gun that also covers the trigger.

MODEL B 1000 SHOT - BB/.175 cal., 1,000 shot. Mfg. 1910.

courtesy Beeman Collection

✳ *Variant 1* - nickel finish, cast iron rear sight, brass barrel, steel buttplate.

	100%	95%	90%	80%	60%	40%	20%
	$400	$275	$195	$150	$115	$85	$65

✳ *Variant 2* - similar to Variant 1, except w/sheet metal barrel w/o buttplate.

	100%	95%	90%	80%	60%	40%	20%
	$350	$225	$150	$125	$100	$75	$65

✳ *Variant 3* - similar to Variant 2, except w/sheet metal rear sight w/o buttplate.

	100%	95%	90%	80%	60%	40%	20%
	$350	$225	$150	$125	$100	$75	$65

✳ *Variant 4* - similar to Variant 3, except blue finish.

	100%	95%	90%	80%	60%	40%	20%
	$350	$225	$150	$125	$100	$75	$65

MODEL B 500 SHOT - BB/.175 cal., without steel buttplate. Mfg. 1910-23.

✳ *Variant 1* - nickel finish, cast iron rear sight, brass barrel, steel buttplate.

	100%	95%	90%	80%	60%	40%	20%
	$350	$225	$150	$125	$100	$75	$65

✳ *Variant 2* - similar to Variant 1, except with sheet metal barrel.

	100%	95%	90%	80%	60%	40%	20%
	$350	$225	$150	$125	$100	$75	$65

✳ *Variant 3* - similar to Variant 2, except with sheet metal rear sight.

	100%	95%	90%	80%	60%	40%	20%
	$350	$225	$150	$125	$100	$75	$65

✳ *Variant 4* - similar to Variant 3, except has blue finish.

	100%	95%	90%	80%	60%	40%	20%
	$350	$225	$150	$125	$100	$75	$65

MODEL H SINGLE SHOT - BB/.175 cal., nickel finish mfg. 1913-20, blue finish mfg. 1921-23.

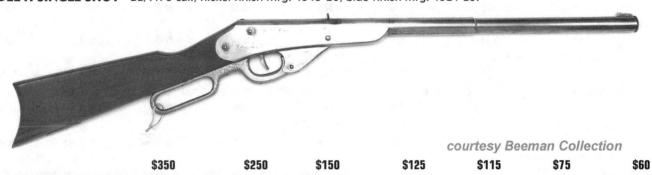

courtesy Beeman Collection

	100%	95%	90%	80%	60%	40%	20%
	$350	$250	$150	$125	$115	$75	$60

Add 20% for nickel finish.

Historical Note: This specimen, and several other illustrated BB rifles, engraved W.R.A. with date, were formerly in the Winchester Repeating Arm collection.

MODEL H REPEATERS - BB/.175 cal., 500-shot nickel finish mfg. 1914-17, 350-shot nickel finish mfg. 1921-32, 350-shot blue finish mfg. 1918-20.

	100%	95%	90%	80%	60%	40%	20%
	$200	$150	$125	$115	$85	$65	$50

GRADING	100%	95%	90%	80%	60%	40%	20%

MODEL 3 SERIES B "DAISY SPECIAL" - BB/.175 cal., 1000-shot, black nickel finish, in lithograph box. Mfg. 1904-08.

	$1,500	$800	$500	$350	$250	N/A	N/A

Add 10% for poor original box.
Add 20% for restored original box.
Add 100% or more for excellent original box.

MODEL 27 (500 SHOT) - BB/.175 cal., 500-shot, blue finish. Mfg. 1927-32.

	$225	$150	$125	$100	N/A	N/A	N/A

MODEL 27 (1000 SHOT) - BB/.175 cal., 1000-shot, nickel finish. Mfg. 1927-32.

	$300	$200	$175	$150	$125	N/A	N/A

MODEL 50 GOLDEN EAGLE - BB/.175 cal., commemorates 50th anniversary of Daisy, special copper-plated model, similar to No. 195 Buzz Barton, pistol grip stock and curved lever, easily identified by black painted stock with red, white, and blue federal eagle decal, and sight tube mounted on top of gun, hooded front sight. Mfg. 1936-1940. Very scarce.

	$400	$300	$200	$150	$100	N/A	N/A

Originally sold for $2.34 by Sears Roebuck & Co. in 1937.

MODEL 75 SCOUT RIFLE - BB/.175 cal., 500-shot, painted finish. Mfg. 1954-58.

	$110	$75	$40	N/A	N/A	N/A	N/A

MODEL 80 - BB/.175 cal., 1000-shot repeater, with scope and canteen, painted. Mfg. 1954-57.

	$150	$125	$100	$75	$50	N/A	N/A

✳ *MODEL 80/155* - over stamp. Mfg. 1955.

MODEL 83 - BB/.175 cal., 350-shot, scope. Mfg. 1961-63.

	$300	$175	$125	$100	$75	N/A	N/A

MODEL 86 SERIES 70 SAFARI MARK 1 - BB/.175 cal., 240-shot repeater. Mfg. 1970-76.

	$130	$85	$50	N/A	N/A	N/A	N/A

Add 20% for factory box with large game poster.

MODEL 88 HUNTER - BB/.175 cal., 1000-shot, 2X scope, plastic stock, painted finish. Mfg. 1959-60.

	$100	$85	$75	$65	$50	N/A	N/A

✳ *Sears Variant* - BB/.175 cal., Sears number 799.19920, Golden Hunter - J.C. Higgins. Mfg. 1957-58.

	$125	$75	$50	N/A	N/A	N/A	N/A

MODEL 90 SPORTSTER - BB/.175 cal., 700-shot, safety, plastic stock, painted finish. Mfg. 1973-78.

	$75	$50	$45	N/A	N/A	N/A	N/A

MODEL 95 - BB/.175 cal., 700-shot, early versions: wood stock, plastic forearm; later version: wood/wood, painted finish. Mfg. 1962-76.

	$50	$45	$40	$35	N/A	N/A	N/A

Quick Kill version - see Model 2299 Quick Kill listing.

✳ *Model 95A* - BB/.175 cal., 700-shot, plastic stock, painted finish. Mfg. 1979-80.

	$50	$45	$40	$35	N/A	N/A	N/A

✳ *Model 95 Timberwolf* - BB/.175, .177 cal., LA, spring air, 325 FPS, 700-shot, black finish, stained wood stock, crossbolt trigger block safety, adj. rear sight, 2.4 lbs. Mfg. 2002-04.

	$39	$32	$25	$20	N/A	N/A	N/A

✳ *Model 95 Pony Express* - similar to Timberwolf. Mfg. 1999.

	$35	$30	$25	$20	N/A	N/A	N/A

✳ *Model 95 Gold Rush* - similar to Pony Express. Mfg. 1999.

	$35	$30	$25	$20	N/A	N/A	N/A

MODEL 96 - BB/.175 cal., LA, 700-shot, painted finish. Mfg. 1963-73.

	$85	$55	$45	$40	N/A	N/A	N/A

MODEL 97 SADDLE GUN - BB/.175 cal., LA, 650-shot, ricochet sound device, painted finish, plastic stock. Mfg. 1961 only.

	$135	$95	$60	N/A	N/A	N/A	N/A

MODEL 98 - BB/.175 cal., 700-shot, plastic or wood stock. Mfg. 1974 only.

	$85	$70	$60	N/A	N/A	N/A	N/A

Add 20% for wood stock.

MODEL 98 DAISY EAGLE - BB/.175 cal., 2X scope, plastic stock, painted finish, leather sling, Plymouth or Rogers addresses. Mfg. 1955-60.

	$150	$105	$75	N/A	N/A	N/A	N/A

Add 20% for Plymouth address.

✳ *Model 98 Golden Eagle* - similar to Model 98 Daisy Eagle, with scope. 1957.

	$100	$75	$50	N/A	N/A	N/A	N/A

✳ *Model 98 Golden Hunter* - similar to Model 98 Daisy Eagle, with scope. 1958.

	$100	$75	$50	N/A	N/A	N/A	N/A

GRADING	100%	95%	90%	80%	60%	40%	20%

MODEL 99 TARGET SPECIAL - BB/.175 cal., painted finish.

   ✱ **Variant 1** - gravity-fed magazine. Mfg. only 1959.

	$135	$90	$60	$50	N/A	N/A	N/A

   ✱ **Variant 2** - spring-fed magazine. Mfg. 1960-1970.

	$100	$70	$50	$40	N/A	N/A	N/A

MODEL 99 CHAMPION - mfg. 1967.

	$100	$75	$50	N/A	N/A	N/A	N/A

      Add 10% for peep sight.

MODEL 99 LUCKY MCDANIELS INSTINCT SHOOTER - BB/.175 cal., mfg. 1960 only.

	$350	$225	$125	$100	N/A	N/A	N/A

MODEL 102 CUB - BB/.175 cal., 350-shot, blue finish, wooden stock. Mfg. 1952-78.

courtesy Howard Collection

	$85	$65	$50	N/A	N/A	N/A	N/A

MODEL 103 SCOUT - BB/.175 cal., plastic stock, painted finish. Mfg. 1964-65 (disc. circa 1990).

	$75	$50	$30	N/A	N/A	N/A	N/A

MODEL 104 GOLDEN EAGLE - BB/.175 cal., 500-shot, plastic stock, peep sight, gold or black paint. Mfg. 1966-74.

	$75	$55	$25	N/A	N/A	N/A	N/A

MODEL 105 BUCK - BB/.175, .177 cal., LA, SP, 275 FPS, 400-shot, black finish, stained wood stock, crossbolt trigger block safety, fiberoptic fixed sights, 1.6 lbs.

MSR $36	$32	$25	$20	N/A	N/A	N/A	N/A

MODEL 105 CUB - BB/.175 cal., 350-shot, painted finish. Mfg. 1979-81, 1982-90.

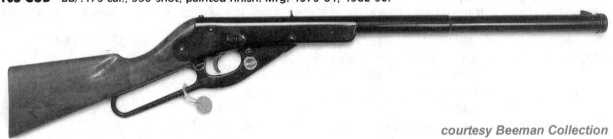

courtesy Beeman Collection

	$45	$30	$25	N/A	N/A	N/A	N/A

MODEL 108 SERIES 39 LONE SCOUT - BB/.175 cal., lightning loader, blue finish. Mfg. 1939 only.

	$500	$400	$250	N/A	N/A	N/A	N/A

   ✱ **Model 108 Series 39** - BB/.175 cal., lightning loader, adj. or fixed rear sight, blue finish. Mfg. 1939-42 and 1945.

	$200	$125	$65	N/A	N/A	N/A	N/A

MODEL 110 AIR FORCE ROCKET COMMAND - BB/.175 cal., LA. Mfg. 1959 only.

	$300	$225	$175	$150	$125	N/A	N/A

MODEL 111 WESTERN CARBINE - BB/.175 cal., 700-shot, plastic stock, straight cocking lever. Mfg. 1963-78.

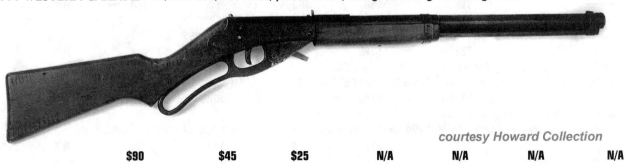

courtesy Howard Collection

	$90	$45	$25	N/A	N/A	N/A	N/A

GRADING	100%	95%	90%	80%	60%	40%	20%

MODEL 111-B AMERICAN YOUTH - BB/.175 cal., wood stock, die-cast cocking lever, stock laser engraved with the logo of a young boy proud to hold his first Daisy air rifle, production number stamped on the butt, gold silk screen words "American Youth" inscribed on the receiver, includes color print of an "American Youth" Bill of Rights. Approx. 1,000 mfg. 1998.

	$200	$160	$125	N/A	N/A	N/A	N/A

This is the lowest number of guns Daisy has ever produced in their collector series. Daisy discovered 1,000 die-cast cocking levers in an old warehouse, and used them to produce this limited edition. Prior to the "American Youth," Daisy had not made an air rifle with a die-cast cocking lever in twenty-five years.

MODEL 155 - BB/.175 cal., repeater, blue finish (painted finish 1953), stamped "1000 shot", cast iron cocking lever 1946, aluminum lever 1947-49. Mfg. 1931. Reintroduced 1952-53.

	$180	$125	$95	N/A	N/A	N/A	N/A

MODEL 299 - BB/.175 cal., 1000-shot, peep sight. Gravity-fed version of Model 99. Mfg. 1975-76.

	$100	$65	$50	N/A	N/A	N/A	N/A

MODEL 400 - BB/.175 cal., five-shot Roto-clip, .177 cal. pellet. Mfg. 1971-72.

	$100	$75	$55	N/A	N/A	N/A	N/A

MODEL 403 - BB/.175 cal., five-shot Roto-clip, .177 cal. pellet. Status of this model not clear. Mfg. 1973-76.

	$125	$85	$60	N/A	N/A	N/A	N/A

MODEL 404 - BB/.175 cal., five-shot Roto-clip, .177 cal. pellet. Mfg. 1974-76.

	$125	$85	$60	N/A	N/A	N/A	N/A

MODEL 450 - BB/.175 cal., five-shot Roto-clip, .177 cal. pellet. Mfg. 1972-73.

	$75	$65	$50	N/A	N/A	N/A	N/A

MODEL 452 - BB/.175 cal., five-shot Roto-clip, .177 cal. pellet. Mfg. 1973 only.

	$125	$85	$60	N/A	N/A	N/A	N/A

MODEL 453 - BB/.175 cal., five-shot Roto-clip, .177 cal. pellet. Mfg. 1974-76.

	$75	$65	$50	N/A	N/A	N/A	N/A

MODEL 454 - BB/.175 cal., five-shot Roto-clip, .177 cal. pellet. Mfg. 1974-76.

	$110	$75	$55	N/A	N/A	N/A	N/A

MODEL 499 - BB/.175 cal., target single shot, plastic or wood stock. Mfg. 1976-79.

	$125	$85	$60	N/A	N/A	N/A	N/A

AVANTI MODEL 499 CHAMPION - BB or .177 (4.5 mm steel shot) cal., SP, SS muzzle loading, lever action smoothbore steel BBL, 240 FPS, hooded front with aperture inserts and adj. rear peep sights, Monte Carlo stained hardwood stock and forearm with weight compartments, 36.25 in. OAL, 3.1 lbs. New 2003.

MSR $90	$85	$75	$65	$55	N/A	N/A	N/A

MODEL 770 SUPER - .177 cal. pellet, UL, SP, single-stroke cocking. Mfg. 1978-80.

	$115	$85	$55	N/A	N/A	N/A	N/A

MODEL 1000 - BB/.175 cal., Western Auto. Mfg. 1957-58.

	$90	$75	$50	N/A	N/A	N/A	N/A

MODEL 1105 - BB/.175 cal., 500-shot, safety. Mfg. 1975-79.

	$50	$40	$25	N/A	N/A	N/A	N/A

MODEL 1201 - BB/.175 cal., gold finish, blond stock, Western Auto. Mfg. 1976-77.

	$125	$75	$50	N/A	N/A	N/A	N/A

MODEL 1205 - BB/.175 cal., economy version of Model 1200, sixty-shot. Mfg. 1979-81.

	$100	$60	$40	N/A	N/A	N/A	N/A

MODEL 1776 GOLDEN EAGLE - BB/.175 cal., 500-shot, peep sight, gold paint finish. Mfg. 1968-72.

	$200	$125	$75	N/A	N/A	N/A	N/A

MODEL 1894 WESTERN CARBINE - BB/.175 cal., forty-shot, grey painted finish, metal buttplate, plastic stock. Mfg. 1961-86.

	$125	$90	$50	N/A	N/A	N/A	N/A

Subtract 40% for missing factory box.

  ✳ *Model 1894 Western Carbine And Pistol Set* - BB/.175 cal., valued as a set. Mfg. 1970-80.

	$250	$125	$75		N/A	N/A	N/A

Subtract 40% for missing factory box.

  ✳ *Model 1894 Commemorative Wells Fargo Limited Edition* - BB/.175 cal. Mfg. 1975-76.

	$300	$200	$125	N/A	N/A	N/A	N/A

Subtract 40% for missing factory box.

  ✳ *Model 1894 Commemorative 1894-1994 Limited Edition* - BB/.175 cal., octagon barrel. Mfg. 1994.

	$140	$100	$70	N/A	N/A	N/A	N/A

Subtract 40% for missing factory box.

GRADING	100%	95%	90%	80%	60%	40%	20%

✳ *Model 1894 Buffalo Bill 150th Anniversary Model* - BB/.175 cal., Winchester Model 94 style rifle, wood stock, wood forearm, gold style coin in stock. Approx. 2,500 mfg. 1996.

	$195	$170	$150	$100	$75	N/A	N/A

Subtract 40% for missing factory box.

✳ *Sears Variants of the Daisy 1894 Carbine Number 799.19052* - 1894 Commemorative, Winchester-style, octagon barrel, marked "Replica Centennial Rifle, Crafted by Daisy" or "Crafted by Daisy" on the barrel, gold paint finish, Sears. Mfg. 1969-73.

	$100	$50	$25	N/A	N/A	N/A	N/A

Subtract 40% for missing factory box.

✳ *Sears Variants of the Daisy 1894 Carbine Number 799.19120* - regular 1894 Winchester-style, octagon barrel, gold paint or brass frame, Sears. Mfg. 1969-73.

	$120	$85	$40	N/A	N/A	N/A	N/A

Subtract 40% for missing factory box.

✳ *Sears Number 799.19210 Cactus Carbine* - J.C. Higgins. Mfg. 1960-70.

	$100	$50	$25	N/A	N/A	N/A	N/A

✳ *Sears Variants of the Daisy 1894 Carbine Number 799.19250* - BB/.175 cal., J.C. Higgins. Mfg. 1952-55.

	$100	$50	$25	N/A	N/A	N/A	N/A

Subtract 40% for missing factory box.

MODEL 2299 QUICK SKILL - civilian version of the U.S. Govt. Quick Kill, no sights, in box with safety glasses, aerial targets. Mfg. 1968-72.

	$125	$75	$50	N/A	N/A	N/A	N/A

Subtract 35% for missing box.

MODEL 2299 QUICK KILL U.S. GOVERNMENT ISSUE - no sights, used with fluorescent BBs to teach instinct shooting to troops in the Vietnam war, U.S. Govt. marking stamped into, or stenciled onto, stock. Mfg. 1968-70.

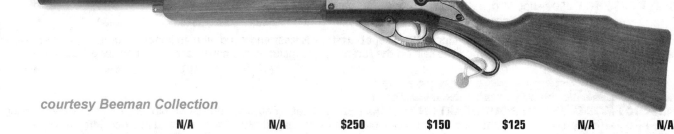

courtesy Beeman Collection

	N/A	N/A	$250	$150	$125	N/A	N/A

MODEL 3030 WESTERN CARBINE BUFFALO BILL SCOUT - forty-shot, saddle ring on forearm or receiver. Mfg. 1969-73.

	$150	$110	$85	$70	$55	N/A	N/A

MODEL 5179 NRA CENTENNIAL COMMEMORATIVE PISTOL/RIFLE SET - two guns, matching serial numbers, value given for pair. Mfg. 1971-72.

	$400	$350	$300	$225	$150	N/A	N/A

MODEL 5694 TEXAS RANGERS COMMEMORATIVE RIFLE & PISTOL - mfg. 1973-74.

	$600	$450	$275	N/A	N/A	N/A	N/A

MODEL 5894 NRA CENTENNIAL COMMEMORATIVE CARBINE - mfg. 1971-72.

	$200	$150	N/A	N/A	N/A	N/A	N/A

MODEL 5994 WELLS FARGO COMMEMORATIVE RIFLE & PISTOL - mfg. 1974-75.

	$350	$230	$175	N/A	N/A	N/A	N/A

NO. 3 MODEL 24 - BB/.175 cal., thousand-shot, nickel plated. Mfg. 1924-26.

	$1,000	$800	$500	$350	$250	$200	$150

NO. 11 MODEL 24 - BB/.175 cal., 350-shot, nickel finish. Mfg. 1924-28.

	$225	$150	$125	$100	N/A	N/A	N/A

NO. 11 MODEL 29 - BB/.175 cal., 350-shot, nickel finish. Mfg. 1929-32.

	$225	$150	$125	$100	$75	N/A	N/A

NO. 12 MODEL 24 - BB/.175 cal., single-shot, blue finish. Mfg. 1924-28.

	$225	$150	$125	$100	N/A	N/A	N/A

NO. 12 MODEL 29 - BB/.175 cal., single-shot, blue finish. Mfg. 1929-32.

	$225	$150	$125	$100	$75	N/A	N/A

NO. 24 MODEL 30 - BB/.175 cal., 500-shot, blue finish. Mfg. 1924-26.

	$1,000	$700	$400	$250	$175	N/A	N/A

NO. 30 MODEL 24 - BB/.175 cal., 500-shot, blue finish. Mfg. 1924-26.

	$250	$175	$150	$125	$100	N/A	N/A

GRADING	100%	95%	90%	80%	60%	40%	20%

NO. 101 MODEL 33 - BB/.175 cal., "Daisy for a Buck," SS, blue finish. Mfg. 1933-35.

	$130	$100	$75	N/A	N/A	N/A	N/A

NO. 102 MODEL 33 - BB/.175 cal., 500-shot, nickel finish, wooden stock. Mfg. 1933-35.

	$175	$125	$100	$75	$50	N/A	N/A

NO. 101 MODEL 36 - BB/.175 cal., SS, blue finish. Mfg. 1936-42.

	$75	$60	$45	N/A	N/A	N/A	N/A

NO. 102 MODEL 36 - BB/.175 cal., 500-shot, nickel (1936-40), blue (1941-42 and 1945-47), or painted (1953) finish, wood stock (plastic stock 1954), aluminum lever 1950 (none mfg. 1947-49).

	$95	$80	$65	N/A	N/A	N/A	N/A

NO. 111 WESTERN CARBINE - BB/.175 cal., 700-shot, plastic stock, straight, uncurved cocking lever. Mfg.1963-78.

	$150	$125	$100	$100	$75	N/A	N/A

BENNETT 1000 SHOT - BB/.175 cal., thousand-shot, nickel. Mfg. 1903-09.

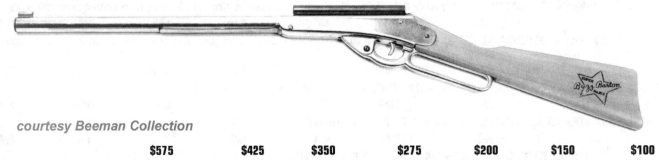

courtesy Beeman Collection

	$1,250	$850	$650	$500	$350	$300	$250

BENNETT 500 SHOT - 500-shot. Mfg. 1905-09.

	$1,800	$1,200	$750	$600	$450	$400	$350

FIREFIGHTER - BB/.175, .177 cal., similar to Model 95, except buttstock is laser engraved with an image of antique pumper wagon and "The Firefighter" with "going beyond the call" on the forearm, also included is a certificate of authenticity. Mfg. 2003-04.

MSR $60	$60	$50	$40	N/A	N/A	N/A	N/A

RIFLES: LEVER ACTION, BUZZ BARTON SERIES

NUMBER 103 MODEL 33 SUPER BUZZ BARTON SPECIAL - BB/.175 cal., thousand-shot LA on Model 27 frame, easy to recognize Buzz Barton series by rear sight tube, bright nickel plate and star-shaped "Buzz Barton" brand in stock. Mfg. 1933-37.

courtesy Beeman Collection

	$575	$425	$350	$275	$200	$150	$100

Add 10% for mahogany stock.

NO. 195 MODEL 32 BUZZ BARTON SPECIAL - BB/.175 cal., LA, thousand-shot, straight barrel and plunger housing with a patch shoulder underneath, blue, cast iron lever, rear sight tube, walnut stock with brand "Buzz Barton Special No. 195" inside lariat with two cowboys. Paper label 1932.

	$450	$300	$250	$200	$150	$100	$75

Add 50% for paper label.

This is a Markham/King design based upon the King No. 55.

✳ *No.195 Model 33* - BB/.175 cal., similar to Model 32 except has brand on stock, mfg. 1933-35.

	$450	$300	$250	$200	$150	$100	$75

Add 50% for paper label.

This is a Markham/King design based upon the King No. 55.

✳ *No. 195 Model 36* - BB/.175 cal., similar to Model 36 except has larger frame, mfg. 1936-41.

	$450	$300	$250	$200	$150	$100	$75

Add 50% for paper label.

This is a Markham/King design based upon the King No. 55.

GRADING	100%	95%	90%	80%	60%	40%	20%

RIFLES: LEVER ACTION, DEFENDER SERIES

NO. 40 MILITARY MODEL ("WWI MILITARY MODEL") - full-length, one-piece wood stock, no bolt handle, 10 in. rubber-tipped metal bayonet, web sling.

* **Variant 1** - adj. front sight, extended shot tube with knurled end extends about .25 in. beyond muzzle. Mfg. 1916-18.

courtesy Beeman Collection

	$950	$850	$700	$500	$300	N/A	N/A

Subtract $300 if without bayonet.
Subtract $100 if without sling.

* **Variant 2** - fixed front sight, standard no. 25 shot tube. Mfg. 1919-32.

	$850	$750	$600	$400	$200	N/A	N/A

Subtract $300 if without bayonet.
Subtract $100 if without sling.

The metal bayonets were often taken away from children, and subsequently either lost or thrown away. Bayonet alone may sell for $300-$400.

NO. 140 DEFENDER ("WWII DEFENDER") - BB/.175 cal., military-style two-piece wooden stock with extended forearm, blue finish, bolt handle (acts as auto safety), gravity-fed, web sling, no bayonet. Very rare. Mfg. 1942 only.

	$600	$500	$450	$375	$300	$200	N/A

NO. 141 DEFENDER ("KOREAN WAR DEFENDER") - similar to No. 140, except with plastic stock and forearm, web sling, blue or painted finish, fifty-shot spring-fed repeater. Mfg. 1951-53.

	$200	$100	$75	N/A	N/A	N/A	N/A

Add 50% for variation with wood stock.

NO. MODEL 142 DEFENDER - same military style, thousand-shot, gravity-fed, blue or painted finish. Mfg.1954, painted, blue, mfg. 1957.

	$250	$125	$95	N/A	N/A	N/A	N/A

RIFLES: LEVER ACTION, DEMOULIN INITIATION SERIES

MODEL B - first DeMoulin initiation guns have external water tubing on Daisy Bennett model and no markings on stock, rifles (pair). Mfg.1910-18.

	$1,500	$1,250	$1,000	$800	$700	$600	N/A

Special Daisy BB gun adapted to shoot water. Used as part of the Rough Masonic Initiation ceremony. Usually sold in pairs; one of the pair shot water forward; the other shot water backwards into the face and eyes of the shooter. (Contrary to previous reports, these guns were also sold individually). Stocks are stamped "DeMoulin Bros. & Co, Greenville, Illinois".

MODEL 3 SERIES 24 - (pair) mfg. 1924-26.

	$2,000	$1,500	$1,000	$900	$800	$700	N/A

Special Daisy BB gun adapted to shoot water. Used as part of the Rough Masonic Initiation ceremony. Usually sold in pairs; one of the pair shot water forward; the other shot water backwards into the face and eyes of the shooter. (Contrary to previous reports, these guns were also sold individually). Stocks are stamped "DeMoulin Bros. & Co, Greenville, Illinois".

MODEL 27 (WATER SHOOTER) - (pair) mfg. 1926-35.

courtesy Beeman Collection

Rear Squirt Tube   **No Squirt Tube**

	$2,000	$1,750	$1,250	$1,100	$1,000	$900	N/A

Special Daisy BB gun adapted to shoot water. Used as part of the Rough Masonic Initiation ceremony. Usually sold in pairs; one of the pair shot water forward; the other shot water backwards into the face and eyes of the shooter. (Contrary to previous reports, these guns were also sold individually.) "Stocks are stamped: DeMoulin Bros. & Co, Greenville, Illinois".

GRADING	100%	95%	90%	80%	60%	40%	20%

RIFLES: LEVER ACTION, RED RYDER SERIES

This grouping contains the Red Ryder models manufactured beginning 1939-1940.

MODEL 1938 - BB/.175 cal., Red Ryder similar to Number 111 Model 40, wood stock and forearm, logo stamped on left side of stock, narrow barrel bands, saddle ring staple does not go completely through side of receiver, blue paint finish, screws are slotted. Mfg. 1972-78.

	100%	95%	90%	80%	60%	40%	20%
	$150	$115	$90	$75	N/A	N/A	N/A

Survival rate on these later models is very slim due to excessive use. Examples in 100% condition are extremely rare.

MODEL 1938 B DUCKS UNLIMITED - BB/.175 cal., special Red Ryder edition for Ducks Unlimited, walnut stock, right side of receiver stamped "Limited Edition", stamping lines filled with gold paint, walnut look rack with brass plaque. Mfg. 1975.

	100%	95%	90%	80%	60%	40%	20%
	$175	$150	$125	$100	N/A	N/A	N/A

MODEL 1938 A-B - BB/.175 cal., Red Ryder, marked "1938 A-B" in gold paint on right side of receiver, loading gate on left side of barrel near muzzle, no muzzle band, plastic saddle ring staple, fake loading tube, plastic front sight and muzzle plug, trigger safety, hole in left side of receiver. Mfg. 1978.

	100%	95%	90%	80%	60%	40%	20%
	$150	$100	$90	N/A	N/A	N/A	N/A

MODEL 1938 B - BB/.175 cal., Red Ryder similar to Model 1938 A-B but with no hole on left side of receiver, stamped "1938-B". New 1979.

	100%	95%	90%	80%	60%	40%	20%
	$40	$35	$30	$25	N/A	N/A	N/A

MODEL 1938 B BUFFALO BILL - export model, plastic loading port, plain Red Ryder stock, gold stencil. Mfg. 1980-85.

	100%	95%	90%	80%	60%	40%	20%
	$125	$90	$80	$65	N/A	N/A	N/A

MODEL 1938 "LAND OF BUFFALO BILL" RED RYDER MODEL - styled by Bill Cody, sold only from William Cody Museum, plastic stock. Mfg. about 1977.

	100%	95%	90%	80%	60%	40%	20%
	$150	$100	$60	N/A	N/A	N/A	N/A

MODEL 1938 B CHRISTMAS STORY - BB/.175 cal., Red Ryder model manufactured due to interest in 1984 film *A Christmas Story*, similar to standard "B" Model, but with large compass and sundial on left side of stock. Mfg. 1984.

	100%	95%	90%	80%	60%	40%	20%
	$350	$275	$150	$100	$75	N/A	N/A

Values equal with small compass.

A Christmas Story author Jean Sheperd invented this model, and Daisy followed his lead. An example in 100% condition must be unopened in original cellophane wrapped display box. To complete *A Christmas Story* set, collectors also need a movie poster, the movie (video tape or DVD), and the small cardboard stand-up display card. Note: Due to the popularity of this model, there unfortunately are a handful of counterfeit Christmas Story BB guns in circulation. (These are made up from regular Red Ryder guns by substituting factory stocks leftover from the production of true Christmas Story models.) Originals have "DAISY" marked in black on a white compass. What no one seems to be able to counterfeit, however, is the original cellophane wrapper! According to a few collectors (who have them and will not part with them at any price), values are still on the conservative side.

MODEL 1938 B - LES KOUBA - BB/.175 cal., standard "B" model Red Ryder, but has extra fancy American walnut stock and forearm, gold forearm band, gold medallion on right side of stock showing a boy with his first Red Ryder. Stamped "Limited Edition", printing filled with gold paint, plastic lever, walnut-look wall rack in box, brass plaque. Includes Les C. Kouba print in cardboard tube marked with the same number as the air rifle. Mfg. 1986.

	100%	95%	90%	80%	60%	40%	20%
	$350	$300	$225	N/A	N/A	N/A	N/A

Add 50% for guns with artist's proofed and signed print.

Only 1,100 Les Kouba guns were produced. The print series numbers from 1 to 2500. The first 250 prints are artist proofed and hand signed on lower left side. There are counterfeit Les Kouba posters and guns which were not produced by Daisy. It is advised that you consult with a qualified expert before making a purchase.

NUMBER 1938 B 50TH ANNIVERSARY - Red Ryder, BB/.175 cal., similar to standard Model B, except has walnut stock and forearm, brass medallion on right side of stock, fifty-year warranty. Mfg. 1988.

	100%	95%	90%	80%	60%	40%	20%
	$125	$90	$60	N/A	N/A	N/A	N/A

MODEL 1938 "DIAMOND ANNIVERSARY" COMMEMORATIVE - BB/.175 cal., commemorates the 60th anniversary of the introduction of the Red Ryder BB gun, limited edition white scroll on the receiver, burnished forearm band, and special lariat logo in the stock. Mfg. 1998.

	100%	95%	90%	80%	60%	40%	20%
	$65	$35	$25	N/A	N/A	N/A	N/A

MODEL 1938 GOLD RUSH COMMEMORATIVE - BB/.175 cal., commemorates the 150th anniversary of the California Gold Rush, "Gold Rush" stamped on the top of the gold-painted barrel, natural finish walnut stock and forearm, countersunk in the stock is a 1-in. gold-colored medallion with a prospector panning for gold, forearm is laser engraved with the gun's production number. Approx. 2,500 mfg.

	100%	95%	90%	80%	60%	40%	20%
	$125	$100	$85	N/A	N/A	N/A	N/A

MODEL 1938 MILLINEUM EDITION COMMEMORATIVE - BB/.175 cal., commemorates the year 2000 with engraving on stock, natural finish walnut stock and forearm, barrels were numbered. Manufactured for one year in 2000.

	100%	95%	90%	80%	60%	40%	20%
	$65	$35	$25	N/A	N/A	N/A	N/A

GRADING	100%	95%	90%	80%	60%	40%	20%

MODEL 1938 RED RYDER - BB/.175, .177 cal., LA, SP, 280 FPS, 650-shot, black finish, stained wood stock/forearm with lariat logo and burnished forearm band, crossbolt trigger block safety, adj. rear sight, saddle ring with leather thong, 2.2 lbs.

	MSR $45	$38	$32	$25	N/A	N/A	N/A	N/A

MODEL 1938 (MFG. 1978) - BB/.175 cal., Red Ryder similar to Model 1938 but with logo on right side of stock, screws are Phillips type. Mfg. 1978.

	$100	$75	$60	$45	N/A	N/A	N/A

MODEL 1938 B (MFG. 1995) - "It´s A Daisy" Red Ryder Limited Edition. Mfg. 1995.

	$150	$100	$75	N/A	N/A	N/A	N/A

MODEL 94 CARBINE - BB/.175 cal., 850-shot, plastic stock and forearm, gold (paint) embossed long horn and logo on left side of stock, dummy hammer on stock with leather boot, bright finish forearm band, high front sight, combo peep or open rear sight, blue paint finish, Plymouth and Rogers addresses. Mfg. 1955-62.

	$250	$150	$100	$60	N/A	N/A	N/A

Subtract 50% for missing boot or barrel band.

Add 20% for Plymouth address.

NO. 111 MODEL 40 RED RYDER VARIANT 1 - BB/.175 cal., thousand-shot, LA, copper plated forearm and barrel bands, front barrel band pinched into place, wood stock and forearm, saddle ring with leather thong, Red Ryder brand burned into left side of stock, cast iron lever, small screw through top of stock, adj. rear sight. This is the "copper band" model shown (with modified stock) in *A Christmas Story* movie. Mfg. 1940-41.

	N/A	$450	$350	$300	$250	$200	$150

NO. 111 MODEL 40 ("1942" MODEL) VARIANT 2 - BB/.175 cal., barrel bands either prick-pinched or welded into place, wood stock and forearm, logo burned into left side of stock, cast iron lever (blue), small original size screw through the top of stock, fixed rear sight. Steel shortage due to WWII caused production to stop in early 1942. Mfg. 1941-42.

	N/A	$225	$200	$175	N/A	N/A	N/A

Extreme rarity precludes accurate pricing on this model.

NO. 111 MODEL 40 VARIANT 3 - BB/.175 cal., blue barrel bands, wood stock and forearm, Red Ryder logo silk screened onto stock with black paint on red background (because of temporary breakdown of regular stock marking equipment), fixed sights. About 1,000 mfg. The very rarest of all Red Ryder Models. Mfg. 1941.

Extreme rarity precludes accurate pricing on this model.

NO. 111 MODEL 40 VARIANT 4 - BB/.175 cal., large screw through top of stock. Mfg. 1946.

	N/A	$250	$200	$150	$125	N/A	N/A

NO. 111 MODEL 40 VARIANT 5 - BB/.175 cal., wood stock, plastic forearm, logo stamped on left side of stock, black painted cast aluminum lever, fixed sights. Mfg. 1947.

	N/A	$200	$175	$150	$100	N/A	N/A

Note: Steel shortage of 1947 forced use of aluminum in cocking lever.

NO. 111 MODEL 40 VARIANT 6 - BB/.175 cal., wood stock, plastic forearm, logo stamped on left side of stock, black painted cast aluminum lever, fixed sights, plastic forearms. Mfg. 1952.

	N/A	$200	$175	$150	$125	N/A	N/A

Plastic forearms on pre-1966 models had a tendency to warp.

NO. 111 MODEL 40 VARIANT 7 - BB/.175 cal., plastic stock and forearm, logo molded into left side of stock, blue painted finish, painted aluminum lever, fixed or adj. rear sight.

	N/A	$150	$125	$100	$75	N/A	N/A

First use of batch registration numbers in 1952.

NO. 111 MODEL 40 VARIANT 8 - BB/.175 cal., plastic stock, painted finish, white filled checkering on stock.

	$200	$175	$150	$125	$100	N/A	N/A

NO. 311 - Red Ryder set, gun similar to Number 111, except set with scope, bell target, cork firing tube, corks, etc., in large box. Mfg.1947-50.

	$550	$450	$350	$300	$250	$200	$100

CHRISTMAS MORNING - BB/.175, .177 cal., similar to Model 1938 Red Ryder, except gunstock is laser engraved with an image of Santa Claus placing a BB gun under a Christmas tree, also included in the full color package is a laser engraved wooden Christmas ornament (same image).

	$70	$55	$45	N/A	N/A	N/A	N/A

ROY/DALE LIMITED EDITION COMMEMMORATIVE - BB/.175, .177 cal., similar to Model 1938 Red Ryder, except walnut stock has gold color medallion of Roy Rogers and Dale Evans inserted, forearm is laser engraved with their signatures and the gun´s serial number, second rifle in the Roy Rogers Series, 2,500 to be mfg.

	$70	$55	$38	N/A	N/A	N/A	N/A

ROY ROGERS/GABBY HAYES COMMEMORATIVE - BB/.175, .177 cal., similar to Model 1938 Red Ryder, except walnut stock has gold color medallion of Roy Rogers and Gabby Hayes inserted, forearm is laser engraved with Gabby´s signature phrase "Yer durn tootin" and gun´s serial number, third rifle in the Roy Rogers Series, 2,500 to be mfg.

	$70	$55	$38	N/A	N/A	N/A	N/A

GRADING	100%	95%	90%	80%	60%	40%	20%

MODEL 9938 RED RYDER KIT - BB/.175, .177 cal., LA, SP, kit includes Model 1938 Red Ryder rifle, shooting glasses, two Shatter-Blast stakes, eight ShatterBlast targets, PrecisionMax BBs, Red Ryder tin of BBs, and Daisy gun case.

	100%	95%	90%	80%	60%	40%	20%
MSR $69	$65	$55	$50	$40	$30	N/A	N/A

RIFLES: PNEUMATIC & CO₂ POWERED

This grouping contains models powered by CO_2 or compressed air.

MODEL 22SG - .22 cal., multi-pump, UL, SS, 550 FPS, die-cast metal receiver, rifled steel barrel, black finish, hardwood stock and forearm, fiberoptic front and adj. rear sights, 4.5 lbs. New 2002.

	100%	95%	90%	80%	60%	40%	20%
MSR $110	$105	$90	$80	$60	$50	N/A	N/A

MODEL 22X - .22 cal., multi-pump, UL, SP, SS, 550 FPS, die-cast metal receiver, rifled steel barrel, black finish, hardwood stock and forearm, fiberoptic front and adj. rear sights, dovetail mount and 4x32 scope, 4.5 lbs. Disc. 2002.

	100%	95%	90%	80%	60%	40%	20%
	$95	$75	$65	$50	$40	N/A	N/A

MODEL 126 EL GAMO - .177 cal., SSP, match style. Mfg. in Spain by El Gamo, 1984.

	100%	95%	90%	80%	60%	40%	20%
	$75	$50	$40	N/A	N/A	N/A	N/A

MODEL 126 EL GAMO SUPER MATCH TARGET RIFLE - .177 cal., SSP, 590 FPS, adj. sights, hardwood stock, match style. 10.6 lbs. Mfg. in Spain by El Gamo. Disc. 1994.

	100%	95%	90%	80%	60%	40%	20%
	$470	$400	$300	N/A	N/A	N/A	N/A

Last MSR was $765.

MODEL 128 GAMO OLYMPIC - .177 cal., similar to El Gamo 126 Super Match Target, except has adj. cheekpiece and buttplate, high quality European diopter sight. Mfg. in Spain by El Gamo.

	100%	95%	90%	80%	60%	40%	20%
	$440	$375	$300	N/A	N/A	N/A	N/A

Last MSR was $735.

MODEL 177X - .177 cal., multi-pump, ULP, SS, 550 FPS, die-cast metal receiver, rifled steel barrel, black finish, hardwood stock and forearm, fiberoptic front and adj. rear sights, 4.5 lbs. New 2003.

	100%	95%	90%	80%	60%	40%	20%
MSR $80	$75	$60	$50	$40	N/A	N/A	N/A

MODEL 300 - BB/.175 cal., CO_2 semi-auto, futuristic styling, plastic stock, five-shot repeater. Mfg. 1968-75.

	100%	95%	90%	80%	60%	40%	20%
	$85	$75	$70	$45	N/A	N/A	N/A

✳ *Model 300 Sears Variant* - Sears number 799.19062 - similar to Model 300 except gold painted receiver and buttplate.

	100%	95%	90%	80%	60%	40%	20%
	$95	$85	$80	$55	N/A	N/A	N/A

MODEL 822 - .22 cal., pneumatic, rifled barrel. Mfg. 1976-78.

	100%	95%	90%	80%	60%	40%	20%
	$75	$60	$40	N/A	N/A	N/A	N/A

MODEL 836 POWERLINE - BB/.175, or .177 cal. Mfg. 1984-85.

	100%	95%	90%	80%	60%	40%	20%
	$75	$60	$40	N/A	N/A	N/A	N/A

MODEL 840 - BB/.175, or .177 cal., SSP. Mfg. 1978-89.

	100%	95%	90%	80%	60%	40%	20%
	$75	$60	$40	N/A	N/A	N/A	N/A

MODEL 840 GRIZZLY/MODEL 840B GRIZZLY - BB/.175, or .177 cal., SSP, 320 FPS (BB/.175 cal.), smooth bore steel barrel, 350-shot (BB/.175 cal.) or SS (.177 cal.), black finish, adj. rear sight, molded woodgrain with checkering stock and forearm, crossbolt trigger block safety, 2.25 lbs.

	100%	95%	90%	80%	60%	40%	20%
MSR $48	$45	$35	$25	$20	$15	N/A	N/A

✳ *Model 840C Grizzly* - BB/.175, or .177 cal., similar to Model 840 Grizzly, except has Mossy Oak Break Up camouflage stock and forearm.

	100%	95%	90%	80%	60%	40%	20%
MSR $55	$50	$45	$35	$25	$20	N/A	N/A

Add $15 for kit (Model 5840).

✳ *Model 3840 Grizzly* - BB/.175, or .177 cal., kit includes Model 840C Grizzly rifle, safety glasses, Truglo fiberoptic sights, 350 BBs, 250 pellets, pad of targets, and Daisy's Right Start to Shooting Sports video.

	100%	95%	90%	80%	60%	40%	20%
MSR $70	$65	$60	$50	$40	N/A	N/A	N/A

Add $15 for kit (Model 5840).

✳ *Model 4841 Grizzly* - BB/.175, or .177 cal., includes Model 840C Grizzly rifle, shooting glasses, 4x15 scope, two ShaterBlast stakes with eight ShaterBlast targets, PrecisionMax pellets and BBs.

	100%	95%	90%	80%	60%	40%	20%
MSR $75	$65	$55	$45	$35	N/A	N/A	N/A

Add $15 for kit (Model 5840).

MODEL 845 TARGET - similar to Model 840, except has peep sights. Mfg. 1980-89.

	100%	95%	90%	80%	60%	40%	20%
	$75	$60	$40	N/A	N/A	N/A	N/A

GRADING	100%	95%	90%	80%	60%	40%	20%

MODEL 850 POWERLINE - BB/.175, or .177 cal., SSP, rifled barrel, black die-cast metal, adj. rear sight, hand-wiped checkered woodgrain finished stock, buttplate, BB 520 FPS, 4.3 lbs. Mfg. 1982-84.

courtesy Howard Collection

	$75	$60	$40	N/A	N/A	N/A	N/A

MODEL 851 POWERLINE - BB/.175, or .177 cal., similar to Model 850 Powerline, except has select hardwood stock. Mfg. 1982-84.

	$110	$60	$40	N/A	N/A	N/A	N/A

MODEL 853 TARGET - .177 cal., SSP. Mfg. 1984.

	$250	$180	$140	N/A	N/A	N/A	N/A

MODEL 856 POWERLINE - .177 cal. (early versions .177 pellet SS/BB repeater combination), multi-pump pneumatic, SS, 670 FPS, rifled steel barrel, black finish, molded wood grain sporter style stock and forearm, crossbolt trigger block safety, adj. rear sight, 2.7 lbs.

courtesy Beeman Collection

	$40	$30	$20	N/A	N/A	N/A	N/A

Add 25% for combination pellet and BB gun.

✳ *Model 856F Powerline* - .177 cal., similar to Model 856 Powerline, except has fiberoptic sights. Disc. 2004.

	$45	$35	$25	N/A	N/A	N/A	N/A

Last MSR was $50.

Add 25% for Model 808 4x15 scope (Model 7856).

✳ *Model 856C Powerline* - .177 cal., similar to Model 856 Powerline, except has fiberoptic sights and Mossy Oak Break Up Camo stock and forearm. Disc. 2004.

	$55	$40	$30	$20	$15	N/A	N/A

Last MSR was $60.

MODEL 860 POWERLINE - BB/.175, or .177 cal. Mfg. 1984-85.

	$75	$60	$40	N/A	N/A	N/A	N/A

MODEL 880 POWERLINE - BB/.175, or .177 cal., pellet, multi-stroke pump pneumatic. Mfg. 1972-89.

courtesy Beeman Collection

	$65	$40	$30	N/A	N/A	N/A	N/A

Add 100% for early models with metal receiver, metal pumping arm, no warnings printed on the guns – the "pure" original version.
Add 50% for metal receiver.

MODEL 880 POWERLINE (CURRENT) - BB/.175, or .177 cal., UL, multi-pump pneumatic, 685 FPS (BB), 75-125 (BB) or SS (pellet), dodecahedral rifling suited to pellet or steel BBs, steel barrel, black finish, molded Monte Carlo-style stock and forearm, adj. rear sight, crossbolt trigger block safety, 3.7 lbs. New 1990.

MSR $61	$55	$40	$30	$20	$15	N/A	N/A

Add $5 for fiberoptic front sight.
Add $15 for Model 808 4x15 scope (Model 1880).

GRADING	100%	95%	90%	80%	60%	40%	20%

MODEL 5880 POWERLINE - BB/.175, or .177 cal., UL, multi-pump pneumatic, kit includes shooting glasses, 4x15 scope, targets and ammo. New 2004.

	100%	95%	90%	80%	60%	40%	20%
MSR $61	$55	$40	$30	$20	$15	N/A	N/A

Add $5 for fiberoptic front sight.
Add $15 for Model 808 4x15 scope (Model 1880).

MODEL 881 POWERLINE - similar to Model 880, rifled barrel. Mfg. 1973-83.

	$75	$60	$40	N/A	N/A	N/A	N/A

MODEL 882 CENTENNIAL - similar to Model 880, rifled barrel. Mfg. 1975-76.

	$75	$60	$40	N/A	N/A	N/A	N/A

MODLE 900 SNAP SHOT - .177 cal., auto-fed, clip. Mfg. 1986.

	$95	$70	$50	N/A	N/A	N/A	N/A

MODEL 901 - BB/.175, or .177 cal., UL, multi-pump pneumatic, 750 FPS (BB), 50 (BB) or SS (pellet), rifled steel barrel, black finish, molded composite stock and forearm, fiberoptic front and adj. rear sight, crossbolt trigger block safety, 37.5 in. OAL, 3.7 lbs. New 2005.

	100%	95%	90%	80%	60%	40%	20%
MSR $67	$60	$50	$40	$30	N/A	N/A	N/A

Add $5 for fiberoptic front sight.
Add $15 for Model 808 4x15 scope (Model 1880).

MODEL 917 - .177 cal., multi-stroke pneumatic, five-shot clip. Mfg. 1979-82.

	$95	$70	$50	N/A	N/A	N/A	N/A

MODEL 920 - multi-stroke pump pneumatic, similar to Model 922 except has wood stock and forearm, five-shot clip. Mfg. 1978-89.

	$130	$105	$80	$65	N/A	N/A	N/A

MODEL 922 - pneumatic, multi-stroke, five-shot clip. Mfg. 1978-89.

	$95	$70	$50	N/A	N/A	N/A	N/A

MODEL 953 TARGETPRO - .177 cal., SSP, ULP, SS, 560 FPS, die-cast metal receiver, rifled steel barrel, black finish, black composite stock and forearm, fiberoptic front and adj. rear sights, 39 3/4 in. OAL, 6.4 lbs. New 2004.

	100%	95%	90%	80%	60%	40%	20%
MSR $90	$80	$65	$50	$40	N/A	N/A	N/A

MODEL 953 U.S. SHOOTING TEAM - .177 cal., single-stroke pneumatic. Mfg. 1984-85.

	$195	$150	$100	N/A	N/A	N/A	N/A

MODEL 9953 TARGETPRO - .177 cal., SSP, ULP, SS, kit includes shooting glasses, ShatterBlast targets and stakes, Shoot-N-C targets, and pellets. New 2004.

	100%	95%	90%	80%	60%	40%	20%
MSR $148	$125	$95	$70	$50	N/A	N/A	N/A

MODEL 977 - similar to Model 880, except has rifled barrel, peep sight. Mfg. 1980-83.

	$100	$75	$50	N/A	N/A	N/A	N/A

MODEL 1880 - similar to Model 880, except with scope. Mfg.1978-80.

	$100	$75	$60	N/A	N/A	N/A	N/A

MODEL 1881 POWERLINE - BB/.175 or .177 cal., pneumatic pump. Mfg. 1978-80.

	$115	$90	$65	N/A	N/A	N/A	N/A

MODEL 1917 POWERLINE - .177 cal., five-shot clip, scope. Mfg. 1978-80.

	$115	$90	$65	N/A	N/A	N/A	N/A

MODEL 7840 BUCKMASTER - BB/.175, or .177 cal., SSP, 320 FPS (BB/.175 cal.), smooth bore steel barrel, 350 (BB/.175 cal.) or SS (.177 cal.), black finish, adj. rear sight and electronic point sight, molded woodgrain with checkering stock and forearm, crossbolt trigger block safety, 2.25 lbs. New 2003.

	100%	95%	90%	80%	60%	40%	20%
MSR $55	$50	$40	$33	$25	$20	N/A	N/A

AMERICAN SPIRIT - BB/.175, or .177 cal., CO_2 similar to Model 840 Grizzly, except stock and forearm are finished in stars and stripes design. Mfg. 2002.

	$50	$40	$33	$25	$20	N/A	N/A

AVANTI MODEL 753 ELITE - .177 cal., SSP, 480 FPS, competition sights, hardwood stock, high cheekpiece, adj. trigger, Lothar Walther rifled barrel, 6 lbs. 8 oz.

	100%	95%	90%	80%	60%	40%	20%
MSR $558	$385	$325	$265	$215	$170	N/A	N/A

AVANTI MODEL 853 LEGEND - .177 cal., SSP, 480 FPS, Lothar Walther barrel, adj. sights, 5 lbs. 8 oz.

	100%	95%	90%	80%	60%	40%	20%
MSR $387	$225	$205	$175	$145	$125	N/A	N/A

AVANTI MODEL 853C LEGEND EX - .177 cal., similar to Model 853 Target, except has five-shot mag.

	100%	95%	90%	80%	60%	40%	20%
MSR $405	$230	$205	$175	$145	$125	N/A	N/A

AVANTI MODEL 888 MEDALIST - .177 cal., CO_2 2.5 oz. cylinder, 500 FPS, SS bolt action, Lothar Walther rifled steel target barrel, hooded front sight with changeable aperture inserts, micrometer adj. rear sight, multi-color laminate three-position sporter style hardwood stock, adj. trigger, 6.9 lbs. New 2001.

	100%	95%	90%	80%	60%	40%	20%
MSR $495	$300	$250	$200	$150	$130	N/A	N/A

GRADING	100%	95%	90%	80%	60%	40%	20%

AVANTI PREMIO PRECISION MODEL XP 30 - .177 cal., CO_2, 580-600 FPS, built-in gauge in the cylinder, 19.8 in. Lothar Walther rifled steel barrel, Hämmerli precision target sights, hardwood laminate stock with adj. cheek piece and buttplate, fully adj. trigger, 8.5 lbs. Mfg. 2001-2002.

	$799	$720	$610	$490	N/A	N/A	N/A

AVANTI TROFEO PRECISION MODEL XT 10 - .177 cal., compressed air, 580-600 FPS, built-in gauge in the cylinder, 23.54-in. Lothar Walther rifled steel barrel, Anschütz precision target sights, hardwood laminate stock with carbon fiber finish, fully adj. cheek piece and buttplate, fully adj. trigger, 11.42 lbs. Mfg. 2001-2002.

	$1,600	$1,440	$1,225	$980	N/A	N/A	N/A

AVANTI VALIANT MODEL XS 40 - .177 cal., compressed air, 580-590 FPS, built-in gauge in the cylinder, 19 in. rifled steel target barrel, front globe sight with changeable aperture inserts, rear diopter sight with micrometer click adjustments for windage and elevation, hardwood stock with adj. cheek piece and buttplate, adj. trigger, 7 lbs. New 2001.

MSR $881	$700	$550	$450	$350	N/A	N/A	N/A

AVANTI VITTORIA PRECISION MODEL XV 20 - .177 cal., compressed air, 580-600 FPS, built-in gauge in the cylinder, 23.54-in. Lothar Walther rifled steel barrel, Anschütz precision target sights, fully adj. target stock with adj. cheek piece and buttplate, fully adj. trigger, 11.42 lbs. New 2001-2002.

	$1,200	$1,080	$915	$730	N/A	N/A	N/A

RIFLES: PUMP/SLIDE ACTION

This grouping contains models that use a mechanical pump/slide action to cock the spring.

MODEL 25 SERIES - BB/.175 cal. elbow-slide pump action cocking, large takedown knurled-head bolt, MV to 450 FPS, internal spring-fed magazine, about 45 rounds, no safety. About 58 variants, 1914 to 1979.

* ❋ *Model 25 Variant 1 ("1914")* - short lever, slide handle with five grooves, straight stock, solder patch, adj. front sight (slides from side to side), black over nickel finish (never sold in bright nickel). Mfg. 1914 only.

	N/A	$250	$175	$125	N/A	N/A	N/A

* ❋ *Model 25 Variant 2 ("1916")* - similar to variation 1 except blue, adj. sights.

	N/A	$200	$150	$125	N/A	N/A	N/A

* ❋ *Model 25 Variant 3* - short lever, straight stock, fixed front sight. Mfg. date unknown.

courtesy Beeman Collection

	N/A	$225	$150	$100	N/A	N/A	N/A

* ❋ *Model 25 Variant 4* - long lever, five-grooved slide handle, straight stock, fixed front sight.

courtesy Beeman Collection

	$225	$150	$100	N/A	N/A	N/A	N/A

* ❋ *Model 25 Variant 5* - pistol grip stock, small takedown screw.

	$225	$150	$100	N/A	N/A	N/A	N/A

* ❋ *Model 25 Variant 6 ("1932")* - pistol grip stock, six-groove slide handle.

	$200	$125	$100	N/A	N/A	N/A	N/A

GRADING	100%	95%	90%	80%	60%	40%	20%

✳ *Model 25 Variant 7 ("1936")* - pistol grip stock, stamped "engraving" with gold paint. Mfg. 1936-42 and 1945-51.

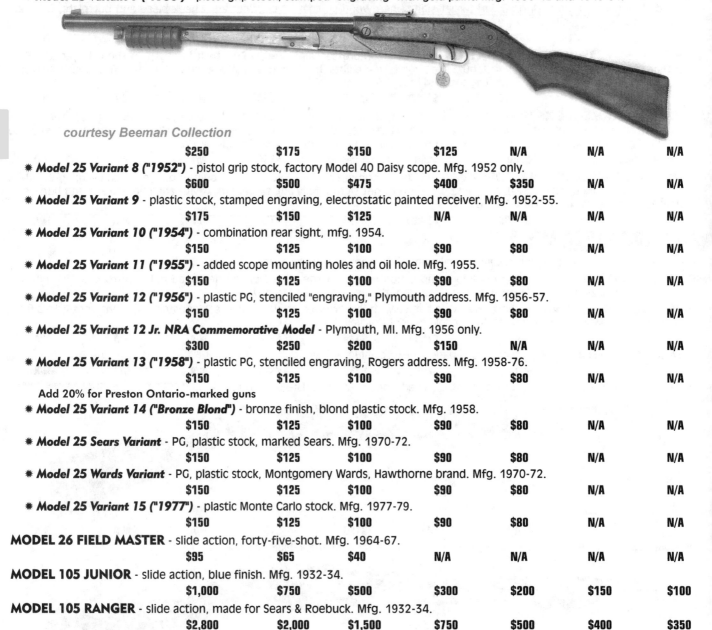

courtesy Beeman Collection

	100%	95%	90%	80%	60%	40%	20%
	$250	$175	$150	$125	N/A	N/A	N/A

✳ *Model 25 Variant 8 ("1952")* - pistol grip stock, factory Model 40 Daisy scope. Mfg. 1952 only.

	$600	$500	$475	$400	$350	N/A	N/A

✳ *Model 25 Variant 9* - plastic stock, stamped engraving, electrostatic painted receiver. Mfg. 1952-55.

	$175	$150	$125	N/A	N/A	N/A	N/A

✳ *Model 25 Variant 10 ("1954")* - combination rear sight, mfg. 1954.

	$150	$125	$100	$90	$80	N/A	N/A

✳ *Model 25 Variant 11 ("1955")* - added scope mounting holes and oil hole. Mfg. 1955.

	$150	$125	$100	$90	$80	N/A	N/A

✳ *Model 25 Variant 12 ("1956")* - plastic PG, stenciled "engraving," Plymouth address. Mfg. 1956-57.

	$150	$125	$100	$90	$80	N/A	N/A

✳ *Model 25 Variant 12 Jr. NRA Commemorative Model* - Plymouth, MI. Mfg. 1956 only.

	$300	$250	$200	$150	N/A	N/A	N/A

✳ *Model 25 Variant 13 ("1958")* - plastic PG, stenciled engraving, Rogers address. Mfg. 1958-76.

	$150	$125	$100	$90	$80	N/A	N/A

Add 20% for Preston Ontario-marked guns

✳ *Model 25 Variant 14 ("Bronze Blond")* - bronze finish, blond plastic stock. Mfg. 1958.

	$150	$125	$100	$90	$80	N/A	N/A

✳ *Model 25 Sears Variant* - PG, plastic stock, marked Sears. Mfg. 1970-72.

	$150	$125	$100	$90	$80	N/A	N/A

✳ *Model 25 Wards Variant* - PG, plastic stock, Montgomery Wards, Hawthorne brand. Mfg. 1970-72.

	$150	$125	$100	$90	$80	N/A	N/A

✳ *Model 25 Variant 15 ("1977")* - plastic Monte Carlo stock. Mfg. 1977-79.

	$150	$125	$100	$90	$80	N/A	N/A

MODEL 26 FIELD MASTER - slide action, forty-five-shot. Mfg. 1964-67.

	$95	$65	$40	N/A	N/A	N/A	N/A

MODEL 105 JUNIOR - slide action, blue finish. Mfg. 1932-34.

	$1,000	$750	$500	$300	$200	$150	$100

MODEL 105 RANGER - slide action, made for Sears & Roebuck. Mfg. 1932-34.

	$2,800	$2,000	$1,500	$750	$500	$400	$350

MODEL 107 BUCK JONES SPECIAL - slide action, blue finish, sundial markings on wooden stock, needle or floating compass, Daisy marked on compass dial, sixty-shot gravity-fed magazine. Mfg. 1934-42.

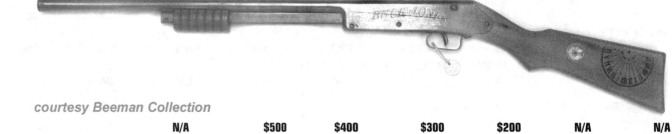

courtesy Beeman Collection

	100%	95%	90%	80%	60%	40%	20%
	N/A	$500	$400	$300	$200	N/A	N/A

MODEL 107 - trombone action, 500-shot, plastic stock, Plymouth. Mfg. 1957-58.

	$80	$55	$35	N/A	N/A	N/A	N/A

MODEL 225 - pump action, plastic Monte Carlo stock, plastic barrel cap. Mfg. 1991-93.

	$65	$50	$40	N/A	N/A	N/A	N/A

GRADING	100%	95%	90%	80%	60%	40%	20%

MODEL 325 - Model 25 rifle with scope set, target, and extra cork ball barrel. Mfg. 1936-37.

	$400	$300	$250	N/A	N/A	N/A	N/A

MODEL 572 FIELD MASTER - slide action, forty-five-shot. Mfg. 1968-72.

	$95	$65	$40	N/A	N/A	N/A	N/A

MODEL 799 - There really aren´t any "Model 799" guns. Rather, 799 is the prefix that Sears uses for all its Daisy airguns. Some of the Sears guns are listed as variations in the appropriate Daisy sections (i.e. 799.10275 is a Sears variation of the Daisy Model 25).

A crossover listing (see "Storebrand Cross-Over List") has been provided in the back of this text .

MODEL 1922 POWERLINE - .22 cal., pneumatic, multi-stroke. Mfg. 1978-80.

	$75	$50	$40	N/A	N/A	N/A	N/A

CENTENNIAL MODEL - replica, straight wood stock. Mfg. 1986 only.

	$150	$125	$75	N/A	N/A	N/A	N/A

RIFLES: VL SERIES

MODEL VL - .22 cal., combination airgun/firearm rifle designed to use special Daisy VL caseless ammunition. Mfg. 1968-69.

Clearly an underlever, spring-piston airgun, which will fire as just an airgun, but which is designed to have its typical airgun action supplemented by the ignition of a propellant mass molded on the base of special 29-grain bullets, i.e., caseless cartridges. Ignition is due to the high temperature normally developed by spring-piston airguns at the moment of firing (adiabatic compression) – not friction in the barrel as usually reported. MV is 1150 FPS.

Developed at Daisy by Jules van Langenhoven (= VL), but apparently the unique valve system, which seals the gun against the back pressure of ignition, was invented by M.R. Kovarik, and some other German engineers. Richard Daniel, former president of Daisy, reported that 25,000 guns had been made and were ready for a promotional launch just as U.S. President J.F. Kennedy was assassinated. The public backlash against firearms was seen as a threat to Daisy´s excellent public image, so the project was immediately dropped. When considering the question of whether this gun is an airgun or not, remember that power augmentation is not new in the airgun world. The Weihrauch Barakuda used ether to boost its power, and many airgunners, most notably the Brits, have been jacking up airgun power by dripping low flashpoint oil into their spring-piston guns for over a century.

The resulting diesel explosion can add real zest to the shot -- and real strain to the gun. This is why so many originally beautiful, originally tight, BSA and Webley airguns sound like a bag of bolts when you shake them. (Collectors and shooters beware.) In final analysis, the VL does not fit cleanly into any group; it definitely is both a firearm and an airgun!

* **V/L Standard Rifle** - .22 V/L cal. (caseless air-ignited cartridge), UL, SP airgun action, 1500 FPS, 18 in. barrel, plastic stock, not particularly accurate. Approx. 19,000 mfg. 1968-69.

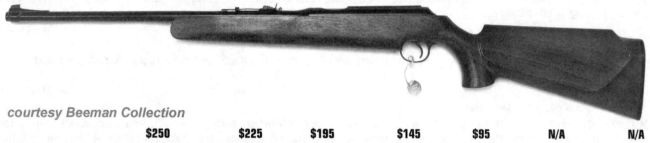

courtesy Beeman Collection

	$250	$225	$195	$145	$95	N/A	N/A

Add 50% for early version shown with checkered underlever, cheekpiece, Monte Carlo stock.

* **V/L Collector´s Kit** - comes with case, gun cradles, 300 rounds of ammo, and gold plated brass buttplate with owner´s name and serial number of gun. Approx. 4,000 mfg., available only by direct factory order.

	$550	$475	$425	$350	$275	N/A	N/A

Last MSR was $125.

* **V/L Presentation** - similar to Collector´s Kit, except does not have owner´s name inscribed on buttplate, walnut stock. 4,000 mfg. for dealers.

courtesy Beeman Collection

	$300	$275	$250	$200	$150	N/A	N/A

Last MSR was $125.

GRADING	100%	95%	90%	80%	60%	40%	20%

DAYSTATE LTD

Current manufacturer located in Stone, Staffordshire, England. Imported exclusively by Daystate America/Precision Airgun Distribution, Gilbert, AZ. Dealer sales. Previously imported and distributed by Airguns of Arizona, located in Mesa, AZ. Founded 1973.

Although often reported as starting with captive bolt cattle killers, the company made only three specimens of such guns. Initially concentrating on tranquilizer guns, Daystate generally is now recognized as the founder of modern PCP airguns, producing PCP air rifles by 1973. By 1987, high precision PCP rifles had become their main line. The publisher and authors of the *Blue Book of Airguns* wish to thank Tony Belas, Sales Manager at Daystate, for assistance with this section.

PISTOLS

FIRST MODEL - PCP, SS, single stage trigger, no trigger guard, approx. 20 made to order circa 1980. Specs may vary as all were made to order, but these are not prototypes.

Value of well-worn specimens from animal control companies about $700.

COMPETA - .177 or .22 cal., PCP, SS, based on Huntsman PCP rifle, breech loading, 8.0 in. barrel, 14 in. OAL, 2.9 lbs. ca. 425 fps in .177 cal., sliding 2-stage trigger, most handmade, no safety. Mfg. 1980-1995. To 1990 guns w/o SN or up to SN 50.

	100%	95%	90%	80%	60%	40%	20%
	$750	$625	$525	$425	$350	N/A	N/A

Last MSR was $730.

Serial numbers are standard after 1993.

RIFLES

FIRST PELLET RIFLE - .22 cal., SS, PCP, no safety, SN 1-42. Mfg. 1975-78.

Current values not yet determined.

These were Daystate's first pellet rifles, made while "still on the farm" by applying 42 surplus .22 cal. barrels which had been removed from Brno .22 rifles when they modified those firearms to 13 mm tranquilizer firearms.

FIREFLY - similar to Mirage except 36 in. OAL, 6 lbs., manual rocker safety. 50 rifles mfg. March to Dec. 2002.

Last MSR was $930.

Current values not yet determined.

CR 94 - all steel action, specialized Field Target rifle, no safety, 60 guns mfg. 1994-1996.

Current values not yet determined.

Successor to Model 2000.

CR 97 - similar to CR 94 except has improved and restyled breech block, cocking bolt and lighter alloy cylinder, improved regulator, no safety. Mfg. 1996-1998.

Last MSR was $1,750.

Current values not yet determined.

✳ **CR 97 Special Edition** - special Silver gun production with improved regulator and new, highly adjustable match trigger, no safety. 50 mfg. 1998-1999.

Last MSR was $1,900.

Current values not yet determined.

CR-X - .177, .20, or .22 cal., PCP, BA, SS, 20.5 in. barrel, blue-black matte finish, two-stage adj. trigger, improved breechblock and other refinements, field target competition wood stock with adj. cheek piece and butt, no safety, 43 in. OAL, 9.6 lbs. Mfg. 1999-2003.

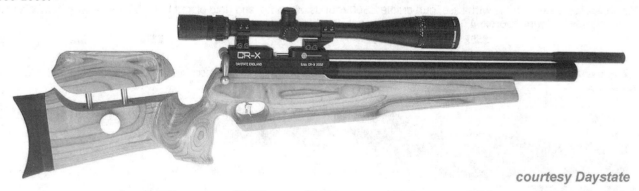

courtesy Daystate

	100%	95%	90%	80%	60%	40%	20%
	$1,795	$1,600	$1,295	$850	$650	N/A	N/A

Last MSR was $2,055.

Add 10% for .20 or .25 cal.

Several stock options available. Harrier-style blue-black matte finish (last ten rifles with gloss finish).

✳ **CR-MM** - an special version of the CR-X. Made of pure titanium. May be the most expensive sporter/FT air rifle made in the 20th century.

GRADING	100%	95%	90%	80%	60%	40%	20%

CR-X ST - .177, .20, or .22 cal., PCP, BA, SS, similar to CR-X, except all steel action, improved breechblock and other refinements, no safety 9.6 lbs. Mfg. 1999-2003.

	100%	95%	90%	80%	60%	40%	20%
	$2,150	$1,895	$1,600	$1,295	$850	N/A	N/A

Last MSR was $2,055.

Add 10% for .20 or .25 cal.

All-steel action version of Model CR-X manufactured for USA only.

MK3 RT/MK3 FT/MK3 SPORT - .177 or .22, PCP, BA, ten-shot rotary mag., 16 1/4 in. BBL, MFC, matt black finish, Harper patent Capacitive Discharge Technology (CDT) electronic firing system includes adj. trigger with electronic lock and MK3 CDT electronic rotary safety. Early A type: "on" light in stock behind action, brass trigger blade, UK only. Current B type: "on" light in the action, alloy trigger blade, keyed power switch in trigger guard, pneumatic regulator, checkered pistol grip (MK3 Sport), thumbhole (MK3 RT), or thumbhole with adj. cheek piece and buttplate (MK3 FT), walnut stock, 37.5 in. OAL, 8 lbs. New 2003.

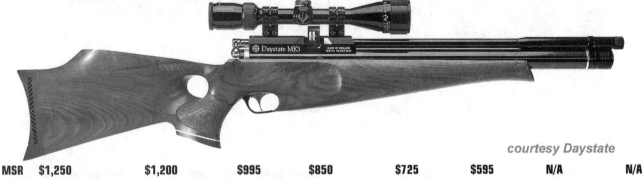

courtesy Daystate

MSR	$1,250	95%	90%	80%	60%	40%	20%
		$1,200	$995	$850	$725	$595	N/A	N/A

Add 20% for MK3 RT.
Add 30% for MK3 FT.

Imported to USA as three different models: MK3 RT, MK3 FT (field target stock) and MK3 Sports (matte finish body tube). MSR: A type = $1430. B type $1500-1610. Sports $1250. 37.5 in. OAL, 8 lbs. New 2003.

HARRIER - .177, .20, .22, or .25 cal., PCP, BA, SS, 16 in. barrel, alloy breech block, matt black finish, adj. trigger, ambidextrous beech or walnut stock, manual rocker safety, Extra Short (XS) variant (for Spanish market where most tanks will be hand filled), silencer, 35 in. OAL, 7 lbs. Mfg. 1997-2002.

courtesy Daystate

	100%	95%	90%	80%	60%	40%	20%
	$625	$550	$475	$395	$325	N/A	N/A

Last MSR was $855.

Add 10% for .20 or .25 cal.
Add 5% for walnut stock.
Add 15% for XS variant.
Add 10% for thumbhole walnut stock.

Basically a Huntsman shortened by two inches with a new alloy breech block.

* ***Harrier SE*** - .177, .20, .22, or .25 cal., PCP, similar to Harrier, except has satin chrome finish on steel parts, Gary Cane handmade walnut stock, manual rocker safety, 38 in. OAL, 8.6 lbs. Mfg. 1997-2002.

	100%	95%	90%	80%	60%	40%	20%
	$890	$815	$725	$600	$495	N/A	N/A

Last MSR was $900.

Add 10% for .20 or .25 cal.

* ***Harrier PH6*** - .177, .20, .22, or .25 cal., PCP, similar to Harrier, except has stainless steel six-shot rotary mag., Muzzle Flip Compensator (MFC), cylinder rotates counter-clockwise away from loading point, manual rocker safety. 38 in. OAL. 8.4 lbs. Mfg. 1998-2002.

	100%	95%	90%	80%	60%	40%	20%
	$1,015	$895	$750	$625	$525	$425	$350

Last MSR was $1,050.

Add 10% for .20 or .25 cal.
Add 50% for SE version. (like Harrier SE).

Designed with Paul Hogarth. Several stock and finish options were available.

GRADING	100%	95%	90%	80%	60%	40%	20%

❋ *Harrier PH6 SE* - .177, .20, .22, or .25 cal., PCP, similar to Harrier SE, except has stainless steel six-shot rotary mag. and is fitted with MFC. 8.6 lbs. Mfg. 2003.

	100%	95%	90%	80%	60%	40%	20%
	$1,150	$950	$715	$625	$500	N/A	N/A

Last MSR was $1,260.

❋ *Harrier X* - .177 or .22 cal., PCP, BA, ten-shot rotary mag. 15.8 in. BBL, MFC, matte black finish, adj. two-stage trigger, rotary manual safety, 35 in. OAL, 7.5 lbs. Mfg. 2003-2004.

courtesy Daystate

	100%	95%	90%	80%	60%	40%	20%
	$835	$625	$550	$475	$395	N/A	N/A

Last MSR was $835.

Add 10% for walnut stock.

Add 25% for thumbhole walnut stock.

HUNTSMAN MIDAS - .22 cal., PCP, SS, two-piece cylinder, square breechblock, pressed steel, single- or two-stage trigger designed by Barry McGraw, manual cross-bolt safety, Midas Mk2 variant -- HM prefix on SN and rocker safety. Mfg. 1983-1992.

	100%	95%	90%	80%	60%	40%	20%
	$890	$815	$725	$600	$495	N/A	N/A

Last MSR was $900.

Add 5% for brass body tube or two-stage trigger.

Add 15% for stainless steel body tube.

Add 10% for Huntsman Midas Mk2 variant.

Very early guns made for animal control companies have stainless steel body tube. Later versions with brass body tube gave rise to the Midas name which is still used for blued models. High power versions prefix SN with HH (Huntsman High) prefix, low power version with HL prefix.

HUNTSMAN MK I - .22 cal., PCP, SS, round tubular breechblock - early versions with loaded port as scallop on right side, later versions with loading port cut completely across, higher pressure valve intro. April 1994. Final version with square breechblock, single stage trigger, manual rocker safety, barrels by BSA. Mfg. 1988-1995.

courtesy Daystate

	100%	95%	90%	80%	60%	40%	20%
	$625	$550	$475	$395	$325	N/A	N/A

Less expensive version of Midas, designed by Rob Thompson.

GRADING	100%	95%	90%	80%	60%	40%	20%

HUNTSMAN MK II - .177, .20, .22, or .25 cal., PCP, bolt action, SS, new version of Mk I, MK II engraved on breech, lighter body tube reduced wt. 2 lbs., adj. two-stage trigger, beech or walnut stock, several finish options, manual rocker safety. Three versions: 1. Heavy Air Tube Variant - used Mk 1 air tube, figure of dart protrudes from engraved logo. 2. BSA Barrel Variant - deeply concave muzzle crown, unchoked, early. 3. Walther Barrel Variant - Lothar Walther choked barrel - later. 8.4 lbs. Mfg.1995 -2002.

courtesy Fred Liady

	$800	$735	$650	$525	$425	$325	$250

Last MSR was $810.

Add 10% for walnut stock.
Add 10% for "TH" (thumbhole version).
Add 10% for .20 or .25 cal.
Add 250% for solid brass construction, two manufactured in .22 cal., 10.3 lbs.

* ***Huntsman MK II PH6*** - .177, .20, .22, or .25 cal., similar to Huntsman MK II, except has stainless steel six-shot rotary mag., 8.4 lbs. Disc. 2003.

	$1,015	$895	$750	$625	$525	N/A	N/A

Last MSR was $1,040.

Add 10% for .20 or .25 cal.
Several stock and finish options available.

LR90 (LIGHT RIFLE 1990) - .177 cal., PCP, SS, BA, 930 FPS, similar to Huntsman except has one-inch diameter body tube, smooth or hand checkered stock, adj. trigger, manual safety, 7.3 lbs., 38.5 in. OAL. Mfg. 1995-99.

	$825	$700	$550	$450	$325	N/A	N/A

Last MSR was $900.

Add 50% for FT model with checkered thumbhole stock.
Same as Beeman Mako.

MIRAGE XLR (EXTRA LIGHT RIFLE) - .177, .20, .22, or .25 cal., PCP, bolt action, SS, 16 in. BBL, aircraft aluminum cylinder, matte blue finish, adj. trigger, beech or walnut stock, 36 in. OAL. 4.2 lbs. Mfg. 1999-2002.

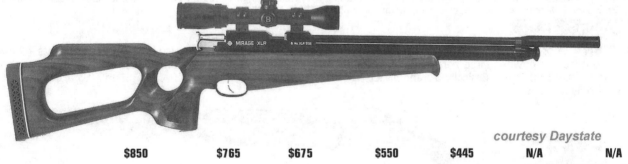

courtesy Daystate

	$850	$765	$675	$550	$445	N/A	N/A

Last MSR was $895.

Add 5% for walnut stock.
Add 10% for .20 or .25 cal.
Several stock and finish options available.

MIRAGE MK2 - .177 or .22 cal., PCP, SS, BA, improved version of Mirage with steel LR90 air cylinder, more robust breech block, new valve design, scope grooves, no sights, manual rocker safety, 1000/860 FPS, 37 in. OAL, 5.5 lbs. Mfg. 2002-2004.

	$825	$700	$550	$450	$325	N/A	N/A

Last MSR was $895.

Same as Beeman Mako 2.

MODEL 2000 - .177 or .22 cal., PCP, SS. Similar to Huntsman with added regulator, manual rocker safety. 41 in. OAL, 9 3/4 lbs. Mfg. 1990-1994.

Last MSR was $1,400.

Current values not yet determined.
Regulators for 12 ft./lb. British versions did not work, but rifle could fire at a reduced force. Most specimens now have an aftermarket regulator or have removed the regulator.

GRADING	100%	95%	90%	80%	60%	40%	20%

QC (QUICK CHANGE) - .22 cal., PCP with removable 16-in. air cylinder. Mfg. 1997-1998.

Current values not yet determined.

✷ *QC 2* - improved version of QC w/ alloy air cylinder. Mfg. 1992-1996.

Last MSR was $875.

Current values not yet determined.

SPORTSMAN - .22 cal., SS, UL, multi-pump pneumatic, Monte Carlo stock w/o cheekpiece, manual safety. FAC models fire to 855 FPS on 9-10 pumps. Non-FAC multi-pump models require six strokes. 38.5 in. OAL, 7.9 lbs. Mfg. 1980-86.

	$1,000	$900	$800	$700	$600	$500	$400

Last MSR was $375.

SPORTSMAN MK II - .22 cal. SS, side-lever SSP for British market, two-stroke pneumatic for unrestricted markets, no safety. Mfg. 1996-98.

Last MSR was $570.

Current values not yet determined.

TRANQUILIZER AIRGUN - .50 in. (13 mm) cal., SS, PCP, Daystate's first airguns,. PCP tranquilizer gun. 1973-78.

Current values not yet determined.

X2 AMBI/X2 SPORTS/X2 PRESTIGE - .177, or .22 cal., PCP, BA, SS, 16 in. barrel, alloy breech block, satin finish, adj. trigger, ambidextrous beech (X2 Ambi), RH or LH synthetic (X2 Sports), or thumbhole extra grade American walnut (X2 Prestige) stock, manual rocker safety, moderator, 38 in. OAL, 7 lbs. New 2004.

courtesy Daystate

MSR	$865	$825	$700	$550	$450	$325	N/A	N/A

Add 20% for regulated versions, less desirable in USA.

Add 35% for Prestige variant with Gary Cane stock.

Most are marked "Daystate X2", a few early guns are marked "Harrier X2". Sports Variant: black synthetic stock, black bolt handle (also, in British market regulated version, chrome bolt handle, limited to 25 ft./lb. ME).

SHOTGUNS

SHOTGUN - .38 or .50 (?) caliber smoothbore, SS, PCP, designed for controlling pests, such as small birds and rats in grain storage, without lead or powder. Fired hard, silver-colored, BB-shaped, candy cake decorations (in UK ="Dragees" or "Rainbow Pearls") from tubular brass case. Basically a tranquillizer barrel built onto a Huntsman air rifle. OAL 45 in., 8.3 lbs, barrel 24.3 in. Mfg. 1987 only 17 guns.

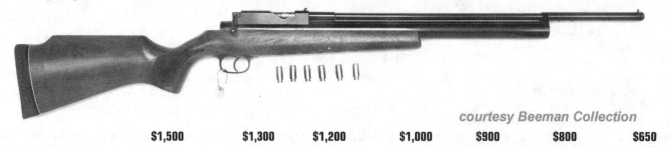

courtesy Beeman Collection

	$1,500	$1,300	$1,200	$1,000	$900	$800	$650

DECKER

Previous trademark of Decker Manufacturing Company located in Detroit, Michigan from about 1891 to 1899.

Decker Manufacturing Company, formerly produced sheet metal BB guns. The company used tools and materials apparently purchased by Charles Decker from defunct Plymouth Air Rifle Company of Plymouth, Michigan which had produced a cast iron BB gun under the name Magic about 1890-91. Decker produced some cast iron guns under the Decker name around 1898, but quickly cheapened and simplified the designs into perhaps three models under the Bijou name. The last Bijou model seems to have been the Model B, named for the large B on the grip frame. This model was all sheet metal of rather poor construction. Survival of specimens has been predictably low, but the numbers produced evidently resulted in more Bijou specimens surviving than Magic, Decker, or the later Hexagon models. Charles Decker and his brother, Frederick Decker, and associate Frank Trowbridge, formed the Hexagon Air Rifle Company which produced the Hexagon air rifles about 1900-1901. These BB guns featured a hexagon shaped barrel cover and an unusual BB reservoir (not properly called a magazine) in the buttstock. .Despite a cast iron grip, the Hexagon rifles did not stand up and are rarely found. Prices of the various Decker produced airguns now may run from about $300 to over $1000 depending on model and condition.. Additional details about the guns and their values are subject to further study and information for future editions of the Blue Book of Airguns. Ref. Dunathan (1957).

DIANAWERK GmbH & CO. KG, MAYER & GRAMMELSPACHER

Current manufacturer located in Rastatt, Germany. Currently imported exclusively by Dynamit Nobel RWS Inc., located in Closter, NJ. Dynamit Nobel is now a division of RUAG AmmoTec GmbH, located in Furth, Germany. Dealer and consumer direct sales.

Dynamit Nobel RWS, Inc. also imports airguns manufactured by Air Arms, BSA, Gamo, and Shinsung/Career. Please refer to their respective listings under this section for pricing.

The authors and publisher wish to thank Ulrich Eichstädt, Mike Driskill, and John Atkins, for their valuable assistance with the following information in this edition of the *Blue Book of Airguns*. Because of the destruction of records in two World Wars, it was not possible to verify all information. Additional information and corrections will be made in future editions. Such information is actively solicted. Please send inputs directly to BlueBookEdit@Beemans.net.

This section covers only the real Dianawerk airguns, made by Mayer & Grammelspacher of Rastatt, Germany. It DOES NOT INCLUDE British "Diana" airguns. For British made "Diana" airguns, see the Millard Brothers section.

Despite the company´s 110 year history, the trademark with the hunting goddess Diana has become more famous than the official name of its company: "Mayer & Grammelspacher Dianawerk GmbH & Co. KG." One of the founders, Jakob Mayer, born in 1866, worked as a toolmaker at the Eisenwerke ("Ironworks") Gaggenau, in Gaggenau, Germany before he left to start his new company in 1890 in nearby Rastatt on the German/French border.

Mayer was the technical director of the new company; his friend, Josef Grammelspacher, financed it. Almost nothing is known of Josef Grammelspacher. He seems to have left the company by 1901 and the Grammelspacher family died out about 70 years ago. All documents concerning the family were lost during the two World Wars.

Around 1892, Mayer presented his first air pistol, which showed a great resemblance to a Gaggenau patent taken on the Haviland & Gunn patent design of 1872. Composed chiefly of a single piece of cast iron, it housed its mainspring in the grip and was marked only with the cast letters "MGR". The MGR trademark, representing Mayer & Grammelspacher in Rastatt, apparently was first used with the MG over the R and later was combined, at least in printed materials, with a target and a smiling boy´s face. It is not known exactly when the famous Diana trademark, showing the hunting goddess Diana holding her air rifle aloft while standing on her discarded bow and arrows, was first used.

One of Mayer´s many patents was issued in 1901 for a spring-loaded wedge mechanism to serve as a detent lock on barrel-cocking airguns. This mechanism, which has appeared on millions of airguns, is still in common use. Production of a number of models of airguns and toy guns developed rapidly during the 1890 to 1910 period, but, again, wars have destroyed most of the records. The toy guns, shooting corks and suction cup darts, were produced under the trademark "Eureka."

Trying to look back through the mists of time, what we do seem to see of the period around the start of the 20th century is a company that did not seem to have a focus. Like so many other airgun makers, they were adding, without particular distinction, to the seemingly endless flow of GEM airguns and toy guns. The advent of the solid MGR "First Model" pistols and rifles, both incorporating superb patent features of Jakob Mayer, seems to been the developmental and economic base, for the future of the company. However, the rapidly growing success of Dianawerk probably was due, as with contemporary Daisy, and even recent airgun company success stories, to aggressive marketing efforts and skills of a visionary, in this case, Jakob Mayer. The creation of the Diana name and logo was the first major step in this marketing.

In the "roaring twenties" the demand of military air rifle trainers was replaced by airgun shooting as a new family game and leisure-time sport. The quality and performance of these first Diana "adult air rifles," like the models 25 and 27, was increased. In 1930, a Model 25 was offered for 25 Marks, while the extra high quality LG 58 was available for 90 Marks. A tin of the newly invented "diabolo" pellets sold for 3.40 Marks. Unfortunately, the catalogs of that period did not mention velocities of the airguns and most of the specimens in collections are not capable of their original power, so we don´t know the potential of those "adult airguns."

By 1933, the emerging NAZI government had had a bad effect on DIANAWERK. Decreasing sales forced withdrawal from the Leipzig trade fair and export to 28 countries was forbidden for political reasons. By 1936, Rastatt had become a center for housing troops and in 1940 all civilian production was halted when the company was forced to produce gun parts for the Mauser factory in Oberndorf. (Dianawerk´s military production was marked with the secret code "lxr.") This military activity resulted in extremely heavy bombing of Rastatt by the British. In 1945, the French occupied the area and DIANAWERK was completely dismantled. As production of air rifles was then subject to a death penalty, the French were glad, to sell, at a donative price (in the spirit of war reparations), all of the company, including its machinery, old parts, and Diana trademark, to London-based Millard Bros. Ltd. With the abbreviated name "Milbro," the operation was moved to Motherwell in Scotland. The first Scottish "Dianas" were produced in 1949.

The Allied Control Council again allowed production of airguns in 1950. By September, the Mayers began production of airguns in their old factory in Rastatt. The loss of their world-famous "Diana" trademark hit them very hard. Within Germany the air rifles were sold as "Original." To commonwealth countries Diana exported "GECADO" models; "Condor," "Firebird," or "Original Diana" was used for Dianawerk guns in England. Many large foreign companies contracted for Diana models, or special variations including different cosmetics and features, under the names of Winchester, Hy-Score, Beeman, Peerless, etc. By 1982, despite the advantage of the trademark, Milbro, using Dianawerk´s old machinery and materials, had gone out of business. Dianawerk repurchased their trademark in 1984.

Although DIANAWERK never became a major force in the growing market of match airgun production like Walther and Feinwerkbau, they had a major effect on that market. Kurt Giss, the chief designer in Rastatt, invented the double piston system at the end of 1950s. This design used two pistons, connected and synchronized by a gear rod. The forward piston compressed the air for pellet propulsion. The second piston moved backward and eliminated recoil. The Giss System resulted in the production of the first recoilless match-guns: the LP 6 air pistol in 1960 and then in 1963 the LG 60 air rifle. The introduction of recoilless airguns caused a revolution in the design of match airguns and established Germany as the leader in this field.

A complete family of airguns with the double piston system followed. However, production of the numerous parts was very expensive and maintenance was very difficult. In the mid-1960s, Dianawerk, like many gun companies, began to simplify the construction and materials of

GRADING	100%	95%	90%	80%	60%	40%	20%

their guns. By the mid-1970s competitors Feinwerkbau, Anschütz and Walther had eclipsed Dianawerk. Dianawerk continued to concentrate on the production of economy-level, leisure-time models and they continued to concentrate on reducing production and material costs. A few attempts to get back into the "match market," with the LG 100 (a single-stroke pneumatic rifle), and match grade smallbore rifles, failed. A 1972 German gun law severely restricted air rifles with power over 7.5 joules; only about 5.5 ft./lb. or 575 FPS in .177 caliber! The British limit is 12 ft./lb. This led to a deepening crisis within the company. The 1979 to 1982 discontinuance of key Diana airgun models by Beeman Precision Airguns in the USA, one of their largest potential markets, may also have had a further disastrous effect. However, as of April 1, 2002, the German airgunners have a new lease on life: they now can have air rifles (over 60 cm) up to 16.3 joules (12 ft./lb.) for field target competition and even more powerful ones on a hunting license permit.

So at the beginning of the 1990s, directors Peter Mayer, the last descendant of the Diana founder, and Hans-Günther Frey faced serious decisions. More than five hundred employees had worked in the huge halls at Karlstraße, but now the halls were empty, and rumors went out that M & G desperately needed a buyer to keep the last hundred employees. No competitor, who was interested in the still successful Diana line, wanted to take the high risk of also buying the buildings. So Dianawerk began to rescue itself. Several production processes were outsourced. Retiring employees were no longer replaced. Models were slightly altered to use standard, plastic, and interchangeable parts. Stock making was discontinued. And a large browning/blueing machine was purchased, which, by drawing work from other companies, could profitably be used to full capacity.

German airgun shooting received a huge boost from the introduction of field target shooting. Firms like Diana, Weihrauch, Dynamit Nobel, and Haendler & Natermann cooperated to help form the first clubs and establish rules which considered the special German situations. Development of separate classes for air rifles above and below the 7.5 joule limit and also for precharged and spring-piston air rifles helped the shooters who had to document a need for high power air rifles. Now many different kinds of airguns and shooters could find shooting opportunities ranging from local fun to serious international competition.

Despite rumors to the contrary, the firm entered 2003 owned 100% by the Frey family (with relatives left from the Mayer and Dorf clans). Now with ninety employees and seven apprentices, Dianawerk was back in the black, beginning its 111th year without old headaches, looking forward to what the future might bring.

At the current time, Dianawerk airguns present a usually good collecting opportunity and challenge. These guns generally are under appreciated and under valued. There is a great deal yet to be learned about Dianawerk airguns. Certainly a major matter is how to designate the many different guns which bear the same factory model number!

Numbering of Diana models is somewhat confusing. Not only were model numbers not issued in chronological order, but sometimes the same model number has been issued to very different guns at different historical periods. Letters shown ahead of and after the model numbers generally do not appear on the guns themselves. Production dates may be stamped on gun in very small type – the date may be the key to the model variation.

DIANA COMPARABLE MODEL NUMBERS

For information on Diana airguns manufactured for other trademarks, see the Dianawerk Comparable Model Numbers chart in the Store Brand Cross-Over List at the back of this text.

Important note:

Comparable models often have vary different values due to different demand by collectors, different levels of rarity, and because distributors of private label guns often specified different power levels (for different markets, and not just mainspring differences), stock design, stock material and quality, calibers, sights, trigger mechanisms, etc. may be different from the basic manufacturer´s model. Beeman and pre-1970 Winchester-marked guns generally sell for a premium. Early models of the same number may differ from more recent models.

HANDGUNS

MGR FIRST MODEL - .177 cal., SP, slugs, pellets, or darts, 6.7 in. BBL, frame, sights, barrel, and grip of single piece are cast iron, spring piston in grip cocked by attaching separate tool to pull action bar, loaded via screw-in breech plug with leather seal, adjustable trigger, no trigger guard, black lacquer or completely nickel-plated finish, integrally cast floral design on sides of frame with cast letters MG over R, for Mayer & Grammelspacher in Rastatt, the company's early trademark, smoothbore barrel, later versions with brass liner, 1.3 lbs., 7.9 in. OAL, Mfg. circa 1892-1905. Ref: Gilbart, Guns Review, Nov. 1988, Atkins, Airgunner, July 1976.

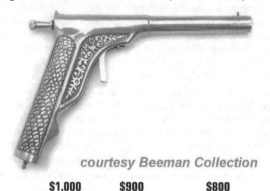

courtesy Beeman Collection

	NA	$1,000	$900	$800	$750	$725	$700

Add 20% for nickel-plated version.

Add 20% for early version with original separate cocking tool.

Add 30% for original wood box with papers and accessories.

Probably Dianawerk's first air pistols. Sold as the Tahiti by A.W. Gamage Ltd. of England, but this name should not be applied to this model in general. Evidently Dianawerk also provided Gamage, circa 1909/11, with a large BC, SP air pistol, like a cut-down Diana 20 air rifle, under the private label of Holborn.

GRADING	100%	95%	90%	80%	60%	40%	20%

MODEL 1 - .177 cal., 5 3/4 in. barrel, similar to MGR First Model, except economy version with pressed sheet metal, tubular brass barrel in sheet metal housing, spring piston in grip, several minor variations. Mfg. 1924-1940.

courtesy Beeman Collection

	$200	$180	$160	$135	$110	$85	$60

MODEL 2 (PRE-WWII MODEL) - .177 cal., push-barrel cocking, with shaped sheet steel frame, nickel finish, 7.9 in. smoothbore telescopic two-part steel barrel, removable knurled knob at back end of receiver for loading pellets or darts, marked "DIANA" on left grip, "Model 2" marked on barrel, fixed sight, 10.6 oz. Pre-WWII variant, approx. 100,000 mfg. 1931-1940.

courtesy Beeman Collection

	$125	$110	$100	$85	$60	$50	$40

✳ *Model 2 Improved* - similar to Model 2, except has adj. sights and riveted wooden grips. Mfg. 1955-1985.

courtesy Beeman Collection

	$85	$75	$65	$55	$45	$35	$25

GRADING	100%	95%	90%	80%	60%	40%	20%

MODEL 3 - .177 cal., BBC, 7.1 in. rifled barrel, blue finish, plastic grips, adj. rear sight, 325 FPS, 2.4 lbs. New 1991.

courtesy Diana

MSR	$97	$95	$85	$75	$65	$55	$45	$35

MODEL 5 ("V") - .177 cal., BBC, SP, rifled or smoothbore 7.5 in. barrel, hand checkered wood grip, 13.3 in. OAL. Mfg. 1933-1945.

	$200	$170	$135	$100	$70	N/A	N/A

Probably the only Dianawerk airgun with circle "D" trademark. Not related to post-WWII Model 5 listed below.

MODEL 5 - .177 or .22 cal., BBC, 7.3 in. tapered barrel, 450/300 FPS, metal trigger guard, adj. rear sight, hooded front sight, adj. trigger and wood grip until 1960, light gray plastic grip in early 1970s, later dark brown, safety, 15.75 in.OAL, 2.4 lbs. Mfg. 1958-1978.

courtesy Beeman Collection

	$110	$95	$85	$75	$65	$55	$45

Add 40% for wooden grip versions with tapered barrel.
Add 5% for gray grips.
Add 10% for "Beeman´s Original" markings -- the rarest version.

✳ *Model 5FO* - fiberoptic sight inserts.

	$145	$115	$95	$85	$75	$65	$55

✳ *Model 5G/GS* - .177 or .22 cal., BBC, 450/300 FPS, 7 in. barrel, improved version of Model 5, precision-cast alloy frame, smaller plastic grip (right/left-handed) with grip angle of 125°, receiver with plastic end cap, two-stage adj. trigger, GS Model equipped with factory scope, 16.5 in. OAL, 2.5 lbs. Mfg. beginning in 1978. Disc.

courtesy Diana

	$170	$135	$100	$70	$50	N/A	N/A

Last MSR was $260.

Add 20% for GS.
Add 20% for GN with matte nickel plating.

✳ *Model 5GM (Magnum)* - .177 cal., BBC, SP, SS, 700 FPS, blue finish, molded black grips, adj. rear sight, adj. trigger. New 2003.

MSR	$226	$195	$157	$115	$80	$65	N/A	N/A

GRADING	100%	95%	90%	80%	60%	40%	20%

❋ **Model P5 Magnum** - .177 or .22 cal., BBC, SP, SS, 568/422 FPS, 9 in. BBL, blue finish, molded black grip, fiberoptic adj. rear sight, 2.64 lbs. Mfg. 2001-03.

courtesy Diana

	$200	$170	$135	$100	$70	N/A	N/A

Last MSR was $250.

MODEL 6 - .177 cal., BBC, similar to Model 5, recoilless Giss double contra-piston system, 7.1 in. tapered barrel, wood grip, adj. trigger, 16.5 in. OAL, 2.9 lbs. Mfg. 1960-1978.

courtesy Beeman Collection

	$200	$170	$135	$100	$70	N/A	N/A

Sometimes misread as "Model 8."

❋ **Model 6G** - .177 cal., BBC, 450 FPS, 7 in. barrel (professional target), alloy frame, separate plastic grip similar to Model 5. Mfg. 1978-2000.

	$300	$275	$230	$195	$150	N/A	N/A

Add 5% for gray grips.

Add 20% for "Beeman's Original" markings - the rarest version.

❋ **Model 6GS** - .177 cal., BBC, 450 FPS, 7 in. barrel (professional target), equipped with factory scope and scope rail, muzzle weight, plastic sport or wooden palm rest grip, 3 lbs. Importation disc. 1995.

	$360	$315	$275	$230	$195	N/A	N/A

Last MSR was $445.

Add 15% for palm rest grips.

❋ **Model 6M** - .177 cal., BBC, 450 FPS, 7 in. barrel (professional target), match style, plastic sport or wooden palm rest grip, rotating barrel-shroud from Model 10 without sight hood. Mfg. 1978-1999.

	$400	$350	$300	$250	$210	N/A	N/A

Last MSR was $620.

Add 15% for palm rest grips.

GRADING	100%	95%	90%	80%	60%	40%	20%

MODEL 10 - .177 cal., BBC, recoilless Giss double contra-piston system, 7.1 in. barrel, 450 FPS, adj. trigger and rear sight, open front sight with adj. width 0.1 in. to 0.2 in., rotating barrel shroud covered front sight during cocking and carried a special designed additional weight, matte phosphate finish, adj. wooden grip, eccentric rotating plastic sleeve around rear of receiver to secure shooting hand on early variant, 7 in. barrel, 16.1 in. OAL, 2.5 lbs. Mfg. 1974-1989.

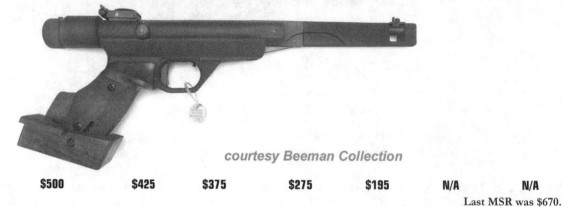

courtesy Beeman Collection

	100%	95%	90%	80%	60%	40%	20%
	$500	$425	$375	$275	$195	N/A	N/A

Last MSR was $670.

Add 15% for cased model.
Add 10% for left-hand variation.
Add 10% for eccentric rotating plastic sleeve.

RIFLES

MGR FIRST MODEL - The airguns which probably are Dianawerk's first airguns are known as MGR models. They are marked M&G over R, for Mayer & Grammelspacher, Rastatt, instead of Diana. All are very rare. Ref: Larry Hannusch, *US Airgun* Oct. 1995, or in *Pneumatic Reflections* by Larry Hannusch, 2001.

Probably first air rifle of the Diana line.

✳ **1901 Variant** - .177 cal., BC, SP, 19 in. smoothbore octagonal blued barrel, rest of gun is nickel plated, complex cast spring cylinder projects straight ahead of trigger, guard, fixed rear sight, side-barrel latch, quarter length straight grip buttstock with cheekpiece, 41.3 in. OAL, 5.3 lbs. M&G German Sept. 1901 patent no. 135599. Mfg. 1901-1904/05.

100%	95%	90%	80%	60%	40%	20%
N/A	N/A	N/A	$1,500	$1,400	$1,300	$900

✳ **1904 Variant** - .177 cal., BC, SP, 18.9 in. rifled octagonal blued barrel, rest of gun is nickel plated, complex cast spring cylinder projects straight ahead of trigger, guard, side-mounted barrel latch, wedge-shaped detent, quarter length straight grip buttstock with cheekpiece, 42.6 in. OAL, 7.1 lbs. M&G German Aug. 1904 patent no. 163094. Mfg. 1904/05.

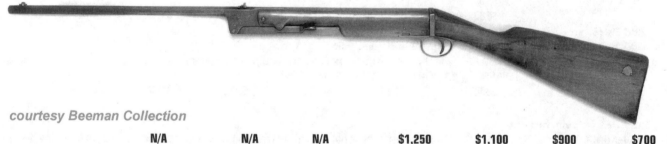

courtesy Beeman Collection

100%	95%	90%	80%	60%	40%	20%
N/A	N/A	N/A	$1,250	$1,100	$900	$700

GEM MODELS - from about 1895 Mayer and Grammelspacher produced many Gem-style air rifles (copied from Haviland and Gunn designs), reportedly including a "Ladies" model and MGR "Patent Repeating Air Gun," capable of 100 shots per loading, around end of 19th century. (See Gem in the "G" section.)

MODEL 0 - .177 cal., SL, SP, blue finish, revmovable smoothbore barrel for darts, balls, and pellets, fires corks with barrel removed, wood halfstock, fixed sights, 29.5 in.OAL, 1.5 lbs. Mfg. 1950-52.

courtesy Beeman Collection

100%	95%	90%	80%	60%	40%	20%
$400	$275	$195	$155	$95	N/A	N/A

GRADING	100%	95%	90%	80%	60%	40%	20%

MODEL 1 (JUNIOR) - .177 cal., BBC, SP, blue finish, tinplate construction, wooden buttstock, Diana goddess trademark above the trigger, fixed sights, loaded via removable rifled barrel (darts or balls), 31.5 in. OAL, 2 lbs. Mfg. 1913-1940.

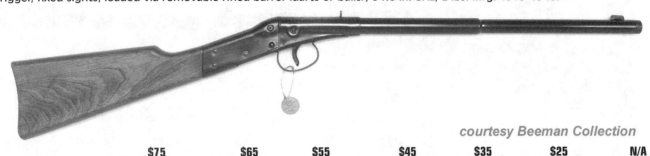

courtesy Beeman Collection

	$75	$65	$55	$45	$35	$25	N/A

✳ *Model LG 1 Improved* - .177 cal., BBC, SP, blue finish, an unspecified major improvement was made, per factory newsletter, after March 1, 1933. Readers determining the improvement should advise *Blue Book of Airguns*. Reported about 60,000 made per year from Nov. 1952 to 1960s, often with various private brand marks.

	$50	$45	$35	$25	$20	$15	N/A

MODEL 2 - .177 cal., BBC, SP, blue finish, fixed sights, underlever, rotating loading tap. Mfg. circa 1910-1940.

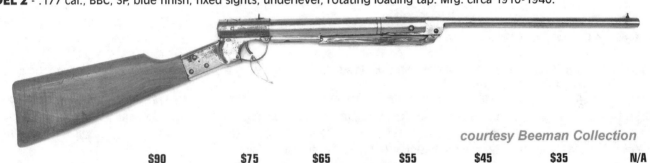

courtesy Beeman Collection

	$90	$75	$65	$55	$45	$35	N/A

MODEL 3 - .177 cal. blue finish, gallery-type trigger-guard cocking lever ("Bügelspanner"), break barrel to load, fixed sights, 35.4 in.OAL, 5.3 lbs. Mfg. 1913-1940.

courtesy Beeman Collection

	$135	$115	$90	$75	$65	$55	N/A

✳ *Model 3L* - .177 cal., blue finish, 34.6 in. OAL, 4.4 lbs.

	$135	$115	$90	$75	$65	$55	N/A

MODEL 3 (MFG. 1927-1940) - .177 or .22 cal., BBC, SP, blue finish, smoothbore or rifled barrel, developed as training rifle for smallbore rifle shooters, two-stage trigger (special order: set trigger), beech stock with pistol grip, finger grooves in forearm, screw-in rear sight, bead front sight. 43.3 in. OAL, 6.6 lbs. Mfg. 1927-1940.

	$225	$185	$150	$105	$75	N/A	N/A

MODEL 6 - .177 cal., BBC, SP, blue finish, less powerful version of Model 3, fixed sights, octagon steel barrel, cylinder and trigger guard nickel plated, walnut stock, 33.5 in. OAL, 4 lbs.

	$110	$85	$65	$55	$45	$35	N/A

MODEL 10 - .177 cal., BBC, SP, blue finish, 29.9 in. OAL, 2 lbs. Mfg. 1950-52.

	$125	$100	$75	$60	$50	$40	N/A

✳ *Model 10DL* - .177/BB cal. SP, SS, SL, 4.8 in. barrel removes for breech loading of BB or dart.

Add 200-300% for side lever version.

Side lever versions of these tiny youth air rifles are very rare.

MODEL 14 - .177 cal., bolt-action-style cocking, SP, blue finish, fixed sights, 38.2 in. OAL, 3.5 lbs. Mfg. 1913-1940.

	$150	$115	$85	$65	$55	$45	N/A

✳ *Model 14A* - .177 cal., military style full stock, contained cleaning rod looked like a bayonet.

	$300	$225	$175	$125	$80	$50	N/A

GRADING	100%	95%	90%	80%	60%	40%	20%

MODEL 15 (MFG. 1930-1940) - .177 cal., BBC, SP, smoothbore, blue finish, tinplate design, lighter and shorter child´s version of Model 16, without forestock. Mfg. circa 1930-1940.

courtesy Beeman Collection

	$90	$75	$65	$55	$45	$35	N/A

MODEL 15 (MFG. 1951-1980) - .177 cal., BBC, SP, blue finish, tinplate, stamped construction, beech buttstock, 12 in. rifled barrel inside sheet steel body tube, two-stage trigger, bead front sight, adj. rear sight, 32.5 in. OAL, 2.4 lbs. Mfg. 1951-1980.

	$50	$45	$35	$25	$20	$15	N/A

MODEL 16 (MFG. 1922-1940) - .177 cal., BBC, SP, smoothbore blue finish octagon barrel, all other metal parts nickel plated, beech buttstock and forearm, rear sight adj. for elevation, no safety, 37.8 in. OAL, 4.4 lbs. Approx. 25,000 per year mfg. 1922-1940.

	$90	$75	$65	$55	$45	$35	N/A

✳ *Model 16 Special Order Variation* - completely blued, matte oiled stock.

	$145	$115	$90	$75	$65	$55	N/A

✳ *Model 16 (Mfg. 1950-1985)* - .177 cal., BBC, SP, blue finish, similar to pre-WWII Model 16, stamped until 1984 with "Original Diana 16", 33 in. OAL, 2.7 lbs. Mfg. 1950-1985.

	$45	$35	$25	$20	$15	$10	N/A

MODEL 17 - .177 cal., BBC, SP, blue finish, similar to Model 16, except 41 in. OAL, 5.5 lbs. Mfg. 1922-1940.

	$75	$60	$50	$40	$30	$20	N/A

✳ *Model 17P* - .177 cal., BBC, SP, blue finish, similar to Model 17, except has pistol grip.

	$110	$90	$75	$65	$55	$45	N/A

MODEL 18 - .177 cal., BBC, SP, blue finish, similar to Model 16, except 41.3 in. OAL, 6.6 lbs. Mfg. 1922-1940.

	$75	$60	$50	$40	$30	$25	N/A

✳ *Model 18P* - .177 cal., BBC, SP, blue finish, similar to Model 18, except has pistol grip.

	$95	$80	$70	$60	$50	$40	N/A

MODEL 19 - .177 cal., BBC, SP, blue finish octagon barrel, all other metal parts nickel plated, beech buttstock, adj. rear sight, 37.4 in. OAL, 6.6 lbs. Mfg. 1922-1940.

	$95	$80	$70	$60	$50	$40	N/A

✳ *Model 19 Special Order Variation* - similar to Model 19, except completely blued, matte oiled walnut stock.

	$125	$100	$85	$75	$65	$55	N/A

✳ *Model 19P* - similar to Model 19, except with pistol grip.

	$110	$90	$75	$65	$55	$45	N/A

✳ *Model 19S* - similar to Model 19, except with safety.

	$110	$90	$75	$65	$55	$45	N/A

✳ *Model 19PS* - .177 or .22 cal., BBC, SP, blue finish, 14 in. barrel, 36 in. OAL, 3.75 lbs. Mfg. 1953-1985. Similar to Model 19, except with both pistol grip and safety.

	$120	$95	$80	$70	$60	$50	N/A

MODEL 20 (MFG. 1910-1911) - .177 cal., UL, tinplate construction, 12.6 in. smoothbore brass barrel, all metal parts nickel plated, beech buttstock, 20 in. OAL, 2.7 lbs. Mfg. circa 1910-11.

	$170	$145	$115	$90	$75	$65	N/A

NOTE: These Model 20 air rifles are not related to each other.

GRADING	100%	95%	90%	80%	60%	40%	20%

MODEL 20 YOUTH - .177 cal., BBC, SP, youth model, all-metal parts are nickel plated, walnut buttstock, date of mfg. stamped on heel, 35 in. OAL, 2.7 lbs. Tens of thousands mfg. 1912-1940.

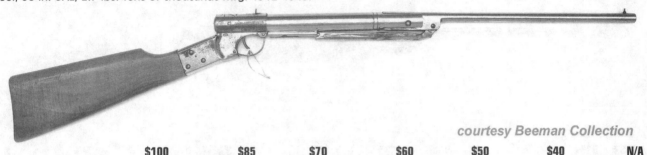

courtesy Beeman Collection

	$100	$85	$70	$60	$50	$40	N/A

Add 10% for early versions with simple rear sight mounted on receiver tube.
Add 20% for stamping "Foreign" instead of "Made in Germany" (just prior to WWII).
Add 20% for specimens w/o model markings but marked "Diana Luft-Gewehr Schutzenmarke".
NOTE: These Model 20 air rifles are not related to each other.

MODEL 20 ADULT - .177 cal., BBC, SP, 480 FPS, 17 in. barrel, black finish, hardwood stock, hooded front and adj. rear sights, 5.5 lbs. Mfg. 1991-2003.

courtesy Diana

	$95	$75	$55	$45	$35	N/A	N/A

Last MSR was $120.

NOTE: These Model 20 air rifles are not related to each other.

MODEL 21 - .177 cal., BBC, 460 FPS, 16.5 in. barrel, black finish, black composit stock, Truglo adj. sights, 5.8 lbs. New 2005.

NO MSR	$130	$105	$85	$65	$45	N/A	N/A

MODEL 22 (MFG. 1927-1940) - .177 cal., BBC, SP, blue finish, youth model, walnut stock, brass barrel either smooth or rifled in sheet steel body tube, adj. rear sight, 35.8 in. OAL. Mfg. 1927-1940.

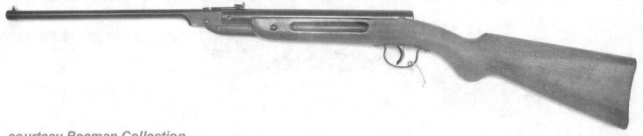

courtesy Beeman Collection

	$115	$90	$75	$65	$55	$45	N/A

NOTE: These Model 22 air rifles appear somewhat similar, but they are completely unrelated with virtually no common parts.

MODEL 22 (MFG. 1953-1985) -

	$65	$55	$45	$35	$25	$15	N/A

NOTE: These Model 22 air rifles appear somewhat similar, but they are completely unrelated with virtually no common parts.

MODEL 23 (DISC. 1940) - .177 cal., BBC, SP, blue finish, smoothbore or rifled barrel, 35.8 in. OAL. 4.2 lbs. Disc. 1940.

	$115	$90	$75	$65	$55	$45	N/A

NOTE: These Model 23 air rifles appear somewhat similar, but they are completely unrelated with virtually no common parts.

MODEL 23 (MFG. 1951-1983) - .177 or .22 cal., BBC, SP, blue finish, 14 in. smoothbore or rifled barrel, bead front and adj. spring-leaf rear sights, 36 in. OAL, 4.25 lbs. Mfg. 1951-1983.

	$65	$55	$45	$35	$25	$15	N/A

Subtract 20% for post-1965 versions with thicker stocks without forearm grooves, with stamped checkering, shallow cheekpieces, front sights as screwed-on ramps or clamped-on tunnels, plastic rear sights.
NOTE: These Model 23 air rifles appear somewhat similar, but they are completely unrelated with virtually no common parts.

GRADING	100%	95%	90%	80%	60%	40%	20%

MODEL 24/24C - .177 or .22 cal., BBC, 700/400 FPS, 13.5 (Model LG 24C) or 17 in. barrel, black finish, hardwood stock, hooded front and adj. rear sights 5.6 lbs. New 1984.

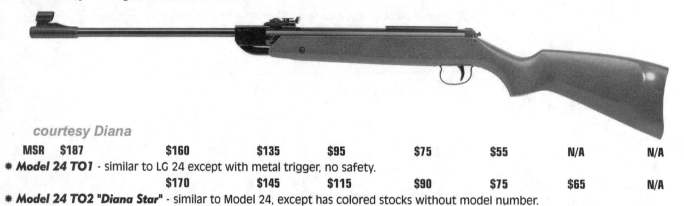

courtesy Diana

	100%	95%	90%	80%	60%	40%	20%
MSR $187	$160	$135	$95	$75	$55	N/A	N/A

✳ *Model 24 TO1* - similar to LG 24 except with metal trigger, no safety.

	$170	$145	$115	$90	$75	$65	N/A

✳ *Model 24 TO2 "Diana Star"* - similar to Model 24, except has colored stocks without model number.

	$120	$95	$80	$70	$60	$50	N/A

MODEL 25A - .177 cal., BBC, SP, blue finish, solid steel parts, walnut stock with finger grooves in forearm, adj. rear sight, no safety, 38.5 in. OAL. Mfg. 1925-1934.

courtesy Beeman Collection

	$115	$90	$75	$65	$55	$45	N/A

NOTE: These Model 25 air rifles appear somewhat similar, but they are completely unrelated with virtually no common parts.

✳ *Model 25 Improved* - .177 or .22 cal., BBC, SP, blue finish, smoothbore or rifled barrel, slightly longer forestock, metal rear sight, 39.7 in. OAL, Mfg. 1933-1940 and 1950-1986.

	$65	$55	$45	$35	$25	$15	N/A

Add 30% for pre-WWII version.

Subtract 20% for post-1965 versions with thicker stocks without forearm grooves, with stamped checkering, shallow cheekpieces, front sights as screwed-on ramps or clamped-on tunnels, plastic rear sights.

NOTE: These Model 25 air rifles appear somewhat similar, but they are completely unrelated with virtually no common parts.

MODEL 25D - .177 or .22 cal., BBC, ball trigger sear 525/380 FPS, 15.75 in. smooth or rifled barrel, 5.75 lbs. Disc. 1986.

courtesy Beeman Collection

	$120	$95	$70	$55	$40	N/A	N/A

Last MSR was $120.

✳ *Model 25DS* - .177 or .22 cal., similar to Model 25D, except has two-piece cocking lever, trigger block manual safety, angular stock styling. Disc. 1986.

	$150	$120	$90	$70	$50	N/A	N/A

Subtract 20% for post-1965 versions with thicker stocks without forearm grooves, with stamped checkering, shallow cheekpieces, front sights as screwed-on ramps or clamped-on tunnels, plastic rear sights.

Approx. ten million Model LG 25 have been sold; this model group is one of the world's most successful air rifles.

NOTE: These Model 25 air rifles appear somewhat similar, but they are completely unrelated with virtually no common parts.

MODEL 26 YOUTH - .177 cal., BBC, SP, blue finish, youth model, no safety. Mfg. 1913-1933.

	$350	$275	$215	$185	$145	N/A	N/A

NOTE: These Model 26 air rifles are not related to each other.

GRADING	100%	95%	90%	80%	60%	40%	20%

MODEL 26U - similar to Model 26 Youth, except UL cocking and loading tap, 38.2 in. OAL, 5 lbs. Mfg. 1933-1940.

	$300	$225	$165	$135	$95	N/A	N/A

NOTE: These Model 26 air rifles are not related to each other.

MODEL 26 - .177 or .22 cal., BBC, SP, 750/500 FPS, "Millita"-style, 17.25 in. barrel, 6 lbs. Importation 1984-1992.

courtesy Beeman Collection

	$150	$125	$95	$75	$55	N/A	N/A

Last MSR was $195.

NOTE: These Model 26 air rifles are not related to each other.

MODEL 27L - .177 cal., BBC, SP, blue finish, 18.5 in. smoothbore or rifled barrel, beech stock with metal buttplate, adj. trigger, no safety, 42.5 in. OAL, tens of thousands mfg. 1910-1936.

	$110	$90	$75	$65	$55	$45	N/A

Add 20% for pre-1923 version with octagonal to round barrel.

One of the most successful barrel cocking adult air rifles of all time.

NOTE: These Model 27 air rifles appear somewhat similar, but they are completely unrelated with virtually no common parts.

MODEL 27A - .177 or .22 cal., BBC, SP, blue finish, 17.5 in. smoothbore or rifled barrel, two-stage trigger, adj. rear sight, triangular front sight, wooden half stock, 41.3 in. OAL, 6.2 lbs. Mfg. 1936-1940.

	$135	$115	$90	$75	$65	$55	N/A

Add 20% for smoothbore.

NOTE: These Model 27 air rifles appear somewhat similar, but they are completely unrelated with virtually no common parts.

MODEL 27E - .177 or .22 cal., BBC, SP, blue finish, checkered beech stock with pistol grip.

	$245	$195	$145	$105	$75	$65	N/A

NOTE: These Model 27 air rifles appear somewhat similar, but they are completely unrelated with virtually no common parts.

MODEL 27S - .177 or .22 cal., BBC, SP, blue finish, two-piece cocking lever, trigger block safety, angular stock styling.

	$190	$160	$125	$95	$65	$55	N/A

NOTE: These Model 27 air rifles appear somewhat similar, but they are completely unrelated with virtually no common parts.

MODEL 27 - .177 or .22 cal., BBC, SP, 550/415 FPS, 17.25 in. smoothbore or rifled barrel, pre-1965 version with ball trigger sear, 6 lbs. Disc. 1987.

courtesy Beeman Collection

	$125	$100	$85	$75	$65	$55	N/A

Last MSR was $150.

Subtract 20% for post-1965 versions with thicker stocks without forearm grooves, with stamped checkering, shallow cheekpieces, front sights as screwed-on ramps or clamped-on tunnels, plastic rear sights.

NOTE: These Model 27 air rifles appear somewhat similar, but they are completely unrelated with virtually no common parts.

MODEL 28 (MFG. 1913-1940) - .177 cal., BBC, SP, blue finish, adj. rear sight, smoothbore or rifled barrel, no safety, 46.5 in. OAL, 7 lbs. Mfg. 1913-1940.

courtesy Diana

	$225	$185	$150	$105	$75	N/A	N/A

GRADING	100%	95%	90%	80%	60%	40%	20%

* ***Model 28 Improved*** - .177 cal., BBC, SP, blue finish, improved version after 1923, sight moved to base of barrel and made adjustable.

| | $185 | $150 | $100 | $75 | $55 | N/A | N/A |

* ***Model 28 (Mfg. 1985-1992)*** - .177 or .22 cal., BBC, SP, 15.75 in. barrel, 750/500 FPS, automatic safety, 6.75 lbs. Importation 1985-1992.

| | $185 | $150 | $100 | $75 | $55 | N/A | N/A |

Last MSR was $205.

MODEL 30B (BUGELSPANNER) - .25 cal., gallery-type with trigger-guard cocking system ("Bügelspanner"), beech buttstock with cheekpiece, octagon blued barrel, nickel finish, adj. rear sight, no safety, 41.7 in. OAL, 6.2 lbs. Mfg. 1913-1935.

| | $850 | $750 | $600 | $450 | $350 | N/A | N/A |

Note: These Model 30 air rifles are not related to each other. The suffix letters have been added to distinguish these models; these letters do not appear on the guns.

MODEL 30M (MILITARY) - .177 cal., UL, cocking lever hidden in forearm, military-style full stock with top hand guard, fixed barrel with loading tap, two-stage trigger, wing safety, front and rear sights similar to the Mauser 98k carbine, 41.7 in. OAL, 5.5 lbs. Mfg. 1935-1940.

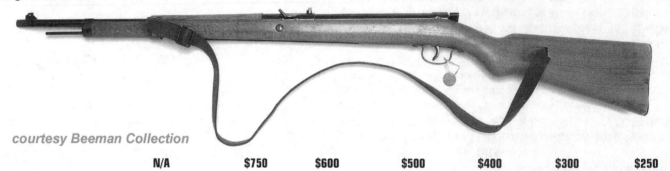

courtesy Beeman Collection

| | N/A | $750 | $600 | $500 | $400 | $300 | $250 |

Note: These Model 30 air rifles are not related to each other. The suffix letters have been added to distinguish these models; these letters do not appear on the guns.

MODEL 30R (REPEATER) - 4.4mm (RWS #7) round ball cal., bolt-action cocking system, ball shot repeater, fixed barrel, 16.9 in., mechanical shot-counter in left side of forearm for gallery use, capacity 125 balls, beech stock with rubber buttplate, two-stage trigger, manual safety, adj. rear sight, triangular front sight, 43.3 in. OAL. 7.25 lbs. Limited mfg. 1972-2000.

courtesy Beeman Collection

| | N/A | $575 | $495 | $425 | $350 | N/A | N/A |

Last MSR was $1,025.

Special orders still possible in 2003.

Note: These Model 30 air rifles are not related to each other; the suffix letters have been added to distinguish these models; these letters do not appear on the guns.

MODEL 32 - .177 cal., BBC, SP, blue finish, similar to Model LG 27, except with more power, 42.5 in. OAL, 6.6 lbs. Mfg. 1936-1940.

| | $225 | $185 | $150 | $105 | $75 | N/A | N/A |

MODEL 33 - .177 cal., BBC, SP, blue finish, checkered wood stock with pistol grip, 42.9 in. OAL, 6.6 lbs. Mfg. 1928-1940.

| | $250 | $215 | $165 | $135 | $80 | N/A | N/A |

MODEL 34 (MFG. 1928-1940) - .177 cal., BBC, SP, blue finish, similar to LG 33, except with British market style stock and pistol grip. Mfg. 1928-1940.

| | $250 | $215 | $165 | $135 | $80 | N/A | N/A |

NOTE: These Model 34 air rifles are not related to each other.

GRADING	100%	95%	90%	80%	60%	40%	20%

MODEL 34/34BC/34C/34N - .177, .20 or.22 cal., BBC, blue, matte nickel (Model 34N), or matte black finish, hardwood stock or black epoxy finish stock (Model 34BC), 920/690 FPS, 15.5 (carbine, Model 34C) or 19 in. barrel, approx. 7 lbs. New 1984.

courtesy Diana

	100%	95%	90%	80%	60%	40%	20%
MSR $261	$225	$185	$150	$105	$75	N/A	N/A

Add 5% for the hundred-year Diana Commemorative Model (new 1990).
Add 25% for .20 cal. model.
Add 15% for Model 34N matte nickel finish.
Add 50% for matte black finish and 4x32 airgun scope.
Add 100% for black epoxy finish stock and 4x32 airgun scope.
Add 15% for "Sport Mfg." without model number.
NOTE: These Model 34 air rifles are not related to each other.

MODEL 35 (MFG. 1953-1964) - .177 or .22 cal., BBC, SP, 665/540 FPS, 19 in. barrel, Monte Carlo stock with shallow cheekpiece, stamped checkering, globe front sight, plastic or metal click adj. rear sight with four-notch insert, plastic or stamped trigger blade, ball sear, 8 lbs. Mfg. circa 1953-1964.

courtesy Beeman Collection

✳ *Model 35 Standard Variant 1* - sporting stock, alloy trigger blade, fixed post front sight, simple rear sight in transverse dovetail.

	$225	$185	$150	$105	$75	N/A	N/A

✳ *Model 35A Variant 2* - like Model 35 Standard except has hooded front sight with four posts on rotating star, click adj. trear sight with four-notch insert, extra dovetail on rear of receiver.

	$250	$215	$165	$135	$80	N/A	N/A

✳ *Model 35B Variant 3* - like 35A except aperture attachment replaces rear sight notch assembly, allowing rear sight to mount on receiver dovetail for match shooting.

	$275	$225	$175	$145	$90	N/A	N/A

✳ *Model 35M Variant 4* - like 35B except has match stock with cut checkering.

	$275	$225	$175	$145	$90	N/A	N/A

About 1964 these were replaced with a simpler version with three variations in addition to standard model.

MODEL 35 (MFG. 1965-1987) - .177 or .22 cal., BBC, SP, 665/540 FPS, 19 in. barrel, 8 lbs. Mfg. 1965-1987.

	$120	$95	$80	$60	$40	N/A	N/A

Last MSR was $160.

Add 10% for metal rear sight or solid alloy trigger blade.
Subtract 20% for post-1965 versions with thicker stocks without forearm grooves, with stamped checkering, shallow cheekpieces, front sights as screwed-on ramps or clamped-on tunnels, plastic rear sights.

✳ *Model 35 Centennial* - commemorative model.

	$160	$135	$105	$85	$65	N/A	N/A

✳ *Model 35M* - target stocked version. Mfg. 1958-1964.

	$150	$125	$95	$75	$55	N/A	N/A

Add 10% for metal rear sight or solid alloy trigger blade.
Subtract 20% for post-1965 versions with thicker stocks without forearm grooves, with stamped checkering, shallow cheekpieces, front sights as screwed-on ramps or clamped-on tunnels, plastic rear sights.

✳ *Model 35S* - two-piece cocking lever, trigger block safety, angular stock styling.

	$150	$125	$95	$75	$55	N/A	N/A

Add 10% for metal rear sight or solid alloy trigger blade.
Subtract 20% for post-1965 versions with thicker stocks without forearm grooves, with stamped checkering, shallow cheekpieces, front sights as screwed-on ramps or clamped-on tunnels, plastic rear sights.

GRADING	100%	95%	90%	80%	60%	40%	20%

MODEL 36/36C/36S - .177 or .22 cal., BBC, SP, 1000/800 FPS, 15.5 (Model 36C) or 19.5 in. barrel, 8 lbs.

courtesy Diana

MSR $350	$300	$245	$215	$185	$145	N/A	N/A

Add $40 for 36S Model with scope.

Subtract $10 for muzzle brake model without factory sights.

MODEL 37 - .177 cal., BBC, SP, blue finish, beech buttstock without forearm, simple rear sight, bead front sight, no safety, 42.9 in. OAL, 6 lbs. Mfg. 1922-1940.

	$250	$215	$165	$135	$80	N/A	N/A

✳ *Model LG 37E* - British market-style stock.

	$300	$225	$165	$135	$95	N/A	N/A

MODEL 38 (MFG. 1922-1940) - .177 cal., BBC, SP, Deluxe version of the Model 36, similar to Model 37, except 7 lbs. Mfg. 1922-1940.

	$200	$175	$150	$125	$80	$50	N/A

NOTE: These Model 38 air rifles are not related to each other.

MODEL 38E - British market-style stock.

	$250	$215	$165	$135	$80	N/A	N/A

NOTE: These Model 38 air rifles are not related to each other.

MODEL 38 (MFG. DISC. 1998) - .177 or .22 cal., BBC, 919/689 FPS, 19.5 in. barrel, beech stock, 345.3 in. OAL, 8 lbs. Importation Disc. 1998.

courtesy Diana

	$275	$225	$175	$145	$90	N/A	N/A

Last MSR was $345.

NOTE: These Model 38 air rifles are not related to each other.

MODEL 40 - .177 or .22 cal., BBC, SP, 950/780 FPS, 19 in. rifled barrel with muzzle brake, blue finish, hardwood stock with buttpad, adj. trigger, 7.5 lbs. New 2002.

MSR $282	$245	$195	$145	$105	$75	N/A	N/A

MODEL 42 - .177 or .22 cal., UL, SP, blue finish, similar to Model 27, except 19.1 in. fixed barrel, adj. rear sight, bead front sight, adj. trigger, 40.9 in. OAL, 6.8 lbs. Mfg. 1927-1940.

	$250	$215	$165	$135	$80	N/A	N/A

✳ *Model 42E* - British market-style stock.

	$275	$225	$175	$145	$90	N/A	N/A

MODEL 43 - .177 or .22 cal., UL, SP, blue finish, similar to Model 42, except has additional checkering, pistol grip, and manual safety. Mfg. 1928-1940.

	$275	$225	$175	$145	$90	N/A	N/A

MODEL 44 - .177 or .22 cal., UL, SP, blue finish, similar to Model 48, except 43.7 in. OAL, 7 lbs. Mfg. 1928-1940.

	$235	$195	$160	$115	$75	N/A	N/A

MODEL 45U - .177 or .22 cal., UL, SP, blue finish, loading tap, similar to Model 26 (and simpler version of the later Model LG 58), 40.2 in. OAL, 7 lbs. Mfg. 1927-1940.

	$295	$235	$185	$155	$105	N/A	N/A

GRADING	100%	95%	90%	80%	60%	40%	20%

MODEL 45/45S DELUXE (MFG. 1978-1988)

MODEL 45/45S DELUXE (MFG. 1978-1988) - .177, .20, or .22 cal., BBC, SP, 790/550 FPS, 19. in. barrel, blue finish, two-stage adj. trigger, adj. rear sight, front sight with inserts, hardwood stock with rubber butt pad, 8 lbs. Mfg. 1978-1988.

courtesy Beeman Collection

	$220	$185	$145	$100	$65	N/A	N/A

Add 15% for Deluxe version.

Add 25% for .20 caliber.

Add 20% for LG 45S Model with scope and sling.

Add 10% for original long safety (recalled), within metal flap below, not marked (use guns with original safety with caution).

Subtract 20% for RWS 45 or Crosman Challenger 6100 markings, less desirable sight and stock systems; inferior handling to standard Diana 45. Ref: Walther, *The Airgun Book*.

✳ *Model 45 Jubilaums Modell* - commemorative model with special Rastatt factory plates in stock.

	$295	$235	$185	$155	$105	N/A	N/A

MODEL 45/45S DELUXE/45 TO1 (CURRENT MFG.)

MODEL 45/45S DELUXE/45 TO1 (CURRENT MFG.) - .177, .20, or .22 cal., BBC, SP, basically a restocked Model 34, 1000/800 FPS, 19. in. barrel, blue finish, two-stage adj. trigger, adj. rear sight, front sight with inserts, hardwood stock with rubber butt pad, 8 lbs. Mfg. 1988-2004.

courtesy Diana

	$220	$185	$145	$100	$65	N/A	N/A

Last MSR was $350.

Add 20% for Deluxe version.

Add 35% for Model 45S with scope and sling.

The post-WWII Model 45 is not related to the pre-WWII Model 45 and the post-WWII model 45 was replaced, still using the Model 45 designation, about 1988 with a restocked Model 34!

MODEL 46

MODEL 46 - .177 or .22 cal., UL, SP, 950/780 FPS, 18 in. barrel, blue finish, auto-safety, adj. trigger, extended scope rail, Monte Carlo stock with checkered forearm and grip (Model 46), recoil pad, 8.2 lbs. New 1998.

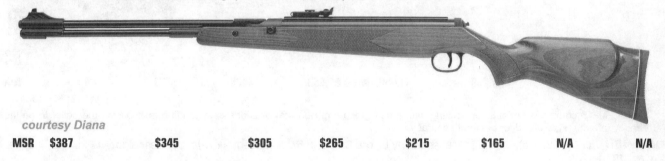

courtesy Diana

MSR	$387	$345	$305	$265	$215	$165	N/A	N/A

GRADING	100%	95%	90%	80%	60%	40%	20%

✳ *Model 46C* - .177 or .22 cal., UL, SP, similar to Model 46, except shorter. New 1998.

courtesy Diana

	MSR $387	$345	$295	$225	$175	$125	N/A	N/A

✳ *Model 46 Stutzen* - .177 or .22 cal., UL, SP, similar to Model 46, except full length Mannlicher-style stock. New 1998.

courtesy Diana

	MSR $491	$445	$385	$295	$245	$195	N/A	N/A

✳ *Model 46 Stutzen Luxus* - .177 or .22 cal., UL, SP, similar to Model 46 Stutzen, except has deluxe stock. New 1998.

courtesy Diana

$895	$815	$685	$625	$565	N/A	N/A

Last MSR was $975.

✳ *Model 46 Stutzen Prestige* - .177 or .22 cal., UL, SP, similar to Model 46, except engraved. New 1998.

courtesy Diana

$1,750	$1,450	$1,250	$995	$795	N/A	N/A

Last MSR was $2,000.

The Model 46 combines under-lever cocking with a flip-up loading port that provides easy loading, and allows the pellet to be inserted directly into the rifled barrel for pinpoint accuracy.

MODEL 48U - 177 or .22 cal., UL, SP, unlicensed copy of the British Jeffries pattern air rifle, adj. rear sight, 46 in. OAL, 7.5 lbs. Mfg. circa 1920-1940.

$350	$275	$215	$185	$145	N/A	N/A

✳ *Model 48E* - English-style stock.

$350	$275	$215	$185	$145	N/A	N/A

GRADING	100%	95%	90%	80%	60%	40%	20%

MODEL 48/48A/48B/48SL - .177, .20, .22, or .25 (new 1994) cal., SL, SP, 950/575 FPS, 17 in. barrel, adj. cheekpiece (Model 48SL), 8.5 lbs.

courtesy Diana

	MSR $375	$335	$295	$245	$195	$135	N/A	N/A

Add 10% for .25 cal.

Add 15% for .20 cal.

Add 5% for Model 48B with black matte finish stock (new 1995).

Add 20% for Model 48A.

MODEL 50 - .177, or .22 cal., UL, SP, two-piece cocking lever, angular stock styling, trigger block safety about two years after the introduction of angular stock styling. 1952-65.

courtesy Beeman Collection

* **Model 50 Standard Variant 1** - sporting stock, alloy trigger blade, fixed post front sight, simple rear sight in transverse dovetail.

	$200	$175	$150	$125	$80	N/A	N/A

* **Model 50A Variant 2** - similar to Model 50 Standard, except hooded front sight with four posts on rotating star, click adj. rear sight with four-notch insert, extra dovetail on rear of receiver.

	$220	$195	$170	$145	$100	N/A	N/A

* **Model 50B Variant 3** - similar to Model 50A, except with match aperture sight mounted on receiver dovetail for match shooting, 45.3 in. OAL, 8.38 lbs.

	$245	$220	$195	$170	$145	N/A	N/A

* **Model 50M Variant 4** - similar to Model 50B, except multi-purpose rear sight, match stock with cheekpiece and deep rubber buttplate 45.3 in. OAL, 10.6 lbs.

	$255	$230	$205	$180	$155	N/A	N/A

MODEL 50S - replaced regular Model 50 about 1965 with a simplified version without the ball sear trigger.

	$175	$150	$120	$95	$80	$70	N/A

MODEL 50T/T01 - .177, .22, or .25 cal., UL, SP, 745/600 FPS, 18.5 in. barrel, ball trigger sear, 8 lbs. Mfg. 1952-1987.

* **Variant 1** - standard with sporting stock, blued finish, sporting front sight with interchangeable posts.

	$285	$235	$185	$155	$110	N/A	N/A

Add 10% for .25 cal.

Add 25% for T01 Model.

Subtract 20% for post-1965 versions with thicker stocks without forearm grooves, with stamped checkering, shallow cheekpieces, front sights as screwed-on ramps or clamped-on tunnels, plastic rear sights.

* **Variant 2** - military with parkerized finish, military front sight with fixed post and protective wings.

	$260	$210	$165	$135	$95	N/A	N/A

Last MSR was $210.

Add 10% for .25 cal.

Add 25% for T01 Model.

Subtract 20% for post-1965 versions with thicker stocks without forearm grooves, with stamped checkering, shallow cheekpieces, front sights as screwed-on ramps or clamped-on tunnels, plastic rear sights.

GRADING	100%	95%	90%	80%	60%	40%	20%

MODEL 52/52 DELUXE - .177, .22, or .25 cal., SL, SP, 950/550 FPS, 17 in. barrel, walnut-stained beech Monte Carlo stock, checkering on forend and pistol grip, ventilated rubber butt pad, 8.5 lbs.

courtesy Diana

	100%	95%	90%	80%	60%	40%	20%
MSR $440	$405	$355	$315	$250	$185	N/A	N/A

Add 10% for .25 cal.

Add 55% for Deluxe version with handcrafted walnut stock, patterned checkering on forend and pistol grip, ornamental black wood insert in forend and base of pistol grip.

MODEL 54 - .177 or .22 cal., SL, SP, recoilless action, 950/780 FPS, 17 in. barrel, match type trigger safety catch with additional cocking guard, adj. front and rear sights, beechwood Monte Carlo stock with rubber butt pad, hand-checkered forend and pistol grip, 9 lbs.

courtesy Diana

	100%	95%	90%	80%	60%	40%	20%
MSR $626	$585	$510	$405	$325	$250	N/A	N/A

MODEL 58 - .177 or .22 cal., UL, SP, three main variations, "Dianawerk's pre-WWII flagship." Mfg. 1915-1940.

courtesy Beeman Collection

✱ *Model 58/1915 First Variant* - .177 or .22, cal., UL, SP, 625/500 FPS, set trigger, steel turn bolt, Walnut buttstock with PG, steel buttplate. 45.25 in. OAL, 8.25 lbs. Mfg. 1915-16.

		95%	90%	80%	60%	40%	20%
	N/A	$1,400	$1,250	$995	$850	$725	$600

✱ *Model 58/2 Second Variant* - .177 or .22, cal., UL, SP, 641 FPS (.177), different design: turn bolt replaced by knurled knob at the end of the receiver, checkered pistol grip stock with finger groove forearm, $70 in Stoeger´s 1937 catalog, when the Winchester Model 12 shotgun was $42.50, 47.25 in. OAL, 8.8 lbs. Mfg. early 1920s-1935.

		95%	90%	80%	60%	40%	20%
	N/A	$1,300	$1,150	$875	$675	$475	$275

✱ *Model 58/3 Third Variant* - .177 or .22, cal., UL, SP, adj. trigger, no outer trigger cocking device, 45.25 in. OAL, 7.9 lbs. Mfg. circa 1936-1940.

		95%	90%	80%	60%	40%	20%
	N/A	$900	$750	$650	$550	$450	$300

MODEL 60/60T - .177 cal., Giss double contra-SP system, 17.9 in. barrel, beech, Tyrolean (Model LG 60T) or walnut stock with rubber buttplate, match diopter rear and tunnel front sight with inserts, adj. trigger, optional barrel weight (tube), 42.7 in. OAL, 9.9 lbs. Mfg. 1963 to circa 1982 (Tyrolean stocks gone by 1980).

courtesy Beeman Collection

	100%	95%	90%	80%	60%	40%	20%
	$550	$455	$385	$295	$235	$185	$145

Add 30% for Model 60T.

GRADING	100%	95%	90%	80%	60%	40%	20%

MODEL 64 - .177 cal., records not yet clear about this model - if it existed, it probably was only a restocked Model 34. Mfg. circa 1986-89.

MODEL 65/65T - .177 cal., BBC, Giss double contra-SP system with radial lock lever, beech, Tyrolean (Model 65T), or walnut stock with rounded forearm, rubber butt pad, automatic safety, match diopter rear and tunnel front sight with inserts, adj. trigger, 43.3 in. OAL, 10.6 lbs. Mfg. 1968-1989 (Tyrolean stocks gone by 1980).

	$500	$405	$325	$255	$205	$145	$105

Add 35% for Model 65T.

MODEL 66/66M - .177 cal., BBC, similar to Model 65, except squared and deeper forestock, modified pistol grip and vertically adjustable rubber buttplate. Mfg. 1974-1983.

courtesy Beeman Collection

	$425	$365	$295	$235	$185	N/A	N/A

MODEL LG 68 - variant of Models 34/36/38 action with different stock.

Values TBD

MODEL 70 - .177 cal., BBC, 450 FPS, 13.5 in. barrel, youth dimensions. Mfg. 1979-1994.

	$130	$105	$85	$65	$45	N/A	N/A

Last MSR was $190.

MODEL 72 - .177 cal., similar to Model 70, except with Giss recoilless action. A rifle version of Model 6 pistol. Mfg. 1979-1993.

courtesy Beeman Collection

	$205	$160	$130	$100	$70	N/A	N/A

Last MSR was $340.

MODEL 75/75HV/75K/75S/75U/75TO1 MATCH MODEL - .177 cal., SL, 580 FPS, 19 in. barrel, micrometer-adj. rear sights, adj. cheekpiece, adj. recoil pad, 43.3 in. OAL, 11 lbs.

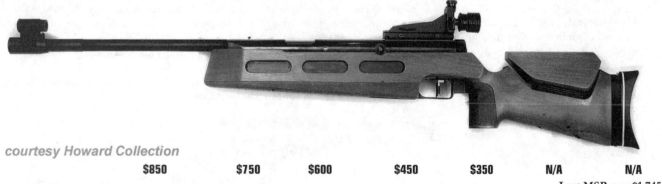

courtesy Howard Collection

	$850	$750	$600	$450	$350	N/A	N/A

Last MSR was $1,745.

Subtract 10% for left-hand version.

Premiums may exist for variations Model 75 mfg. 1977-1983, Model 75B mfg. 1988-1994, Model 75HV and Model 75TO1 mfg. 1983-88, Model 75K was disc. in 1990, Model 75S mfg. beginning in 1999, now disc., Model 75U mfg. 1982-86.

GRADING	100%	95%	90%	80%	60%	40%	20%

MODEL 100 - .177 cal., SSP, 580 FPS, 18.9 in. barrel, adj. cheekpiece, target model, 42.9 in. OAL, 11 lbs. Mfg. 1989-1998.

	100%	95%	90%	80%	60%	40%	20%
	$995	$800	$640	$480	$395	N/A	N/A

Last MSR was $1,950.

MODEL 350 MAGNUM - .177 or .22 cal., BBC, SP, 1175/970 FPS, 19.5 in. barrel, hooded front sight, adj. rear sight, checkered Monte Carlo beech stock with cheekpiece, 48 in. OAL, 8 lbs. New 2001.

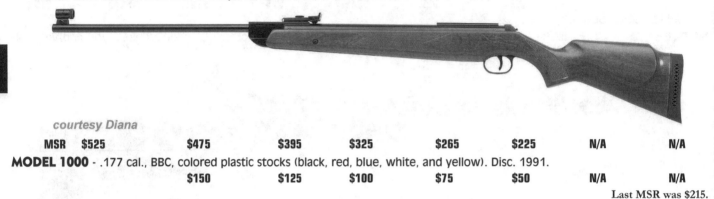

courtesy Diana

MSR	$525	$475	$395	$325	$265	$225	N/A	N/A

MODEL 1000 - .177 cal., BBC, colored plastic stocks (black, red, blue, white, and yellow). Disc. 1991.

	100%	95%	90%	80%	60%	40%	20%
	$150	$125	$100	$75	$50	N/A	N/A

Last MSR was $215.

Model 1000 was the sport model of the standard Model 34.

MODEL 300 - .177 or .22 cal., UL, SP, 900/700 FPS, 11 in. barrel, blue finish, adj. rear sight, auto-safety, Monte Carlo stock with checkered forearm and grip (Model 46), recoil pad, 29.2 in. OAL, 7.9 lbs. New 2005.

courtesy Diana

MSR	$537	$485	$425	$365	$315	$265	N/A	N/A

DOLLA

The Dolla name appeared about 1927 as a general designation for a number of push barrel air pistols with a cast one-piece grip and frame of distinctive shape but typically with no maker's name.

Most apparently were produced in Germany between WWI and WWII and may have been produced by several makers. They were especially promoted by Darlow of Bedford, England and Midland Gun Company of Birmingham, England. All are very solid and have very low power. The name came from the fact that the guns were priced at about the equivalent of an American dollar at the time of their introduction (SP, SS, .177 cal.).

Noted European airgun historian, John Atkins, indicates that the term Dolla, strictly speaking, should be applied only to models produced after 1927. Earlier, similar appearing pistols, perhaps first produced about the 1890s by the Langenhan and Gaggenau (formerly aka "Eisenwerke") factories in Zella Mehlis, Germany, never had this name applied to them while they were in production. The recent Dolla pistols typically have a trigger guard with a completely rounded opening while the similar, older, pre-Dolla versions typically had the upper rear area of the trigger guard opening with a distinct right angle profile. The pre-Dolla versions are worth significantly more.

Push barrel air pistols with sheet metal trigger guards, as made by Anschütz, and perhaps others, as early as 1930, had graduated to the designation of Dolla Mark II.

Dolla values range from about $100 to $500 depending on model, condition, and case. Typical specimens marked "British Cub" and "Cub" are illustrated here: The Anschütz Dolla Mark II has sold to $500 with original purple box. Ref: AG Jan. 2005.

courtesy Beeman Collection

GRADING		100%	95%	90%	80%	60%	40%	20%

DONG IL

Current manufacturing/marketing group in Seoul, Korea whose products include airguns.

RIFLES

M1 CARBINE MODEL 106 - .177 cal., SP, SL, full-scale replica air rifle of the U.S. Model M1 Carbine complete with military sling stock slots and bayonet base.

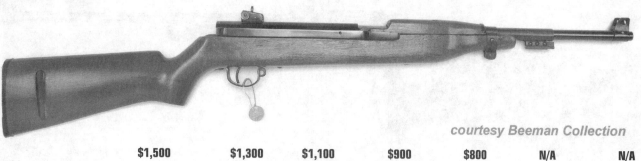

courtesy Beeman Collection

		$1,500	$1,300	$1,100	$900	$800	N/A	N/A

DREIBUND

For information on Dreibund airguns, see Philippines Airguns in the "P" section.

DRULOV

Current manufacturer located in Litomysl, Czech Republic. Currently imported and distributed by Top Gun Air Guns Inc. located in Scottsdale, AZ.

PISTOLS

DRULOV DU-10 CONDOR - .177 cal., CO_2, five-shot mag., adj. sights, blue finish, wood grip.

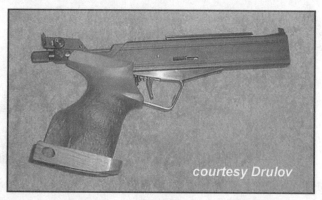

courtesy Drulov

MSR	$405	$375	$300	$250	$150	N/A	N/A	N/A

DRULOV LOV-21 - .177 cal., CO_2, SS, black plastic frame, 6 in. rifled steel BBL, 420 FPS, adj. sights, 11.3 in. OAL. New 2004.

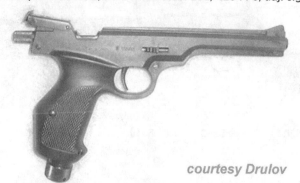

courtesy Drulov

MSR	$119	$110	$95	$75	$50	N/A	N/A	N/A

DRULOV RADA PISTOL - 9mm cal., CO_2, SS, adj. sights, rifled steel BBL, 210 FPS, blue finish, wood grip and forend, detachable wire shoulder stock. New 2004.

MSR	$430	$395	$325	$250	$150	N/A	N/A	N/A

Add 10% for Rada Convertible with longer BBL.

GRADING	100%	95%	90%	80%	60%	40%	20%

RIFLES

DRULOV 10 EAGLE - .177 cal., CO_2, five-shot mag., 525 FPS, 15.75 or 19.7 in. barrel, adj. sights, blue finish, wood stock.

	MSR $418	$400	$350	$300	$250	N/A	N/A	N/A

DRULOV 10 SOKOL - .375 or 9mm cal., CO_2, SS, adj. sights, blue finish, wood stock.

courtesy Howard Collection

	MSR $430	$430	$360	$310	$260	N/A	N/A	N/A

DUK IL

Current manufacturing group in Seoul, Korea whose products include pre-charged pneumatic airguns. Distributed in USA by Air Rifle Specialists.

PISTOL

HUNTING MASTER AR-6 - .22 (.177 or .20 special order) cal., PCP, SS, 12 in. rifled steel barrel, six-shot rotary mag., approx. twenty shots at 20 ft./lb. ME on one charge. 18.3 in. OAL, 3 lbs. Disc.

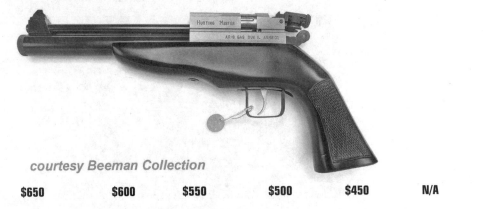

courtesy Beeman Collection

$650	$600	$550	$500	$450	N/A	N/A

RIFLE

HUNTING MASTER 900 - 9mm cal., PCP, 26.8 in. BBL, 900 FPS, wood stock. Disc. 1999.

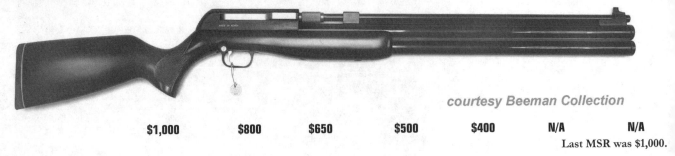

courtesy Beeman Collection

$1,000	$800	$650	$500	$400	N/A	N/A

Last MSR was $1,000.

E SECTION

EM-GE

Previous trademark manufactured by Moritz & Gerstenberger located in Zella-Mehlis, Thüringen, Germany circa 1922-1940, for airguns, starting pistols, blank-firing guns, and flare pistols. Re-established as Gerstensberger & Eberwein located in Gerstetten-Gussenstadt, Germany about 1950. Company seems to have vanished circa 1997.

Moritz & Gerstenberger apparently produced products for the German military program during WWII under the code "ghk." Now known mainly for rather low grade airpistols and teargas and blank-firing pistols; some of their pre-WWII products, such as the very interesting top-lever Zenit air pistol (SP) were quite good. Among their older products is a BBC, SP pistol, without model markings, which is very similar to a pre-WWII Diana Model 5. (probably an early version of the EmGe LP3A). Research is ongoing with this trademark, and more information will be included both in future editions and online. Ref: AR2: 16-20.

GRADING	100%	95%	90%	80%	60%	40%	20%

PISTOLS

MODEL 3 - .22 cal., BC, SS, fixed sights, 7.4 in. stepped, rifled steel BBL, all steel receiver, blue finish, checkered wood grips, no safety, 15.5 in. OAL, 2.6 lbs. Mfg. pre-WWII.

EM-GE LP3A
courtesy Beeman Collection

	100%	95%	90%	80%	60%	40%	20%
	$250	$225	$200	$150	$100	$65	N/A

Rear sight at back end of receiver.

MODEL LP 3 - .177 or .22 cal. BC, SS, 5.8 in. rifled seel BBL, adj. trigger, adj. sights, no safety, checkered brown plastic, grips, anodized blue finish on zinc barrel cover, receiver, and other zinc die-cast metal parts, 12.4 in. OAL, 2.7 lbs. Mfg. circa 1957-1975.

	100%	95%	90%	80%	60%	40%	20%
	$150	$125	$100	$65	$40	N/A	N/A

Subtract 25% for LP3A (top of receiver and BBL ribbed). Ref: GR, Aug. 76. Ca. 1975-1980.

Branded as HyScore 822T in USA. Ref: GR Dec. 74.

MODEL 100 - Specs and values TBD.

HERKULES - .177 cal, BC, SS, fixed sights, rear sight on breech end of barrel, blue finish, wood grips, no safety.

	100%	95%	90%	80%	60%	40%	20%
	$275	$225	$175	$125	$85	N/A	N/A

ZENIT - .177 cal., TL, SS, fixed sights, smoothbore or rifled steel BBL, blue finish, wood grip, (marked "gez"), no safety. Ref: AR2:16-20. Mfg. circa 1937-1940.

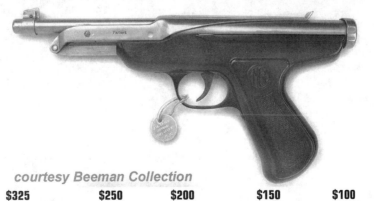

courtesy Beeman Collection

	100%	95%	90%	80%	60%	40%	20%
	$325	$250	$200	$150	$100	N/A	N/A

Add 25% or nickel finish.

Add 50-100% for ten-shot repeater (if with mag.).

Rumored to also have been made after WWII in Russia.

GRADING	100%	95%	90%	80%	60%	40%	20%

EASTERN ENGINEERING CO.

Previous manufacturer located in Syracuse, NY.

PISTOLS

GAMESTER - .177 or .25 caliber. SP, SS, push-barrel action suggestive of the Hubertus air pistol of Germany. Bronze frame, blued steel body tube, silver colored thin barrel. No marks on gun but fitted cardboard factory box with illustrated information inside cover makes identification certain and indicates a production item. 5.5 in. BBL, 11 in. OAL, 2.1 lbs. Date not known, but production must have been short as there has only been one known specimen as of March 2004.

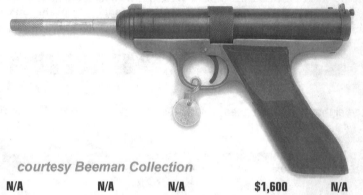

courtesy Beeman Collection

N/A	N/A	N/A	$1,600	N/A	N/A	N/A

Add 20% for illustrated factory box.

Factory information indicates that .177 barrel and supplied mainspring is for "semi-harmless use" while an optional .25 cal. barrel and stronger mainspring was available for pest control.

EDISON GENERAL ELECTRIC

Previously manufactured by Edison General Electric Appliance Co., Chicago, IL.

These are large airguns which simulated heavy machine guns for training gunners during WWII. Used in simulated combat with back projected images of enemy planes flying at different speeds and angles. Edison General Electric Appliance became General Electric after WWII. "Hotpoint" was their appliance brand. Mfg. circa 1943-45.

TRAINER MACHINE GUNS

Gunnery trainer machine guns -- fully automatic, powered via hose from air compressor. .375 cal. bakelite ball ammo, magazine tube above and parallel to shorter true barrel, magazine loaded by unscrewing cap at muzzle end and attaching loader which mates with projectile exit opening below. Loader filled from separate projectile hopper. 115v/60 cycle firing mechanism, painted black. There are three known models.

ANTI-AIRCRAFT MACHINE GUN MODEL 9 - .375 cal., ground to air gunnery trainer, dual hand grips, massive steel plate pivoting/swiveling base, barrel sleeve about 4 3/4 in. diameter to simulate water-cooled barrel jacket of .50 cal. machine gun; marked with Edison General Electric Appliance Company name but without Hotpoint brand marking, 67 in. OAL, 78 lbs.

courtesy Beeman Collection

$2,125	$2,000	$1,875	$1,675	$1,550	$1,400	$1,250

Add 10% for loading funnel, hopper.

GRADING	100%	95%	90%	80%	60%	40%	20%

AERIAL GUNNERY MACHINE GUN MODEL E10 - .375 cal., side gunner version for training gunners in U.S. bombers, dual hand grips; barrel sleeve simulates barrel sleeve of air-cooled machine guns, small steel pin support base, marked with Hotpoint brand and Edison General Electric Appliance Company name 57.5 in. OAL, 41 lbs.

courtesy Beeman Collection

	100%	95%	90%	80%	60%	40%	20%
	$850	$800	$750	$675	$625	$575	$500

Add 10% for loading funnel, hopper.

AERIAL GUNNERY MACHINE GUN MODEL E11 - .375 cal., remote control version of E10, no hand grips; probably mounted in pairs in remote gun turrets, marked with Hotpoint brand and Edison General Electric Appliance Company name, 48 in. OAL, 24 lbs.

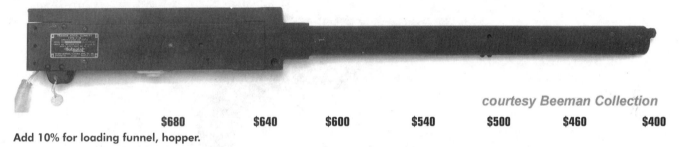

courtesy Beeman Collection

	100%	95%	90%	80%	60%	40%	20%
	$680	$640	$600	$540	$500	$460	$400

Add 10% for loading funnel, hopper.

EISENWERKE GAGGENAU (GAGGENAU IRONWORKS)

See Gaggenau Ironworks in the "G" section.

EL GAMO

For information on El Gamo airguns, see Gamo in the "G" section.

ELMEK

Previously unknown maker, presumed Danish, mid-twentieth century.

RIFLES

ELMEK RIFLE - .25 cal., smoothbore, SP, UL, SS, 21.5 in. BBL, blue/nickel finish, iron cocking lever behind trigger with unique attached wooden pistol grip, downswing of underlever causes breech block, which contains the mainspring and piston, to move back as a unit – exposing barrel breech for direct loading – upswing causes compression chamber tube only to move forward, leaving piston cocked, and closing breech – similar to the complex, fully opening breech system in the Feinwerkbau 300 and 65 airguns, receiver body is brass with nickel plating, hexagon containing the word "ELMEK" is stamped on lower edge of receiver.

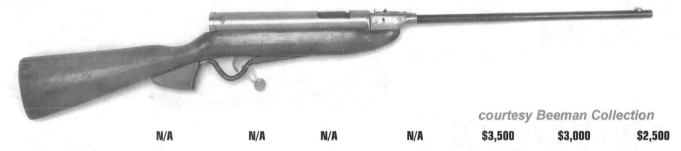

courtesy Beeman Collection

	100%	95%	90%	80%	60%	40%	20%
	N/A	N/A	N/A	N/A	$3,500	$3,000	$2,500

ENSIGN ARMS CO., LTD.

Previous international distributors for Saxby Palmer Airguns located in Newbury, England. Previously imported until 1988 by Marksman Products, located in Huntington Beach, CA.

Ensign Arms previously distributed the Saxby Palmer line of airguns into the U.S. Please refer to the Saxby Palmer section for these guns. Ensign-designated models were trademarked by Ensign Arms Co., Ltd.

ERMA

Previously manufactured by Erma-Werke GmbH, located in München-Dachau, Germany.

Erma produced their only airgun, the ELG 10, in 1981, which was discontinued in the 1990s. Apparently related to pre-WWII Erfurter Maschinenfabrik. Erma (= ER-Furter MA-Schinenfabrik) was relocated from Erfurt to Bavaria after WWII like the other companies (which mostly went to the Baden-Wurtemmberg region, Ulm, etc.). Having the same origin in the 1990s, Erma went back to Suhl (after near insolvency and a management buyout). In 1998, the company was officially closed. Some models and spare parts were bought and distributed by Frankonia Jagd, Würzburg (wholesaler).

Makers of blowback copies of the Luger-style firearms, such as the Beeman P-08 and MP-08 in .22 LR and .380 ACP, respectively, and copies of the U.S. M1 carbine in .22 LR (and in .22 WMR, famous as the "Jungle Carbine" in banana republics). They also produced some very little-known electro-optical shooting guns, including a version of the ELG 10, known as the EG 80 Ermatronic, and an Ermatronic copy of a Colt revolver.

For more information and current values on Erma-Werke firearms, please refer to the *Blue Book of Gun Values* by S.P. Fjestad (also available online).

REVOLVERS

MODEL ER 83 - optical shooting version of Smith & Wesson revolver. Beautifully made of blued gun steel with hand checkered grips.

courtesy Beeman Collection

$400	$350	N/A	N/A	N/A	N/A	N/A

MODEL PEACEMAKER ER - optical shooting version of Colt Peacemaker. Beautifully made of blued gun steel with fine walnut grips.

courtesy Beeman Collection

$400	$350	N/A	N/A	N/A	N/A	N/A

RIFLES

ELG 10 - .177 in. cal., SP, SS, LA, manual safety, copy of the Winchester 1894, 38 in. OAL, 6.4 lbs.

courtesy Beeman Collection

$550	$450	$350	$295	$250	N/A	N/A

EG 80 - optical shooting version of the ELG 10.

$400	$350	$295	$250	$195	N/A	N/A

EUSTA

Previous trademark used by Alpina-Werk M&M Vorwerk GmbH & Co., KG,8950 Kaufbeuren, Germany on inexpensive sheet metal air pistols.

The authors and publisher wish to thank Dr. Trevor Adams for his valuable assistance with the following information in this edition of the *Blue Book of Airguns*. Trademark registered in Germany on October 13, 1965. Gun design invented by Walter Ussfeller, A. Weber, and H. Witteler. Most notable for the concentric piston design. Distributed by Hans Wrage & Co. of Hamberg, Germany,1968-76.

PISTOLS

LP 100 - .177 cal., SP, TL, SS, sheet metal frame with plastic grips, concentric piston, 6.3 in rifled steel barrel, 8 in. OAL, 1.5 lbs. Mfg. 1965-68.

	100%	95%	90%	80%	60%	40%	20%
	$350	$300	$250	$200	$150	$100	$50

Add 20% for factory box and papers.
Patented in Germany by Walter Ussfeller on Sept. 24, 1969.

LP 210 - .177 cal., SP, TL, SS, similar to LP 100, except there's a change in the top lever catch, , breech-end of cylinder sloped forward, and has two-piece trigger. Mfg. 1968-1971.

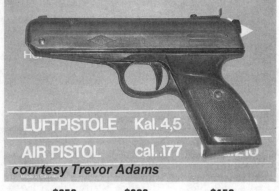

LUFTPISTOLE Kal.4,5
AIR PISTOL cal..177
courtesy Trevor Adams

	100%	95%	90%	80%	60%	40%	20%
	$300	$250	$200	$150	$100	$65	$35

Add 20% for factory box and papers.
Based on Alpina Werk patent of Nov. 5, 1970.

EXCELLENT

Previous manufacturer, Exellent Gevaret AB of Stockholm, Sweden and several different makers and owners circa 1905-1974. The authors and publisher wish to thank Kenth Friberg for his valuable assistance with the following information in this edition of the *Blue Book of Airguns*.

Note that C1 and CI, etc. are different models! The models with Roman numerals have heavier stocks with pistol grips. Additional research is underway concerning this group, and any updates will be available through online subscriptions and in future editions.

PISTOLS

MODEL 1950 CONCENTRIC PISTON PISTOL - .177 cal., TL, SP, SS. Barrel lift cocking like Webley Tempest. Concentric piston. Marked "EXCELLENT" but without model marking. 8.1 in. rifled BBL, no safety. 8.5 in. OAL, 2.0 lbs. About 25 specimens known. Mfg. 1946-59. Ref: AGNR Apr. 1989.

courtesy Beeman Collection

	100%	95%	90%	80%	60%	40%	20%
	$650	$550	$450	$350	$300	N/A	N/A

Add 20% for factory box.

GRADING	100%	95%	90%	80%	60%	40%	20%

PHANTOM "REPETER" PISTOL - .173 (4.4 mm) lead balls cal., SP, repeater, UL, zinc metal cast frame, "Phantom" cast into LHS frame. Cocking lever consists of front of grip and trigger guard. No safety. 7.1 in. OAL, 1.5 lbs. About six specimens are known to exist, mfg. 1953-59.

courtesy Beeman Collection

	$550	$450	$350	$250	$175	N/A	N/A

RIFLES

MODEL AE - .22 cal., smoothbore heavy barrel, pump pneumatic, 35.4-39.4 in. OAL, 3.5-4.4 lbs. Two versions, one specimen known, mfg. 1904-12.

   Current values not yet determined.

MODEL C1 - .22 cal., smoothbore, pump pneumatic, slim stock with no pistol grip, 39.4 in. OAL, 4.4 lbs. 1905-1939.

   Values approximate Model C2.

MODEL CI - .22 cal., smoothbore, pump pneumatic, large buttstock with pistol grip, 38.2 in. OAL, 5.1 lbs. 1945-52.

   Values approximate Model C2.

MODEL C2 - .22 cal., rifled, SS, trombone-style pump pneumatic with wooden slide handle, breech block swings to left to load, rifled 22.5 in. round BBL blue and nickel finish, slim stock with no pistol grip, no safety, 39.4 in OAL, 4.4 lbs. Mfg. 1905-39.

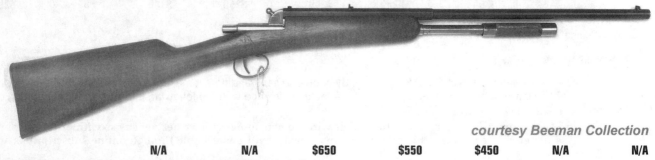

courtesy Beeman Collection

	N/A	N/A	$650	$550	$450	N/A	N/A

   Add 20% for early version with checkered metal slide handle.
   See also Bahco in the "B" section of this guide.

MODEL CII - .22 cal., trombone-style pump pneumatic, swinging breech block, various sight versions, large buttstock with pistol grip, 38.2 in. OAL, 5.1 lbs. mfg. 1945-52.

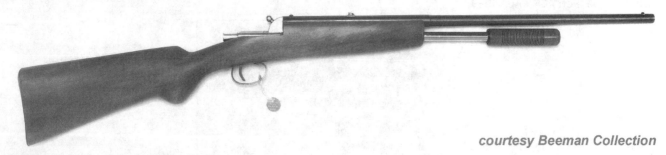

courtesy Beeman Collection

   Values are approximate to the Model C2.

MODEL CIIK - similar to Model C2, except .22 in. cal, trombone-style pump pneumatic, with faucet tap loading breech, similar to Model C2, large buttstock with pistol grip, 22.3 in. rifled round BBL, no safety, 38.2 in. OAL, 4.6 lbs. Mfg. 1953-67.

	$650	$500	$400	$300	$225	N/A	N/A

MODEL CIII - .22 cal., pump pneumatic, Mauser mechanism, rifled or smoothbore, 39.8 in. OAL, 5.5 lbs. No specimens known. Mfg. 1907-?

MODEL CIV - .25 cal., CO_2, 39.8 in. OAL, 5.5 lbs. No known specimens, mfg. circa 1912-?

GRADING	100%	95%	90%	80%	60%	40%	20%

MODEL C5 - .22 cal., CO$_2$, slim stock with no pistol grip, 39.8 in. OAL, 5.5 lbs. one specimen known, mfg. 1907-?

MODEL CVI - .22 cal., CO$_2$, rifled or smoothbore, 39.8 in. OAL, 5.5 lbs. no known specimens, mfg. 1907-?

MODEL CF - .177 cal., SP, SS, BBC, rifled BBL, slim stock with very small pistol grip, 39.4 in. OAL, 4.4 lbs., mfg. 1933-48.
    Value about 50% of Model C2.
    Subtract 25% for later version (c. 1949-?) with heavier stock and pistol grip.

MODEL F1 - .177 cal., SS, TL, SP, smoothbore, 39.8 in., 4.4 lbs. mfg. c. 1919-?
    Current values not yet determined.

MODEL F2 - .177 cal., smoothbore, SS, TL, SP, checkered metal pad on each side of receiver, forward bolt slides to open breech for loading, similar to F1, no safety. Very early model. 38.2 in. OAL, 4.1 lbs. Mfg. c. 1919-?

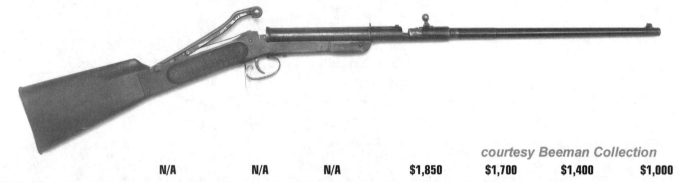

courtesy Beeman Collection

	100%	95%	90%	80%	60%	40%	20%
	N/A	N/A	N/A	$1,850	$1,700	$1,400	$1,000

MODEL F3 - .177 cal, SS, SP, TL, tap loading, 39.4 in OAL, 4.4 lbs. One specimen known, mfg. 1925-?
    Current values not yet determined.

MODEL MATCH - .22 cal. lead balls, short tubular, gravity-fed magazine loads tap loading breech block, trigger guard swings to cock the action, trombone-style pump pneumatic, pistol grip, wooden slide handle, no safety. 38.6 in. OAL, 5.9 lbs., mfg. 1967-74.

courtesy Beeman Collection

	100%	95%	90%	80%	60%	40%	20%
	N/A	$850	$700	$600	$500	$400	$300

NOTES

_____

_____

_____

_____

_____

_____

_____

Bellows Airguns: powered by a bellows, not unlike a fireplace bellows, hidden within the beautiful, hollowed-out buttstocks. Created only in a small area of central Europe during the late 18th or early 19th centuries, Bellows airguns may have been designed as nostalgic replicas of wheel-lock firearms made in the "good old days" of the 1600s. They fired darts, up to .50 caliber, which were used over and over, at indoor targets. The elaborate design and beautiful engraving suggest wealthy or royal owners. Photo by R. Valentine Atkinson for Gray's Sporting Journal, Sept. 1992. Guns courtesy of Beeman Collection. (The air pump, balls, and tools in the lower part of the picture belong to our Mortimer butt-reservoir air rifle; they were added here by the photographer for artistic balance.)

F SECTION

FARAC

Previous manufacturer of spring piston airguns located in Buenos Aires, Argentina circa 1990s.

GRADING	100%	95%	90%	80%	60%	40%	20%

RIFLES

SUPER VALIANT - .177 lead ball cal., SP, UL, vertical loading tap with tubular magazine, blue finish, hardwood stock, 42.6 in. OAL, 9.6 lbs.

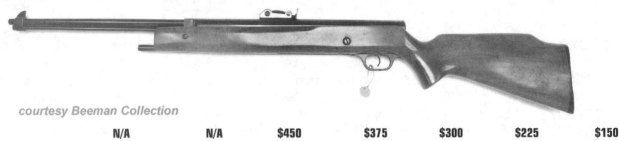

courtesy Beeman Collection

	N/A	N/A	$450	$375	$300	$225	$150

FAS

Current manufacturer located in Milan, Italy. Previously imported by Airguns of Arizona, located in Mesa, AZ, by Beeman, then located in Santa Rosa, CA, by Nygord Products, located in Prescott, AZ, and Top Gun Air Guns Inc., located in Scottsdale, AZ.

Research is ongoing with this trademark, and more information may be included both in future editions and online.

For more information and current pricing on both new and used FAS firearms, please refer to the *Blue Book of Gun Values* by S.P. Fjestad (also available online).

PISTOLS

FAS 400 - .177 cal., TL, SSP, similar to Model 604, except without dry fire feature.

	$195	$150	$100	$80	$60	N/A	N/A

FAS 604 - .177 cal., TL, SSP, adj. trigger, adj. sights, target model.

courtesy Beeman Collection

MSR $350	$300	$265	$195	$150	$100	N/A	N/A

FAS 606 - .177 cal., TL, SSP, 7.5 in. barrel, adj. trigger, adj. sights, UIT target model, walnut grips, 2 lbs. 3 oz. Disc. 1994.

No MSR	$395	$325	$295	$225	$150	N/A	N/A

FAS 609 - .177 cal., PCP, 7.5 in. barrel, adj. trigger, adj. sights, UIT target model, adj. walnut grips. New 1997.

No MSR	$550	$425	$345	$250	$175	N/A	N/A

FB RECORD (BARTHELMS, FRITZ)

Current manufacturer located in Heidenheim-Oggenhausen, Germany.

Founded by Fritz Barthelms in 1948 and now owned by his son, Martin Barthelmes. Production of airguns began in the late 1960s. The specialty of the company is producing economical air pistols using alloy and plastic casting methods that have minimal labor involvement. Annual production in the mid-1980s was about 40,000 air pistols, produced by only twenty workers.

In the 1980s, the Record brand began to include more substantial and interesting air pistols. The little, strangely named Jumbo features one of the most interesting mechanisms in the airgun field, a very compact concentric piston design. The extremely unexpected oval profile of the piston forces perfect piston alignment.

PISTOLS

FB RECORD LP 1 - .177 cal., smoothbore, SP, BBC, SS, fixed sights, brown plastic grips with RH thumbrest, no safety, 10.9 in. OAL, 1.6 lbs.

	$40	$35	$30	$25	$20	N/A	N/A

GRADING	100%	95%	90%	80%	60%	40%	20%

FB RECORD LP 2 - .177 cal., rifled, SP, BBC, SS, adj. sights, white plastic grips with RH thumbrest, no safety, 11.5 in. OAL, 1.7 lbs.

courtesy Beeman Collection

	100%	95%	90%	80%	60%	40%	20%
	$50	$45	$40	$35	$30	$25	$20

FB RECORD LP 3 - .177 cal., rifled, SP, BBC, SS, adj. sights, brown plastic grips with RH thumbrest, no safety, 11.5 in. OAL, 1.9 lbs.

	$60	$55	$45	$40	$35	$30	$25

FB RECORD 68 - .177 cal., rifled, SP, BBC, SS, adj. sights, brown plastic grips with RH thumbrest, no safety, 14.6 in. OAL, 3.1 lbs.

	$90	$85	$80	$75	$70	$60	$50

FB RECORD 77 - .177 cal., rifled, SP, BBC, SS, adj. sights, tan plastic grip with RH thumbrest, trigger guard and bar molded in front of grip, ventilated rib on barrel, anti-bear trap, no safety, 12.4 in. OAL, 2.1 lbs.

courtesy Beeman Collection

	$65	$60	$50	$45	$40	$30	$25

FB RECORD CHAMPION - .177, SP, TL, SS, styling like Beeman P1 or BSA 240, blue finish, hardwood grips, 6 in. round barrel. New c. 2001.

courtesy Beeman Collection

	$250	$200	$150	$95	$65	N/A	N/A

FB RECORD JUMBO - .177, 260 FPS, rifled, TL, SS, oval-shaped concentric piston, fixed sights, contoured walnut grips, may be marked with "Mauser U90/U91", 7.3 in. OAL, 1.9 lbs. Mfg. 1980s.

courtesy Beeman Collection

	$150	$130	$115	$100	$90	$80	$75

Add 10% for Target model, adj. sights (intro. 1983).

Add 10% for Deluxe model, oakleaf carving on walnut grips.

This air pistol is very compact, well balanced, may be marked with "Mauser U90/U91" (not made by Mauser). Previously imported by Beeman Precision Airguns, then located in San Rafael, CA.

GRADING	100%	95%	90%	80%	60%	40%	20%

FEG

Current manufacturer located in Hungary (FEG stands for Fegyver es Gepgyar) since circa 1900. Previously imported by K.B.I. Inc. (formerly Kassnar Imports). Dealer sales.

Research is ongoing with this trademark, and more information will be included both in future editions and online.

For more information and current pricing on both new and used FEG firearms, please refer to the *Blue Book of Gun Values* by S.P. Fjestad (also available online).

PISTOLS

MODEL GPM-01 - .177 cal., CO_2 cartridge or bulk fill, 425 FPS, 10.25 in. barrel, 2 lbs. 7 oz.

MSR	$525	$425	$360	$315	$235	$165	N/A	N/A

The Model GPM-01 has been imported as the Daisy Model 91.

RIFLES

CLG-62 - .177 cal., match rifle. Disc.

courtesy Beeman Collection

		$425	$360	$315	$235	$165	N/A	N/A

CLG-462 - .177 or .22 cal., CO_2 cartridge or cylinder charge, 490-410 FPS, 16.5 or 24 (.22 cal. only) in. barrel, 5 lbs. 8 oz.

		$400	$350	$270	$215	$145	N/A	N/A

Last MSR was $550.

CLG-468 - .177 or .22 cal., CO_2 cartridge or cylinder charge, 705-525 FPS, 26.75 in. barrel, 5 lbs. 12 oz.

		$450	$380	$300	$225	$150	N/A	N/A

Last MSR was $600.

F.I.E.

Previous importer (F.I.E. is the acronym for Firearms Import & Export) located in Hialeah, FL until 1990.

For more information and current pricing on F.I.E. firearms, please refer to the *Blue Book of Gun Values* by S.P. Fjestad (also available online).

PISTOLS

TIGER - .177 cal., BBC, SP, SS, black enamel finish, black plastic grip frame, marked "Made in Italy" (by Gun Toys?), 12.6 in. OAL, 1.7 lbs.

courtesy Beeman Collection

		$50	$45	$40	$35	$30	N/A	N/A

Add 10% for factory box with new targets.

Factory box bears the letters "MAM" in raised foam, thus probably eliminating Mondail as the maker, as their initials are MMM.

FLZ

For information on FLZ air pistols, see Langenhan in the "L" section.

GRADING	100%	95%	90%	80%	60%	40%	20%

FX AIRGUNS

Current manufacturer located in Hova, Sweden. Currently imported and distributed by Airguns of Arizona, located in Mesa, AZ. Dealer and consumer direct sales.

RIFLES

CYCLONE - .177 or .22 cal., PCP, biathlon style BA, eight-shot rotary mag., 19.7 in. Lothar Walther match grade barrel, blue finish, two-stage adj. trigger, synthetic stock with rubberized PG, grooved receiver for scope mounting, adj. power, built-in pressure gauge, removable air cylinder, 6.6 lbs.

	100%	95%	90%	80%	60%	40%	20%
MSR $921	$895	$765	$675	$505	$425	N/A	N/A

Add 15% for walnut stock.

SUPER SWIFT - .177 or .22 cal., PCP, self-closing Biathlon style action, eight-shot rotary mag., 19.7 in. Lothar Walther match grade barrel, blue finish, two-stage adj. trigger, black thumbhole synthetic stock, grooved receiver for scope mounting, external power adjuster, built-in pressure gauge, 40.5 in. OAL, 5.3 lbs. New 2004.

	100%	95%	90%	80%	60%	40%	20%
MSR $980	$895	$750	$675	$595	$445	N/A	N/A

TARANTULA - .177, or .22 cal., PCP, BA, eight-shot rotary mag., 19.7 in. Lothar Walther match grade barrel with threaded muzzle weight, blue finish, two-stage adj. trigger, checkered grade three hand rubbed oil finished Turkish Circassian walnut (Tarantula) stock, ventilated recoil pad, grooved receiver for scope mounting, adj. power, built-in pressure gauge, 6 lbs., 39.5 OAL.

	100%	95%	90%	80%	60%	40%	20%
MSR $876	$850	$750	$665	$580	$475	N/A	N/A

Add 15% for grade four walnut stock.

TARANTULA SPORT - .177, or .22 cal., PCP, BA, similar to Tarantula, except grade two English walnut stock, 6 lbs., 39.5 in. OAL.

	100%	95%	90%	80%	60%	40%	20%
MSR $815	$795	$695	$515	$450	$375	N/A	N/A

TIMBERWOLF - .22 cal., PCP, bolt action, two-shot mag., 19.7 in. Lothar Walther match grade barrel, blue finish, two-stage adj. trigger, checkered beech or grade two walnut stock, ventilated recoil pad, grooved receiver for scope mounting, adj. power, built-in pressure gauge, 6.5 lbs. Disc. 2005.

	100%	95%	90%	80%	60%	40%	20%
	$515	$425	$350	$275	$225	N/A	N/A

Last MSR was $578.

Add $42 for walnut stock.

ULTIMATE - .177 or .22 cal., PCP, pistol grip pump action, eight-shot rotary mag., 19.7 in. Lothar Walther match grade barrel, blue finish, two-stage adj. trigger, synthetic stock, grooved receiver for scope mounting, built-in pressure gauge, 6.6 lbs.

	100%	95%	90%	80%	60%	40%	20%
MSR $729	$650	$575	$495	$415	$345	N/A	N/A

XTERMINATOR - .177 or .22 cal., PCP, forearm pump action, eight-shot rotary mag., 19.7 in. Lothar Walther match grade barrel, blue finish, two-stage adj. trigger, synthetic stock, grooved receiver for scope mounting, built-in pressure gauge, 4.4 lbs.

	100%	95%	90%	80%	60%	40%	20%
MSR $1,206	$1,095	$925	$750	$675	$595	N/A	N/A

FALCON

Current trademark manufactured by Falcon Pneumatic Systems Limited located in Birmingham, England. Falcon Pneumatic Systems has been manufacturing air guns since 1993, when it took over air gun production from Titan Enterprises. Currently imported and distributed by Airhog Inc. located in Dallas, TX. Dealer and consumer direct sales.

Falcon name also used by Beeman for economy-level Spanish air rifles. See Beeman in the "B" section.

PISTOLS

SINGLE SHOT PISTOL MODELS (FN6-PG, FN6-WG, FN8-PG, FN8-WG) - .177, .20, or .22 cal., PCP, SS, 6 (FN6, disc. 2004) or 8 (FN8) in. Walther rifled barrel, grooved receiver for adj. rear sight or scope, high gloss blue finish, checkered hardwood (PG) or walnut with stippled palm swell (WG) grip, 2.7 lbs., 12-13.5 in. OAL.

	100%	95%	90%	80%	60%	40%	20%
MSR $554	$495	$435	$375	$295	N/A	N/A	N/A

Add 5% for left-hand variation.
Add 10% for open front and adj. rear sights.
Add 20% for walnut grip with stippled palm swell (WG).

HAWK PISTOL MODELS (FN6-PGH, FN6-WGH, FN8-PGH, FN8-WGH) - .177, or .22 cal., PCP, eight-shot mag., 6 (FN6, disc. 2004) or 8 (FN8) in. Walther rifled barrel, grooved receiver for adj. rear sight or scope, high gloss blue finish, checkered hardwood (PGH) or walnut with stippled palm swell (WGH) grip, 2.9 lbs., 12-15 in. OAL.

	100%	95%	90%	80%	60%	40%	20%
MSR $650	$585	$525	$465	$395	N/A	N/A	N/A

Add 5% for left-hand variation.
Add 10% for open front and adj. rear sights.
Add 20% for walnut grip with stippled palm swell (WGH).

RAPTOR PISTOL MODELS (FN6-PGR, FN6-WGR, FN8-PGR, FN8-WGR) - .177, or .22 cal., PCP, similar to Hawk Pistol, eight-shot mag., 6 (FN6, disc. 2004) or 8 (FN8) in. Walther rifled barrel, grooved receiver for adj. rear sight or scope, high gloss blue finish, checkered hardwood (PGR) or walnut with stippled palm swell (WGR) grip, 2.9 lbs., 12-15 in. OAL.

	100%	95%	90%	80%	60%	40%	20%
MSR $664	$595	$535	$485	$395	N/A	N/A	N/A

Add 5% for left-hand variation.
Add 10% for open front and adj. rear sights.
Add 20% for walnut grip with stippled palm swell (WGR).

GRADING	100%	95%	90%	80%	60%	40%	20%

RIFLES

SINGLE SHOT RIFLE MODELS (FN19-SB, FN19-SW, FN19-TW, FN19-WS, FN19-SL) - .177, .20, .22, or .25 cal., PCP, SS, 19 in. Walther rifled barrel, grooved receiver for adj. rear sight or scope, high gloss blue finish, checkered beech pistol grip sporter (SB), checkered walnut pistol grip sporter (SW), walnut thumb hole with stippled palm swell and forend (TW), walnut skeleton (WS), or laminate skeleton (SL) stock, ventilated (SB, SW) or adj. (TW, WS, SL) butt pad, 5.8-6.5 lbs., approx. 37.5 in. OAL.

MSR $665	$615	$545	$465	$395	$325	N/A	N/A

Add 5% for left-hand variation.

Add 10% for open front and adj. rear sights.

Add 15% for walnut sporter stock (SW).

Add 25% for walnut thumbhole stock (TW).

Add 20% for walnut skeleton stock (WS).

Add 30% for laminate skeleton stock (SL).

SINGLE SHOT CARBINE MODELS (FN12-SB, FN12-SW, FN12-TW, LIGHTHUNTER 12W, LIGHTHUNTER 8W, LIGHTHUNTER 12L, LIGHTHUNTER 8L) - .177, .20, .22, or .25 cal., PCP, SS, 8 or 12 in. Walther rifled barrel, grooved receiver for adj. rear sight or scope, high gloss blue finish, checkered beech pistol grip sporter (SB), checkered walnut pistol grip sporter (SW), walnut thumb hole with stippled palm swell and forend (TW), walnut skeleton (Lighthunter W), or laminate skeleton (Lighthunter L) stock, ventilated (SB, SW) or adj. (TW, Lighthunter W, Lighthunter L) butt pad, 4.75-5.9 lbs., 26.5-30.5 in. OAL.

MSR $665	$615	$545	$465	$395	$325	N/A	N/A

Add 5% for left-hand variation.

Add 10% for open front and adj. rear sights.

Add 15% for walnut sporter stock (SW).

Add 25% for walnut thumbhole stock (TW).

Add 20% for walnut skeleton stock (Lighthunter W).

Add 30% for laminate skeleton stock (Lighthunter L).

HAWK RIFLE MODELS (FN19-HB, FN19-HW, FN19-HT, FN19-HS, FN19-HL) - .177, .20, .22, or .25 cal., PCP, similar to Single Shot Rifle, except has eight-shot mag., 5.8-6.6 lbs., 37.5 in. OAL.

MSR $786	$745	$625	$550	$475	$395	N/A	N/A

Add 5% for left-hand variation.

Add 5% for open front and adj. rear sights.

Add 10% for walnut sporter stock (HW).

Add 20% for walnut thumbhole stock (HW).

Add 15% for walnut skeleton stock (HS).

Add 25% for laminate skeleton stock (HL).

HAWK CARBINE MODELS (FN12-HB, FN12-HW, FN12-HT, FN12-HS, FN12-HL) - .177, .20, .22, or .25 cal., PCP, similar to Single Shot Carbine, except has eight-shot mag., 5.5-6.3 lbs., 30.5 in. OAL.

MSR $786	$745	$625	$550	$475	$395	N/A	N/A

Add 5% for left-hand variation.

Add 5% for open front and adj. rear sights.

Add 10% for walnut sporter stock (HW).

Add 20% for walnut thumbhole stock (HW).

Add 15% for walnut skeleton stock (HS).

Add 25% for laminate skeleton stock (HL).

RAPTOR RIFLE MODELS (FN19-RB, FN19-RW, FN19-RT, FN19-RS, FN19-RL) - .177, .20, .22, or .25 cal., PCP, similar to Hawk Rifle, eight-shot mag., 5.8-6.6 lbs., 37.5 in. OAL.

MSR $806	$785	$695	$595	$495	$395	N/A	N/A

Add 5% for left-hand variation.

Add 5% for open front and adj. rear sights.

Add 10% for walnut sporter stock (RW).

Add 20% for walnut thumbhole stock (RW).

Add 15% for walnut skeleton stock (RS).

Add 25% for laminate skeleton stock (RL).

RAPTOR CARBINES MODELS (FN12-RB, FN12-RW, FN12-RT, FN12-RS, FN12-RL) - .177, .20, .22, or .25 cal., PCP, similar to Hawk Carbine, eight-shot mag., 5.5-6.3 lbs., 30.5 in. OAL.

MSR $806	$785	$695	$595	$495	$395	N/A	N/A

Add 5% for left-hand variation.

Add 5% for open front and adj. rear sights.

Add 10% for walnut sporter stock (RW).

Add 20% for walnut thumbhole stock (RW).

Add 15% for walnut skeleton stock (RS).

Add 25% for laminate skeleton stock (RL).

GRADING	100%	95%	90%	80%	60%	40%	20%

TARGET RIFLE MODELS (FN19-FSJ, FN19-FSP, FN19-FSPL, FN19-TR, FN19-TRL, FN19-PTB, FN19-PTL) - .177, or, .22, cal., PCP, SS, 19 in. Walther rifled barrel, grooved receiver for adj. rear sight or scope, high gloss blue finish, beech (FSJ or PTB), walnut (FSP or TR), or laminated (FSPL, TRL, or PTL) target stock with adj. cheek piece and butt pad, adj. match trigger, 6.3-8.7 lbs., 35.5-38 in. OAL.

MSR $819	$795	$705	$605	$505	$405	N/A	N/A

Add 5% for left-hand variation.

Add 5% for open front and adj. rear sights.

Add 25% for walnut stock Field Star Pro-Target Rifle (FN19-FSP).

Add 35% for laminated stock Field Star Pro-Target Rifle (FN19-FSPL).

Add 25% for walnut stock Field Target Rifle (FN19-TR).

Add 35% for laminated stock Field Target Rifle (FN19-TRL).

Add 35% for beech stock 10 Metre Target Rifle (FN19-PTB).

Add 45% for laminated stock 10 Metre Target Rifle (FN19-PTL).

FALKE AIRGUN

Previous manufacturer located in Wennigsen, Germany 1951-1958.

The authors and publisher wish to thank Mr. Trevor Adams for assistance with the following information in this edition of the *Blue Book of Airguns*.

In February 1949, Albert Föhrenbach founded the engineering firm of Falkewerke in Wennigsen near Hanover, Germany. It provided maintenance for conveyer belt machines, a service vital to the industrial recovery of post-WWII Germany. Very soon their conveyer belt expertise was extended to making shooting arcade games. By mid-1951 they started production of a variety of air rifles and one air pistol under the brand of Falke (German for Falcon). The rifles were superior copies of guns made by Dianawerk, Haenel, BSA, and Will. The one air pistol, the Falke 33, apparently was a Falke original. Despite the excellence of Falke products, the firm failed to prosper. The advertising and marketing strengths of larger manufacturers such as Mayer & Grammelspacher, BSA, and Webley prevented Falke from becoming a well-known brand. Financial difficulties led to cessation of production in 1958, and in 1961 Falkewerke went into airgun history. Due to their very limited production run during only seven years and their special quality of manufacture, Falke airguns now are of considerable interest to both collectors and shooters.

The production period of each model isn't known. An early 1953 catalog describes all models and *Smith´s Encyclopaedia of Air Gas & Spring Guns*, published in 1957, notes the full range of models as available – just one year before the end of production. Special Reference: John Walter, *Guns Review,* April 1988.

PISTOLS

MODEL 33 - .177 cal., trigger guard swings forward to cock, SP, rifled barrel, beech grip with Falcon badge on each side, 11.25 in. OAL, 1.75 lbs.

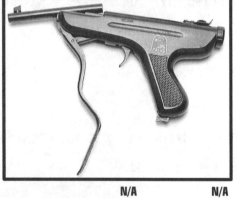 

courtesy Beeman Collection

N/A	N/A	N/A	$200	$175	$150	$100

RIFLES

MODEL 10 - .177 cal., BBC, SP, tinplate, smoothbore, wood buttstock, 30.5 in. OAL.

N/A	N/A	N/A	$60	$50	$40	$30

MODEL 20 - .177 cal., BBC, SP, similar to model 10, except has checkered wood forearm.

N/A	N/A	N/A	$100	$80	$60	$50

MODEL 30 - .177 cal., BBC, SP, tinplate, smoothbore, 32 in. OAL.

N/A	N/A	N/A	$70	$60	$50	$40

MODEL 40 - .177 cal., BBC, SP, tinplate, smoothbore, simple post front sight, 35 in. OAL.

N/A	N/A	N/A	$70	$60	$50	$40

MODEL 50 - similar to Model 40, except has seamless tube steel smooth or rifled barrel, ramp rear and blade front sight, 36 in. OAL.

N/A	N/A	N/A	$100	$80	$60	$50

GRADING	100%	95%	90%	80%	60%	40%	20%

MODEL 60 - .177 or .22 cal., BBC, SP, solid steel, rifled, adj. trigger, some mfg. with breech lock, 38 in. OAL.

courtesy Beeman Collection

| | N/A | N/A | N/A | $100 | $80 | $60 | $50 |

MODEL 70 - .177 or .22 cal., BBC, SP, adj. trigger, breech lock device, 42.5 in. OAL, 6.6 lbs.

| | N/A | N/A | N/A | $140 | $115 | $90 | $70 |

This is the most frequently encountered Falke rifle.

MODEL 80 - .177 or .22 cal., UL, SP, auto. opening loading tap, micrometer rear sight, interchangeable insert front sight, elm stock, 44.5 in. OAL, 8.25 lbs. approx. 400 mfg.

| | N/A | N/A | N/A | $425 | $350 | $275 | $200 |

Add 10% for diopter sight.

MODEL 90 - .177 or .22 cal., UL, SP, similar to Model 80, except has walnut stock, micrometer and diopter rear and interchangeable insert front sight, sling swivels, 44.5 in. OAL, 9.5 lbs., approx. 200 mfg.

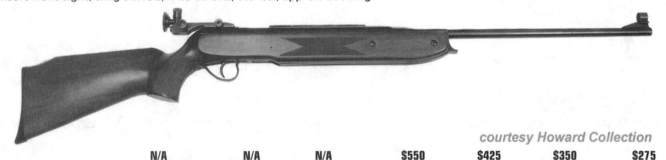

courtesy Howard Collection

| | N/A | N/A | N/A | $550 | $425 | $350 | $275 |

MODEL 100 - .177, .22, or .25 cal., trigger guard cocking gallery gun, blue finish with nickel action, barrel drops for loading, 42 in. OAL, 7 lbs.

| | N/A | N/A | N/A | $350 | $275 | $200 | $150 |

FAMAS

Currently imported by Century International Arms, Inc., located in St. Albans, VT.

RIFLES

FAMAS MODEL - .177 cal., CO_2, semi-auto, copy of French-made MAS .223, used for military training, clip-fed.

| No MSR | $395 | $350 | $285 | $195 | $125 | N/A | N/A |

FARCO

Current manufacturer located in the Philippines. Previously imported by ARS located in Pine City, NY. Dealer or consumer direct sales. Ref: AR 2:10.

RIFLES

FARCO FP SURVIVAL - .22 or .25 cal., footpump action multi-pump pneumatic, SS, 22.75 in. barrel, nickel finish, hardwood stock, fixed sights, 5.75 lbs. Disc. 2001.

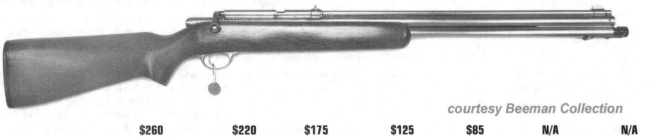

courtesy Beeman Collection

| | $260 | $220 | $175 | $125 | $85 | N/A | N/A |

Last MSR was $295.

GRADING	100%	95%	90%	80%	60%	40%	20%

LONG CYLINDER RIFLE - .22 or .25 cal., CO_2, similar to Short Cylinder Rifle except gas cylinder extends to end of barrel. Approx. 25 mfg. Disc. 2001.

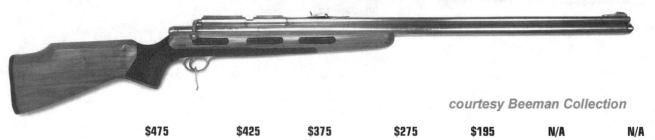

courtesy Beeman Collection

	$475	$425	$375	$275	$195	N/A	N/A

Last MSR was $460.

FARCO SHORT CYLINDER RIFLE - .22 or .25 cal., CO_2, charged from bulk fill 10 oz. cylinder, stainless steel, adj. rear sight, Monte Carlo hardwood stock, hard rubber buttplate, approx. 7 lbs. Disc. 2001.

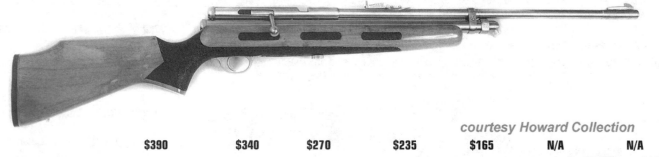

courtesy Howard Collection

	$390	$340	$270	$235	$165	N/A	N/A

Last MSR was $460.

SHOTGUNS

FARCO SHOTGUN - 28 ga., CO_2, 30 in. barrel, charged from bulk fill 10 oz. cylinder, hardwood stock, 7 lbs. Importation 1988- 2001.

courtesy Howard Collection

	$400	$350	$280	$215	$145	N/A	N/A

Last MSR was $460.

Add $20 for extra CO_2 cylinder. (Caution, use only recently mfg. stainless steel cylinders!)

Add $1 for each extra brass shells (12 included with gun).

FEINWERKBAU WESTINGER & ALTENBURGER GmbH

Current manufacturer established circa 1951, and located in Oberndorf, Germany. Currently imported and distributed by Marksman (marked Beeman), located in Huntington Beach, CA, and Brenzovich Firearms & Training Center located in Ft. Hancock, TX, also distributed by Pilkington Competion Equipment LLC located in Monteagle, TN. Dealer and consumer direct sales.

The authors and publisher wish to thank Mr. Ulrich Eichstädt for his valuable assistance with the following information in this edition of the *Blue Book of Airguns*.

Feinwerkbau, an airgun industry leader, has been responsible for developing many of the current technical innovations used in fabricating target air pistols and rifles. In 1992, Feinwerkbau swept the Olympic competition. Feinwerkbau guns are prized by both match shooters and those who just enjoy fine guns – especially ones that they can shoot indoors!

"Feinwerkbau" means "fine work factory" and was just a brand name. For many years it was only a prefix to the actual company name (named for its founders): Westinger & Altenburger. Gradually, the word Feinwerkbau (and the abbreviation FWB) came to be an equivalent term for this airgun maker and their products. So, you find this text under "F" instead of "W" in this book.

Although the Westinger & Altenburger company never used big advertising campaigns or sponsored top shooters, their products are on top: the first recoilless match air rifle with a fixed barrel was the Feinwerkbau Model 150. Introduced in 1961, it soon forced the UIT (Union Internationale de Tir, now known as the International Shooting Sports Federation or ISSF) to reduce the size of their targets. This success was repeated in 1965 with the introduction of the FWB model 65 match air pistol. This pistol was in production and pretty much ruled air pistol competition for more than three decades. The Feinwerkbau 600 series have simply owned this title since 1984. The pre-charged successor to the FWB 600 series, the FWB P 70, wins one title after another (including the world record with the maximum score of 600 out of 600 points).

The firm was founded by two engineers, Ernst Altenburger and Karl Westinger. They both worked in the famous Mauser factory in Oberndorf/Neckar, which has been the leading gun manufacturing city in Germany since 1870. After WWII, the factory fell into the French occupation zone. The French authorities ordered the disassembly of all Mauser´s machines. Metal processing was forbidden, and the two engineers desperately sought a new way to use their technical knowledge. In 1948, they were allowed to establish a small workshop in Dettingen. It was not far away, but because the French military authority had poor maps, they did not realize that they had allowed the establishment of a shop across the line in the adjoining Hohenzollern territory, which was not under French control.

With the help of a small punch machine they produced wooden wheels for children´s scooters, wooden casings for pencils, and even wooden spoons. Stealthily, in the attic of what is now Oberndorf College, they designed their first prototype of an electro-mechanical calculator. In 1948, after the Allies again allowed metal processing companies in that region, Feinwerkbau Westinger & Altenburger became a registered company. Their new calculator went into production at the Olympia-Werke in Wilhelmshaven, Germany. Thousands of their machines were sold internationally. Later they produced textile mandrels, counters, and, for IBM, a small device to cut letters out of paper punchcards. Today, a part of the company manufactures vital, but undisclosed, parts for "Formula-One" race cars.

In 1951, the German Shooting Federation was re-established. Starting in 1952, the production of rifled barrels was again allowed. The 1950s was the decade of the Carl Walther Company in Ulm. Their barrel-cocking air rifles Model 53 and, later, Model 55, were used by almost every competitive European air rifle shooter. However, many of the top marksmen believed that wear at the hinge point in these barrel-cocking guns caused reduced accuracy.

In 1961, Walter Gehmann, one of the top marksmen in Germany before WWII and also a famous inventor, came to visit his old friend Ernst Altenburger, with whom he had worked in the legendary Mauser R & D department. (Together they had invented the Mauser "Olympia" smallbore rifle, which was the predecessor of all modern .22 match rifles.) Soon the company started to design air rifles with the barrel rigidly fixed to the receiver.

Anschütz also presented a fixed barrel air rifle, their side-lever Model 220. Feinwerkbau replied with their Model 100. It was immediately successful. Helmut Schlenker, the reigning German shooting champion, took the German championship with this gun in 1961 – this is especially significant because that was the year of the German Shooting Federation´s centennial.

Feinwerkbau exceeded that success with the Model 150. This gun featured an elegantly simple, very effective recoil-elimination device which made Feinwerkbau rifles almost unbeatable during the next decade: When the trigger was released, the entire rigid, upper action and barrel was released to ride on concealed steel rails and thus absorb the recoil. The basic mechanism was based on a recoil control mechanism that Westinger and Altenburger had developed, when working for Mauser, for controlling machine gun recoil. All the succeeding FWB spring-piston match airguns used this mechanism. It was covered by patent 1,140 489, awarded in February of 1961 to Westinger and Altenburger and their chief engineer, Edwin Wöhrstein. Walter Gehmann was honored for his input with a gift of the Model 150 with serial number "000001."

The 1966 World Shooting Championship in Wiesbaden, Germany was a turning point for air rifle shooting. Here the world was introduced to precision match air rifles. While the first world championship was won by Gerd Kuemmet with a non-production, prototype Anschütz Model 250, Feinwerkbau would come into its glory with world championships by Gottfried Kustermann (1970), Oswald Schlipf (1978), Walter Hillenbrand (1979), Hans Riederer (1986 and 1990), and Sonja Pfeilschifter (1994).

Feinwerkbau extended their very successful recoilless sledge mechanism to an air pistol in 1965; the FWB Model LP 65. It had special arrangements to block the recoil compensating mechanism and to switch the trigger pull from 500 to 1360 grams. This allowed this air pistol to be used for simulated firearm pistol training. It was produced in several minor variations until 1998. Although other models, such as the LP 80 and the LP 90 (the first air pistol with an electronic trigger), were introduced during that period, the Model 65 reigned supreme. Air pistol shooting became an official international sport in 1969 and Feinwerkbau had come to virtually "own" that field of competition. Model 65 air pistols also had become very popular with non-match shooters, especially in the USA.

At the beginning of the 1980s, two Austrian technicians, Emil Senfter and Viktor Idl revived the century-old French patent by Paul Giffard for a CO_2 pistol with a tubular gas tank under the barrel. The first "Senfter" pistols were very successful in competition and could be shot like a free pistol. Their advantage over the spring-piston air pistols was a lack of movement from a piston during firing and a quicker shot release. When Senfter and Idl parted company, Senfter offered the system to Walther and Idl went to Feinwerkbau. As a result, the first two CO_2 pistols of both companies, the Walther CP 1 and FWB Model 2, respectively, appear to be almost identical. (Some years later a lawsuit awarded the patent and system to Senfter.)

Feinwerkbau took an excursion into producing sporting air rifles in the early 1970s. This was the "Sport" series under the model numbers 120 to 127. These were slim, highly efficient barrel-cocking, spring-piston air rifles. The primary market was the United States where the high power versions were known the Model 124 in 4.5 mm (.177) caliber and the much less popular Model 127 in 5.5 m (.22) caliber. A lower powered version of the 5.5mm caliber model was fairly popular in Great Britain. Limited numbers of the lowest powered version, the Model 121, were made for countries like Germany where there were very strict airgun power limits. Feinwerkbau began a joint effort with Beeman Precision Airguns to develop a 5mm version, with a special stock to Beeman specifications, to be known as the Beeman R5. Regular production was not possible because Feinwerkbau was not able to find suitable 5 mm barrels in the numbers projected for first sales. The Model R5 is now one of the rarest of collectors´ items. Production of the Sport series was halted in the 1980s because Feinwerkbau´s technicians were so tuned to produce limited quantities of match guns with extremely close fitting and quality control that they could not seem to produce such production level items at reasonable cost! Now much sought after by both shooters and collectors, its slender profile and trigger placement make it a favorite for restocking with premium quality custom stocks.

In the USA, Beeman Precision Airguns, Feinwerkbau´s American partner, had taken an unusual step. They created a larger market for match air rifles among America´s quality conscious non-match gun buyers than had existed for America´s much lower concentration of match shooters. So, in America, the sales of FWB match guns continued to exceed those of all other match airguns combined.

In 1973, Walther introduced a new type of recoilless air rifle, the Walther LGR, a single-stroke pneumatic. It had a shorter shot release time than the spring-piston air rifles and was soon adopted, at least in Europe, by most of the top competitive air rifle shooters.

In 1984, Feinwerkbau struck back, from its factory deep in the German Black Forest, with their own single stroke pneumatic rifle, the FWB 600 (named after the 600-point maximum possible score in the new 60-shot international competitions). This rifle featured a reverse cocking lever which closed towards the body, a much easier motion, and had a shorter barrel of only 420mm (16.5 in.), which reduced the shot release time even more. Feinwerkbau again dominated the world of match air rifles. Scores of 600 became so common that the international shooting authorities again had to reduce the size of the ten ring, from one to one/half millimeter (2/100") diameter! However, the FWB 600 shooters soon began to crowd even that incredibly small bullseye with all of their shots. The models FWB 601, 602, and 603, introduced during the

GRADING	100%	95%	90%	80%	60%	40%	20%

1990s, were only slight modifications of FWB´s basic single-stroke pneumatic system.

In air pistol competitions, only a few shooters preferred pneumatic pistols instead of CO_2 models (and later PCP), but the air rifle shooters were more reluctant in choosing the easy-to-shoot carbon dioxide systems: They didn´t want to rely on uncertain CO_2 supplies during competitions in foreign countries and therefore had to tolerate the heavier cocking effort of the single-stroke pneumatic rifles.

That changed again in 1997, when the key manufacturers of precision airguns introduced their pre-charged pneumatic (PCP) match air rifles. These guns did not depend on local supplies of CO_2 and did not have the physical limitations of CO_2 guns. They simply were charged from easily portable tanks of compressed air. Despite the keen competition of Anschütz, Walther, Steyr-Mannlicher, and Hämmerli, the FWB Model P70 PCP match air rifle has maintained the lead in air rifle competition. Using the FWB P70, Gaby Bühlmann from Switzerland fired the first ever maximum of 400, followed by the first 600 score by Tavarit Majchacheep from Thailand.

Today´s leading airguns are the Feinwerkbau P34 PCP air pistol and the Model 603 single-stroke pneumatic and P70 PCP air rifles. These models use a special "Absorber" feature which reduces even the tiny recoil produced by the pellet itself during its acceleration. A five-shot version of the PCP air pistol, known as the P55, was developed for the new ISSF "Falling Targets" event. And, a five-shot PCP rifle, the Model P75, is used in the summer biathlon competitions. Several smaller and lighter versions of these models are designed for young shooters and smaller adults.

Feinwerkbau now also produces some very successful match firearms: The FWB smallbore rifle earned the Olympic gold medal in 1992, the FWB semi-auto .22 caliber pistol, and the AW 93 (based on a Russian patent).

The Feinwerkbau Westinger & Altenburger factory is still located in Oberndorf at the headwaters of the Neckar River in Germany´s Black Forest, and has about two hundred employees. The company is managed by two sons of the founders: Jörg Altenburger and Rolf Westinger, while two other sons, Reiner Altenburger and Gerhard Westinger, respectively, oversee the sales and purchasing departments. Note: Do not depend on dates in importer catalogs for model production dates.

For more information and current pricing on both new and used Feinwerkbau firearms, please refer to the *Blue Book of Gun Values* by S.P. Fjestad (also available online).

PISTOLS

MODEL 2 - .177 cal., CO_2, 425-525 FPS, adj. trigger, adj. sights, UIT target model, 2.5 lbs. Disc. 1989.

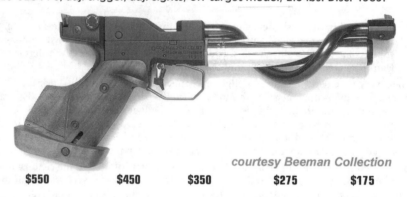

courtesy Beeman Collection

$550	$450	$350	$275	$175	N/A	N/A

Last MSR was $780.

Add $50 for mini.

Subtract $50 for left-hand version.

Add $1,000 for helical barrel (twisted around gas cylinder), 3 mfg. (yes, it shoots accurately!).

MODEL C5 - .177 cal., CO_2, five-shot, 7.33 in. barrel, 510 FPS, 2.4 lbs. Disc. approx. 1993.

$1,000	**$900**	**$800**	**$695**	**$500**	N/A	N/A

Last MSR was $1,350.

Subtract 7% for left-hand variation.

MODEL C10 - .177 cal., CO_2, 510 FPS, adj. trigger, adj. sights, UIT target model, 2.5 lbs. Disc. 1990.

courtesy Beeman Collection

$750	$700	$650	$500	$400	N/A	N/A

Last MSR was $965.

Subtract 5% for left-hand model.

GRADING	100%	95%	90%	80%	60%	40%	20%

MODEL C20 - .177 cal., CO_2, 510 FPS, adj. trigger, adj. sights, UIT target model, 2.5 lbs. Mfg. 1991-95.

	$650	$600	$550	$475	$350	N/A	N/A

Last MSR was $1,160.

Subtract 10% for left-hand model.

This model was intended as a replacement for the Model C2 and the Model C10.

MODEL C25 - .177 cal., CO_2, 510 FPS, CO_2 flask placed directly below action, adj. trigger, adj. sights, UIT target model, 2.5 lbs.

	$750	$700	$650	$500	$350	N/A	N/A

Last MSR was $1,325.

Subtract 10% for left-hand model.

MODEL C55 - .177 cal., CO_2, SS or five-shot, 510 FPS, CO_2 flask placed directly below action for vertical CO_2 feed, up to 225 shots/fill, 2.5 lbs. Mfg. 1994-2001.

	$1,000	$900	$800	$675	$500	N/A	N/A

Last MSR was $1,460.

Subtract 10% for left-hand model.

✱ *Model C55P* - .177 cal., compressed air, five-shot, 8.75 in. barrel, 510 FPS, adj. rear and interchangeable front sights, adj. trigger, swiveling anatomical grip, compressed air cylinder is fitted with integrated manometer, 2.4 lbs. Mfg.2001-04.

	$1,200	$900	$800	$675	$500	N/A	N/A

Last MSR was $1,570.

Subtract 5% for left-hand model.

MODEL P30 - .177 cal., PCP, 515 FPS, adj. match trigger, adj. sights, UIT target model, stippled walnut match grip, 2.4 lbs. Disc.

	$950	$850	$750	$625	$450	N/A	N/A

Last MSR was $1,275.

Subtract 10% for left-hand model.

MODEL P34 - .177 cal., PCP, 515 FPS, adj. match trigger, adj. sights, UIT target model, 7.2 and 9.2 in. (standard) barrel, blue or red air cylinder, stippled walnut match grip, revised version of the P30 with contoured barrel shroud, sliding barrel weight system, valve housing reduced in size, and removable trigger guard, 2.4 lbs. Mfg. 1999-2004.

courtesy Beeman Collection

	$1,400	$1,200	$995	$800	$550	N/A	N/A

Last MSR was $1,640.

Add 5% for left-hand model.

Add 10% for Morini walnut grip and interchangeable trigger unit.

MODEL P40 - .177 cal., PCP, 515 FPS, adj. match trigger, adj. sights, UIT target model, 5.9 in. barrel, two air cylinders with integrated manometer, fully adj. multi-color Morini laminated grip, sliding barrel weight system, 16.1 in. OAL, 2.5 lbs., cased. New. 2004.

MSR 1,815	$1,750	$1,550	$1,350	$1,050	$750	N/A	N/A

Add 5% for left-hand model.

✱ *Model P40 Basic* - .177 cal., PCP, similar to Model P40 except has anatomical adj. Morini walnut grip, no weight system, 16.1 in. OAL, 2.3 lbs. New. 2004.

MSR 1,495	$1,425	$1,300	$1,100	$900	$700	N/A	N/A

Add 5% for left-hand model.

MODEL 65 MK I AND II - .177 cal., SL, SP, 525 FPS, recoil compensating mechanism may be locked, adj. trigger pull may be instantly switched from 500 to 1360 grams, adj. sights, UIT target model, 2.6-2.9 lbs., MKII Model has shorter barrel. M-65 MK I. Approx. 145,000 mfg. 1965-1998.

	$675	$600	$550	$400	$300	N/A	N/A

Last MSR was $1,070.

Subtract 10% for left-hand model.
Add 7% for adj. grips.

GRADING	100%	95%	90%	80%	60%	40%	20%

MODEL 80 - .177 cal., SL, SP, 475-525 FPS, similar to Model 65, except has stacking barrel weights and fine mechanical trigger, adj. sights, UIT target model, 2.8-3.2 lbs. Approx. 48,000 mfg. 1977-1983.

	$675	$600	$500	$400	$350	N/A	N/A

Last MSR was $625.

Add 100% for factory gold plating.

MODEL 90 - similar to Model 80, except has electronic trigger. Approx. 20,000 mfg. 1982-1992.

	$600	$525	$475	$375	$300	N/A	N/A

Last MSR was $1,155.

Add 5% for short barrel.
Subtract 10% for left-hand model.

MODEL 100 - .177 cal., pneumatic action, adj. trigger, adj. sights, UIT target model, 460 FPS, 2.5 lbs. Disc. 1992.

	$675	$600	$450	$350	$250	N/A	N/A

Last MSR was $1,100.

Subtract 10% for left-hand variation.

MODEL 102 - similar to Model 100, except has two cocking levers. Mfg. 1992.

	$900	$800	$700	$500	$350	N/A	N/A

Last MSR was $1,555.

Subtract 10% for left-hand variation.

MODEL 103 - .177 cal., detachable UL, pneumatic, 6.38 in. BBL, 475/508 FPS, adj. trigger, adj. sights, adj. Morini grip (new 2005), 10.5 in. OAL, 3 lbs.

courtesy Beeman Collection

MSR	$1,750	$1,475	$1,150	$995	$750	$550	N/A	N/A

Add 5% for left-hand variation.

RIFLES

MODEL 110 - .177 cal., SP, SL, SS, similar to Model 150 but no recoil-compensating mechanism, less than 200 made March 1962- March 1964. Extremely rare, esp. in good condition.

	$1,800	$1,400	$1,000	$800	$600	N/A	N/A

Most existing specimens heavily used by individuals or shooting club members.

MODEL 121 - .177 or .22 cal., basic European version of the Models 124 and 127, 465 mm barrel, plain beechwood stock without buttplate or high comb. 7.2 lbs.

courtesy Beeman Collection

	$350	$295	$250	$195	$150	N/A	N/A

Add 20% for Deluxe version with checkered beechwood stock, buttplate, high comb.
This low-velocity model was not distributed in the USA.

GRADING	100%	95%	90%	80%	60%	40%	20%

MODEL 124 - .177 cal., BBC, SP, 780-830 FPS, 7.2 lbs. Disc. 1989. Ref: AR3: 61-62.

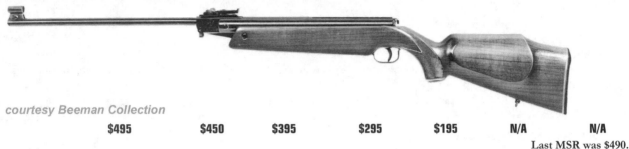

courtesy Beeman Collection

	100%	95%	90%	80%	60%	40%	20%
	$495	$450	$395	$295	$195	N/A	N/A

Last MSR was $490.

Add 150% for factory 5mm marked "5mm/.22 Cal." (4 mfg., see Beeman section).
Add 15% for Beeman markings.
Add 15% for deluxe.
Add 5% for San Rafael address.
Add 5% for "Jnc." Instead of "Inc." on Beeman guns (only 20).
Add 40% for factory deluxe with walnut stock.
Add 10% for left-hand deluxe version (rare).
Add 100% for custom select.
Add 100% for custom fancy.
Add 110% for custom extra fancy.
Deduct 10% for no Wundhammer palm swell on Deluxe models.

MODEL 127 - .22 cal., BBC, SP, 620-680 FPS, 6 lbs./7 lbs. 1 oz. Disc. 1989.

	100%	95%	90%	80%	60%	40%	20%
	$495	$450	$395	$295	$195	N/A	N/A

Last MSR was $490.

Add 125% for factory 5mm (only four mfg.).
Add 15% for Beeman markings.
Add 15% for deluxe version.
Add 5% for San Rafael address.
Add 35% for factory deluxe with walnut stock.
Add 10% for left-hand deluxe variation (rare).
Add 100% for custom select.
Add 100% for custom fancy.
Add 120% for custom extra fancy.

MODEL 150 - .177 cal., SL, SP, first FWB airgun with the patented recoil-compensation sledge system, 20 in. (510 mm) barrel, 450 FPS. Disc. 1968. Very scarce.

	100%	95%	90%	80%	60%	40%	20%
	$1,000	$800	$600	$475	$300	N/A	N/A

Add 60% for Tyrolean stock.
Most existing specimens heavily used by individuals or shooting club members.

MODEL 200 - similar to Model 300 but without recoil-compensation mechanism.

MODEL 300 - .177 cal., SP long SL, recoil-compensation system, 460 FPS, rubber buttplate, rounded forearm, match aperture sight. Disc. 1972.

	100%	95%	90%	80%	60%	40%	20%
	$650	$600	$500	$400	$250	N/A	N/A

✳ *Model 300S* - .177 cal., SP, SL, 640 FPS, 8.8/10.8 lbs. Disc. circa 1996.

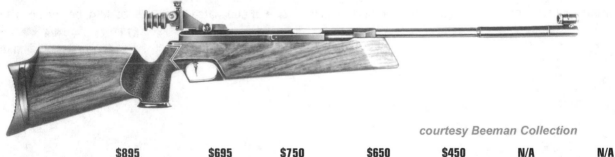

courtesy Beeman Collection

	100%	95%	90%	80%	60%	40%	20%
	$895	$695	$750	$650	$450	N/A	N/A

Last MSR was $1,235.

Add 50% for Tyrolean stock.
Add 10% for Running Boar stock configuration or Universal Model.
Add 10% for figured walnut.
Subtract 10% for left-hand variation (all styles).
Add 10% for junior stock.

GRADING	100%	95%	90%	80%	60%	40%	20%

MODEL 600 - .177 cal., SL, SSP, recoilless top-of-the-line match rifle with aperture sights, unique hardwood laminate stock, 585 FPS, 10.5 lbs. Disc. 1988.

	$800	$700	$600	$500	$300	N/A	N/A

Last MSR was $900.

Subtract 10% for left-hand variation.

This model was also available in a Running Boar variation with an extra-long barrel cover that unscrewed for transporting.

MODEL 601 - .177 cal., SL, SSP, 10.5 lbs.

	$850	$750	$650	$600	$400	N/A	N/A

Last MSR was $1,750.

Add 5% for 5454 diopter sight.

Subtract 10% for left-hand variation.

This model replaced the Model 600, and a Running Target Model was also available (add 25%).

MODEL 602 - .177 cal., SL, SSP.

	$900	$800	$700	$650	$450	N/A	N/A

Last MSR was $1,875.

Subtract 10% for left-hand variation.

This model replaced the Model 601.

MODEL 603/603 JUNIOR - .177 cal., SL, SSP, recoilless top-of-the-line match rifle with aperture sights, unique hardwood laminate stock, 570 FPS, 43 in. OAL, 10. lbs.

courtesy Beeman Collection

MSR	$2,375	$2,250	$2,100	$1,750	$1,300	$895	N/A	N/A

Add 5% for left-hand variation.

Add 10% for multicolored laminated stock.

Add 15% for left-hand multicolored laminated stock.

Subtract 20% for FWB 603 Junior.

This model replaced the Model 602.

MODEL C60 - .177 cal., CO_2, 570 FPS, similar to Model 600, 9.2-10.6 lbs.

	$1,000	$900	$800	$700	$550	N/A	N/A

Last MSR was $1,675.

A Running Target Model was also available.

MODEL C62 - .177 cal., CO_2, similar to Model C60.

	$1,100	$1,000	$900	$800	$650	N/A	N/A

Last MSR was $1,750.

C60 MINI - .177 cal., CO_2, quick change cylinder (bottle), mini version of C60 Match Rifle, 7.75 lbs. Mfg. beginning in 1991. Disc.

	$1,150	$1,050	$950	$850	$700	N/A	N/A

Last MSR was $1,675.

GRADING	100%	95%	90%	80%	60%	40%	20%

MODEL P70 - .177 cal., PCP, lever cocking, match model, 17 in. barrel, adj. trigger, 570 FPS, laminated wood or multicolor stock with fully adj. cheekpiece and buttplate, 10.6 lbs. New 1998.

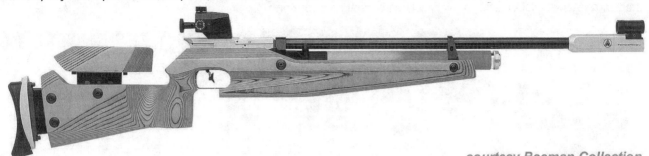

courtesy Beeman Collection

	MSR	$1,935	$1,795	$1,695	$1,395	$1,095	$895	N/A	N/A

Add 5% for left-hand variation.
Add 10% for multicolored stock.
Add 45% for right-hand P70 variation with aluminum stock (Field Target).
Add 50% for left-hand P70 variation with aluminum stock.
Subtract 10% for right-hand Running Target model with laminated wood stock.
Add 1% for left-hand Running Target model with laminated wood stock.

✳ *Model P70 Junior* - .177 cal., similar to Model P70, except has youth dimensions. New 1998.

	MSR	$1,595	$1,350	$1,225	$995	$850	$650	N/A	N/A

MODEL P75 BIATHLON - .177 cal., PCP, five-shot mag., match model, 17 in. barrel, repeat lever trigger system cocks trigger and transports magazine simultaneously, 570 FPS, laminated wood stock with fully adj. cheekpiece and buttplate. New 2000.

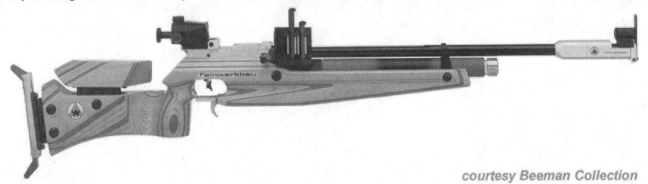

courtesy Beeman Collection

	MSR	$2,995	$2,875	$2,595	$2,195	$1,695	$1,295	N/A	N/A

MODEL P700 ALUMINUM - .177 cal., PCP, SS, match model, 10.8 in. barrel, interior vibration absorber, 570 FPS, aluminum stock with fully adj. cheekpiece, grip, and buttplate, adj. match trigger, 43.3-46.25 in. OAL, 10.8 lbs. New 2004.

	MSR	$2,875	$2,750	$2,595	$2,150	$1,850	$1,550	N/A	N/A

✳ *Model 700 Aluminum Junior* - .177 cal., PCP, SS, match model, 10.8 in. barrel, interior vibration absorber, 570 FPS, aluminum stock with fully adj. cheekpiece, grip, and buttplate, adj. match trigger, 39.4-43.3 in. OAL, 9.7 lbs. New 2004.

	MSR	$2,685	$2,550	$2,395	$1,950	$1,650	$1,350	N/A	N/A

MODEL P700 UNIVERSAL - .177 cal., PCP, SS, match model, 10.8 in. barrel, interior vibration absorber, 570 FPS, laminated wood stock with fully adj. cheekpiece, grip, and buttplate, adj. match trigger, 43.7 in. OAL, 9.9 lbs. New 2004.

	MSR	$2,465	$2,250	$2,025	$1,850	$1,650	$1,250	N/A	N/A

✳ *Model 700 Junior* - .177 cal., PCP, SS, match model, 10.8 in. barrel, interior vibration absorber, 570 FPS, laminated wood stock with fully adj. cheekpiece, grip, and buttplate, adj. match trigger, 39.4-43.3 in. OAL, 7.5 lbs. New 2004.

	MSR	$2,030	$1,995	$1,895	$1,550	$1,350	$950	N/A	N/A

FELTMAN PRODUCTS

Previous manufacturer of pneumatic machine guns for shooting galleries located in Scotch Plains, NJ, from the 1930s to 1990s. Company sold to Starr of New Jersey.

Production of a final 100 of the Tommy Gun model was taken over by the Vintage Pneumatics Company, but that firm closed in 1994. It is not known if all 100 were ever produced.

ARCADE AUTOMATIC

FELTMAN PNEUMATIC MACHINE GUNS – various styles, fashioned after Browning air cooled machine guns and other full automatic weapons are known. Information and pictures for future editions of this book are actively solicited by the authors at BBA6@Beemans.net.

GRADING	100%	95%	90%	80%	60%	40%	20%

FELTMAN PNEUMATIC MACHINE GUN/STARFIRE AIR MACHINE GUN - no. 2 shot cal., fully automatic, gravity-fed hundred-shot mag., fired with hose-fed compressed air, Tommygun-style with ribbed barrel or M-16 style with top handle and perforated barrel sleeve, black crackle or nickel-plated central receiver finish.

courtesy Beeman Collection

$1,200	$1,000	$900	$750	$575	$450	$375

Add 5% for actual carnival tie-down chain.

No one who has ever tried to "shoot out the red star" will ever forget these guns! Firing one hundred rounds of birdshot, fully automatic, at close range, it seemed that it would be easy, but despite various shooting plans of the shooters it just never seemed possible to get that last bit of red!

FIRE BALL (FIREBALL)

For information on Fire Ball (Fireball) airguns, see Apache in the "A" section.

FIREFLY

For information on Firefly air pistols, see Anson, E. & Co. in the "A" section.

FLÜRSCHEIM

For information on Flürscheim, see Gaggenau.

G SECTION

GAGGENAU IRONWORKS (EISENWERKE GAGGENAU)

Previous airgun manufacturer located in Gaggenau, Germany circa 1879-1900. (See also Dianawerk, Gem, Haviland & Gunn and Lincoln sections in this text.)

The authors and publisher wish to thank Mr. Ulrich Eichstädt for much of the following information in this edition of the *Blue Book of Airguns.*

The Gaggenau Ironworks (Eisenwerke Gaggenau) was noted as a "very old company" in a letter dated 1680. Gaggenau is a small town near Rastatt in the middle of the German Black Forest, an area traditionally famous for gunmaking (Feinwerkbau, Dianawerk, Heckler & Koch, and Mauser). The ironworks were not very successful during the 17th century. Although they had cheap power from the nearby Murg-creek, the distance to iron ore forced them to use scrap metal as raw material. Their fortunes were changed in the mid-1800s with the addition of a new casting furnace and especially by their connection, via the Murgtal railroad, to Rastatt and the modern rail system spreading across Europe. By the end of the century, they were producing structural steel, bridges, railings, gas regulators, crushing and paint mills, enamel advertising signs, and bicycles. In 1873, Michael Flürscheim (1844-1912) purchased the works with its forty workers. Flürscheim added a joiners' shop, a tool shop, metal-plating equipment, and a wood processing division to produce rifle stocks. The staff grew to 390 in 1882 and 1041 in 1889.

Theodor Bergmann (later famous with Louis Schmeisser as a designer of self-loading cartridge pistols) joined Flürscheim as managing partner in 1879. One year earlier Flürscheim had been granted a patent for an air pistol, and in 1879, he patented two air pistol improvements. Thus, the company's first air pistol, sometimes known as the "Bergmann Air Pistol" is more properly the Flürscheim air pistol. The Flürscheim air pistol may be Germany's oldest production air pistol. Actually, this pistol, right down to the detail of its disassembly/cocking tool, seems to be a clear copy of the Haviland and Gunn pistol patented in the USA in 1872. At that time, companies outside of the USA were more interested in local monopoly than they were worried about overseas lawsuits.

Jakob Mayer worked in the Gaggenau Ironworks before he founded Dianawerk in nearby Rastatt in 1890. It comes as no surprise that he used the same basic design for his first MGR air pistol (see Dianawerk section). Around 1905, the same design again appeared in Belgium, shamelessly marked "Brevet" (French for "Patent!"). Possibly the same unknown maker also made the virtually identical "Dare Devil Dinkum" air pistol which later appeared on the British market based on George Gunn's 1872 invention in far-off Ilion, New York. As noted in the Lincoln section of this book, the same design led to the Lincoln air pistols and the famous Walther LP 52/53.

By 1891, the "gun division" in Gaggenau produced hunting and military rifles, air rifles and air pistols, gun barrels, reloading tools, and clay-target traps. Production of airguns had become significant, especially of Gem-style air rifles. Pellets and darts were made by automatic machines at about 20,000 pellets per hour.

From 1885 to 1898, the official brand of Gaggenau was two crossed Flürscheim air pistols, usually with the letter "E" above and "G" below. Apparently, many guns made by Gaggenau were not marked, probably so that they could be sold under other trade names.

Two other Flürscheim patents for airguns are known: Patent no. 399962 covers a combination air rifle/.22 firearm apparently derived from George Gunn's combination airgun/rimfire rifle or its derivatives, the Quackenbush Model 5 and Gem air rifles. The second patent, no. 42091 from June 5, 1887, covers a repeating air rifle with a spring-fed magazine for pointed pellets.

Production of Gaggenau airguns apparently ceased about 1900. (However, some airguns bearing the Bergmann name or "Th.B." may date from 1880 to as late as 1920.) Today the Gaggenau company is one of the largest manufacturers of built-in kitchen appliances in Germany and sells to fifty countries on all five continents. The former question as to whether the company should be called "Eisenwerke," which simply means "Iron Works" in German (no more descriptive than "Manufacturing Works" or just "Factory"), or "Gaggenau," has been resolved by the company which calls itself "Gaggenau." "With a name like Gaggenau, it has to be good." Refs: Atkins, AG July 1990; Hannusch, AAG Jan-May 1992.

GRADING	100%	95%	90%	80%	60%	40%	20%

PISTOLS

FLUERSCHEIM - several calibers including .181 cal., smooth bore for darts, SP, mainspring in grip, barrel and grip of gray cast iron, outer parts nickel plated, deeper parts of raised floral patterns and checkering painted black, separate cocking device has two small hooks which grip protruding piston shaft knob during cocking, two prongs at other end of this tool serve as a spanner wrench for removing mainspring retainer ring, later version of the pistol has large T-shaped handle at the end of the piston shaft to allow cocking without a separate tool, fitted wooden cases, incorrectly known as the Bergman air pistol. Mfg. circa 1878-1898.

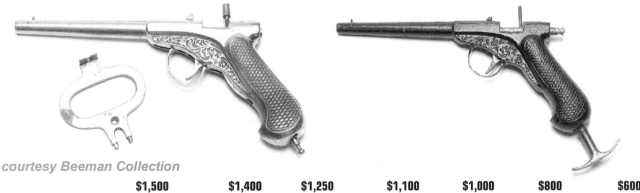

courtesy Beeman Collection

$1,500	$1,400	$1,250	$1,100	$1,000	$800	$600

The wooden cases almost surely were also made by Gaggenau; the company had a box factory producing nearly 300,000 special wooden boxes per year for tools, guns, cigars, etc. Reference: Dr. Bruno Brukner

GRADING	100%	95%	90%	80%	60%	40%	20%

PEERLESS - .21 cal., SP, rear cocking ring or "T"-shaped handle, one-piece wood grip and forearm, nickel plated.

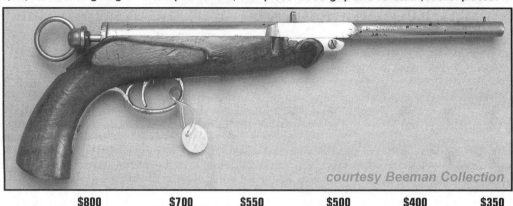

courtesy Beeman Collection

	$800	$700	$550	$500	$400	$350	$300

CONTRACT MODELS - evidently a large variety of air pistols, esp. push-barrel models as illustrated, were made under other brands or without brand markings. Values generally run from about $50 to $300.

PP TARGET PISTOL ("PATENT-PRÄCISIONS") - .180 cal., SP, BBC, SS, small, LHS "push-lever" lock barrel release lever assembly, one-piece hardwood grip and forearm, carved flutes on grip, Schnabel forearm, complex cocking leverage system, cocking plunger exposed under barrel, marked "PATENT" and with Gaggenau crossed-pistols logo on barrel, almost identical mechanism and styling as Gaggenau rifles marked "COLUMBIA". Nickel-plated/blued. 8.7 in. smoothbore, octagonal BBL, 18.3 in. OAL, 2.8 lbs. Mfg. circa 1890s.

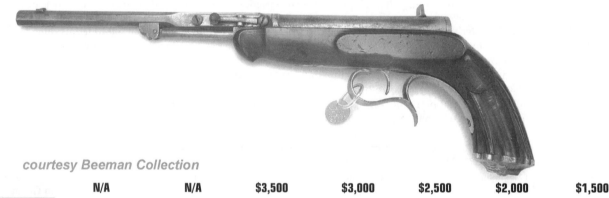

courtesy Beeman Collection

	N/A	N/A	$3,500	$3,000	$2,500	$2,000	$1,500

RIFLES

MODEL 1 GALLERY RIFLE - .25 in. cal., SP, UL, SS, 23.5 in. smoothbore blued BBL, nickel-plated metal work, the forward end of the cocking lever has a very distinctive, trigger-guard-like loop just behind the real trigger guard loop. 42.5 in. OAL, 6 lbs. circa 1881-87. Values TBD. Ref: AAG - Jan. 1992.

Ref: Hannusch AAG Jan-March 1992.

MODEL 2 COLUMBIA - .21 cal., SP, BBC, SS, rear sight slides as barrel release, smoothbore octagonal barrel, one-piece hardwood buttstock, sweeping cheekpiece, and Schnabel forearm, complex cocking leverage system, cocking plunger exposed under barrel, marked "PATENT" and with Gaggenau crossed-pistols logo and "COLUMBIA" on barrel (some not marked "COLUMBIA"). Nickel-plated/blued. 8.7 in. smoothbore, octagonal BBL. Circa 1860s.

courtesy Beeman Collection

	N/A	N/A	$3,750	$3,000	$2,500	$2,000	$1,000

Subtract 10% if not marked "COLUMBIA" (U.S. market name).

GRADING	100%	95%	90%	80%	60%	40%	20%

MODEL 3 GEM - (see Gem section) especially the distinction between combo rimfire firearm/airgun and airgun-only models (see figures here and in the Gem section).

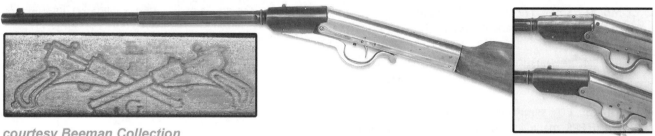

courtesy Beeman Collection

LH insert shows Gaggenau logo stamped on the barrel. It depicts a crossed pair of Flürscheim air pistols.
Upper gun in RH insert is a combination rimfire and air gun. Note the side wings of the cartridge case extractor.

GALWAY

Previous trademark of Galway Arms Co. located in Leicestershire, England, founded in 1964.

The Galway Arms Co. manufactured high grade firearm silencers and introduced the first airgun silencers (requiring a $200 transfer tax in USA). In 1983 they developed and produced in limited numbers the Fieldmaster Mark 2 PCP rifle with adjustable power levels and easily interchanged barrels in .177, .20, or .22 cal. Excellent condition specimens sell in the $2,000 range.

GAMO PRECISION AIRGUNS

Current trademark manufactured by Industrias El Gamo, located in Barcelona, Spain. Currently imported by Gamo USA, Corp., located in Ft. Lauderdale, FL. Previously imported by Stoeger Industries, located in Wayne, NJ, and by Dynamit Nobel, RWS, Inc., located in Closter, NJ. Some models were also sold by Daisy (see Daisy El Gamo 126 and Daisy Model 128 Gamo Olympic). Dealer sales.

One of the oldest manufacturers of lead products in Europe, Gamo was founded during the late 1880s in Barcelona, Spain, as Antonio Casas, S.A. Sixty years ago, the company changed its name to Industrias El Gamo, and expanded into the manufacturing of high-quality airgun pellets and precision airguns. Today, Gamo is one of the largest airgun manufacturers in Europe.

HANDGUNS

F-10 - .177 cal., pneumatic, 430 FPS, 7 in. barrel, 1 1/4 lbs. Importation disc. 1993.

	100%	95%	90%	80%	60%	40%	20%
	$75	$60	$45	$35	$25	N/A	N/A

Last MSR was $115.

AUTO 45 - .177 cal., CO$_2$, DA, 12 BB magazine or SS with pellets, 410 FPS, 4.3 in. rifled steel BBL, 1.1 lbs., manual safety. Mfg. 1999-2004.

	100%	95%	90%	80%	60%	40%	20%
	$70	$55	$45	$35	$25	N/A	N/A

Last MSR was $100.

CENTER - .177 cal., UL, SP, 400-435 FPS, 14 in. barrel, 2 lbs. 8 oz.

courtesy Tim Saunders

	100%	95%	90%	80%	60%	40%	20%
	$90	$75	$55	$45	$35	N/A	N/A

COMPACT TARGET - .177 cal., SSP, 400 FPS, 9 1/4 in. rifled steel barrel, adj. match trigger, fully adj. rear sight, anatomical walnut grip with heavy stippling and adj. palm shelf, 1.94 lbs.

	100%	95%	90%	80%	60%	40%	20%
MSR $250	$215	$185	$150	$125	$90	N/A	N/A

FALCON - .177 cal., UL, SP, 430 FPS, 7 in. barrel. ABS plastic grips, 2 7/8 lbs. Importation disc. 1993.

	100%	95%	90%	80%	60%	40%	20%
	$70	$55	$40	$30	$20	N/A	N/A

Last MSR was $105.

GRADING	100%	95%	90%	80%	60%	40%	20%

P-23 - .177 cal., CO_2, DA, 12 BB magazine or SS with pellets, 410 FPS, 4.25 in. rifled steel barrel, manual safety, 1.0 lbs.

	MSR $90	$65	$55	$45	$35	$25	N/A	N/A

P-23 COMBO LASER - .177 cal., CO_2, DA, 12 BB magazine or SS with pellets, 410 FPS, 4.25 in. rifled steel barrel, 650Nm laser sight mounted under frame, manual safety, 1.1 lbs.

	MSR $140	$105	$85	$65	$50	$35	N/A	N/A

PR-45 - .177 cal., pneumatic, 9 1/4 in. barrel, 1 lb. 9 oz.

		$100	$85	$70	$50	$40	N/A	N/A

Last MSR was $13

PT-80 - .177 cal., CO_2, semi-auto, SA or DA, tilt-up barrel for quick loading of the eight-shot rotary magazine, 4.25 in. rifled steel barrel, 410 FPS, manual safety, adj. three-dot sights, 1.2 lbs. New 2001.

	MSR $110	$75	$65	$55	$45	$35	N/A	N/A

Add $10 for wood grips (new 2002).

PT-80 LASER - .177 cal., CO_2, semi-auto, SA or DA, tilt-up barrel for quick loading of the eight-shot rotary magazine, 4.25 in. rifled steel barrel, 410 FPS, manual safety, adj. three-dot sights, 650Nm laser sight mounted under frame, 1.2 lbs. New 2001.

	MSR $160	$125	$95	$75	$55	$45	N/A	N/A

Add $10 for wood grips (new 2002).

PT-90 - .177 cal., CO_2, semi-auto, SA or DA, tilt-up barrel for quick loading of the eight-shot rotary magazine, 4.25 in. rifled steel BBL, 410 FPS, blue or chrome finish, manual safety, adj. three-dot sights, 1.2 lbs. New 2002.

	MSR $115	$80	$65	$55	$45	$35	N/A	N/A

Add $5 for chrome finish.

PX-107 - .177 cal., CO_2, semi-auto, fifteen-shot BB magazine also holds CO_2 cylinder in grip, 425 FPS, rifled steel BBL, black chrome finish, adj. rear three-dot sight, manual safety, 7.9 in. OAL , 0.8 lbs. New 2005.

	MSR $90	$65	$55	$45	$35	$25	N/A	N/A

Add $10 for chrome finish.

R 357 - .177 cal., CO_2, SA or DA revolver, 5.7 in. Lothar Walther barrel, target-style front sight adj. rear sight, plastic grips. Mfg. 1997-2001.

		$100	$70	$55	$45	$35	N/A	N/A

Last MSR was $13

R-77 CLASSIC/COMBAT 2.5/COMBAT 4 - .177 cal., SA or DA revolver, CO_2 (12-gram cartridge in grip housing), checkered walnut (Classic) or Santoprene (Combat) grips, swing-out cylinder holds eight pellets, 2.5 (R-77 2.5), 4 (Combat) or 6 in. rifled steel barrel, 400 FPS, adj. rear sights, cross-bolt hammer block safety, 1.5 lbs., 8-11.6 in. OAL.

	MSR $100	$70	$55	$45	$35	$25	N/A	N/A

Add $20 for R-77 Classic.

R-77 COMBAT LASER - .177 cal., SA or DA revolver, CO_2 (12-gram cartridge in grip housing), checkered walnut (Classic) or Santoprene (Combat) grips, swing-out cylinder holds eight pellets, 2.5 (R-77 2.5), 4 (Combat) or 6 in. rifled steel BBL, 400 FPS, adj. rear sights, cross-bolt hammer block safety, R77 Laser has built-in grip-pressure activated 650 Nm beam laser mounted in barrel shroud.

	MSR $200	$170	$155	$115	$85	$65	N/A	N/A

V-3 - .177 cal., CO_2, semi-auto, fifteen-shot BB magazine also holds CO_2 cylinder in grip, 425 FPS, rifled steel barrel, black or chrome finish, adj. rear three-dot sight, manual safety, skeletonized trigger, 7.6 in. OAL, 1.1 lbs.

	MSR $100	$70	$55	$45	$35	$25	N/A	N/A

Add $10 for chrome finish.

V-3 LASER - .177 cal., CO_2, semi-auto, fifteen-shot BB magazine also holds CO_2 cylinder in grip, 425 FPS, rifled steel barrel, black chrome finish, adj. rear three-dot sight, 650Nm laser sight mounted under frame, manual safety, skeletonized trigger, 7.6 in. OAL, 1.1 lbs.

	MSR $140	$115	$95	$75	$55	$35	N/A	N/A

Add $10 for chrome finish.

PX-107 LASER - .177 cal., CO_2, semi-auto, fifteen-shot BB magazine also holds CO_2 cylinder in grip, 425 FPS, rifled steel barrel, black or chrome finish, adj. rear three-dot sight, 650Nm laser sight mounted under frame, manual safety, 7.9 in. OAL, 0.8 lbs. New 2005.

	MSR $140	$125	$95	$75	$55	$35	N/A	N/A

Add $10 for chrome finish.

GRADING	100%	95%	90%	80%	60%	40%	20%

RIFLES

ANTONIO CASAS BB GUN - .173/BB cal., SP, Winchester-style lever action, decal on RHS has Casas' initials around a deer and an ad for El Gamo lead "Diabolo" pellets, 6.2 in. BBL. Mfg. circa 1930.

courtesy Beeman Collection

	N/A	N/A	N/A	$400	$350	$300	$200

CF 20 - .177 or .22 cal., UL, SP, 790-625 FPS, 17.75 in. barrel, checkered stock, 6 lbs. 6 oz. Importation disc. 1993.

	$155	$125	$100	$65	$50	N/A	N/A

Last MSR was $190.

CF-30 - .177 cal., UL, SP, 950 FPS, rifled steel barrel with scope mount rail, micrometer rear sight with four-position interchangeable windage plate, two-stage trigger, manual cocking and trigger safeties, Monte Carlo-style walnut stained beech stock with checkered grip, ventilated rubber butt pad, 6.4 lbs. Disc. 2001.

	$215	$180	$145	$105	$75	N/A	N/A

Last MSR was $270.

CFX - .177 cal., UL, SP, 1000 FPS, rifled steel barrel with scope mount rail, Truglo adj. rear sight, two-stage trigger, manual cocking and trigger safeties, synthetic stock, ventilated rubber butt pad, 44 in. OAL, 6.6 lbs. New 2003.

MSR $230	$175	$140	$105	$75	$55	N/A	N/A

Add 70% for CF-X Royal with Deluxe hardwood stock (new 2004).

CFX COMBO - .177 cal., UL, SP, 1000 FPS, similar to CFX except with BSA 2-7x32 scope. New 2004.

MSR $270	$210	$180	$135	$95	$75	N/A	N/A

CFX ROYAL - .177 cal., UL, SP, 1000 FPS, similar to CFX except with deluxe wood stock. New 2004.

MSR $300	$250	$210	$175	$125	$95	N/A	N/A

CADET - .177 cal., BBC, SP, 570 FPS, beechwood stock, 5 lbs.

	$70	$55	$45	$35	$25	N/A	N/A

CONTEST - .177 cal., SL, SP, 543 FPS, beechwood stock, 10.1 lbs.

	$100	$80	$60	$45	$35	N/A	N/A

CUSTOM 600 - .177 or .22 cal., BBC, SP, 690 FPS, 17.75 in. barrel, two-stage adj. trigger, checkered stock, 6 lbs. 3 oz.

	$130	$105	$80	$65	$45	N/A	N/A

Last MSR was $170.

DELTA - .177 cal., BBC, SP, 525 FPS, 15.75 in. barrel, two-stage trigger, automatic safety, adj. sights, plastic stock, 5 lbs. 5 oz.

MSR $90	$65	$50	$40	$30	$20	N/A	N/A

Add $10 for 4x15 scope, rings, and 1000 rounds ammo (Delta Combo).

EUROPIA - .177 cal., SL, SP, 625 FPS, adj. sights, Monte Carlo stock.

	$165	$145	$115	$90	$60	N/A	N/A

EXPO - .177 or .22 cal., BBC, SP, 625 FPS, adj. trigger, special sights, 5 lbs. 8 oz. Disc. 1994.

	$80	$65	$50	$40	$30	N/A	N/A

Last MSR was $130.

EXPO 24 - .177 cal., BBC, SP, 560 FPS, 15.7 in. rifled steel BBL with non-glare polymer coating, two-stage trigger, automatic anti-beartrap safety, manual trigger safety, adj. rear sight, hardwood beech stock with black ABS buttplate, 4.2 lbs.

	$70	$55	$45	$35	$25	N/A	N/A

Last MSR was $120.

EXPOMATIC - .177 cal., BBC, SP, repeater, 575 FPS, adj. trigger, 5 lbs. 5 oz. Disc. 1997.

	$120	$100	$80	$60	$40	N/A	N/A

Last MSR was $170.

EXPO 2000 - .177 cal., BBC, SP, 625 FPS, 17 in. barrel, Monte Carlo-style stock, 5 1/2 lbs. Mfg. 1992-1994.

	$90	$75	$55	$45	$35	N/A	N/A

Last MSR was $135.

GRADING	100%	95%	90%	80%	60%	40%	20%

GAMO 68 - .177 or .22 cal., BBC, SP, 600 FPS, 6 lbs. 8 oz.

	100%	95%	90%	80%	60%	40%	20%
	$80	$65	$50	$40	$30	N/A	N/A

GAMATIC 85 - .177 cal., BBC, SP, 560 FPS, 17.75 in. BBL, two-stage trigger, pistol grip stock, 6 lbs. 3 oz.

	100%	95%	90%	80%	60%	40%	20%
	$75	$65	$55	$45	$35	N/A	N/A

Last MSR was $160.

G-1200 - .177 cal., CO$_2$ cylinder, 560 FPS, 17.75 in. barrel, 6 lbs. 6 oz.

	100%	95%	90%	80%	60%	40%	20%
	$165	$145	$115	$90	$60	N/A	N/A

Last MSR was $185.

HUNTER 220/220 COMBO - .177 cal. or .22 cal., BBC, SP, 1000 FPS, rifled steel BBL, adj. barrel-mounted rear sight or BSA 4x32 scope (Hunter 220 Combo), hooded front sight, manual cocking and trigger safeties, matte finish beechwood stock, black buttplate, 6.2 lbs.

MSR	$190	100% $140	95% $110	90% $90	80% $65	60% $40	40% N/A	20% N/A

Add $20 for Hunter 220 Combo.

HUNTER 440/440 COMBO - .177 or .22 cal., BBC, SP, 1000/750 FPS, 18 in. rifled steel BBL, two-stage adj. trigger, fully adj. rear sight or BSA 4x32 scope (Hunter 440 Combo), wood Monte Carlo-style stock with checkered grip, rubber ventilated butt pad, 6.6 lbs.

MSR	$230	$185	$140	$105	$75	$55	N/A	N/A

Add $20 for .22 cal.
Add $50 for Hunter 440 Combo.

HUNTER REALTREE/REALTREE COMBO - .177 cal., BBC, SP, 1000 FPS, 18 in. rifled steel barrel, two-stage adj. trigger, fully adj. rear sight or BSA 4x32 scope (Hunter Realtree Combo), Realtree impregnated wood Monte Carlo-style stock with checkered grip, rubber ventilated butt pad, 6.6 lbs. Disc. 2004.

	100%	95%	90%	80%	60%	40%	20%
	$225	$175	$140	$105	$75	N/A	N/A

Last MSR was $250.

Add $30 for Hunter Realtree Combo.

HUNTER 890S - .177 cal. or .22 cal., BBC, SP, 1000/750 FPS, 18 in. rifled steel BBL with muzzle brake, two-stage adj. trigger, manual safety and automatic anti-beartrap safety, walnut-stained beech Monte Carlo-style stock with checkered grip, rubber ventilated butt pad, includes BSA 3-12x44 mm air rifle scope, 7.5 lbs.

MSR	$300	$275	$245	$205	$175	$125	N/A	N/A

HUNTER 1250 HURRICANE - .177 cal., BBC, SP, 1250 FPS, rifled steel BBL with muzzle brake, two-stage adj. trigger, hand-finished walnut stained beech Monte Carlo-style stock, checkered grip, ventilated rubber butt pad, 7.5 lbs. New 1999.

MSR	$400	$320	$275	$220	$165	$125	N/A	N/A

MAGNUM 2000 - .177 or .22 cal., BBC, SP, 820-660 FPS, 17.75 in. barrel, adj. two-stage trigger, checkered stock, 7 lbs. 2 oz.

	100%	95%	90%	80%	60%	40%	20%
	$165	$145	$115	$90	$60	N/A	N/A

Last MSR was $200.

MAXIMA - .177 cal., BBC, SP, 1000 FPS, rifled steel BBL with muzzle brake, manual safety and automatic anti-beartrap safety, walnut-stained beech Monte Carlo-style stock with checkered grip, rubber ventilated butt pad, includes BSA 3-12x40 mm air rifle scope, 46.3 in. OAL, 6.8 lbs. New 2005.

MSR	$280	$255	$225	$185	$155	$115	N/A	N/A

MAXIMA COMBO - .177 cal., BBC, SP, 1000 FPS, similar to Maxima except includes BSA 3-12x40 mm air rifle scope, 46.3 in. OAL, 6.8 lbs. New 2005.

MSR	$320	$295	$265	$225	$185	$135	N/A	N/A

MULTISHOT - .177 cal., BBC, SP, eight-shot rotary mag., 750 FPS, rifled steel BBL with polymer-coated finish, adj. rear sight, hooded front sight, dovetail grooves for scope, adj. trigger, cocking and trigger safeties, beech stock, hard rubber butt pad, 6.4 lbs. Mfg. 2001-04.

	100%	95%	90%	80%	60%	40%	20%
	$170	$145	$115	$80	$60	N/A	N/A

Last MSR was $190.

SHADOW 640 - .177 cal., BBC, SP, 640 FPS, rifled barrel, two-stage trigger, automatic safety, Truglo adj. sights, synthetic stock, 41 in. OAL, 5.3 lbs. Mfg. 2003-04.

	100%	95%	90%	80%	60%	40%	20%
	$115	$90	$65	$50	$40	N/A	N/A

Last MSR was $140.

SHADOW 1000/HUNTER BLACK/SILVER/SILVER SUPREME/COMBO - .177 or .22 cal., BBC, SP, SS, 1000/722 FPS, rifled steel BBL with black polymer-coated or nickel (Silver/Silver Supreme) finish, adj. rear fiberoptic sight, BSA 4x32 scope (Shadow/Silver Combo) BSA 30mm red dot scope (Hunter Black), or BSA 3-12x50 scope (Silver Supreme), dovetail grooves for scope, adj. trigger, cocking and trigger safeties, synthetic stock, hard rubber butt pad, 6.6 lbs. New 2002.

MSR	$190	$170	$145	$115	$80	$60	N/A	N/A

Add $40 for Silver Shadow (new 2003).
Add $30 for Shadow Combo (new 2003).
Add $60 for Silver Shadow Combo (new 2003).
Add $150 for Silver Shadow Supreme (new 2003).
Add $50 for Shadow Hunter Black (new 2003).

GRADING	100%	95%	90%	80%	60%	40%	20%

SPORTER - .177 cal., BBC, SP, 760 FPS, rifled steel BBL with polymer coated finish, adj. rear sight, hooded front sight, adj. trigger, cocking and trigger safeties, Monte Carlo-style beech stock, ventilated rubber butt pad, 5.5 lbs. Disc. 2004.

	$120	$95	$80	$65	$50	N/A	N/A

Last MSR was $160.

STINGER - .177 cal., BBC, SP, eight-shot mag., 750 FPS, rifled steel barrel, fully adj. rear sight, cocking and trigger safeties, Monte Carlo-style beech stock, hard rubber butt pad, 6.4 lbs. Disc. 2001.

	$145	$115	$90	$60	$45	N/A	N/A

Last MSR was $190.

STUTZEN - .177 cal., UL, SP, 950 FPS, micrometer rear sight with a four-position interchangeable windage plate, rifled steel BBL, one-piece, full-length hardwood Mannlicher stock, hand-carved cheekpiece, and ventilated rubber butt pad. New 2000.

MSR $380	$325	$285	$225	$180	$125	N/A	N/A

SUPER - .177 cal., SL, SP, 593 FPS, 10 lbs. 8 oz.

	$145	$115	$90	$60	$45	N/A	N/A

TROOPER RD CARBINE - .177 cal., BBC, SP, 560 FPS, rifled steelBBL with polymer coated finish, muzzle brake, two-stage trigger, manual safety, automatic anti-beartrap safety, Gamo red dot sight, black synthetic stock with cheekpiece and checkered grip, 5.3 lbs.

	$90	$65	$55	$45	$35	N/A	N/A

Last MSR was $120.

TWIN - .177 or .22 cal., BBC, SP, 675 FPS. adj. sights, barrel insert tubes to change from .177 to .22 cal., hardwood stock.

	$140	$110	$85	$70	$45	N/A	N/A

Last MSR was $165.

VARMINT HUNTER - .177 cal., BBC, SP, SS, 1000 FPS, rifled steel BBL with black polymer coated finish, 4x32 scope, laser, flashlight, dovetail grooves for mounting all three on special bracket, cocking and trigger safeties, ambidextrous synthetic stock, deluxe recoil pad, 43.8 in. OAL, 6.2 lbs. New 2005.

MSR $230	$195	$175	$135	$95	$75	N/A	N/A

YOUNG HUNTER/COMBO - .177 cal., BBC, SP, 640 FPS, 17.7 in. rifled steel BBL, adj. rear sight, hooded front sight, two-stage adj. trigger, manual trigger safety, automatic anti-beartrap safety, Monte Carlo-style beech stock, ventilated rubber butt pad.

MSR $130	$85	$75	$60	$45	$30	N/A	N/A

Add $40 for Young Hunter Combo with 4x32 scope.

560 CARBINE - .177 cal., BBC, SP, 560 FPS, rifled steel barrel with muzzle brake, blue finish, ambidextrous black synthetic stock, two-stage trigger, automatic safety, 4x20 scope with mounts, 42.1 in. OAL, 5.2 lbs. New 2005.

MSR $90	$65	$50	$40	$30	$20	N/A	N/A

640 CARBINE - .177 cal., BBC, SP, 640 FPS, rifled steel barrel with muzzle brake, blue finish, ambidextrous black synthetic stock, two-stage trigger, automatic safety, 4x28 scope with mounts, 42.1 in. OAL, 5.3 lbs. New 2005.

MSR $100	$85	$65	$50	$40	$30	N/A	N/A

850 CARBINE - .177 cal., BBC, SP, 850 FPS, rifled steel barrel with muzzle brake, blue finish, ambidextrous black synthetic stock, two-stage trigger, automatic safety, 4x32 scope with mounts, 43.1 in. OAL, 5.3 lbs. New 2005.

MSR $120	$99	$85	$65	$50	$40	N/A	N/A

GAMESTER

For information on Gamester, see Eastern Engineering Co. in the "E" section.

GARCO

For information on Garco airguns, see Philippines Airguns in the "P" section.

GAT

Previous trademark of T. J. Harrington & Son located in Walton, Surrey, England.

For information on GAT airguns, see Harrington in the "H" section.

GECADO

Previous tradename used on sporting goods made by Mayer and Grammelspacher (Dianawerk).

Gecado was used by G.C. Dornheim of Suhl, Germany until 1940 and was used in certain German and other markets for guns made by Mayer and Grammelspacher. For more information see Dianawerk in the "D" section of this book.

GECO

Previous tradename used on sporting goods by Gustav Genschow & Co. located in Berlin prior to 1959.

This company was purchased by Dynamit Nobel in 1959, the present owners of Mayer and Grammelspacher. For more information see Dianawerk in the "D" section of this book.

GEM

A general term sometimes used like a brand name. See also Haviland & Gunn, Gaggenau Ironworks, and Dianawerk (Mayer & Grammelspacher).

The term "Gem" has been used to refer to an enormous number of spring piston air rifles. Although a great variety of airguns fall into this category, they have a general similarity in appearance characterized by having the compression chamber in the slanted wrist of the gun rather than ahead of the trigger, and a one-piece wooden buttstock behind the compression chamber. Apparently all are derived from a USA patent issued to George Gunn on April 18, 1871 as modified by a USA patent issued to Asa Pettengill on May 28, 1878. The original Gunn patent is the basis for the drop-barrel cocking mechanism so popular among spring piston airguns throughout the world for over a century. George Peck Gunn combined the wrist-cylinder with the drop-barrel mechanism in his USA patent of March 9, 1886.

Patents properly licensed to Henry Quackenbush in the United States were further licensed to Eisenwerke Gaggenau in Europe, where production of European Gems began in the 1880s. Other early makers, eager for monopoly control of their own markets and simply ignoring prior foreign patents, often copied the basic Gunn and Pettengill patterns or added minor features. Most guns so produced are airguns, but some are combination firearm/airgun designs derived from the Haviland & Gunn designs which became the Quackenbush Model 5.

Gem-type guns were made by many manufacturers from circa 1885 until the 1930s and were at least distributed from many countries and companies, esp. Eisenwerke Gaggenau, Langenham, and Mayer & Grammelspacher (Dianawerk) in Germany, an unidentified Belgian gunmaker (using an encircled "M" as a mark), Arbebz, Sugg, Lane Bros, Baker & Marsh in England, and Coirier of France. They range from crude to excellent in quality and often are "notoriously difficult to classify." Ref: GR March 1974.

Most Gems are small to medium size with octagonal, smoothbore barrels ranging from .177/4.5mm to .25/6.35mm caliber. Current values typically run from about $50 to $100 with few exceeding $250.

Gem Air Rifle. Typical shape and design with angled body tube which serves as mainspring/piston housing and pistol grip. This Jewel Model by Lane of England is special for its "Lane-style" barrel latch and because it is a .177 cal. smoothbore shotgun, designed to fire Lane's Patent Shot Cartridges, filled with No. 7 or No. 9 lead birdshot.

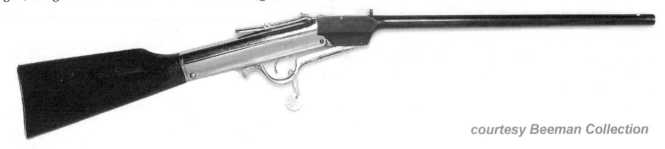

courtesy Beeman Collection

GIFFARD

Previous trade name of airguns manufactured in succession, by Rivolier & Fils and Sociéte d´Stephanoise d´Armes, and Manufacture Française d´Armes et Cycles located in St. Étienne, France. Paul Giffard (1837-1897) was the designer of pump pneumatic and CO_2 air rifles and pistols.

Giffard´s 1862 patent for a pump pneumatic with an in-line pump built under the barrel is often credited with being the basis of virtually all pump pneumatics of the present time. The basic design quickly appeared (1869) in far-off America as Hawley´s Kalamazoo air pistol.

The first production CO_2 guns were patented by Giffard in 1873. Giffard, and many military experts of the time, predicted that the CO_2 guns would produce a major revolution in warfare; perhaps even lead to an end of warfare! Very small quantities of a hammerless CO_2 rifle were made by International Giffard Gun Company Ltd. in London. Giffard also patented (1872) and produced an air cartridge rifle which is similar to the Saxby-Palmer air cartridge system introduced in England in the 1980s.

PISTOLS

PNEUMATIC PISTOL - .177 cal., in-line pneumatic pump along underside of 8 in. barrel, Faucet loading tap with RH oval turning tab, walnut forearm and grip continuous, grip fluted, floral craving on forearm, moderate engraving on all metal parts except barrel and pump, blue finish, no safety, 16.3 in. OAL, 1.8 lbs. 1860s.

courtesy Beeman Collection

	N/A	$4,000	$3,000	$2,500	$2,200	$1,800	$1,500

Add 150% for matched pairs of pistols.

GRADING	100%	95%	90%	80%	60%	40%	20%

GAS PISTOL - .177 cal., CO_2 with removable gas cylinder affixed horizontally under the 10 in. round barrel of single diameter or stepped midway to smaller diameter, SS, BA tap-loading, exposed hammer rests on power adjustment wheel, arched walnut grip with fine checkering and ornate blued steel grip cap, deep blue finish, no safety. 17.9 in. OAL, 3.0 lbs. Mfg. late 1870s.

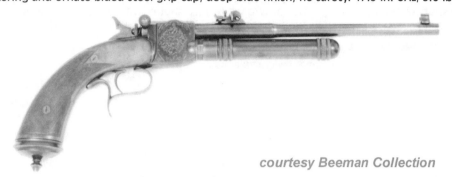

courtesy Beeman Collection

	N/A	$3,250	$3,000	$2,550	$2,150	$1,695	$995

Add 25% for hand guards, reportedly designed to reduce injuries during "dueling practice" with wax projectiles.

RIFLES

PUMP PNEUMATIC RIFLE - 6mm or 8mm cal., in-line pneumatic pump along underside of 19.3-20.3 in. barrel, SS, faucet-loading tap with RH folding or rigid bi-lobed turning tab, external hammer, walnut forearm with deep floral engraving or smooth raised panels and English grip finely checkered or smooth, plain or deeply engraved on all metal parts except barrel and pump, blue or blue with German Silver on receiver and steel buttplate finish, "Giffard-style" guard. No safety, 36.3-38.0 in. OAL, 4.1-4.6 lbs. Mfg. 1860s.

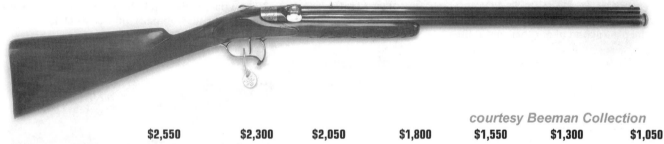

courtesy Beeman Collection

	$2,550	$2,300	$2,050	$1,800	$1,550	$1,300	$1,050

Add 50% to 100% for engraving, German silver, stock carving, etc.

GAS RIFLE (EXTERNAL HAMMER MODEL) - 6mm or 8mm cal., CO_2 removable and rechargeable gas cylinder with decorative knurled rings affixed horizontally under the 24.4-24.9 in. round barrel, SS, exposed hammer rests on power wheel, rotating loading tap, operated by bolt or small lever on surface of receiver which exposes rectangular or round loading port, simple or complex rear sight, slim walnut stock, English grip with fine checkering and ornate blued steel grip cap, Giffard name and maker´s name may be stamped or inlaid in gold, deep blue finish, simple or ornate "Giffard style" trigger guard, no safety, 41.6-42.6 in. OAL, 5.4 lbs. Mfg. late 1870s.

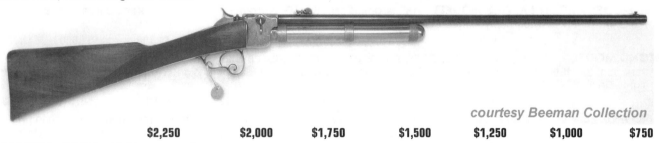

courtesy Beeman Collection

	$2,250	$2,000	$1,750	$1,500	$1,250	$1,000	$750

Add 50% to 100% for highly engraved.

Also known in a pneumatic version with hand pump – may not be original.

GRADING	100%	95%	90%	80%	60%	40%	20%

GAS RIFLE (HAMMERLESS MODEL) - 8mm cal. conical lead projectile, CO_2 with removable, 10.2 in. rechargeable gas cylind
affixed horizontally under the round barrel, SS, gas cylinder with flats for removal, top-loading tap operated by trigger gua
acting as a cocking lever, LHS receiver marked "The Giffard Gun Company Limited London", advertised by maker as "A gun shoc
ing three hundred shots without reloading," with or w/o white-face shot counter (to 200), English-style walnut stock with fir
checkering, tang manual safety, light engraving, blue steel parts. Mfg. late 1880s to early 1890s.

courtesy Beeman Collection

| | $2,550 | $2,300 | $2,050 | $1,800 | $1,550 | $1,300 | $1,050 |

Add 5% for shot counter.

Again showing the confusion in describing the number of projectiles held within a repeater and the number of shots which a single sh
airgun can produce from a single charge of air or gas.

GLOBE

Trade name of BB rifles previously manufactured by J.A. Dubuar Manufacturing Company of Northville, MI circa 1890-1908.

The Globe airguns were invented by Merritt F. Stanley, a former Markham Air Rifle Company employee. Stanley set up
small machine shop in the second story of the Ely Dowell Manufacturing Company in Northville, MI. Apparently unable
make a go of machine work by himself, he moved into a larger shop in the J.A. Dubuar Manufacturing Company and appa
ently began making the first Globe air rifles in 1890. Stanley had three BB gun patents issued to him; one for a lever action gu
which evidently was never produced. Stanley's patents went to Daisy Manufacturing Company in 1908 as Daisy closed dow
the production of another competitor.

courtesy Beeman Collection

RIFLES

All have smoothbore barrels and are without safeties.

FIRST MODEL – (IRON LATTICE MODEL) - .180 large BB cal., BO, SP, SS, frame and diamond lattice pattern stock of cast iro
Nickel finish. Brass smoothbore barrel. Globe design at body hinge. Circa 1890-91.

| | N/A | N/A | N/A | $1,200 | $1,100 | $1,000 | $900 |

SECOND MODEL - .180 large BB cal., BO, SP, SS, similar to first model, except has wood stock with metal parts marked "GLOB
Pats. Jan. 28, 1890" on both sides. Nickel finish. Brass smoothbore barrel. Globe design at body hinge. Peep sight, post fro
sight. Circa 1892-97.

| | N/A | N/A | N/A | $1,050 | $950 | $875 | $800 |

THIRD MODEL ("G" MODEL) - .180 large BB cal., BO, SP, SS. Similar to first model. Cast iron frame, more ornate than first mod
Pine wood stock with oval containing "J.A. Dubuar" and address. Nickel finish. Sheetmetal smoothbore barrel with full leng
external patch. Grip frame marked "GLOBE" and large "G". Circa 1894.

| | N/A | N/A | N/A | $1,000 | $900 | $825 | $750 |

GENERAL CUSTER - no known specimens.

MICHIGAN - no known specimens.

SPECIAL (PUSH BARREL MODEL) - .180 large BB cal., SP, SS. Push-barrel cocking. Cast iron frame, sheet metal plunger housin
Plunger housing marked "GLOBE SPECIAL". Wood stock with oval containing "J.A. Dubuar" and address, deep crescent bu
Nickel finish. Brass tube smoothbore barrel. Grip frame with checkered pattern. Circa 1897-99.

| | N/A | N/A | N/A | $1,000 | $900 | $825 | $750 |

WARRIOR - .180 large BB cal., BO, SP, SS. Sheet metal frame, barrel shroud, sights. Pine wood stock without stamping. Nickel finis
Sheetmetal smoothbore barrel. Grip frame marked "GLOBE" and J.A. Dubuar address. Circa 1900-08.

| | N/A | N/A | N/A | $600 | $500 | $450 | $400 |

GRADING	100%	95%	90%	80%	60%	40%	20%

✳ *Repeater Version* - .180 cal., similar to Warrior, except repeater. Mfg. circa 1908.

	N/A	N/A	N/A	$750	$625	$550	$475

Subtract 25% if not complete.
These are usually missing parts.

✳ *Barrel Lug Version* - .180 cal., similar to Warrior, except with lug under barrel near muzzle. Circa 1908.

	N/A	N/A	N/A	$550	$450	$400	$350

✳ *Embossed Version* - .180 cal., similar to Warrior, except sides with embossed design. Dubuar stock stamp. Circa 1901.

	N/A	N/A	N/A	$575	$475	$425	$375

✳ *Buster Brown Version* - .180 cal., similar to Warrior, except has Dubuar oval logo on buttstock with "BUSTER BROWN SHOES". Spring loaded shot cup under barrel. Circa 1908.

	N/A	N/A	N/A	$650	$550	$500	$450

GOLONDRINA

For information on Golondrina airguns, see Venturini in the "V" section.

GREENER, W.W., LIMITED

Previous manufacturer located in Birmingham, England, since 1829. No current U.S. importation.

Producers of many guns from sub-machine guns to fine shotguns and a unique spring piston air rifle. The rifle was based on British patent 411,520, issued 8 June 1934, to Charles Edward Greener, for a cam mechanism to tightly seal the breech area.

For more information and current pricing Greener firearms, please refer to the *Blue Book of Gun Values* by S. P. Fjestad (also available online).

RIFLES

GREENER - .177 or .22 cal., BBC, SP, SS, usually distinguished by a large cam lever on the left forward end of the compression tube, this lever swings forward to cause the barrel to move forward of the breech block for opening and loading the breech, moving it back cams the barrel tightly shut, buttstock similar to BSA designs with top ridge for the shooting hand´s web, no wood forward of trigger, 43 in. OAL, 7.5 lbs. Mfg. 1934 to 1960s.

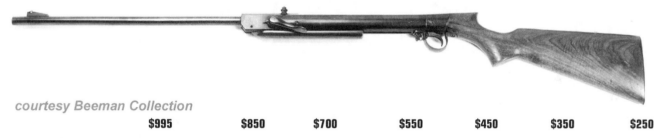

courtesy Beeman Collection

$995	$850	$700	$550	$450	$350	$250

GUN POWER STEALTH

Previous trademark manufactured by AirForce Airguns, located in Ft. Worth, TX.

See listing for AirForce Airguns in the "A" section.

GUN TOYS SRL

Current manufacturer of inexpensive barrel cocking air pistols and pistol/carbines located in Miliano, Italy beginning about early 1970.

Gun Toys SRL also privately labeled airguns to Scalemead and Sussex Armory of Britain.

PISTOLS/CARBINES

RO-71 - .177 cal., SP, BBC, SS, die-cast metal and plastic parts, black plastic buttstock, about 250 FPS, 13.3 in. OAL, 2.1 lbs. Mfg. circa 1973.

courtesy Beeman Collection

$50	$40	$35	$30	$20	$10	N/A

Sold as Scalemead Hotshot Standard, Sussex Armory Panther, Classic, IGI202, and Bullseye. Also known as IGI 202 (IGI became FAS about 1980). Ref: AW Dec. 2004.

GRADING	100%	95%	90%	80%	60%	40%	20%

RO-72 - .177 cal., SP, BBC, SS, similar to RO71, except has one-piece black plastic buttstock, 300 FPS, 14.2 in. OAL, 2.3 lbs.

	$55	$45	$40	$35	$25	$15	N/A

Also sold as Scalemead Hotshot Deluxe, Sussex Armory Panther Deluxe, Classic Deluxe, and IGI203.

RO-76 - .177 cal., SP, BBC, SS, similar to RO-72, except has hardwood buttstock and separate pistol grip.

	$55	$45	$40	$35	$25	$15	N/A

RO-77 - .177 cal., SP, BBC, SS, similar to RO-76, except has longer barrel and shoulder stock rod screwed directly into end cap of receiver.

	$55	$45	$40	$35	$25	$15	N/A

RO-80 - .177 cal., SP, BBC, SS, similar to RO-72, except has plain receiver end cap and grey buttstock.

	$55	$45	$40	$35	$25	$15	N/A

H SECTION

HS

Previous trademark of Herbert Schmidt located in Ostheim an der Röhn, Germany. Manufacturers of cartridge and blank firing pistols and air pistols including the HS 71A, a side lever BB repeater, and the HS 9A, a push barrel model of the type known to the British as a "Gat."

GRADING	100%	95%	90%	80%	60%	40%	20%

PISTOLS

HS 9A - .177 cal., push-barrel cocking, SP, screw-in breech plug for loading, smoothbore barrel, port in right side of frame to allow lubrication of mainspring and piston seal, hard plastic coated frame, approx. 250 FPS, no safety, 5-7.8 in. OAL, 0.5 lbs.

courtesy Beeman Collection

	100%	95%	90%	80%	60%	40%	20%
	$40	$35	$30	$25	$20	N/A	N/A

HS 71A - .177 cal. lead balls, SL, SP, spring-fed hundred-shot magazine. Composition stock and forearm. 6 in. BBL, circa 1970s.

courtesy Beeman Collection

	100%	95%	90%	80%	60%	40%	20%
	$250	$200	$175	$150	$125	$100	N/A

Add 20% for factory box and accessories.

HAENEL

Previous manufacturer located in Suhl, Germany. Previously imported by Pilkington Competition Equipment LLC located in Monteagle, TN, Cape Outfitters, located in Cape Girardeau, MO, and G.S.I., located in Trussville, AL.

The Haenel Company was founded in 1840 by Carl Gottlieb Haenel. The company originally produced military weapons, then sporting guns and later airguns. The company was sold around 1890 and the Haenel brand name has changed hands many times since then. Haenel airguns were most recently made by Suhler Jagd-und Sportwaffen GmbH, Suhl, Germany. Waffentechnik in Suhl currently has control. Identity of the company itself and all of the records were lost when the firm was integrated into the communist state-run firearms industry in the late 1940s. Therefore, accurately dating and identifying every Haenel airgun is not always possible.

Haenel guns are all stamped with the Haenel name and model number. The 1926 catalog only lists the models I, II, III, and IV air rifles and no air pistols. The 1937 catalog lists the model 10 and IV ER and VR, and four air pistols including the 28R and 50.

The Luger-style Model 28 air pistol and the Model 33 air rifle are Haenel's most famous models. Designed by Hugo Schmeisser, of sub-machine gun fame, the model 33 was the basis for the later Haenel 49, 310,400, 510, LP55R and the Anschütz 275. The Schmiesser brothers worked at the factory for about twenty years.

Haenel had been noted for exceptionally high quality, but standards seemed to almost vanish under the state-owned operation. Quality improved some after the unification of Germany.

The key reference on post-WWII Haenel airguns was compiled by Ernst Dieter (a pseudonym) (2002), a former top engineer at Haenel: *Luftgewehre und Luftpistolen nach 1945 aus Suhl und Zella-Mehlis*.

GRADING	100%	95%	90%	80%	60%	40%	20%

Spare parts and repairs for some discontinued Haenel air rifles may be available at:

WTS Waffentechnik in Suhl GmbH, Lauter 40, 98528 Suhl, Germany

phone: + 49 (0) 36 81 / 46 15 21, fax: + 49 (0) 36 81 / 80 57 66, e-Mail: wts@trimm.de

http://www.gunmaker.org/englisch/index_e.htm

For more information and current pricing on used Haenel firearms, please refer to the *Blue Book of Gun Values* by S.P. Fjestad (also available online).

PISTOLS

MODEL 26 - .177 cal. pellets, SP, SS, smoothbore or rifled barrel, cocks by lifting receiver tube up from trigger guard and grip frame, loaded by tipping breech open, black enamel finish, ribbed black plastic or hardwood grips with straight line checkering, resembles Luger military pistol, no safety, 10 in. OAL, 1.5 lbs. Circa 1926-late l930s.

courtesy Beeman Collection

N/A	$225	$175	$145	$105	$85	$50

Add 30% for factory box.

MODEL 28 - .177 or .22 cal pellets, SP, SS, smoothbore or rifled barrel (rifled barrel indicated by asterisk after caliber marking), cocks by lifting receiver tube up from trigger guard and grip frame, loaded by tipping breech open, blue finish, synthetic or wood grips with brass Haenel medallion, Luger styling, no safety, 10 in. OAL, 2.5 lbs. Famous as German military trainer. Circa 1929-late 1930s.

courtesy Beeman Collection

N/A	$185	$150	$!25	$100	$75	$50

Add 30% for factory box.
Add 15% for Super 28 markings.

MODEL 28R - .177 or .22 cal. pellets, SP, similar to Model 28, except repeating mechanism, twenty rounds of .177 or fifty rounds of .22, rifled barrel, manual safety, 10.5 in. OAL, 2.6 lbs. Magazine knob projection from rear of receiver immediately identifies this gun. 1930-1940s.

courtesy Beeman Collection

N/A	$285	$235	$185	$135	$100	$75

Add 30% for factory box.

GRADING	100%	95%	90%	80%	60%	40%	20%

MODEL 50/51 - .174 cal. (4.4 mm lead balls), SP, repeater, fifty-shot gravity-fed magazine (Model 51 - lighter, SS), smoothbore barrel, nickel finish, hardwood grips with or without Haenel brass medallion, no safety, 8.8 in. OAL, 2.6 lbs. Circa late 1932 to 1937.

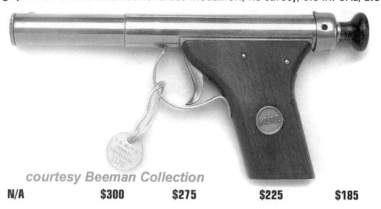

courtesy Beeman Collection

	N/A	$300	$275	$225	$185	$145	$110

Add 30% for factory box.

MODEL 100 - .174 cal. (4.4 mm lead balls), SP, cocked by pulling ring on base of grip to release grip-backstrap cocking lever, fifty-shot gravity-fed magazine, smoothbore barrel, nickel or blued finish, no safety. Circa 1934-1938.

courtesy Beeman Collection

	N/A	$300	$275	$225	$185	$145	$110

Add 30% for factory box.

RIFLES

MODEL 1 - .177 or .22 cal., SS, BBC, SP, smoothbore or rifled barrel, beech stock, small pistol grip, blue finish, no safety, 38.3 in. OAL, 4.6 lbs. Mfg. 1925-1939. (Listed in 1939 Stoeger Catalog as their Model 3100).

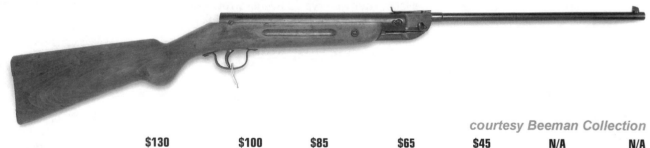

courtesy Beeman Collection

$130	$100	$85	$65	$45	N/A	N/A

Add 30% for factory box.
Add 20% for Stoeger markings.

MODEL 1-53 - .177 in. cal., SS, BBC, SP, rifled barrel with lock similar to Haenel II and III, beech stock, small pistol grip, manual safety, blue finish, 38.3 in. OAL, 4.6 lbs. 1949-1969.

$150	$125	$100	$80	$60	N/A	N/A

Add 30% for factory box.

MODEL II/MODEL III - .177 or .22 cal. pellets, rifled (eight grooves) or smoothbore, SS, BBC, SP, barrel release lever LHS of breech. 43.3 in. OAL, sight radius 17.7 in., 6.6 lbs. Numbers stamped under barrel may be manufacturing date and serial number. Model II with only wood buttstock. Model III with full stock with integral finger-grooved forearm. Circa 1925 to 1939

	N/A	$225	$200	$160	$120	$80	$40

Add 30% for factory box.

MODEL III-53/III-56/III-60/III-284/3.014 - .177 or .22 cal. pellets, SS, BBC, SP. Five variations of Model III made from 1950 to 1993. 568 FPS (173 MPS) for .177, 400 FPS (122 MPS) for .22, 43.3-44.3 in. OAL, 19 in. barrels with 12-groove rifling. Walnut finish beech or laminated stocks. Open or micrometer sights. 6.8 to 7.7 lbs. East German quality problems and very limited distribution outside of East Germany preclude determination of market values at this time (estimated $50 to $150).

GRADING	100%	95%	90%	80%	60%	40%	20%

MODEL IV - .177 or .22 cal. pellet, SS, SP, UL, wood buttstock behind trigger guard (Millita-style), 43.3 in. OAL, sight radius 17. inches, 6.6 lbs. Model IV-E - repeater, drum magazine on top of breech. Ca. 1927-39.

	N/A	$300	$250	$225	$190	$140	N/A

Add 30% for factory box.
Add 100% for Repeater.

MODEL IV/M - .177 cal. pellet, SP,SS, TL, match rifle, characteristic top cocking bolt pivots at rear sight. Available in 1958 and 1959 became the IV/M in 1960. 43 in. OAL, 6.75 lbs.

	N/A	$275	$250	$225	$200	$170	N/A

Add 30% for factory box.
Add 100% for Repeater.

MODEL VIII - .177 or .22 cal. pellets, UL, SP, smoothbore or rifled, Wooden buttstock behind grip. Blued. 42.9 in. OAL, sight radius 17.3 in., 5.7 lbs. Mfg. ca. 1925-39.

	$130	$100	$85	$65	$45	N/A	N/A

Add 30% for factory box.

MODEL 10 (X) - .177 cal. smoothbore, SP, SS, BO, slab-sided wood buttstock behind grip area, sheetmetal "tinplate construction" (may have been made by Dianawerk; this model is not listed in Dieter's book), nickel-plated, 1.3 lbs., 31 in. OAL, date stamp o under edge of stock. German variation: stamped rippling on air chamber, stamped 'MADE IN GERMANY", blued finish. Mfg. ca mid-1930s-1939.

	N/A	N/A	$180	$135	$105	$80	$55

Add 50 % for German variation.

MODEL 15 (XV) - .177 cal., BBC, SP, SS, smoothbore barrel, loaded by removing brass inner barrel from sheetmetal barrel shroud sheetmetal/tinplate construction, beech buttstock behind grip area, blued or nickel. 32.5 in. OAL, 2 lbs. 7 oz. Model XV (Mode VA) similar but with wood forearm side slabs, more complex barrel lock, 2.75 lbs. 1929 to late 1930s.

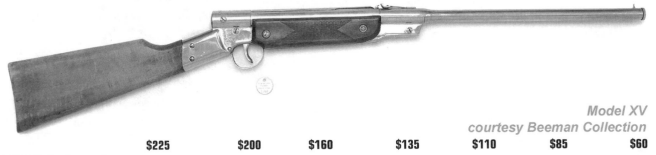

*Model XV
courtesy Beeman Collection*

	$225	$200	$160	$135	$110	$85	$60

Add 30% for factory box.
Add 30% for Model XV/VA.

MODEL 20 (XX) - .177 cal. smoothbore, similar to Model 15, except direct breech loading, thin inner barrel within sheetmetal barrel shroud, early versions with round Haenel logo; later with typical Haenel arrow logo, late 1930s rear sight moved from boc tube to barrel, nickel or blued finish, 34.5 in. OAL, 3.2 lbs. Mfg. ca. mid-1920s-1930s.

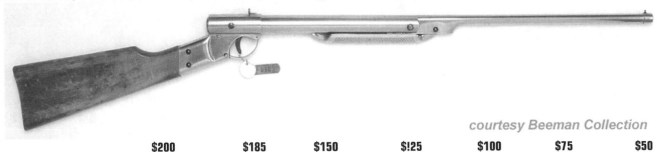

courtesy Beeman Collection

	$200	$185	$150	$!25	$100	$75	$50

Add 20% for round Haenel logo.
Subtract 10% for rear sight on barrel.
Add 30% for factory box.

GRADING	100%	95%	90%	80%	60%	40%	20%

MODEL 30 (XXX) - .177 cal., similar to Model 20, except rifled or smoothbore, full stock with pistol grip and grooved forearm, no buttplate, no safety, 34.5 in. OAL, 3.1 lbs.

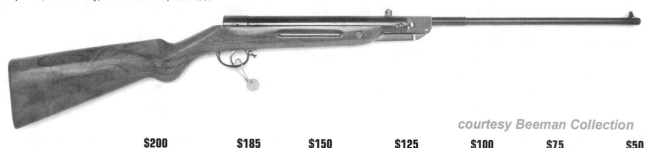

courtesy Beeman Collection

	$200	$185	$150	$125	$100	$75	$50

MODEL 33/33 JUNIOR - .174 cal. (4.45 mm lead balls), SP, bolt lever cocking, paramilitary-style with bayonet lug and stock slot for sling, detachable spring-fed 8 or 12 (Model 33) or 6 or 12 (Model 33 Junior) round box magazines, Mauser type wing manual safety, 44 in. OAL, 7.5 lbs. (Model 33), 40 in. OAL, 5.3 lbs (Model 33 Junior). Model 33 sling on side of stock. 33 Junior sling on bottom of stock. Ca. 1933-early 1940s. Production may have been resumed in 1950s. Schmeisser's Patent.

courtesy Beeman Collection

	N/A	N/A	$350	$300	$250	$200	$150

Add 30% for factory box.

The Model 28 air pistol and the Model 33 air rifle are Haenel´s most famous models. Designed by Hugo Schmeisser, of sub-machine gun fame, this model was the basis for the later Haenel 310 and the Anschütz 275.

MODEL 40 - .177 cal., SP, BBC, SS, similar to Model 30 (XXX) except solid 14.8 in. barrel, pistol grip stock with finger grooved forearm, no buttplate, no safety, 35.5 in. OAL, 3.75 lbs. Mfg. 1930s to 1939.

	$150	$130	$110	$100	$80	$60	$40

MODEL 45 - .177 cal. only, SP, BBC, SS, solid steel rifled or smoothbore barrel, straight grip stock with no forearm, 35 in. OAL, 3.6 lbs. Mfg.1930s to 1939.

	$150	$130	$110	$100	$80	$60	$40

MODEL 49/MODEL 49a - .174 cal. (4.4 mm lead balls), SP, rocking-bolt lever cocking, Sporter version of Model 33, detachable spring-fed six-, eight-, or twelve-shot round ball box magazines, Mauser-type wing manual safety, date stamp on steel buttplate. OAL Model 49 41.5 in., Model 49a 41.75 in., 5.9 lbs. Model 49 sight radius: 16.2 in., Model 49a sight radius:18.5 in. Mfg. ca. 1949-1960.

courtesy Beeman Collection

	N/A	N/A	$350	$300	$250	$200	$150

Add 30% for factory box.

MODEL 85 (KI 1) - .177 cal. Importation disc. 1993.

	$100	$80	$70	$50	$40	N/A	N/A

Last MSR was $130.

MODEL B96 BIATHLON TRAINER - .177 cal., PCP, SS or five-shot repeater using one-round and five-round magazines, Fortner-type action, adj. match trigger, adj. sights, competition stock with adj. cheekpiece, 39.4 in. OAL, 9.6 lbs.

	$1,435	$1,290	$1,050	$800	$600	N/A	N/A

Last MSR was $1,595.

Add 10% for semi-auto conversion.

This model is designed as a trainer for Biathlon rifle disciplines.

GRADING	100%	95%	90%	80%	60%	40%	20%

MODEL 100/MODEL 510 - .177 cal., SS, BBC, small pistol grip, blue finish, 38.3 in. OAL, 4.6 lbs. Model. 510: 1989-1991; Model 100: 1991-1993.

	$150	$125	$100	$80	$60	N/A	N/A

Number change for Model 300.

MODEL 110/MODEL 520 - .177 cal. pellets, Model 110:1992-1993. Model 520:1991-1993.

	$125	$100	$85	$65	$45	N/A	N/A

Improved deluxe versions of Model 303.

MODEL 300 - .177 cal., SS, BBC, small pistol grip, blue finish, 38.3 in. OAL, 4.6 lbs. Mfg. 1969-1989.

	$150	$125	$100	$80	$60	N/A	N/A

Became Model 510 in 1989. Became Model 100 in 1991.

MODEL 302 - .177 or .22 cal., SS, BBC, larger version of Model 300, several versions with minor changes. Production began in 1966.

	$150	$100	$85	$80	$60	N/A	N/A

MODEL 303 (KI)/MODEL 303-8 SUPER - .177 or .22 cal., similar to Model 302 with minor improvements. Production began 1969. Presumably replaced Model 302. USA importation discontinued ca. 1993. Unusual variation: Model 303-8 Super with target stock and aperture sights.

	$125	$100	$85	$65	$45	N/A	N/A

Last MSR was $190.

Add 75% for 303-8 Super.

MODEL 304 - similar to Model 303, except with plastic stock. Mfg. after 1976.

	$125	$100	$85	$65	$45	N/A	N/A

MODEL 308-8 - .177 cal., SP, SS. Importation disc. 1993.

	$225	$175	$145	$125	$95	N/A	N/A

Last MSR was $300.

Not well known outside of former iron curtain countries.

MODEL 310 (KI 104) - 4.4 mm round lead ball. SP, rocking-bolt lever cocking, sportier version of Model 49/49a, detachable, spring-fed six-, eight-, or twelve-shot round ball box magazines. Push pull safety at rear of compression tube. Numerous versions differ mainly in sights and stock. Fifth version (4.5 [.177] cal) has horizontal seven-shot drum repeating mechanism mounted horizontally over top of breech. Mfg. 1960-1989.

	$175	$140	$110	$85	$50	N/A	N/A

Last MSR was $200.

Add 100% for repeater version 310-5.

MODEL 311 (KI 102) - .177 cal. pellets, SS, SP, top action bolt cocking handle, tap loader. Open or aperture sight. 43.75 in. OAL, 7.2 lbs. Mfg. 1964-1992.

	N/A	$225	$175	$125	$95	N/A	N/A

Last MSR was $395.

Numerous variations mainly are minor stock changes.

MODEL 312 - .177 cal., SL, SP, multiple spring/rubber buffer recoil-reduction system, tap-loading. 42.5 in. OAL, 10.8 lbs. Mfg. early 1970s-1990s.

courtesy Beeman Collection

	N/A	$200	$175	$150	$125	$100	$50

MODEL 400/MODEL 570 - upgrades of model 310. Model 570 is 1989 model number change for Model 310. Model 400 is 1991 model number change for Model 570. Detachable spring-fed six-, eight-, or twelve-round box magazines for 4.4 mm round lead balls.

	$175	$140	$110	$85	$50	N/A	N/A

MODEL 410/MODEL 580 - 4.4 mm lead balls, SP, unique lever action repeater. Same magazine system as Models 400 and 570. Dummy in-line magazine below barrel resembles tubular .22 in cal. rimfire magazine.

	$175	$140	$110	$85	$50	N/A	N/A

MODEL 600 - .177 or .22 cal., SP. SS. SL, Match rifle, open or aperture sights, adj. buttplate, 42.13 in. OAL, 8.8 lbs.

	$250	$225	$200	$175	$150	$125	$50

Replaced Model 312.

GRADING	100%	95%	90%	80%	60%	40%	20%

MLG 550 (KI 101) - .177 cal, SP, SS, tap-loading, SS top lever mechanism, 25.6 in. BBL, recoilless match rifle, the MLG (Meister-schafts-Luftgewehr) approx. 500 FPS, match trigger. 42.8 in OAL, 10.8 lbs. USA importation disc. 1993.

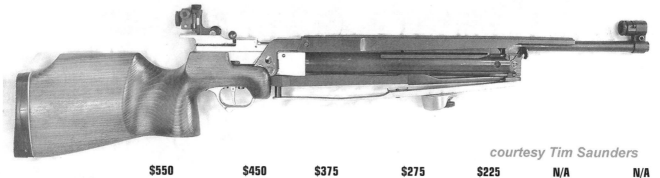

courtesy Tim Saunders

$550	$450	$375	$275	$225	N/A	N/A

Last MSR was $695.

Small numbers made for Soviet bloc international match competitors.

MODEL 800 - .177 cal. SS, SP, match rifle, characteristic top-cocking bolt pivots at rear sight. Mfg. ca. 1990-1992.

$450	$400	$350	$250	$200	N/A	N/A

Replaced Model 550-1.

HAKIM

For information on this Egyptian military training air rifle, please refer to Anschütz in the "A" section of this text.

HÄMMERLI AG

Current manufacturer located in Lenzburg, Switzerland, with most manufacturing actually done in Schaffhausen in the old SIG factory. They are now separate from SIG, but owned by San Swiss AG which also owns J.P. Sauer und Sohn, Blaser, B. Rizzini, and SIG. Currently imported by Larry´s Guns, located in Portland, ME, Wade Anderson (Hämmerli Pistols USA), located in Groveland, CA, and George Brenzovich located in Fort Hancock, TX. Previously imported until 1995 by Champion´s Choice, located in LaVergne, TN, Gunsmithing, Inc., located in Colorado Springs, CO., and 10 Ring Service Inc. located in Jacksonville, FL. Dealer and consumer direct sales.

The Hämmerli CO_2 rifles and pistols were the first true precision CO_2 guns in the world. This is only a partial listing of models, with preliminary information. Additional research is underway and more information will be presented about Hämmerli airguns in future editions of this guide.

A devastating fire in 1977 destroyed the production lines for precision CO_2 guns. Some recent airguns bearing the Hämmerli name have been built to much more economical standards than the pre-1977 models. Hämmerli recently has served as a distributor of BSA and El Gamo airguns, but the claims that any of the Hämmerli brand airguns were made by other companies evidently is not true.

For more information and current pricing on both new and used Hämmerli AG firearms, please refer to the *Blue Book of Gun Values* by S.P. Fjestad (also available online).

PISTOLS

DUELL - .177 cal., CO_2 cylinder, five-shot manual, spring-fed magazine horizontal on top of receiver feeds pop-up loading block, black crinkle and blued finish, composition checkered RH thumbrest grip. 16.1 in. OAL, 2.6 lbs. Mfg. 1967-70.

courtesy Beeman Collection

$1,000	$950	$900	$700	$500	$350	$250

Add 10% for factory box.

GRADING	100%	95%	90%	80%	60%	40%	20%

MASTER - .177 cal., CO_2 (bulk fill or capsules), adj. sights and trigger, UIT target model, no safety, 15 9 in. OAL, 2.4 lbs. Mfg. 1964-1977.

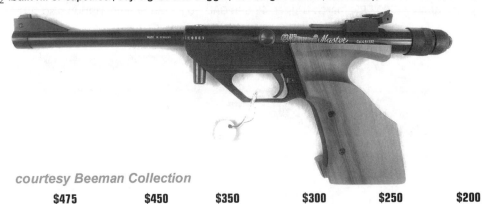

courtesy Beeman Collection

	$475	$450	$350	$300	$250	$200	$150

Add 15 % for wood grips.
Add 15% for fitted factory case.
This model won the German National Championships in 1965, 1966, and 1967.
Additional information and values was not available at time of printing.

PRINZ - .177 cal., CO_2 cylinder, five-shot manual, spring-fed, vertical magazine replaces pop-up loading block, black crinkle and blued finish, composition checkered RH thumbrest grip. Not marked Hammerli (identified by box), the only marking is "MOD 5/1". 11.8 in. OAL, 2.2 lbs. Mfg. 1967-70.

courtesy Beeman Collection

	$850	$800	$650	$500	$300	$225	$200

Add 20% for factory box.

RAPID - .174/BB lead ball cal., CO_2, five-shot semiautomatic, adj. sights and trigger, training pistol for UIT rapid fire, 13 in. OAL, 3.4 lbs. Mfg. 1966-69.

courtesy Beeman Collection

	$750	$650	$550	$450	$350	N/A	N/A

Add 10% for wood grips.

GRADING	100%	95%	90%	80%	60%	40%	20%

SINGLE - .177 cal., CO_2 (bulk fill or capsules), adj. sights and trigger, pop-up breech loading plug. no safety, 13.8 in. OAL, 2.2 lbs. Junior target model. Mfg. 1961-1970s.

courtesy Beeman Collection

	$325	$275	$225	$175	$100	N/A	N/A

Add 10 % for wood grips.

Add 15% for fitted factory case.

Declining velocity is prevented by two measures: 1. Constant pressure metering sytem. 2. Pressure vented to atmosphere when a set low pressure level is reached.

SPARKLER - .175/BB and .177 cal., CO_2 "Sparkler" cartridge, manual repeater five-shot magazine. Two versions: R and RD. The RD can fire lead balls as a repeater and pellets as a SS, 13.7 in. OAL, 2.7 lbs. Mfg. 1958-1961.

courtesy Beeman Collection

	$750	$650	$550	$475	$400	$350	$250

Add 10 % for wood grips.

Add 25% for RD version.

Add 15% for fitted factory case.

MODEL 480 - .177 cal., CO_2 or PCP, fixed cylinder, adj. grips, UIT target model, adj. sights, adj. trigger, adj. grip, up to 320 shots per full compressed air tank, approx. 2.25 lbs. Mfg. 1994-99.

	$500	$400	$350	$300	$250	N/A	N/A

Last MSR was $1,355.

Add $145 for walnut grips.

MODEL 480K - .177 cal., CO_2 or PCP, similar to Model 480, except has detachable cylinders.

	$650	$550	$475	$400	$350	N/A	N/A

Add $145 for walnut grips.

MODEL 480K2 - .177 cal., CO_2 or PCP, similar to Model 480, except has detachable cylinders. Mfg. 1998-2000.

	$800	$680	$550	$475	$400	N/A	N/A

Add $145 for walnut grips.

MODEL AP 40 MATCH - .177 cal., PCP (tank with integral pressure gauge), adj. rear target sights, integral front sight with three different sight widths, fully adj. trigger system, optional adj. "Hi-Grip," blue or gold breech and cylinder, 9.85 in. barrel, includes case and replacement tank, 2.2 lbs. Mfg. in Switzerland. New 2001.

MSR $1,538	$1,370	$1,150	$995	$795	$650	N/A	N/A

Add $59 for ported BBL.

✳ MODEL AP 40 Junior - .177 cal., PCP (tank with integral pressure gauge), adj. rear target sights, integral front sight with three different sight widths, fully adj. trigger system, optional adj. "Hi-Grip," blue breech and cylinder, includes case and replacement tank, 14.82 in. OAL, 1.9 lbs. Mfg. in Switzerland.

MSR $1,150	$1,000	$895	$725	$595	$450	N/A	N/A

GRADING	100%	95%	90%	80%	60%	40%	20%

RIFLES

AIR GUN TRAINER - .174 cal. precision steel balls, SP, SS. SL. A side-lever, spring piston powered insert designed to instantly replace the bolt in the Swiss Kar. 31 service rifle, with its own barrel which fits into the firearm barrel. Uses the frame, stock, trigger mechanism, and sights of the host rifle; its cocking action mimics that of this straight pull bolt action rifle. Developed in the late 1950s; machined and blued Ref.: Smith (1957, pp. 155-166, 168). 28 in. OAL (fits into K31 rifle w/ OAL of 43 in.), 1.0 lbs. ca. 250 fps. Marked Hammerli Trainer, SN, and model of host firearm. A 6 shot, gravity fed, CO_2 version definitely was also patented and developed for the German Kar. 98 service rifle, but actual production may not have been commenced; SN 10 is the highest number reported to Blue Book as of March 2005. A number of experimental and prototype versions apparently were made for other rifles and even pistols such as the German P38. Evidently actually produced only for the Mauser 98 and the Swiss Kar. 31 firearms. Extremely rare, most specimens surviving WWII reportedly were lost in a fire. Estimated value, about $1500. Ref: W.H.B Smith (1957).

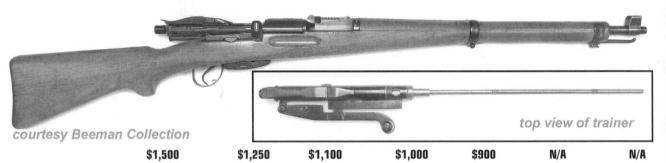

courtesy Beeman Collection

top view of trainer

$1,500	$1,250	$1,100	$1,000	$900	N/A	N/A

Subtract 20% for trainer w/o equal or better condition K31 rifle. (Note that the rifle w/ airgun trainer insert still is subject to USA firearm regulations because the firearm receiver is intact.)
Values of versions other than K31: TBD.

CADET REPEATER (MEHRLADER) - .174/BB cal., CO_2 cylinder, BA, spring-fed eighty-shot magazine, derived from a previous Single Cadet Model, no safety, 41.5 in. OAL, 6 lbs. Mfg. 1968-69.

courtesy Beeman Collection

$500	$375	$350	$275	$240	$200	$150

Add 20% for older Cadet SS model.

JUNIOR - similar to the Match, except uses disposable CO_2 cartridges, does not have a rubber buttplate or barrel sleeve, and is scaled down in size, no safety aperture sight/base swing forward for charging. 41.5 in. OAL, 6 lbs. Mfg. 1962-1970.

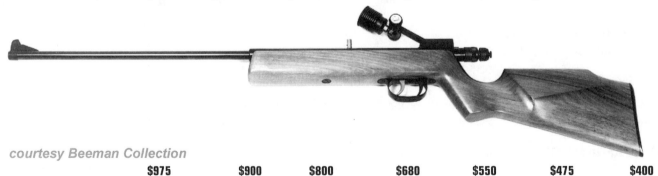

courtesy Beeman Collection

$975	$900	$800	$680	$550	$475	$400

GRADING	100%	95%	90%	80%	60%	40%	20%

MATCH - .177 cal., CO$_2$ filled from storage tank, SS, cocking the gun by pushing the cocking knob forward automatically pops up the loading block, heavy barrel sleeve, extremely angular stock lines and cheekpiece, no safety. 41.5 in. OAL, 9.6 lbs. Mfg.1962-67.

courtesy Beeman Collection

	$1150	$975	$900	$800	$680	$550	$475

MODEL 3 (OR PUMA 496) - .177, SL, SP, SS, rotary tap, intended for match shooting, but provided with fixed sights, barrel-like weight under barrel, no safety, w/o barrel wgt., 44.3 in. OAL, 7.5 lbs. Mfg. 1971-74.

courtesy Beeman Collection

	$200	$185	$150	$125	$100	$75	$50

Side lever may be very dangerous as it has sharp edges and no anti-beartrap mechanism (Models 1, 2,4, and 10 are similar rifles in the Puma 490 series with different sights, barrel wgts., etc.), all the 490 series were replaced by a 400 series circa 1974 which has an anti-bear trap mechanism and manual safety. The 490 series included Models 401, 402, 403 and the strange military-style 420 with a greenish plastic stock with pistol grip handle and dummy cartridge magazine.

MODEL 403 - .177 cal., SL, SP, 700 FPS, adj. sight target model, 9.25 lbs.

	$325	$275	$225	$175	$100	N/A	N/A

Last MSR was $400.

MODEL 420 - .177 cal., SL, SP, 700 FPS, plastic stock, 7.5 lbs.

	$225	$195	$155	$115	$75	N/A	N/A

Last MSR was $300.

MODEL 450 - .177 cal., TL, SP, adj. target sight and cheekpiece, target model. Imported 1994-2001.

	$1,230	$1,020	$795	$595	$425	N/A	N/A

Last MSR was $1,400.

Add $40 for walnut stock.

MODEL AR 30 - .177 cal., PCP, fully adj. rear precision peep sight, hooded front sight, polygon rifling, adj. trigger system, aluminum adj. stock in silver finish, interchangeable pistol grips, 8.6 lbs. New 2005.

MSR	$980	$925	$825	$695	$500	N/A	N/A	N/A

MODEL AR 50 - .177 cal., PCP, fully adj. rear precision peep sight, hooded front sight, 19.5 in. polygon rifling, adj. trigger system, wood laminated or four-piece all aluminum fully adj. stock in blue or silver finish, interchangeable pistol grips (aluminum stock), 10.5 lbs. New 2001.

MSR	$1,750	$1,675	$1,450	$1,150	$900	$650	N/A	N/A

Add 15% AR 50 Alu Pro.
Subtract 10% for AR 50 Junior.

STUTZEN - Hämmerli marked Stutzen-style long forearm SP air rifle. Apparently a private brand production by BSA of their Stutzen model.

For more information on this air rifle see BSA in the "B" section of this text.

HAMMOND, KEN

Current custom airgun maker located in Ontario, Canada. Direct sales only.

Ken Hammond makes custom airguns with a military look, even using military spec M-16 parts to mimic the firearm. His airguns feature a "spool valve" of his own design which doubles as the intermediate air reservoir. The back of the valve is at atmospheric pressure and thus requires very little force to open. This allows for a simple trigger design with a low trigger release pressure.

GRADING	100%	95%	90%	80%	60%	40%	20%

RIFLES

HAMMOND WASP - 9mm cal., PCP or CO_2 up to 3000 PSI. 850 FPS, SS with interchangeable barrels of any caliber. Uses a "cartridge" which holds a standard bullet and acts as connector between valve and barrel. 44 in. OAL, 10 lbs.

courtesy Fred Liady

	$2,500	$2,250	N/A	N/A	N/A	N/A	N/A

HARLIE

For information on Harlie airguns, see Philippines Airguns in the "P" section.

HARPER CLASSIC GUNS

Previous manufacturer located in Buckingham, England. Previously imported by Beeman Precision Airguns, Santa Rosa, CA. Introduced about 1985.

Products include air canes and pistols. Some Harper pneumatics, based on the Saxby-Palmer rechargeable air cartridges. More recent airguns, including electronic trigger guns, will be considered in future editions of this guide. See Brocock introduction in the "B" section of this guide for information on the 2004 ban on production and sale of air cartridge airguns.

PISTOLS

CLASSIC MICRO PISTOL - .177 cal., air cartridge forms the body of the gun, SS, manual firing block, includes separate 9.6 in. air pump, which uses a special chamber to fill the air cartridge without connecting to the cartridge, 2.3 in. OAL, 0.8 oz.

courtesy Beeman Collection

	$350	$295	N/A	N/A	N/A	N/A	N/A

Subtract 40% for missing pump.

This model was created to be the world´s smallest air pistol and, unlike true miniatures, it is a full size caliber. Brass collection ID tag in illustration is 7/8 inches in diameter. Under their anti-airgun-cartridge law, this gun is now illegal in England as a dangerous weapon!

CLASSIC PISTOL - .22 or .25 cal., Harper Air Cane rifle action, walnut handle, brass barrel, concealed fold-out trigger, 300 FPS, 6.5 OAL, 4 oz. Mfg. 1989 only.

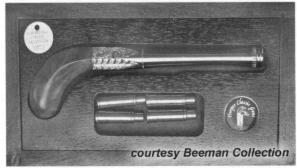

courtesy Beeman Collection

	$595	$495	$375	$295	$225	N/A	N/A

Last MSR for a cased pair was $700.

GRADING	100%	95%	90%	80%	60%	40%	20%

Add 50% if cased.
Add 10% for .25 cal.
Add 10% for deluxe.
Add 50%-75% for rare specimens of air pistols in the form of smoking pipes, ball-point pens, etc.
Only six were imported into U.S. Under their anti-airgun-cartridge law, this gun is now illegal in England as a dangerous weapon!

LASSIC PEPPERBOX - .22 cal., PCP, similar to Beeman/Harper Classic Pistol, 9.8 oz. Mfg. 1989 only.

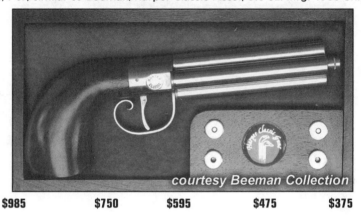

courtesy Beeman Collection

$985	$750	$595	$475	$375	N/A	N/A

Last MSR was $575.

Only three were imported into the U.S. Under their anti-airgun-cartridge law, this gun is now illegal in England as a dangerous weapon!

AIR CANES

LASSIC AIR CANE - .22 or .25 cal., pneumatic (reusable gas cartridge), 650 FPS, reproduction of 19th century Walking Cane Gun, 1 lb. Mfg. circa 1980s.

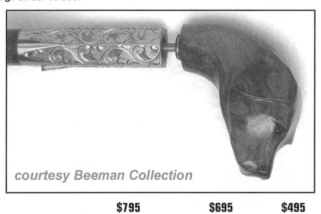
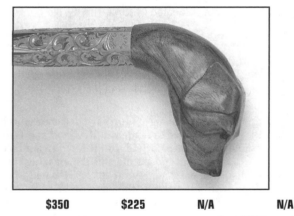

courtesy Beeman Collection

$795	$695	$495	$350	$225	N/A	N/A

Last MSR was $595.

Add $55 for decorative head piece.
Only ten of these models were imported into the U.S. Under their anti-airgun-cartridge law, this gun is now illegal in England as a dangerous weapon!

HARRINGTON

Current Trade name of T.J. Harrington & Sons Ltd. of Walton, Surrey, England. Made about one million spring-piston, push-barrel airguns (based on the 1877 H.M. Quackenbush patent) from 1937 to 1940 and 1947 to 2000. Sold to Marksman Products of Huntington Beach, CA about 2000 with production continuing.

The GAT is a low cost, mostly cast alloy, pop-out type pistol. This gun enjoyed enormous popularity for decades. In fact, most airgunners outside of the USA probably cut their teeth on a GAT. It was first introduced in 1937, production ceased during the war but recommenced postwar and still carries on. The design of the GAT drew heavily upon an H. M. Quackenbush patent of 1877. All GATs have a smoothbore .177 barrel. Many are also fitted with a muzzle device that enables corks, as well as pellets and darts, to be fired.

The GAT design has undergone few variations; the most significant one would be the addition of a safety catch in 1982, to make the gun acceptable on the U.S. market.

In 1987 a smoothbore long gun version of the GAT was produced and marketed with little success.

The authors and publisher wish to thank Trevor Adams and John Atkins for their valuable assistance with the following information in this edition of the *Blue Book of Airguns*.

GRADING	100%	95%	90%	80%	60%	40%	20%

PISTOLS

GAT - .177 darts, slugs, waisted pellets, or corks, SP, SS, push-barrel cocking, cast alloy and (later) plastic, smoothbore barrel. Muzzle nut for shooting corks. Safety added in 1982 for USA market. Initially black or bright chrome finish, then black paint or polished (buffed bare metal) and finally black paint only.

courtesy Beeman Collection

	$40	$30	$20	$10	N/A	N/A	N/A

Add 25% for bright nickel finish.
Add 50% for original green factory box.
Add 20% for other factory boxes.

RIFLES

GAT RIFLE - .177 cal. darts, balls, or pellets, SP, SS, push-barrel cocking similar to Gat Pistol, except long gun version. Current retail values in the $50 to $75 range depending on condition. Mfg. 1987.

HATSAN ARMS CO.

Current manufacturer located in Izmir, Turkey. No current importation.

HAVILAND AND GUNN (G.P. GUNN COMPANY)

Previous airgun designers and manufacturers located in Ilion, NY circa 1871-1882. Then the company was purchased by H.M. Quackenbush. (See also Gem and Quackenbush sections).

The authors and publisher wish to thank Mr. John Groenwold for the following information in this edition of the *Blue Book of Airguns*.

The airgun designs of George Gunn have had enormous impact on the development of modern airguns. Patent number 113766, dated April 18, 1871, registered to Benjamin Haviland and George Gunn, was the basis for not only the Haviland & Gunn barrel-cocking air rifles and the resulting, wonderful H.M. Quackenbush Model 5 rifles, but led to the great variety of air rifles known as the Gem airguns in Europe and indeed most of the amazing number and variety of barrel-cocking air rifles and pistols which have been developed since then! Patent number 126954, dated May 21, 1872, also registered to Haviland and Gunn, for an air pistol with the mainspring within the grip, is the basis for another more than century-long parade of airguns, including some early Gaggenau air pistols, the MGR air pistols, the Lincoln air pistols, and even the Walther LP 53 made famous by James Bond!

George P. Gunn was born in Tioga County, PA in 1827. He was a gunsmith in North Ilion, NY. He first he marketed an airgun under his own name while working for Remington Arms Company and then another after leaving their employ. These guns, based on his first patents, were marked "G. P. GUNN, ILION, NY, PAT. APR. 18, 1871".

About the time of Gunn´s first patent, he joined with Benjamin Haviland to form the firm of Haviland and Gunn. Benjamin Haviland (1823-1920) had been involved with the grocery, commission, and freighting fields. His position as senior partner in the new firm evidently resulted from bringing essential marketing skills and financial backing. Throughout the 1870s the firm of Haviland and Gunn was engaged in the manufacture of airguns at the Ilion Depot, on the New York Central Railroad, in Ilion, NY.

Most of the rifles produced by Gunn or Haviland & Gunn were combination guns which could function as either an air rifle or as a .22 rimfire firearm. Some models were strictly air rifles and some may have been strictly rimfire. A "patch box" in the buttstock of the combination guns stored the firing pin and/or breech seal. When used as a rimfire gun, the firing pin was installed in the air transfer port on the front of the cylinder face. When the trigger was pulled, the piston moved forward, without significant air compression and struck the firing pin which in turn crushed and detonated the primer of the rimfire cartridge. The patch box on the Haviland and Gunn rifles underwent several changes in shape, style, lid type and functioning, and location, finally ending up as round on the right side of the stock.

A traditional "tee bar" breech latch is found on most Haviland and Gunn air rifles and combination rifles. A side swinging breech latch on smooth bore air rifles probably was an earlier design.

Haviland & Gunn developed numerous "improved" modifications of their various models during the 1870s. They produced their last catalog in 1881. In 1882, H.M. Quackenbush purchased at least part of the Haviland and Gunn Company, including patent rights, machinery, existing stock, and equipment related to gun and slug manufacture. George Gunn agreed to work for H.M. Quackenbush but Benjamin Haviland did not.

In 1884, Quackenbush offered exactly the same gun as the Haviland and Gunn "Improved 1880" as the Quackenbush Model 5. The parts were the same but not all were interchangeable. Quackenbush soon began offering it with an increased number of options. The

GRADING	100%	95%	90%	80%	60%	40%	20%

stronger marketing by Quackenbush contributed to a much increased success of the Number 5 Rifle.

While working for H. M. Quackenbush, George Gunn considered a repeating version of the combination rifle known as the Hurricane. Apparently it exists only in the papers of patent number 337,395 of March 9, 1886. That Henry Marcus Quackenbush´s name does not appear on this patent, filed August 12, 1885, may be related to George Gunn leaving the Quackenbush firm in that year.

A mechanical target, as produced by Haviland and Gunn for many years, was improved with several Quackenbush patents and became an important item in the Quackenbush line. A reversible "iron face" plate with a hole in the center created the "bullseye." When the shooter struck the bullseye, a figure popped up on the top of the target and/or a bell sounded. These targets are known only unmarked or with Quackenbush markings.

George Gunn also invented the felted airgun slug, patenting the process for manufacturing them on December 18, 1883. Quackenbush was granted United States patent 358,984, on March 8, 1887, for improvements in their manufacturing process. The felted slug was so superior to the burred slug that its sales immediately surpassed those of the burred slug, but Quackenbush continued selling the burred slugs until 1947.

Entries in H.M Quackenbush´s personal diary indicate that George Gunn was ill, on and off, for quite some time after joining the Quackenbush Company. The last record of his employment by Quackenbush was August 12, 1885, at which time he was working on the Quackenbush Safety Rifle.

After leaving Quackenbush, George Gunn invented another airgun and started the Atlas Gun Company, in Ilion, NY to market it. He died on March 2, 1906 when he was hit by a train while walking home from the Central Depot in Ilion, NY.

PISTOLS

1872 MODEL - .177 cal., SP, SS, breech loading, mainspring within grip. It is cocked by inserting the breech block hook into a hole in the piston rod projecting from the base of the grip, has cast iron body with smooth surface or cast checkered grip, trigger blade with strap guard, smoothbore, may be unmarked except for patent date of May 21, 1872 stamped onto surface of mainspring retaining ring (this may not be visible if retaining ring has been installed backwards). This design was also apparently licensed for Morers patent improved air pistol.

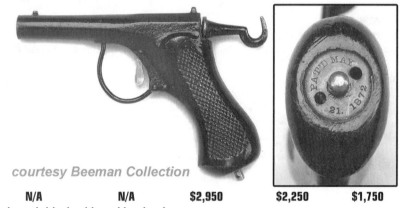

courtesy Beeman Collection

	N/A	N/A	$2,950	$2,250	$1,750	$1,250	$850

Subtract 20% for missing breech block with cocking hook.

RIFLES

All models are breech-loading airguns with walnut buttstocks and no forearms unless otherwise noted. Smoothbore models had a brass-lined barrel to fire darts, slugs, or shot. Rifled barrels were designed for burred or felted slugs. A tee bar breech latch is found on most guns; a side swinging latch is less common, presumably an earlier style. Except for the Parlor rifle, the H&G guns were finished in nickel plating or browning.

STRAIGHT LINE MODEL - .22 cal., BBC, SP, SS, receiver/spring chamber in straight line with barrel, metal stock wrist does not contain mainspring, receiver nickel plated, barrel brown finish.

	N/A	N/A	$3,500	$3,000	$2,200	$1,000	$500

NEW MODEL - combination air rifle/.22 rimfire gun, "patch box" of various shapes in buttplate holds firing pin or breech seal when other is in use, spring chamber angled down from barrel to form wrist of stock above trigger.

courtesy Beeman Collection

	N/A	N/A	$3,000	$2,500	$1,800	$1,000	$500

Add 10% for browned finish.
Add 25% for side swinging breech latch.

GRADING	100%	95%	90%	80%	60%	40%	20%

NEW IMPROVED 1880 MODEL - combination air rifle/.22 caliber rimfire rifled gun (rare version: smoothbore air rifle only), predecessor to the Quackenbush Model 5, spring chamber angled down from barrel to form wrist of stock above trigger, patch box for firing pin only in lower edge of buttstock, serial number stamped on rear of barrel, under barrel latch, trigger. Barrel base only under lower half of barrel.

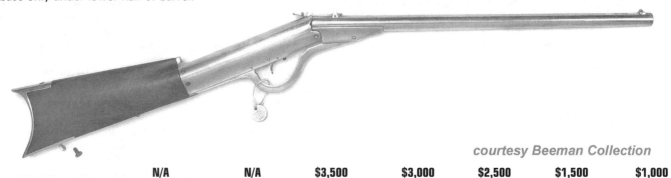

courtesy Beeman Collection

| | N/A | N/A | $3,500 | $3,000 | $2,500 | $1,500 | $1,000 |

Add 10% for browned finish.
Add 20% for nickel finish.
Add 25% for smoothbore airgun only.

IMPROVED JUNIOR MODEL - .22 cal., BBC, SP, SS, spring chamber angled down from barrel to form wrist of stock above trigger, rifled or smoothbore barrel. Minor differences in barrel lengths and patch box locations, airgun action only so "patch box" served no real purpose.

| | N/A | N/A | $3,000 | $2,500 | $1,800 | $1,000 | $500 |

Add 10% for browned finish.
Add 25% for smoothbore airgun only.

PARLOR MODEL - .22 cal., piston cocked by pulling plunger ring within wire skeleton stock, 17.8 in. smoothbore barrel, heavy cast iron receiver, black and gilt (black Japan enamel and bright nickel) finish, other colors are known but have no factory documentation.

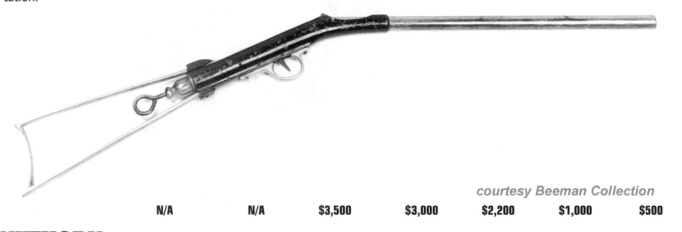

courtesy Beeman Collection

| | N/A | N/A | $3,500 | $3,000 | $2,200 | $1,000 | $500 |

HAWTHORN

Previous Store Brand name used by Montgomery Wards.

For the original manufacturer and model name/number of Hawthorn Brand airguns see the Store Brand Cross-Over List at the back of this text.

HEALTHWAYS, INC.

Previous trademark manufactured and distributed by Healthways, Inc., Compton, CA into the 1970s. CO_2 versions designed by Richard Kline and Kenneth Pitcher in 1955-56; patented in late 1950s. Healthways was purchased by Marksman.

For additional information on Plainsman Model airguns, see Challenger Arms Corp. in the "C" section.

PISTOLS

PLAINSMAN MODEL 9400 - BB/.175 cal. steel only, CO_2 (12 gm. CO_2 cylinders mounted in grip; 8 gm. with adapter) semi-auto with coin-slotted, three-position power switch, hundred-shot gravity-fed mag., manual thumb safety, black plastic (later Marksman production had simulated woodgrain) grips, black epoxy finish, 5.9 in. rifled barrel, 350 FPS. 1.72 lbs.

| $90 | $75 | $65 | $55 | $45 | $35 | $25 |

1977 retail was approx. $30.

Add 25% for box, accessories, and factory papers.

GRADING	100%	95%	90%	80%	60%	40%	20%

PLAINSMAN MODEL 9401 - BB/.175 cal., similar to Model 9400, except smoothbore.

	100%	95%	90%	80%	60%	40%	20%
	$90	$75	$65	$55	$45	$35	$25

1977 retail was approx $30.

Add 25% for box, accessories, and factory papers.

PLAINSMAN MODEL 9404 "SHORTY" - .22 cal. for lead-coated steel round balls, CO_2 (8 gm. or 12 gm), forty-shot magazine, similar to Model 9400, except 3.9 in. barrel, 1.65 lbs.

courtesy Beeman Collection

	100%	95%	90%	80%	60%	40%	20%
	N/A	$100	$85	$75	$55	$45	$35

1977 retail was approx $35.

Add 30% for box, accessories, and factory papers.

PLAINSMASTER MODEL 9405 - BB/.175 cal., CO_2, 9.4 in. rifled barrel, black epoxy finish, detachable walnut wood-grain plastic thumbrest grip and forend, adj. rear sight, thumb safety, three-position power switch, hundred-round capacity, approx. 2.54 lbs.

	100%	95%	90%	80%	60%	40%	20%
	$90	$75	$65	$55	$45	$35	$25

1977 retail was approx $45.

Add 25% for box, accessories, and factory papers.
Subtract 75% for missing forearm and hand grip.

PLAINSMASTER MODEL 9406 - .22 cal. for lead-coated steel round balls, similar to Model 9405, except smoothbore.

courtesy Beeman Collection

	100%	95%	90%	80%	60%	40%	20%
	N/A	$90	$75	$65	$55	$45	$35

1977 retail was approx $45.

Add 25% for box, accessories, and factory papers.
Subtract 75% for missing forearm and hand grip.

PLAINSMAN MODEL MA 22 - .22 cal. lead covered steel balls, CO_2, approx. 350 FPS, gravity-fed fifty-shot mag., manual safety, styled like Colt Woodsman. Mfg. 1969-1980.

courtesy Beeman Collection

	100%	95%	90%	80%	60%	40%	20%
	$135	$100	$85	$65	$45	N/A	N/A

GRADING	100%	95%	90%	80%	60%	40%	20%

PLAINSMAN MODEL ML 175 - .175/BB cal., CO_2, approx. 350 FPS, gravity-fed fifty-shot mag., manual safety, metal grips, styled like Colt Woodsman, black finish, plastic grips, 6 in. BBL, 9.3 in. OAL, 1.9 lbs. Mfg.1969-1980.

courtesy Beeman Collection

	$80	$65	$55	$45	$35	N/A	N/A

Add 25% for chrome finish.

PLAINSMAN WESTERN - .175/BB cal., CO_2, spring-fed magazine (approx. fifteen shots), no safety, styled like Colt Peacemaker SA revolver. 11.5 in. OAL, 2.1 lbs.

courtesy Beeman Collection

	$95	$80	$70	$55	$45	$35	$25

TOPSCORE MODEL 9100 - BB/.175 cal., lifting-barrel spring air action, 6.5 in. smoothbore barrel, approx. 200 FPS, fifty-shot gravity-fed mag., manual thumb safety, die-cast one-piece grip/frame, 1.7 lbs.

	$75	$60	$50	$45	$40	$30	$25

1977 retail was approx $20.

Add 25% for box, accessories, and factory papers.

PLAINSMAN TOPSCORE 175 - .177 BB cal., CO_2, repeater, 10.5 in. OAL, 2.2 lbs.

	$75	$60	$50	$45	$40	$30	$25

PLAINSMAN SHARP SHOOTER 175 - .177 BB cal., CO_2, repeater.

Values and dates not available at the time of publication.

RIFLES

PLAINSMAN MODEL MX175 - BB/.175 cal., CO_2 12 gm., 20 in. barrel, scope rail cast in top, low power, beech stock. 4 lbs.

courtesy Beeman Collection

	$65	$55	$50	$40	$35	$30	$20

Add 20% for box, accessories, and factory papers.

PLAINSMAN MODEL MC22 - .22 cal., lead coated steel round balls, similar to Model MX175.

	$75	$65	$55	$50	$40	$35	$30

Add 20% for box, accessories, and factory papers.

HEGMANS, THEO

Current craftsman located in Kerken, Germany.

Theo Hegmans is a German who can only be described as a craftsman genius - although he is a graduate economist and computer specialist, he retreats to an old-fashioned shop in his barn to make too many things to describe, but all wonderful. These creations include the most unusual firearms and astonishing airguns. His inventions include a version of the old large bore German airguns, or Windbüchsen. This Windbüchse is most unusual in that it uses a percussion cap to open the air valve to a charge of stored air and push a 200-grain, .45 caliber lead bullet out at great velocity. Ref: VISIER, March 2005.

PISTOLS

HEGMANS MCAIRROW CLASSIC - soda straw cal, the only Hegmans airgun ever made in quantity. The straw projectiles are fitted with a rubber tip and some fins cut from other straws. The projectile is shoved over the concealed barrel - the missile is around the barrel rather than in it! Two to twelve pumps power the gun. On full power it fires up to 230 FPS to a range of 30 or 40 yards! Original retail price equaled about $125. Rarity precludes accurate pricing.

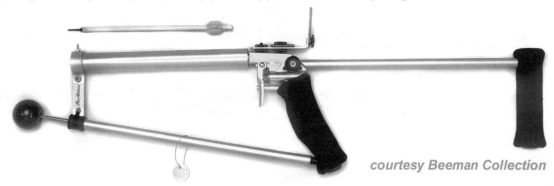

courtesy Beeman Collection

In 1999, this started out as a toy for his then nine-year-old nephew, made from a bicycle tire pump, a grease gun, and garden soaker hose! As projectiles, he used plastic drinking straws from an international fast food firm whose name may be suggested by the name of this gun. The fast food firm was not pleased and he was pressured to stop production after only exactly fifty specimens had been made over three years.

RIFLES

AIR TWIN - .177 or .22 cal., SxS double-barrel, SP, SS, mainsprings around the barrels, 18.5/33.4 ft./lb. ME, 41.3 in. OAL, 8.8 lbs. Rarity precludes accurate pricing.

courtesy Theo Hegmans

Each BBL holds 10mm group ctc at 25 yds, together 20 mm ctc.

CHIP MUNK - .22 cal., SS, PCP, real BBL hidden under false barrel air reservoir, 25 shots per charge, 52 ft./lb. ME 41.3 in OAL, 7.0 lbs. Rarity precludes accurate pricing.

courtesy Theo Hegmans

GO WEST - .177 cal., PCP, real BBL hidden under false barrel air reservoir, eight-shot repeater with lever activated cylinder, 32 sho @ 14.8 ft./lb. ME, 16 shots @ 11.4 ft./lb. ME, 40.6 in. OAL, 9.3 lbs. Rarity precludes accurate pricing.

courtesy Theo Hegmans

GRANDPA - .45 cal., PCP, muzzle loader, walnut stock, 297 ft./lb. ME at 3000 PSI with 250 gr. bullet, 900 PSI, 89 ft./lb. ME, 47.2 OAL, 9.7 lbs. Rarity precludes accurate pricing.

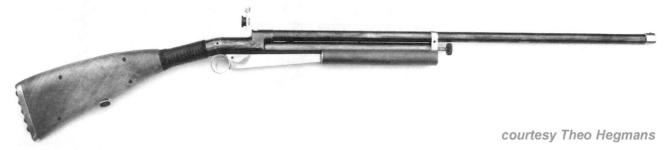

courtesy Theo Hegmans

HOW STUFF WORKS - .177 cal., BBC, SP, SS, butt reservoir, all operating elements on the outside of the gun, 40 shots per charg @ 18 ft./lb. ME. 43.3 in. OAL, 6.2 lbs. Rarity precludes accurate pricing.

HEILPRIN MANUFACTURING CO.

For information on Heilprin Manufacturing Co. airguns, see Columbian in the "C" section.

HEIRINKAN

Previous trade name of Heirinkan Co. located in Tokyo, Japan.

Heirinkan airguns were designed by the company's founder, the late Ueda Shoji (1918-81). Former producer of high pow pneumatic air rifles. These rifles were made only in small numbers and for a very short time in the 1970s. Reportedly most the rifles remaining in Japan were destroyed by the government and ownership is forbidden without a special need – such professional pest control. Collection as such is not allowed. Much sought by collectors and shooters because of their hi power, accuracy, and high quality. Reportedly in production 1953-81, information not confirmed. Research is ongoing with th trademark, and more information will be included both in future editions and online.

RIFLES

MODEL A - .177 cal., swinging arm, multi-pump pneumatic, sporter model, 6.6 lbs, 36.6 in. OAL. Rarity precludes exact pricing.

courtesy Beeman Collection

Rarity precludes accurate pricing. A very good specimen sold for $1,500 in 1996.

MODEL SS - Apparently similar to Model A with telescopic sight.

Rarity precludes accurate pricing.

MODEL Z - no information at this time.

Rarity precludes accurate pricing.

MODEL 120 - Apparently similar to Model A but w/ thumbhole stock.

Rarity precludes accurate pricing.

HEXAGON

For information on Hexagon airguns, see Decker in the "D" section.

HEYM WAFFENFABRIK GmbH

Current manufacturer established in 1865 and located in Gleichamberg, Germany since 1995. Made airguns from 1949-52.

Currently firearms are imported beginning 1999 by New England Custom Gun Service, Ltd., located in Plainfield, NH. During 1998, Heym underwent a management change. Previously manufactured in Muennerstadt, Germany circa 1952-1995 and Suhl, Germany between 1865 and 1945. Originally founded in 1865 by F.W. Heym. Previously imported by JagerSport, Ltd. located in Cranston, RI 1993-94 only, Heckler & Koch, Inc. (until 1993) located in Sterling, VA, Heym America, Inc. (subsidiary of F.W. Heym of W. Germany) located in Fort Wayne, IN, and originally by Paul Jaeger, Inc. 1970-1986.

For more information and current pricing on both new and used Heym firearms, please refer to the *Blue Book of Gun Values* by S.P. Fjestad (also available online).

PISTOLS

LP 103 - .177 cal., SP, SS, push-barrel Gat-style air pistol, white plastic checkered grips, 7.8 in. OAL, 12 oz. Estimated value in average condition about $35.

courtesy Beeman Collection

RIFLES

Research is ongoing for this rifles section, and more information will be included both in future editions and online. Three models are known: LG 100 (about 3000 produced), LG 101 (repeater version of LG 100), and LG 103 (junior version of LG 100).

HILL & WILLIAMS

Previous manufacturer located in Staffordshire, England, circa 1905-1911.

The Hill & Williams air rifle, in .22 cal., is a barrel-cocking, spring-piston design cocked by pushing forward a barrel latch at the breech and then pivoting the barrel downward. British patent number 25222/'05 was issued to Arthur Henry Hill and Walter F. Williams on 16 July 1908 for the design. Hill´s address was 28 Leyton Road, Handsworth, Staffordshire, England. Walter notes that the gun may not have been made by Hill and Williams until about 1908. It was probably too complicated and expensive to compete with the Lincoln Jeffries design underlever rifles from BSA. Production ended by 1911. Apparently about two hundred guns were produced.

This gun evidently was one of the pioneer production designs, along with the somewhat similar MGR First Model Rifle, developed at the very beginning of the 20th century. Specimens in good condition should have a retail value in the $2,500 range. Refs: *Airgunner* April 1986, Dec. 1986, and *Guns Review*, Aug. 1978.

courtesy Beeman Collection

HOLBORN

For information on Holborn airguns, see Dianawerk in the "D" section.

HOTSHOT

For information on Hotshot airguns, see Gun Toys SRL in the "G" section.

GRADING	100%	95%	90%	80%	60%	40%	20%

HOWA

Current manufacturer located in Tokyo, Japan, and previously located in Nagoya, Japan.

Howa Machinery Limited, formerly manufacturers of Japanese defense force assault rifles, Weatherby Vanguard rifle actions, and rifles and shotguns for Smith & Wesson. Also produced small numbers of extremely high grade CO_2 rifles (styled like the Weatherby Mark V semi-auto rifle, reportedly to induce Weatherby to distribute them in the USA) in the mid-1970s.

For more information and current pricing on both new and used Howa firearms, please refer to the *Blue Book of Gun Values* by S.P. Fjestad (also available online).

RIFLES

MODEL 55G - .177 cal., two CO_2 cylinders back-to-back, BA feeds five pellets from spring-fed magazine, blue finish, highly polished steel parts with highly finished and detailed hardwood or synthetic stocks, 38.7 in. OAL, 6.0 lbs. Mfg. circa 1975.

courtesy Beeman Collection

$800	$700	$600	$500	$400	$300	N/A	N/A

This model is very rarely seen anywhere in the world, esp. outside of Japan.

User's note and warning: bolt will not close after magazine delivers its last pellet until the charging rod is retracted.

HUBERTUS

Previously manufactured by Jagdwaffenfabrik, in Suhl, Germany. (Other addresses may include Molin, Germany.)

PISTOLS

HUBERTUS - .177 or .22 cal., push-barrel, spring-piston action, single shot (barrel must be pulled back out before loading and firing), blue steel receiver, plain barrel, both front and rear sights on receiver, marked "D.R.G.M. Deutsches Reichs-Gebrauch-Muster" (a low level patent notice). Small frame variant: smoothbore, 8.5 in. OAL, forward breech ring ribbed, early production. Large frame variant: rifled, 10.5 in. OAL, about 1.5 lbs., patented 1925, probably mfg. to mid-1930s. See *Guns Review*, May, 1973 and Dec. 1975.

small frame

large frame

courtesy Beeman Collection

N/A	$200	$160	$140	$120	$100	$90

Add 40% for factory box and papers.

Add 40% for cocking aid and pellet tin.

Add 40% for spare barrel.

Add 60% for small frame version.

Add 25% for .22 caliber.

The large version was distributed as the Snider Air Pistol for a short time in the USA by E.K. Tryon & Co, Philadelphia, PA.

HY-SCORE ARMS CORPORATION

Previous distributor and importer located in Brooklyn, NY.

The American Hy-Score CP (Concentric Piston) air pistols are well-made airguns by a unique American company. As spring piston airguns, especially with their unusual concentric piston design, they stand in bold contrast to the pump and CO_2 guns that were the standard in the USA.

Steven E. Laszlo founded the S.E. Laszlo House of Imports of Brooklyn, NY in 1933. The company imported many items, including airguns, ammunition, black powder firearms, binoculars, telescopes, magnetic compasses, and movie camera lenses. The S.E. Laszlo House of Imports served as the umbrella company for the Hy-Score Arms Corporation, whose main claim to fame was their development and manufacture of a unique series of concentric piston spring air pistols. The company originally was located at 25 Lafayette St. in Brooklyn, NY. In October 1965, the firm moved to 200 Tillary Street, Brooklyn, NY, where it remained until Steve Laszlo´s death in 1980.

Steve Laszlo was an expert marketer, but he was not a designer. About 1940, he asked his brother, Andrew Lawrence (nee Laszlo), an engineer in applied mechanics, to develop a compact, modern high-powered air pistol.

Andrew designed the gun to be produced without the forgings and leather seals typical of contemporary air pistols, to have a light, good trigger action, and to look like a firearm. A desire for easy cocking, no pumping, and reliability dictated a spring piston powerplant. His Stanford University research paper, which outlined the development of this pistol, discussed the pros and cons of the Zenit, Webley, Diana, and Haenel spring piston airguns. He settled on the concentric piston design found in the English Acvoke, Warrior, Westley Richards, and Abas-Major air pistols. These pistols are conspicuous by their lack of any mention in Andrew´s paper and he dismissed consideration of English patents as "too costly."

Concentric piston airguns use the barrel as a guide for a piston snugly fitted around it. The concentric powerplant allowed for a very long, powerful mainspring and a long barrel, conducive to both high power and accuracy, in a rather compact pistol. World War II delayed production until about 1946. Hy-Score advertised their new pistols as the world´s most powerful airguns, with the accuracy of an air rifle, and the looks and feel of a Luger.

Andrew was skilled in automotive engineering; so instead of the conventional leather seals, the first Hy-Score CP pistols used automotive-type steel piston rings made by the Perfect Circle Co., expected to be good for a lifetime of normal use. (The seals were later changed to o-rings when the steel piston rings proved to be a maintenance problem.) The solid, durable grips were made of Tenite, a new plastic from General Electric. Steel blocks cast into the grip provided excellent heft and balance.

The trigger system is unique and deserves special mention. Rather than having the full pressure of the mainspring bear on the sear, Lawrence designed a special "servo-mechanism" to enable the shooter to apply relatively little pressure to very smoothly release the shot. A "dry practice" feature allowed the shooter to slightly open the gun, without cocking the mainspring, to set the trigger for practice trigger pulls.

Lawrence´s genius is revealed by the loading mechanism. The loading gate is a very ingenious camera-shutter system, which, in the repeater version, is coupled with one of the cleverest projectile feeding mechanisms in the world of gun design. When the breech cap is turned by the shooter, six little steel cylinders cam their way around, like bumper cars at a carnival, to each feed their contained pellet into the firing chamber. This mechanism apparently has never been duplicated in any other gun.

The body tube is a very sturdy, drawn steel tube which, in the later models, is smoothly tapered down to form the barrel profile. The frame is a smooth stamping. Engraving-style, stamped scroll markings were added to the frame at approximately serial number 850,000. An excellent blue finish was standard. Chrome plating was an extra cost option and is rarely seen.

The various Hy-Score CP air pistol models all used the same basic mechanism and frame. The key differences were in single vs. repeater mechanism, finish, grip color, barrel style, and barrel length. The 700 and 800 model series appear to be fixed long-barrel single-shots, although what appears to be the visible barrel in the Model 700 is just a large-bore tube extending forward from the frame which contains a short barrel. The 802 is a fixed long-barrel repeater. The 803 Sportster is a short interchangeable-barrel single-shot. The 804 is a short fixed-barrel repeater. An "R" on the repeaters or an "S" on the Sportster models precedes serial numbers in the 800,000 range. Serial numbers over 900,000 are without the prefixes.

In 1970, Hy-Score discontinued marketing of the Hy-Score CP air pistols, perhaps due to increased legal and political pressure for a safety mechanism. The cost and effort of converting the design to appease these pressures may not have been of interest to Steve Laszlo in that stage of his life. He had started to import other airguns as early as 1950. From 1970 until his death in 1980, he concentrated on selling airguns made by overseas factories.

The American Hy-Score CP air pistols were produced for only about twenty-five years, but they form one of the most interesting groups of airguns for collectors who appreciate their unique nature.

In 1989, the Hy-Score concentric-piston design returned full circle to England when the Hy-Score brand became British. Richard Marriot-Smith purchased the trademark, plans, and what remained of the long idle Hy-Score factory machinery and Hy-Score pistol parts. Operating under the name of the Phoenix Arms Co., in Kent, England, he began production of the "New Hy-Score" Single-Shot pistol using original Hy-Score machinery and many original American parts. The general appearance was that of the Model 803 Sportster with the muzzle threaded for a moderator. It was a rather expensive, unfamiliar style for the English market and regular exports to the USA were precluded by the lack of a safety mechanism. Production was extremely limited; almost as soon as Phoenix Arms had arisen from the ashes of Marriot-Smith´s other gun enterprises, it disappeared, having created instant collectibles.

Hy-Score Comparative Model Numbers

Most of Hy-Score´s airgun imports were made by Dianawerk of Rastatt, Germany. (See the comparative model chart in the Dianawerk section.) Various other airguns were made for Hy-Score by BSF, Hämmerli, Anschütz, Baikal, Em-Ge, Slavia, and FN. Important note: Comparable models often have different values due to varying degrees of rarity, different demand by collectors, and because distributors of private label guns often specified different power levels (for different markets, not just mainspring differences), stocks, calibers, sights, trigger mechanisms, etc. from the basic manufacturer´s model. Early models of the same number may differ from more recent models.

Hy-Score imports not made by Dianawerk:

Hy-Score 822T Pistol - Made by Em-Ge in Germany.

Hy-Score 821, 833SM, 894 sidelever rifle - Made by Hämmerli of Germany.

Hy-Score 824M Pistol - Hämmerli "Master" CO_2.

Hy-Score 823M Pistol - Hämmerli "Single" CO_2.

Hy-Score 817M Pistol - BSF (Wischo) CM w/o front sight hood.

Hy-Score 818 Pistol - toy-like pistol from Anschütz, etc. (8¾ ounces).

GRADING	100%	95%	90%	80%	60%	40%	20%

Hy-Score 833 - Hämmerli Model 10 (Puma Model 497).
Hy-Score 870 Mark III - Izhevsk Vostok IZh022 (Baikal).
Hy-Score 894 or 894 Sport - Hämmerli Model 4 (Puma Model 490).

PISTOLS

All models feature no safety.

MODEL 700 TARGET SINGLE SHOT - .177 or .22 cal., rifled short barrel within the frame, what appears to be the visible barrel i only a tube for cosmetic purposes, angular step where false barrel base is pinned to the separate compression tube, rear sigh attached with screw, Tenite grips (walnut, petrified wood, ivory, or onyx), blue finish. Not marked with model number but a Model 700 serial numbers begin with a seven. Approx. 2500 mfg 1947 only.

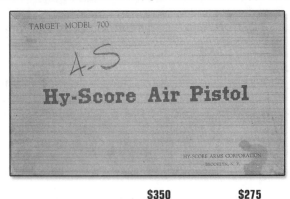

courtesy Beeman Collection

$350	$275	$240	$200	$150	$125	$90

Add 10% for grip colors other than walnut.
Add 50%-60% for box and instruction sheet (box must say "700" on it).
Subtract 5% for missing rear sight riser.

MODEL 800 TARGET SINGLE SHOT - BB/.175 smoothbore, .177 or .22 rifled cal., 10.25 in. barrel, barrel cover and compressio chamber a single smoothly tapered unit, dovetailed rear sight, Tenite grips (walnut, petrified wood, ivory, or onyx), blue o chrome finish. Mfg. 1948-1970.

courtesy Beeman Collection

$180	$130	$100	$90	$80	$60	$40

Add 75% for chrome finish ("C").
Add 10% for grip colors other than walnut.
Add 30%-50% for box and instruction sheet.
Add 10% for BB smoothbore barrel (model 800BB).
Add 5%-10% for Hy-Score holster.
Subtract 5% for missing rear sight riser.

GRADING	100%	95%	90%	80%	60%	40%	20%

MODEL 802 TARGET REPEATER - BB/.175 smoothbore, .177 or .22 rifled cal., 10.25 in. barrel, six-shot, cammed rotation magazine, barrel cover and compression chamber a single smoothly tapered unit, dovetailed rear sight, Tenite grips (walnut, petrified wood, ivory, or onyx), blue or chrome finish. Mfg. 1949-1970.

courtesy Beeman Collection

$230	$195	$150	$135	$120	$90	$60

Add 80% for chrome finish ("C").
Add 10% for grip colors other than walnut.
Add 30%-50% for box and instruction sheet.
Add 10 % for BB smoothbore barrel (model 802BB).
Add 5%-10% for Hy-Score holster.
Subtract 5% for missing rear sight riser.

MODEL 803 SPORTSTER SINGLE SHOT - BB/.175 smoothbore, .177 and .22 rifled cal., interchangeable 7.75 in. barrels, short design, dovetailed rear sight, blue or chrome finish. Mfg. 1952-1954.

courtesy Beeman Collection

$250	$190	$170	$150	$125	$90	$75

Add 60% for chrome finish ("C").
Add 25%-40% for box and instruction sheet.
Add 10%-15% for each extra barrel.
Add 70% for five-in-one gun kit, blue, two extra barrels, ammo, and accessory tin (Model 803 SB).
Add 100% for five-in-one gun kit, chromed, two extra barrels, ammo, and accessory tin (Model 803 SC).
Subtract 5% for missing rear sight riser.

MODEL 804 SPORTSTER REPEATER - BB/.175 smoothbore, .177 or .22 rifled cal., fixed 7.75 in. barrel, short design, six-shot cammed rotation magazine, dovetailed rear sight, blue or chrome finish. Mfg.1953-1954.

courtesy Beeman Collection

$325	$305	$285	$255	$230	$210	$190

Add 35% for chrome finish ("C").
Add 30%-50% for box and instruction sheet.
Add 10% for BB only smoothbore barrel.
Subtract 5% for missing rear sight riser.

GRADING	100%	95%	90%	80%	60%	40%	20%

NEW HY-SCORE SPORTER SINGLE SHOT - .177 cal., rifled barrel, semi-compact design with flat sided fixed barrel, threaded the muzzle for moderator, rear sight adjustable for windage only or fully adjustable, blue finish. Made by Phoenix Arms Co England. 1989-1990.

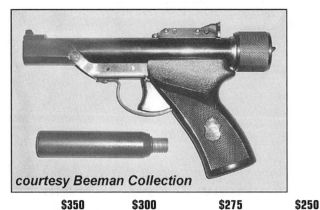

courtesy Beeman Collection

	N/A	$350	$300	$275	$250	$175	$125

Add 10% for fully adjustable rear sight (Mk II Model).

Add 20% for factory box and literature.

Add 10% for extra interchangeable barrel (modified original Hy-Score 803 barrels).

Add 25% for repeater.

Add 50% for chrome finish and white grips.

Add 20% for Fake Moderator (apparently a non-functional expansion chamber).

Add 100% or more for functional silencer/moderator with transferable $200 federal permit (required in U.S.).

I SECTION

IAR, INC.

Current importer and distributor located in San Juan Capistrano, CA.

Previously imported of Chinese air rifles.

GRADING	100%	95%	90%	80%	60%	40%	20%

RIFLES

MODEL B-19 - .177 cal., BBC, SP, SS, rifled steel barrel, 900 FPS, blue finish, hardwood Monte Carlo-style stock with recoil pad, hooded front and adj. rear sight, push/pull safety, 5.5 lbs.

	100%	95%	90%	80%	60%	40%	20%
No MSR	$90	$65	$50	$40	$30	N/A	N/A

MODEL B-21 - .177 cal., SL, SP, SS, rifled steel barrel, 1000 FPS, blue finish, hardwood Monte Carlo-style stock with recoil pad, hooded front and adj. rear sight, dovetail scope base, push/pull safety, 9.9 lbs.

	100%	95%	90%	80%	60%	40%	20%
No MSR	$150	$115	$80	$65	$50	N/A	N/A

MODEL B-22 - .22 cal., SL, SP, SS, rifled steel barrel, 800 FPS, blue finish, hardwood Monte Carlo-style stock with recoil pad, hooded front and adj. rear sight, dovetail scope base, push/pull safety, 9.9 lbs.

	100%	95%	90%	80%	60%	40%	20%
No MSR	$150	$115	$80	$65	$50	N/A	N/A

IGA

For information on IGA airguns, see Anschütz in the "A" section.

IGI

For information on IGI airguns, see Gun Toys SRL in the "G" section.

IMPERIAL AIR RIFLE CO.

Previous manufacturer of the Double Express, a double barrel airgun manufactured by Mike Childs in the UK, who subsequently produced the Skan airguns.

Many components produced by Helston Gunsmiths in Helston, Cornwall, England.

RIFLES

DOUBLE EXPRESS - .177, .22, or .25 cal., DB, multiple-pump pneumatic DT, flip-open breech block loading, blue finish, walnut stocks, 10 ft./lb. ME, no sights, scope rail on valve housing, 40.5 in. OAL, 7.4 lbs. Mfg. 1987.

courtesy Vic Thompson

100%	95%	90%	80%	60%	40%	20%
$1,500	$1,250	$1,000	N/A	N/A	N/A	N/A

Add 10% for mixed calibers.

Twenty four guns produced, most were .22 cal.

IN KWANG

Previous manufacturing or marketing group in Seoul, Korea whose products include pre-charged pneumatic airguns.

GRADING	100%	95%	90%	80%	60%	40%	20%

RIFLES

MIRACLE GLS - .22 cal., PCP, six-shot revolving cylinder, 42.4 in. OAL, 8.3 lbs. Disc.

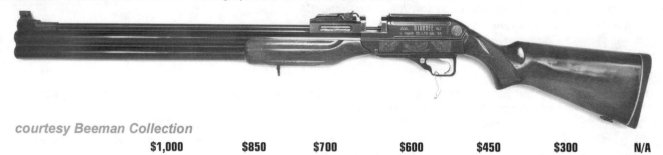

courtesy Beeman Collection

	$1,000	$850	$700	$600	$450	$300	N/A

INDUSTRY BRAND

Current trademark manufactured by Shanghai located in Shanghai, China. Currently imported by Compasseco, located in Bardstown, KY, and Air Gun Inc. located in Houston, TX.

See Compasseco listing.

ISAAC

For information on Isaac airguns, see Philippines Airguns in the "P" section.

IZH

Please refer to the Baikal section in this text.

J SECTION

JBC

For information on JBC airguns, see Philippine Airguns in the "P" section.

JAGUAR ARMS

Previous trademark manufactured in the mid-1970s by Jaguar Arms of Batavia N.Y.

Tiny, compact CO_2 pistols, produced as "the smallest CO_2 gun ever made." Very low power, inaccurate, and the finish was not durable. Thus, only a small number were sold and survived. They are sought-after collectors items, especially in excellent condition.

GRADING	100%	95%	90%	80%	60%	40%	20%

PISTOLS

CUB - .177 or .22 cal., use 8-gram disposable CO_2 cylinders, black painted finish, brown or white grips.

courtesy Beeman Collection

	100%	95%	90%	80%	60%	40%	20%
	$225	$150	$125	$100	$75	$55	$45

Add 30% for box and papers.
Add 60% for .22 cal.

BICENTENNIAL CUB - .177 or .22 cal., similar to Cub, except has chrome-plated finish, brown or white grips.

courtesy Beeman Collection

	100%	95%	90%	80%	60%	40%	20%
	$300	$225	$185	$150	$100	$80	$65

Add 30% for box and papers.
Add 60% for .22 cal.

JAPANESE MILITARY TRAINER

Previously produced by unknown maker or makers in Osaka, Japan during WWII.

SS, air powered version of Japanese service rifles. Muzzle 193 in, original ammo not known, but fires .177 pellets well. Straight-pull bolt action cocks on pull, spring piston completely built into bolt. Well machined bolt, trigger guard, bbl bands, and heavy, nickeled buttplate. Functional bayonet lug; fake cleaning rod. Marked w/ various Japanese characters (inc. Osaka address), JAPAN OSAKA, bomb symbol containing letters HA, and stamped with large AFC under sunburst on forward receiver ring. SN of specimen shown: L93497. 19.8 in. smoothbore bbl., 38.2 in. OAL, 13.1 in. stock pull, ca. 8 lb. trigger pull, wgt. 4.8 lbs. Very rare; Japanese wartime production efforts desperately had to turn to production of only actual firearms. Very

GRADING	100%	95%	90%	80%	60%	40%	20%

heavy wear is to be expected of military trainers, – average specimens valued about $1000.

courtesy Beeman Collection

JELLY

For information about the Jelly mark on airguns, see Relum Limited in the "R" section.

JIFRA

Current manufacturer located in Guadalajara, Jalisco, Mexico beginning about 1980.

RIFLES

Model 700 - BB/.174 cal., SP, LA, repeating BB gun of classic Daisy styling, finished in bright color paints or nickel plated, may have fake telescope tube, riveted tinplate construction, 32.8 in. OAL.

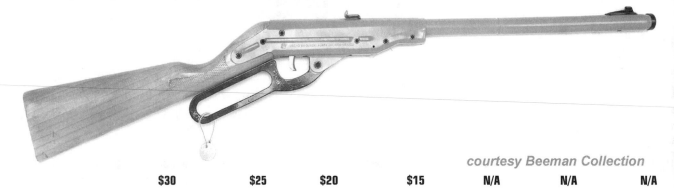

courtesy Beeman Collection

$30	$25	$20	$15	N/A	N/A	N/A

JOHNSON & BYE

Previous trade name of the Johnson & Bye Co. located in Worchester, MA.

Iver Johnson was the co-patentee, with Martin Bye, on U.S. patents 176,003 and 176,004 of April 11, 1876. These two Norwegian immigrants had developed an air pistol in which the barrel rotates to form a T-shaped cocking handle. Iver Johnson started his small gunsmithing shop about 1867 and then joined with Bye to form Johnson and Bye about 1875. In 1883 the company became Iver Johnson & Company and soon changed to Iver Johnson Arms & Cycle Works which became famous for inexpensive revolvers.

As noted elsewhere, Johnson, Bye, Bedford, Walker, and Quackenbush all were close associates. Their production, distribution, and ownership is confusing at times: H.M. Quackenbush recorded selling 69 Champion air pistols in 1884. It is not clear who made those 69, or how the total production of Champion air pistols was divided. And Albert Pope of Boston apparently was the main seller of Champion air pistols and also marketed air pistols, made by Quackenbush, under the Pope name. The Bedford & Walker air pistol production started in the Pope plant, then went to the Bedford & Walker plant, and finally transferred to the H.M. Quackenbush factory.

For more information and current pricing on Iver Johnson firearms, please refer to the *Blue Book of Gun Values* by S.P. Fjestad (also available online).

GRADING	100%	95%	90%	80%	60%	40%	20%

PISTOLS/RIFLES

CHAMPION - .21 cal., SP, SS, barrel turns to form cocking handle, 8.3 in. smoothbore barrel, Japan black lacquer, nickel plated, or nickel plated with rosewood grips finish, a standard, or perhaps optional, feature, was a fitted wooden case with a wire shoulder stock, 100 slugs, six targets, a dart pulling claw, and a wrench, 15.5 in. OAL, 1.6 lbs. Mfg. 1875-1883.

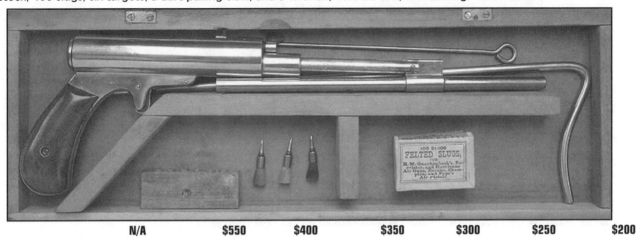

N/A	$550	$400	$350	$300	$250	$200

Add 10% for nickel plating.
Add 10% for wire shoulder stock.
Add 20% for deluxe model with nickel plating and rosewood grip plates.
Add 20% for original fitted wood case with some accessories.

JOHNSON AUTOMATICS, INC.

Previous manufacturer located in Providence, RI. Johnson Automatics, Inc. moved many times during its history, often with slight name changes. M.M. Johnson, Jr. died in 1965, and the company continued production at 104 Audubon Street in New Haven, CT as Johnson Arms, Inc. mostly specializing in sporter semi-auto rifles in .270 Win. or 30-06. For more information and current pricing on both new and used firearms, please refer to the Blue Book of Gun Values by S.P. Fjestad (also available online).

For information on Johnson Automatics, Inc. airguns, see Johnson Indoor Target Rifle in this section.

JOHNSON INDOOR TARGET RIFLE

Previous trade name believed to be used by Johnson Automatics, Inc. located in Providence, RI.

Johnson Automatics, Inc. was famous for the production of the Johnson Automatic semi-automatic rifles and machine guns. Evidently also produced the Johnson Indoor Target Rifle about 1936-38.

RIFLES

JOHNSON INDOOR TARGET RIFLE - #6 lead birdshot cal., catapult rifle, hundred-shot, spring-fed magazine, 28.7 in. OAL.

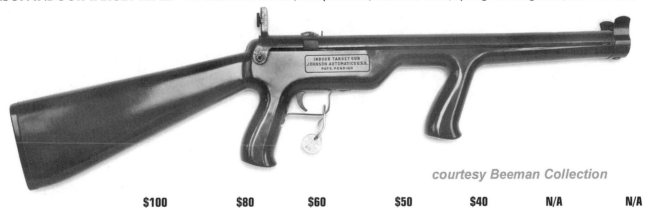

courtesy Beeman Collection

$100	$80	$60	$50	$40	N/A	N/A

Add 20% for original factory shooting range box.
Originally available with shooting gallery setup in factory cardboard box.

JONES, TIM

Current custom airgun maker located in Hawley, PA.

Designs include large bore air rifles with unique nineteenth century traditional styling.

GRADING	100%	95%	90%	80%	60%	40%	20%

RIFLES

395 LONG RIFLE - .395 cal., 850 FPS, SS, PCP (3000 PSI), tiger maple Kentucky-styled stock, steel barrel and cylinder, cast bra[] furniture, 7.2 lbs. New circa 2000.

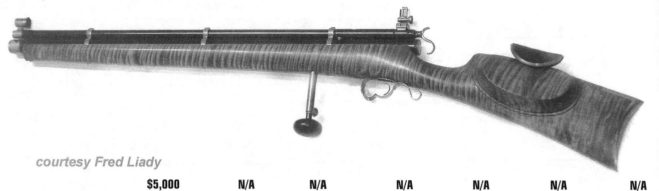

courtesy Fred Liady

	$5,000	N/A	N/A	N/A	N/A	N/A	N/A

JONISKEIT

Current manufacturer Detlef Joniskeit located in Allmersbach im Tal, near Stuttgart.

Developed the Waffentechnik Joniskeit sidelever match air pistol in 1983.

PISTOLS

WAFFENTECHNIK JONISKEIT - .177 cal., SP, SL, SS, match grips, left-hand cocking lever lifts barrel for loading. A sligh[] improved version; the "Joniskeit Hurrican" was introduced in 1990. Special international distribution included Beeman Precisi[] Airguns in USA ceased in the 1980s, but the pistol is still made to order. Experiments with the very low 120 m/s velocity of th[] pistol revealed that differences in lock time between low and high velocity pistols are far below the human reaction tim[] which is around 15 milliseconds.

Value is about $2000.

JONISKEIT FINALE - .177 cal., SS, PCP and/or CO_2, modified and vented version of the Tau 7 air pistol from Aeron, a daught[] company of CZ in Czechia introduced in 1991> Many variations: Finale PCP, Finale CO_2, and Finale Super (hybrid) in various ba[] rel lengths, compensators, etc. Works at 300 bar pressure.

Value from about $500 to $650, plus shipping and duty.

Test review in 1991 VISIER.

K SECTION

KAFEMA

Previous trademark of Industria Argentina, Buenos Aires, Argentina circa pre-WWII.

Research is ongoing with this trademark, and more information will be included both online and in future editions.

courtesy Beeman Collection

GRADING	100%	95%	90%	80%	60%	40%	20%

RIFLES

KAFEMA - .177 cal., BBC, SS, SP, hardwood stock with fluted forearm, no buttplate.

	100%	95%	90%	80%	60%	40%	20%
	$200	$175	$150	$115	$85	$50	N/A

KALAMAZOO

Previously manufactured in Kalamazoo, MI about 1871.

The Kalamazoo Air Pistol is an especially significant gun; it evidently is America's first commercial pneumatic pistol. Based on a patent granted to Edwin H. Hawley in 1869 and an improvement patented in 1871 to E.H. Hawley and G.H. Snow (U.S. Patent 118,886). Predated many other airguns in having a pneumatic pump located under the barrel. Percussion-style hammer. The patent improvement included making the front sight by turning up a section of the front barrel band. It appears that the original patent design was never manufactured.

PISTOLS

KALAMAZOO - .25, .32, or possibly other cals., smoothbore, pneumatic, SS, breech-loading pistol. Longitudinal pump with handle at the muzzle may have used a simple piece of rod as a pumping handle. Cast iron grip with black Japan finish contains air reservoir. Front sight formed by turning up part of the front barrel band. Extremely rare, values are estimated. (See *Airgun World*, Nov. 1979, USA July 1995).

courtesy Howard Collection

N/A	$1,500	$1,000	$800	$550	$400	$300

Add 40% for unusual triangular purple box.
Add $125 for original instruction sheet.

KEENFIRE

For information on Keenfire airguns, see Anschütz in the "A" section.

KESSLER

Previous trade name of Kessler Rifle Company, located in Buffalo, Rochester, and Silver Creek, NY, circa 1948-50. Ref: AR 1: pp 18-21.

GRADING	100%	95%	90%	80%	60%	40%	20%

RIFLES

ONE-PIECE STOCK MODEL - .22 cal., swinging arm pump pneumatic, BA, SS, Crosman Model 101-like styling, except apparently descended from the Rochester airgun, ball exhaust valve apparently derived from the Sheridan Supergrade, 36 in. OAL.

courtesy Beeman Collection

$275	$235	$200	$175	$150	$125	$95

Variation 1: Small Stock Version - black barrel, body tube, and cocking knob.

Variation 2: Large Stock Version - chromed barrel, body tube, and cocking knob. Large walnut stock with checkpiece; stock styled like Sheridan Super Grade.

TWO-PIECE STOCK MODEL - .177 cal., swinging arm pump pneumatic, BA, SS, similar to Rochester air rifle with two-piece stock (see Rochester in the "R" section of this guide), except stamped "KESSLER" on the barrel, 38 in. OAL.

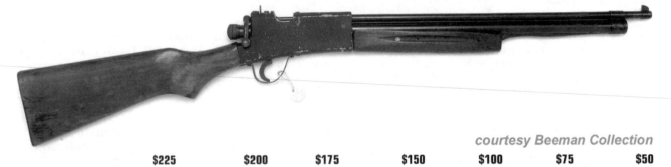

courtesy Beeman Collection

$225	$200	$175	$150	$100	$75	$50

This model may have been distributed as a private label by Kessler before they developed their own model.

Factory installed, stamped metal front sight indicates that this was not just a Rochester airgun with a Kessler stamped barrel.

KOFFMANZ

For information on Koffmanz airguns, see Philippine Airguns in the "P" section.

KRICO

Current trademark manufactured by Kriegeskorte Handels GmbH Co, located in Pyrbaum, Germany. Previously located in Stuttgart-Hedelfingen, Germany.

Manufacturers of spring piston air rifles after WWII and quality firearms since the mid-1950s. Krico firearms previously were imported by Beeman Precision Arms Inc., Santa Rosa, CA in the 1980s. Only one basic model of airgun was made circa 1946-1953.

For more information and current pricing on both new and used Krico firearms, please refer to the *Blue Book of Gun Values* by S.P. Fjestad (also available online).

RIFLES

MODEL LG 1 - .177 or .22 cal., BBC, SP, SS, rifled barrel, grooved forearm, no buttplate.

courtesy Beeman Collection

$350	$300	$250	$200	$150	$100	$75

MODEL LG 1S - .177 or .22 cal., BBC, SP, SS, similar to Model LG 1, except has buttplate, checkered pistol grip and grooved forearm.

$400	$350	$300	$250	$200	$150	$100

GRADING	100%	95%	90%	80%	60%	40%	20%

MODEL LG 1 LUXUS - .177 cal. only, similar to LG 1S, except heavier stock, better sights, and heavy checkered forearm.

	$450	$400	$350	$300	$250	$200	$150

KÜNG (KUENG) AIRGUNS

Current tradename of Dan Küng (Kueng) located in Basel, Switzerland.

Working in Switzerland, Dan Kueng builds high-end, side-lever, spring-piston, recoilless magnum air rifles and is in the final stages of developing a spring piston air pistol that will produce over 10 ft./lb. ME. His website, at http://www.blueline-studios.com/kuengairguns.com, gives a great deal of technical airgun information and beautifully illustrates the products. Production is based almost entirely on components made in-house, thus production is still very limited. Costs up to $6000 for guns like those illustrated on the website are expected to be considerably reduced.

KYNOCH LIMITED

Current manufacturer located in Witton, Brimingham, Warwickshire England, founded in 1862.

Manufacturers of sporting rifle and shotgun cartridges, previously produced the Swift air rifle. Also produced the Mitre airgun slug and the Lion, Match, and Witton diabolo airgun pellets.

RIFLE

SWIFT - .177 or .25 cal., BBC, SP, SS, BBC, SP, snap hook on each side of the breech, plain walnut buttstock, based on the 1906 patents of George Hookham and Edward Jones. About 1908.

courtesy Beeman Collection

	$1,000	$900	$800	$650	$500	$400	$300

NOTES

_____

_____

_____

_____

_____

_____

Four Antique PCPs (left to right):

a) Mortimer butt-reservoir airgun with inte[r] changeable rifle and shotgun barrels. Th[e] buttstock air reservoirs of such British a[ir] rifles generally were covered with sharkski[n]. This unusually elegant specimen from gu[n] maker T.J. Mortimer was made with a reservo[ir] covered with smooth calfskin. Late 1800s.

b.) Pneumatic shotgun with ball air reservo[ir] Made by Bate in London with fake flintlo[ck] mechanism. Mid-1800s.

c.) Massive pneumatic .58 caliber "flintloc[k]" style air rifle by Bate. The air reservoir is a f[ull] length brass cylinder positioned concent[ri] cally around the barrel. A pump is built into t[he] buttstock. The cocking hammer serves as [a] loading tap to receive those huge lead bal[ls] from the internal magazine and to cock t[he] mechanism. About 1780.

d.) Girandoni Military Repeating Pneumat[ic] Rifle. 22 shot, 46.2" OAL. Photo by R.V. Atki[n] son, Beeman collection.

L SECTION

LD AIRGUNS

Previous manufacturer located in Mandaluyong City, Manila, Philippines 1968-2001.

As discussed in the Philippine Airguns section of this guide, the unexpected development of powerful, bulk-fill CO_2 guns for hunting primarily was due to one man, president/dictator Ferdinand Edralin Marcos, who declared martial law and outlawed civilian firearms in the Philippines in 1972.

There had been a few airgun makers around before martial law hit, but one soon came to the foreground. That was the shop of Eldyfonso Cardoniga which had opened in 1968 in Mandaluyong City, a part of metropolitan Manila.

Eldyfonso Cardoniga (or "Eldy" or just "LD") was born in 1930 in Navotas, Rizal, then a fishing port north of Manila. Reportedly, he made his first airgun at eight years of age by welding together various worn out guns. He studied architecture at the excellent Mapua University in Manila and worked as an architectural assistant for a while, and then as a skilled mechanic and welder. He started the LD airgun factory in 1968 from a design that he had developed. This was the LD 380, a combo rifle/shotgun. The key features were the multi-caliber barrel system, a breech block that swings to the side for loading, and an external hammer for releasing the exhaust valve. This breech system, now known as the "hammer swing action," has been basic to perhaps most of the Philippine airguns. To overcome the power limits of the Crosman hammer-valve system, the LD designs used a larger valve and valve stem activated by a stronger and heavier hammer arrangement. The result was exactly what the market needed: a dependable airgun that was economical to produce and use and of unprecedented POWER! [1]

Of the Philippine airguns, those made by LD certainly are the best known and among the very best quality. The innovation represented by the LD airguns is well demonstrated by the "Rancher" version of the LD 380S. This .50 caliber air rifle is provided with insert barrels of several calibers for pellets, balls, darts, arrows, spears, and shot charges. Some versions of this model were equipped with spinning reels, from the fishing equipment trade, to provide for retrieval of arrows and spears. The .50 caliber barrel could fire large tranquilizer syringes or even fearful "torpedoes" consisting of finned brass projectiles containing a shaped charge of TNT! When Eldy visited the Beemans in California in the 1980s he told us that these torpedoes were very effective, but presented the problem of sometimes "blowing away one quarter of the water buffalo!" (Times have changed - note: he had some of these loaded torpedoes with him, carried on the plane in his coat pocket!)

The factory grew rapidly and Eldy brought in his son Mandy as an apprentice and then as a partner. As his skill grew, Mandy developed the MC TOPGUN line of precision match guns and moved to a nearby separate shop to concentrate on these models. However, this market was too limited due to the high cost of the guns and the diminished ranks of match shooters. He returned to work with his father on the powerful hunting guns and inherited the shop when Eldy passed away in September 1998. During those thirty years, Eldy is credited with at least thirty airgun designs, including several full auto ball shooters. The LD airguns developed and maintained a reputation as dependable, innovative, and powerful. The quality of the rifling in LD guns is believed to be due to the barrels being imported from a precision barrel manufacturer in Japan.

Mandy Cardoniga, now a master gunmaker in his own right, continued to produce LD airguns until sometime in 2001 when the tooling was changed to produce stainless steel industrial accessories, especially equipment for the baking industry. The LD airguns became history.

All Philippine hunting airguns are relatively scarce. Production ran from an average of less than one hundred guns per month for LD, evidently the largest maker, down to a few guns a month from a custom maker such as JBC. Perhaps 70 to 99% of most production runs stayed in the Philippines. Most American and European airgun factories, and large importers, figure on several thousand or tens of thousands of guns per month.

Values have yet to be established for many LD airguns, but in the Philippines it is said that excellent specimens sell for about triple their original cost. Good specimens are about double and poor specimens go for about their original cost.

I felt that it was important to chronicle this amazing line of airguns before the information faded away. Having jumped in and made this first listing, I recognize that much of this information needs improvement and augmentation. This must not be considered as a complete nor final list. We actively solicit your positive input at bluebookedit@beemans.net or at Blue Book Publications.

The authors and the publisher wish to thank Guillermo Sylianteng Jr. and Mandy Cardoniga for their assistance with this section of this edition.

[1] Eldy reported that one tuned specimen fired a single charge of three .380 cal. steel balls, combined wgt 180+ grains of 800 FPS MV. Three groups of three balls all punched through both sides of a 55 gallon steel drum (18 ga.) at 5 meters. Used with #4 or #6 lead shot for duck hunting.

GRADING	100%	95%	90%	80%	60%	40%	20%

PISTOLS

LD M45 - .22 cal., CO_2 bulk fill, SS, close replica of M1911A1 Colt U.S. military pistol, slide action and manual safety like original firearm, 4.3 in. rifled brass BBL, Narra wood grips, black nickel or satin nickel finish, adj. sights, 8 in. OAL, 2.5 lbs. Mfg. circa 1990s. 9,000 units.

courtesy Beeman Collection

	$295	$250	$225	$200	$150	$100	N/A

Add 20% for Colt 80 Mark V markings.

LD M45 REPEATER - .25 cal., CO_2 bulk fill, close replica of M1911A1 Colt U.S. military pistol, slide action and manual safety like original firearm, spring-fed magazine in slide for 6-8 .25 in. ball bearings or #3 lead buck shot balls, manual repeating action, 4.3 in. rifled brass BBL, Narra wood grips, black nickel or satin nickel finish, adj. sights, 8 in. OAL, 2.5 lbs. Mfg. circa 1990s.

	$395	$350	$315	$280	$225	N/A	N/A

LD BERETTA 9M - .22 cal., CO_2 bulk fill, SS, close replica of Beretta 92SB-F U.S. military pistol, slide action and manual safety like original firearm, 4.3 in. rifled brass BBL, Narra wood grips, black nickel or satin nickel finish, adj. sights, 8 in. OAL, 2.7 lbs. Mfg. circa 1990s. 1,500 units.

courtesy Beeman Collection

	$350	$325	$300	$250	$225	$200	$150

LD GLOCK - .22 cal., CO_2 bulk fill, SS, close replica of Glock Model 19 semi-auto pistol, slide action like original firearm, blued steel slide, polymer frame, rifled brass BBL, exact copy of Glock logo on LHS grip, shipped in actual Glock plastic case, 7.4 in. OAL, 2.2 lbs. Mfg. circa 1990s. About 1,800 units.

courtesy Howard Collection

	$295	$250	$200	$180	$160	$140	$100

Subtract 15% for "politically correct" specimens with Glock logo not legible.

GRADING	100%	95%	90%	80%	60%	40%	20%

LD LONG PISTOL (REPEATER) - .22/.380 cal. combo, CO_2 bulk fill, hammer swing action, adj. trigger, deluxe Narra grip with forearm, dark wood grip cap, black nickel finish, smoothbore .380 shot barrel with rifled brass barrel .22 cal. insert, (fires pellets, lead or steel balls, shot cartridges, short arrows, and spears, etc.), threaded muzzle ring for suppressor and/or barrel retaining insert, spring-fed tubular magazine LHS for about ten .22 cal. lead balls, see-through scope mounts, 21.1 in. OAL, 3.6 lbs.

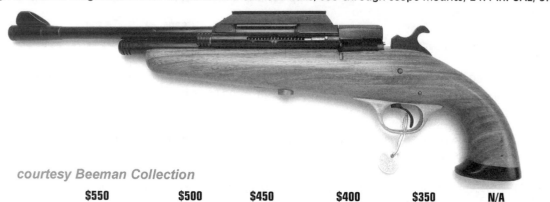

courtesy Beeman Collection

	$550	$500	$450	$400	$350	N/A	N/A

LD LONG PISTOL (SINGLE SHOT) - .177/.380 cal. combo, CO_2 bulk fill, hammer swing action, SS, adj. trigger, deluxe Narra grip with forearm, dark grip cap, black nickel finish, smoothbore .380 shot barrel rifled brass barrel .177 cal. insert, (fires pellets, lead or steel balls, shot cartridges, short arrows, and spears, etc.), threaded muzzle ring for suppressor and/or barrel retaining insert, regular scope base, 20 in. OAL, 2.7 lbs.

courtesy Beeman Collection

	$500	$450	$400	$350	$300	N/A	N/A

LD M100 - .22/.380 cal. combo, CO_2 bulk fill, hammer swing action, SS, adj. trigger, deluxe Narra grip with forearm, dark grip cap, black nickel finish, smoothbore .380 shot barrel rifled brass barrel .22 cal. friction-fit insert (fires pellets, lead or steel balls, shot cartridges, short arrows, and spears, etc.), no scope base, extended gas tube under barrel gives over/under appearance, heavy aluminum trigger guard, nickel satin finish, 17.1 in. OAL, 2.6 lbs.

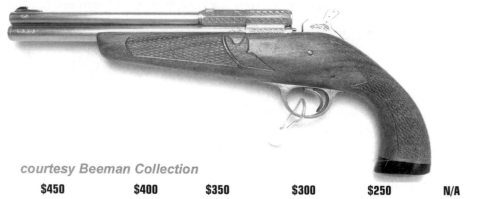

courtesy Beeman Collection

	$450	$400	$350	$300	$250	N/A	N/A

LD MC 87 - target pistol, info. not available at time of printing. 700 units.
   Values TBD.

RIFLES

Note: Some of the guns listed below may be combination (combo) calibers, but this could not be determined at time of writing. Degrees of metal engraving, stock shaping, stock decorations, and special features will affect pricing from 10% to 100%.

LD LC 3000 - .22 cal., CO_2 bulk fill, SS, hammer swing action, two-stage trigger, double cock hammer, deluxe Narra Monte Carlo stock, ambidextrous cheekpieces, rubber buttplate, black nickel or satin nickel finish, 27 in. rifled brass barrel, 42 in. OAL. 8600 units.
   Values TBD.

GRADING	100%	95%	90%	80%	60%	40%	20%

LD M 300 M - .22/,380 cal. combo, CO_2 bulk fill, SS, hammer swing action, two-stage trigger, double cock hammer, gas tube extended to end of barrel, deluxe Narra Monte Carlo stock, thumbhole grip (for RH only), ambidextrous cheekpieces, rubber buttplate, smoothbore .380 shot barrel rifled brass barrel .22 cal. insert (fires pellets, lead or steel balls, shot cartridges, short arrows and spears, etc.), threaded muzzle ring for suppressor and/or barrel retaining insert, black nickel or satin nickel finish, 42.8 in. OAL, 5.8 lbs. 8500 units.

	100%	95%	90%	80%	60%	40%	20%
	$1,150	$1,000	$750	$600	$450	$375	$300

LD 500 - hunting rifle. Info not available at time of printing. 1,000 units.
Values TBD.

LD STINGER - .22 cal., CO_2 bulk fill, SS, SL action, adj. power, exotic carbine-style Narra stock like a pistol with shoulder stock, separate Narra forearm, adj. open sights and scope grooves, 19 in. rifled brass barrel, gold, black nickel, or satin nickel finish, 42 in. OAL, 11 lbs. 300 units.
Values TBD.

LD MATCH - .177 cal., CO_2 bulk fill, SS, hammer swing or SL action, micrometer aperture sights, Narra match stock with adj. high cheekpiece and buttplate, 27 in. rifled brass barrel, 42 in. OAL, 11 lbs.
Values TBD.

LD 600 SPORTER - .177 or .22 cal., CO_2 bulk fill, SS, hammer swing action, adj. two-stage trigger, adj. power, deluxe Narra Monte Carlo stock, rubber buttplate, black nickel or satin nickel finish, 27 in. rifled brass barrel, 44 in. OAL.
Values TBD.

LD SPORTER - .22 cal., CO_2 bulk fill, SS, hammer swing or SL action, adj. trigger, deluxe Narra Monte Carlo stock, rubber buttplate, black nickel finish, 24 in. rifled brass barrel, 42 in. OAL, 5.5 lbs.
Values TBD.

LD 380/380S (SPECIAL) - evidently all variations had these features in common: multiple caliber barrel inserts, CO_2 bulk fill, SS, hammer swing action, two-stage trigger, double cock hammer, deluxe Narra Monte Carlo stock with rubber buttplate and sling swivels, black nickel or satin nickel finish, rifled brass barrel insert, threaded muzzle ring for suppressor and/or barrel retaining insert. Two of the many variations suggest the range of features, calibers, size, and weights possible.

courtesy Beeman Collection

This was Eldy's first and highest production model. During the thirty years of production from 1966 to 1996, 17,500 guns were produced. They probably had more variations and custom features than any other model.

✳ *Rancher* - four caliber combo: .50 smoothbore, .380 smoothbore insert, .22 rifled insert, .177 rifled insert cal. Laminated two-tone Narra stock with RH cheekpiece and RH Windhammer swell grip, standard scope mount base. 44.6 in. OAL, 9.0 lbs.

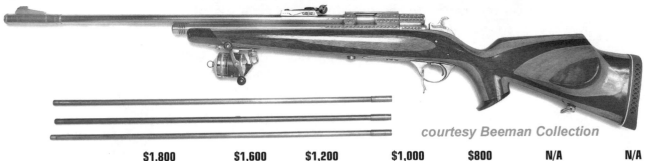

courtesy Beeman Collection

	100%	95%	90%	80%	60%	40%	20%
	$1,800	$1,600	$1,200	$1,000	$800	N/A	N/A

Add 20% for thumbhole stock.

Subtract 20% if stock is not laminated

Add 50% for .50 caliber (less than one hundred were made).

This caliber range gave the Rancher amazing flexibility: it could project .177 or .22 cal. pellets, .38 cal. shot charges, .38 cal. bullets or lead or steel balls, arrows without fletching, expanding tip spears, multi-prong spears, .50 in. tranquilizer darts, and even shaped TNT charges in brass "torpedoes." A spinning reel mounted under the forearm enhanced fishing and frog hunting. (Perhaps less than five hundred of this Special variation were produced. Many were elaborately engraved and given special stock checkering and treatment.)

GRADING	100%	95%	90%	80%	60%	40%	20%

✳ **Barbarella** - three caliber combo: .380 smoothbore, .22 cal. rifled insert, .177 cal. rifled insert. Could fire: .177 or .22 cal. pellets, .38 cal. shot charges, .38 cal. bullets or lead balls, arrows w/o fletching, expanding tip spears, and multi-prong spears. SS, ambidextrous checkered Narra stock with both cheekpieces and thumbhole grip (top of the stock has a saddle-like appearance), metal engraving, blackened design areas on the stock, see-through scope mount base. 41.5 in. OAL, 6.8 lbs.

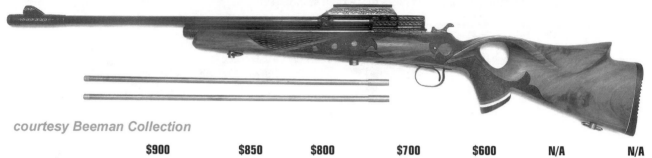

courtesy Beeman Collection

	100%	95%	90%	80%	60%	40%	20%
	$900	$850	$800	$700	$600	N/A	N/A

Subtract 30% for single caliber (.22, .25, or .380).
Subtract 20% for no thumbhole.
Add 30% for retractable wire stock.

LD 300 SS PHANTOM - hunting rifle. Info not available at time of printing. 2,500 units.
Values TBD.

LD 380 SS PHANTOM - .22 cal., CO_2 bulk fill, SS, hammer swing, action, two-stage trigger, double cock hammer, Narra cruiser-style stock ends at pistol grip, retractable stainless steel folding wire shoulder stock, sling swivels, black nickel or satin nickel finish, 22 in. rifled barrel, see-through scope base, muzzle ring covers suppressor threads, 27 in. OAL, retracted. 5,000 units.

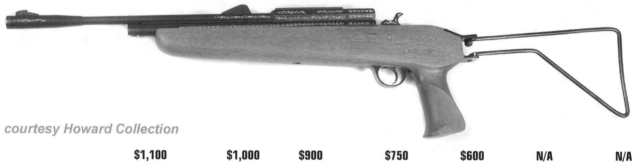

courtesy Howard Collection

	100%	95%	90%	80%	60%	40%	20%
	$1,100	$1,000	$900	$750	$600	N/A	N/A

LD 700 - .32 or .40 (10 mm) cal., CO_2 bulk fill, bolt action, styled after Remington Model 700 big bore rifle. SS, rifled. Deluxe Narra stock with semi-ambidextrous cheekpiece. Threaded for suppressor, satin nickel finish. Manual safety. 39.3 in. OAL, 6.6 lbs. 24 units made (17 RH 10mm, 4 LH 10mm, 1 RH .32, 2 LH .32) – all to order, may not be marked LD.

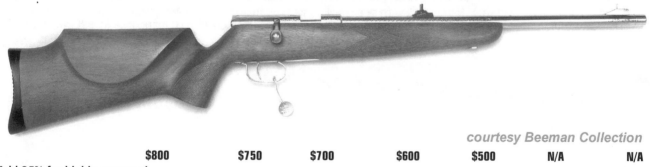

courtesy Beeman Collection

	100%	95%	90%	80%	60%	40%	20%
	$800	$750	$700	$600	$500	N/A	N/A

Add 25% for highly engraved.
Add 50% for PCP (only one was made).
Suppressor requires $200 Federal Transfer Tax in USA.

LD MC 2400 - bolt action sporter rifle. Info not available at time of printing. 320 units.
Values TBD.

LD MC 2800 - lever action sporter rifle. Info not available at time of printing. 180 units.
Values TBD.

GRADING	100%	95%	90%	80%	60%	40%	20%

LD HOME DEFENSE REPEATER - .380/.22 cal. combo., CO_2 bulk fill, SS, 24 in. barrel with .22 cal. rifled insert, .380 steel ball smoothbore manual repeater, probably seven-shot, spring-fed, tubular magazine attached along left side of barrel. Not marked. Hammer swing action. Cruiser-style stock with pistol grip and extendable heavy wire shoulder stock. Machined trigger guard. Threaded muzzle cap. Light engraving plus recessed panels of unique engraving designs. Open sights, no scope grooves, 41.1 in. OAL (32.8 in. retracted), 6.7 lbs. Costs 45% more than standard LD 380.

courtesy Beeman Collection

	$1,300	$1,200	$1,100	$900	$850	$800	$750

Confirmed by Mandy Cardoniga as work of Eldy Cardoniga.

LD SLIDE ACTION REPEATER - .22 (and .25 and .380?) cal. ball repeater, CO_2 bulk fill, slide action; spring-fed, fixed tubular magazine ca. 10 balls; two-stage trigger, double cock hammer, Narra Monte Carlo stock with ambidextrous cheekpieces, rubber buttplate, sling swivels on Narra wood buttstock and separate wood cocking slide, satin nickel finish, scope grooves, cast aluminum trigger guard. Light engraving plus recessed panels of unique engraving designs. 22.5 in. BBL, 39.5 in. OAL, 6.1 lbs. Circa 1980s, rare, less than 1500 total; most stayed in the Philippines.

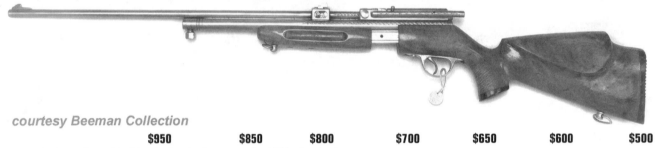

courtesy Beeman Collection

	$950	$850	$800	$700	$650	$600	$500

Not marked; confirmed by Mandy Cardoniga as work of Eldy Cardoniga.

SHOTGUNS

See also Rifles – the .380 and .50 cal. models served as both shotguns and rifles.

LD 20 GAUGE - 20 ga., CO_2 bulk fill, SB shotgun, block hammer action, scope rails, nickel black finish, uses 1.8 in. aluminum tubes with wad in each end to hold shot, Narra stock with skip checkering, Wundhammer swell RHS pistol grip, 46.1 in. OAL, 6.9 lbs. Only 18 made, plus four double barrel specimens. All special order, therefore not marked with LD mark. 29.8 in. BBL, 46 in. OAL, 7.1 lbs.

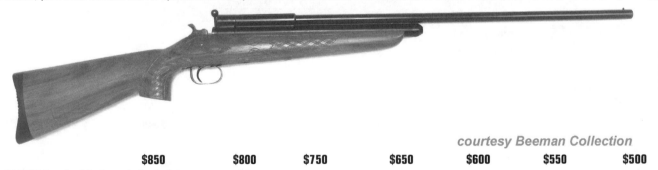

courtesy Beeman Collection

	$850	$800	$750	$650	$600	$550	$500

Add 50% for double barrels (only four were made).
Add 10% for rifled barrel inserts (.22, .32, .38, and .40 cal.).

LANGENHAN

Previous manufacturer of firearms and airguns. Founded by Valentin Friedrich Langenhan in Zella Mehlis, Germany in 1842. Moved to adjacent Zella St. Blasii in 1855.

About 1900, they started production of airguns, apparently making huge numbers of them under a wide variety of their own and private labels. The most definitive mark is FLZ (i.e. Friedrich Langenhan in Zella-Mehlis) with the letters in a three-segmented circle. Other labels include Ace, Favorit, and FL. Among the most commonly encountered Langenhan airguns are the militia-style air rifles (commonly imported into England from Germany by Martin Pulverman & Company of London circa 1900) and the rifle-like break-barrel, spring-piston FLZ pistols, made circa 1920s. Langenhan finally succumbed to competition

GRADING	100%	95%	90%	80%	60%	40%	20%

from Mayer und Grammelspacher, Weihrauch, Haenel, etc. Trading ended circa 1945.

The FLZ pistols generally sell in the $200 range; more for excellent specimens. (The FLZ air pistols range from about 1.6 to 1.9 lbs, and from about 16.7-18.0 in. OAL). The British Cub, which may have been made by another maker for Langenhan, will have a retail value in the $125 range for very good specimens. Ref: AGNR - Oct. 1985.

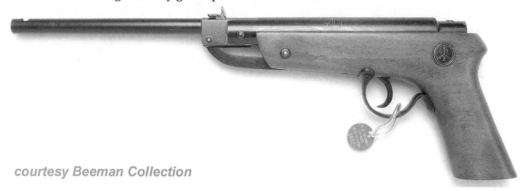

courtesy Beeman Collection

LARC

Previous trade name of LARC International located in Miami, FL.

Previous manufacturer of freon-charged, fully automatic BB sub-machine guns designed by LARC president Russell Clifford circa 1974-80.

RIFLES

MODEL 19A - .174/BB cal., powered from removable can of freon gas, fully automatic, 3000-round gravity-fed magazine, rate of fire about 2500 RPM. 400-450 FPS, plastic body, aluminum smoothbore barrel black with white or red/brown insert plates, early models may have heavy wire shoulder stock; fake suppressor, later models with plastic shoulder stock bar or none, 23.5-33 OAL, 1.0 lbs - 0.8 lbs.

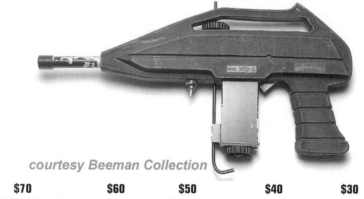

courtesy Beeman Collection

$70	$60	$50	$40	$30	N/A	N/A

Add 150% for early Model 19 with pressure hose and hose for BB magazine.
Add 100% for metal body.
Add 20% for fitted case.

LINCOLN JEFFRIES

Previous designer and gunmaker located in Birmingham, England circa 1873-1930s.

The authors and publisher wish to thank Mr. John Groenwold and John Atkins for valuable assistance with the following information in this edition of the *Blue Book of Airguns*. Lincoln Jeffries was born in Norfolk, England in 1847. By 1873 he had established a well regarded gun business in Birmingham producing shotguns and breech loading and muzzle loading air canes. The firm also put their name on a variety of imported break barrel, smoothbore air rifles – generally Gem-style copies of Haviland & Gunn designs and rifled militia-style (not military!) airguns. In 1904, he patented a fixed-barrel, under-lever, tap-loading, rifled air rifle which was the forerunner of the enormously successful BSA underlever air rifles. These rifles were manufactured for Jeffries by the Birmingham Small Arms factory. They were branded Lincoln Jeffries and later as BSA. These airguns are discussed and listed in the BSA section.

The Lincoln Jeffries firm continued to market the Lincoln Jeffries air rifles until the line of models came completely under the BSA label. By 1921, Lincoln Jeffries, Jr. had been issued a patent for a Lincoln air pistol with the mainspring housed in the gun's grip. Two versions of this unusual, all-metal air pistol were produced in very small numbers during the 1920s, with a few special pistols being individually made by Lincoln Jeffries, Jr. until circa 1927. The first version had a lever in the back of the grip which was pulled down to compress the mainspring and cock the gun. The second type was a barrel cocking air pistol which used the forward part of the trigger guard as a link to compress the mainspring. This was based on the American Haviland and Gunn patent. The Walther LP52 and LP53 air pistols were clearly derived from this gun. The all-metal Lincoln differed from the Walther mainly by not having grip plates and in having an exposed slot in the forward part of the grip which

GRADING	100%	95%	90%	80%	60%	40%	20%

could take flesh samples from a shooter unlucky enough to have his fingertips in that groove when the piston head rushed upward during firing.

The grandsons of Lincoln Jeffries, Messrs. A.H. Jeffries, and L.G. Jeffries were still operating the company in the 1990s, but now only to produce Marksman brand airgun pellets. Ref: *Guns Review,* Dec. 87.

PISTOLS

BISLEY BACKSTRAP COCKING MODEL - .177 cal., SP, SS, all-metal construction, fixed trigger guard, lever along backstrap of grip for cocking mainspring in the grip, blued finish, approx. 150 mfg. circa 1918 to the early 1920s. Ref: AG. Rotary lock variant - lever for locking the cocking lever, about one inch long, projects to the right on the upper rear corner of gun. Circa 1918. Side latch variant - side latch for locking cocking lever. Circa 1922.

courtesy Beeman Collection

N/A	$3,800	$3,500	$3,000	$2,500	$2,000	$1,600

Add 20% for rotary lock variant.

A handful of other variations exist. These may be experimental, special order, or prototypes. SN 3 has grip safety on forward side of grip and dull nickel finish. A larger specimen based on the 1910-11 patents, with top loading tap, brass frame, and walnut grip plates, is known. Values of these special forms cannot be estimated at this time.

BARREL-COCKING MODEL - .177 cal. (one known in .22 cal.), BBC, SP, SS, all-metal construction, trigger guard is cocking link between barrel and piston assembly in grip, approx. Standard version: .177 cal., large knurled screw head on take-down screw linking barrel block and cocking arm, receiver steps up in thickness just above trigger, spring chamber cap top at angle to barrel, thick trigger, crowded trigger guard area, point on inside of trigger guard ahead of trigger Grip cylinder typically about 5.5 in., but several specimens with extended cylinders known. Rare. Large version: .177 cal., receiver uniform in thickness, spring chamber cap top in line with axis of barrel, thin trigger, uncrowded trigger guard area, trigger guard/cocking lever with only smooth curves, grip cylinder over 5.5 in. long, max. (diagonal) OAL about 14.9 in. Small head on takedown screw. Very rare. Giant version: .177 and .22 cal., larger diameter grip cylinder, 15.5 in. max. OAL. Extremely rare, only one known in .22 cal. 1500 mfg. circa 1910-1927. Ref: AG.

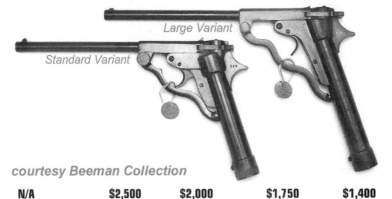

Large Variant

Standard Variant

courtesy Beeman Collection

N/A	$2,500	$2,000	$1,750	$1,400	$1,200	$900

Add 10% for standard versions with extended grip cylinder.

Add 30% for large version.

Other experimental and special order versions known. Values not estimated yet.

RIFLES

All rifles sold by Lincoln Jeffries were rifled and stamped "H THE AIR RIFLE" or "L THE LINCOLN AIR RIFLE". The meaning of the "H" and "L" letters has yet to be clearly determined. The guns stamped "H" are larger than the guns stamped "L", but the theory that these letters refer to "Heavy" and "Light" is not strong. All single shot.

GEM STYLE - H THE AIR RIFLE/L THE LINCOLN AIR RIFLE - various cals., SS, BBC, SP, mainspring in grip similar to Haviland and Gunn air rifle design, from various European makers, sizes varied. Mfg. late 1800s-very early 1900s.

	$300	$250	$200	$160	$120	$90	$60

GRADING	100%	95%	90%	80%	60%	40%	20%

MILITIA STYLE - H THE AIR RIFLE/L THE LINCOLN AIR RIFLE - various cals., BBC, SS, SP, from various European makers (although Militia actually was a Langenhan/Pulvermann air rifle brand or model, "Militia" is commonly used to represent a barrel cocking type of air rifle that does not have wood forward of the grip area), sizes varied. Mfg. late 1800s and first few years of 1900s.

courtesy Beeman Collection

	$300	$250	$200	$160	$120	$90	$50

UNDERLEVERS - H THE AIR RIFLE/L THE LINCOLN AIR RIFLE - various cals., SS, SP, UL (bayonet style), made on the Lincoln Jeffries 1904 Patent by BSA and sold as Lincoln Jeffries air rifles (as sold by BSA as The BSA Air Rifle - see BSA in the "B" section), faucet tap loading. The bayonet type underlever was the original Lincoln Jeffries design. The front end of this lever bears a small handle, or "bayonet" dropping down from, but parallel to the barrel. Original bayonet underlevers just had a bend where they engaged the latch mechanism. Variation H: The Air Rifle model, marked "H", 43.5 in. OAL. Mfg. 1904-1908. Variation L: The Lincoln Air Rifle, 39 in. OAL, marked "L", sometimes referred to as the "Ladies" or "Light" version. Mfg. 1906-1908.

courtesy Beeman Collection

	$500	$450	$400	$325	$275	$200	$100

LOGUN

Current manufacturer located in Willenhall, West Midlands, UK beginning 1998. Currently distributed by Straight Shooters Precision Airguns located in St. Cloud, MN and Crosman Corporation located in East Bloomfield, NY.

RIFLES

AXSOR - .177 or .22 cal., PCP, Supa Glide BA, eight-shot rotary magazine, equipped for scope mounts, two-stage adj. trigger, 19.5 in. rifled steel barrel, blue finish, 1000 FPS, English gloss walnut Monte Carlo stock, checkered grip and forearm (with pressure gauge), rubber recoil pad, 40 in. OAL, 6.8 lbs. New 2004.

MSR N/A	$850	$695	$550	N/A	N/A	N/A	N/A

While first advertised during 2001, this model was first imported into the USA during 2004.

DOMIN8OR - .177 or .22 cal., PCP, Side Speed side lever action, eight-shot rotary mag., two-stage adj. trigger, equipped for scope mounts, 19.7 in. rifled steel barrel, blue finish, checkered synthetic thumbhole stock, rubber recoil pad, 490 cc Buddy Bottle incased in butt stock, 40.5 in. OAL, 5.3 lbs. New 2004.

MSR N/A	$800	$700	$495	N/A	N/A	N/A	N/A

EAGLE - .177 or .22 cal., PCP, ambidextrous Versa Glide action, SS or eight-shot manual mag., two-stage adj. trigger, equipped for scope mounts, 17.5 in. rifled steel barrel, blue finish, molded synthetic thumbhole PG stock, rubber recoil pad, 36 in. OAL, 5.6 lbs. New 2005.

As this edition went to press, retail pricing had yet to be established.

GEMINI - .177 or .22 cal., PCP, BA, multi-shot magazine (two shots: .177 or .22), equipped for scope mounts, English gloss walnut Monte Carlo stock, checkered grip and forearm, rubber recoil pad, 37.75 in. OAL, 7.1 lbs.

MSR N/A	$695	$595	$495	N/A	N/A	N/A	N/A

GLADI8OR - .177 or .22 cal., PCP, Side Speed side lever action, eight-shot rotary mag., two-stage adj. trigger, equipped for scope mounts, 19.7 in. rifled steel barrel, blue finish, checkered pistol grip, rubber recoil pad, 490 cc Buddy Bottle, 41.5 in. OAL, 7.8 lbs. New 2004.

MSR N/A	$950	$850	$595	N/A	N/A	N/A	N/A

LG-MKII PROFESSIONAL - .177 or .22 cal., PCP, Supa Glide BA, nine-shot inline magazine, equipped for scope mounts, 21 1/4 in. rifled steel barrel, blue finish, 1050 FPS, English gloss walnut Monte Carlo stock, checkered grip and forearm (with pressure gauge), rubber recoil pad, 45 in. OAL, 8.25 lbs. New 2004.

MSR N/A	$1,425	$1,225	$995	N/A	N/A	N/A	N/A

While first advertised during 2001, this model was first imported into the USA during 2004.

GRADING	100%	95%	90%	80%	60%	40%	20%

S-16s (SWEET SIXTEEN) - .22 cal., PCP, Supa-Speed BA, 400cc buddy bottle, sixteen-shot (two eight-shot rotary) mag., equipped for scope mounts, two-stage adj. trigger, 14.5 in. rifled steel shrouded BBL, blue finish, checkered synthetic grip and forearm (with pressure gauge), cross over safety, 34.5-38 in. OAL, 8.5 lbs. New 2004.

	100%	95%	90%	80%	60%	40%	20%
MSR N/A	$800	$725	$575	N/A	N/A	N/A	N/A

SOLO - .177 or .22 cal., SS or eight-shot manual mag., PCP, BA, equipped for scope mounts, checkered English gloss walnut Monte Carlo stock, rubber recoil pad, 41 in. OAL, 6.1 lbs.

	100%	95%	90%	80%	60%	40%	20%
MSR N/A	$575	$495	$395	N/A	N/A	N/A	N/A

LUCZNIK

Previous tradename probably used by the Polish state firearms company, Zaklady Metalowe Lucznik.

As with most "Iron Curtain" guns, the construction is more sturdy than precise. The guns are infamous for unavailability of parts. Formerly imported into UK by Viking Arms Company. Dates not known.

PISTOLS

PREDOM-LUCZNIK 170 - .177 cal., BBC, SP, SS, a copy of the Walther LP 53, 12.2 in. OAL, 2.6 lbs. Mfg. circa 1975-1985.

	100%	95%	90%	80%	60%	40%	20%
	$550	$500	$400	$350	$300	N/A	N/A

Add 10% for factory box w/ test target.

RIFLES

MODEL 87 - .177 in. cal., BBC, SP, SS, simple hardwood stock with fluted forearm.

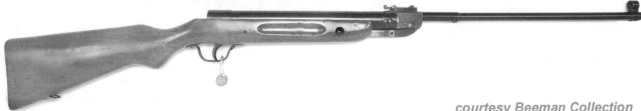

courtesy Beeman Collection

	100%	95%	90%	80%	60%	40%	20%
	$180	$160	$150	$125	$100	$75	$50

MODEL 141 - .177 in. cal., BBC, SP, SS, 14.5 rifled steel barrel, adj. rear sight, hardwood stock with fluted forearm, 36.5 in. OAL. Mfg. 1970s.

	100%	95%	90%	80%	60%	40%	20%
	$80	$60	$50	$40	$30	$20	$10

MODEL 188 - .177 in. cal., BBC, SP, SS, similar to Model 87 except, larger stock w/ cheekpiece and grooved forearm.

	100%	95%	90%	80%	60%	40%	20%
	$220	$200	$180	$150	$120	N/A	N/A

M SECTION

MC

For information on MC airguns, see Philippine Airguns in the "P" section.

MGR

For information on MGR, see Dianawerk in the "D" section.

MMM - MONDIAL

Previous tradename of Modesto Molgora located in Milano, Italy circa 1950s to 1990s.

Most Molgora products are toys and blank-firing guns, but there are several youth/adult airguns. Research is ongoing with this trademark, and more information will be included both online and in future editions.

GRADING	100%	95%	90%	80%	60%	40%	20%

PISTOLS

OKLAHOMA - .177 cal., BBC, SP, SS, 6.3 in. rifled BBL, 200 FPS, fixed sights, with only minor variations, resembles the Steiner air pistol, black or nickel finish, plastic or hardwood grips, no safety, 12.3 in. OAL, 1.9 lbs.

	$45	$40	$35	$30	$25	$20	$15

ROGER - .173/BB cal., CO_2, semi-auto, styled after Colt Woodsman, smoothbore BBL, adj. sights, DA trigger, hundred-shot gravity-fed magazine, manual safety, black finish, die-cast parts, 10.9 in. OAL, 2.3 lbs.

courtesy Beeman Collection

	$50	$45	$40	$30	$25	$20	$15

Add 100% for gun in factory shooting kit.

MACGLASHAN AIR MACHINE GUN CO.

Previous manufacturer in Long Beach, CA.

The MacGlashan Air Machine Gun Company began production in early 1937 with a single shot BB air rifle. During WWII, they produced two models of the now famous air machine gun trainer, used to train gunners in U.S. bombers. In 1945, they returned to making airguns for arcades with a pump action .24 cal rifle. In 1947, they produced a .24 cal. semi-automatic carbine, followed by an improved and lighter version in 1951.

RIFLES: SEMI-AUTO

SEMI-AUTOMATIC CARBINE ARCADE GUN - .24 cal. round lead shot, twenty-five-shot semi-auto, magazine parallel to barrel, wood stock, cross-bolt feed, 600 FPS at 1500 PSI. First Model: fiber fore grip, 35.75 in. overall, 6 lbs. Improved Model: wood fore grip, 37.5 in. OAL, 5 lbs.

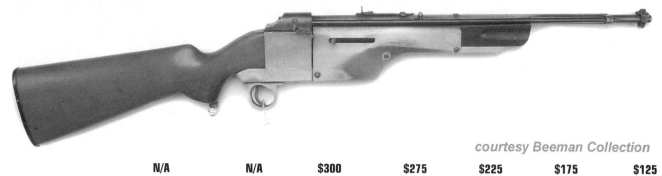

courtesy Beeman Collection

	N/A	N/A	$300	$275	$225	$175	$125

Add 10% for First Model.

GRADING	100%	95%	90%	80%	60%	40%	20%

RIFLES: SLIDE ACTION

"DRICE" SLIDE ACTION RIFLE - .24 cal. round lead shot, pump action twenty-five-shot magazine parallel to barrel, 40.5 in. long, 750 FPS at 1500 PSI (can operate at CO_2 pressures also), rifled barrel, blue finish, walnut stock and "tootsie roll" slide, designed to compete with .22 cal firearms in arcades, 6.6 lbs.

courtesy Beeman Collection

N/A	N/A	$350	$300	$250	$200	$150

RIFLES: TRAINER/ARCADE AUTOMATIC

MODEL E-3 B-B MACHINE GUN - SIDE GUNNER TRAINER - full auto, dual hand grips, low velocity; magazine parallel to body of gun, 30.75 in. long, blue finish, front and rear sight, 12v solenoid operated air valve, used in WWII to train side gunners on B17 bombers with back projected images of enemy planes flying at different speeds and angles, 16 lbs.

courtesy Beeman Collection

N/A	N/A	$750	$675	$625	$550	$400

MODEL E-13 B-B MACHINE GUN - TURRET GUNNER TRAINER - full auto, no hand grips, magazine vertical to receiver, 29.75 in. overall, blue finish, no sights, same mechanism as E-3, used to train turret gunners on U.S. bombers in two-gun remote control mock-up as above, 13 lbs.

courtesy Beeman Collection

N/A	N/A	$600	$525	$475	$400	$250

GRADING	100%	95%	90%	80%	60%	40%	20%

"TOMMY GUN" - SUB-MACHINE ARCADE GUN - BB cal., full auto, magazine under barrel, electrically interrupted solenoid air valve as on E-3, wood stock, styled after Thompson sub-machine gun.

courtesy Beeman Collection

	N/A	N/A	$450	$375	$300	$225	$175

MAGIC

For information on Magic airguns, see Decker in the "D" section.

MAHELY

Previous trademark of Giachetti Gonzales & CIA, located in Buenos Aires, Argentina. Not regularly exported. About 1950s-1990s.

PISTOLS

MAHELY 51 - .177 cal., SP, SS, BBC, 8.2 in. rifled barrel, plastic or wooden vertically grooved grips. 2.3 lbs. Mfg. 1950s. Ref: Hiller (1993).

	N/A	N/A	$375	$250	$175	$125	$350

RIFLES

MAHELY 1951 - .177 cal., SP, UL, SS, wood handle on underlever looks like a pump action handle, 39.4 in. OAL, 7.2 lbs. Disc. about 1950s.

courtesy Beeman Collection

	$450	$400	$350	$300	$250	$200	$150

MAHELY R 0.1 - .177, SP, BBC, SS, thumbhole stock. Disc. late 1990s.

courtesy Beeman Collection

	$375	$325	$300	$250	$200	$150	$100

MANU-ARMS

Previous French trademark of confusing origin and association. ManuArm is a French company formed in 2000, but both of the airguns below are from the 1980s. An association with Manufacture Française d'Armes et de Cycles de Saint Etienne, a.k.a. Manufrance, has been suggested. The original company was the producer of Paul Giffard's famous CO_2 guns in the 1880s and Manufrance was a household name in France, selling almost every form of consumer hard goods until the firm closed in 1986.

GRADING	100%	95%	90%	80%	60%	40%	20%

PISTOLS

MANU-ARMS AIR PISTOL - .177, BBC, SP, SS, very similar to the Dianawerk Model 5, black or brightly colored paint finish, receiver is marked "MANU ARMS", 14.3 in. OAL, 2.7 lbs.

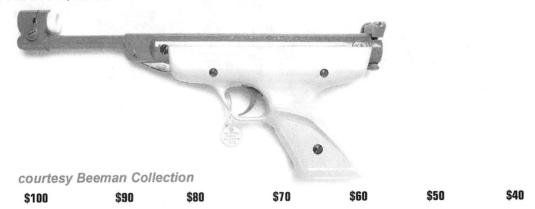

courtesy Beeman Collection

$100	$90	$80	$70	$60	$50	$40

RIFLES

MANU-ARMS AIR RIFLE - .177., BBC, SP, SS, wood stock, beavertail forearm.

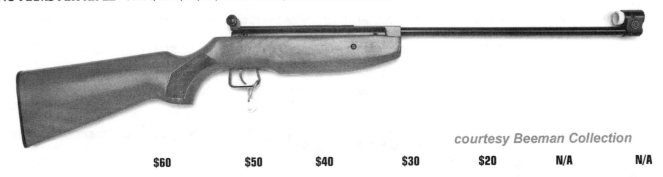

courtesy Beeman Collection

$60	$50	$40	$30	$20	N/A	N/A

MARKHAM-KING

Previous manufacturer located in Plymouth, MI. Circa 1887-1941. Owned and operated by Daisy Manufacturing Company from 1916.

The Markham Air Rifle Company has been credited with the development of the first commercially successful toy BB airgun. Dunathan's *American BB Gun* (1971) reported two BB rifles with the Challenger name as the first models made by Markham. However, the gun listed there as an 1886 Challenger actually represents only a single patent model without any markings and almost surely not made by Markham. The second gun, listed as an 1887 Challenger, actually was marked "Challenge" and was made in small numbers, but, again, probably not by Markham. There seems to be no justification for referring to either one under the Challenger name or as Markhams. The "Chicago" model, which appeared about 1887, made mainly of wood, probably was Markham's first real model.

The story of how the company grew to producing over 3,000 guns per day in 1916 is one of the great stories of airgun development and production. However, the company did little promotion and eventually was absorbed into the emerging airgun giant, Daisy. The history and models of Markham-King and Daisy became inseparably intertwined for a quarter of a century. Although Daisy ownership began in 1916, the Markham King models continued for decades and the sub-company gradually became known as King. In 1928, Daisy officially changed the company name to King. The advent of WWII probably caused Daisy to issue the last King price list on Jan. 1, 1942. Much of the model information in Dunathan's book has now been superseded, but this pioneering work absolutely is still required reading.

There are many variations of the early Markham air rifles. All minor variations cannot be covered in this guide. Variations may include changes in type or location of sights, location and text of markings, muzzle cap design, etc.

The authors and publishers wish to thank Robert Spielvogel and Dennis Baker for assistance with this section of the *Blue Book of Airguns*.

RIFLES: NO ALPHA-NUMERIC MARKINGS

All models have smoothbore barrels and are without safety.

CHICAGO - .180 large BB cal., darts, BC, SP, SS, exterior all maple wood with rosewood stain, double cocking rods pass through the stock. Stock stamped: "Chicago Air Rifle – Markhams Patent" on two lines. 9.8 in. brass barrel liner. 32 in. OA, circa 1887-1910. Patch Box Variation: Wooden "Patch Box" (dart storage?), 2.4 in. diameter, on LH side of stock. Stock stamped on left side with logo printed "Markham Air Company, Plymouth, Michigan, Chicago, patented" or "CHICAGO AIR RIFLE, MARKHAM'S PATENT". Considered by some to be the oldest version. Circle Logo Variation: slight change in stock shape, stock stamped "Markham Air Rifle

GRADING	100%	95%	90%	80%	60%	40%	20%

Co. – Plymouth Mich." and "CHICAGO – Patented" in circle.

courtesy Beeman Collection

	N/A	N/A	$600	$450	$350	$250	$175

Add 10% for BB clearing rod.

Add 15% for patch box variation.

Subtract 10% for circle logo variation.

Subtract 15% for cracked stock (common fault).

1890 KING - .180 large BB cal., darts, BC, SP, SS, cast iron frame, brass barrel, screw-on muzzle cap, button barrel release on side of receiver, nickel finish. "KING" cast in grip frame. 31 in. OAL. Mfg. circa 1890-1893.

	N/A	N/A	$2,500	$1,700	$1,000	$600	$400

1892 KING - .180 large BB cal., darts, BC, SP, SS, sheet metal frame, brass barrel, screw-on muzzle cap, barrel release button on side of receiver, flat sided stock with oval King logo, 31 in. OAL. Mfg. circa 1892.

	N/A	N/A	$1,500	$1,000	$750	$500	$300

1896 NEW KING SINGLE SHOT - .180 large BB cal., darts, BC, SP, SS, sheet metal frame, sheet metal barrel shroud, metal patch soldered over seam under shroud, muzzle cap over barrel shroud. Red stained stock stamped: "New King Patent Number 483159" in oval logo on slab sided stock. 31 in. OAL. Mfg. circa 1896-1905.

courtesy Beeman Collection

	N/A	N/A	N/A	$1,000	$700	$450	$250

1896 NEW KING REPEATER - .180 large BB cal., BC, SP, sheet metal frame, 150-shot magazine, domed muzzle cap lever allows BBs to be fed one by one from magazine to shot tube. Barrel release button on top of frame. Soldered patch under full length of barrel shroud. Shaped stock (oval in cross section) with logo. Later versions with flush muzzle cap and slab-sided stock. Variation: foreign patent numbers on stock. 31 in. OAL. Mfg. circa 1896-1904

	N/A	N/A	N/A	$1,200	$900	$600	$300

Add 20% for shaped stock.

Subtract 10% for flush muzzle cap.

1900 NEW KING SINGLE SHOT - .180 large BB cal., darts, BC, SP, SS, first use of "friction latch barrel": a section of rear frame snaps over raised part of trigger guard part of frame – holding gun together by friction; this replaced barrel release button of previous King air rifles. Fixed muzzle cap over outside of barrel shroud. (Variations: rounded muzzle cap.) Slab-sided stock stamped: "New King" on one side and patent dates on other side. Nickel plated. 31 in. OAL. Mfg. circa 1900-1904.

	N/A	N/A	N/A	$750	$550	$350	$200

There may have been a repeater version.

1900 PRINCE SINGLE SHOT - .180 large BB cal., darts, BC, SP, SS, sheet metal frame, sheet metal barrel shroud, friction barrel latch. Marked "Prince". Nickel finish. No trigger guard. Walnut stock with oval profile, crescent butt. Ref: AR4. (Sears Roebuck advertised a New Rival version, but no specimens are known.)– 1900-07. Variation: "Dandy," made by Markham for private label sales, marked "DANDY" with Markham patent dates (not marked "Markham"), not sold directly by Markham.

	N/A	N/A	N/A	$1,000	$800	$400	$250

Add 100% for Dandy variation.

1900 PRINCE REPEATER - similar to Prince Single Shot but with 150-shot magazine, BB release button on muzzle cap. Not a true repeater. Mfg. circa 1900-07.

	N/A	N/A	N/A	$1,200	$900	$600	$350

1900 PRINCE (TRIGGER GUARD MODEL) - .180 large BB cal., darts, BC, SP, SS, sheet metal frame wraps completely around wrist, sheet metal barrel shroud, separate sheet metal trigger guard. Variant: Marked "Boy's Own", premium gun. Mfg. circa 1900-07.

Values TBD.

GRADING	100%	95%	90%	80%	60%	40%	20%

1900 QUEEN - .180 large BB cal., darts, BBC, SP, SS, removable pins were substituted for rivets to allow gun to be taken down to three pieces, no trigger guard, similar to 1900 Prince Single Shot. Circular markings on wrist: "Markham Air Rifle Co. Plymouth, Mich" plus two patent numbers, advertised as the "Queen Take Down," but not marked "Queen", nickel finish, 33 in. OAL. Mfg. 1900-07.

	N/A	N/A	N/A	$450	$375	$335	$225

1903 NEW KING SINGLE SHOT - .180 large BB cal., darts, BC, SP, SS, friction barrel latch. Fixed muzzle cap within barrel shroud. Stock stamped: "New King" on one side and patent dates on other of slab sided stock. Nickel plated. 31 in. OAL. Mfg. circa 1903-1904.

	N/A	N/A	N/A	$750	$550	$350	$200

1904 SINGLE SHOT - .180 in large BB cal., BBC, SP, SS, friction barrel latch, Domed muzzle cap with sight. Patch under barrel shroud. Slab sided stock marked: "King Markham Air Rifle Co." Later versions with oval shaped stocks, without markings. Early versions had name stamping on small area on top of receiver; later name stamping was on barrel shroud. Mfg. circa 1904.

courtesy Beeman Collection

	N/A	N/A	$600	$500	$400	$300	$150

1904 REPEATER - 180 large BB cal., BBC, SP, friction barrel latch, spring release at muzzle like 1896 New King Repeater. Later versions had oval-shaped stocks without markings. Mfg. circa 1904.

	N/A	N/A	$750	$600	$450	$350	$250

RIFLES: WITH ALPHA-NUMERIC MARKINGS

MODEL C (SINGLE SHOT) - .180 BB or .177 lead air rifle shot cal., SP, BC, SS. Smooth contour Polley patent sheet metal frame wraps around wrist, barrel shroud with step, nickel finish, walnut stock with oval profile and deep crescent butt. Domed muzzle cap allows a BB to be shaken from BBs stored in barrel shroud into the shot tube (true barrel). Not a true repeater. Oval stock. 32 in. OAL. Mfg. 1905-09.

	N/A	N/A	$600	$500	$400	$350	$250

MODEL C (REPEATER) - .180 BB or .177 in. lead air rifle shot CAL., SP, BC, gravity-fed 500-shot storage. Smooth contour Polley patent sheet metal frame wraps around wrist, barrel shroud with step, nickel finish, walnut stock with oval profile and deep crescent butt, stock stamped "King 500 Shot Repeater". Not a true repeater. 33 in. OAL. Mfg. circa 1906-09.

	N/A	N/A	$700	$550	$450	$350	$300

MODEL D (SINGLE SHOT) - .180 BB caliber or .177 in. lead air rifle shot cal., SP, BC, muzzle loading SS, barrel tube retained by spring clip, muzzle cap not removable. Smooth contour Polley patent sheet metal frame wraps around wrist, barrel shroud with step, marked "KING MODEL D, THE MARKHAM AIR RIFLE CO., PLYMOUTH, MICH., U.S.A.", nickel finish, walnut stock with oval profile and deep crescent butt. 9.5 in barrel, 31 in. OAL. Mfg. circa 1907-09.

courtesy Beeman Collection

	N/A	N/A	$600	$500	$400	$350	$300

MODEL D (REPEATER) - .180 BB or .177 in. lead air rifle shot cal., SP, BC, 350-shot gravity-fed magazine, barrel tube removes to load, shot tube with oval cap. Smooth contour Polley patent sheet metal frame wraps around wrist, barrel shroud with step, marked "KING MODEL D, THE MARKHAM AIR RIFLE CO., PLYMOUTH, MICH., U.S.A.", nickel finish, walnut stock with oval profile and deep crescent butt. 9.5 in barrel, 31 in. OAL. Mfg. circa 1907-09.

	N/A	N/A	$700	$550	$450	$350	$300

MODEL E (REPEATER) - .180 large BB cal., darts, BC, SP, Model D frame with straight (no step down) Prince type barrel, muzzle lever repeater, gravity-fed, smooth profile (Polley Patent) sheet metal frame, sheet metal barrel shroud, full length solder patch, walnut stock with oval profile, deep crescent butt. Nickel finish. 32 in. OAL. Dates not known.

	N/A	N/A	N/A	$600	$500	$400	$350

GRADING	100%	95%	90%	80%	60%	40%	20%

NUMBER 1 - .180 large BB cal., darts, BC, SP, SS, similar to Model D, removable shot tube, barrel marked "KING NO. 1", 31 in. OAL. Mfg. 1910-14.

	N/A	N/A	$500	$400	$350	$250	$200

NUMBER 2 - .180 large BB cal., darts, BC, SP, 350-shot repeater, loading port below front sight, side of grip stamped "KING 350 SHOT NO. 2", 31 in. OAL. Mfg. 1910-14.

	N/A	N/A	$750	$600	4500	$400	$300

NUMBER 4 - .177 lead air rifle shot cal., SP, lever action, gravity-fed 500-shot magazine, one-piece sheet metal frame and half-round, half-octagonal barrel shroud, frame with scroll stamping "King 500 Shot" with Markham address and patent dates, nickel finish, walnut stock with deep crescent butt, 34 in. OAL. Mfg. circa 1908-15. Smooth variation: no scroll stamping on frame. Mfg. 1910-14. Blued finish mfg. 1914-22.

courtesy Beeman Collection

	N/A	N/A	$700	$600	$500	$400	$300

Add 5% for smooth variation.
Subtract 15% for blued finish.
Markham's first lever action repeater.

NUMBER 5 LEVER ACTION - .177 lead air rifle shot cal., SP, LA, gravity-fed 1000-shot magazine, one-piece sheet metal frame and half-round, half-octagonal barrel shroud, blue or nickel finish, walnut stock with deep crescent butt, 36 in. OAL, 2.5 lbs. Mfg circa 1908-22.

	N/A	N/A	$700	$600	$500	$400	$300

✳ Scroll Side Variant - frame with scroll stamping "King 1000 Shot" with Markham address and patent dates, nickel finish, walnut stock with deep crescent butt. Mfg. circa 1908-22.

courtesy Beeman Collection

	N/A	N/A	$800	$675	$550	$450	$350

✳ Plain Side Variant - markings on top, no scroll stampings on side, nickel finish, mfg. 1910-14.

	N/A	N/A	$850	$700	$600	$500	$400

✳ Blued Variant - blue finish, mfg. 1914-22.

	N/A	N/A	$675	$575	$475	$375	$275

NUMBER 5B SPECIAL LEVER ACTION - .177 lead air rifle shot cal., SP, lever action, gravity-fed magazine, one-piece sheet metal frame and half-round, half-octagonal barrel shroud, Frame with scroll stamping "King 1000 Shot" with Markham address and patent dates, special black nickel finish on metal, special finish on walnut stock with deep crescent butt. Hinged gift box with color lithographing. 36 in. OAL. Mfg. circa 1908-16.

	N/A	N/A	$950	$800	$700	$550	$400

Deduct 25% for missing gift box.

NUMBER 5 SLIDE ACTION - .177 lead air rifle shot cal., SP, sixty-shot gravity-fed magazine, six-groove wooden cocking slide, pistol grip stock, 36 in. OAL (same design used by Daisy for Daisy No. 105 Junior Pump Gun and Daisy No. 107 Buck Jones Special). Mfg. 1932-36.

	N/A	N/A	$450	$400	$300	$250	$200

GRADING	100%	95%	90%	80%	60%	40%	20%

NUMBER 10 JUNIOR - .177 air rifle shot cal., SP, BC, SS. Sheet metal frame. Flat sided walnut stock with crescent butt. Cast iron trigger guard (E.S. Roe patent) extends into wrist and provides cocking action fulcrum. Nickel or blued finish. 29 in. OAL. Variation 1: cast iron trigger guard and conventional trigger. One-piece barrel. Nickel finish. Variation 2: cast iron trigger guard and conventional trigger. Stepped barrel. Blued finish. Variation 3: ring trigger, one-piece barrel, blue finish. Variation 4: stepped barrel, blue finish. Mfg. 1909-41.

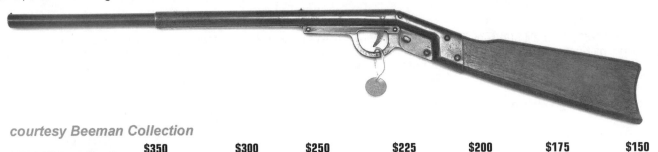

courtesy Beeman Collection

	100%	95%	90%	80%	60%	40%	20%
	$350	$300	$250	$225	$200	$175	$150

Subtract 25% for variation two.

Subtract 50% for variations three and four.

NUMBER 11 JUNIOR (THREE IN ONE GUN) - .177 air rifle shot or darts cal., or corks fired with shot tube removed, SP, BC, SS. Sheet metal frame and straight one-piece barrel shroud. Flat-sided walnut stock with crescent butt. Cast iron trigger guard (E.S. Roe patent) extends into wrist and provides cocking action fulcrum. Nickel finish. 29 in. OAL. Mfg. 1910-16.

	N/A	N/A	$450	$400	$350	$300	$250

NUMBER 17 BREECH LOADER - .177 lead air rifle shot or darts cal., SP, SS, sheet metal frame and barrel shroud, blued finish, BC action with two external cocking rods similar to Chicago Model. 12 in. BBL, 31 in. OAL. Mfg. circa 1917-32.

	N/A	N/A	$350	$300	$250	$175	$150

Add 20% for ammo box variant.

Ammo box variant – small ammo storage chamber below barrel pivot. Bears June 13, 1922 patent date.

NUMBER 21 SINGLE SHOT - .177 lead air rifle shot or darts cal., SP, SS, removable shot tube, lever action, cast iron lever, sheet metal frame and barrel shroud, blue or nickel finish. "NO. 21, KING MANUFACTURING Co., PLYMOUTH, MICH., SINGLE SHOT" plus patent dates marked on gun. 31 in. OAL. Mfg. circa. 1913-32. Variation one: earlier production with scroll stamped receiver marked "KING SINGLE SHOT No. 21, THE MARKHAM AIR RIFLE CO." with 1907 to 1913 patent dates. Variation two: blued finish, plain receiver. Variation Three: nickel finish, plain receiver.

	N/A	N/A	$200	$175	$150	$125	$100

Add 50% for variation one.

Note: The dash in the following four-digit model numbers does not appear on the guns themselves – but is added here to highlight the two-digit date of introduction which is added to the basic two-digit model number (i.e. Number 2123 is shown as Number 21-33 to indicate that it is a variation of No. 21 introduced in 1933).

MODEL 21-33 SINGLE SHOT - .177 lead air rifle shot or darts cal., SP, SS, removable shot tube, lever action, cast iron lever, sheet metal frame and barrel shroud, blue finish. Barrel marked "KING MFG. CO" and with Markham address. 31 in. OAL. Mfg. 1933-35.

	N/A	N/A	$200	$175	$150	$100	$75

NUMBER 21-36 SINGLE SHOT - .177 air rifle shot cal., SP, SS, cast iron cocking lever, sheet metal frame and barrel shroud, removable shot tube, blued finish. Straight grip stock. 32 in. OAL. Mfg. circa 1936-41.

courtesy Beeman Collection

	N/A	N/A	$200	$175	$150	$100	$75

NUMBER 22 REPEATER - .177 inch air rifle shot, SP, same as Number 21 gun but with 500-shot gravity-fed magazine repeater. Lever action, cast iron lever, sheet metal frame and barrel shroud, blue or nickel finish. Markham address on barrel. Loading port below front sight. 31 in. OAL. Mfg. circa 1916-1932.

	N/A	N/A	$220	$195	$170	$140	$115

NUMBER 22-33 REPEATER - .177 air rifle shot, SP, 500-shot gravity-fed magazine repeater, lever action, cast iron lever, sheet metal frame and barrel shroud, blue finish. Marked "King". Markham address on barrel. Loading port on RH side. 32 in. OAL. Mfg circa 1933-35.

	N/A	N/A	$175	$150	$125	$100	$80

GRADING	100%	95%	90%	80%	60%	40%	20%

NUMBER 22-36 500 SHOT REPEATER - .177 lead air rifle shot cal., SP, lever action, gravity-fed magazine, one-piece sheet metal frame and barrel shroud, cast iron lever, blued finish, straight grip wood stock. Daisy design influence, replaced King Number 22-33. 32 in. OAL. Mfg. circa 1936-1941.

	100%	95%	90%	80%	60%	40%	20%
	$125	$100	$75	$65	$50	$35	$25

NUMBER 23 KADET ARMY - .177 air rifle shot cal., SP, gravity-fed 500-shot magazine repeater, lever action, cast iron lever, sheet metal frame and barrel shroud, nickel finish. Frame marked "King Kadet". Markham address on barrel. Military type rear sight, rubber tipped bayonet. Web sling. 31 in. OAL (38 in. with bayonet). Mfg. circa 1915-16.

	100%	95%	90%	80%	60%	40%	20%
	N/A	N/A	$650	$550	$450	$350	$250

Subtract 30% for missing bayonet.
Subtract 10% for missing sling.

NUMBER 24 NEW CHICAGO - .177 lead air rifle shot or darts cal., SP, SS, BC. Barrel marked "New Chicago Number 24" and Markham address. Bolt action locking device. Blued finish. 36 in. OAL. Mfg. 1917 only. Ref: AR 2.

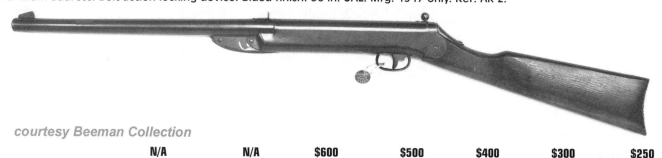

courtesy Beeman Collection

	100%	95%	90%	80%	60%	40%	20%
	N/A	N/A	$600	$500	$400	$300	$250

NUMBER 55 REPEATER - .177 lead air rifle shot or .174 in. steel BB cal., SP, lever action, gravity-fed 1000-shot magazine, one-piece sheet metal frame and barrel shroud, cast iron lever, blued finish. Markham address on top of barrel. Variation one: straight walnut stock. Variation two: pistol grip model with curved lever. 35 in. OAL. Mfg. 1923-1931.

	100%	95%	90%	80%	60%	40%	20%
	N/A	N/A	$180	$160	$140	$120	$100

Add 30% for variation two.

NUMBER 55-32 SINGLE SHOT - .177 lead air rifle shot or 174 in. steel BB cal., SP, lever action, one piece sheet metal frame and barrel shroud, cast iron lever, blued finish, pistol grip wood stock. Uses Number 55 frame. Loading port LH side. 35 in. OAL. Mfg. 1932 only.

	100%	95%	90%	80%	60%	40%	20%
	$100	$85	$65	$50	$35	$25	$20

NUMBER 55-33 1000 SHOT REPEATER - .174 steel BB cal., SP, lever action, 1,000 shot gravity feed magazine, new frame with Daisy type spring anchor and rear sight, straight grip stock, blued finish. 35 in. OAL. Mfg. 1933-35.

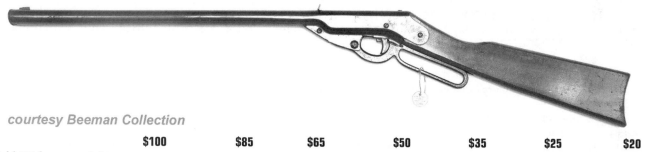

courtesy Beeman Collection

	100%	95%	90%	80%	60%	40%	20%
	$100	$85	$65	$50	$35	$25	$20

Add 5% for peep sight.
Also available with peep sight.

NUMBER 55-36 1000 SHOT REPEATER - .174 BB cal., SP, lever action gravity-fed magazine, one-piece sheet metal frame and barrel shroud, cast iron lever, blued finish, pistol grip wood stock. Daisy design influence, similar to Daisy Red Ryder and Number 155. 36 in. OAL. Mfg. circa 1936-41.

	100%	95%	90%	80%	60%	40%	20%
	$125	$100	$75	$65	$50	$35	$25

Add 5% for peep sight.

MARKSMAN PRODUCTS

Current manufacturer and importer located in Huntington Beach, CA. Marksman is a division of S/R Industries. Dealers and consumer direct sales.

Morton Harris, operating as Morton H. Harris Inc. in Beverly Hills and then Los Angeles, CA, developed a simple spring piston pistol during 1955-57. The firm continued as Marksman Products in Torrance, CA with airguns and expanded to slingshots and accessories. They later acquired Healthways, the manufacturer of some of the airguns sold under the Plainsman label. They also formerly imported Milbro Diana from Scotland, BSA from England, and Weihrauch/BSF, and Anschütz spring piston air rifles from Germany. Most of these imports were not special Marksman models and many were not marked with the Marksman name and thus generally are not covered here. Marksman produced the Model 1010 air pistol under private labeling via Milbro of Scotland. Today Marksman Products operates in Huntington Beach, CA as a division of S/R Industries of Maryland.

GRADING	100%	95%	90%	80%	60%	40%	20%

PISTOLS

MODEL MP (MARKSMAN PISTOL) - .175/ BB or .177 cal. pellet or dart. SS, SP, one-stroke cocking by sliding top of receiver, 2.5 in. smoothbore BBL, black paint or chrome finish, die-cast body. Morton Harris markings. Variation one: rotating cover in left grip over an ammunition storage area; marked "Beverly Hills, Calif." Apparently produced only in 1955 in very limited numbers. Variation two: without ammunition storage area; marked "Los Angeles, Calif." 1.5 lbs., 8.75 in. OAL. Mfg. 1955-57.

courtesy Beeman Collection

	$75	$60	$45	$30	N/A	N/A	N/A

Add 100% for factory box, ammo samples, and literature.

Subtract 50% for variation two.

Add 100% for chrome finish.

Add 200% for Dillingham Industries, Los Angeles, Calif. markings.

MSR was $6.95 for black finish, $8.95 for chrome finish.

MODEL MPR (MARKSMAN PISTOL REPEATER) - .175/ BB or .177 cal. pellet or dart, SP-slide cocking, smoothbore 2.5 in. BBL, die-cast, twenty-shot spring-fed BB magazine, forerunner of nearly identical Model 1010, black paint or chrome finish, early production marked "Los Angeles 25", later ones may be marked "Torrance, Calif." Sears Model 1914 with "Sears" cast into side-plate instead of "Marksman". Styrofoam box base appeared in 1967. 1.7 lbs, 8.75 in. OAL. Mfg. 1958-1977.

	$15	$10	N/A	N/A	N/A	N/A	N/A

Add 10% for Los Angeles address.

Add 50% for box, ammo samples, and paperwork.

Add 35% for chrome finish.

Add 100% for Sears markings.

MSR was $8.95 for black, $12.95 for chrome.

MODEL 1010/1010C/1010H/1010HC - .175/ BB or .177 cal. pellet or dart, slide action cocking, SP, smoothbore, 200 FPS, die-cast, twenty-shot spring-fed BB magazine, black paint, brass, or chrome finish (Model 1010C), fixed sights, and holster (Model 1010H). Mfg. 1977-present.

MSR $23	$20	$17	$13	N/A	N/A	N/A	N/A

Add 20% for models other than basic 1010.

Add 50% for box and literature (later versions clamshell packaging, no premium).

Add 50% for chrome.

Add 200% for gold color plating, presentation box.

Add 100% for original presentation case.

Model 1015 Special Edition - "combat" styling. Model 1300 with "Shootin' Darts" set. Model 1320 "Shootin' Triangles" with self-contained tar-get box.

MODEL 1010X - similar to Model 1010, except has full nickel plating and black plastic grip panels with inlaid silver colored Marks-man logos.

	$22	$18	$15	N/A	N/A	N/A	N/A

MODEL 1015 - similar to Model 1010, except has full nickel plating and brown plastic grip panels with inlaid silver colored Marks-man logos.

	$18	$13	$10	N/A	N/A	N/A	N/A

MODEL 1020 - BB/.175 cal., slide action, SP, black finish, eighteen-shot reservoir (BB), 200 FPS, fixed sights.

MSR $21	$18	$13	$8	N/A	N/A	N/A	N/A

MODEL 1049 (PLAINSMAN) - BB/.174 cal., CO_2 (12 gram), repeater, hundred-shot BB gravity-fed reservoir, adj. 300-400 FPS.

	$40	$30	$25	$15	N/A	N/A	N/A

Discontinued in 1990s. See Healthways in the "H" section of this guide.

MODEL 1399 - BB/.175 cal. and .177 pellet, darts, or bolts, slide action, SP, silver chrome finish, gravity-fed twenty-four-shot BB reservoir, 230 FPS, fiberoptic front sight, extended barrel, includes dartboard and twelve darts.

MSR $26	$23	$18	$13	N/A	N/A	N/A	N/A

GRADING	100%	95%	90%	80%	60%	40%	20%

MODEL 2000 - BB/.175 cal., slide action, SP, 200 FPS similar to Model 1010C, except has silver chrome finish and squared trigger guard.

| MSR $25 | $22 | $17 | $12 | N/A | N/A | N/A | N/A |

Add 25% for Model 2000K, kit includes safety glasses, speed loader, and BB/pellet/dart samples.

MODEL 2004 DELUXE - .177 pellet, SSP, over-cocking, polymer frame with finger grooves and cast aluminum slide, black finish, 410 FPS, adj. rear sight, squared trigger guard, automatic trigger safety, 9.5 in. OAL, 1.7 lbs. New 2005.

| MSR $45 | $40 | $35 | $30 | N/A | N/A | N/A | N/A |

MODEL 2005 - BB/.175 cal. and .177 pellet, darts, or ballistic bolt, slide action, SP, silver chrome finish, twenty-four-shot BB reservoir, 260 FPS, "Laserhawk" fiberoptic front sight, extended barrel, squared trigger guard.

| MSR $26 | $23 | $17 | $13 | N/A | N/A | N/A | N/A |

RIFLES

JUNIOR MODEL 28 - .177 cal., BBC, SP, 600 FPS, 16.75 in. barrel, blue finish, 6 lbs. Mfg. for Marksman by Weihrauch.

| | $135 | $120 | $95 | $75 | $50 | N/A | N/A |

Last MSR was $225.

MODEL 29/30 - .177 or .22 cal., BBC, SP, 800/625 FPS, 18.5 in. barrel, blue finish, 6 lbs. Mfg. for Marksman by BSA. Disc. 1991.

| | $135 | $120 | $95 | $75 | $50 | N/A | N/A |

Last MSR was $200.

MODEL 40 - .177 cal., BBC, SP, 720 FPS, 18.4 in. barrel, blue finish, 7 lbs. 5 oz.

| | $145 | $125 | $105 | $85 | $55 | N/A | N/A |

Last MSR was $250.

MODEL 45 - .177 cal., BBC, SP, 900-930 FPS, 19.2 in. barrel, blue finish, 7.15 lbs. New 1993.

| | $125 | $110 | $80 | $60 | $40 | N/A | N/A |

Last MSR was $195.

MODEL 55 (RIFLE) & 59 CARBINE - .177 cal., BBC, SP, 925 FPS, 19.75 (rifle) or 14 (carbine) in. barrel, blue finish, 7.5 lbs. Mfg. for Marksman by Weihrauch, using B.S.F. tooling.

| | $195 | $160 | $125 | $80 | $60 | N/A | N/A |

Last MSR was $300.

MODEL 56/56K - .177 cal., BBC, SP, 925 FPS, 19.6 in. barrel, blue finish, adj. cheekpiece and trigger, 8.7 lbs.

| | $300 | $250 | $225 | $165 | $115 | N/A | N/A |

Add 50% for 56K Model with Marksman Model 6941 scope.
The Model 56/56K is manufactured for Marksman by Weihrauch, using B.S.F. tooling.

MODEL 58/58K - .177 cal., BBC, SP, 925 FPS, 16 in. heavy bull barrel, blue finish, adj. trigger, designed for silhouette shooting, 8 lbs. 8 oz. Importation disc. 1993.

| | $250 | $205 | $165 | $125 | $85 | N/A | N/A |

Last MSR was $390.

Add 50% for 58K Model with Marksman Model 6941 scope.
Manufactured for Marksman by Weihrauch, using B.S.F. tooling.

MODEL 60/61 CARBINE - .177 cal., UL, SP, blue finish, 810-840 FPS, 8 lbs. 12 oz.

| | $300 | $250 | $225 | $165 | $115 | N/A | N/A |

Last MSR was $490.

This model is a modified version of HW77 by Weihrauch manufactured for Marksman using B.S.F. tooling.

MODEL 70 - .177, .20, or .22 cal., BBC, SP, 19.75 in. barrel, blue finish, 925/760 FPS, 8 lbs.

| | $235 | $185 | $145 | $105 | $65 | N/A | N/A |

Last MSR was $355.

Add 10% for .20 cal.
Mfg. for Marksman by Weihrauch using B.S.F. tooling.

MODEL 72 - .177, .20, or .22 cal., BBC, SP, similar to Model 70.

| | $235 | $185 | $145 | $105 | $65 | N/A | N/A |

Last MSR was $355.

Add 10% for .20 cal.
Mfg. for Marksman by Weihrauch using B.S.F. tooling.

MODEL 746 - .177 cal., BBC, SP, SS, rifled barrel, 580 FPS, 42 in. OAL.

| | $125 | $85 | $60 | $45 | $30 | N/A | N/A |

Marksman private branding of Diana Milbro G79 from Scotland.

MODEL 1700 - .177/BB cal., pump action cocking, SP, 275 FPS, twenty-shot spring-fed mag., blue finish.

| | N/A | $18 | $13 | $10 | N/A | N/A | N/A |

GRADING	100%	95%	90%	80%	60%	40%	20%

MODEL 1702 - .177/BB cal., pump action cocking, SP, 275 FPS, twenty-shot spring-fed mag., blue finish, adj. rear and fiberoptic front sights.

	MSR $26	$23	$18	$13	N/A	N/A	N/A	N/A

MODEL 1705 - .177/BB cal., similar to Model 1702, except has three-position length adj. stock.

	MSR $30	$27	$22	$17	N/A	N/A	N/A	N/A

MODEL 1710 (PLAINSMAN) - .177/BB cal., pump action cocking, SP, 275 FPS, twenty-shot spring-fed mag., blue finish.

$20	$15	$10	N/A	N/A	N/A	N/A

MODEL 1740 - .177/BB cal., BBC, SP, 450 FPS, eighteen-shot reservoir, blued finish.

N/A	$35	$25	$15	N/A	N/A	N/A

MODEL 1745 - .177/BB cal., BBC, SP, 450 FPS, eighteen-shot reservoir, blued finish, ambidextrous Monte Carlo plastic stock.

N/A	$27	$22	$17	N/A	N/A	N/A

Add 20% for Model 1745S with factory installed Marksman 1804 scope.

MODEL 1750 - .177/BB cal., BBC, SP, similar to Model 1740, except skeletonized.

N/A	$30	$20	$10	N/A	N/A	N/A

MODEL 1780 - .177/BB cal., BBC, SP, 450 FPS, single shot version of Model 1740.

N/A	$30	$20	$10	N/A	N/A	N/A

MODEL 1790 (BIATHLON TRAINER) - .177/BB cal., BBC, SP, 450 FPS, plastic stock.

N/A	$60	$50	$40	N/A	N/A	N/A

MODEL 1792 - .177 cal., BBC, SP, 450 FPS, similar to Model 1790.

N/A	$45	$35	$25	N/A	N/A	N/A

MODEL 1795 - .177/BB cal., UL, SP, bolt action loading, 450/500 FPS, ten-round spring-fed magazine.

N/A	$50	$40	$30	N/A	N/A	N/A

Add 10% for Model 1795S with factory installed Marksman 1804 scope.

MODEL 1798 - .177 cal., BBC, SP, similar to Model 1790 Biathlon Trainer, except has "Laserhawk" sighting system.

N/A	$50	$40	$30	N/A	N/A	N/A

MODEL 2015/2015K - .177/BB cal., similar to Model 1705, except has "Laserhawk" sighting system, BB speed loader, and targets (Model 2015K only).

	MSR $42	$39	$33	$27	N/A	N/A	N/A	N/A

Add 10% for Model 2015K with all accessories.

MARS

Previous trade mark manufactured by Venus Waffenfabrik located in Thüringen, Germany.

The Mars military-style air rifles were listed with many models of Tell airguns in old Venus Waffenfabrik factory catalogs. It presently is assumed that VWF were the makers. For more information on Mars airguns, see Tell in the "T" section.

MATCHGUNS srl

Current manufacturer located in Parma, Italy. Previously imported and distributed by Nygord Precision Products, located in Prescott, AZ.

For more information and current pricing on Matchguns srl firearms, please refer to the *Blue Book of Gun Values* by S.P. Fjestad (also available online).

PISTOLS

MODEL MG I - .177 cal., PCP, SS, 9.36 in. barrel, black finish, 625 FPS, adj. anatomical wood grip, adj. electronic trigger, fully adj. sights, adj. stabilizer, 10.7 in. OAL, 2.42 lbs.

No MSR	$825	$750	$695	N/A	N/A	N/A	N/A

MODEL MG I LIGHT - .177 cal., PCP, SS, similar to Model MG 1 except, standard grip and no stabilizers, 10.7 in. OAL, 2.42 lbs.

courtesy Matchguns srl

As this edition went to press, retail pricing had yet to be established.

GRADING	100%	95%	90%	80%	60%	40%	20%

MATCHLESS

Previous trade name of BB rifles manufactured by Henry C. Hart Company located in Detroit, MI, circa 1890 to 1900.

These were spring piston BB rifles using a top lever for cocking; similar in this function to the First Model Daisy introduced in 1889. Cast iron parts made them more substantial and heavier than contemporary BB rifles. Promoted as the only repeating BB guns on the market, they actually were single shots, which, like some of the early Daisy "repeaters," could be fed BBs one at a time from a built-in magazine.

RIFLES

FIRST MODEL - .180/large BB cal., SP, TL, sixty-five-shot gravity-fed magazine, cast iron frame with black paint finish, blued steel barrel, marked "MATCHLESS" in a curving line on the side of the grip frame, top cocking lever w/o knob, no safety, 35.5 in. OAL, 2.5 lbs. Mfg. 1890-95.

courtesy Beeman Collection

	N/A	N/A	$2,000	$1,650	$1,300	$995	$600

Add 30% if not missing any parts.

Commonly the rear sight, magazine latch, and/or loading gate at the muzzle have been lost.

SECOND MODEL - similar to First Model, except "MATCHLESS" is name much smaller and in a straight line on the side of the breech area of the receiver, seamless brass, nickel-plated barrel, top cocking lever with false-hammer knob. Mfg. 1895-1900.

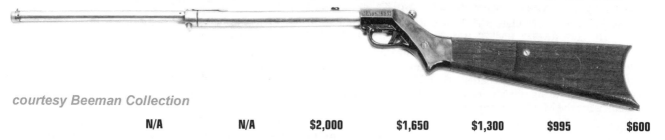

courtesy Beeman Collection

	N/A	N/A	$2,000	$1,650	$1,300	$995	$600

MAUSER

Current trademark manufactured in Europe by various subcontractors. No current U.S. importation. Mauser airguns are not manufactured by Mauser-Werke. Previously imported and distributed by Beeman Precision Airguns located in San Rafael, CA, and Marksman, located in Huntington Beach, CA.

For more information and current pricing on both new and used Mauser firearms, please refer to the *Blue Book of Gun Values* by S.P. Fjestad (also available online).

PISTOLS

U90/U91 JUMBO AIR PISTOLS - for information on this model, see FB Record (Fritz Barthelms) in the "F" section.

RIFLES

MATCH 300SL/SLC - .177 cal., UL, SP, 550/450 FPS, adj. sights and hardwood stock, 8 lbs. 8 oz.

$200	$165	$120	$85	$55	N/A	N/A

Last MSR was $330.

Add 25% for SLC Model with diopter sights.

This model was mfg. in Hungary.

MAYER AND GRAMMELSPACHER

For information on Mayer and Grammelspacher, see Dianawerk.

MEIER

Previously produced by Jeff Meier of Miami, FL.

PISTOLS

MEIER SLUG/SHOT PISTOL - .38 cal. smoothbore, fires .375 slugs or .38 shot shells built on Crosman 2240 frame, 18.5 in OAL. Circa 1990. Estimated value in 90% condition about $275.

courtesy Beeman Collection

MENALDI

Current tradename of Menaldi Armas Neumaticas located in Cordoba, Argentina.

In 2004 Luis Mendaldi started development of a line of CO_2 rifles of high end quality for both target and hunting. At time of printing only a few handmade samples had been made and digital illustrations were not available. Additional information on this line will be provided in future issues of this guide. Best current source of information is the Menaldi website at www.menaldi.com.ar.

MENDOZA S.A. de C.V.

Current manufacturer Productas Mendoza, S.A. located in Xochimilco, Mexico. Currently imported and distributed under the Benjamin and Crosman names by Crosman Corp., located in East Bloomfield, Airgun Express, Inc. located in Montezuma, IA, also distributed by Compasseco located in Bardstown, KY, and by Airgun Express located in Montezuma, IA.

For information on Models RM622 and RM777, see Benjamin Air Rifle Co. in the "B" section. For information on Models RM177, RM277, RM522, RM577, RM677, RM877, and RM 650 BB Scout, see Crosman Corp. in the "C" section.

The Mendoza brand has an exotic history, beginning in 1911 when engineer Rafael Mendoza established the company to develop a unique 7 mm two-barrel machine gun and then an "improved" Mauser-type bolt action rifle. Mendoza produced machine guns and hand grenades, 35 and 37 mm field artillery cannons, and field heliographs for General Francisco Villa (Pancho Villa) during the Mexican Revolution. In 1934, the Mendoza 1934 C model rifle/machine gun was selected as standard ordnance for the Mexican Army and Navy.

In the 1950s, Mendoza began production of an interesting variety of BB guns including the Model 50 double barrel BB gun – a gun considerably rarer than the Daisy double barrel BB guns. In 1971, still owned by the family, the Mendoza Company moved from exclusive production of guns to six different product lines, including sophisticated pellet guns such as the RM 2003 with its quick change calibers and dual component safety trigger (RM, in case you hadn't guessed, stands for Rafael Mendoza.)

A wide variety of airguns has been produced by Mendoza. This is a first, preliminary model list. There presently is confusion regarding the designation, specifications, and dates for several models Additional research is being done on this brand and results will appear in future editions of this guide and on the web. Information is actively solicited from Mendoza collectors. Please contact Blue Book Publications or send inputs to BlueBookEdit@Beemans.net .

The authors and publisher of *Blue Book of Airguns* wish to express their appreciation to Ralph Heize Flamand of the Mendoza Company for his assistance with this section in this edition.

RIFLES

MODEL 4 - .177 or .22 cal., SP, UL, SS, mahogany or habillo wood stock, rubber buttplate.

courtesy Mendoza

Values TBD.

GRADING	100%	95%	90%	80%	60%	40%	20%

MODEL 5 - deluxe version of Model 4.

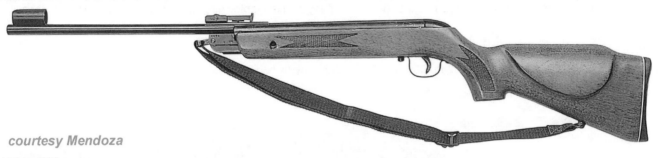

courtesy Mendoza

Values TBD.

MODEL 25 - .177/BB cal., BBC, tinplate construction, nickel plated. Mfg. circa 1950.

courtesy Mendoza

Values TBD.
Mendoza's first airgun.

MODEL 50 DOUBLE BARREL BB GUN - double barrel version of Model 25; extremely rare. Mfg. circa 1954.

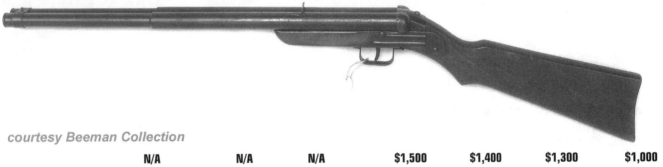

courtesy Beeman Collection

	N/A	N/A	N/A	$1,500	$1,400	$1,300	$1,000

MODEL 50 LEVER ACTION BB GUN - .174/BB cal., SP, Winchester-style cocking lever, tinplate BB gun-type construction. Separate wood buttstock and forearm.

Values TBD.
No other information or value available at time of printing.

MODEL 85 LEVER ACTION BB GUN - .174/BB cal., SP, Winchester-style cocking lever, tinplate BB gun-type construction. Separate wood buttstock and forearm.

Values TBD.
No other information or value available at time of printing.

MODEL COMPETITION - BB, SP, SS, mahogany or habillo wood Monte Carlo stock, checkered grip and forearm, buttplate with white line spacer, sling swivels, rear body tube cap styled like Webley Airsporter, blued finish, pellet holder at base of BBL. 1980s.

Values TBD.
No other information or value available at time of printing.

MODEL HM-3 - .177 BB, SP, UL, thirty-five-shot spring-fed magazine, folding metal stock, nickel plated. Mfg. 1957-60.

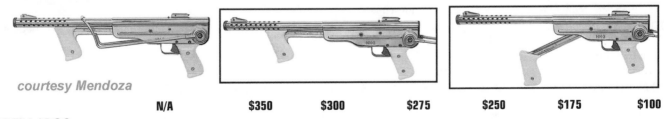

courtesy Mendoza

	N/A	$350	$300	$275	$250	$175	$100

MODEL LARGO

No other information or values available at time of printing.

GRADING	100%	95%	90%	80%	60%	40%	20%

MODEL MAGNUM - BB, SP, SS, "high velocity," mahogany or habillo wood Monte Carlo stock, checkered grip and forearm, butt-plate with white line spacer, sling swivels, rear body tube cap styled like Webley Airsporter, blued finish, pellet holder at base of BBL. 1980s.

Values TBD.

No other information or value available at time of printing.

MODEL RM 10 - .22 cal., SP, BBC, SS, 14.2 in. BBL, 450 FPS, mahogany or habillo wood Monte Carlo stock, sling, 35.4 in. OAL, 5.94 lbs. New 1986.

courtesy Mendoza

MSR	N/A	$127	$100	$75	$50	N/A	N/A	N/A

MODEL RM 65 - .174/BB cal., SP, Winchester-style cocking lever, 11.8 in. BBL, 250 FPS, tinplate BB gun-type construction, separate Monte Carlo-style wood buttstock and forearm, blue finish, 35.83 in. OAL, 3.08 lbs. New 1986.

courtesy Mendoza

Values TBD.

No other information or value available at time of printing.

❊ **Model RM 650** - similar to RM 65, except with 500-shot magazine.

MODEL RM 100 - .177 or .22 cal., SP, BBC, SS, 19 in. BBL, 750/675 FPS, mahogany or habillo wood Monte Carlo stock, sling, 41 in.OAL, 6.6 lbs. New 1986.

courtesy Mendoza

Values TBD.

No other information or values available at time of printing.

MODEL RM 200 - .177 or .22 cal., BBC, SP, SS, 19 in. BBL, mahogany or habillo wood Monte Carlo stock, RH cheekpiece, swivels and sling, 41 in. OAL, 6.6 lbs.

MSR	N/A	$162	$130	$100	$70	N/A	N/A	N/A

Add $51 for Model RM-200 Combo with 4x32mm scope.

MODEL RM 450C/450L - .177 cal., BBC, SP, SS, 18.5 in. BBL, 600 FPS, mahogany or habillo wood Monte Carlo stock, RH cheekpiece, deep belly forearm, swivels and sling. 40.16-42.5 in. OAL, 6.82 lbs.

Values TBD.

No other information available at time of printing.

MODEL RN 600 - .22 cal., BBC, SP, SS, 18.5 in. BBL, 900 FPS, mahogany or habillo wood Monte Carlo stock, RH cheekpiece, swivels and sling, 45.28 in. OAL, 7.7 lbs.

MSR	N/A	$200	$165	$125	$85	N/A	N/A	N/A

Add $49 for Model RM-600 Combo with 4x32mm scope.

Add $75 for Model RM-600 Combo with 3-9x32mm scope.

GRADING	100%	95%	90%	80%	60%	40%	20%

MODEL RM 800 - .177 or .22 cal., SP, BBC, SS, 18.5 in. BBL, 1050/900 FPS, laminated wood, thumbhole stock, nylon sling, rubber pellet holder on barrel, manual safety, blue finish, 20.5 in. round barrel, 45.28 in. OAL, 7.92 lbs. New 1986.

	$350	$325	$300	$250	$225	$200	$175

MODEL RM 1000 - .22 cal., SP, BBC, seven-shot repeater, 19 in. BBL, 650 FPS, mahogany or habillo wood Monte Carlo stock, 45.28 in. OAL, 7.7 lbs. New 1986.

Values TBD.

No other information or values available at time of printing.

MODEL RM 2000 - .22 cal., BBC, SP, SS, 18.5 in. BBL, 850 FPS, mahogany or habillo wood Monte Carlo stock, RH cheekpiece, swivels and sling, 45.28 in. OAL, 7.7 lbs.

MSR	N/A	$241	$205	$175	$135	N/A	N/A	N/A

Add $47 for Model RM-2000 Combo with 4x32mm scope.

MODEL RM 2003 ADVANCE - .177 or .22 cal., SP, BBC, SS, 18.5 in. BBL, 1200/1000 FPS, mahogany or habillo wood Monte Carlo stock, instant change barrels with dual caliber muzzle brake, double blade safety trigger. 45 in. OAL, 7.7 lbs. New 2003.

courtesy Mendoza

MSR	N/A	$271	$230	$185	$145	N/A	N/A	N/A

Add $45 for Model RM-600 Combo with 4x32mm scope.

Add $86 for Model RM-600 Combo with 3-9x32mm scope.

MODEL 2800 - .22 CAL., BBC, SP, SS, 18.5 in. BBL, 1150/950 FPS, mahogany or habillo wood Monte Carlo thumbhole stock, RH cheekpiece, swivels and sling, 45.28 in. OAL, 7.7 lbs.

Values TBD.

No other information or values available at time of printing.

MODEL SHORT M6 - BB, SP, SS, mahogany or habillo wood Monte Carlo stock, buttplate with white line spacer, sling swivels, rear body tube cap styled like Webley Airsporter, blued finish, pellet holder at base of BBL. Mfg. circa 1980s.

Values TBD.

No other information available at time of printing.

MODEL SUPER V-57 - .177/BB cal., gravity-fed magazine, Daisy-style lever action cocking, tinplate construction, nickel plated.

courtesy Mendoza

Values TBD.

No other information or values available at time of printing.

MODEL TI MEN - .177/BB cal., gravity-fed magazine, Daisy-style lever action cocking, tinplate construction, blued.

courtesy Mendoza

Values TBD.

No other information or values available at time of printing.

MODEL VAQUERO - appears to be a copy of Beeman C1 hunting carbine, BB, SP, SS, mahogany or habillo wood straight shotgun-style stock without pistol grip, buttplate with white line spacer, rear body tube cap styled like Webley Airsporter, blued finish. Mfg. 1980s.

Values TBD.

No other information available at time of printing.

PISTOLS

MODEL M-56 - tinplate copy of Colt Single Action Army revolver. No additional info at this time; please submit info to BBAinput@Beemans.net.

MILBRO

Previous trade name of Millard Brothers located in Motherwell, Lanarkshire, Scotland

The name Milbro is derived from 'Millard Brothers' a family owned business founded in 1887; apparently the senior figure was David W Millard.

Milbro began producing airguns in 1949, using machinery and equipment taken as WW2 war reparations from the Mayer and Grammelspacher Company (DIANAWERK) in Rastatt, Germany in 1945. Milbro also received the brand name DIANA and even the Diana logo showing the goddess of hunting, Diana, discarding her bow and arrow in favor of an airgun, held high above her head. This resulted in today's collectors having both German and British airguns bearing the Diana name and logo! In 1950, DIANAWERK again began the production of airguns. in their old factory in Rastatt. They were forced to use names other than "Diana." Within Germany the Dianawerk airguns were sold as "Original." The brand "Original Diana" was used for Dianawerk guns in England. Dianawerk repurchased their trademark in 1984 after Milbro ceased airgun production. After 1984 all Diana airguns were again made in Rastatt, Germany (see Dianawerk section). For greater detail on this aspect, see DIANAWERK in the "D" section of this book.

Milbro produced airguns under both their own name and the acquired Diana brand. Most of these guns were close copies of the German pre-war models; many bore the same model number as their German pre-war siblings. This even while Dianawerk in Germany had resumed production of some of the same models under the same model numbers (but under the Original or Original Diana labels); some with modifications or improvements! .Milbro made airguns for other firms in the shooting trade including Umarex in Germany, Daisy in the USA, and Webley & Scott and Phoenix Arms in England. The Webley Jaguar was manufactured by Milbro and. the virtually identical Webley Junior may also have been a Milbro product. Some of the Milbro airguns did not bear the Diana name, but were marked "Milbro Foreign" which indicates that they may have been made for Milbro of Scotland by Dianawerk in Germany in the pre-WW2 period when German markings were not in favor in England.

Milbro was sold in 1970 to Grampian Holdings who also owned businesses making fishing tackle, golf clubs, and other items. During the mid-1970s Milbro sold airguns to mail order catalog retailers. By 1982, despite the advantage of the famous old Diana trademark, Milbro, using Dianawerk´s old machinery and materials, had ceased making airguns. The machinery was sold to El Gamo. Some remaining guns were sold to a Swiss firm for mail order sales.

Milbro began making airgun pellets in 1950. The pellet business was sold to former Milbro employee Jim Mark. Milbro pellets, under the names of Caledonian, Jet, Rhino, Clipper, Match and TR are still made in Motherwell, Scotland.

The authors and publisher wish to thank Tim Saunders and Jim Mark for their valuable assistance with the following information in this edition of the *Blue Book of Airguns*. Ref.: Dennis Hiller´s British based "The Collectors´ Guide to Air Rifles" and "The Collectors' Guide to Air Pistols". Much of the following is based on those books. Additional information is actively sought from readers; direct info to BBAinfo@Beemans.net.

PISTOLS

DIANA G2 - .177 cal., pellets or darts. SP, SS, derived from German Diana Model 2 but w/ 2 pc. black plastic grips. "Gat" style push-barrel cocking. Mfg. late 1950s to early 1960s.

courtesy Beeman Collection

	$55	$45	$35	$25	$20	N/A	N/A

Add 50% for factory box.

GRADING	100%	95%	90%	80%	60%	40%	20%

DIANA MODEL 2 - .177 cal., pellets or darts, SP, SS, "Gat" style push-barrel cocking, similar to German Diana Model 2 push-barrel pistolexcept, w/ wood grips. Mfg. late 1950s to early 1960s.

courtesy Beeman Collection

	$55	$45	$35	$25	$20	N/A	N/A

Add 50% for factory box.

MILBRO MK II - .177 cal., SP, TL, SS, based on 1937 patent of German Em-Ge Zenit, single stage trigger, one piece wooden stock, 11 in. OAL, 1.5 lbs.

	$160	$125	$110	$90	$80	$60	$40

Add 60% for original six sided box.
Add 30% for original four sided box.

DIANA MK II (G4) - .177 cal., SP, TL, SS,based on 1937 patent of German Em-Ge Zenit,single stage trigger, one piece wooden stock w/ medallion of Diana logo or Diana name, 11 in. OAL, 1.5 lbs.

	$150	$120	$105	$85	$75	$55	$35

Add 25% for factory box.

MILBRO CUB - 2.41 mm lead balls (No.7 lead birdshot) caL., fired by a quick squeeze on the rubber bulb in the grip, gravity feed 500 shot magazine, one piece cast alloy construction; no moving parts, purple anodized finish or polished zinc alloy. Mfg.began during late 1940s.

courtesy Beeman Collection

	$300	$250	$175	$125	$75	$50	N/A

Add 50% for factory box.

"World's Weakest Air Pistol". Shot sold by Milbro in packets marked "Spare charges". Patented in France 1948 and also produced in France in all plastic version.

MILBRO G10 - .177 cal., SP, slide pulls to load and cock, 20 shot repeater w/ BBs, SS w/ pellets or darts, may be various finishes, markings, and accessories. Mfg. 1952-1982.

	$35	$30	$25	$20	$20	N/A	N/A

A private branding of Marksman 1010 air pistol from California.

GRADING	100%	95%	90%	80%	60%	40%	20%

DIANA SP50 - .177 cal., SP, SS, push barrel design, 400 fps., styled like an automatic pistol, cast alloy frame, darts or pellets loaded at the rear, sold in polystyrene cartons complete with packets of .177 darts and pellets. Mfg.1970s -1982. OAL 7 in., weight 1.6 lbs.

courtesy Beeman Collection

	$55	$45	$35	$25	$15	N/A	N/A

Add 5% for factory box.

Identical pistol marketed by Phoenix Arms Company, Eastbourne, East Sussex, England as G50until at least 1989. Also sold as Perfecta SP50.

MILBRO COUGAR - .177 or .22 cal., SP, BBC, SS, similar to BSA Scorpion, grips and barrel pivot cover plates of simulated wood, blue steel body tube and barrel, black finished cast metal receiver, 18.5 in. OAL. Mfg. 1978-1982.

	$175	$150	$125	$95	$75	N/A	N/A

Add 20% for box with shoulder stock, sight blades, scope ramp, and pellets.

MILBRO BLACK MAJOR - .177 or .22 cal., SP, BBC, SS, similar to Milbro Cougar except, skeletal shoulder stock, reflector sight system. Mfg. 1981-82.

	$200	$165	$135	$100	$70	N/A	N/A

MILBRO TYPHOON - .177 cal., push-barrel, aluminum pistol, similar to Harrington "GAT", beech grip, 6.8 in OAL. Mfg.1950s.

Current values not yet determined.

Name conflict w/ Webley Typhoon air pistol and Relum Typhoon air rifle.

RIFLES

Early models may have date stamp on the lower edge of the stock.

DIANA MODEL 1 - .177 in., BBC, SP, SS, similar to pre-WW2 German Diana Model 1, removable smoothbore barrel, tinplate construction. Mfg. circa 1949-1959.

	$75	$50	$35	$25	$15	N/A	N/A

DIANA MODEL 15 - .177 cal., BBC, SP, SS, similar to pre-WW2 German Diana Model 1, tinplate construction, smoothbore barrel. Mfg. 1950s–1980.

	$90	$75	$60	$45	$30	N/A	N/A

DIANA MODEL 16 - .177 cal., BBC, SP, SS, similar to pre-WW2 German Diana Model 16, tinplate construction, smoothbore barrel, later models w/ scope ramp spot welded to body.cylinder. Mfg. late 1940s -1974.

courtesy Beeman Collection

	$110	$90	$75	$60	$45	N/A	N/A

Also sold in USA as Winchester 416, HyScore 805, Daisy 160.

GRADING	100%	95%	90%	80%	60%	40%	20%

DIANA MODEL 22 - .177 cal., BBC, SP, SS, similar to pre-WW2 German Diana Model 22, tinplate construction, smoothbore barrel. Mfg. late1940s- early 1970s.

courtesy Beeman Collection

	100%	95%	90%	80%	60%	40%	20%
	$125	$100	$85	$70	$55	N/A	N/A

MILBRO MODEL 22 - .177 cal., BBC, SP, SS, similar to English Diana Model 22, tinplate construction, smoothbore barrel, recognizable by sweeping curve of stock up behind rear of cylinder, Mfg. late1940s- early 1970s.

	$125	$100	$85	$70	$55	N/A	N/A

Add 10% for box.
Gave rise to Webley Jaguar and Junior.

DIANA MODEL 23 - .177 cal., BBC, SP, SS, similar to pre-WW2 German Diana Model 23, solid barrel version of Model 22, 37 in. OAL. Mfg . late 1940s- approx. 1960.

	$150	$125	$95	$75	$50	N/A	N/A

Became Milbro G23.

MILBRO G23 - .177 cal., BBC, SP, SS, similar to English Diana Model 23, 37 in OAL, 3.5 lbs. Mfg. circa 1970s.

	$150	$125	$100	$85	$70	N/A	N/A

DIANA 25 - .177 or .22 cal., BBC, SP, SS, similar to pre-WW2 German Diana Model 25, rifled or smoothbore., 38.3 in. OAL, 5 lbs.

	$120	$95	$75	$55	$40	N/A	N/A

DIANA COMET - .177 or.22 cal., BBC, SP, SS, kit version, similar to pre-WW2 German Diana Model 25. Mfg. early 1960s- 1963.

	$250	$215	$185	$150	$125	N/A	N/A

DIANA G25 - 177 or .22 cal., BBC, SP, SS, similar to English Diana Model 25, 38 in. OAL, 5 lbs. Mfg. 1963-66.

	$130	$115	$95	$80	$65	N/A	N/A

DIANA 27 - .177 or .22 cal., BBC, SP, SS, similar to pre-WW2 German Diana Model 27, smoothbore or rifled bbl., 5.8 lbs. Mfg. circa 1950s- 1963.

	$120	$95	$80	$65	$50	N/A	N/A

DIANA G27 - .177 CAL., smoothbore/rifled BBL, .22 rifled cal., similar to English Diana 27 except, with manual safety (early production may lack safety.), 41.5 in. OAL, 5.9 lbs. Mfg. circa 1963-67.

	$125	$95	$80	$65	$50	N/A	N/A

DIANA G36 - .177 or .22 cal. BBC, SP, SS, manual safety, 41.5 in OAL, Mfg. 1966-early 1970s.

	$120	$95	$80	$65	$50	N/A	N/A

DIANA G44 (TARGETMASTER) - .177 or .22 cal., BBC, SP, SS, similar to British Diana Model 25, rifled or smoothbore, manual safety, aperture sight, 42 in. OAL, 6.3 lbs. Mfg. circa 1967- early 1970s.

	$250	$215	$185	$155	$115	N/A	N/A

DIANA G46 (TARGETMASTER) - .177 or .22 cal., BBC, SP, SS, similar to British Diana Model 27, rifled or smoothbore in .177; rifled only in .22, aperture sight, manual safety. Mfg. circa 1967- early 1970s.

	$250	$115	$85	$65	$50	N/A	N/A

DIANA 55/G55 - .177 or .22 cal. UL, SP, SS, similar to German Original Model 50, faucet tap loading, 42 in. OAL, 7.2 lbs. Mfg. Ca. late 1950s- early 1960s.

	$375	$325	$265	$215	$165	N/A	N/A

DIANA SERIES 70 - .177 or .22 cal., BBC, SP, SS. MFG. Ca. 1971-1980s.

  ✱ **Model 71** - .177 cal., BBC, SP, SS, rear manual safety, deluxe Monte Carlo stock w/ white line buttpad, checkering, BBL w/ outer sleeve, 42.8 in. OAL. MFG. Ca. 1971-1982.

	$225	$185	$155	$115	$85	N/A	N/A

  ✱ **Model 74 (G74)** - .177 cal. BBC, SP, SS, similar to German Original Model 16 except, improved stock, tinplate construction, smoothbore barrel, 32.5 in. OAL, 3 lbs. Mfg. early 1970s- late 1970s.

	$50	$40	$30	$20	N/A	N/A	N/A

  ✱ **Model 75** - .177 cal., BBC, SP, SS, similar to Diana Series 70, Model 74 except, rifled barrel, tinplate construction, 32.5 in. OAL, 3 lbs. Mfg. Ca. 1980-1982.

	$60	$50	$40	$30	N/A	N/A	N/A

GRADING	100%	95%	90%	80%	60%	40%	20%

✷ *Model 76* - .177 or .22 cal., BBC, SP, SS, semi- tinplate construction, rifled barrel, 400/300 fps., 37 in. OAL, 5.3 lbs. Mfg. Ca. 1972-1980s.

	$120	$95	$70	$55	$40	N/A	N/A

✷ *Model 77* - .177 or .22 cal., BBC, SP, SS, rifled barrel. 400/300 fps., 38.5 in. OAL, 6 lbs. Mfg. Ca. 1972- 1980s.

	$120	$95	$70	$55	$40	N/A	N/A

✷ *Model 78 (Standard)/Model 79 (Deluxe)* - .177 in. cal. BBC, SP, SS, manual safety on side, 38.5 in. OAL. Mfg. Ca. 1978–1980s.

	$120	$95	$70	$55	$40	N/A	N/A

DIANA G80 - .177 or .22 cal., BBC, SP, SS, 625/500 FPS, sloping forearm as of 1980, 42 in. OAL, 6.8 lbs. Mfg. early 1977-82.

	$150	$115	$95	$70	$45	N/A	N/A

DIANA G85 (BOBCAT) - .177 cal., BBC, SP, SS, smoothbore barrel. 33 in. OAL, 3.8 lbs. Mfg. Ca. 1978-82.

	$120	$95	$75	$55	$40	N/A	N/A

Similar to DIANA Series 70, Model 74 –(G74) , and updated version of Model 16.

MILBRO SCOUT - .177cal., BBC, SP, SS, similar to pre-WW2 German Diana Model 1 except, 2 ball detents to hold barrel shut.

	$35	$30	$25	$20	$15	N/A	N/A

MILLARD BROTHERS

For information on Millard Brothers airguns, see Milbro in the this "M" section.

MONDIAL

For information on Mondial airguns, see MMM - Mondial in this section.

MONOGRAM

For information on Monogram, see Accles & Shelvoke Ltd. in the "A" section.

MONTGOMERY WARD

Catalog sales/retailer that has subcontracted various domestic and international manufacturers to private label various brand names under the Montgomery Ward conglomerate.

Montgomery Ward airguns have appeared under various labels and endorsers, including Western Field and others. Most of these models were manufactured through subcontracts with both domestic and international firms. Typically, they were "spec." airguns made to sell at a specific price to undersell the competition. Most of these models were derivatives of existing factory models with less expensive wood and perhaps missing the features found on those models from which they were derived. Please refer to the Store Brand Crossover Section in the back of this book under Montgomery Ward for converting models to the respective manufacturer.

To date, there has been limited interest in collecting Montgomery Ward airguns, regardless of rarity. Rather than list Montgomery Ward models, a general guideline is that values generally are under those of their "first generation relatives." As a result, prices are ascertained by the shooting value of the airgun, rather than its collector value.

MORINI COMPETITION ARM SA

Current manufacturer located in Bedano, Switzerland. Currently imported and distributed Pilkington Competition Equipment, located in Monteagle, TN, and by Champion´s Choice, located in LaVergne, TN. Previously imported 1993-2004 by Nygord Precision Products, located in Prescott, AZ.

For more information and current pricing on both new and used Morini Competition Arm SA firearms, please refer to the *Blue Book of Gun Values* by S.P. Fjestad (also available online).

PISTOLS

MODEL 162E - .177 cal., PCP, UIT pistol with fixed cylinder, electronic trigger, adj. sights, adj. grips.

	$795	$600	$450	$300	$225	N/A	N/A

Last MSR was $1,000.

MODEL 162EI/162EI SHORT - .177 cal., PCP, SS, match pistol, 7.41 (Short) or 9.36 in. Lothar Walther barrel, two detachable cylinders, black finish, Morini anatomical adj. wood grip, adj. electronic trigger, adj. sights, 2.2 lbs.

MSR	$1,400	$1,095	$950	$850	$750	$650	N/A	N/A

MODEL 162MI/162MI SHORT - .177 cal., similar to Model 162EI, except has mechanical trigger.

MSR	$1,400	$1,095	$950	$850	$750	$650	N/A	N/A

N SECTION

NATIONAL (KOREA)

Current status not known. Beeman Precision Airguns imported examples of one model in the mid-1970s.

GRADING	100%	95%	90%	80%	60%	40%	20%

RIFLES

NATIONAL VOLCANIC - .25 cal., SS, swinging lever pump pneumatic, with sliding loading port system identical to Yewha 3B air shotguns, requires same plastic shot tubes. Rifled barrel. No markings. Blued barrel and body tube, parkerized trigger guard. Excellent construction; much more detailed than Yewha. May have some association with Yewha or Tong II. 37 in. OAL, 6.6 lbs. Extremely rare in USA. Ref: AA Oct. 1987 (reprinted as Hannusch, 2001).

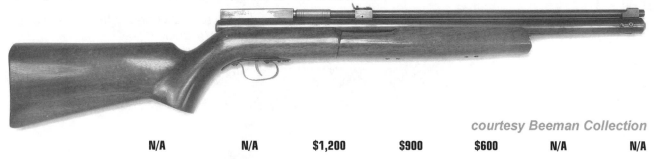

courtesy Beeman Collection

	100%	95%	90%	80%	60%	40%	20%
	N/A	N/A	$1,200	$900	$600	N/A	N/A

NATIONAL RIFLES LTD. (INDIA)

Current maker located in Ahmedabad, India. Distributed by Indian Hume Pipe Co. Ltd., Bombay, India.

India's leading airgun manufacturer; production based on German machinery and airgun designs. Walter (1984) reported that National produced a National Cadet CO_2 bulb rifle version of the Hammerli Cadet CO_2 rifle under a 1968 license from Hammerli and the National 25, as a simpler version of the Dianawerk Model 25.

NORICA FARMI S.A.L.

Current trademark manufactured by Norica-Farmi, S.A.L., located in Eibar, Spain. No current U.S. importation. Previously imported by American Arms, Inc., located in North Kansas City, MO, K.B.I., located in Harrisburg, PA, and by S.A.E., located in Miami, FL.

Norica produces several economy level, private label airguns. Norica airguns imported by American Arms, Inc. will appear under the American Arms, Inc. heading in this text.

RIFLES

MODEL 47 - .177 cal., SL, SP, 600 FPS, black pistol grip, 5.5 lbs.

	100%	95%	90%	80%	60%	40%	20%
	$120	$90	$65	$45	$35	N/A	N/A

MODEL 61C - .177 cal., BBC, SP, 600 FPS, 5.5 lbs.

	$85	$70	$50	$35	$25	N/A	N/A

MODEL 73 - .177 or .22 cal., BBC, SP, 580/525 FPS, 6 lbs. 4 oz.

	$110	$85	$60	$45	$30	N/A	N/A

MODEL 80G - .177 or .22 cal., BBC, SP, 635/570 FPS, 7 lbs. 2 oz.

	$140	$120	$80	$60	$40	N/A	N/A

MODEL 90 - .177 cal., BBC, SP, 650 FPS, includes scope.

	$130	$100	$75	$55	$40	N/A	N/A

MODEL 92 - .177 cal., SL, SP, 650 FPS, 5.75 lbs.

	$125	$95	$70	$55	$40	N/A	N/A

NORICA YOUNG - .177 cal., BBC, SP, 600 FPS, colored stock.

	$85	$70	$50	$35	$25	N/A	N/A

BLACK WIDOW - .177 or .22 cal., BBC, SP, 500/450 FPS, black plastic stock, 5 lbs.

	$120	$90	$65	$45	$35	N/A	N/A

GRADING	100%	95%	90%	80%	60%	40%	20%

NELSON PAINT COMPANY

Paint company located in Iron Mountain, MI, previous manufacturers of paintball markers founded in 1940.

Marketed the first paintball guns (invented by James C. Hale of Daisy, U.S. patent 3,788,298, Jan 29, 1974). Originally marketed to ranchers and foresters for marking cattle and trees. Undoubtedly, one day, a cowboy or ranger was holding a Nelson marking gun when he saw his partner, not too far away, bend over to pick something up. At that moment, the paintball combat game market was born! The first organized paintball game in 1981 used Nelson 007 pistols. The first paintball game gun was the Splatmaster (U.S. patent 4,531,503, Robert G Shepherd, July 30, 1985), also rather collectible, values $25 to $40.

Paintball markers are now a huge specialized field onto themselves (http://apg.cfw2.com/article.asp?content_id=7282) and thus will not be covered in this guide except where the models have historical connections with the regular airgun field.

Nelson tree markers today are specialized paint spraying devices, but the company continues to produce paintballs.

PISTOLS

NEL-SPOT 007 - .68 cal. paintball, 12 gm. CO_2 cylinder, eight- (ten with threaded ball tube) shot gravity-fed, bolt action, steel and brass construction, black paint finish, 3 lbs., 11 in. OAL. Mfg. by Daisy beginning 1974. Disc.

courtesy Beeman Collection

$200	$150	$100	$75	$50	N/A	N/A

Add 5% for holster.

Add 100% for early versions without removable barrel sleeve, magazine tube threaded inside to accept threaded aluminum paint ball tubes. Plastic pellet stop snapped into magazine center holes.

NEL-SPOT 707 - .68 cal. paintball, CO_2, six-ball gravity-fed magazine along LHS of receiver, blue finish, 11.6 in. OAL, 3.2 lbs. unloaded. Disc.

courtesy Beeman Collection

$400	$325	$250	$175	$100	N/A	N/A

Add 5% for holster.

Briefly made by Crosman, apparently before the 007.

O SECTION

O´CONNELL GAS RIFLE

Previous trade name manufactured by the George Robinson Co. located in Rochester, NY circa 1947-49. See George Robinson Co. in the "R" section.

OKLAHOMA

For information on Oklahoma airguns, see MMM – Mondial in the "M" section.

NOTES

Elegant double barrel, .40 caliber combination powder/air rifle apparently built in Austria in mid 1800s. The left barrel is part of a muzzle-loading percussion fire arm system. Right barrel is part of a breech-loading, pneumatic air gun system. Pushing a lever within the trigger guard causes a breech block, its incredibly finely fitted surface outline hidden by the deep engraving, to pop up for loading a lead ball. The airgun system is cocked by pulling back the right hammer. Note that there is no percussion cap nipple on right side of the receiver as there is on the left. A power adjustment lever marked to IV represents game levels such as "wild boar, deer, fox, rabbit." Very deeply engraved and deeply inlaid with gold. Photo by R.W. Atkinson, Beeman collection.

P SECTION

PAFF

Previous tradename used by the merchant Henry Schuermans located in Liege, Belgium.

In 1890, Henry Schuermans registered the bow and arrow trademark, with the letters "PAFF", found on the airgun discussed here. Schuermans was the producer and/or distributor for the Paff air rifle patented by L. Poilvache of Leige under Belgian patents – number 76743 (March 1887), 79663 (November, 1887) and 84461 (December, 1888). This most unusual barrel-cocking, spring piston, .177 cal. air rifle has a 3.5 in. long air chamber which resembles the cylinder on a Colt revolving rifle. This chamber contains three concentric mainsprings which power a hollow piston. 37.7 in. OAL, 5.1 lbs. Retail values will be in the $1,000-$2,000+ range. Ref: John Atkins, AG, Feb. 2003.

PAINTBALL

For information on Paintball, see Nelson in the "N" section.

PALMER

Previous trade name used by Frank D. Palmer Inc., Chicago, IL.

Frank D. Palmer Inc., Chicago, IL, maker of carnival machine guns. Research on this brand is ongoing and additional material will be published in this guide series and on the web as available. Information is actively solicited at BBA6info@Beemans.net.

MACHINE GUN

"CONEY ISLAND" MACHINE GUN - .174 BB cal., not known if steel or lead, or both, electric drive of horizontally rotating feeding disc which is gravity fed from top BB hopper, approximately one hundred balls, dual spade handle grips with RH trigger built in. 69 in. tall, 20 in. wide, about 300 pounds on original steel stand, black paint finish, marked with eagle shaped logo plate bearing Palmer name.

courtesy Beeman Collection

Value in good condition about $2000.

PALMER CHEMICAL AND EQUIPMENT CO.

Current manufacturer of tranquilizer guns located in Douglasville, GA.

Manufacturers of Palmer CapChur tranquilizer guns, generally based on CO_2 models of Crosman airguns. Generally use a small explosive charge in the syringe dart to force out the contents into the target, but the guns themselves are not firearms. Please contact the company directly for more information and prices of current products (see Trademark Index listing).

GRADING	100%	95%	90%	80%	60%	40%	20%

PISTOLS

STANDARD CAPCHUR PISTOL - .50 cal. tranquilizer darts, SS, CO_2, bolt action, contained small explosive charge for injecting the contents of the syringe dart into the animal to be subdued. Mid-twentieth century.

courtesy Beeman Collection

	100%	95%	90%	80%	60%	40%	20%
	$250	$200	$150	$100	$75	N/A	N/A

GRADING	100%	95%	90%	80%	60%	40%	20%

VET 4X CHAPCHUR PISTOL - more recent version of Standard CapChur pistol.

courtesy Beeman Collection

	$200	$150	$100	$85	$65	N/A	N/A

RIFLES

RED'S SPECIAL - .50 cal. tranquilizer darts, SS, CO_2, bolt action, contained small explosive charge for injecting the contents of the syringe dart into the animal to be subdued. Mid-twentieth century.

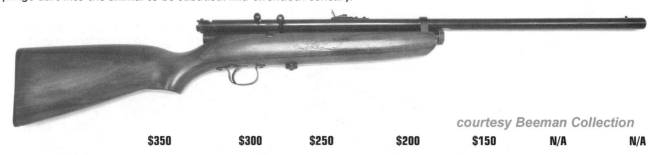

courtesy Beeman Collection

	$350	$300	$250	$200	$150	N/A	N/A

PAMPANGA

For information on Pampanga airguns, see Philippine Airguns in this "P" section.

PANTHER

For information on Panther airguns, see Gun Toys SRL in the "G" section.

PARDINI, ARMI S.r.l.

Current manufacturer located in Lido di Camaiore, Italy. Currently imported by Larry's Guns, located in Portland, ME. Previously imported by Nygord Precision Products, located in Prescott, AZ, by MCS, Inc.

For more information and current pricing on both new and used Pardini firearms, please refer to the *Blue Book of Gun Values* by S.P. Fjestad (also available online).

PISTOLS

MODEL K-2 - .177 cal., CO_2, (250-shot capacity), UIT model, 10 in. barrel, adj. trigger, adj. walnut grip.

	MSR	$999	$950	$750	$650	$550	$450	N/A	N/A

MODEL K-2S - .177 cal., similar to Model K-2, with PCP system.

	MSR	$999	$950	$775	$675	$575	$475	N/A	N/A

MODEL K58 - .177 cal., UL, 9 in. barrel, UIT model, 2 lbs. 6 oz.

	MSR	$799	$650	$575	$450	$350	$275	N/A	N/A

MODEL K60 - .177 cal., CO_2, 9.5 in. barrel, 2 lbs. 4 oz. Disc. 1997.

		$500	$450	$400	$325	$250	N/A	N/A

Last MSR was $795.

Add 20% for pre-charged pneumatic.

MODEL K90 - .177 cal. CO_2, youth model, 7.25 in. barrel, 1.85 lbs.

	$450	$375	$300	$250	$175	N/A	N/A

Last MSR was $580.

MODEL P10 - .177 cal., UL, 7.75 in. barrel, 2 lbs. 3 oz. Disc. 1990.

	$400	$350	$300	$250	$175	N/A	N/A

Last MSR was $560.

GRADING	100%	95%	90%	80%	60%	40%	20%

PARK RIFLE COMPANY

Current manufacturer located in Kent, England. No current U.S. importation.

RIFLES

RH93/93W/93-800 - .177 or .22 cal., UL, 12ft./lb. energy, 37 or 38 (Model 93-800) in. barrel. 9 lbs. 10 oz.

	MSR	$500	$400	$350	$275	$200	$135	N/A	N/A

Add $100 for thumbhole walnut stock.

PARKER-HALE

Parker was the previous tradename of the A.G. Parker Company located in Birmingham, England, which was formed from a gun-making business founded in 1890 by Alfred Gray Parker. The company became the Parker-Hale company in 1936. Purchased by John Rothery Wholesale about 2000.

This firm made an air pistol designed by Alfred Hale and Ernest Harris and Lee-Enfield sporter firearm rifles. For more information and current pricing on Parker-Hale firearms, please refer to the *Blue Book of Gun Values* by S.P. Fjestad (also available online).

PISTOLS

These guns are often referred to as the "Parker-Hale" air pistols. However, this is not correct, as these pistols were made about 1921 and the Parker-Hale Company did not come into existence until 1936.

PARKER PATENT PRECISION AIR PISTOL - .177 cal,. SP, SS, fixed rifled 9.6 in. BBL, piston moves rearward during firing. Cocked by turning a large crank on the RHS 3.5 turns; crank remains attached to gun at all times but disengages internally for firing; blued finish. Loaded by unscrewing a large knurled screw on the breech block and swinging the loading gate downward. A built-in pellet seater could help swage the pellet into place. Later production had a two-diameter compression cylinder/body tube, there was a larger diameter area between the barrel support and about the middle of the wooden grip. Serial numbers known to 215. 10.6 in. OAL, 3.3 lbs. Ref: John Atkins, AG, April 1992: 65.

courtesy Beeman Collection

	N/A	N/A	$1,750	$1,500	$1,250	$1,000	$750

Add 10% for first version with single-diameter body tube.

RIFLES

PHOENIX MK 1 - .177 or .22 cal., PCP, detachable air cylinder in buttstock, ten-shot BSA Superten magazine, lever action cocking, beech stock. Mfg. circa 1998-99.

Current values not yet determined.

Designed by Graham Bluck.

PHOENIX MK 2 - .22 cal., PCP, detachable air cylinder in buttstock, new repeater magazine, other design improvements, deluxe walnut stock. Intro. 2004.

courtesy Tim Saunders

Current values not yet determined.

DRAGON - .177 or .22 cal., SSP, SS, walnut sporter stock (about twelve with large FT stocks). Mk1 and Mk 2 variants: identical except for hardened valve in Mk 2, 40 in. OAL. Made about 1995.

	$400	$350	$275	$195	$150	N/A	N/A

Designed by Graham Bluck.

GRADING	100%	95%	90%	80%	60%	40%	20%

PARRIS MANUFACTURING COMPANY

Previous manufacturer located in Savannah, TN.

Company began in Iowa in 1943 making toy guns (pop guns, cork guns, Kadet training rifles, etc). Made a few bolt action military training firearm rifles during WW2. Moved to Savannah, TN circa 1953. BB guns manufactured circa 1960 - 1970 when the company became a Division of Gayla Industries. All BB rifles with decal, on RHS buttstock, usually marked "Kadet" or "Trainer" but w/o model number. Additional research is underway on this complex group. Information given here must be considered as tentative. Information and illustrations is solicited at BBA6info@Beemans.net . The authors and publisher wish to thank John Groenewold for his valuable assistance with the following information in this edition of the Blue Book of Airguns.

PISTOLS

KADET 507 - .174 cal., SP, SS, BB or Cork, 11 in. OAL.

	100%	95%	90%	80%	60%	40%	20%
	$150	$140	$120	$100	$80	$60	$40

RIFLES

KADET 500 - .174 cal., SP, LA, "Selector Loader" mechanism at muzzle holds 50 BBs; twisting it releases 1 to 6 BBs to be fired together at one time, magnetic shot retainer holds BBs until fired, one piece wood stock, 30 in. OAL, 2.6 lbs.

courtesy Beeman Collection

	100%	95%	90%	80%	60%	40%	20%
	$150	$140	$120	$100	$80	$60	$40

KADET 501 - .174 cal. BB or cork., SS, SP, LA, 32 in. OAL, 2.6 lbs.

	100%	95%	90%	80%	60%	40%	20%
	$150	$140	$120	$100	$80	$60	$40

Add 40% for shooting kit model 501WT.

KADET 502 - .174 cal., SP, LA, "Selector Loader" mechanism at muzzle holds 50 BBs; twisting it releases 1 to 6 BBs to be fired together at one time, magnetic shot retainer holds BBs until fired, one piece wood stock, 37.5 in. OAL, 3.2 lbs.

courtesy Beeman Collection

	100%	95%	90%	80%	60%	40%	20%
	$150	$140	$120	$100	$80	$60	$40

Add 40% for shooting kit model 502WT.

KADET 504 - similar to Kadet 502 except, army style stock and 1 inch sling.

	100%	95%	90%	80%	60%	40%	20%
	$200	$175	$150	$125	$100	$75	$50

Add 40% for shooting kit model 504WT.

KADET "X" (MODEL NO. UNKOWN) - .174 cal., SP, LA, plastic muzzle piece and rectangular assembly under the barrel near muzzle houses safety, 37 in. OAL, 2.9 lbs. Mfg. circa 1969-1970.

courtesy Beeman Collection

	100%	95%	90%	80%	60%	40%	20%
	$250	$225	$200	$175	$150	$125	$100

Probably last configuration of BB gun made by Parris Manufacturing Company.

GRADING	100%	95%	90%	80%	60%	40%	20%

PAUL

Previously trademark manufactured by William Paul located in Beecher, IL.

Pump pneumatic SS shotgun with bicycle-type pump under barrel. To charge, fold out the foot pedal on the forward end of pump rod held to ground, and gun moved up and down for about seventy strong strokes. Additional strokes needed between shots. See *Airgun Journal* 4(1) - 1983, AGNR - Apr. 1987.

SHOTGUNS

MODEL 420 - .410 cal., smoothbore barrel slides forward for breech loading, nickel plated brass receiver, barrel, and pump; cast aluminum buttplate, and trigger guard; 43 in. overall, walnut stock, shotshells are brass tubes with wad at each end, cardboard shotshells illustrated on cover of cartridge box not known, each shell contains about 32 pellets number 6 birdshot (1/6 oz.). Jan. 1924 patent shows cocking rod in pistol grip (apparently never produced). Production followed Sept. 1924 patent with cocking rod projecting from forearm. Two variants (with small variations within each type): 6.5 lbs., approx. 1,000 mfg. mid-1920s to mid-1930s.

❋ *Ringed Variant* - barrel and pump tube connected by soldered rings, barrel flat spring soldered to body tube.

courtesy Beeman Collection

N/A	$1,250	$995	$895	$795	$650	$400

Add 25% for original shotshell loading kit.

❋ *Banded Variant* - barrel and pump tube connected by soldered bands, barrel flat spring clamped to body tube.

courtesy Beeman Collection

N/A	$1,000	$900	$850	$750	$700	$600

Add 25% for original shotshell loading kit.

MODEL 420 REPLICA - excellent replicas of the Paul Shotgun were made by Dennis Quackenbush (See Quackenbush Air Guns in the "Q" section). Approx. 10 mfg. 1994.

courtesy Beeman Collection

N/A	$850	$750	$700	$600	$500	$400

Add 50% for "Mule" version with pressure gauge on compression chamber for experimental studies by the maker.
Add 30% for early version.

PEERLESS

Previous tradename used pre-WWII by Stoeger Arms of New York for airguns imported from Germany, probably all from Dianawerk, using original Dianawerk model numbers. See Dianawerk in the "D" section of this book for more information.

PENNY'S, J.C.

Catalog sales/retailer that has subcontracted manufacturers to private label airguns.

To date, there has been limited interest in collecting J.C. Penny's airguns, regardless of rarity. Rather than list models, a general guideline is that values generally are under those of their "first generation relatives." As a result, prices have been ascertained by the shooting value of the airgun, rather than its collector value. See "Store Brand Crossover List" located in the back of this text.

GRADING	100%	95%	90%	80%	60%	40%	20%

PERFECTA

Apparently a private brand name used for at least a copy of the Milbro Diana SP50 air pistol.

Perfecta was a brand name for spring piston airguns made by Oskar Will of Zella Mehlis, Germany in the 1920s for the Midland Gun Company of Birmingham, England, so it may have been resurrected by Midland Gun Company, or another company, for use on this pistol which was made in the British Diana form from the mid-1970s to 1982.

PISTOL

PERFECTA SP50 - .177 cal., darts or pellets, push barrel SP, SS, die-cast body, black paint finish.

courtesy Beeman Collection

	$25	$20	$15	$10	N/A	N/A	N/A

Same as the Milbro Diana SP50.

PHILIPPINE AIRGUNS

There has been a thriving production of airguns in the Philippines for many years – most of these are especially powerful, bulk fill CO_2 guns for hunting.

There has been a thriving production of airguns in the Philippines since the 1970s. The reason for this and why the spring piston airgun revolution largely bypassed the Philippines basically was due to one man: President/Dictator Ferdinand Edralin Marcos. In 1972 [1], Marco declared martial law and all gun importations were stopped, including importation of airguns. All firearms were confiscated except for those belonging to people who were able to get a special license only for pistols under 9mm, .22 rimfire rifles, and shotguns. Even those guns became hard to get because of the ban on importation. Local supplies of American airguns, like the popular Crosman 114 and 160, and precision European airguns, quickly dried up. The Squires Bingham Company tried to resurrect the Crosman 160, but this failed and, in any case, that gun was not up to the hunting standards of Philippine shooters. Airgun clubs dedicated to the precision shooting sports closed because of the halt in the importation of precision airguns; there were no precision airguns produced locally. Philippine shooters suddenly needed airguns, but mainly they wanted power for hunting. Spring piston airguns and guns using soda pop cartridges were not up to their needs, and PCP guns were not a viable choice due to the difficult filling requirements. Bulk fill CO_2 was the answer for this new hunter-driven market. Bulk fill CO_2 guns were light and easy to fill from a 10 oz. tank on the shooter's belt and the cylinders could be filled easily and cheaply at many places. So the Philippines became a hunter's airgun market, not a precision airgun market!

The most interesting things about Philippine airguns are their power, freewheeling designs, and their variety. Separate sections of this guide now give an introduction to some of the main Philippine brands found in the USA: Some of the best known makers are LD, Farco, MC Topgun, Valesquez, Valiente, Rogunz, Koffmanz, JBC, Harlie, Isaac, Garco, Centerpoint, Trident, Dreibund, Armscor (SB), and Spitfire. Some especially interesting guns are the beautifully made sidelever "Pampanga-type" CO_2 guns.

It is reported that the majority of the Philippine airguns that have come into the USA were brought via service men who purchased them in the Philippines. This was especially true of the LD airguns; apparently about 20% to 25% of their production came in via that route. Several models of Philippine airguns also have been imported into the USA by Air Rifle Specialties in New York and Bryan and Associates in South Carolina. (Dave Schwesinger, owner of Air Rifle Specialties in New York, used to live in the Philippines and spent a lot of time in the LD airgun shop).

All Philippine hunting airguns are relatively scarce. Production ran from an average of less than one hundred guns per month for LD, evidently the largest maker, down to a few guns a month from a custom maker such as JBC. Perhaps 70% to 99% of most production runs stayed in the Philippines. Most American and European airgun factories, and large importers, figure on several thousand or tens of thousands of guns per month. Thus Philippine hunting airguns are very desirable from an airgun hunter's or collector's standpoint.

[1] By interesting coincidence, this was just about the time that the adult airgun market in the USA got its first significant commercial start, based primarily on spring-piston airguns. (See www.beemans.net/adult_airguns_in_america.htm.)

A sampling of Philippine airguns is given below. See the "L" section for LD airguns and the "F" section for Farco airguns.

JBC/LD/PAMPANGA/ROGUNZ/VALESQUEZ/UNKNOWN MAKERS

Selected brands (all are CO_2 bulk fill and in calibers .177 to .25 as specified by buyer):

JBC - High end, small maker. Valve body and stem aluminum or brass. 12-groove rifling. Expansion chambers.

✳ ***Monkey Gun*** - .22 cal., SS, BA rifle, thumbhole stock, 33.9 in. OAL, 6.3 lbs, approx. 725 FPS. Serial numbers up to 3 are known. 1987. Value approx. $1250.

courtesy Beeman Collection

LD - For more info and other LD models, see LD Airguns in the "L" section of this guide.

✳ ***LD 380 (Rancher)*** - four caliber combo: .50 in. smoothbore, .380 smoothbore insert, .22 cal. rifled insert, .177 cal. rifled insert. This caliber range gave the Rancher amazing flexibility: it could project .177 or .22 cal. pellets, .38 cal. shot charges, .38 cal. bullets or lead balls, arrows w/o fletching, expanding tip spears, multi-prong spears, .50 in. tranquilizer darts, and even shaped TNT charges in brass "torpedoes." A spinning reel mounted under the forearm enhanced fishing and frog hunting. Laminated two-tone Narra stock.

PAMPANGA - This is not a brand, but a geographical group of guns made in the central Luzon section of the Philippines in the region of the former U.S. Clark Air Force Base. This area was turned into hundreds of square miles of desert by the massive Pinatubo volcanic explosion. The Pampanga guns are especially designed for hunting the wild dogs and ducks which now abound there. The identifying characteristics are: 1) extensive use of red Narra wood (very decorative, but too heavy according to some); 2) finely made stainless steel parts; brass or stainless steel valve parts; 3) removeable CO_2 reservoirs extended under the barrel; 4) straight-pull bolt action or a modified LD-type hammer swing action. 5) unusually good fitting of parts; 6) lack of an expansion chamber so that these guns may dump CO_2 as fast as possible for maximum power; 7) twelve-groove rifling. Not all Pampanga guns have the above features. Some are high end copies of LD, JBC, Rogunz, and other brands. The best way to identify unmarked Philippine bulk fill CO_2 guns is to count the rifling grooves; the Pampanga guns almost always have twelve grooves while most of the main line Philippine guns have seven- or eight-groove rifling. Also, Pampanga guns have brass or stainless steel valves, while others have only brass valve bodies (or brass or aluminum, in the case of JBC guns) with Teflon valve stems (white for LD, colored for Rogunz).

There are very few shops in the Pampanga area, especially in the City of San Fernando, that specialize in acquiring these guns from very small makers (two- or three-man operations) who do not produce more than five or six guns a month. Pampanga airguns are the most expensive airguns in the Philippines, but generally are the finest and most desired of all Philippine airguns. Values begin circa $1250. Because they are made for the retailers, they generally do not bear any conspicuous sign of the maker. However, close examination of the reservoir and areas hidden by the stock often reveals small marks of the actual maker.

✳ ***Pampanga Rifle*** - .22 cal., 47.3 in. OAL, straight pull bolt action.

courtesy Beeman Collection

✳ ***Pampanga Shotgun*** - 20 ga., 57.4 in. OAL, straight pull bolt action, almost entirely stainless steel.

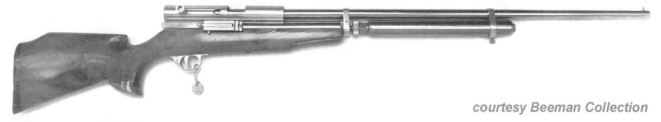

courtesy Beeman Collection

ROGUNZ - Major maker. Seven- or eight-groove rifling, valve body of Tiger brass; value stem of Teflon, lock ring (bolt retaining ring) is always knurled. Expansion chambers.

✳ *Falcon 1-132* - SS, hammer swing match rifle. Value about $750.

courtesy Beeman Collection

✳ *Match Model* - .22 cal., turning bolt, robust match stock with decorative panels cut in forearm, lateral easy-feed magazine on RHS. Expansion chamber.

courtesy Beeman Collection

UNKNOWN MAKERS - Perhaps as a result of subcontracting gun construction, many of the Philippine airguns are not marked. An example is this well made, bulk fill, long range pistol, made in .22 and .25 calibers, hand checkered black ebony wood grips, no maker's name, two specimens marked only "1" and "2" on hidden grip frame area. 14.6 OAL.

courtesy Beeman Collection

Value estimated at $295 in 90% condition.

VALESQUEZ - seven or eight-groove rifling, valve body of Tiger brass; valve stem of Teflon. Expansion chambers.

✳ *Brass Beauty* - .22 in. cal., SS, bolt action, barrel and most metal parts are brass. Value about $850.

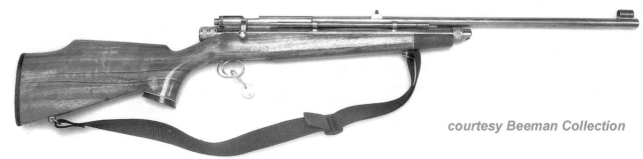

courtesy Beeman Collection

✳ *Bolt Action Match Rifle* - value about $700.

courtesy Beeman Collection

GRADING	100%	95%	90%	80%	60%	40%	20%

PIPER

Current manufacturer located in Lanposa, TX beginning circa 1999. Piper Precision Products, founded by Paul Piper, currently manufactures CO_2 driven, fully automatic airguns (and softair guns).

Research is ongoing with this trademark, and more information will be included both online and in future editions.

RIFLES: AUTOMATIC

MINI-VULCAN - .174/steel BB cal., CO_2, portable 12 oz. tank mounted in center axis of six rotating barrels, laser sight, powered by onboard DC motor, 1200 rounds per minute, portable gun fired from arm sling, machined aluminum and steel, some optional features. 24 in. OAL, 22 lbs. 20 mfg. Ref: AR4: 75-76.

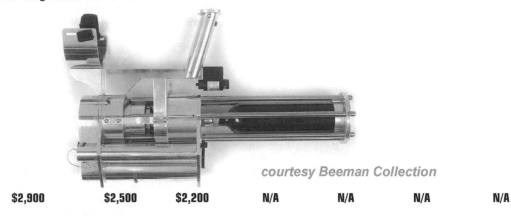

courtesy Beeman Collection

	100%	95%	90%	80%	60%	40%	20%
	$2,900	$2,500	$2,200	N/A	N/A	N/A	N/A

PLYMOUTH AIR RIFLE COMPANY

Previous manufacturer of cast iron BB guns located in Plymouth, Michigan circa 1891.

Apparently based on patents of Merritt Stanley and/or G.W. Sage. Guns were produced under the MAGIC label only during one year, after which the patents, tools ,and supplies were sold to George Decker who formed the Decker Manufacturing Company in Detroit, Michigan. For more information on Plymoth Air Rifle Co. airguns, see Decker in the "D" section.

PNEUDART, INC.

Current marketers of tranquilizer guns located in Williamsport, PA.

Manufacturers of tranquilizer guns Models 176 (CO_2) and 178 (pneumatic) single shot rifles plus the models 179 and 190 CO_2 pistols. They also supply firearm dart projectors and tranquilizer supplies. Guns and parts made by Benjamin/Crosman. Crosman parts diagrams and Crosman parts numbers. Evidently, repeating air "projectors" are no longer available. Please contact the company directly for more information and prices of their products (see Trademark Index listing).

RIFLES

MODEL 167 - .50 in. cal., three-shot sliding magazine repeater, CO_2 charged. Blue steel, hardwood stock, 37.2 in. OAL, 6.6 lbs.

courtesy Beeman Collection

	100%	95%	90%	80%	60%	40%	20%
	$350	$300	$250	$200	$150	N/A	N/A

PODIUM

Previous trademark of Sportil S.A. Portal De Gamarra, Vitoria, Spain.

From 1983 to 1987, Sportil manufactured and distributed three CO_2 powered guns. Each bore an uncanny resemblance to an obsolete Crosman model, but this firm says that Sportil did not manufacture under license. Although they were well made and very reliable, Podium gas guns had a very limited international distribution. The authors and publisher wish to thank Trevor Adams thank for his valuable assistance with the following information in this edition of the *Blue Book of Airguns*.

GRADING	100%	95%	90%	80%	60%	40%	20%

PISTOLS

MODEL 284 - BB cal., CO_2, repeating pistol and a clone of the Crosman Model 454.

	$80	$55	$40	$30	N/A	N/A	N/A

RIFLES

MODEL 186 - BB cal., CO_2, BA, fires a single pellet or BBs from a magazine, outwardly resembling the Crosman 766 pneumatic rifle, powerlet concealed beneath the forearm.

	$100	$80	$65	$50	$35	N/A	N/A

MODEL 286 - BB cal., CO_2, BA, similar to Crosman Model 70, fires either a single lead pellet or BBs from an eight-shot mag., powerlet lies in the forearm, knurled ring, halfway along the plastic barrel shroud, helps prevent barrel warp in the noonday sun (maybe).

	$120	$95	$80	$65	$50	N/A	N/A

POPE

Previous tradename of Pope Brothers located in Boston, MA.

At least part-time producers and sellers of a spring piston air pistol invented by H.M. Quackenbush. Patented in 1874, this was not Quackenbush´s first air pistol, as sometimes reported, but it was the basis for the Bedford, Bedford & Walker, Johnson and Bye, and later Quackenbush air pistols and other airguns. Produced from at least 1871. Pope received the rights to the gun in 1874, but abandoned the original Quackenbush design later, allowing Quackenbush to have the patent reissued to him. Quackenbush reported sales of seventy-four Eureka air pistols in 1884. Some of the never-to-be-completely-unraveled features of the relationship of Pope and other makers of this time and place in America are summarized in the Johnson & Bye listing in the "J" section of this guide.

PISTOLS/RIFLES

POPE PISTOL/RIFLE - .210 cal., SP, SS, pull-barrel cocking and loading, Japan black enamel or nickel finish, hole in grip base for wire shoulder stock, 12 in. OAL. Mfg. circa 1871-1885.

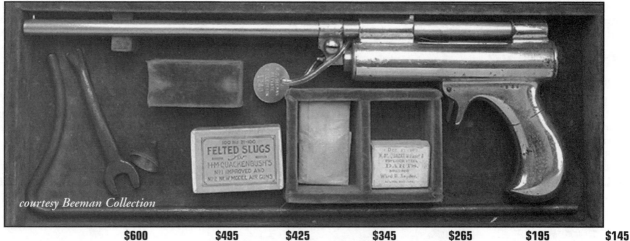

courtesy Beeman Collection

	$600	$495	$425	$345	$265	$195	$145

Add 10% for H.M. Quackenbush name stamped on gun, with patent dates.
Add 10% for nickel finish.
Add 10% for wire shoulder stock.
Add 20% for factory fitted wooden case.

POWERLINE

For information on Powerline, see Daisy in the "D" section.

PRECHARGE AB

Current manufacturer located in Hova, Sweden.

During 2002 PRECharge AB changed its name to FX Airguns AB. PRECharge AB are the manufacturers of FX trademark airguns imported and/or distributed by ARS, Airguns of Arizona, RWS, and Webley & Scott. See FX Airguns AB listing in the "F" section.

RIFLES

FX EXCALIBRE - .177 or .22 cal., PCP, bolt action, eight-shot rotary mag., 21 in. choked Lothar Walther rifled barrel, high gloss blue finish, checkered walnut Monte-Carlo style stock with Schnabel forend and recoil pad, adj. trigger, receiver grooved for scope, 7 lbs.

No MSR	$995	$800	$700	$575	N/A	N/A	N/A

Add 20% for deluxe Turkish walnut stock.

GRADING	100%	95%	90%	80%	60%	40%	20%

PREDOM

For information on Predom airguns, see Lucznik in the "L" section.

PRODUSIT

Previous manufacturer located in Birmingham, England.

Produsit Ltd., previous makers of a concentric piston air pistol very similar to the Tell II in design, but somewhat larger.

PISTOLS

THUNDERBOLT JUNIOR - .177 cal, SP, SS, concentric piston design, cocked with lever which includes the backstrap, rear loading cover, brown plastic grips marked with "THUNDERBOLT JUNIOR", a lightning bolt, and "MADE IN ENGLAND", 6.7 in. OAL. Approx. 8000 mfg. circa 1947-49.

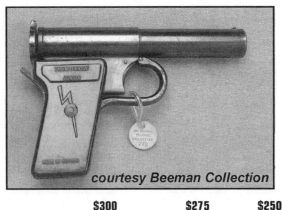

courtesy Beeman Collection

	100%	95%	90%	80%	60%	40%	20%
	$300	$275	$250	$175	$135	$100	$75

RIFLES

BIG CHIEF - .174/BB cal., SS, SP, break action, folded metal construction, slab sided hardwood stock with colored decal: "BIG CHIEF AIR GUN BRITISH MADE". No other markings. Patented Feb.13, 1952, blue steel finish, 31.7 in. OAL, 2.5 lbs. Ref: Trevor Adams, Dec. 1991, New Zealand Guns Magazine. (Also known with Abbey Alert decal on stock and "Prov Pat 33207" on frame. May have been a premium gun and may appear with other labels.). 1950s.

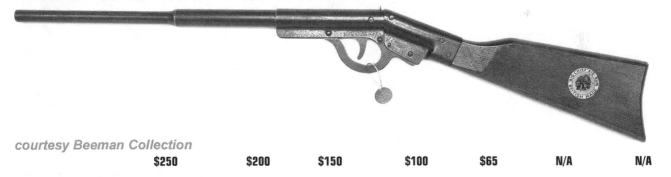

courtesy Beeman Collection

	100%	95%	90%	80%	60%	40%	20%
	$250	$200	$150	$100	$65	N/A	N/A

PYRAMYD AIR INTERNATIONAL

Current importer and distributor located in Pepper Pike, OH.

Pyramyd Air International imports and markets the largest caliber air rifle in mass production, the Big Bore 909, manufactured in Korea by Sam Yang.

Pyramyd Air International also imports Air Arms, China Shanghai, Umarex, Gamo, IZH-Baikal, Rutten, Tau Brno, Walther, Webley & Scott Ltd./Venom, and Weihrauch airguns. Please refer to these individual listings in this text

RIFLES

MODEL 909 BIG BORE 44 - .45 cal., PCP, 550-775 FPS (670 FPS with cast .454 190 gr. SWC), 670 FPS, 22.25 in. rifled barrel, carved and checkered walnut stock, 7.5 lbs. Mfg. 2000-04.

	100%	95%	90%	80%	60%	40%	20%
	$525	$450	$350	$300	$150	N/A	N/A

Last MSR was $585.

MODEL 909S BIG BORE 45 - .45 cal., PCP, 550-775 FPS (670 FPS with cast .454 190 gr. SWC), 670 FPS, 21.65 in. rifled barrel, carved and checkered walnut stock, 42.1 in. OAL, 7.15 lbs. New 2005.

		100%	95%	90%	80%	60%	40%	20%
MSR	$600	$500	$425	$350	$300	$150	N/A	N/A

DRAGON MODEL - .50 cal., PCP, SS, BA, 22. in. rifled barrel, adj. trigger, checkered hardwood stock, rubber butt pad. New 2004.

		100%	95%	90%	80%	60%	40%	20%
MSR	$650	$575	$495	$450	$350	$250	N/A	N/A

NOTES

Q SECTION

QUACKENBUSH, DENNIS

Current manufacturer located in Urbana, MO beginning in 1992.

In addition to the listed models, Dennis Quackenbush has also produced a wide variety of single order items and some excellent replicas of antique airguns, such as External Lock ("Liege Lock") Air Rifles and Paul Air Shotguns (see Paul in the "Q" section of this guide). See a wider range and notice of current products at www.quackenbushairguns.com or contact Mr. Quackenbush at quackenbushairguns@yahoo.com.

GRADING	100%	95%	90%	80%	60%	40%	20%

PISTOLS

These pistols were custom manufactured action and barrel conversions for the Crosman Models SSP 250 and 2240 pistols.

PISTOL - .25, 9mm, or .375 cal., CO_2 or PCP, SS, BA, 8-11 in. rifled barrel, blue finish, adj. rear sight. Approx. 450 mfg. Disc.

courtesy Beeman Collection

	$250	$200	$125	$75	$50	N/A	N/A

Add 100% for shotshell version (four made).

OUTLAW - .25, .308, 9mm, .45, or .50 (limited) cal., PCP, SS, BA, 10-14 in. rifled barrel, approx. 850/500 FPS, blue finish, adj. rear sight. New 2005.

	$500	$500	$400	$300	N/A	N/A	N/A

Add $10 for carbine buttstock.

RIFLES

XL - .22 cal., CO_2 or PCP, SS, removable bottle, Lothar Walther barrel, 650-850 FPS, blue finish, walnut stock, 35 in. OAL, 6.75-7 lbs. Mfg. beginning in 1994. Disc.

	$425	$350	$285	$225	$175	N/A	N/A

BANDIT - .50 cal., PCP, SS, fixed reservoir, 26 in. rifled steel barrel, 780 (.50 cal.) FPS, blue finish, American walnut stock, 43 in. OAL, 7.25 lbs. New 2000.

MSR	$535	$495	$425	$375	$295	N/A	N/A

Add 5% for Standard grade with deluxe blue.
Add 10% for Select grade with deluxe blue and select stock.
Add 15% for Superior grade with deluxe stock or master blue.

BRIGAND - .375 cal., CO_2 (128 mfg.) or PCP (10 mfg. 1998-99), SS, fixed reservoir, rifled steel barrel, 600-800 FPS, blue finish, walnut stock, 41 in. OAL, 7.25 lbs. Mfg. 1996-99.

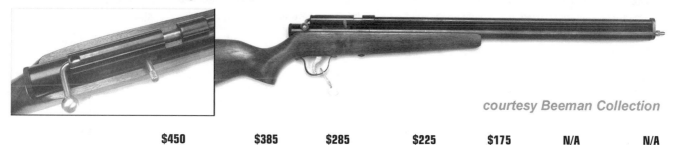

courtesy Beeman Collection

	$450	$385	$285	$225	$175	N/A	N/A

Add 20% for PCP.

EXILE - .308 cal., PCP, SS, fixed reservoir, 26 in. rifled steel barrel, 780 (.50 cal.) FPS, blue finish, American walnut stock, 43 in. OAL, 7.25 lbs. New 2000.

MSR	$495	$495	$425	$375	$295	N/A	N/A

Subtract 5% for service grade.
Add 5% for select grade.

GRADING	100%	95%	90%	80%	60%	40%	20%

LAIDY SPECIAL - .22 cal., uses Brocock-type air cartridges (large style, about size of 20 ga. Shotgun cartridge), BA, SS. No oper sights, grooved for scope. No markings. 41.8 in OAL, 5.3 lbs. with scope. One specimen known, about 1997.

courtesy Beeman Collection

	$450	N/A	N/A	N/A	N/A	N/A	N/A

LIGHT SPORTER - .22 cal., CO_2 or PCP, SS, fixed reservoir, Lothar Walther barrel, 650-850 FPS, blue finish, walnut stock, 35 in. OAL 6.75-7 lbs. Mfg. circa 1995-96.

	$425	$350	$285	$225	$175	N/A	N/A

ROGUE - .44 cal., PCP, SS, fixed reservoir, rifled steel barrel, 800 FPS, blue finish, walnut stock, 41 in. OAL, 7.25 lbs. Approx. 40 mfg in 1999 only.

	$550	$485	$385	$325	$275	N/A	N/A

QUACKENBUSH, H.M. AIR RIFLES

Previous manufacturer located in Herkimer, NY from 1871 to 1943.

The first airguns made by Henry. M. Quackenbush were air pistols. (See Bedford & Walker, Johnson & Bye, and Pope sections of this guide.) They are not included here because they were not marked with model identification or serial numbers, thus are very difficult to identify.

The authors and publisher wish to thank Mr. John Groenewold for his valuable assistance with the following information in this edition of *Blue Book of Airguns*.

The H.M. Quackenbush factory began air rifle production in 1876. The airguns sold from 1929 to 1943 were assembled from parts on hand. During that time no parts manufacturing occurred, only airgun assembly. Some airguns made after 1903 had two-part serial numbers, separated by a hyphen. The number to the left of the hyphen is the model number. These guns were available in several different types of boxes. The Model 1 came with a combination wrench and a cast iron dart removal tool. The other airguns came with a steel dart removal tool. Airguns with these accessories will command significantly more than the listed prices.

H.M. Quackenbush also produced airgun ammunition, rimfire rifles, and targets. For precise identification of all models and more information on the guns and accessories manufactured by H.M. Quackenbush, see the book *Quackenbush Guns*, by John Groenewold. Price adjustments for "original bluing" below mean factory bluing or browning applied instead of nickel plating before the gun left the factory. Reblued or replated guns are substantially lower in value.

For more information and current pricing on used Quackenbush firearms, please refer to the *Blue Book of Gun Values* by S.P. Fjestad (also available online).

Square loading port detail   *Spoon shape loading port detail*   *Round loading port detail*   *Model 9/10 muzzle cap detail*

courtesy Beeman Collection

RIFLES

MODEL EXCELSIOR - .21 cal., spring powered, SS, smooth bore, nickel-plated, walnut stock, action is very similar to the Johnson and Bye Champion pistol (see the Johnson and Bye section of this book), very low powered, sequential serial number is usually found on the bottom rear of the compression tube, some not serial numbered, 35 in. OAL, 3.5 lbs. Approx. less than 1,000 mfg circa 1887-1891.

	N/A	N/A	4,000	3,500	3,000	2,500	2,000

Many parts are interchangeable with the Champion and other Quackenbush air guns.

GRADING	100%	95%	90%	80%	60%	40%	20%

MODEL 0 (LIGHTNING) - .21 cal., smooth bore rubber band powered SS, nickel-plated, walnut stock, 32 in. OAL, weight 4 pounds. The only rubber band powered air rifle made by H.M. Quackenbush. Only made in 1884.

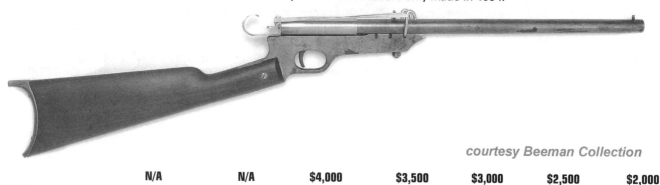

courtesy Beeman Collection

	N/A	N/A	$4,000	$3,500	$3,000	$2,500	$2,000

Add 50% for original box and literature.

MODEL 1 - .21 cal., push-barrel, SP, SS, smooth bore, nickel finish, walnut stock. Designed to shoot round shot, felted slugs, burred slugs, or darts. Loads through rectangular loading port in front part of receiver. Easily identified by the two-part receiver and simple, single loop trigger guard. Eleven variations of the Model 1 are distinguished by various features. The serial number can be used to approximate these variations. Later versions not listed below can be valued by listed prices unless special circumstances exist. Mfg. 1876-1938.

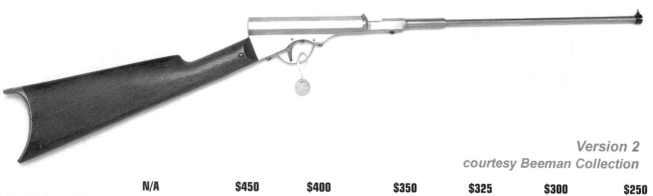

Version 2
courtesy Beeman Collection

	N/A	$450	$400	$350	$325	$300	$250

Add 10% for original bluing.
Add 50% for original wood box and literature.
Add 25% for original cardboard box and literature.
Add 100% for Version 1, no serial number, round receiver, and no name.
Add 60% for Version 2, serial number 1 to 300 or w/o number, octagon receiver.
Add 40% for Version 3, serial number 301 to 1000.
Add 20% for Version 4, serial number 1001 to 7500.
Add 10 % for Version 5, serial number 7501 to 12484.
Versions 6 to 11, serial number 12485 to 36850 – use prices listed above.

MODEL 2 - .21 cal., push-barrel, SP, SS, smooth bore, nickel finish, walnut stock. Distinguished from Model 1 by much heavier, one-piece receiver. Versions 1 and 2 with rectangular loading port ahead of rear sight; other versions with spoon shaped loading port behind rear sight. Version 1 with single loop, simple trigger guard; later versions with forward end of trigger guard much extended and with another loop. Designed to shoot round shot, felted slugs, burred slugs, or darts. Five versions distinguished by various features. The serial number can be used to approximate these variations. Mfg. 1879-1918.

Version 2
courtesy Beeman Collection

	N/A	$650	$575	$500	$365	N/A	N/A

Add 10% for original bluing.
Add 35% for original cardboard box and literature.

GRADING	100%	95%	90%	80%	60%	40%	20%

Add 35% for Version 1, serial number 1 to 5500.
Add 30% for Version 2, serial number 5501 to 20000.
Add 25% for Version 3, Model 83, serial number 1 to 8000 (number sequence started over).
Add 10% for Version 4, serial number 1 to 8000 (number sequence started over).
Version 5 serial number 8001 to 16823.

MODEL 3 - .21 cal., round ball, push-barrel, SP, SS, smooth bore, nickel finish, walnut stock. Round loading port/hole in top of receiver behind rear sight. Five versions are distinguishable by various features. The serial number can be used to approximate these variations. Values for Version 5 are listed. Mfg. 1881-1919.

	N/A	$750	$625	$500	$450	N/A	N/A

Add 10% for original bluing.
Add 50% for original box and literature.
Add 35% for Version 1, serial number 1 to 1300.
Add 30% for Version 2, serial number 1300 to 2600.
Add 25% for Version 3, serial number 2600 to 8000.
Add 10% for Version 4, serial number 8000 to 88700.

MODEL 4 - .21 cal., round ball, push-barrel, SP, smooth bore, nickel finish, walnut stock, gravity-fed in-line magazine repeater. Three variations distinguished by various features. The serial number can be used to approximate these variations. Version 3 values are listed. Mfg. 1882-1910.

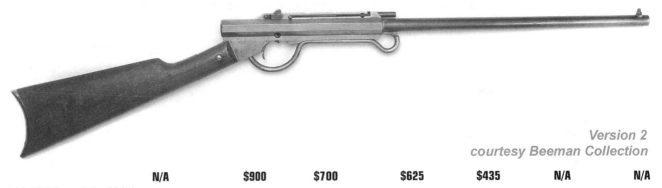

Version 2
courtesy Beeman Collection

	N/A	$900	$700	$625	$435	N/A	N/A

Add 10% for original bluing.
Add 50% for original box and literature.
Add 10% for Version 1, serial number 1 to 1000.
Add 5% for Version 2, serial number 1001 to 1425.

MODEL 5 (COMBINATION GUN) - .22 cal., BBC, SP, smooth bore, nickel finish, walnut stock. The smooth bore version did not have an extractor and operated only as an airgun. Designed to shoot round shot, felted slugs, burred slugs, or darts. Another version, rifled and with an extractor, could operate as an air rifle or fire .22 caliber rimfire ammunition. A removable firing pin was stored in a "patch box" on the right side of the buttstock. To function as a firearm, the firing pin was installed in place of the breech seal. (Replacement firing pins are available from John Groenewold.) Four variations are distinguished by various features. The serial number can be used to approximate these variations. Prices below are for the 22-inch barrel version. Mfg. 1884-1913.

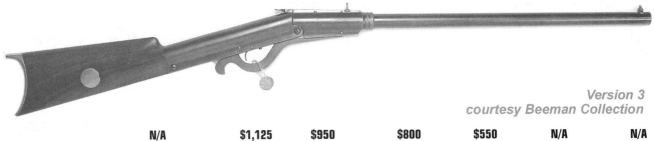

Version 3
courtesy Beeman Collection

	N/A	$1,125	$950	$800	$550	N/A	N/A

Subtract 20% for rifled barrel.
Subtract $50.00 for missing firing pin.
Add 10% for 18-inch barrel.
Add 20% for original bluing.
Add 20% for optional hooded front sight and flip-up rear aperture sight.
Add 35% for original cardboard box and literature.
Add 50% for original wood box and literature.
Add 15% for Version 1, serial number 1 to 100.
Add 10% for Version 2, serial number 101 to 1350.
Add 5% for Version 3, serial number 1351 to 2850.

GRADING	100%	95%	90%	80%	60%	40%	20%

MODEL 6 - BB/.175 cal., push-barrel, SP, smooth bore, blue finish, one-piece walnut buttstock/forearm, breech loading SS, sheet metal barrel housing, almost same general appearance as Number 7 except for round cocking stud in "2" slot under barrel instead of flat rectangular lug. Early versions with Z-shaped slot for cocking stud. Later versions with J shaped slot. No serial numbers. Mfg. 1907 to approximately 1911.

courtesy Beeman Collection

	100%	95%	90%	80%	60%	40%	20%
	N/A	N/A	$1,600	$1,300	$1,000	N/A	N/A

Add 50% for original box and literature.

MODEL 7 - BB/.175 cal., push-barrel, SP, smooth bore, blue finish, one-piece walnut buttstock/forearm, breech loading SS, sheet metal barrel housing, flat, rectangular cocking lug in slot running almost full length of underside of barrel shroud (housing). No serial numbers. Mfg. 1912-1936.

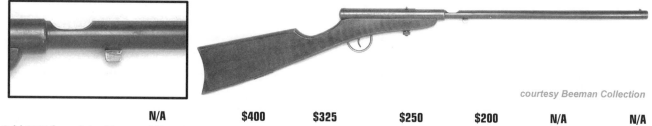

courtesy Beeman Collection

	100%	95%	90%	80%	60%	40%	20%
	N/A	$400	$325	$250	$200	N/A	N/A

Add 35% for original box and literature.

MODEL 8 - BB/.175 cal., push-barrel, SP, SS, muzzle loader, smooth bore, blue finish, walnut stock, similar to Models 6 and 7, except no cocking lug/stud or open slot on underside of barrel housing. Sheet metal barrel housing. No serial numbers. Mfg. 1918-1920.

	100%	95%	90%	80%	60%	40%	20%
	N/A	N/A	$2,200	$1,750	$1,400	N/A	N/A

Add 50% for original box and literature.

MODEL 9 - BB/.175 caliber, push-barrel, spring piston, smooth bore, felted slugs and darts, nickel-plated finish, walnut stock. Similar to Model 2 (with spoon shaped loading port), except for .175 caliber and a sheet metal barrel shroud with knurled muzzle piece to support shot tube at muzzle. Two-part serial numbers, e.g., 9-16620. Sold from 1920-1941.

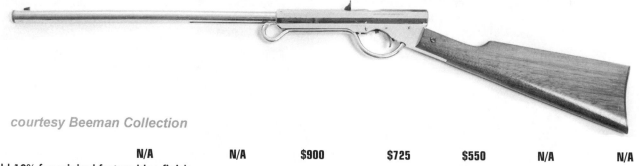

courtesy Beeman Collection

	100%	95%	90%	80%	60%	40%	20%
	N/A	N/A	$900	$725	$550	N/A	N/A

Add 10% for original factory blue finish.
Add 35% for original box and literature.

MODEL 10 - BB/.175 cal., push-barrel, spring piston, smooth bore, nickel planted finish, walnut stock. Similar to Model 3 (with round loading port), except for .175 caliber and sheet metal barrel shroud with knurled muzzle piece to support shot tube at muzzle. Two-part serial numbers, e.g., 10-16000. Sold from 1919-1943.

	100%	95%	90%	80%	60%	40%	20%
	N/A	N/A	N/A	$1,825	$1,500	$1,100	N/A

Add 10% for original factory blue finish.
Add 35% for original box and literature.

MODEL 83 - see Model 2, version 3.

NOTES

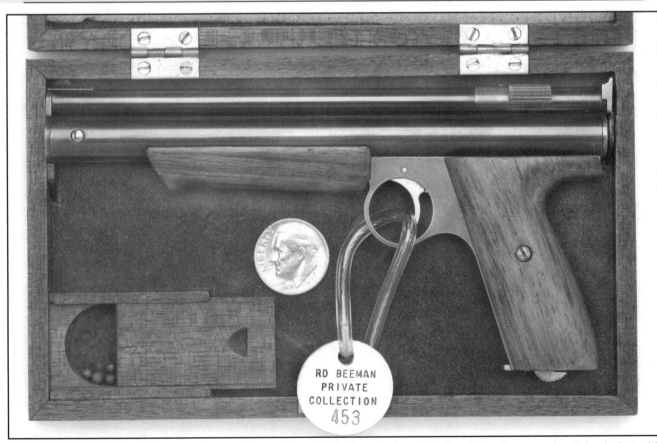

Miniature Crosman pump air pistol: Beautifully built and fully functioning, this specimen fires number 9 lead shot with sharp report and surprising force. Note US dime for scale; Beeman collection disk is 22 mm. Beeman collection.

R SECTION

RWS PRECISION PRODUCTS

Current trademark imported and distributed by Dynamit Nobel-RWS (Rheinisch Westfalische Spregstoff-Fabriken) Inc. located in Closter, NJ. Dealer sales only.

RWS imports the Dianawerk, Mayer and Grammelspacher airguns, these models are listed in the "D" section of this book.

For more information and current pricing on both new and used RWS firearms, please refer to the *Blue Book of Gun Values* by S.P. Fjestad (also available online).

GRADING	100%	95%	90%	80%	60%	40%	20%

PISTOLS

MODEL 9B/9N - .177 cal., SL, SP, SS, 550 FPS, black or nickel finish, molded black grips, adj. rear sight. Mfg. 2002-2004.

	100%	95%	90%	80%	60%	40%	20%
	$115	$80	$65	$50	$35	N/A	N/A

Last MSR was $157.

MODEL C-225 - .177 cal., CO$_2$, semi-auto, SA or DA, 385 FPS., 4 or 6 in. barrel, eight-shot rotary clip, styled after a modern handgun, interchangeable 4 or 6 in. barrels, adj. rear sight, black or nickel finish. Disc. 2001.

	100%	95%	90%	80%	60%	40%	20%
	$175	$150	$125	$95	$65	N/A	N/A

Last MSR was $210.

Add $10 for nickel finish.
Add $10 for 6 in. barrel, $25 for nickel model.

MODEL C-357 - .177 ca., CO$_2$ revolver, 380 FPS, eight-shot cylinder, 6 in. rifled barrel. Mfg. 1998-99.

	100%	95%	90%	80%	60%	40%	20%
	$150	$115	$90	$65	$45	N/A	N/A

Last MSR was $170.

MODEL CP-7 - .177 cal., match/sport SS, CO$_2$ refillable from tank or 12-gram capsule, 425 FPS, adj. rear sight, adj. trigger, adj. counter weight, 8.27 in. barrel, includes hard case and accessories, 2.23 lbs. Mfg. 1999-2001.

	100%	95%	90%	80%	60%	40%	20%
	$345	$295	$235	$165	$115	N/A	N/A

Last MSR was $450.

Subtract $50 for left-hand model.

MODEL CP95 - .177 and .22 cal. match grade SS, CO$_2$ refillable from tank or 12-gram capsule, 425 FPS, adj. rear sight, adj. trigger, adj. barrel weight, adj. pistol grip, 10.24 in. Lothar Walther barrel, 2.31 lbs. Disc. 2001

	100%	95%	90%	80%	60%	40%	20%
	$405	$345	$275	$205	$145	N/A	N/A

Last MSR was $525.

This model includes UIT regulations for international match shooting.

MODEL CP96 - .177 cal. match grade five-shot, CO$_2$ refillable from tank or 12-gram capsule, 425 FPS, adj. rear sight, adj. trigger, adj. barrel weight, adj. pistol grip, 10.24 in. Lothar Walther barrel, 2.23 lbs. Mfg. 1999-2001.

	100%	95%	90%	80%	60%	40%	20%
	$490	$415	$335	$255	$175	N/A	N/A

Last MSR was $635.

Subtract $100 for left-hand model.
This model includes UIT regulations for international match shooting.

RIFLES

MODEL 92 - .177 cal., BBC, SP, SS, 700 FPS, black finish, beech stock, grooved receiver for scope, rifled barrel, adj. rear sight, automatic safety. Mfg. in Spain. Mfg. 2002-04.

	100%	95%	90%	80%	60%	40%	20%
	$95	$75	$55	$45	$35	N/A	N/A

Last MSR was $122.

MODEL 93 - .177 or .22 cal., BBC, 850 FPS (.177 cal.), beech stock, adj. trigger, grooved receiver for scope, rifled barrel, adj. rear sight, hooded front sight, manual safety. Mfg. in Spain. Mfg. 2001-04.

	100%	95%	90%	80%	60%	40%	20%
	$160	$135	$110	$85	$55	N/A	N/A

Last MSR was $172.

MODEL 94 - .177 or .22 cal., BBC, SP 1000 FPS (.177 cal.), beech stock, adj. trigger, grooved receiver for scope, rifled barrel, adj. rear sight, hooded front sight with interchangable inserts, automatic safety. Mfg. in Spain. Mfg. 2001-04.

	100%	95%	90%	80%	60%	40%	20%
	$195	$160	$125	$95	$65	N/A	N/A

Last MSR was $227.

MODEL 312 - .177 cal., BBC, SP, SS, 900 FPS, black finish, beech stock, hooded front and adj. rear sights, automatic safety. Mfg. 2002-04.

	100%	95%	90%	80%	60%	40%	20%
	$70	$55	$45	$35	$25	N/A	N/A

Last MSR was $87.

GRADING	100%	95%	90%	80%	60%	40%	20%

MODEL 320 - .177 cal., BBC, SP, SS, 1000 FPS, black finish, beech stock, hooded front and adj. rear sights, manual safety. New 2002.

MSR $152	$130	$105	$85	$55	$45	N/A	N/A

MODEL 512 - .177 cal., BBC, SP, SS, 490 FPS, 17.7 in. barrel, black finish, synthetic stock, hooded front and adj. rear sights, scope rail, automatic safety. 6.2 lbs. Mfg. 2002-04.

	$80	$60	$50	$40	$30	N/A	N/A

Last MSR was $97.

MODEL 514 - .177 cal., SLC, SP, SS, 490 FPS, five-shot mag., 17.8 in. barrel, black finish, adj. black synthetic pistol grip stock, hooded front and adj. rear sights, automatic safety. 6.4 lbs. Mfg. 2002-04.

	$90	$70	$60	$50	$40	N/A	N/A

Last MSR was $106.

MODEL 516 - .177 cal., BBC, SP, SS, 1000 FPS, 17.7 in. barrel, black finish, synthetic stock, hooded front and adj. rear sights, scope rail, automatic safety. 6.2 lbs. Mfg. 2002-04.

	$115	$90	$70	$60	$50	N/A	N/A

Last MSR was $147.

MODEL CA 100 - .177 cal., PCP, 22 in. barrel, diopter sight, match trigger, adj. laminated stock, 11 lbs. 6 oz. Disc. 1998.

	$1,000	$750	$600	$450	$300	N/A	N/A

Last MSR was $2,200.

MODEL CA 200 TARGET - .177 cal., PCP, 22 in. barrel, adj. rear sight, hooded front sight, match trigger, laminated stock with adj. cheekpiece, adj. recoil pad, available in right- or left-hand variation, 11 lbs. 6 oz.

	$350	$275	$200	$135	$95	N/A	N/A

Last MSR was $570.

This model was also listed as CR 200 in some catalogs.

CA-707 - .22, .25, or 9mm cal., PCP, LA, eight-shot repeater or side-loading single shot, 1200 FPS at high-power setting, three-position power setting, built-in pressure gauge to monitor remaining shots, 16 (carbine) or 23 in. barrel, Western-style straight heel stock, high-gloss blue finish, Indonesian walnut stock with checkered forearm and hand grip, 7.75 lbs. New 1999.

courtesy Howard Collection

MSR $730	$560	$475	$380	$290	$195	N/A	N/A

CA-710T - .22, or .25 cal., PCP, LA, eight-shot repeater or side-loading single shot, similar to Model CA-707, except has interchangeable cylinder, 16 (carbine) or 19 in. barrel, Western-style straight heel stock, high-gloss blue finish, Indonesian walnut stock with checkered forearm and hand grip, 7 lbs. New 2000.

MSR $850	$630	$535	$440	$350	$225	N/A	N/A

CA-715 - .22 cal., CO_2 refillable from tank or 12-gram capsule, BA, SS, 1200 FPS, 20 in. barrel, open rear sight fully adj., hooded front sight with post, Indonesian walnut stock with rubber buttplate, raised cheekpiece, hand checkered hand grip, includes ten rechargeable cartridges, pellet seater, cartridge holder to refill cartridge with air, optional adaptor for scuba tank or pump, 6.5 lbs. Mfg. 1999-2000.

	$500	$425	$340	$270	$165	N/A	N/A

Last MSR was $685.

RA-800 BREAKBARREL (BY THEOBEN) - .177, .20, or .22 cal, 1110-1150 FPS, 12.25 in. barrel with integral extended muzzle brake, two-stage adj. trigger (from 1.75 to 3.25 lbs.), Deluxe African Hyedua stock with high cheekpiece and fine checkering on pistol grip and forearm. Mfg. 2000-2001.

	$1,000	$800	$600	$450	$300	N/A	N/A

Last MDSR was $1,400.

This gas-spring model was built in conjunction with Theoben, and featured a match grade Anschütz barrel.

RADCLIFFE

Previously manufactured by C.H. Radcliffe, located in Chicago, IL.

RIFLES

RADCLIFFE - appears to be a .25 cal. air rifle, but it is designed to shoot water back into the eyes of the shooter, 20.5 in. barrel, walnut buttstock with heavy steel buttplate, marked "Patd. June 17, 1902. No. 702478". For Masonic initiation rites; it predates the light (2.8 lbs.), little Daisy "back squirters," 38.5 in. OAL, 5.8 lbs. Value over $1,000.

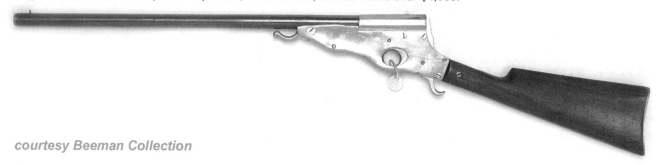

courtesy Beeman Collection

RANCO

For information on Ranco, see "Targ-Aire" in the "T" section.

RANDALL BROTHERS

Previous trademark manufactured by Myron Randall located in Waupaca, WI, circa 1924-29 under U.S. patent #1,509,257 (9/23/24).

Very high quality and design. Estimated production 20-25 guns. Extreme rarity prevents current price evaluation. Ref: AI, Oct. 2002.

RIFLES

RANDALL REPEATER AIR RIFLE - .22 cal., SP, LA moves sliding breech block, tapered steel barrel, tubular magazine under barrel for ten diabolo pellets, blue finish, walnut quarter stock with steel buttplate, walnut forearm, unmarked except for serial number stamped in several places, 38 in. OAL, 6 lbs. Current retail values are in the $1,000-$2,000+ range.

courtesy Hannusch Collection

RANDALL SINGLE SHOT AIR RIFLE - similar to repeater, except without magazine. Current retail values are in the $1,000-$2,000+ range.

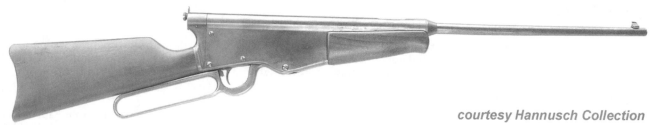

courtesy Hannusch Collection

RANGER

Previous tradename of American Tool Works located in Chicago, IL.

For information on Ranger, see American Tool Works in the "A" section.

Also used as a tradename for Erma ELG-10 lever action air rifles sold under the Webley brand, circa 1980s.

RAPIDE

For information on Rapide airguns, see Relum Limited in this section.

RAPID

For information on Rapid, refer to Cycloid/Rapid in the "C" section.

RECORD

For information on Record, refer to FB Record in the "F" section.

GRADING	100%	95%	90%	80%	60%	40%	20%

RELUM LIMITED

Previous London distributor of several lines of Hungarian products including airguns, founded by George Muller in 1954.

Relum is a reverse version of the name Muller. Brands included Relum, Jelly, FEG Telly (sometimes misread as Jelly), Rapide, Taurus, and Super Tornado. Most are heavily built economy line air rifles with .177 MV in the 500 FPS area. Still in business as of 1980. Resale values generally well under $100.

REMINGTON ARMS COMPANY, INC.

Current manufacturer established in 1816, with factory currently located in Ilion, NY. Originally founded by E. Remington, and previously located in Litchfield, Herkimer County, NY circa 1816-1828. Remington moved to Ilion, NY in 1828, where they continue to manufacture a variety of sporting arms. Corporate offices were moved to Madison, NC in 1996.

For more information and current pricing on both new and used Remington firearms, please refer to the *Blue Book of Gun Values* by S.P. Fjestad (also available online).

RIFLES

MODEL 26 REPEATING AIR RIFLE - .177 cal. for lead shot (early) or steel, SS pump action, spring air rifle with unique geared system, 21 1/8 in. barrel, adj. rear sight, blue (early) or black painted finish, plain varnished walnut pistol grip buttstock, ten-groove forearm, 4 lbs. Approx. 19,646 total mfg. circa 1928-1930.

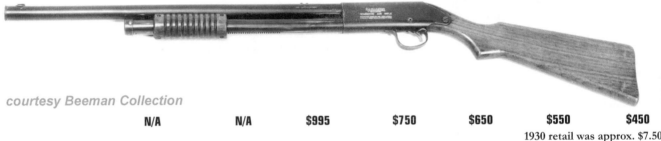

courtesy Beeman Collection

	N/A	N/A	$995	$750	$650	$550	$450

1930 retail was approx. $7.50.

Add 10% for blue finish.
Add 15% for first model.

AIRMASTER MODEL AM77 - BB.175 or .177 cal., pump pneumatic, 20.8 in. barrel, 725 FPS, adj. rear sight, brushed nickel barrel and black reciever finish, black synthetic pistol grip buttstock, imported, 39.75 in. OAL. New 2003.

MSR	$103	$90	$70	$55	$45	N/A	N/A	N/A

GENESIS 1000 MODEL R1K77PG/R1K77PGX - .177 cal., BBC, SP, SS rifled steel barrel, two stage adj. trigger, 1000 FPS, adj. rear sight, 3-9X40 scope (Model R1K77PGX new 2005), blue finish, ergonomic soft synthetic pistol grip stock, vented recoil pad. New 2004.

MSR	$230	$190	$160	$125	$95	N/A	N/A	N/A

Add 25% for 3-9x40 scope (Model R1K77PGX).

RIPLEY RIFLES

Current manufacturer of PCP rifles, located in Derbyshire, United Kingdom.

The authors and publisher wish to thank Tim Saunders for his valuable assistance with the following information in this edition of the *Blue Book of Airguns*. Owned and operated by Steve Wilkins, son of late Joe Wilkins who manufactured the Predator rifle and had a significant role in developing the modern PCP. High end regulated PCP rifles, mainly FT. Sporting rifles were available as XL series, .22 cal. SS or with nine-shot rotary magazine (XL9) or twenty-five-shot version (XL25) with spring-loaded linear magazine feeding the rotary magazine.

Most production is custom; all typical airgun calibers. Many actions fitted with very high end stocks from Paul Wilson and other custom stockmakers. Finishes include blue, nickel, colored, and camo. These air rifles typically will retail in the $1,500-$2,000 range.

courtesy Neil MacKinnon

RO

For information on RO airguns, see Gun Toys SRL in the "G" section.

ROBINSON, GEORGE CO.

Previous manufacturer of the O´Connell Gas Rifle located in Rochester, NY circa 1947-49.

During WWII, the Robinson Co. produced munitions for the U.S. Government. Shortly after the company turned to the production of toy tools, an engineer by the name of O´Connell approached George Robinson with a design for a single shot CO_2 rifle. At about the same time, Crosman Arms Corporation was promoting their CG (Compressed Gas) series rifles via indoor shooting leagues, one of which was in East Rochester, NY. It is probably no coincidence that the O´Connell rifle so closely resembles a Crosman CG rifle that collectors who have seen one of these very rare rifles often think that it a prototype or a version of the Crosman CG rifles. The complete lack of any markings on the O´Connell rifles helps promote this error. However, the internal design is considerably different and the quality is higher.

RIFLES

O´CONNELL GAS RIFLE - .22 cal., CO_2, SS, rifling barrel, with removable, vertically attached 4 oz. CO_2 tank (tanks are not interchangeable with Crosman CG guns), aperture rear sight only, safety gas by-pass lever on right side of receiver, breech loading by pulling a knob at the rear of the receiver, valve similar to a Schimel gas pistol, approx. 540 FPS, dark stained hardwood stock, machined steel parts, 41.5 in. OAL, 6 lbs. Approx. 100-200 mfg. 1947-49.

courtesy Beeman Collection

N/A	$1,000	$750	$650	$550	N/A	N/A

ROCHESTER

Previous tradename of air rifles previously manufactured by the Monroe Gasket and Manufacturing Company located in Rochester, NY circa 1948.

The Rochester Air Rifle is the only model known, a swinging air pump pneumatic, BA, SS, two-piece wooden stock, with a black crackled paint finish. Probably the direct ancestor of the Kessler Two Piece Stock Model (see Kessler in the "K" section) with which it is identical except for the names stamped on the barrel. Research is ongoing with this trademark, and more information will be included both online and in future editions. Average original condition specimens are typically priced in the $250-$300 range. MSR was $10.

courtesy Beeman Collection

ROGER

For information on Roger airguns, see MMM - Mondial in the "M" section.

ROGUNZ

For information on Rogunz airguns, see Philippine Airguns in the "P" section.

courtesy Beeman Collection

GRADING	100%	95%	90%	80%	60%	40%	20%

RÖHM GmbH

Current manufacturer located in Sontheim an der Benz, Germany. Currently imported by Airguns of Arizona located in Mesa, AZ.

For more information and current pricing on both new and used Röhm firearms, please refer to the *Blue Book of Gun Values* by S.P. Fjestad (also available online).

PISTOLS

TWINMASTER ACTION CO2 MODEL - .177 cal., CO_2, eight-shot mag. repeater, 8.58 in. rifled Walther barrel, black frame with brushed barrel finish, molded grip, adj. trigger, adj. rear sight, trigger safety, 1.96 lbs.

	MSR	$412	$390	$315	$250	$195	N/A	N/A	N/A

TWINMASTER ALLROUNDER MODEL - .177 cal., PCP, eight-shot mag. repeater, 8.58 in. rifled steel Walther barrel, black frame with brushed barrel finish, molded grip, adj. trigger, adj. rear sight, trigger safety, built-in gauge, 2 lbs.

	MSR	$577	$545	$485	$395	$325	N/A	N/A	N/A

TWINMASTER COMBAT TRAINER CO2 MODEL - .177 cal., CO_2, eight-shot mag. repeater, 8.58 in. rifled Walther barrel, black frame with brushed barrel finish, universal contoured grip, adj. trigger, adj. rear sight, trigger safety, 11 in. OAL, 2.4 lbs. New 2005.

	MSR	$510	$480	$425	$350	$295	N/A	N/A	N/A

TWINMASTER MATCH MODEL - .177 cal., PCP, SS, 8.58 in. rifled steel Walther barrel, black frame and barrel finish, adj. walnut grip, adj. trigger, adj. rear sight with extra blades, trigger safety, built-in gauge, balance weights, tool kit, hard case, 2 lbs. New 2005.

	MSR	$948	$895	$845	$750	$675	N/A	N/A	N/A

TWINMASTER MATCH TRAINER CO2 MODEL - .177 cal., CO_2, eight-shot mag. repeater, 8.58 in. rifled Walther barrel, black frame with brushed barrel finish, adj. laminate grip, adj. trigger, adj. rear sight, trigger safety, 11 in. OAL, 2.4 lbs. New 2005.

	MSR	$581	$548	$495	$425	$365	N/A	N/A	N/A

TWINMASTER SPORT MODEL - .177 cal., PCP, SS, 8.58 in. rifled steel Walther barrel, black frame and barrel finish, adj. molded grip, adj. trigger, adj. rear sight with extra blades, trigger safety, built-in gauge, balance weights, tool kit, hard case, 2 lbs.

	MSR	$845	$800	$745	$650	$575	N/A	N/A	N/A

TWINMASTER TOP MODEL - .177 cal., PCP, eight-shot mag. repeater, 8.58 in. rifled steel Walther barrel, black frame with brushed barrel finish, adj. wood grip, adj. trigger, adj. rear sight, trigger safety, built-in gauge, 2 lbs.

	MSR	$680	$641	$575	$475	$395	N/A	N/A	N/A

RUBI

For information on Rubi airguns, see Venturini in the "V" section.

RUTTEN AIRGUNS SA

Current manufacturer located in Herstal-Liege, Belgium. Previously imported on a limited basis by Pyramyd Air, located in Pepper Pike, OH. Previously imported by Cherry´s Fine Guns, located in Greensboro, NC, and by Compasseco, located in Bardstown, KY.

The Browning Airstar, built by Rutten, was the first air rifle with a battery-powered electronic cocking system. Less than 800 were manufactured. Please refer to the Browning section in this text for more information. Rutten also builds three other models sold through selected Rutten dealers.

For more information and current pricing on both new and used Rutten firearms, please refer to the *Blue Book of Gun Values* by S.P. Fjestad (also available online).

PISTOLS

J&L RUTTEN WINDSTAR HS550 TARGET PISTOL - .177 cal., BBC, SP, SS, 550 FPS, automatic safety, fully adj. rear sight, checkered beech grips, 2.35 lbs. Disc. 2002.

		$200	$190	$155	$115	$75	N/A	N/A

Last MSR was $235.

RIFLES

BROWNING AIRSTAR - please refer to the Browning section.

AIRSTAR - .177 cal., electronic cocking mechanism powered by rechargeable Ni-Cad battery (250 shots per charge), 780 FPS, flip-up loading port, warning light indicates when spring is compressed, electronic safety with warning light, 17.5 in. fixed barrel, hooded front sight with interchangeable sight inserts, adj. rear sight, frame grooved for scope mount, beech wood stock, 9.3 lbs.

	MSR	$490	$375	$325	$265	$215	$175	N/A	N/A

J&L RUTTEN WINDSTAR MACH 1 D.E. - .177 cal., UL, SP, SS, 870 FPS, safety integrated with cocking lever, 18 in. barrel, hooded front sight with interchangeable inserts, fully adj. rear sight, frame grooved for scope mount, beechwood stock, 9.7 lbs. Disc. 2002.

		$450	$405	$335	$275	$225	N/A	N/A

Last MSR was $525.

J&L RUTTEN WINDSTAR PRO 2000 D.E. TARGET - .177 cal., UL, SP, SS, 570 FPS, safety integrated with cocking lever, 18 in. barrel, hooded front sight with interchangeable inserts, fully adj. rear peep sight, frame grooved for scope mount, beechwood target stock with adj. buttplate, 10 lbs.

	MSR	$510	$465	$420	$345	$280	$230	N/A	N/A

S SECTION

S G S (SPORTING GUNS SELECTION)

Previous trademark imported by Kendell International.

GRADING	100%	95%	90%	80%	60%	40%	20%

RIFLES

DUO 300AP - .177 or .22 cal., TL, SP, 455/430 FPS.

	100%	95%	90%	80%	60%	40%	20%
	$135	$115	$70	$50	$40	N/A	N/A

DUO 300AR - .177 or .22 cal., TL, SP, 455/430 FPS, with extra stock and barrel assembly to create a three-in-one gun.

	100%	95%	90%	80%	60%	40%	20%
	$195	$135	$85	$65	$50	N/A	N/A

SAINT LOUIS

For information on Saint Louis airguns, see Benjamin in the "B" section.

SAVAGE ARMS

Current manufacturer and importer located in Westfield, MA.

A century-old manufacturer of rifles and shotguns (more than two hundred different models since 1895), Savage brought its expertise to air rifles in 1999 with five imported sporting models in .177 caliber.

For more information and current pricing on both new and used Savage Arms firearms, please refer to the *Blue Book of Gun Values* by S.P. Fjestad (also available online).

RIFLES

PLAY RIFLE - .38 cal., SP, pump action, sheet metal construction, spring-fed tubular magazine, fixed sights, marked "SAVAGE" in large letters on RHS of receiver, with SVG in circle, barrel stamped: "SAVAGE PLAY RIFLE MANUF. BY SAVAGE ARMS CORP, UTICA, N.Y. PAT. APPLIED FOR", black Japan finish, 34.1 in. OAL, 3.0 lbs.. Mfg. circa 1920-1930s, may be up to three variations.

courtesy Beeman Collection

	100%	95%	90%	80%	60%	40%	20%
	N/A	N/A	$225	$200	$185	$165	$145

MODEL 560F - .177 cal., BBC, SP, two-stage trigger with manual safety, adj. rear sight, grooved receiver, 18 in. rifled steel barrel, velocity 560 FPS, black polymer stock with metallic finish, 5.5 lbs. Mfg. 1999-2001.

	100%	95%	90%	80%	60%	40%	20%
	$73	$62	$50	$35	$25	N/A	N/A

Last MSR was $93.

MODEL 600F - .177 cal., similar to Model 600FXP, except without scope and rings, 6 lbs. Mfg. 1999-2001.

	100%	95%	90%	80%	60%	40%	20%
	$100	$85	$70	$45	$30	N/A	N/A

Last MSR was $128.

MODEL 600FXP - .177 cal., BBC, SP with twenty-five-shot mag., two-stage trigger with manual safety, adj. rear sight, hooded front sight, grooved receiver, includes 2.5x20 scope and rings, 18 in. rifled steel barrel, 600 FPS, black polymer stock with lacquer finish and rubber recoil pad, 6.5 lbs. Mfg. 1999-2001.

	100%	95%	90%	80%	60%	40%	20%
	$105	$90	$70	$50	$35	N/A	N/A

Last MSR was $135.

MODEL 1000G - .177 cal., similar to Model 1000GXP, except without scope and rings, 7.1 lbs. Mfg. 1999-2001.

	100%	95%	90%	80%	60%	40%	20%
	$145	$125	$100	$85	$65	N/A	N/A

Last MSR was $186.

MODEL 1000GXP - .177 cal., BBC, SP with anti-bear trap mechanism, two-stage adj. trigger with manual safety, adj. rear sight, hooded front sight, grooved receiver, includes 4x32 scope and rings, 18 in. barrel, 1000 FPS, walnut stained hardwood stock with vent. rubber recoil pad, 7.5 lbs. Mfg. 1999-2001.

	100%	95%	90%	80%	60%	40%	20%
	$169	$144	$119	$95	$70	N/A	N/A

Last MSR was $216.

GRADING	100%	95%	90%	80%	60%	40%	20%

SAXBY PALMER

Previous manufacturer located in Stratford-Upon-Avon, England. Previously imported/distributed by Marksman Products, located in Huntington Beach, CA.

Saxby Palmer developed a cartridge loading air rifle. This is not a CO_2 or other type of compressed gas gun. The cartridges are pressurized (2250 PSI) and reusable, facilitating speed of loading and much greater velocities. Rifles were supplied with the table pump (for reloading brass or plastic cartridges) and ten cartridges. These accessories are necessary in order to operate air rifles or pistols. See Brocock introduction in the "B" section for information on the British 2004 ban on production and sale of air cartridge airguns.

REVOLVERS

Subtract 50% if without accessories.

ORION AIR REVOLVER - .177 cal., six-shot, compressed air cartridges (reusable), 550 FPS, 6 in. barrel, 2.2 lbs. Disc. 1988.

courtesy Beeman Collection

N/A	$450	$375	$300	$225	$150	$95

Add 20% for chrome finish.

This model was manufactured by Weihrauch of Germany and included a Slim Jim pump and twelve reusable cartridges. It also came with a 30 grain .38 cal. zinc pellet to allow cartridges to be used in a .38 Special pistol for practice.

MODEL 54 - .177 cal., five-shot, compressed air cartridges (reusable), 4 in. barrel, 1.35 lb. Disc. 1988.

courtesy Beeman Collection

$195	$145	$110	$85	$65	N/A	N/A

This model was manufactured by Weihrauch of Germany and included a Slim Jim pump and twelve reusable cartridges.

WESTERN 66 - .177 or .22 cal., compressed air cartridge, styled after Colt SAA (Peacemaker), blue finish, 11.6 in. OAL, 2.4 lbs.

courtesy Beeman Collection

N/A	$450	$395	$295	$225	$150	N/A

GRADING	100%	95%	90%	80%	60%	40%	20%

RIFLES

Subtract 50% if without accessories.

ENSIGN ELITE - .177 or .22 cal., compressed air cartridge, BA, 1000/800 FPS automatic safety.

	$225	$150	$120	$95	$75	N/A	N/A

Last MSR was $175.

ENSIGN ROYAL - .177 or .22 cal., compressed air cartridge, BA, 1000/800 FPS automatic safety, walnut stock.

	$195	$145	$110	$85	$65	N/A	N/A

Last MSR was $275.

GALAXY - .177 or .22 cal., compressed air cartridge, BA, 1000/800 FPS, automatic safety, walnut stained, hardwood stock, 6.5 lbs.

	$175	$125	$90	$75	$65	N/A	N/A

SATURN - .177 or .22 cal., compressed air cartridge, BA, 1000/800 FPS, automatic safety, black polymer stock, 6.5 lbs. Disc. 1987.

	$165	$115	$80	$65	$55	N/A	N/A

Last MSR was $175.

SBS

For information on SBS, see Shark.

SCALEMEAD

For information on Scalemead airguns, see Gun Toys SRL in the "G" section.

SCHIMEL

Previous trademark manufactured by Schimel Arms Company located in California circa 1952-54, and A.C. Swanson located in Sun Valley, CA, circa 1956-58.

The Schimel was the first of a series of pistols made from the same general design by Orville Schimel. Due to undercapitalization and a number of design flaws in the Schimel, the small company went bankrupt. In 1955, the manufacturing fixtures were acquired by the American Weapons Corporation, headed by Hy Hunter. The unsatisfactory seals were replaced by a one-seal unit and an ingenious eight-shot magazine for .22 cal. lead balls was added. The improved design was marketed as the American Luger. Stoeger arms had U.S. ownership of the Luger trademark and quickly forced these "American Lugers" from the market, making them very rare pistols.

PISTOLS

Smith (1957) heralds these as the first American-made CO_2 production pistol and the first to use disposable CO_2 cylinders.

MODEL GP-22 - .22 cal., CO_2, SS, close copy of the German Luger, toggle action, 6 in. barrel, die-cast body, blue finish, 9.3 in. OAL, 2.5 lbs.

courtesy Beeman Collection

	$225	$195	$160	$125	$100	$60	$40

Add 15% for factory box.

Subtract 5% for Model P-22 marking.

Subtract 40% for broken back strap.

A pneumatic version, the Model AP-22 was presented in catalogs but no specimens are known.

Compressed fiber washer ("paper seals" are a myth). Two U-shaped cup seals highly prone to failure.

GRADING	100%	95%	90%	80%	60%	40%	20%

AMERICAN LUGER - .22 cal., CO_2, similar to Model GP-22, except is an eight-shot repeater. Ref: AGNR - Jan. 1989.

courtesy Beeman Collection

	$950	$800	$700	$600	$500	$350	$275

Add 15% for factory box.
Subtract 15% for black Schimel grips.

Information sheet included in box with "American Luger" guns may refer to Model V822 and Model HV822, however the guns are marked "American Luger" on the LHS and have the "AL" logo on each grip.

CARBO JET - Smith (1957) and others have reported a repeating CO_2 pistol, supposedly related to the American Luger. Smith illustrates a Schimel and an American Luger as the Carbo Jet. Despite almost a half century of looking, no verified specimens of the CarboJet are known.

SCOUT

For information on Scout airguns, see Milbro in the "M" section.

SEARS ROEBUCK AND CO.

Catalog merchandiser that, in addition to selling major trademark firearms, also private labeled many configurations of airguns and firearms (mostly longarms) under a variety of trademarks and logos (i.e., J.C. Higgins, Ted Williams, Ranger, etc.). Sears discontinued the sale of all firearms circa 1980, and the Ted Williams trademark was stopped circa 1978.

A general guideline for Sears Roebuck and related labels (most are marked "Sears, Roebuck and Co." on left side of barrel) is that values are generally lower than those of the major factory models from which they were derived. Remember, 99% of Sears Roebuck and related label airguns get priced by their shootability factor in today's competitive marketplace, not collectibility. A crossover listing (see "Storebrand Cross-Over List") has been provided in the back of this text for linking up the various Sears Roebuck models to the original manufacturer with respective "crossover" model numbers.

SELECTOR

Previous trademark used by SGL Industries of Rockville, MD (formerly GL Industries in Westville, NJ) for Special Purpose CO_2 pistols. Circa 1969-1970.

PISTOL

SELECTOR - .68 cal., CO_2, 6 shot semi-automatic, fires special purpose projectiles, mainly for law enforcement work. Projectiles include: Stinger, noise/confusion, CN tear gas, CS tear gas, and Fluorescent Dye.

courtesy Beeman Collection

	$125	$100	$90	$80	N/A	N/A	N/A

Add 20% for SGL factory box.
Add 30% for GL factory box.

SETRA

Previous trademark of unknown maker in Spain, less than 200 imported into England after WWII, a few of these went to New Zealand.

RIFLES

AS 1000 - .22 cal., pump pneumatic, SS, similar in design to American-made Sheridan air rifles, checkered pump handle and pistol grip, 37.3 in. OAL.

courtesy Beeman Collection

		100%	95%	90%	80%	60%	40%	20%
		$375	$325	$275	$225	$175	N/A	N/A

AS 2000 - .22 cal., bulk fill CO_2 or cartridge.

	100%	95%	90%	80%	60%	40%	20%
	$375	$325	$275	$225	$175	N/A	N/A

SETTER

Previous trademark for 28 gauge pneumatic shotgun made by Armibrescia, Italy ca. 1935-1947. Ref: Hannusch (2001).

There may be a pneumatic rifle version. Additional information is solicited from readers, please contact BBAinput@Beemans.net. Late 1930s.

SHARK MANUFACTURING CO.

Current manufacturer located in Buenos Aires, Argentina. Currently imported by Sunshine Airguns located in FL.

The authors and publisher wish to thank Mr. Eduardo Poloni for much of the following information in this edition of the *Blue Book of Airguns*.

Shark began in 1975, producing underwater spear guns, using elastic bands or a gas-spring mechanism. The great power and ease of power regulation in the underwater gas-spring guns led to the development of air rifles for use on land. Two years of research resulted in the Shark Model CD 455 (Caño Deslizable de 455mm or "455mm Sliding Barrel") in .22/5.5mm caliber. The barrel of this rifle slides through a bushing when an underlever is activated to move the piston back and compress the gas spring. As with the Theoben gas-spring airguns (sometimes inappropriately referred to as gas ram airguns), independently developed later in England, the mainspring consists of a trapped body of gas. The gas, in this case air, which does not exit with the shots, is supplied from a separate manual air pump. This system was granted Argentina patent number 213,908 (application 22 June 1978, granted 30 March 1979) and USA patent number 4,282,852 (granted 11 August 1981).

To take advantage of the great power, special Shark ogival projectiles of 1.6 grams were developed. With these projectiles, muzzle velocity could be adjusted to more than 300 MPS at various levels suitable for the smallest game at close range or larger game to more than 50 meters.

In 1979, a unique application of this gas-spring mechanism was used in the development of the Shark CQ air rifles which use a conventional barrel cocking system but have a very interesting, special multiple cocking capability. A single barrel-cocking stroke compresses the gas-spring to ordinary power potential; two strokes triples the power.

In 1985, Shark introduced an unusual CO_2 powered rifle/shotgun combination. These were charged from separate CO_2 storage bottles. It features instantly interchangeable .22 cal., (5.5mm) rifle and 13 mm shotgun barrels. In the shotgun mode it uses shot charges in plastic or metal cases and is claimed to be effective to 25 meters for hunting of birds and small mammals. In 2003 this model was produced with a horizontally attached buddy-style CO_2 bottle. Caliber .25 (6.35mm) and a rifled 13 mm barrel were also made available. This gun has been used, with arrow projectiles, to take water buffalo in Argentina!

In the early 1990s, Shark switched most of its production to a light, handy CO_2 carbine with a Mauser-type bolt in either .22 (5.5mm) or .25 (6.35mm) caliber. Sturdy, handy SP pistols of the same arrangement were also produced in much smaller numbers.

In 1997, Shark began production of a semiautomatic carbine powered by a horizontally attached buddy-style CO_2 bottle. A 17.5mm paintball version was produced for the newly arrived paintball games.

The Shark airguns have been virtually handmade in a small plant which has grown to only ten employees. Because of this extremely limited production and the fact that these guns normally are produced only for Argentina and Chile, they are rarely seen in most countries. Their rarity and unusually interesting, very well built mechanisms make them highly desirable to collectors. The early, independently developed, complex gas-spring mechanism is especially interesting. Shark guns with the gas spring system now are of special interest to collectors because the factory has decided that they are too expensive to make more of them.

Only a very few of the total production runs of Shark airguns have ever left Argentina. Local specimens may show extremely hard usage.

GRADING	100%	95%	90%	80%	60%	40%	20%

PISTOLS

MODEL SP 95 STANDARD - .177 or .22 (13mm new 2002) cal., CO_2, quick change barrel. Approx. 700 mfg. 1995 to date.

courtesy Beeman Collection

	N/A	$395	$325	$250	N/A	N/A	N/A

MODEL SP 95 MAGNUM - .25 cal., CO_2. Approx. 185 mfg. 2002 to date.

courtesy Beeman Collection

	N/A	$350	$300	$250	N/A	N/A	N/A

MODEL SP 95 REPEATER - .174/BB cal., spring-fed internal magazine.

courtesy Beeman Collection

	$500	$425	$350	$275	$200	N/A	N/A

RIFLES

MODEL CD 405 - .22 cal., GS, hand pump, 16 in. barrel. Approx. 519 mfg. 1980-85.

courtesy Beeman Collection

	$650	$600	$550	$500	$475	$450	$400

GRADING	100%	95%	90%	80%	60%	40%	20%

MODEL CD 455 - .22 or 8mm (shot) cal., GS, hand pump, 17.9 in. barrel. Approx. 1252 mfg. 1979-85.

courtesy Beeman Collection

	$800	$750	$700	$650	$600	$550	$525

MODEL CQ-1E - .22 cal., GS, single cocking action with hand pump, identified by rear of receiver being a large flat disc. with a large coin slot, removing the disc exposes the charging valve. Approx. 636 mfg. 1997-2001.

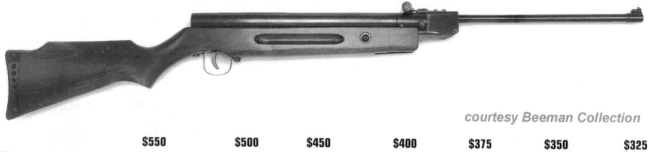

courtesy Beeman Collection

	$550	$500	$450	$400	$375	$350	$325

I Estapa = 1 step

MODEL CQ-2E - .22 cal., GS, double cocking action (one cocking action provides standard power, two cocking actions provide maximum power) allowed by the captive charge of the gas spring system, rear end of receiver is conical with visible opening for air charging with hand pump. Approx. 850 mfg. 1982-86.

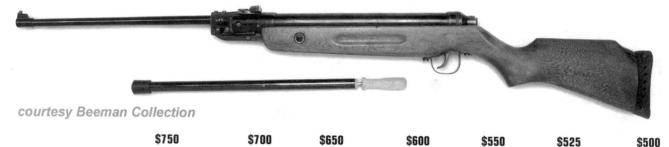

courtesy Beeman Collection

	$750	$700	$650	$600	$550	$525	$500

2 Estapas = 2 steps

MODEL CARBINE CERROJO - .22 or .25 (new 2002) cal., CO_2, manual slide action. Approx. 8350 mfg. 1991 to date.

	$250	$200	$180	$170	$150	$125	$75

MODEL REPEATING CARBINE - .22 or 13 mm (dart) cal., CO_2, interchangeable barrels, Mauser-style bolt action. Approx. 4500 mfg. 1993 to date.

	$250	$200	$180	$170	$150	$125	$75

Also made in 17.5 mm paintball and tranquilizer versions.

MODEL SEMI-AUTOMATIC CARBINE - .22 cal., CO_2, thirty shots. Approx. 650 mfg. 1998-2003.

courtesy Beeman Collection

	$250	$200	$180	$170	$150	$125	$75

GRADING	100%	95%	90%	80%	60%	40%	20%

MODEL SEMI-AUTO QC - all basic airgun cals., similar to Semi-Auto Model except has quick change barrels, bolt slot RHS of stock., approx. thirty shots. New 2004.

courtesy Beeman Collection

	$325	$275	$225	$175	N/A	N/A	N/A

MODEL BOLT ACTION - .25 cal., BA, CO_2, ambidextrous Monte Carlo stock with rubber recoil pad, sling swivels, scope grooves, no safety, 37.4 in. OAL, 4.8 lbs. New 2004.

	$250	$200	$175	$125	$85	N/A	N/A

SHOTGUNS

MODEL SHOTGUN - .22, .25 (new 2003) pellet or 13 mm (shot) cal. CO_2, quick change rifled barrels. Approx. 3000 mfg. 1989-90. Reintroduced in 2003.

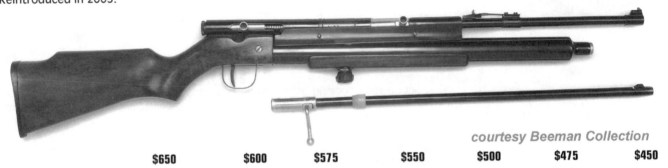

courtesy Beeman Collection

	$650	$600	$575	$550	$500	$475	$450

Add 25% for pre-1990 version.

SHARP

Current tradename of Sharp Rifle Manufacturing Company, Tokyo, Japan. Current manufacturer of air rifles and pistols. Previously imported by Beeman Precision Airguns, then of San Rafael, CA, and perhaps by others.

Founded by Kensuke Chiba, an airgun marksman and inventor, in 1952 as the Tokyo Rifle Laboratory. Name changed in 1955 to Tokyo Rifle Company and then to Sharp Rifle Manufacturing Company in 1960. Over twenty models of gas and pneumatic guns have been developed by this firm; most of these were produced for Asian markets. Research is ongoing with this trademark, and more information will be included both online and in future editions. Ref: AAG - Jan. 1999.

PISTOLS

MODEL U-FP - .177 cal., 545 FPS, CO_2, SS, black finish, hardwood grips, 8 in. BBL, 12 in. OAL. Intro. 1969.

courtesy Beeman Collection

	$650	$600	$550	$425	$350	N/A	N/A

Add 10% for factory box.

GRADING	100%	95%	90%	80%	60%	40%	20%

RIFLES

ACE SPORTER - .177 or .22 cal., swinging forearm pump pneumatic, BA, SS, leaf rear sight, hardwood stock, rubber buttplate with white spacer, 23.9 in. BBL, 920/750 FPS, manual safety catch, 38.4 in. OAL, 6.3 lbs. Mfg. circa 1981-1987. Ref: AR1 (1997): pp. 36-38.

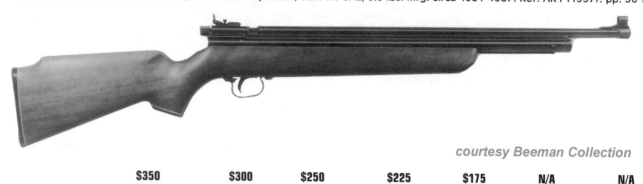

courtesy Beeman Collection

	100%	95%	90%	80%	60%	40%	20%
	$350	$300	$250	$225	$175	N/A	N/A

Last MSR was $295.

ACE TARGET - .177 or .22 cal., SL, BA, SS, similar to Ace Sporter except, sidelever, more massive stock, adjustable buttplate, and match diopter sights. Mfg. circa 1981-1987. Ref: AR1 (1997): pp. 36-38.

	100%	95%	90%	80%	60%	40%	20%
	$525	$450	$375	$300	$225	N/A	N/A

Last MSR was $450

GR-75 - .177, CO_2, pump action loading repeater, two 12 gm CO_2 cylinders, 19.6 in. rifled bbl., deep blue steel parts, wood stock, grip cap and buttplate w/ white line spacers, manual cross bolt safety, 39 in. OAL, 6.7 lbs.

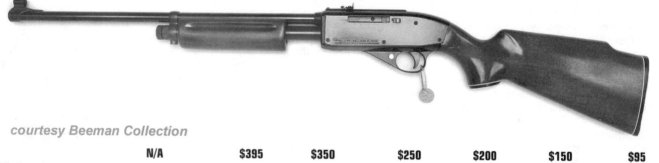

courtesy Beeman Collection

	100%	95%	90%	80%	60%	40%	20%
	N/A	$395	$350	$250	$200	$150	$95

Highest SN known is 1933.

INNOVA - .177 or .22 cal, swinging forearm pump pneumatic, BA, SS, 20 in. BBL, 920/720 FPS, smooth wood stock and forearm, bolt catch serves as safety. 34.6 in. OAL, 4.3 lbs. Disc. 1988. Innova Special has side lever pump handle and one-piece stock. New 1985.

courtesy Beeman Collection

	100%	95%	90%	80%	60%	40%	20%
	$250	$200	$165	$115	$80	N/A	N/A

Last MSR was $175.

GRADING	100%	95%	90%	80%	60%	40%	20%

TIGER 500 TARGET - similar to Ace, except has double set trigger, palm rest, special match sights and thumbhole match stock, adj. buttplate, match sling, and fitted case.

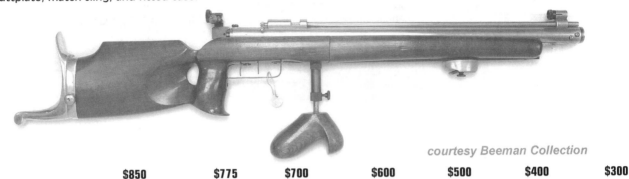

courtesy Beeman Collection

	$850	$775	$700	$600	$500	$400	$300

USL - .177 cal., CO_2, BA, SS, plastic slab-sided stock, approx. 620 FPS, 32 in. OAL. Mfg. beginning 1969.

	$200	$175	$150	$100	$70	N/A	N/A

SHARPSHOOTER

For information on Sharpshooter airguns, see Bulls Eye in the "B" section.

SHERIDAN PRODUCTS, INC.

Previous manufacturer located in E. Bloomfield, NY.

In 1994 through 1995, after their purchase by Crosman Air Guns, some of the separate lines of the Benjamin and Sheridan airgun companies were merged into one.

The Sheridan Company of Racine, WI was started in 1945 by E.H. Wackerhagen, who teamed up with fellow airgun enthusiast Robert Kraus, who had engineering skills. He stated that their objective was to best the Benjamin Air Rifle Company by producing what they planned would be the best possible pneumatic air rifle. Mr. Kraus related to Robert Beeman that they felt that, because that Wackerhagen and Kraus would not be too catchy a name for an air rifle, they named the company after Sheridan Street, a road in Racine which they traversed almost daily as they went between their respective garages during the development of the new gun. Their first model, the Model A, was produced in March 1947. The first paid advertisements evidently appeared about 1948. The perfection of the Model A required a retail price of $56.50 in 1948, equivalent to over $500 in the year 2001. Sales were very poor. A less expensive model, the Model B, introduced in October 1948 at a retail price of $35 (equivalent to about $247 today), was even less successful. Good sales did not begin until after the introduction of the Model C, which sold for $19.95 in 1949 (equivalent to about $145 today).

See the introduction to the Benjamin section for information on manufacturing locations and the names under which these guns have been marketed in the 1990s.

All Sheridan air rifles and pistols are single shot, bolt action, breech-loading, and .20 (5 mm) caliber. Muzzle velocity figures are for Sheridan´s standard weight pellets of 14.3 grains.

For more information and current pricing on the Sheridan firearms, please refer to the *Blue Book of Gun Values* by S.P. Fjestad (also available online).

PISTOLS

Values listed below assume good working order with no missing parts. If finish has been removed, and the brass polished, the value is reduced to approximately one half of the 90% value.

MODEL E - .20 cal., 12 gm CO_2 cylinder, 5.85 in. barrel, 400 FPS, high polish nickel finish, walnut grips, special serial range of E00xxxx. Limited mfg. 1990 only.

	$135	$110	$95	$85	$65	N/A	N/A

Add 25% for box and owner´s manual.

MODEL EB - .20 cal., 12 gm CO_2 cylinder, 5.85 in. barrel, 400 FPS, matte black finish, brown plastic grips. Mfg. 1977-1989.

courtesy Beeman Collection

	$85	$75	$65	$55	$50	N/A	N/A

Add 25% for Sheridan box and owner´s manual.

GRADING	100%	95%	90%	80%	60%	40%	20%

❊ **Dart Pistol** - .50 (13mm) cal., CO_2, SS, similar to Model EB except is tranquilizer dart version, matte black finish.

courtesy Beeman Collection

	$200	$175	$150	$125	$100	N/A	N/A

MODEL HB - .20 cal., matte black finish, walnut forearm, brown plastic grips, multiple stroke forearm pneumatic, 8.75 in. barrel, 400 FPS, marked "Sheridan 1982-1990". Mfg. in Racine, WI until 1994, and in E. Bloomfield, NY from 1995 to 1998.

	$100	$90	$75	$65	$55	$50	$45

Add 15% for Sheridan box and owner´s manual.

Add 5% for later box and owner´s manual.

This design has been marketed under the Sheridan name, the Benjamin/Sheridan name, and the Benjamin name. Also marketed as the Sheridan HB20, it cannot be distinguished from identical pistols under the Benjamin HB20 heading in the Benjamin section (please refer to names used in the 1990s in the introduction to the Benjamin section).

MODEL H20PB - .20 cal., multiple stroke forearm pneumatic, polished brass plated, 5.85 in. barrel, 400 FPS, commemorates the 50th Anniversary of Sheridan. Mfg. 1998 only.

	$160	$145	$120	$100	$75	N/A	N/A

Add 15% for box and owner´s manual.

This model was marketed only under the Sheridan name.

RIFLES

Values listed below assume good working order with no missing parts. If finish has been removed, and the brass polished, value is reduced by approx. 50%.

MODEL A SUPER GRADE - .20 cal. (first specimen of the Model A may be .22 cal.), multiple stroke forearm pneumatic, blue finish, walnut half stock with raised cheekpiece, aluminum receiver, peep sights, 20.15 in. barrel, 700 FPS. Approx. 2,130 mfg. 1947-1953. Ref: AR 1 (1997): pp. 41-42.

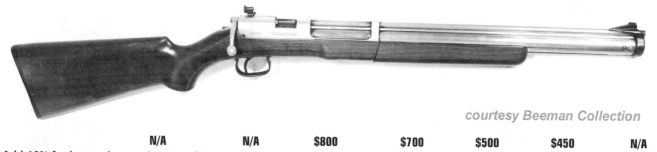

courtesy Beeman Collection

	N/A	N/A	$800	$700	$500	$450	N/A

Add 60% for box and owner´s manual.

Add 15% for first production version without serial numbers, Sheridan logo engraved, felt lining in forearm cocking handle.

Serial numbers on this model were not consecutive, up to about no. 4000 have been observed.

MODEL A-B TRANSITION - intermediate form between Models A and B. Solid rib under barrel, ramp front sight, and forward cap over body tube as in Model A, forward receiver ring does not go over barrel, rear sight attached on both sides of receiver as in Model B. Less than 10 observed.

courtesy Beeman Collection

Rarity precludes accurate pricing.

GRADING	100%	95%	90%	80%	60%	40%	20%

MODEL B SPORTER - .20 cal., multiple stroke forearm pneumatic, black painted finish, walnut half stock, soldered, "ventilated" barrel/pump tube construction, heavy aluminum receiver, peep sights, 20.15 in. barrel, 700 FPS, not serial numbered. Approx. 1,051 mfg. 1948-1951.

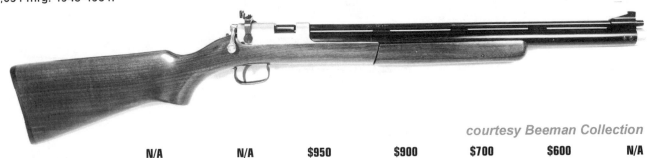

courtesy Beeman Collection

	N/A	N/A	$950	$900	$700	$600	N/A

Add 60% for box and owner´s manual.

MODEL C SILVER STREAK/MODEL CB BLUE STREAK - .20 cal., multiple stroke forearm pneumatic, nickel or black finish, walnut full stock, open sights, 19.5 in. barrel, 675 FPS, rotating safety. Ref: AR (1997): pp. 22-24.

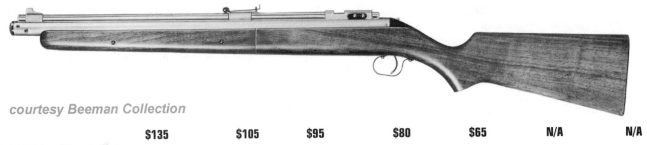

courtesy Beeman Collection

	$135	$105	$95	$80	$65	N/A	N/A

Add 5% for Silver Streak.

Add $20 for Williams peep sight.

Add 15% for Sheridan box and owner´s manual.

Add 20% highly polished original finish, plus 20% for box and owner´s manual.

Add 25% for "hold-down" automatic safety models (mfg. 1952-1963 only), and 25% for box and owner´s manual.

Subtract 25% for disabled automatic safeties; such guns should be repaired or put into non-firing condition.

Add 250% for early Silver Streaks with knurled windage knobs (mfg. 1949-1952) and 30% for box and owner´s manual.

Add 125% for earliest Silver Streak "slab stock" model (mfg. in 1949 only), add 35% for original box and owner´s manual.

Add 150% for left-handed models, approx. 400 mfg.

This model was marked "Sheridan" from 1949 to 1990. Serial numbering began in 1972 with #000000. Also marketed as the Sheridan C9 Silver Streak and the CB9 Blue Streak. (See introduction of Benjamin section for information on manufacturing locations and names used in 1990s.)

MODEL C9 SILVER STREAK - .20 cal., multi-pump pneumatic, BA, SS, 19.38 in. rifled brass barrel, 675 FPS, nickel finish, adj. rear sight, American hardwood stock and forearm, 6 lbs.

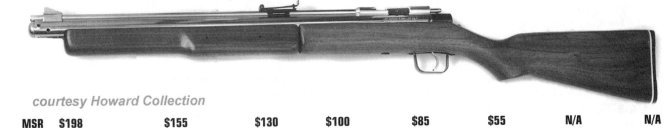

courtesy Howard Collection

MSR	$198	$155	$130	$100	$85	$55	N/A	N/A

✳ *Model C9 Blue Streak* - .20 cal., multi-pump pneumatic, BA, SS, 19.38 in. rifled brass barrel, 675 FPS, black finish, adj. rear sight, American hardwood stock and forearm, 6 lbs.

MSR	$183	$145	$120	$90	$75	$45	N/A	N/A

GRADING	100%	95%	90%	80%	60%	40%	20%

MODEL C9PB - .20 cal., polished brass plating, multiple stroke forearm pneumatic, 675 FPS, medallion inset into stock (1998 only) to commemorate the 50th Anniversary of Sheridan. 1999-2000.

courtesy Howard Collection

	$150	$125	$110	$90	$70	N/A	N/A

Add 20% for medallion in stock.

Add 20% for box and owner´s manual.

This model was marketed only under the Sheridan name.

MODEL F/FB - .20 cal., 12 gm CO_2 cylinder, nickel (Model F) or black (Model FB) finish, walnut half stock, open sights, 19.5 in. barrel, 515 FPS, rotating safety.

courtesy Howard Collection

	$110	$95	$85	$80	$60	N/A	N/A

Add 100% for Model F.

Add 25% for early production, highly polished original finish.

Add 15% for Sheridan box and owner´s manual.

Add 300% for left-handed models.

Add $30 for Williams 5D-SH peep sight.

This model was marked "Sheridan 1975-1990". It was later marketed as the Model F9 under the Benjamin/Sheridan name. (See information on 1990s marketing in the introduction to the Benjamin section.)

SHIN SUNG INDUSTRIES CO. LTD.

Current manufacturer located at 201-6, Samjung-Dong, Ohjeong-Ku, Buchon-City, Kyungki-Do, Korea. Currently imported and distributed by RWS Precision Products located in Closter, NJ, also distributed by ARS located in Pine City, NY.

Manufacturer of a wide variety of amazing, usually very large, pre-charged pneumatic airguns, often of great power, ranging from the exact trumpet look-alike confetti/ribbon-shooting, eye-popping polished brass Celebration which advertises that "It is real action for your unforgettable moment" up to large bore rifles, such as Career 707, Ultra, Carbine, Tanker Carbine, and Fire 201 for which the maker claims: "It is a rearl action to chase the fascinated target" or "Become an explorer in the jungle, run for the freedom with your instinct." The guns are very well built and as interesting as the copy. The shiny brass Celebration trumpet model has a current value above $1,200 in excellent condition. Several simple versions without the trumpet's slide and mouthpieces are known. For more information on these airguns, also see ARS in the "A" section, and RWS in the "R" section.

RIFLES

ADVENTURE DB - .22 cal., PCP, removable mag., PG stock, 41.3 in OAL, 8.2 lbs. Mfg. 1990s.

courtesy Beeman Collection

$550	$500	$450	$350	$275	N/A	N/A

GRADING	100%	95%	90%	80%	60%	40%	20%

VAN STAR 505 - .22 cal., BA, SS, Brocock-type air cartridges (about size of 20 ga. shell), barrel concentric with receiver. 46.2 in. OAL, 6.7 lbs.

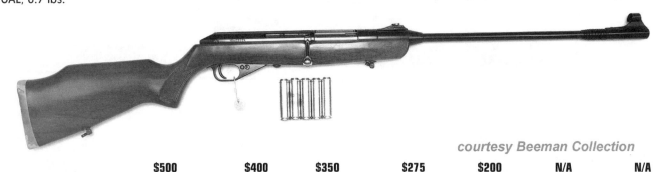

courtesy Beeman Collection

	$500	$400	$350	$275	$200	N/A	N/A

CAREER ULTRA - 9 mm, PCP, SS, under lever cocks gun and moves transverse loading bar, adj. power dial, pressure gauge, hand checkered high grade stock, cross bolt manual safety, 9.4 lbs.

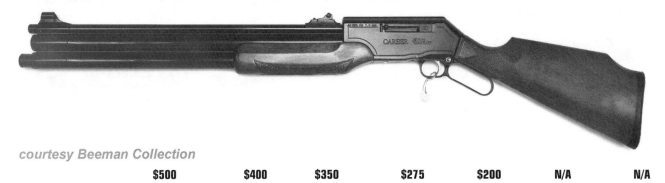

courtesy Beeman Collection

	$500	$400	$350	$275	$200	N/A	N/A

SHUE

Previous trademark of Shue High Pressure Air Rifle Company located in Milwaukee, WI circa 1912-14. Ref: AR2:57-60.

RIFLES

SHUE HYPRESURE AIR RIFLE - .173 steel/ 4.4 lead balls cal., BBC, SP, SS, 423 FPS with steel BB, sheet metal, break action BB gun 33.4 in. OAL, 2.6 lbs. Ref: AR 2 (1998): pp. 57-60.

Rarity precludes accurate pricing.

Only two specimens are known: one fine, one poor.

SIMCO

For information on Simco airguns, see Apache in the "A" section.

SKAN AR

Current manufacturer located at PO Box 3342, White Colne, Colchester CO6 2RA, England 1991 to present.

Current manufacturer of chronographs (chronoscopes) and bullpup PCP air rifles. Owned and operated by Mike Childs. Extruded aluminium frames with small air reservoir in, or forming, the buttstock. Stock parts usually plastic or rubber; walnut offered from 1995.

RIFLES

Skan rifles vary greatly. Older versions will be detailed in later issues of this guide. Models included: Mk 1 with flat 'pipe organ' magazines holding stacked pellets, cocked with side knob. Mk 2 with horizontal, cylindrical magazine with chambers holding about ninety pellets. From 1992 to 1998 cocked with sliding forearm. Forearm cocking discontinued due to concern that British government would ban such actions as slide action weapons. Normally set to UK 12 ft./lb. limit. Single stage trigger on all but most recent guns. Black or brushed anodized silver finishes.

R32 MILLENIUM - .177 or .22 cal., PCP, thirty-two-shot mag., Bullpup style, air cylinder in walnut stock, extended forearm with flush fitting bipod, grey anodised aluminium, nickel finished steel components, removable silencer, 33 in. OAL, 7.5 lbs. 10 mfg. 1999.

MSR	$1,800	$1,550	$1,150	$895	$750	$600	N/A	N/A

Add 5% for case.

MINI M32 MK3 - .177 or.22 (cal., PCP, two vertical drums total thirty-two-shot mag., bullpup style, bottle forms part of buttstock, rubber fittings, two-stage adj. trigger, rear grip slides backwards and forwards to cycle action, built-in sound moderator, bipod, 25 in. OAL, 0.75 lbs.

MSR	$1,125	$950	$775	$650	$495	$375	N/A	N/A

Add 15% for laser sight.

Add 5% for case.

GRADING	100%	95%	90%	80%	60%	40%	20%

R32 ULTRA - .177 or .22 cal., PCP, thirty-two-shot mag., similar to Mini except with walnut fittings, leather cover on bottle, built-in laser, spare magazine slot under buttstock.

MSR $1350	$1,095	$895	$750	$625	$500	N/A	N/A

Add 5% for case.

SLAVIA

For information on Slavia, see CZ in the "C" section.

courtesy Beeman Collection

SMITH & WESSON

Current manufacturer located in Springfield, MA. Dealer sales.

In 1965, Smith & Wesson was purchased from the Wesson family by the conglomerate Bangor Punta. A major diversification program led to the in-house design of an airgun line. With the aid of a former Crosman engineer, four airgun models were developed: the Models 77A, 78G, 79G, and 80G ("A" for "air"; "G" for "gas"). The Model 77A was a .22-caliber pump pneumatic pellet rifle with a less-than-sleek wood stock and forearm-pump lever.

The Model 78G was a single-shot .177 caliber pellet pistol designed to resemble the popular Smith & Wesson Model 41 target automatic. The Model 79G is the .22 caliber version. Both had adjustable rear sights and power. Early versions had non-adjustable triggers; later models had good adjustable trigger mechanisms, adjustable for pull weight. A few problems included gas leakage through porous frame castings.

Smith & Wesson´s Air Gun Division introduced their fourth and final model in 1972, the Model 80G rifle. It was designed by Roger Curran, formerly with Remington. This autoloader fired .175 caliber BBs from a tubular magazine below the barrel. In 1973 the Air Gun Division moved from Springfield, Massachusetts to Tampa, Florida. Some early Model 80G rifles are marked with the Springfield address, as are some Model 77A rifles.

In 1978, the Air Gun Division returned to Springfield in a part of the former Westinghouse complex and the Model 77A was dropped. Due to changing from a sprayed paint finish to a baked powder-coat finish, Springfield production pistols have a duller, more uniform finish than earlier production. Also around this time, Curran began to develop a CO_2 pellet revolver, although Smith & Wesson was not destined to complete development of this model.

Around 1980, Bangor Punta decided that Smith & Wesson should concentrate more on its core handgun business. The Air Gun Division was sold to Daisy. Daisy reportedly was most interested in the pellet revolver project, but had to take the entire airgun division. Daisy renamed the Smith & Wesson Models 78G and 79G as the Daisy Powerline Models 780 and 790. A nickel-plated model .177 caliber version was introduced as the Power Line Model 41 – in honor of the original Smith & Wesson Model 41 firearm.

Smith & Wesson again entered the airgun field in 1999, when they introduced two models made for them by Umarex of Germany: the .177 caliber ten-shot CO_2 pellet revolvers, Models 586 and 686. These were close copies of the .357 Magnum Smith & Wesson revolvers bearing the same numbers.

For more information and current pricing on both new and used Smith & Wesson firearms, please refer to the *Blue Book of Gun Values* by S.P. Fjestad (also available online).

PISTOLS

MODEL 78G - .22 cal., CO_2, SS, styled after S&W Model 41 semiautomatic pistol, gun blue finish, brown plastic grips, 8.5 in. barrel, fully adj. sight, 42 oz. Mfg. 1971-80.

courtesy Beeman Collection

$135	$115	$100	$85	$60	N/A	N/A

Last MSR was $53.45.

Add 50% for orig. box with can of S&W pellets and box of CO_2 cylinders.

GRADING	100%	95%	90%	80%	60%	40%	20%

Add 30% for orig. box with plastic envelope of pellets and CO_2 cylinders.

Add 25% for early pistols with adj. trigger.

Add 10% for Model 78G guns stamped "80G".

MODEL 79G - .177 cal., CO_2, SS, styled after S&W Model 41 semiautomatic pistol;, gun blue finish, brown plastic grips, 8.5 in. barrel, fully adj. sight, 42 oz. Mfg.1971-80.

	100%	95%	90%	80%	60%	40%	20%
	$135	$115	$100	$85	$60	N/A	N/A

Last MSR was $53.45.

Add 50% for orig. box with can of S&W pellets and box of CO_2 cylinders.

Add 30% for orig. box with plastic envelope of pellets and CO_2 cylinders.

Add 25% for early pistols with adj. trigger.

REVOLVERS

MODEL 586B4/586B6/586B8 - .177 cal., CO_2, SA and DA, ten-shot cylinder, 450 FPS, replica of Smith & Wesson Model 586 .357 Mag. revolver, high gloss black finish, black rubber grips, 4, 6, or 8 (disc. 2004), in. interchangeable barrels, 40-48 oz. New 1999.

	100%	95%	90%	80%	60%	40%	20%
MSR $225	$170	$145	$115	$85	$70	N/A	N/A

Add $25 for 6 in. barrel Model 586B6.

Add $29 for 8 in. barrel Model 586B8.

MODEL 686N4/686N6/686N8 - .177 cal., CO_2, SA and DA, ten-shot cylinder magazine, 450 FPS, replica of Smith & Wesson Model 686 .357 Mag. revolver, 4 (disc. 2004), 6, or 8 (disc. 2004), in. interchangeable barrel, satin nickel finish, checkered black rubber grips, 40-48 oz. New 1999.

	100%	95%	90%	80%	60%	40%	20%
MSR $281	$215	$165	$125	$105	$70	N/A	N/A

Add $12 for 6 in. barrel Model 686N6.

Add $22 for 8 in. barrel Model 686N8.

RIFLES

MODEL 77A - .22 cal., swinging forearm, multi-stroke pump pneumatic, wood buttstock and forearm/pump handle, sliding wedge elev. adj. rear sight, trigger guard drops for loading breech, SS, black oxide blue finish, 22 in. rifled barrel, 6.5 lbs. Mfg. 1971-78.

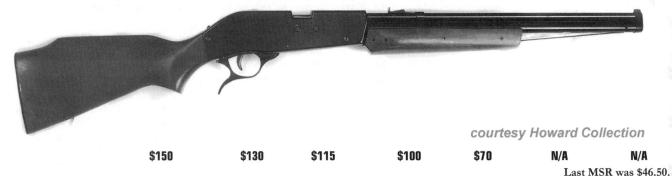

courtesy Howard Collection

	100%	95%	90%	80%	60%	40%	20%
	$150	$130	$115	$100	$70	N/A	N/A

Last MSR was $46.50.

Add 10% for Springfield address.

MODEL 80G - .175/BB cal. CO_2, semi-automatic, brown plastic stock, sliding wedge elev. adj. rear sight, 22 in. barrel. Mfg. 1972-80.

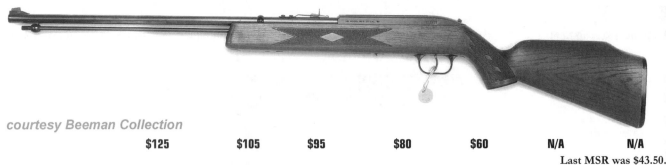

courtesy Beeman Collection

	100%	95%	90%	80%	60%	40%	20%
	$125	$105	$95	$80	$60	N/A	N/A

Last MSR was $43.50.

Add 10% for Springfield address.

SNYDER, RUSS

Current highly noted model and tool maker.

Manufactured twelve each museum quality firing replicas of the original St. Louis 1899 and 1900 air rifles.

GRADING	100%	95%	90%	80%	60%	40%	20%

RIFLES

In 1997, collector Marv Freund persuaded Russ Snyder, a highly noted model maker and toolmaker, to make only twelve masterpiece replicas - museum quality, firing copies of his original St. Louis 1899 air rifle. On a whim, Snyder also made five double-barrel versions of the airgun – something that had never existed in the historical record. In 2002, Russ Snyder produced just a dozen copies of the St. Louis 1900 model air rifle for the purchasers of the 1899 model reproductions. Ref: AR 2 (1998): 76-78.

ST. LOUIS 1899 REPLICA - these replicas are virtually perfect copies of the original, right down to the St. Louis Air Rifle Company logo impressed into the wooden buttstock. Eleven were finished with the original black Japan enamel and nickel plating. One replica was given special decoration, including gold plating. Original maker´s price $750. Ref: ARZ: 1976-78.

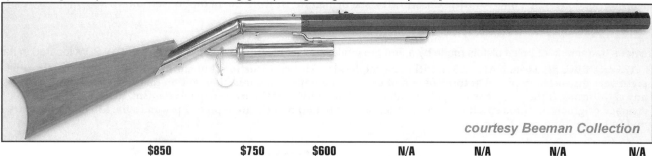

courtesy Beeman Collection

$850	$750	$600	N/A	N/A	N/A	N/A

ST. LOUIS 1900 REPLICA - these are complete with an exact copy of the original St. Louis Air Rifle Company logo stamped into the LHS of the slab sided wooden stock. 33.8 in. OAL. Original price was $850.

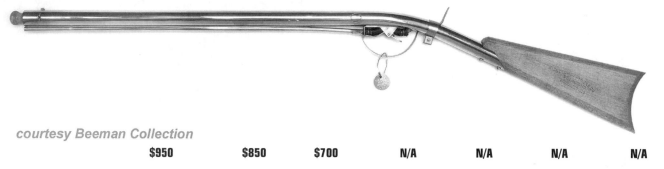

courtesy Beeman Collection

$950	$850	$700	N/A	N/A	N/A	N/A

SPITFIRE

For information on Spitfire airguns, see Philippine Airguns in the "P" section.

SPLATMASTER

For information on Splatmaster tranquilizer guns, see Palmer Chemical & Equipment Co. in the "P" section.

SPORTSMATCH

Current manufacturer of scope mounts located in Leighton Buzzard, Bedfordshire, UK.

Sportsmatch started around the early 1980s by founder John Ford. Sportsmatch is now run by his son, Matthew Ford.

In its day, the GC2 was probably the most coveted rifle a shooter could own; it was akin to owning a Ferrari. Most were sold for use in UK field target competitions, but some were fitted with sporting stocks. The name was derived from 'Gerald Cardew', the famous airgun engineer who designed the GC2 air regulating mechanism. 'GC1' was a testbed for the regulator and not a production rifle. The GC2 was produced in three marks from 1986 to 1993. In all, around 350 guns were produced, some were sold as 'action only' and were married to custom-built stocks from the likes of John Welham. Weight varies accordingly, but these guns have alloy cylinders and are quite light for their size. The two-stage flat blade trigger is fully adjustable. The Lothar Walther barrel was fitted with a fluted muzzle brake to prevent barrel lift on firing. Most were .177 caliber, although any caliber was available. A bullpup version called the Scimitar was available, although only twelve were made.

The GC2 value is in the $1,750 range with basic walnut stock. Add up to 100% for finest quality custom walnut. The Scimitar value is in the $2,100 range.

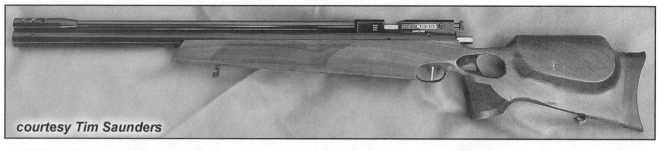

courtesy Tim Saunders

STANLEY AIR RIFLE COMPANY

Previous manufacturer located in Northville, MI circa 1889.

Merritt Stanley, a former employee of the Markham Air Rifle Company was granted at least three patents for BB guns, starting in 1890. He produced a BB gun under his own name circa 1889 in Northville, Michigan, then moved into the Dubuar Manufacturing Company of Northville which produced the Globe air rifles from the early 1890s. In 1908 Daisy consumed the Stanley and Dubuar BB gun production. Stanley may also have been involved in producing designs used by the Plymouth Air Rifle Company. See the Plymouth, Globe, and Decker sections of this guide. Input on existing specimens is actively sought by the authors and publisher. Contact Blue Book Publications or BBA6input@Beemans,net. Ref. Dunathan (1957).

ST. LOUIS AIR RIFLE CO.

For information on St. Louis Air Rifle Co. air rifles, see Benjamin Air Rifle Co. in the "B" section.

STEINER

Previous trademark for pellet pistols made by a firm presently known only from markings on the guns as BBM located in Italy.

- .177 cal., BBC, SP, 14 in. OAL, 7.25 in. rifled barrel, SS. Die-cast construction, but sturdily built. Brown plastic grips. Front sight very distinctively placed at forward end of receiver, perhaps in the mistaken notion that consistent sight alignment has any significance if the barrel has irregular positioning. No safety or anti-barrel snap mechanism. Black or bright nickel finish. Average original condition specimens on most common (Steiner) models are typically priced in the $35 range for black finish and $40 range for nickel finish.

courtesy BeemanCollection

STELLA

Previous trademark of Kovo AS of Prague, Czechoslovakia.

This firm mainly made spring piston, barrel-cocking air rifles in the early 1950s. The line may have moved into the Slavia brand.

PISTOLS

MODEL 551 - .177 cal., smoothbore, BBC, SP, SS, marked with "STELLA" (pierced by an arrow) and "Made in Czechoslovakia" on top of the barrel, 7.9 in OAL, 1.7 lbs. Mfg. circa 1950.

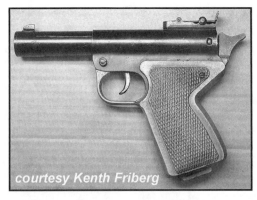

courtesy Kenth Friberg

Rarity precludes listing a value at this time.

GRADING	100%	95%	90%	80%	60%	40%	20%

GAT STYLE - .177 in. cal., smoothbore, push-barrel cocking, folded metal construction, blued, SP, SS. Marked "STELLA" in round logo on grip and "Made in Czechoslovakia" on side of the barrel.

courtesy Beeman Collection

Estimated value about $65 in 90% condition.

STERLING

Previous trademark manufactured by Sterling in England.

Design and trademark purchased by the Benjamin Air Rifle Company, located in East Bloomfield, NY, in 1994. After Benjamin was purchased by Crosman Air Guns in 1994, the manufacture of the Sterling line was discontinued.

RIFLES

HR 81 - .177, .20, or .22 cal., UL, SP, 700/660 FPS, adj. V-type rear sight, 8.5 lbs.

	100%	95%	90%	80%	60%	40%	20%
	$250	$200	$155	$115	$80	N/A	N/A

Last MSR was $250.

Add $50 for original English markings.
Add $10 for .22 cal.
Add $20 for .20 cal.

HR 83 - .177, .20, or .22 cal., UL, SP, 700/660 FPS, adj. Williams (FP) peep sight, walnut stock, 8.5 lbs.

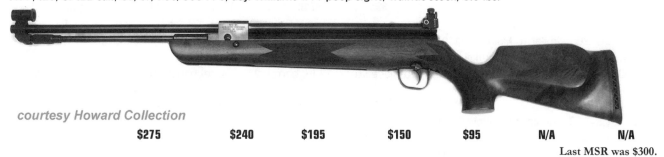

courtesy Howard Collection

	100%	95%	90%	80%	60%	40%	20%
	$275	$240	$195	$150	$95	N/A	N/A

Last MSR was $300.

Add $50 for original English markings.
Add $5 for .22 cal.
Add $20 for .20 cal.

STERLING/UPTON

Previous tradename of American Tool Works located in Chicago, IL. Previous manufacturer of BB guns under the Sterling and Upton names circa 1891-1928.

For information on Sterling and Upton, see American Tool Works in the "A" section.

STEYR SPORTWAFFEN GmbH

Current manufacturer located in Austria. Currently imported by Pilkington Competition Equipment, LLC, located in Monteagle, TN. Previously imported and distributed by Nygord Precision Products, located in Prescott, AZ. Dealer or consumer direct sales.

For more information and current pricing on both new and used Steyr firearms, please refer to the *Blue Book of Gun Values* by S.P. Fjestad (also available online).

PISTOLS

LP-1/LP-1P/LP-C - .177 cal., CO_2 or PCP, UIT pistol with compensator, 15.33 in. overall, 2 lbs. 2 oz. Disc. 2002.

	100%	95%	90%	80%	60%	40%	20%
	$850	$800	$750	$600	$450	N/A	N/A

Last MSR was $995.

Add 10% for colored tank variations (red, blue, green, or silver - marked "LP1-C").
Add 100% for limited edition models.
Subtract 15% for CO_2.

The Limited Edition consists of 250 units, engraved and signed Barbara Mandrell LP-1 USA Shooting Team, in red, white, and blue, and complete with lined walnut presentation case and certificate of authenticity.

GRADING	100%	95%	90%	80%	60%	40%	20%

LP-2 - .177 cal., CO_2 or PCP, SS, UIT pistol, 9 in. BBL with two-port compensator, 530 FPS, two-stage adj. trigger, adj. sights, adj. Morini grip, 15.3 in. OAL, 2 lbs. New 2003.

	MSR $1,150	$1,025	$900	$800	$625	$525	N/A	N/A

Subtract 15% for CO_2.

✳ *LP-2 Junior* - .177 cal., CO_2 or PCP, SS, UIT pistol, similar to LP-2, except 13.2 in. OAL, 1.8 lbs. New 2004.

	MSR $1,045	$995	$875	$750	$600	$500	N/A	N/A

Subtract 15% for CO_2.

LP-5/LP-5P/LP5C - .177 cal., CO_2, PCP (LP-5P), match pistol, five-shot semi-auto.

	$1,000	$900	$800	$650	$500	N/A	N/A

Last MSR was $1,150.

Subtract 15% for CO_2.

LP-10 - .177 cal., CO_2 or PCP, SS, UIT pistol with internal stabilizer, 15.25 in., adj. trigger, adj. sights, adj. Morini grip, four ten-gram barrel weights, 2 lbs. 2 oz. New 1999.

	MSR $1,400	$1,250	$1,075	$900	$775	$625	N/A	N/A

Subtract 15% for CO_2.

LP-50 - .177 cal., PCP, CO_2 or PCP, five-shot semiautomatic, match pistol, similar to LP-5, except LP-10 style BBL shroud with three ports. New 2003.

	MSR $1,500	$1,350	$1,150	$995	$850	$725	N/A	N/A

Subtract 15% for CO_2.

RIFLES

LG-1/LG-1P - .177 cal., SL/SSP (LG-1) or PCP (LG-1P), target model, micrometer sight and adj. stock. Disc. 1998.

	$900	$800	$700	$550	$475	N/A	N/A

Last MSR was $995.

MODEL LG-10/LG-10P - .177 cal., similar to LG-1, except has stabilizer and distinctive anodized red frame. Disc. 2000.

	$1,110	$935	$740	$585	$495	N/A	N/A

Last MSR was $1,139.

MODEL LG-20 - similar to Model LG-110 except with wood stock. New 2005.

As this edition went to press, retail pricing had yet to be established.

MODEL LG-100 - .177 cal., PCP, aluminum two-piece stock, 17 in. barrel, 27 in. steel barrel shroud, 570 FPS, match sight set, 9.5 lbs. New 2001.

	MSR $1,850	$1,665	$1,500	$1,150	$975	$800	N/A	N/A

MODEL LG-110 - similar to Model LG-100. New 2005.

As this edition went to press, retail pricing had yet to be established.

MATCH 88 - .177 cal., CO_2, match rifle with precision receiver sight and adj. buttplate. Mfg. 1991-1995.

	$650	$500	$400	$300	$225	N/A	N/A

MATCH 91 - .177 cal., CO_2, match rifle with precision receiver sight and adj. buttplate. Mfg. 1991-1995.

	$750	$650	$500	$400	$300	N/A	N/A

Last MSR was $1,400.

Add $50 for left-hand variation.
Add $100 for Running Target.

LGB1 BIATHLON - .177 cal., PCP, five-shot repeater, Fortner-type action, adj. match trigger, adj. snow sights, 40 in. OAL, 9.6 lbs. New 2004.

	MSR $2,300	$1,995	$1,750	$1,450	$1,075	N/A	N/A	N/A

Comes with one-shot and five-shot magazine.

STIGA

Previous tradename of Stig Hjelmqvist AB located in Trånas, Sweden.

Makers of firearms, sporting goods, and may be maker or distributor only of a Zenit-style top-lever air pistol. Research is ongoing with this trademark, and more information will be included both online and in future editions.

GRADING	100%	95%	90%	80%	60%	40%	20%

PISTOLS

ZENIT - .177 cal., TL, SP, SS, 5 in. smooth bore barrel. First variant: wood grips with Stiga shield on left-hand side, the name "Zenit" is stamped on the left side of cocking lever, rear side incorporoated in cocking in the rear (back portion of cocking lever), mfg. 1949-1961. Second variant: uses the Zenit action with a brown or blue-grey plastic grips Stiga name molded into bottom of grip on bottom sides, mfg. 1962-65. Third variant: blue-grey plastic grips with heavy-duty reinforced sheet metal cocking lever with wings for easier grip, rear sight is at the end of the action, 11 in. OAL, approx. 1.5 lbs. Mfg. 1965-69. Ref: AR 2 (1998): pp. 16-20.

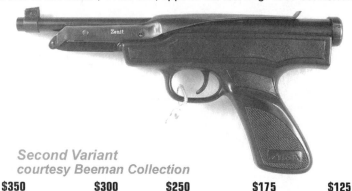

*Second Variant
courtesy Beeman Collection*

	$350	$300	$250	$175	$125	$75	N/A

Very similar to Zenit single shot, top lever air pistol patented by Franz Moller, Zella-Mehlis, Germany for Em-Ge (See the "E" section) in 1937 and discontinued in 1939 due to WWII. (Also copied by Milbro Bros. as the British Diana Model 4.)

CADET - .177 cal., SP, SS, push-barrel, similar to Diana Model 2, loaded from rear of action, 7.9 in. OAL, .66 lbs. Mfg. 1949-1959.

RIFLES

MODEL 99 (JUNIOR) - .177 cal., BBC, SP, SS, smooth bore barrel with sheet metal shroud. Mfg. 1948-1960.
  Current values not yet determined.

MODEL 100 - .177 cal., BBC, SP, SS, 17.4 in. smooth bore solid steel barrel, adj. rear and blade front sights, PG wood stock with Stiga shield on LH side, marked "STIGA TRANAS SWEDEN" on spring tube, 40 in. OAL. Mfg. 1948-1960.
  Current values not yet determined.

ORIGINAL - .177 cal., BBC, SP, SS, 17.4 in. smooth bore solid steel barrel, adj. rear and blade front sights, PG wood stock with Stiga shield on LH side, marked "STIGA TRANAS SWEDEN" on spring tube, 40 in. OAL. Mfg. 1948-1960.
  Current values not yet determined.

SUSSEX ARMORY

For information on Sussex Armory airguns, see Gun Toys SRL in the "G" section.

SUPER TORNADO

For information on Super Tornado airguns, see Relum Limited in the "R" section.

SWISS ARMS MANUFACTURE (SAM)

Current manufacturer located in Davesco, Switzerland. Previously imported and distributed by Nygord Precision Products, located in Prescott, AZ. Dealer or consumer direct sales.

PISTOLS

MODEL M5 JUNIOR - .177 cal., PCP, similar to Model M10, except shorter and lighter.

	$600	$500	$400	$300	$200	N/A	N/A

MODEL M10 - .177 cal., PCP, 492 FPS, 9.50 in. barrel with compensator, adj. trigger, sights and pistol grip, special dry firing mechanism, walnut grips. Mfg. 1998-2000.

	$700	$550	$475	$400	$300	N/A	N/A

MODEL SAM K-9 - .177 cal., PCP, similar to Model K-11, except Junior variation.

MSR	N/A	$675	$535	$465	$385	$295	N/A	N/A

MODEL SAM K-11 - .177 cal., PCP, 492 FPS, 9.45 in. barrel with compensator, adj. trigger, sights and pistol grip, two rod counter-balancing system, special dry firing mechanism, walnut grips, 2.34 lbs. New 2000.

MSR	N/A	$900	$800	$700	$550	$475	N/A	N/A

MODEL SAM K-12 - .177 cal., PCP, 492 FPS, 9.45 in. barrel with compensator, adj. trigger, sights and pistol grip, one rod counter-balancing system, special dry firing mechanism, walnut grips, 2.34 lbs. New 2002.

MSR	N/A	$875	$775	$675	$525	$450	N/A	N/A

SNIDER AIR PISTOL

For information on Snider airguns, see Hubertus in the "H" section.

NOTES

T SECTION

TAHITI

For information on Tahiti airguns, see Dianawerk in the "D" section.

TAIYO JUKI

Current trademark of Miroku Firearms Manufacturing Company (Miroku Taiyo Zuki) located in Kochi, Japan. Airguns manufactured from circa 1970s.

For more information and current pricing on both new and used firearms, please refer to the *Blue Book of Gun Values* by S.P. Fjestad (also available online).

GRADING	100%	95%	90%	80%	60%	40%	20%

RIFLES

BOBCAT - .177 or .22 cal., CO_2, SS, similar to Crosman Model 160.

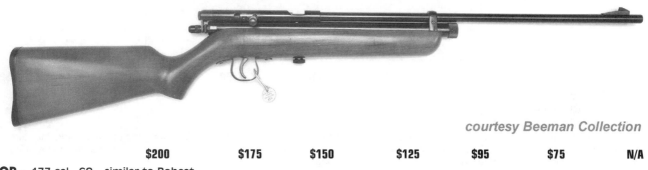

courtesy Beeman Collection

	$200	$175	$150	$125	$95	$75	N/A

JUNIOR - .177 cal., CO_2, similar to Bobcat.

courtesy Beeman Collection

	$200	$175	$150	$125	$95	$75	N/A

GRAND SLAM - .22 cal., CO_2, semiautomatic.

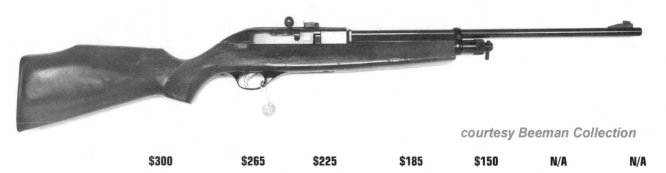

courtesy Beeman Collection

	$300	$265	$225	$185	$150	N/A	N/A

GRADING	100%	95%	90%	80%	60%	40%	20%

TARG-AIRE (AND RANCO)

Previously manufactured by Targ-aire Pistol Co., located at 120 S. La Salla St. Chicago, IL.

PISTOLS

TARG-AIRE PISTOL - .177, or .22 cal., BBC, SP, 4.25 in. rifled barrel, 10.5 in. overall, blue finish, Tenite or cast aluminum grips, backstrap cocking lever, "Targ-aire" molded in circle around grip screw, large protruding thumbrest top left side of grip, 2.8 lbs. Mfg. 1946-47.

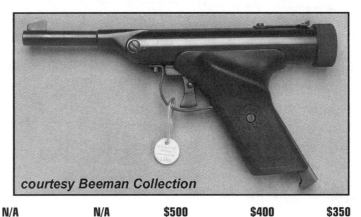

courtesy Beeman Collection

	N/A	N/A	$500	$400	$350	$275	$200

Add 40% for factory box.

Add 10% for cast aluminum grips.

Add 25% for Ranco markings.

When Targ-aire production ceased, Randall Tool Co. continued production of identical guns for short time using existing Targ-aire marked grips and compression tubes. Thus, some Targ-aire marked guns are found in Ranco boxes. Ranco marking began in Nov. 1947. Ranco manufacture ceased in 1951. See Ranco in the "R" section for image.

TAU BRNO, spol. s r.o.

Current manufacturer located in Brno, Czech Republic. Currently imported and distributed by Pilkington Competition Equipment LLC located in Monteagle, TN, Top Gun Air Guns Inc. located in Scottsdale, AZ. Dealer or consumer direct sales.

PISTOLS

TAU-7 - .177 cal., CO_2, SS, UIT target model, attaché case, extra seals, and counterweight, 2.3 lbs. Mfg. by Aeron. Disc. circa 1997.

	$260	$200	$155	$110	$85	N/A	N/A

TAU-7 STANDARD - .177 or .22 cal., CO_2, SS, UIT target model, 10.25 in. barrel, 426 FPS, adj. trigger and sights, attaché case, extra seals, and counterweight, 2.3 lbs. Disc. 2004.

	$265	$200	$155	$110	$85	N/A	N/A

Last MSR was $315.

TAU-7 SPORT - .177 or .22 cal., CO_2, SS, UIT target model, 10 in. barrel, 426 FPS, adj. trigger and sights, attaché case, extra seals, and counterweight, 2.3 lbs.

MSR	$435	$375	$275	$230	$185	$145	N/A	N/A

TAU-7 MATCH - .177 or .22 cal., SS, CO_2, similar to TAU-7 Sport, except has select grade barrel, compensator.

MSR	$500	$435	$360	$265	$225	$185	N/A	N/A

TAU-7 SILHOUETTE - .177 or .22 cal., SS, CO_2, similar to TAU-7 Match, except has 12.6 in. select grade barrel, scope mount, and compensator.

MSR	$550	$475	$395	$295	$255	$200	N/A	N/A

RIFLES

TAU-200 - .177 cal., CO_2, SS, UIT target model, synthetic adj. stock. Mfg. by Aeron. Disc. circa 1997.

	$210	$185	$150	$115	$85	N/A	N/A

TAU-200 JUNIOR - .177 cal., CO_2, SS, UIT target model, 400 FPS, adj. sights, adj. trigger adj. laminated stock, 40 in. OAL, 7 lbs.

MSR	$480	$395	$325	$285	$225	$175	N/A	N/A

TAU-200 ADULT - .177 cal., CO_2, SS, UIT target model, 512 FPS, adj. sights, adj. trigger adj. beech stock, 46 in. OAL, 7 lbs.

MSR	$495	$425	$350	$295	$235	$175	N/A	N/A

TAURUS

For information Taurus on airguns, see Relum Limited in the "R" section.

GRADING	100%	95%	90%	80%	60%	40%	20%

T. DIANA

Probably an illegal trademark previously used by manufacturer of unauthorized copy of the Dianawerk Model 5 air pistol.

The most interesting feature is the logo stamped in the top of the receiver – it shows Diana, the Goddess of Hunting, holding her bow and arrow. (Over the curved stamping: T. DIANA). The maker used this classical view of Diana instead of Dianawerk's humorous and protected trademark which shows Diana holding her air rifle aloft while discarding her bow and arrow. This switch in logos was done either out of ignorance or as a clever attempt to avoid trademark prosecution. Solidly made, blued, two-step barrel, wooden grip with coarse hand checkering. .177 cal., 13.3 in. OAL, BBC, SP, SS. Value of this novel Diana airgun collection item estimated to be about $175.

courtesy Beeman Collection

TELL

Previously manufactured by Venuswaffenwerk, located in Zella, Mehlis, Germany.

Venuswaffenwerk was formed by Oskar Will in 1844, and made both air rifles and pistols for nearly one hundred years. The Tell 1 was most likely designed by Will as a companion to his popular rifles. The design of Tell 2 & Tell 3 are very different and more elegant. They were not companions to any rifle and were designed after Wilhelm Foss took over the company about 1919. The company ceased operations in late 1950s.

PISTOLS

TELL 1 - .177 cal., BBC, SP, rifled 9.75 in. blue barrel, nickel plated body, rounded wood grips, 21 in. overall, nickel plated trigger guard with finger rest. Its ungainly size and style suggests that it was a pistol version of the original Will-style air rifle. At least two versions: one unmarked, the other marked "TELLOW" - for Tell and the initials of Oskar Will. 2.9 lbs.

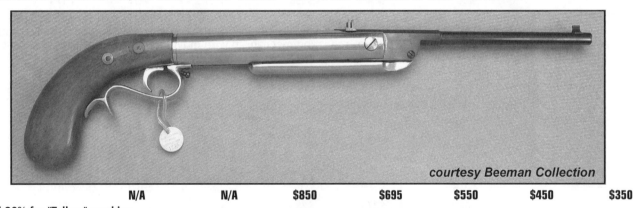

courtesy Beeman Collection

N/A	N/A	$850	$695	$550	$450	$350

Add 20% for "Tellow" marking.

TELL 2 - .177 cal., SP, concentric-piston, 5 in. rifled barrel, 5.75 in. overall, blue or nickel finish, grip backstrap folds out to aid cocking which is accomplished by front of trigger guard engaging piston, checkered wood grips, 0.9 lbs.

courtesy Beeman Collection

N/A	N/A	$300	$250	$200	$150	$100

Add 35% for nickel finish (rare). Add 50% for factory box, pellet tin, and paperwork.
The Tell 2 and the Clarke's Bulldog apparently are the world's smallest spring piston airguns.

GRADING	100%	95%	90%	80%	60%	40%	20%

TELL 3 - .177 cal., BBC, SP, Luger style, unique cocking link above air chamber, 5.38 in. rifled barrel, 10 in. overall, blue finish, brown checkered plastic grips with Tell emblem in center, rare, perhaps fifty exist. 2.2 lbs. Ref: AW - June 2003.

courtesy Beeman Collection

	N/A	N/A	$750	$650	$500	$400	$300

Add 40% for factory box, accessories, and paperwork.

RIFLES

MARS 86 - .177 cal. balls, SP, BA, youth sized, full length hardwood stock, gravity-fed mag. loads through gate on barrel sleeve, swinging safety, 34.1 in. OAL, 3.6 lbs.

courtesy Beeman Collection

	N/A	N/A	$395	$325	$275	$175	N/A

MARS 110 - .173/BB lead ball cal., SP, BA, paramilitary-style trainer based on Schmeisser design of Anschütz Model 275, styled very closely to Mauser 98 paramilitary rifle w/full length stock, top wooden hand guards and side slot in buttstock for leather sling, paramilitary type rear sight marked 6 to 12 meters, repeating mechanism with gravity-fed magazine, Mauser wing-type manual safety, 43 in. OAL, 7.3 lbs.

courtesy Beeman Collection

	$425	$375	$325	$250	$175	$125	$75

Produced for German Hitlerjugend training. Related military-style models reported: 1935-40 (perhaps some later during Soviet occupation, these would be much lower quality).

MILITIA MODEL - .177, BBC, SP, SS, milita-style rifle, part-round/part-octagonal BBL, walnut buttstock, blue steel buttplate. 5.4 lbs.

	$450	$400	$350	$275	$200	N/A	N/A

TELLY

For information on Telly airguns, see Relum Limited in the "R" section.

TEX

For information on Tex, see Slavia in the "S" section.

TEXAN

For information on Texan airguns, see Apache in the "A" section.

GRADING	100%	95%	90%	80%	60%	40%	20%

THEOBEN ENGINEERING

Current manufacturer located in England. Currently imported and distributed by Theoben USA located in Garden Grove, CA beginning 2004 and beginning 1992 by Beeman Precision Airguns, located in Huntington Beach, CA, and previously imported by Air Rifle Specialists located in Pine City, NY. Dealer and consumer direct sales.

Models built for Beeman Precision Airguns can be found in the Beeman section of this text. Please contact Theoben USA directly for more information and prices of their products (see Trademark Index listing).

RIFLES

The U.S. importation of the models listed below was discontinued during 1993 (unless otherwise marked).

Add $150 for Theoben pump applicable for some models listed below.

SIROCCO COUNTRYMAN - .177 or .22 cal., BBC, 1100/800 FPS, pre-charged sealed gas spring, includes scope rings, barrel weight, walnut stained beechwood stock, 7 1/2 lbs. Importation disc. 1987.

	100%	95%	90%	80%	60%	40%	20%
	$360	$285	$175	$125	N/A	N/A	

Last MSR was $585.

SIROCCO DELUXE - similar to Countryman, except has hand checkered walnut stock. Importation disc. 1987.

	100%	95%	90%	80%	60%	40%	20%
	$540	$450	$395	$245	$195	N/A	N/A

Last MSR was $650.

SIROCCO CLASSIC - similar to Sirocco Deluxe, except has updated floating inertia system in piston chamber and automatic safety, 900/1100 FPS. Mfg. 1987.

	100%	95%	90%	80%	60%	40%	20%
	$665	$565	$465	$385	$295	N/A	N/A

Last MSR was $830.

Add $60 for left-hand variation.
This model was available with either a choked or unchoked Anschütz barrel as standard equipment.

SIROCCO GRAND PRIX - similar to the Sirocco Classic, except has checkered walnut thumbhole stock.

	100%	95%	90%	80%	60%	40%	20%
	$750	$655	$565	$430	$345	N/A	N/A

Last MSR was $940.

Add $60 for left-hand variation.
Subtract 50% for older models without safety and new piston design.
In 1987, this model was updated with a floating inertia system in piston chamber, automatic safety, and variable power.
This model was available with either a choked or unchoked Anschütz barrel as standard equipment.

ELIMINATOR - .177 or .22 cal., barrel cocking, 1400/1100 FPS, deluxe checkered thumbhole stock with cheekpiece and pad, 9 1/2 lbs.

	100%	95%	90%	80%	60%	40%	20%
	$825	$750	$490	$410	$325	N/A	N/A

Last MSR was $1,500.

Add $60 for left-hand variation.
This model incorporated an improved barrel design featuring pronounced rifling for the higher velocity pellets.

IMPERATOR - .22 cal., UL, SP, 750 FPS, walnut hand checkered stock, automatic safety. Mfg. 1989.

	100%	95%	90%	80%	60%	40%	20%
	$825	$750	$490	$410	$325	N/A	N/A

Last MSR was $1,500.

IMPERATOR SLR 88 - similar to Imperator, except has a seven-shot magazine. Very limited importation.

	100%	95%	90%	80%	60%	40%	20%
	$1,200	$900	$750	$490	$410	N/A	N/A

Last MSR was $1,680.

RAPID 7 - .22 cal., PCP, 19 in. Anschütz barrel, stippled walnut stock, seven-shot bolt action design, 6 3/4 lbs.

	100%	95%	90%	80%	60%	40%	20%
	$1,000	$850	$750	$650	$550	N/A	N/A

Last MSR was $1,300.

Add $60 for left-hand variation.
Add $120 for scuba tank adaptor.

THUNDERBOLT

For information on Thunderbolt airguns, see Produsit in the "P" section.

TIGER

For information on Tiger airguns, see F.I.E. in the "F" section.

TITAN (CURRENT MFG.)

Current tradename resurrected by a current British airgun maker who seems to have operated under several names and perhaps several ownerships circa 1990 to present.

Products include high quality air rifles and pistols, including PCP and pump pneumatic power plants. Additional research is

GRADING	100%	95%	90%	80%	60%	40%	20%

being done on this maker and their guns. Research is ongoing with this trademark, and more information will be included both online and in future editions. Average original condition specimens on most common Titan models are typically priced in the $400-$1,200 range. See also Beeman and Falcon sections in this edition.

courtesy Beeman Collection

TITAN (DISC.)

Previous trademark of air pistols patented and probably manufactured by Frank Clarke located in Birmingham, England circa 1916-1926.

Note that there are a considerable number of variations from these basic models; variations which do not seem to merit model level status at this time. These model numbers have been proposed by noted airgun researcher John Atkins (Airgun Editor *Airgunner Magazine*) and do not represent model designations of the maker. Numbers on guns probably are not serial numbers. The authors and publisher of the *Blue Book of Airguns* wish to express their appreciation to John Atkins and Ingvar Alm for their valuable assistance with the following information in this edition of the *Blue Book of Airguns*.

PISTOLS

Unless otherwise noted, all air pistols noted below are .177 cal., SP, SS, rear rod-cocking, blue finish steel, with walnut grip plates fitted into the sides of the grip frame.

MARK 1 - 9.25 in BBL, bolt action, nickel finish, one-piece grip frame and breech block with black hard rubber grip plates, front sight sleeves muzzle, rear sight is a notch on the bolt handle, cocking plunger in front of compression chamber, angled hard rubber grip plates with "FC" for Frank Clark and "B" for Birmingham on the right side, and "Titan" imprinted on the left side, a crown is stamped over "MADE IN ENGLAND" on back of breech block, 10 in. OAL. approx. 1.1 lbs. Mfg. 1916-17.

courtesy Loke Collection

Rarity precludes accurate pricing.
To aid cocking, a device, made of twisted steel wire, could be attached to the cocking plunger and then held down by the user's toe.

MARK 2 - similar to Mark 1 except, iron grip frame and air chamber cast in one piece, no grip plates, cocked by plunger rod (apparently removable) from rear, bolt attached to BBL, BBL slides forward to load, nickel plated finish. Mfg. 1917.

Rarity precludes accurate pricing.
The spring is compressed by means of a plunger and rod operated from the rear of the action.

MARK 3 - barrel length similar to Mark 1 and Mark 2 except barrel projects far ahead of body tube, one-piece cast iron compression tube, barrel bands with with rear band acting as sight, and vertical grip frame, front sight on barrel, twist breech block rotated counter-clockwise for loading, cocking rod folds into grooved back strap, three pins mounting trigger guard, black painted finish, cocked by pushing a rod in from the rear. Mfg. 1918.

Rarity precludes accurate pricing.
Establishes the basic Titan pattern of cocking and loading found in all later Titan air pistols.

MARK 4 - similar to Mark 3 except, more streamlined, BBL support lugs cast into body tube, pinned cap at forward end allows forward removal of mainspring. BBL extends far forward of body tube. Vertical grip frame with checkered wood grip plates inset into frame. 10.5 in. OAL. Mfg. 1919-1923.

	N/A	N/A	N/A	$900	$650	$550	$450

GRADING	100%	95%	90%	80%	60%	40%	20%

MARK 5 - similar to Mark 4 except has 7 in. barrel, extends only about one inch forward of body tube, mainspring removes from breech end, front sight cast on top of front barrel band, checkered hard rubber grips, roll stamped LH side compression chamber 'THE "TITAN" AIR PISTOL' over 'PATENT 110999/17', approx. 1.9 lbs. Most common model. Mfg. circa 1920.

courtesy Beeman Collection

	N/A	N/A	N/A	$695	$550	$450	$350

MARK 6 - similar to Mark 5 except, trigger sear adj. screw through rear of trigger guard, four pins mounting trigger and guard, roll stamped LH side 'THE "TITAN" AIR PISTOL' over 'PATENT 110999/17', approx. 1.8 lbs. Mfg. circa 1921.

courtesy Loke Collection

	N/A	N/A	N/A	$695	$550	$450	$350

MARK 7 - similar to Mark 6 except, without trigger sear adj. screw, internal grip safety disengaged when cocking rod is depressed into frame slot, checkered hard rubber grip with "T" inside of a circle molded on top half, roll stamped LH side 'THE "TITAN" AIR PISTOL' over 'PATENT 110999/17', approx. 1.7 lbs. Mfg. circa 1923-1925. Ref: AG July, Aug, Sept 1987, Oct 1988, Oct 1991.

courtesy Loke Collection

	N/A	N/A	N/A	$850	$650	$550	$450

Only turning-breech, folding-cocking-rod Titan w/ slanted grips. Evolved into the Clarke-designed Webley Mk 1 which replaced it.

GRADING	100%	95%	90%	80%	60%	40%	20%

TOK

Previous manufacturer of barrel cocking air rifles, presumably in Japan.

RIFLES

INDIAN - .177 cal., BBC, SP, SS, one-inch dia. receiver tube, copy of BSA barrel cocking air rifle, 17 in. barrel, marked with outline letters "INDIAN" and an Indian head on top of receiver, stamped across receiver: Made by TOK O. 39.4 in. OAL, 3.7 lbs.

courtesy Beeman Collection

Research is ongoing with this trademark, and more information will be included both online and in future editions.

TONG IL

Tong Il Industrial Co. Ltd. of Seoul, South Korea. Apparently active.

Relationship to Yewha and National brands are not clear at this time.

RIFLES

GARAND MODEL MT 1 - .177 cal., SS, UL, swinging lever pump pneumatic, very realistic, slightly oversized replica of Garand military rifle. Same bolt action to load. Flash suppressor. Parkerized finish. Marked "TONG IL MT 1" on top rear of receiver. 28.5 in. round BBL, 46.7 in. OAL, 9.8 lbs.

courtesy Beeman Collection

		N/A	N/A	$1,800	$1,600	$1,400	$1,000	$700

MI CARBINE MODEL CT 2 - .177 cal., SP, SS, SL, sidelever very suggestive of Feinwerkbau 300 side lever. Very realistic replica of US M1 Carbine military rifle. Same bolt action to load. Web sling with oiler sling retainer; some other original M1 parts. Parkerized finish. Marked "MOD. CT 2." 36.3 in. OAL, 7.3 lbs.

courtesy Beeman Collection

		N/A	N/A	$1,500	$1,300	$1,200	$900	$600

TOPGUN

For information on Topgun airguns, see Philippine Airguns in the "P" section.

TRIDENT

For information on Trident airguns, see Philippine Airguns in the "P" section.

TYPHOON

For information on Typhoon airguns, see Milbro in the "M" section and Webley in the "W" section.

GRADING	100%	95%	90%	80%	60%	40%	20%

TyROL

Previous brand name of previous manufacturer, Tiroler Sportwaffenfabrik und Apparatebau GmbH ("TyROL Sport Weapon Makers and Apparatus Factory"), Kufstein, Austria. Circa 1939 to 1970s.

Many airgun collectors think that non-match CO_2 rifles were made only in the United States. Here are some wonderful exceptions. The rifles below bear the same TyROL brand name (in the same unusual font printed in this unique way), same Austrian eagle logo, and "MADE IN AUSTRIA" marking.

Production of these airguns sometimes has been attributed to Tiroler Waffenfabrik ("Tyrol Weapon Makers") Peterlongo, Richard Mahrhold & Sohn, Innsbrück, Austria, founded in 1854 and reportedly still making airguns into the 1970s, but Richard Mahrhold's Waffenlexikon (Weapon Dictionary) edition of 1998 notes that they are the product of the firm presently known as Tiroler Sportwaffenfabrik und Apparatebau GmbH ("Tyrol Sport Weapon Makers and Apparatus Factory Inc.") (aka Tiroler Jagd und Sportwaffenfabrik or "TyROL Hunting and Sport Weapon Makers") of Kufstein, Austria, a gunmaker associated with Voetter & Co. of Vöhrenbach/Schwarzwald ("Black Forest"), Germany. The Tiroler Jagd und Sportwaffenfabrik Company name was established in 1965, but the firm was known as the Tiroler Maschinenbau und Holzindustrie ("TyROL Machine Factory and Wood Works") in the 1950s when the TyROL COmatic and CM1 CO_2 rifles were produced and prior to that as Tiroler Waffenfabrik H. Krieghoff (probably unrelated to H. Kreighoff of Suhl and then Ulm, Germany).

These airguns, especially the M1 Carbine-style trainer, may have been supplied to Voetter & Co. who reportedly was the official supplier of arms to the Austrian Army. Voetter also used the well-known brand name of Voere. The M1 Carbine version known officially as the Österreichischen Übungskarabiner KM 1 or "ÜK" is one of the most sought-after military arms among European arms and airgun collectors.

The association of the Austrian TyROL CO_2 rifles and the Italian Armigas "OLIMPIC" CO_2 rifles is a puzzle. While the civilian COmatic version of the TyROL gas rifle and the Armigas "OLIMPIC" appear to be the same, close examination shows that while virtually every part is similar, with almost identical styling, none actually are the same and they certainly are not interchangeable! Perhaps the TyROL CO_2 repeater was the inspiration for the OLIMPIC from Armigas, or, less likely, the reverse.

The TyROL CO-Matic rifle obviously was also the model for Venturini's Golondrina "COMatic CO_2 pellet rifle, not surprising, considering the past ties of Germany and Argentina. The Golondrina repeater was in turn the model for the Golondrina repeating CO_2 pistol.

The TyROL COmatic and CM1 rifles may have additional special significance in the historical development of airguns as the maker claimed that they were the first semi-automatic CO_2 rifles to be developed commercially. (Ref: Amer. Rifleman Sept 1959:62-3; DWJ March 1992:401-3).

RIFLES

Information on other TyROL models is solicited. Contact BBAupdate@Beemans.net or Blue Book Publications Inc.

TyROL GAS RIFLE ("COmatic" MODEL) - .177 cal., CO_2 bulk feed, charging valve by muzzle, semi-automatic; spring-fed removable sixty-shot magazine for lead balls, combination cocking tab/manual safety cannot be reset to safe after cocking, 21.2 in. rifled barrel, blue finish, date stamped LHS, 38 in. OAL, 5.3 lbs. Mfg. 1959.

courtesy Beeman Collection

$475	$375	$295	$245	$205	$160	$135

Civilian version of the Austrian Army Model CM1.

TyROL AUSTRIAN ARMY MILITARY MODEL CM1 - .177 cal., CO_2 bulk feed, 21 in. barrel, long removable spring-fed magazine for lead balls on right side of barrel, stock styled exactly after U.S. M1 Carbine, complete with web sling retained by regulation oiler tube, military style adj. peep rear and blade protected front sight, LH receiver marked TyROL and with Austrian eagle logo, rear edge of receiver marked 4,5 mm DPH. supplied with four actual M1 carbine magazines loaded with dummy .30 cal. carbine cartridges, gas charging device, cleaning rod, regulation canvas magazine pouches, and canvas case, 36 in. OAL, 5.7 lbs. Approx. only 340 mfg. circa 1950s.

courtesy Beeman Collection

N/A	N/A	$1,200	$1,000	$800	$600	$500

GRADING	100%	95%	90%	80%	60%	40%	20%

Subtract 40% for "demilitarized" versions.

Subtract 25% if missing accessories.

Spring-fed magazine reportedly designed to take approx. the same time to replace as a box magazine of cartridges on the actual U.S. M1 Carbine. Original U.S. M1 carbine magazines fit into the gun in the conventional manner, but did not function. Reportedly used for training of Austrian and Dutch troops who had received large quantities of the U.S. M1 Carbines after WWII, most were destroyed by military authorities. Specimens remaining in Germany usually were modified to a "non-military configuration" by removing the military style sights, regulation sling and oiler, and filling in the sling slot in the stock.

TyROL MODEL 51 - .177 cal., SP, BC, SS, conventional sporter-style stock, open sights, TyROL and eagle logo markings.

	$100	$75	$60	$50	$35	$25	$20

TyROL TOURNIER 53 - .177 cal., SP, BC, SS, 17.7 in. rifled barrel, blue finish, precision diopter (match aperture sight), match style stock with carved grip cap, marked on barrel "Tournier 53", "TyROL" plus a large Austrian eagle logo enclosing a large stylized letter "M" on top of receiver, and "MADE IN AUSTRIA" and serial number on LH side of barrel block, no safety, 42 in. OAL, 9.6 lbs.

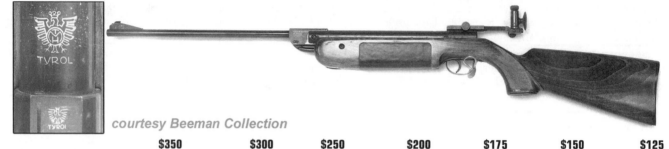

courtesy Beeman Collection

	$350	$300	$250	$200	$175	$150	$125

Stylized letter "M" may indicate an association with Richard Mahrholdt.

U SECTION

ULTI-SHOT

Previous trademark of Ultimate Force in England the manufacturer of UltiShot air shotgun designed by Luke Cammilleri and Martin McManus of Merseyside, England.

Research is ongoing with this trademark, and more information will be included both online and in future editions. Input about this gun is actively solicited by this guide at BBA6@Beemans.net. Ref: AW: Feb. 1996.

GRADING	100%	95%	90%	80%	60%	40%	20%

SHOTGUN

ULTISHOT - .38 caliber air shotgun (or .375 lead balls or .38 cal. 110 gr. HP slugs), PCP, smoothbore. British FAC version produces about 30 ft./lb. ME (9 mm rifled barrel version made in at least prototype form).Tilting breech block, takes .38 cal. Crosman shot cartridges. 37.2 in OAL, 19.3 in BBL, 6.9 lbs, checkered walnut straight grip stock. Appears to be based on Falcon PCP action. Serial numbers to 6 known. Produced only in 1996. Disc.

courtesy Beeman Collection

$1,200	$995	$800	N/A	N/A	N/A	N/A

ULTRA-HI PRODUCTS

Previous Pioneer BB76 BB gun distributor located in Hawthorne, NJ.

Made in Japan.

RIFLES

PIONEER BB76 - 4.4 mm cal. lead balls (bore too large for American steel .173 in BBs), SP, fifty-shot spring-fed magazine similar to Daisy 25, copy of a Kentucky rifle for the 1976 US Bicentennial. Underlever charging lever. 45.0 OAL, 4.1 lbs. Velocity with 7.8 gr lead balls = 304 FPS, with 5.4 gr Daisy Quick Silver BBs 372 FPS.Three stage adjustable trigger. Hammer is the safety. US Patent 238780. Manufactured in 1976 only. Ref: AR 6:7-10.

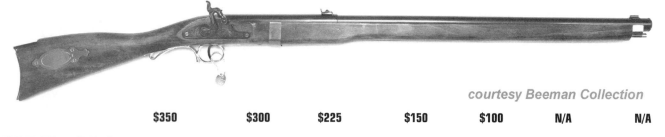

courtesy Beeman Collection

$350	$300	$225	$150	$100	N/A	N/A

UMAREX SPORTWAFFEN GMBH & CO. KG

Current manufacturer located in Arnsberg, Germany. Umarex manufactures private label airguns sold under the Walther, Beretta, Colt, and Smith & Wesson names.

Umarex is the present owner of Walther. Umarex does not sell directly to the general market, and the various private label models produced are listed under their respective trademark names. Please refer to the Beretta, Colt, Smith & Wesson, and Walther listings in this text.

For more information and current pricing on both new and used Umarex firearms, please refer to the *Blue Book of Gun Values* by S.P. Fjestad (also available online).

UNICA

Manufacturer status is unknown at time of printing.

Details of construction, including cast aluminum receiver, indicate that the one known model is a regular production item.

SHOTGUNS

UNICA AIR SHOTGUN - .25 cal., SP, BBC, SS, breech opening. Appears to be an over/under shotgun, but bottom barrel-like tube is open near barrel pivot, side sling swivels, blued steel and aluminum, rib runs full length of barrel and receiver (serves as scope base on receiver), threaded muzzle ring removes to receive muzzle brake or suppressor, walnut stock. "Unica" in molded type and winged eagle logo on white plastic buttplate – matching grip cap. No safety. 18.3 in. BBL, 41.5 in. OAL, 6.5 lbs.

courtesy Beeman Collection

N/A	N/A	$1,100	$850	N/A	N/A	N/A

Information on this gun is actively solicited – please contact BlueBookEdit@Beemans.net or Blue Book Publications.

UPTON

For information on Upton airguns, see Sterling/Upton in the "S" section.

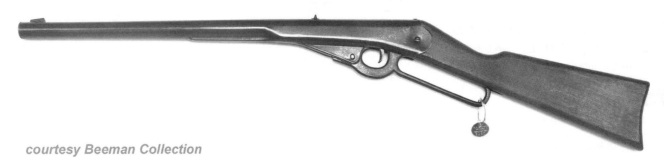

courtesy Beeman Collection

V SECTION

VALESQUEZ

For information on Valesquez airguns, see Philippine Airguns in the "P" section.

VALIENTE

For information on Valiente airguns, see Philippine Airguns in the "P" section.

VALMET

Previous tradename of Valmet Oy located in Jyväskylä, Finland. Manufacture of Valmet firearms was replaced by Tikka circa 1989.

Former governmental engineering works, later famous for fine sporting and military firearms, such as the Model 58 Kalashnikov assault rifle. Fused with Sako in 1987 to become Sako-Valmet. Formerly produced BBC air rifles of especially high quality. For more information and current values on used firearms, please refer to the *Blue Book of Gun Values* by S.P. Fjestad (also available online).

GRADING	100%	95%	90%	80%	60%	40%	20%

RIFLES

AIRIS - .177 cal., BBC, SP, SS, steel parts, fwd. sling swivel mounted into outside of barrel, blue finish, hardwood stock with finger-grooved forearm, 39.5 in. OAL, 5.0 lbs.

courtesy Beeman Collection

	100%	95%	90%	80%	60%	40%	20%
	$425	$375	$325	$250	$200	$150	N/A

VENOM ARMS CUSTOM GUNS

Current manufacturer/customizer located in the Birmingham, England. No current U.S. importation. Venom Arms Custom Guns is a division of Webley & Scott.

Venom Arms specializes in customizing Weihrauch air rifles manufactured in Germany. For more information on their current model lineup, pricing, and U.S. availability, please contact the company directly (see Trademark Index).

See also Weihrauch and Webley & Scott in the "W" section.

Pricing for Venom Arms Custom Guns models may run 100%-300% over the initial cost of a standard gun.

VENTURINI

Previous airgun manufacturer located in Argentine. Produced airguns under Venturini, Rubi, and Golondrina brands. Circa 1970-1980s.

PISTOLS

GOLONDRINA ("C-O-MATIC") - .177 cal., CO_2, repeater, removable spring-fed magazine along barrel, bulk feed, no safety, unusual pistol version of Golondrina "C-O-matic" rifle.

courtesy Beeman Collection

	100%	95%	90%	80%	60%	40%	20%
	$500	$400	$350	$300	$250	$200	N/A

GRADING	100%	95%	90%	80%	60%	40%	20%

RIFLES

GOLONDRINA ("C-O-MATRIC") - .177 cal., CO_2 repeater, removable spring-fed magazine along RH length of barrel, bulk feed almost surely copied from the German Tyrol "C-O-matic" repeater, also similar to the Spanish ArmiGas "Olimpic"!

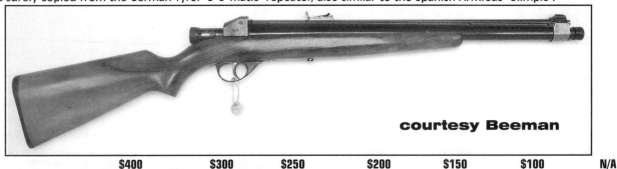

courtesy Beeman

	$400	$300	$250	$200	$150	$100	N/A

RUBI - .177 cal., BBC, SP, SS, birch stock with finger grooved forearm.

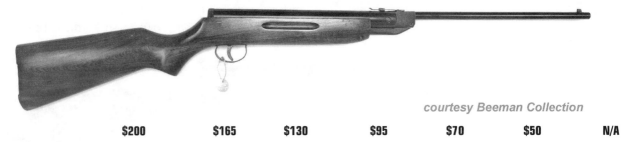

courtesy Beeman Collection

	$200	$165	$130	$95	$70	$50	N/A

VENUSWAFFENWERK

For information on Venuswaffenwerk airguns, see Tell in the "T" section.

VINCENT

Previously manufactured by Frank Vincent, located in Hillsdale, MI.

Metal pump lever handle under barrel. Designed to be pumped to high pressure with seventy strokes. Would shoot many times with one fill, but with diminishing power unless pumped about thirty strokes between shots. Original instructions warned to use only "automobile brake fluid" to lubricate pump. Walnut stocks are handcrafted and metal parts are painted black. Mfg. circa 1930s.

Dennis Quackenbush (see the "Q" section of this guide) has recently manufactured some working replicas of the Vincent airguns.

RIFLES

RIFLE - .177 cal., BA, rifled brass barrel, 39.75 in. OAL, 700+ FPS, 5 lbs.

courtesy Beeman Collection

	N/A	N/A	$1,300	$1,000	$950	$700	$550

SHOTGUNS

SHOTGUN - .410 cal., bolt action, smoothbore steel barrel, 44.6 in. overall, very powerful. With brass shot shells, wad cutter, and shell filling tools, 6.4 lbs.

courtesy Beeman Collection

	N/A	N/A	$1,400	$1,150	$800	$500	N/A

Add 25% for tool kit and spare cartridges.

W SECTION

WAFFENTECHNIK JONISKEIT

For information on Waffentechnik Joniskeit airguns, see Joniskeit in the "J" section.

WALTHER

Current manufacturer located in Ulm, Germany. Currently imported and distributed by Champion´s Choice, located in La Vergne, TN, and by Crosman Corp., located in East Bloomfield, NY. Previously imported by Walther USA located in Springfield, MA, and Interarms, located in Alexandria, VA. Dealer or consumer direct sales.

For more information and current pricing on both new and used Walther firearms, please refer to the *Blue Book of Gun Values* by S.P. Fjestad (also available online).

GRADING	100%	95%	90%	80%	60%	40%	20%

PISTOLS

CP 2 - .177 cal., CO_2, 9 in. barrel, adj. sights and trigger, UIT target model, 2.5 lbs. Mfg. 1985-90.

	100%	95%	90%	80%	60%	40%	20%
	$550	$475	$400	$350	$275	N/A	N/A

Last MSR was $850.

Subtract 10% for left-hand variation.

CP 3 - .177 cal., CO_2, adj. sights and trigger, UIT target model. Importation 1987-93.

	100%	95%	90%	80%	60%	40%	20%
	N/A	$600	$450	$350	$325	N/A	N/A

Last MSR was $1,360.

CP 5 - .177 cal., CO_2, target model. Mfg. 1989-95.

	100%	95%	90%	80%	60%	40%	20%
	$700	$625	$550	$475	$350	N/A	N/A

Last MSR was $1,650.

CP 88 - .177 cal., CO_2, SA and DA, 4 in. rifled barrel, 393 FPS, 8 shot mag., blue or nickel finish, adj. rear sight, 2.25 lbs. New 1996.

	100%	95%	90%	80%	60%	40%	20%
MSR $233	$195	$160	$120	$95	$70	N/A	N/A

Add 10% for nickel finish.
Add 20% for wood grips.

✳ CP88 Competition - .177 cal., similar to CP 88, except has 6 in. barrel with compensator and bridge mount, 426 FPS, adj. rear sight, 2.4 lbs.

	100%	95%	90%	80%	60%	40%	20%
MSR $245	$190	$165	$135	$95	$70	N/A	N/A

Add 10% for nickel finish.
Add 20% for wood grips.
Add 75% for bridge scope mount (New 2005).

CP 99 - .177 cal., CO_2, eight-shot rotary magazine at breech, 320 FPS, 3.3 in. rifled barrel, slide action for first shot or single action firing, single or double action trigger, manual safety and decocking system, black polymer frame and black or nickel slide finish, adj. rear sight, 1.7 lbs. New 2000.

courtesy Beeman Collection

	100%	95%	90%	80%	60%	40%	20%
MSR $190	$165	$130	$90	$70	$50	N/A	N/A

Add 10% for nickel finish slide.
Add 15% for Class III laser (CP99BLS new 2005).
The CP99 is designed for police, military and civilian training, where the actual feel, weight, and action of a firearm are necessary. The CO_2 capsule is loaded in a removable cartridge-style magazine.

✳ CP 99 Military - .177 cal., similar to CP 99, except green polymer frame with black slide finish, adj. rear sight. 1.7 lbs. New 2001.

	100%	95%	90%	80%	60%	40%	20%
MSR $190	$165	$130	$90	$70	$50	N/A	N/A

GRADING	100%	95%	90%	80%	60%	40%	20%

✳ **CP 99 Trophy** - .177 cal., similar to CP 99, except black polymer frame and black or nickel slide finish, includes bridge mount, red dot optical sighting system and case, 1.7 lbs. New 2001.

	MSR $300	$250	$185	$140	$100	$75	N/A	N/A

Add 10% for nickel finish slide.

CPM-1 - .177 cal., CO_2, adj. sights and trigger, UIT target model. New 1992.

	$650	$600	$550	$500	$425	N/A	N/A

CP SPORT(CPS) - .177 cal., CO_2, SA and DA, 3.3 in. rifled barrel, 360 FPS, eight-shot mag., black, orange, or yellow polymer frame with blue slide, adj. rear sight, 1.7 lbs. New 2001.

	MSR $110	$90	$65	$50	$40	$30	N/A	N/A

Add 25% for Class III laser (CP Sport Laser new 2005).

✳ **CPS Trophy** - .177 cal., similar to CPS, except has red dot scope and mount included. New 2002.

	$150	$115	$90	$65	$50	N/A	N/A

LP 2 - .177 cal., SSP using linked lever around trigger and grip. Mfg. 1967-72.

	N/A	N/A	$450	$350	$300	N/A	N/A

Add 25% for fitted case.

LP 3 - .177 cal., SSP, 405 FPS, 2.8-3.0 lbs. Mfg. 1973-85.

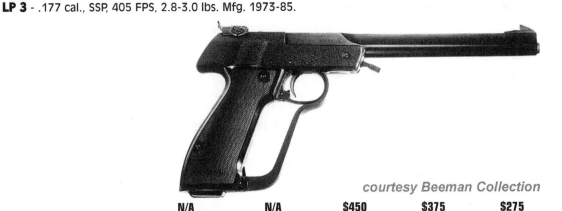

courtesy Beeman Collection

	N/A	N/A	$450	$375	$275	N/A	N/A

Add 15% for shaped barrel (shown) rather than round.

Add 20% for fitted case.

Add 20% for match grade (adjustable wooden grips).

LP 52 - .177 cal., BBC, with SP system in grip, 9.45 in. rifled barrel, adj. rear sight, blue finish, brown plastic grips, wood cocking block, 40.6 oz. Rare early version of LP 53. Mfg. 1952 only.

	$900	$800	$700	$550	$475	N/A	N/A

LP 53 - .177 cal., similar to LP 52, except early versions with curved receiver back, later versions are straight, brown or black plastic grips with Walther logo, smooth blue steel (until circa SN 23,200) then with much more common black crinkle enamel finish adj. sights with two sets of extra inserts. (This pistol was made famous by appearing in a James Bond poster.) Mfg. 1952-83 Ref: AAG - Oct. 1991.

courtesy Beeman Collection

	N/A	$400	$350	$325	$300	N/A	N/A

Add 35% for fitted case, blue and gray inside.

Add 25% for fitted case, maroon inside.

Add 10% for original brown factory cardboard box.

Add 30% for original smooth blue finish.

Add 25% for straight back receiver.

Add 15% for barrel weight.

Subtract 5% for missing sight inserts.

Early versions of the fitted case are blue and gray inside; later versions are maroon.

GRADING	100%	95%	90%	80%	60%	40%	20%

LPM-1 - .177 cal., SSP, 9.15 in. barrel, 2.25 lbs. Mfg. 1990-04.

	$850	$750	$700	$550	$400	N/A	N/A

Last MSR was $1,050.

LP 200/CP 200 - .177 cal., PCP (CO_2 on CP 200, disc. March 1996), 450 FPS., 9 1/8 in. barrel, adj. grips, sights, and trigger, UIT target model, 2.5 lbs.

	$900	$840	$670	$525	$425	N/A	N/A

Last MSR was $1,100.

Subtract 35% for CO_2.

LP 201/CP 201 - .177 cal., PCP (CO_2 on CP201, disc. March 1996), 450 FPS., 9.15 in. barrel, adj. grips, sights, and trigger, UIT target model, 2.5 lbs. New 1990.

	$900	$815	$700	$550	$450	N/A	N/A

Last MSR was $1,065.

Subtract 35% for CO_2.

LP 300 - .177 cal., PCP (integral pressure gauge in cylinder), integrated front sight with three different widths, adj. rear sight, 450 FPS, 9.15 in. barrel, adj. grips, and trigger, UIT target model, 2.2 lbs. New 2001.

MSR $1,295	$1,75	$975	$800	$650	$500	N/A	N/A

✳ **LP 300 Ultra Light** - .177 cal., PCP (integral pressure gauge in cylinder), integrated front sight with three different widths, adj. rear sight, 450 FPS, 8.19 in. barrel, adj. grips, and trigger, UIT target model, 1.9 lbs. New 2004.

MSR $1,140	$965	$865	$675	$525	$375	N/A	N/A

NIGHTHAWK - .177 cal., CO_2, DA, semiautomatic, 3.3 in. rifled steel barrel, 360 FPS, synthetic body, eight-shot mag., red dot sight, 11.5 in. OAL, 1.63 lbs. New 2004.

MSR $202	$189	$155	$120	$85	$65	N/A	N/A

PPK/PPK/S/PPK/S LASER - BB/.175 cal. or .177 cal., CO_2, SA and DA, 3.5 in. smooth bore barrel, 295 FPS, fifteen-shot mag., blue frame with blue or nickel slide, fixed sights, Class III laser (PPK/S Laser new 2005), 1.25 lbs. New 2000.

MSR $88	$70	$55	$45	$30	$20	N/A	N/A

Add 15% for nickel finish slide (PPK/S).
Add 30% for PPK/S Laser (New 2005).

REDSTORM - .177 cal., CO_2, DA, semi-auto, eight-shot mag., 3.3 in. rifled steel BBL, 360 FPS, synthetic body, red dot sight, 7.1 in. OAL, 1.39 lbs. New 2004.

MSR $179	$145	$125	$95	$65	$45	N/A	N/A

RIFLES

CG 90 - .177 cal., CO_2, 18.9 in. barrel, 10 lbs. 2 oz. Mfg. 1989-1996.

courtesy Howard Collection

	$850	$800	$700	$600	$500	N/A	N/A

Last MSR was $1,750.

CGM - .177, CO_2, target model, laminated stock, similar to LGM-2. Disc. 1997.

	$1,000	$950	$850	$750	$650	N/A	N/A

Last MSR was $1,270.

Add 10% for junior model.
Add 10% for running target model.

GRADING	100%	95%	90%	80%	60%	40%	20%

LG 51 - .177 cal., BBC, SP, 17.75 in. smoothbore barrel, adj. rear sight, blue finish, walnut color beech stock, steel (early) or plastic buttplate, grooved forearm, pistol grip, 5.7 lbs. Mfg. 1951-53.

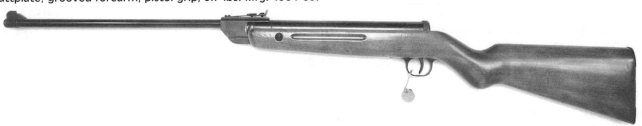

courtesy Beeman Collection

	100%	95%	90%	80%	60%	40%	20%
	$235	$200	$175	$110	$75	N/A	N/A

Approx. 1951 Retail $34.

Add 10% for steel buttplate.
Add 25% for aperture sight.
Add 20% for box, accessories, and factory papers.

✷ LG 51 Z - .177 cal., similar to LG 51, except has rifled barrel. Mfg. beginning in 1953. Disc.

	$200	$175	$110	$75	$50	N/A	N/A

Approx. 1953 Retail $30.

Add 25% for aperture sight.
Add 20% for box, accessories, and factory papers.

LG 52 - .177 cal., BBC, SP, beech stock, grooved forearm, checkered pistol grip, adj. trigger, 17.75 in. barrel, steel buttplate, 15 mm steel post inset in stock behind receiver for optional aperture sight. Mfg. 1953.

	$275	$225	$200	$130	$120	N/A	N/A

Add 20% for box, accessories, and factory papers.
Add 40% for aperture sight.

LG 53 - .177 cal., similar to Model LG 51, except has plastic buttplate. Aperture sight. Mfg. 1952-76.

	$225	$175	$150	$100	$80	N/A	N/A

Add 20% for box, accessories, and factory papers.
Add 40% for aperture sight.

✷ LG 53 M - .177 cal. similar to Model LG 53, except has match-style stock, front sight with interchangeable inserts, stock and barrel weight. Mfg. 1956.

	$325	$275	$250	$180	$150	N/A	N/A

Add 20% for box, accessories, and factory papers.
Add 40% for aperture sight.

✷ LG 53 ZD - .177 cal., similar to Model LG 53, 5.7 lbs. Mfg. 1951-53.

	$325	$275	$250	$180	$150	N/A	N/A

Add 20% for box, accessories, and factory papers.
Add 40% for aperture sight.

LG54 MG - .177 cal. lead balls, similar to Model LG 51, except has round magazine for six lead balls. Mfg. 1954.

	$425	$375	$350	$280	$250	N/A	N/A

Add 20% for box, accessories, and factory papers.
Add 25% for aperture sight.
Add 20% for blank magazine for shooting pellets.

LG 55 - .177 cal., BBC, SP, deep leaded forearm, checkered pistol grip. adj. trigger, aperture sight, cresent rubber buttplate. Mfg 1955-67 (was available through 1974).

courtesy Beeman Collection

	$375	$325	$300	$280	$250	N/A	N/A

Add 20% for box, accessories, and factory papers.
Add 25% for aperture sight.
Add 20% for walnut stock.

GRADING	100%	95%	90%	80%	60%	40%	20%

Add 10% for barrel weight.
Add 100% for Tyrolean stock.

LG 90 - SL, target model, 11 lbs. New 1989. Disc.

	100%	95%	90%	80%	60%	40%	20%
	$850	$750	$700	$600	$500	N/A	N/A

Last MSR was $1,320.

LGM-1 - .177 cal., SL, 19 in. barrel, approx. 10 lbs. Mfg. 1991. Disc.

	$900	$850	$650	$600	$550	N/A	N/A

Last MSR was $1,890.

LGM-2 - .177 cal., SL, similar to LGM-1, laminated stock, 10 lbs. Mfg. 1993-98.

	$900	$850	$650	$600	$550	N/A	N/A

Last MSR was $1,890.

Subtract 15% for junior model.
Add 10% for running target model.

LGR RIFLE - .177 cal., SL, 580 FPS, target model, 10 lbs. 8 oz. Mfg. 1974-89.

courtesy Beeman Collection

	$800	$750	$650	$600	$550	N/A	N/A

Last MSR was $1,250.

Add 15% for Running Boar Model.
Add 15% for universal.
Subtract 10% for left-hand variation.

LGV MATCH RIFLE - .177 cal., BBC, SP, match rifle, barrel latch, heavy barrel sleeve, aperture sight with Walther banner on left, cresent shaped, fixed rubber buttplate, beech stock with cheekpiece and stippled grip. Mfg. 1963-68.

	$775	$700	$650	$550	$450	N/A	N/A

Add 20% for box, accessories, and factory papers.
Add 15% for later version with adjustable buttplate, new style aperture sight with Walther banner on top.
Add 15% for walnut stock.

✳ **LGV Special** - similar to LGV Match Rifle, except more massive beech stock, receiver diameter increased to allow direct milling of aperture sight dovetail, double mainspring system. Mfg. 1968-72 (was available through 1985).

courtesy Beeman Collection

	$775	$700	$650	$550	$450	N/A	N/A

Add 10% for box, accessories, and factory papers.
Add 40% for Tyrolean stock.
Add 10% for Junior version.
Add 15% for Junior 3 position version.

MODEL LG 210 - .177 cal., SL, pneumatic, 16.5 in. barrel, laminated wood stock with anatomic pistol grip, rubber butt plate, adj. cheek piece, inline compensator, chrome-molybdenum steel trigger, and peep sight with twenty-click-adjustment. 11.5 lbs. Mfg.1998-2004.

	$1,175	$950	$825	$700	$600	N/A	N/A

Last MSR was $1,393.

Add $85 for fully adj. light metal buttplate.

GRADING	100%	95%	90%	80%	60%	40%	20%

✳ *LG 210 Junior* - .177 cal., SL, pneumatic, similar to Model LG 210, except scope rail for the three-position competition and an anatomical metal buttplate, 9.92 lbs. Mfg. 1999-2004.

	$1,150	$970	$800	$725	$650	N/A	N/A

Last MSR was $1,314.

MODEL LG 300 - .177 cal., PCP (integral pressure gauge in cylinder), carbon fiber barrel jacket and absorber (dampener) system eliminates perceptible recoil, 16.5 in. barrel, laminated wood stock with adj. cheekpiece, adj. and tiltable alloy buttplate, adj. chrome-molybdenum steel trigger, precision diopter rear sight, 9.7 lbs. New 2001.

MSR $1,586	$1,375	$1,095	$965	$850	$750	N/A	N/A

Add $35 for left-hand model.

Subtract $200 for Beech stock.

✳ *Model LG 300 Alutec* - .177 cal., similar to Model LG 300, except has aluminum stock with adj. cheekpiece, adj. and tiltable alloy buttplate, interchangable, adj. pistol grip, adj. forearm, adj. chrome-molybdenum steel trigger, precision diopter rear sight, 9.7 lbs. New 2001.

MSR $1,950	$1,595	$1,395	$1,095	$995	$875	N/A	N/A

Add $50 for left-hand model.

✳ *Model LG 300 FT Dominator (Field Target)* - .177 cal., similar to Model LG 300, except 19.3 in. barrel and 9.48 lbs. (laminated wood stock or 10.7 lbs. aluminum stock). New 2001.

MSR $1,520	$1,295	$995	$865	$725	$645	N/A	N/A

Add $250 for aluminum stock.

✳ *Model LG 300 Hunter* - .177 cal., similar to Model LG 300, except with brown laminated wood stock with adj. cheekpiece, no sight, 935 FPS, 7.6 lbs. New 2004.

MSR $1,410	$1,195	$975	$795	$695	$595	N/A	N/A

✳ *Model LG 300 Junior* - .177 cal., similar to Model LG 300, except has beech stock with adj. cheekpiece, adj. and tilting alloy buttplate, interchangable, adj. pistol grip, adj. forearm, chrome-molybdenum steel trigger, precision diopter rear sight, 9.7 lbs. New 2001.

MSR $995	$925	$865	$700	$625	$545	N/A	N/A

Add $35 for left-hand model.

✳ *Model LG 300 XT* - .177 cal., similar to Model LG 300, except anti-vibration system, 25.5 in. rifled steel barrel with carbon fiber sleeve, scaled BBL weight, Centra front sight, 41.7 in. OAL, laminated wood or aluminum stock, 10.7 lbs. New 2004.

MSR $1,950	$1,715	$1,495	$1,195	$995	$850	N/A	N/A

Add 35% for Carbontec carbon stock (new 2005).

Subtract 10% for beech stock.

JAGUAR - .177 cal., SL, SP, tap loading, 16.4 in. barrel, stained beech adj. stock (for comb, buttplate, and pull), adj. trigger, adj. rear sight, fixed front sight with interchangeable inserts. 7.5 lbs. New 1994.

	$325	$275	$250	$180	$150	N/A	N/A

Add 25% for aperture sight.

Add 20% for box, accessories, and factory papers.

LEVER ACTION RIFLE - .177 cal., CO_2, eight-shot rotary mag., 18.9 in. rifled steel barrel, 630 FPS, wood stock, adj. front and rear sights, cross bolt safety, 38.3 in. OAL, 7.5 lbs. New 2002.

courtesy Howard Collection

MSR $465	$375	$295	$255	$215	N/A	N/A	N/A

LEVER ACTION CARBINE - .177 cal., CO_2, eight-shot rotary mag., similar to lever action rifle, except with 15 in. rifled steel barrel, 34.5 in. OAL, 7 lbs. Mfg 2003.

	$250	$210	$185	$150	N/A	N/A	N/A

Last MSR was $255.

PANTHER - .177 cal., similar to Jaguar, except barrel cocking. New 1994.

	$275	$225	$175	$110	$75	N/A	N/A

Add 25% for aperture sight.

Add 20% for box, accessories, and factory papers.

WARRIOR

For information on Warrior, see Accles & Shelvoke Ltd. in the "A" section.

WEBLEY & SCOTT, LTD.

Current manufacturer established in 1906, and located in Birmingham, England. Currently imported by Airguns of Arizona, located in Mesa, AZ, by Beeman Precision Airguns, located in Huntington Beach, CA, and by Pyramyd Air International, located in Pepper Pike, OH.

Webley reports that their roots go back to about 1790. The name Webley has been associated with a wide variety of firearms, ranging from early percussion pistols and centerfire revolvers to much later military and police self-loading pistols. The current name dates to 1897, when the company amalgamated with shotgun manufacturers W & C Scott and Sons, becoming The Webley and Scott Revolver and Arms Company Ltd of Birmingham. The name was shortened in 1906 to the now familiar name of Webley and Scott Ltd.

Webley's airgun history began in 1910 when an interesting air pistol, with an in-line spring piston and barrel, was designed and patented by William Whiting, then director of Webley & Scott. At least one working example was constructed, but the gun never went into production. The first production Webley airgun was the Mark I air pistol designed by Douglas Johnstone and John Fearn. It was patented and appeared in 1924 and became an immediate success. Like the Webley & Scott firearms, these pistols were built of interchangeable parts of superior quality and the designs were internationally patented. In these new pistols, placing the barrel over the spring chamber allowed a relatively long barrel in a compact gun. The Mark I was soon followed by a target model, the Mark II Deluxe version. A smaller air pistol, the Junior, was introduced in 1929 to give younger shooters a more economical version. It had a smoothbore barrel for firing reusable darts for economy of use. These young users soon were eager to acquire the more advanced Webley models. Shortly after the Junior air pistol had been launched, Webley & Scott brought out the more powerful Senior air pistol which established a basic pattern for future manufacture. Its improved method for cocking the air chamber piston, plus the use of the stirrup barrel latch, now a Webley hallmark, contributed to the enduring popularity of the design.

Success of the Webley air pistols encouraged Webley to introduce the Mark I air rifle, basically an extended version of the Mark II Target air pistol. The Mark I air rifle was well received but was produced in limited numbers only from 1926 to 1929. A much improved, larger version, the Service Air Rifle Mark II, was introduced in 1932. Acknowledged to be the finest of its type, it dominated the British airgun scene for many years. The new model featured an airtight barrel locking collar and an additional safety sear, but its most outstanding feature was a quick-change barrel system.

A major shift in appearance of the Mark I and Senior air pistols occurred in 1935 when Webley & Scott introduced the "New Model" series. The key difference was an increase in the vertical grip angle from 100 to 120 degrees. This, and a slightly shorter barrel, created a more contemporary look and considerably improved their balance and gave them a much more natural pointing characteristic. The advent of war in 1939 caused a sudden end to commercial manufacture at the Webley plant and created a five-year gap in all commercial manufacture until the production of airguns was resumed in 1946. The New Model pistol styling, but with a grip angle of only 110 degrees, was extended to the Junior air pistol when airgun production resumed.

Post-WWII activities also included new designs for the Webley air rifles. The original barrel-cocking linkage design was replaced in 1947 by an under lever cocking system in the Mark III, Junior, and Jaguar air rifles. These were followed by the introduction of the Ranger air rifle in 1954.

The original Webley factory site at Weaman Street, Birmingham, which had survived two world wars, was vacated during 1958 and the entire operation moved to Park Lane, Handsworth. In 1960, the Senior air pistol was replaced by the Premier. The Premier was virtually identical to its predecessor but featured a series of minor refinements. These series were identified in an alphabetical sequence, starting with model A in 1960 and progressing to model F in 1975. A redesigned version of the Junior air pistol, using new lighter alloy castings, was designated the Junior Mk. II. This was followed by the Premier Mk.II, of similar construction. That model enjoyed only a brief production run.

During the 1970s, Webley introduced the barrel-cocking Hawk, Tomahawk, Victor, Vulcan and Valiant air rifles and the side-lever cocking Osprey and Supertarget air rifles. An improved piston seal development, which helped to reduce piston rebound, was patented in 1979. The improved seal become an important feature of the Vulcan and subsequent rifle models.

To compete with new foreign models, more modern styling was added to the air pistol line in the mid-1970s with the introduction of the Hurricane and its slightly less powerful junior mate, the Typhoon. In 1977, Webley's largest customer at that time, the Beeman Precision Airgun Company in the United States, requested a more compact version. The resulting Tempest, designed by Paul Bednall in the Webley technical department, that more closely followed the size and balance of the more traditional Webley air pistols was introduced in 1979 and soon became the most popular model of the series.

As noted by Walther (1984 - see "Airgun Literature Review" section in the 3rd edition, *Blue Book of Airguns*), Webley and Beeman mutually benefited by forming additional links in the 1980s. Beeman expanded their Webley offerings and helped design some Webley airguns, most notably the Beeman C1 air rifle. Webley incorporated Beeman Silver Jet pellets and several of their accessories, such as special air pistol grips, into the Webley international promotions. The Beeman/Webley association became even closer as Webley's president, Keith Faulkner, became Beeman's vice president and Harold Resuggan, then Webley's very talented head engineer, moved up to head Webley.

A basic shift in Webley's business base was completed in 1979 when the company discontinued the manufacture of all firearms. The manufacture of Webley airguns continued at Handsworth until 1984, when the company moved to a modern industrial site at Rednal, South Birmingham, England. Various additions to the Webley line of air rifles during the 1980s included the Viscount, Tracker, Omega, Airwolf, and Eclipse models, while manufacture of air pistols was limited to the Hurricane and Tempest. These two pistols continue to feature the same forward-swing barrel-cocking system as those produced more than seventy years earlier, a sound testament to its efficiency. In 1994, Webley expanded into the mass market arena by adding completely fresh designs, the Nemesis, a single-stroke pneumatic air pistol and the Stinger, a spring-piston, repeating BB pistol, in 1996.

The twenty-first century finds Webley rapidly evolving. Air rifles, ranging from conventional barrel-cocking, spring piston models to the latest pre-charged pneumatic and CO_2 guns are now the mainstay of the company. The latest state-of-the-art, computer-driven production stations have replaced the cumbersome networks of separate huge machines powered by noisy forests of immense over-

GRADING	100%	95%	90%	80%	60%	40%	20%

head shafts, wheels, and belts.

The main company recently joined with the legendary Venom Arms Company to form the Webley Venom Custom Shop. This shop, operating out of the Webley factory, offers many airgun products and services including custom air rifles and tuning accessories. This new partnership also opens up a host of new manufacturing and design developments and capabilities. The new Webley Venom team claims that no project in the airgun market is too daunting.

The authors and publisher wish to thank Gordon Bruce for his valuable assistance with the air pistols section, as well as John Atkins, Peter Colman, and Tim Saunders for their assistance with the rifle section information in this edition of the *Blue Book of Airguns*. Bruce's 2001 book, *Webley Air Pistols*, is required reading. Ref: Hannusch, 1988 and AGNR – July 1988, Atkins, AG April, May, & June 1996.

For more information and current pricing on Webley & Scott firearms, please refer to the *Blue Book of Gun Values* by S.P. Fjestad (also available online).

PISTOLS

All pistols have rifled barrels, unless otherwise noted. Webley airguns are a large and complex group. This introductory material cannot be complete, and its concise nature may result in some inaccuracies of identification and information. It is strongly advised that you consult the *Webley Air Pistols* book mentioned above for additional details and illustrations.

> **Add 25-40% for original factory box.**
> **Add 100% for fitted case.**
> **Add 100-200% for factory cut-away display models with moving parts.**
> **Add 100% for factory nickel plating, not offered in all models, unless otherwise noted.**
> **Add 25-75% for factory etching.**

GnAT - SP, SS, push barrel cocking, very small inexpensive air pistol similar to Harrington GAT (which is a modern version of the 19th century Quackenbush design). New 2004.

courtesy Beeman Collection

As this edition went to press, retail pricing had yet to be established.

HURRICANE - .177 or .22 cal., TL, SP, SS, 420/330 FPS, plastic grips with RH thumbrest, adj. rear sight with replacement adapter for scope mounting, hooded front sight, aluminum grip frame cast around steel body tube, RH manual safety, black epoxy finish, 8 in. button rifled barrel, 11.2 in. OAL, 38 oz.

✳ *Hurricane Variant 1* - forearm marked "HURRICANE", barrel housing (under front sight) 2.75 in. Mfg. 1975-1990.

	100%	95%	90%	80%	60%	40%	20%
	$225	$185	$145	$100	$60	N/A	N/A

> Add 5% for simulated wood grips (not available in USA).
> Add 10% for wood grips.
> Add 15% for finger groove Beeman "combat" wood grips.
> Add 20% for Beeman factory markings with San Rafael address.
> Add 10% for Beeman factory markings with Santa Rosa address.
> Add 10% for lack of F in pentagon mark ("little hut") which indicated lower power for European market.
> Add 20% for large deluxe factory box with form fitting depressions, including depression for mounted scope, in hard plastic shell with red flocked surface.
> Add 10% for factory box with molded white foam support block.

✳ *Hurricane Variant 2* - forearm marked "WEBLEY HURRICANE", barrel housing 2.187 inches with full length flattop. New 1990.

	100%	95%	90%	80%	60%	40%	20%
No MSR	$220	$195	$150	$115	$90	N/A	N/A

> Add 5% for simulated wood grips (not available in USA).
> Add 10% for wood grips.
> Add 15% for finger groove Beeman "combat" wood grips.
> Add 20% for Beeman factory markings with San Rafael address.
> Add 10% for lack of F in pentagon mark ("little hut") which indicated lower power for European market.
> Add 20% for large deluxe factory box with form fitting depressions, including depression for mounted scope, in hard plastic shell with red flocked surface.
> Add 10% for factory box with molded white foam support block.

GRADING		100%	95%	90%	80%	60%	40%	20%

JUNIOR - .177 cal., TL, SP, SS, metal grips with screw head on RH side, 100-degree grip slant ("straight grip"), fixed rear sight, sliding barrel latch, no safety, 6.5 in. smoothbore barrel for darts, 287 FPS, 7.75 in. OAL, 24 oz. Mfg. 1929-1938.

courtesy Bruce Gordon

	N/A	$325	$200	$165	$120	$85	N/A

Add 20% for adjustable rear sight.

Add 20-50% for original wood grips with vertical grooves, grip screw head on LH side.

Subtract 5% for final version with 6.25 in. barrel (protrudes beyond body tube).

✳ *Junior New Model* - .177 cal., TL, SP, SS, Bakelite grips, 110-degree grip slant, adj. rear sight, sliding barrel latch, 6.125 in. smoothbore barrel for darts, 290 FPS, blued, no safety, 7.75 in. OAL, 24 oz. Mfg. 1945-73.

courtesy Bruce Gordon

	N/A	$200	$175	$125	$95	$75	N/A

Add 5% for early versions with grip plate "spur" that extends about 0.25 inches from the upper forward edge of the Bakelite grip plates.

Add 5% for good condition leather breech seal (barrel joint washer) in pre-1960 production.

Subtract 20% for Suncorite 243 paint finish (post-1970).

Add 40% for factory nickel or chrome finish (uncommon on Junior models).

✳ *Junior Mark II* - .177 cal., TL, SP, SS, aluminum grip frame cast around steel body tube, Bakelite grips, rhombus-shaped logo with "BIRMID" mark and a casting number under grips, stirrup barrel latch, black epoxy coating, adj. rear sight, no safety, 6.125 in. barrel, 290 FPS, 8 in. OAL, 23 oz. Approx. 31,750 mfg. 1973-76.

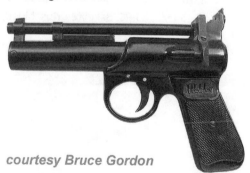

courtesy Bruce Gordon

	N/A	$150	$115	$85	$55	$45	N/A

Add 50% for low rear sight (barrel latch visible thru aperture), caused pre-Sept 1973 pistols to shoot low.

Add 10% for smoothbore (pre-August 1975).

Add 15% for seven-groove broached rifling (special order, pre-August 1975).

Introduced the massive aluminum grip frame cast around steel body tube characteristic of Webley pistols. BIRMID mark for Birmingham Aluminium Casting Company Ltd.

MARK I - .177 or .22 cal., TL, SP, SS, 367/273 FPS, wood grips, adj. rear sight, 100-degree grip slant ("straight grip"), manual safety, 8.5 in. OAL, 30 oz. Mfg. 1924-35.

GRADING	100%	95%	90%	80%	60%	40%	20%

❋ **Mark I First Series - Variant 1** - spring clip barrel catch on right side of breech block, no trigger adj. screw on forward edge of trigger guard.

	N/A	$995	$775	$600	$450	$295	N/A

✦ **_Mark I First Series - Variant 2_** - spring clip barrel catch on each side of breech block, no trigger adj. screw on forward edge of trigger guard.

	N/A	$495	$375	$300	$225	$175	N/A

❋ **Mark I Second Series** - sliding barrel catch on top of breech block, no trigger adj. screw on forward edge of trigger guard.

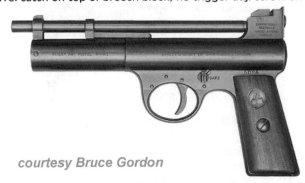

courtesy Bruce Gordon

	N/A	$370	$275	$200	$150	$95	N/A

❋ **Mark I Third Series** - trigger adj. screw on forward edge of trigger guard.

courtesy Beeman Collection

	N/A	$370	$275	$200	$150	$95	N/A

❋ **Mark I Fourth Series** - trigger adj. screw on forward edge of trigger guard, U.S. Patent notice on RS, barrel hinge screw with retainer.

	N/A	$370	$275	$200	$150	$95	N/A

❋ **Mark I Fifth Series** - locking screw on LH side for cone-head trigger adj. screw.

	N/A	$370	$275	$200	$150	$95	N/A

❋ **Mark I Sixth Series** - flanged screw plug at front end of body cylinder provided front end access to mainspring and piston assembly.

	N/A	$370	$275	$200	$150	$95	N/A

MARK I NEW MODEL - .177 and .22 cal., TL, SP, SS, 345/293 FPS, Bakelite grips, blued, adj. rear sight, introduced the "New Model 120-degree angle grip, 8.5 in. OAL, 30 oz. Mfg. 1935-64.

❋ **Mark I New Model Pre-WWII** - blued trigger, barrel without thicker section ahead of rear sight.

courtesy Bruce Gordon

	N/A	$275	$225	$175	$125	$75	N/A

Add 20% for smooth bore barrel.
Add 5% for diamond knurling on barrel. Late 1939.
Add 10% for unmarked rear breech cap with small retaining screw below sight.
Add 10% for black bakelite grips without Webley name.

GRADING	100%	95%	90%	80%	60%	40%	20%

❋ *Mark I New Model Post-WWII* - introduced batch numbers instead of serial numbers (none exceed approx. 6000), barrel with 2.4 in. thicker reinforced section with straight knurling.

	N/A	$185	$155	$125	$95	$55	N/A

Add 5% for unmarked rear breech cap.

MARK II TARGET - .177 or .22 cal., TL, SP, SS, 410/325 FPS, vulcanite grips, adj. rear sight, barrel latch secured by screw instead of pin, 100-degree grip slant ("straight grip"), improved piston seal, sliding barrel latch, manual safety, 8.5 in. OAL, 28 oz. Mfg. 1925-30.

	N/A	$660	$495	$350	$250	$185	N/A

Add 30-50% for minor factory engraving (usually done to hide imperfections).
Add 100-200% for special order models made in 1928, chased with scroll engraving, silver plated, mother-of-pearl grips.

❋ *Mark II Target - First Pattern* - spring guide recessed into front end of body tube, fillister head trigger adj. screw without locking screw.

courtesy Bruce Gordon

	N/A	$660	$495	$350	$250	$185	N/A

Add 30-50% for minor factory engraving (usually done to hide imperfections).
Add 100-200% for special order models made in 1928, chased with scroll engraving, silver plated, mother-of-pearl grips.

❋ *Mark II Target - Standard Pattern* - spring guide with flange to match diameter of front end of body tube, cone head trigger adj. screw with LH locking screw.

	N/A	$450	$395	$350	$250	$185	N/A

Add 30-75% for minor factory etching (usually done to hide imperfections).
Add 100-200% for special order models made in 1928, chased with scroll engraving, silver plated, mother-of-pearl grips.

❋ *Mark II Target - Final Pattern* - walnut grips, Stoeger address on RH side.

courtesy Howard Collection

	N/A	$660	$495	$350	$250	$185	N/A

Add 30-50% for minor factory engraving (usually done to hide imperfections).
Add 100-200% for special order models made in 1928, chased with scroll engraving, silver plated, mother-of-pearl grips.

GRADING	100%	95%	90%	80%	60%	40%	20%

NEMESIS - .177 or .22 cal., TL, SP, SS, 385/300 FPS, two-stage adj. trigger, black or brushed chrome finish, manual safety, adj. sights, integral scope rail, 2.2 lbs. New 1995.

courtesy Bruce Gordon

No MSR	$167	$135	$110	$75	N/A	N/A	N/A

Add 10% for brushed chrome finish.

PREMIER - .177 or .22 cal., TL, SP, SS, 350/310 FPS, Bakelite grips, blued finish, adj. rear sight, no safety, 8.5 in. OAL, 37 oz. Last of the traditional forged steel blued Webley air pistols. Six variation series were produced, fortunately each series was marked with a capital letter, starting with A and ending with F, stamped on the LH side of the frame, usually near the trigger guard. Details of each series are given in Bruce (2001). Plated finishes were not provided by the factory during the period of Premier production. Mfg. 1964-1975.

courtesy Beeman Collection

	N/A	$275	$225	$180	$125	$85	N/A

Subtract 20% for painted finish on series E and F.

☀ **Premier MKII** - .177 or .22 cal., TL, SP, SS, 350/310 FPS, Bakelite grips, blued finish, adj. rear sight, no safety, 8.5 in. OAL, 37 oz, series A through F, production date stamped (LH side of grip frame under grips). Mfg. 1964-1975.

courtesy Beeman Collection

	N/A	$370	$275	$200	$150	$95	N/A

Add 25% for barrel forged from one piece of steel (identified by ring-like raised area about 1 in. behind front sight), only 1,700 produced in 1976. Most production had muzzle end of barrel in a 1.48 in. muzzle shroud which incorporates the front sight.

Add 20% for Beeman factory markings.

SENIOR - .177 or .22 cal., vulcanite grips, blued, adj. rear sight, stirrup barrel latch, 100-degree grip slant ("straight grip"), no safety, 416/330 FPS, 8.5 in. OAL, 33 oz. Mfg. 1930-35.

Introduced the stirrup barrel latch from Webley revolvers to the air pistols.

GRADING	100%	95%	90%	80%	60%	40%	20%

✳ *Senior First Pattern* - trigger adj. screw at forward end of trigger guard.

courtesy Bruce Gordon

	N/A	$450	$375	$265	$185	$125	N/A

Add 25% for A.F. Stoeger marking on RH side of air cylinder with checkered walnut grip.

Add 10% for flat cocking links which obscured hole in top of air cylinder. Replaced by forward link with wings which operated upon wedge-shaped small rear link.

✳ *Senior Second Pattern* - no trigger adj. screw.

courtesy Bruce Gordon

	N/A	$525	$375	$265	$185	$125	N/A

Add 25% for A.F. Stoeger marking on RH side of air cylinder with checkered walnut grip.

Add 10% for flat cocking links which obscured hole in top of air cylinder. Replaced by forward link with wings which operated upon wedge-shaped small rear link.

✳ *Senior New Model* - .177 or .22 cal., TL, SP, SS, 416/330 FPS, Bakelite grips, blue finish, adj. rear sight, no safety, 8.5 in overall, 33 oz. 1935-64.

courtesy Bruce Gordon

Judged to be the best of the pre-WWII Webley air pistols. Over the thirty-year production span of this model, there were at least fourteen variations, different finishes, barrels, etc. Consult Bruce (2001) for details.

✦ *Senior New Model Pre-WWII* - plain exterior of barrel ahead of rear sight - a few 1939 guns had knurled barrels, slim trigger, grips w/o Webley name.

	N/A	$475	$345	$235	$165	$115	N/A

Add 30% for original nickel plating.

Add 5% for unmarked rear breech cap.

Add 30% for extra long target barrel.

✦ *Senior New Model Post-WWII* - cross knurling on barrel, thick trigger, Webley name on grips.

	N/A	$275	$225	$175	$125	$65	N/A

Add 30% for original nickel plating.

Add 5% for unmarked rear breech cap.

Add 30% for extra long target barrel.

GRADING	100%	95%	90%	80%	60%	40%	20%

STINGER - BB/.175 cal., slide action dual-cocking, SP, 220 FPS, forty-five-shot internal mag., smoothbore, fixed sights with integral scope rail, black finish. New 2001.

	100%	95%	90%	80%	60%	40%	20%
No MSR	$60	$45	$35	$30	N/A	N/A	N/A

TEMPEST - .177 or .22 cal., TL, SP, SS, 420/330 FPS, plastic grips with RH thumb rest, adj. rear sight, aluminum grip frame cast around steel body tube, compact version of Hurricane, RH manual safety, 6.87 in. button rifled barrel, black epoxy finish, 9.2 in. OAL, 32 oz.

Tempest bodies were produced by grinding off the rear section of Hurricane castings. Bruce (2001) refers to the Tempest as "the most charismatic of all Webley air pistols." (Webley offered "Beeman Accessories," such as special grips, for the Tempest and Hurricane in their factory leaflets in England and other world markets.)

✳ **Tempest Variant 1** - forearm marked "TEMPEST". Mfg. 1979-1981.

	100%	95%	90%	80%	60%	40%	20%
	N/A	$195	$175	$125	$85	N/A	N/A

Add 5% for simulated wood grips (not sold in USA).

Add 10% for Beeman wood grips.

Add 15% for finger groove Beeman "combat" wood grips.

Add 20% for Beeman factory markings with San Rafael address (rare).

Add 20% for large factory box 11.6 x 8.6 inches, black with logo.

Add 10% for medium factory box 10.2 x 6.6 inches, black with logo.

✳ **Tempest Variant 2** - forearm marked "WEBLEY TEMPEST", Beeman versions of this variation marked with Beeman name and address and "TEMPEST". New 1981.

	100%	95%	90%	80%	60%	40%	20%
No MSR	$205	$175	$135	$105	$85	N/A	N/A

Add 5% for simulated wood grips. (not sold in USA)

Add 10% for Beeman wood grips.

Add 15% for finger groove Beeman "combat" wood grips.

Add 20% for Beeman factory markings with San Rafael address (rare).

Add 10% for Beeman factory markings with Santa Rosa address.

Add 20% for large factory box, 11.6 x 8.6 inches, black with logo.

Add 10% for medium factory box, 10.2 x 6.6 inches, black with logo.

TYPHOON - .177 or .22 cal., TL, SP, SS, similar to Hurricane, except intended for youth and persons with smaller hands, 360/280 FPS, plastic grips, adj. rear sight, 11.2 in. OAL, 37.5 oz. Approx. 14,214 mfg.1987-1992.

courtesy Bruce Gordon

100%	95%	90%	80%	60%	40%	20%
$200	$160	$130	$100	$60	N/A	N/A

Uncommon in USA, not regularly imported. Warning: early versions could fire upon release of safety; guns should be returned to Webley distributor for correction. Corrected guns have a satin chrome finish on the trigger.

RIFLES

AXSOR - .177 or .22 cal., PCP, bolt action loading, eight-shot rotary magazine, 1000/800 FPS, 19.7 in. barrel, walnut or beech Monte Carlo stock, recoil pad, two-stage adj. trigger, integral scope grooves, 39.5 in. overall, 6 lbs. Mfg. 1998-2000.

courtesy Howard Collection

100%	95%	90%	80%	60%	40%	20%
$550	$475	$400	$325	$250	N/A	N/A

Last MSR was $625.

Add 10% for walnut stock.

GRADING	100%	95%	90%	80%	60%	40%	20%

BEARCUB - .177 cal., BBC, SP, SS, 915 FPS, 13 in. barrel, single stage adj. trigger, manual safety, beech stock with PG, cheekpiece, forearm ends at barrel pivot, threaded muzzle weight, PTFE, nylon Spring Tamer spring guide, 37.8 in. OAL, 7.2 lbs. Mfg. for Beeman 1995-1998.

	$255	$215	$175	$135	$100	N/A	N/A

Last MSR was $325.

Muzzle weight threaded for silencer on this model (if silencer/sound moderator is present), transfer to qualified buyer requires $200 federal tax in USA.

ECLIPSE - .177, .22, or .25 cal., SP, UL, SS, fully opening breech loading hatch allows direct seating of pellet in chamber, 975/710/620 FPS MV, deluxe Monte Carlo stock, cut checkering, rubber buttplate and grip cap w/white line spacers, PTFE, muzzle threaded for Beeman Air Tamer or Webley Silencer, automatic safety, 44 in. OAL, 7.9 lbs. Mfg. 1990-96.

	$350	$300	$250	$200	$150	N/A	N/A

Last MSR was $510.

Add 25% for .25 caliber.

Add 10% for Air Tamer (muzzle unit without baffles).

Add 10% for Webley Silencer.

Muzzle threaded for silencer on this model (if silencer is present), transfer to qualified buyer requires $200 federal tax in USA.

EXCEL - .177 or .22 cal., BBC, 870/660 FPS, 11.37 (carbine) or 17.5 in. barrel, integral scope grooves, open sights, beech stock, 7 lbs. Disc. 2000.

	$175	$145	$115	$85	$65	N/A	N/A

Last MSR was $215.

FALCON - .177 or .22 cal., SP, BBC, SS, 550/500 FPS, SN hidden by cocking arm when closed, scope ramp welded to body tube, all metal parts, Webley medallion inletted into LHS buttstock, no safety, 41 in. OAL, 6 lbs. Mfg. 1960-70.

	$150	$130	$110	$100	$80	N/A	N/A

Subtract 10% for no medallion.

FX2000 - .177 or .22 cal., PCP, 1000/800 FPS, bolt action loading, eight-shot magazine, 19.7 in. match quality choked barrel, beech or walnut stock, two-stage adj. trigger, integral pressure gauge, 6.6 lbs. New 2000.

courtesy Howard Collection

No MSR	$1,054	$825	$750	$550	$450	N/A	N/A

Add 15% for walnut stock.

✳ **FX2000 Field Target** - .22 cal., similar to FX2000, except has Field Target competition black walnut stock with adj. cheekpiece and buttplate, 1000 FPS. Mfg. 2002-04.

	$1,100	$875	$700	$575	$475	N/A	N/A

✳ **FX2000 Hunter SK** - .22 cal., similar to FX2000, except threaded for noise suppressor, two-stage adj. trigger, walnut skeleton stock. New 2000.

No MSR	$1,100	$875	$700	$575	$475	N/A	N/A

Add 15% for High-Power model (suppressor requires $200 federal tax in the USA).

HAWK - .177 or .22 cal., BBC, SP, SS, interchangeable barrels, 40-41 in. OAL, approx. 6.5 lbs.

✳ **Hawk Mk I** - angular stock lines, forearm with forward bulge, interchangeable barrels. Mfg. 1971-74.

	$160	$135	$100	$75	$50	N/A	N/A

Add 20% for extra interchangeable barrel.

✳ **Hawk Mk II** - smooth stock lines, interchangeable barrels. Mfg. 1974-77.

courtesy Beeman Collection

	$160	$135	$100	$75	$50	N/A	N/A

Add 20% for extra interchangeable barrel.

Most specimens in USA were diverted by Beeman Company from shipments which failed to reach agents of the Shah of Iran.

GRADING	100%	95%	90%	80%	60%	40%	20%

✳ *Hawk Mk III* - fixed barrel. Mfg. 1977-79.

	100%	95%	90%	80%	60%	40%	20%
	$160	$135	$100	$75	$50	N/A	N/A

JAGUAR - .177 or .22 cal., SP, BBC, SS, 500 FPS .177, sheetmetal "tinplate construction," sheetmetal barrel shroud, scope ramp (early with dumb-bell shape, later with parallel sides), early versions with finger grooves on forearm, no safety, 36.25 in. (early), 39 in. (later) OAL, 3.75 lbs. Mfg. 1940s to late 1970s.

courtesy Beeman Collection

	100%	95%	90%	80%	60%	40%	20%
	$150	$130	$110	$100	$80	N/A	N/A

Subtract 10% for early versions.
Some parts interchangeable with Webley Junior and Milbro Diana 22 air rifles.

JUNIOR - .177 cal., SP, BBC, SS, smoothbore (early) or rifled brass inner barrel, 405 FPS, sheetmetal barrel shroud, sheetmetal "tinplate construction," blued, no safety, 36.25 in. OAL, 3.25 lbs. Mfg. late 1940s to late 1960s.

	100%	95%	90%	80%	60%	40%	20%
	$150	$130	$110	$100	$80	N/A	N/A

Subtract 10% for smoothbore.
May have been made by Millard Bros.

LONGBOW/LONGBOW DELUXE - .177 or .22 cal., SP, BBC, SS, 850 FPS, short cylinder and barrel version of Tomahawk, scope grooves, no sights, Venom designed removable adj. trigger system, beech or walnut (Longbow Deluxe) checkered PG Monte Carlo stock with vented recoil pad, blue finish, ported muzzle brake. 39 in. OAL, 7.3 lbs. New 2003.

	100%	95%	90%	80%	60%	40%	20%
No MSR	$495	$395	$315	$225	$195	N/A	N/A

Add 15% for Longbow Deluxe w/Walnut stock.

MARK I - .177 or .22 cal., BBC, SP, SS, a small rifle version of the Webley Mark I air pistols, barrel swings forward over compression chamber for cocking, interchangeable barrels, wood half stock, 34 in. OAL, 5.3 lbs. Approx. 1500 mfg. 1926-29.

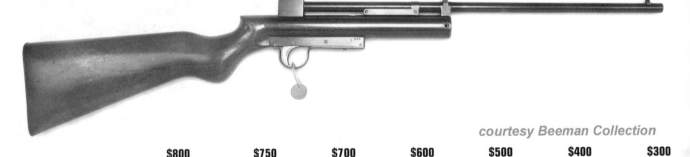

courtesy Beeman Collection

	100%	95%	90%	80%	60%	40%	20%
	$800	$750	$700	$600	$500	$400	$300

MARK II - .177, .22, or .25 cal., similar to Mark I, except larger, quick change barrels, bolt handle turns to open action and to cam barrel back into airtight connection with air vent, wood half stock, typical size: 43.8 in. OAL, approx. 6.8 lbs.

Important Note: there are many variations of the Webley Mark II rifles, rare versions add to the value. Essential information is available in Atkins, AG April, May, and June 1996.

✳ *Version 1* - .177 or .22 cal., L-shaped aperture sight, dovetail mounted barrel, leaf spring ahead of receiver which secures the barrel. S serial number prefix. Approx. 1000 mfg. in 1932.

courtesy Beeman Collection

	100%	95%	90%	80%	60%	40%	20%
	$995	$895	$795	$695	$595	$495	$395

Add 10% for extra .177 or .22 cal. barrel.
Add 100% for original factory box with inserts.
Add 150% for fitted factory case.

GRADING	100%	95%	90%	80%	60%	40%	20%

❋ **Version 2** - .177 or .22 cal., L-shaped aperture sight, side mounted push button for quick release of interchangeable barrels, S serial number prefix. Approx. 1000 guns mfg. early 1933-34, approx. 2000 total of version one and two mfg. circa 1935-38.

	$895	$795	$695	$595	$495	$395	$295

Add 10% for extra .177 or .22 cal. barrel.

Add 20% for extra .25 cal. barrel (as added after 1937).

Add 100% for original factory box with inserts.

Add 150% for fitted factory case.

After 1937 Mark II Version 3 .25 cal. barrels were added to some Mark II Version 2 sets.

❋ **Version 3** - .177, .22, or .25 cal., U-shaped folding aperture sight mounted in center of receiver frame, push button barrel release, S serial number prefix from S2001 forward. Approx. 13,700 mfg. 1934 -1945 (sales ceased during WWII).

courtesy Beeman Collection

	$650	$600	$550	$450	$350	$250	$150

Add 10% for extra .177 or .22 cal. barrel.

Add 20% for .25 caliber (The Webley "Rook and Rabbit Rifle", only mfg. 1937 and later).

Add 100% for original factory box with inserts.

Add 150% for fitted factory case.

MARK III SERIES - .177 or .22 cal., UL, SP, SS, tap loader. 42.25 to 43.5 in OAL, 6.8 lbs. Mfg. 1947-1975.

	$400	$350	$300	$225	$150	$100	$75

Many British airgun enthusiasts consider the Mark III as one of the finest air rifles ever produced. Became less complex and detailed as it evolved. Made in great numbers and great variety, this guide can only introduce this model. Fortunately, the basic variations generally can be identified by serial number. Additional info is available in the literature, esp. Hiller (1985).

❋ **Mark III Series I** - SN 1-2500. Standard: straight grooving in forearm, ribbed butt. Deluxe: hand checkered stock, ribbed butt-plate. Mfg. 1947-49.

	$450	$375	$300	$225	$175	$125	$75

Add 50% for Mark III Series I Deluxe.

❋ **Mark III Series II** - SN 2501-6000. Mfg. 1949-1957.

	$360	$300	$240	$180	$145	$120	$95

❋ **Mark III Series III** - SN 6001-42857. Mfg. 1957-1961.

	$330	$275	$220	$165	$135	$110	$85

❋ **Mark III Series IV** - SN 42858-46289. Mfg. 1961-64.

	$300	$250	$200	$150	$125	$100	$80

❋ **Mark III Late Model Series** - SN 46290 on. Mfg. 1964-1975.

	$300	$250	$200	$150	$125	$100	$80

MARK III SUPERTARGET (MODEL 2) - .177 or .22 cal., UL, SP, SS, tap loader, similar to Mark III, except fitted with Parker Hale micrometer aperture sight, stamped "SUPERTARGET" on receiver (body tube, air chamber), 9.4 lbs. Mfg. 1963-1975.

	$400	$350	$300	$275	$250	$225	$200

NIMBUS - .177 cal., BBC, SP, SS. 570 FPS. Beech stock with contoured comb, plastic buttplate, pressed steel trigger guard. Adj. sights, scope grooves. Push-button manual safety. Junior size, economy level air rifle, imported from China. Intro. 2004.

As this edition went to press, retail pricing had yet to be established.

OMEGA - .177 or .22 cal., SP, BBC, SS, PTFE and O-ring piston seal, 830/675 FPS, scope grooves, auto/manual safety, 42 in. OAL, 7.8 lbs. Mfg. 1989-92.

	$225	$200	$175	$150	$125	N/A	N/A

Last MSR was $430

Add 20% for Beeman marking.

OSPREY - .177 or .22 cal., SL, SP, SS, tap loader, manual safety, 43 in. OAL, 7.3 lbs. Mfg. 1975-1990s.

	$150	$125	$100	$75	$50	$35	N/A

Add 20% for Supertarget version with semi-match style stock, heavier.

PATRIOT - .177, .22 or .25 cal., BBC, 1170/920/820 FPS, 17.5 in. barrel, two-stage adj. trigger, integral scope grooves, low-profile sights, walnut Monte Carlo stock with hand-checkered grip, recoil pad, 9 lbs.

No MSR	$566	$515	$465	$385	$285	N/A	N/A

Add 15% for Venom Edition with black walnut stock and gold plated trigger guard.

GRADING	100%	95%	90%	80%	60%	40%	20%

RAIDER - .177 or .22 cal., PCP, 1000/800 FPS, BA, SS or two-shot magazine (.22 cal. only), Venom Custom designed beech or walnut stock, 7 lbs. New 2000.

No MSR	$495	$425	$350	$275	$195	N/A	N/A

Add 15% for walnut stock.
Add 10% for two-shot version.

RANGER - .177 cal., SP, BBC, SS, rifled or smoothbore steel barrel, scope ramp (late versions), full length stock, no safety, blued, 38.25 in. OAL, 3.5 lbs. Mfg.1950-1970.

	$450	$400	$350	$300	$250	$225	$200

Add 10% for no code or scope ramp.

Variations: four minor changes indicated with code letter stamped LHS barrel: no code = early, A, B, C. Ranger (grip lever cocking). Ranger name also used as a Webley private label version of Erma ELG10 grip lever Winchester-carbine-style pellet rifle: see Erma section.

SPECTRE - .22 cal., PCP, BA, eight-shot rotary magazine indexed and cocked by RHS cocking lever, neoprene pads inletted into grip and forearm, pressure gauge in synthetic stock, two-stage adj. trigger, free floating barrel, 36.2 in. OAL, 5.5 lbs. Mfg. 2004.

	$900	$725	$575	$475	N/A	N/A	N/A

Joint design with Axelsson of Sweden.

STINGRAY RIFLE - .177 or .22 cal., BBC, 870/660 FPS, two-stage trigger, beech or walnut (Deluxe) Monte Carlo-style stock, adj. rear sight, hooded front sight, 44 in. overall. New 2001.

No MSR	$360	$295	$250	$195	$150	N/A	N/A

Add 15% for checkered walnut stock (Deluxe).

❋ **Stingray KS (Carbine)** - .177 or .22 cal., similar to Stingray Rifle, except 38 in. overall. New 2001.

No MSR	$295	$255	$210	$170	$130	N/A	N/A

Add 15% for checkered walnut stock (Deluxe).

SPORT - .22 in. cal., BBC, SP, SS. 490 FPS. Beech stock, plastic buttplate and trigger guard. adj. sights, scope grooves. No safety. Junior size, economy level air rifle, imported from England. New 2004.

	$235	$210	$180	$145	$105	N/A	N/A

Last MSR was $235.

TOMAHAWK - .177 or .22 cal., BBC, 845/622 FPS, 15 in. barrel with Venon designed ported barrel brake, two-stage adj. trigger, automatic safety, beech or walnut (deluxe) stock with dual cheekpiece, 7.5 lbs. New 2001.

No MSR	$463	$405	$325	$260	$215	N/A	N/A

Add 15% for checkered walnut stock (Deluxe).

TRACKER/CARBINE - .177 or .22 cal., SL 750/600 FPS, 11.37 (carbine) or 17.5 in. barrel with removable muzzle weight, single-stage "hunter" adj. trigger, integral scope grooves, Black Nighthunter, Camo Fieldshooter, or beech Monte Carlo stock with recoil pad, optional stocks, 7.2-7.4 lbs. Disc. 2000.

	$240	$195	$165	$125	$85	N/A	N/A

Last MSR was $300.

Add 5% for .22 cal. model.
Add 15% for Black Nighthunter or Camo Fieldshooter stocks.

VENOM VIPER - .177, .20 or .22 cal., PCP, similar to Raider, except 6.2 lbs. New 2001.

No MSR	$784	$675	$550	$485	$405	N/A	N/A

Add 15% for walnut stock.

VICTOR - .177 or .22 cal., SP, BBC, SS, 720/580 FPS, PTFE and O-ring piston seal, no safety, 40.1 in. OAL, 7 lbs. Mfg. 1981.

	$150	$130	$120	$100	$80	$60	$50

Junior version of Vulcan II.

VISCOUNT/VISCOUNT DELUXE - .177 or .22 cal., SP, SL, SS, tap-loading, 830/650 FPS, PTFE and O-ring piston seal, Italian beech or European walnut (Viscount Deluxe) Monte Carlo full stock, black plastic PG cap, rubber buttplate with white line spacer, manual safety. 43.5-43.8 in. OAL, 7.6-7.7 lbs. Mfg. 1982.

	$300	$250	$200	$175	$150	$130	$110

Add 75% for Viscount Deluxe.

Viscount Deluxe included oil-finished European walnut stock with hand checkering, sling swivels, and vent. rubber buttplate. Intro. Aug. 1982.

VULCAN I - .177 or .22 cal., SP, BBC, SS, 810/630 FPS, PTFE and O-ring piston seal, PG beech stock with angular forearm, shallow cheekpiece, black rubber buttplate, adj. trigger (to 3 lbs.) with constant sear engagement, manual safety, 40.8 in. OAL, 7.1 lbs. Mfg. 1979-81.

	$125	$110	$90	$80	$60	N/A	N/A

Introduced "Webley Power Intensification System" PTFE and O-ring piston seal.

❋ **Vulcan I Deluxe** - similar to Vulcan I, except .177 cal. only, special walnut stock, hand checkered forearm and PG, soft rubber buttplate with white line spacer, gold plated trigger and manual safety. 43.8 in OAL, 7.65 lbs. Mfg. 1980-81.

	$350	$295	$225	N/A	N/A	N/A	N/A

GRADING	100%	95%	90%	80%	60%	40%	20%

VULCAN II - .177 or .22 cal., SP, BBC, SS, 830/650 FPS, PTFE and O-ring piston seal, PG beech stock with rounded forearm and plastic grip cap, shallow cheekpiece, ventilated rubber buttpad with white line spacer, adj. trigger (to 3 lbs.) with constant sear engagement, manual safety, 43.6 in. OAL, 7.65 lbs. Mfg.1981-84.

	$175	$150	$125	$100	$75	$N/A	N/A

✳ *Vulcan II Deluxe* - similar to Vulcan II, except special walnut stock, hand cut checkering, sling swivels. Optional: Special Sporter or Tyrolean stocks of select French Walnut, oil finished. 43.8 in OAL, 7.85 lbs. 1981-84.

	$295	$250	$195	N/A	N/A	N/A	N/A

Add 75% for Special Sporter or Tyrolean stocks of select French Walnut, oil finished.

VULCAN III - .177, .22, or .25 (carbine) cal., BBC, 870/660/620 FPS, 11.37 (carbine) or 17.5 in. barrel with threaded muzzle-brake, single-stage "hunter" adj. trigger, integral scope grooves, open sights, beech Monte Carlo stock with recoil pad, 7.6 lbs. Mfg. 1984-2000.

	$225	$195	$165	$125	$95	N/A	N/A

Last MSR was $300.

Add 10% for .25 cal. model.

Add 5% for Carbine version in .177 and .22 cal.

Add 10% for noise suppressor (requires $200 federal tax in the USA).

✳ *Vulcan III Deluxe* - similar to Vulcan III, except has special walnut stock with hand cut checkering and sling swivels.

	$280	$230	$180	N/A	N/A	N/A	N/A

XOCET RIFLE - .177, or .22 cal., SP, BBC, 870/660 FPS, beech Monte Carlo stock, adj. rear sight, hooded front sight, 39 in. overall. New 2001.

No MSR	$290	$250	$195	$160	$130	N/A	N/A

XOCET CARBINE - .177, or .22, cal., similar to Xocet Rifle, except 36 in. overall. New 2001.

No MSR	$290	$250	$195	$160	$130	N/A	N/A

CARBINE C1 - .177 or.22 cal., SP, BBC, SS, 830/660 FPS, slim stock with straight wrist, PTFE, "Spring Tamer" nylon spring guide, rubber buttplate, scope grooves, no safety, 38.2 in. OAL, 6.3 lbs. Mfg. 1981-1996.

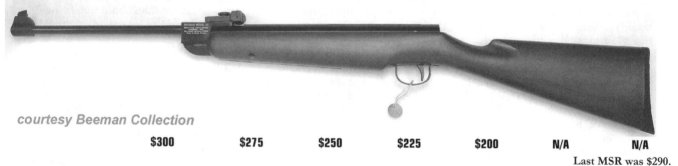

courtesy Beeman Collection

	$300	$275	$250	$225	$200	N/A	N/A

Last MSR was $290.

Subtract 10% for manual safety in later versions.

Designed by Robert Beeman for fast handling in the hunting field. USA serial numbers began at 800,000.

WEIHRAUCH SPORT

Current manufacturer located in Mellrichstadt, Germany. Formerly known as Hans-Hermann Weihrauch. Currently imported and distributed by Beeman Precision Airguns, located in Huntington Beach, CA, and by Pyramyd Air, located in Pepper Pike, OH. Dealer sales.

The authors and publisher wish to thank Mr. Ulrich Eichstädt for valuable assistance with the following information in this edition of the *Blue Book of Airguns*.

The Hermann Weihrauch company was founded in 1899 in Zella-Mehlis, the same small German town where several other famous gun manufacturers such as Walther, Sauer & Sohn, and Anschütz also began. Hermann Weihrauch, Sr. was well-known for making excellent hunting rifles. His three sons, Otto, Werner, and Hermann, Jr., soon joined the family-based company. Several new models were introduced after WWI, including the HWZ 21 smallbore rifle (HWZ stands for Hermann Weihrauch, Zella-Mehlis). This was the first mass-produced German .22 rimfire rifle and soon developed an excellent match record. Double and triple barrel shotguns, over and under shotguns, and large bore hunting rifles rounded out the line and established an excellent reputation for quality.

In 1928, Weihrauch began a large international sale of bicycle parts and mechanical door closers. During WWII, Weihrauch was the only German factory to continue production of spare parts for bicycles. At the end of the war, Zella-Mehlis became part of the Soviet occupation zone. In 1948, the Weihrauchs were forced out of their homes and factories by the communist government.

Otto Weihrauch became a mechanic and later a gunsmith in Zella-Mehlis. Werner went to work at the Jagdwaffenwerk (Hunting Weapon Factory) in nearby Suhl. Hermann Weihrauch, Jr. moved to the little German village of Mellrichstadt in Bavaria. There, with the help of his long-time hunting club friends and former customers, and his son Hans, he started the Weihrauch business all over again in the barracks of a pre-war laundry. Spare parts for bicycles were their first and main products.

When German companies were again allowed to manufacture airguns in the early 1950s, Weihrauch made the their first air rifle, the HW Model 50V. This airgun had to have a smooth bore because the Allied Occupation Government would not allow rifled barrels. Finally, after the German Shooting Federation ("Deutscher Schützenbund") was re-established, the allied government allowed the production of rifled barrels. However, because they were not allowed to produce firearms, they put their efforts into making the finest sporting airguns in the world. Even after the firearm manufacturing ban finally was withdrawn, the Hermann Weihrauch KG company continued to produce sporting air rifles of the highest quality. The little HW 25 was slanted towards the youth market while versions of the HW 30 and HW 50 continued as solid mid-market air rifles. The HW 55 was one of Europe´s leading barrel-cocking target rifles. The rather uncommon HW 55T version with its ornate Tyrolean-style stock, usually sporting fine walnut of exceptional grain, has always been a favorite among offhand shooters and collectors. The big HW 35 sporting air rifle was their main and most successful model.

After Hermann Weihrauch, Jr. died in 1967, a new era in the company began under the leadership of Hans Weihrauch, Sr. (born in 1926 and the father of today´s directors Stefan and Hans-Hermann.) The company celebrated 1970 with the introduction of the HW 70 air pistol.

The company had begun plans, and first production, of a repeating air pistol before WWII, but the war aborted its regular production. Although pre-war HWZ sales literature shows an illustration of that thirty-shot top-lever spring piston air pistol, only one specimen of that HWZ LP-1 air pistol is now known. It had survived both the war and the Russian occupation by having safely gone overseas as a sales sample to the Hy-Score Arms Company in the USA. The Hy-Score president, Steve Laszlo, had given it to his friend, Dr. Robert Beeman. Dr. Beeman surprised Hans, Sr. and Christel Weihrauch, the husband/wife directors of the new HW company, when they were visiting the Beeman home, in San Anselmo, CA, by showing them this Weihrauch airgun which was completely unknown to them!

The close connection between the owners of the Weihrauch company and Beeman Precision Airguns led to one of the first (if not the first) joint ventures between a German-based manufacturer and an American airgun distributor. After a period of importing Weihrauch-designed airguns, the Beemans had decided that they needed to introduce a German-made air rifle with American styling and features. They had determined that their main need, in addition to new styling, was a power level above anything that had been known before in the airgun field. They had been very impressed with the quality of the HW 35, but puzzled by its power, which was lower than that of the Feinwerkbau Model 124. That gun, for which Beeman had developed a large market in the U.S., had a lighter spring and smaller compression chamber.

Based on their computer simulation studies, the Beemans proposed a new air rifle model with the quality of the HW 35. This cooperative development program resulted in the Beeman R1 (sold outside of the USA as the Weihrauch HW 80 in a lower power version with a more European-style stock). The new model quickly became the best-selling adult sporting air rifle; it is credited with bringing the American airgun market into the world of adult airguns. Ironically, due to delivery problems with the longer, more complex R1 stock, the first HW 80 rifles were available some weeks earlier than the R1. This led to the incorrect conclusion made by some that the R1 was a copy of the HW80. Tom Gaylord also has written about that coincidence in his book *The Beeman R1* and pointed out that clearly Dr. Beeman was the main force behind the invention of the R1/HW80 and that Weihrauch did an outstanding job of production engineering and manufacture.

Almost the same thing happened with the introduction of the next Weihrauch air pistol, the very successful Beeman P1 (sold outside of the USA as the Weihrauch HW 45). Although the Beemans provided the full specifications and design features of this pistol, there was an initial misunderstanding about the external appearance. The factory presented a rather bulky, high top, "Desert Eagle-like" design which the Beemans did not think would appeal to the American market. They felt that it should follow the very popular and trim lines of the Colt 1911 automatic pistol. So the Beeman Company quickly made a plaster-of-paris, life-sized 3D model which the Weihrauch technicians used as a model for the final design. Ironically, the Weihrauch engineers were far ahead of their time in a different way because of another misunderstanding: they thought that, because the Beeman plans were blank in the powerplant area, that Beeman had suggested a single-stroke pneumatic air system instead of the desired, more powerful spring-piston action. These pneumatic models came some years later, when the Beeman P2/Weihrauch HW 75 was introduced. The huge commercial success of the P1 design was aided by its many features: high power, accuracy, solid metal construction, three caliber choices, different choices of finish, and especially its great flexibility: the ability to fire at two power levels, integral scope rail, and the availability of a Beeman-designed shoulder stock.

The R1/HW80, and its several variations, gave rise to a lighter, easier to cock model: the R10/HW85. Weihrauch then produced an under-lever spring piston rifle, the HW77. This gun opened fully for loading directly into the breech of the barrel, like a Feinwerkbau match rifle. This was a great improvement over barrel-cocking air rifles which utilized a loading tap from which the pellet had to leap into the barrel. The HW77 and HW77 Carbine, with their rigid barrel and easy cocking and loading, became extremely popular in countries where their lower power was under the legal limit. However, these models had very disappointing sales in the USA, where shooters still preferred the R1/HW80 and R10/HW85 barrel-cockers, by a margin of over 20 to 1, due to their higher power.

The field-style air rifle designs for the American market were a great success because only a very small minority of adult airgun shooters were involved in any competition or group shooting activities. Field target shooting was the most popular of the American group airgun shooting sports, but even that involved much less than one percent of adult airgun shooters. Almost the exact opposite was true of airgun shooters in Germany; there, most such shooters were involved in 10 meter competition. Nevertheless, in 1989, the leading German gun magazine, VISIER, discovered from a survey that a large number of German airgun shooters would be willing to pay more than 500 DM (about 300 U.S. dollars) for an air rifle which was equipped with a sporting-style stock and designed for scope use. Many Germans responding to the poll also submitted useful suggestions for new designs to be added to the many new stock designs being developed by Weihrauch.

The reunification of Germany in 1990 resulted in many changes for every German citizen and manufacturer. Weihrauch began a cooperation with Theoben Engineering in England which resulted in the introduction of the first German/English air rifle design: the Weihrauch HW 90 (the Beeman versions are the RX and RX-1). This was the first Weihrauch rifle using the patented Theoben gas-spring system (sometimes inappropriately called "gas ram"). These new rifles sold very well in Great Britain where field target shooting had originated in the early 1980s and also were well received there and in the USA for small game hunting.

The great optimism of that period of the company´s development was dampened by the unexpected death of Hans Weihrauch, Sr. on April 3, 1990 at the age of only 63. His business accomplishments were so admired that he was posthumously decorated

GRADING	100%	95%	90%	80%	60%	40%	20%

with the Federal Cross of Merit. His wife, Christel, and sons, Stefan and Hans-Hermann, took the reins of the company. Fortunately, Christel Weihrauch had shared the management of the firm for decades and the preparation of the two sons for their expected future management roles was well advanced. Both had been involved with the company all of their lives and had nearly finished their engineering and marketing training as well. Director-to-be Hans-Hermann had even spent several months as an apprentice executive in the Beeman Precision Airguns business in America and had polished his English language skills by living with Robert and Toshiko Beeman in their California home during that time.

The fall of the German wall right by their little village of Mellrichstadt suddenly placed them "in the middle of Germany." This opened new markets for their surface engineering branch. They added new machines for electroless nickel plating and bronzing (and made the floors slip-proof with expanded mesh, stainless-steel fencing panels supplied from the nearby fallen "Iron Curtain!").

When Christel Weihrauch retired in 1998, Stefan and Hans-Hermann took her place. The company was separated into Weihrauch & Weihrauch (single-action revolvers for cowboy action shooting) and Weihrauch Sport (airguns). New airgun models accompanied that change and their centennial ceremonies in 1999; the HW 97 succeeded the HW 77, designed only for use with a scope in field target and hunting. An economy version of the HW 97, the HW 57 features a pop-up loading chamber. A single-stroke pneumatic air pistol, the HW 40 (the Beeman version is the P3), displays the styling of the popular polymer frame firearm pistols and features fully recoilless action for right- or left-hand use.

The world-wide success of Weihrauch airguns is still based on the motto which the company has used for over a century: "Quality – Made in Germany." International gun expert John Walter noted that "Weihrauch is rightly regarded as one of the last bastions of traditional airgunsmithing." It is interesting and instructive to compare the details of their airgun design and quality with any other sporting airguns.

Note that guns stamped with an "F" in a pentagon are low velocity versions intended for the German and other markets with strict power limits. Without that mark the guns generally are designed for the English market with its 12 ft./lb. limit for air rifles and 6 ft./lb. limit for air pistols.

Beeman/Weihrauch guns: For those special models and versions of Beeman brand airguns made by Weihrauch, see the Beeman Precision Airguns section of this book.

For more information and current pricing on Weihrauch firearms, please refer to the *Blue Book of Gun Values* by S.P. Fjestad (also available online).

PISTOLS

MODEL HWZ - LP 1 - .177 lead balls, thirty-shot repeater, TL, SP, walnut single-piece grip, front sight acts as BB magazine retainer, blue finish. Extremely rare. Mfg. 1939.

courtesy Beeman Collection

	N/A	N/A	$3,800	N/A	N/A	N/A	N/A

MODEL HW 40 PCA - .177 cal, CO_2, SSP, SS, styled like semi-auto firearm, 410 FPS, adj. rear sight.

MSR $185	$155	$130	$110	$90	$60	N/A	N/A

MODEL HW 45 LP - .177, .20, or .22 cal, SP, 600/500 FPS, adj. rear sight, blue or matte nickel finish. Developed from Beeman P1.

MSR $400	$340	$290	$230	$195	$150	N/A	N/A

Add 10% for matte nickel finish.

Add 50% for shoulder stock.

MODEL HW 70 - .177 cal., BBC, SP, SS, 410 FPS, 2.25 lbs.

	$155	$130	$110	$90	$60	N/A	N/A

Last MSR was $170.

Add 30% for chrome.

GRADING	100%	95%	90%	80%	60%	40%	20%

✱ *Model HW 70-A* - similar to HW 70, except has improved rear sight suitable for scope mount, improved trigger and safety.

courtesy Beeman Collection

MSR	$225	$185	$160	$140	$115	$90	N/A	N/A

Add 10% for stylized black grip and silver finish.
Add 10% for early versions without safety.

✱ *Model HW 70 LP* - .177 cal., BBC, 440 FPS, 2.25 lbs.

MSR	$225	$185	$160	$140	$115	$90	N/A	N/A

MODEL HW 75 M - .177 cal, SSP, 435 FPS, adj. rear sight, manual safety, walnut target grips.

MSR	$495	$440	$390	$340	$290	$240	N/A	N/A

RIFLES

MODEL HW 25 L - .177 cal., BBC, SP, 590 FPS.

courtesy Beeman Collection

MSR	$220	$185	$155	$125	$95	$75	N/A	N/A

MODEL HW 30 - .177 or .20 cal., BBC, SP, 660/600 FPS, 17 in. barrel, 5.3 lbs.

courtesy Beeman Collection

MSR	$205	$175	$150	$120	$90	$70	N/A	N/A

Add 10% for .20 cal.

✱ *Model HW 30 M/II* - .177 or .22 cal., BBC, SP, 660/450 FPS, match trigger, automatic safety, 17 in. barrel, 5.3 lbs.

MSR	$245	$210	$180	$145	$120	$90	N/A	N/A

Add 15% for Monte Carlo cheekpiece.
Add 20% for Beeman factory markings.

GRADING		100%	95%	90%	80%	60%	40%	20%

* **Model HW 30 S** - .177 or .22 cal., BBC, SP, 660/450 FPS, Rekord match trigger, 17 in. barrel, tunnel front sight.

courtesy Beeman Collection

MSR	$260	$220	$190	$155	$125	$95	N/A	N/A

Add 15% for Monte Carlo cheekpiece.
Add 20% for Beeman factory markings.

MODEL HW 35 - .177 or .22 cal., BBC, SP, 790/600 FPS, Rekord match trigger, walnut, beech or stained beech Safari stock, matte blue finish barrel and receiver.

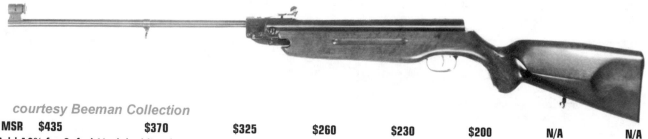

courtesy Beeman Collection

MSR	$435	$370	$325	$260	$230	$200	N/A	N/A

Add 10% for Safari Model with safari finish stock.
Add 25% for walnut stock.
Add 20% for thumbhole stock.
Add 15% for Safari Model - matte blue, safari finish stock.
Add 20% for Beeman factory markings.

* **Model HW 35 EB** - .177 or .22 cal., BBC, SP, walnut stock with special cheek piece, checkered pistol grip with white spacer under grip cap, rubber buttplate, 755/660 FPS, 20 in. barrel, 8 lbs. Disc. 1985.

		$350	$305	$250	$210	$175	N/A	N/A

Last MSR was $450.

Add 20% for chrome.
Add 5% for .22 cal.
Subtract 10% for 35L.
Add 20% for Beeman factory markings.

MODEL HW 50 - .177 or .22 cal., BBC, SP, 705 FPS, 17 in. barrel, 6 lbs. 9 oz.

MSR	$292	$255	$215	$185	$150	$90	N/A	N/A

Add 40% for Beeman factory markings with up-grade stock, and rubber buttplate.

* **Model HW 50 M/II** - .177 or .22 cal., BBC, SP, 850/620 FPS, 17 in. barrel, 6.6 lbs.

courtesy Beeman Collection

MSR	$325	$280	$225	$175	$135	$105	N/A	N/A

Add 10% for HW50S with Rekord trigger.
Add 20% for Beeman factory markings.

GRADING	100%	95%	90%	80%	60%	40%	20%

MODEL HW 50V - .177 cal., smoothbore, BBC, SP, SS, beech stock with rounded grip end, grooves across butt, cast trigger guard, knurled and threaded rear end cap, marked "H.W.50" with image of soaring bird over that marking, no safety, 42.1 in. OAL, 5.6 lbs. Mfg. early 1950s

courtesy Beeman Collection

	N/A	N/A	$1,500	$1,250	$995	$750	N/A

Weihrauch's first airgun, smoothbore because the Allied Occupation Government would not allow German civilians to own rifled guns after WWII.

HW BARAKUDA EL 54 - .22 cal., BBC, SP, SS, power augmented by diesel ignition of ether vapors from ether-injection tube affixed to right side of main body tube, 19.7 in. barrel, approx. 600-700 FPS without ether; much higher with ether, early versions with steel trigger guard and simple steel trigger system, later versions with cast aluminum trigger guards and Rekord trigger system, 8.4 lbs. Mfg. 1954-81.

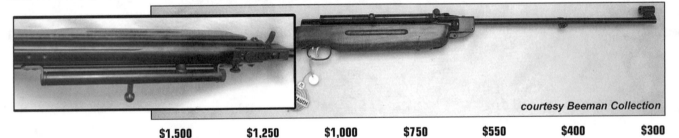

courtesy Beeman Collection

$1,500	$1,250	$1,000	$750	$550	$400	$300

Add 25% for Beeman markings. (Factory stamped with RDB for Robert David Beeman serial number - value N/A.)

Add 30% for high gloss factory chrome plating.

Subtract 20% for Standard Model with beech stock.

Ether injection attachment only = $295.

Only a few hundred were made under cooperation of Weihrauch Company and Barakuda Company in Hamburg, Germany. Twenty specially made for Beeman Precision Airguns in 1981 from last remaining parts.

Caution: Specimens are not authentic unless factory stamped "BARAKUDA". Air rifles with ether-injection tubes, but marked HW 35, or with other model numbers, are fakes; compromised specimens of other models. Handle ether with care.

MODEL 55 - .177 cal., BBC, SP, 660-700 FPS, 7.5 lbs.

courtesy Beeman Collection

	$440	$375	$295	$225	$175	N/A	N/A

Last MSR was $610.

Add 10% for left-hand variation.

Add 20% for Match (squarish forearm with lower line equal to bottom of trigger guard).

Add 30% for Tyrolean stock.

Add 10% for Beeman factory markings.

* **Model HW 55 SM** - .177 cal., BBC, SP, 590 FPS, adj. match target rear sight, hooded front sight, match trigger.

MSR	$540	$460	$390	$315	$235	$185	N/A	N/A

MODEL HW 57 - .177 and .22 cals., UL, SP, beech stock, rubber buttplate, Rekord trigger, 14.2 in. (360 mm) barrel, 820/570 FPS MV, 7 lbs. (3.8 kg). (An economy version of the HW97 with a pop-up loading tap.)

MSR	$365	$295	$245	$195	$150	$115	N/A	N/A

GRADING	100%	95%	90%	80%	60%	40%	20%

MODEL 77/77 CARBINE - .177, .20, or .22 cal., UL, SP, 830/710 FPS, 8.6 lbs.

courtesy Beeman Collection

MSR $435	$385	$330	$250	$175	$125	N/A	N/A

Add 10% for left-hand version.
Add 10% for deluxe version.
Add 10% for .20 cal.
Add 25% for Tyrolean stock.

MODEL HW 80 - .177, .20, .22, and .25 cals., BBC, SP, SS, barrel length 19.7 in. (500 mm) (16.1 in., 410 mm for Carbine), 965-570 FPS, Rekord trigger, beech stock does not cover barrel pivot, checkered pistol grip, rubber buttplate. 8.8 lbs. (4.0 kg).

MSR $454	$395	$350	$295	$245	$175	N/A	N/A

Add 5% for .20 cal.
Add 15% for .25 cal.

MODEL HW 85 - similar to Model HW 80 except 7.7 lbs (3.5 kg) and plain stock.

	$250	$215	$170	$135	$90	N/A	N/A

Add 5% for .20 cal.
Add 20% for .25 cal. in USA.
Add 15% for Deluxe Model with fine checkered pistol grip with cap and white spacers.

MODEL HW 90 - .177, .20, .22, or .25 cal., Theoben gas spring system, 1120/790 FPS.

MSR $640	$545	$460	$370	$300	$250	N/A	N/A

Add 15% for .20 and .25 cal. models.

MODEL HW 97 - .177, .20, .22, and .25 cals., UL, SP, 930 FPS in .177; 9 lbs (4.1 kg), laminated stock, designed for scope use only. Replaced by HW 97K in 2001.

courtesy Beeman Collection

	$465	$395	$310	$250	$195	N/A	N/A

Add 10% for .20 cal.
Add 20% for .25 cal. in USA.

✳ *Model HW 97 K* - .177, .20, .22, and .25 cals. UL, SP, designed for field target and silhouette. 930 FPS in .177 cal., brown laminated stock, 9 lbs. (4.1 kg.).

MSR $550	$465	$395	$310	$250	$195	N/A	N/A

Add 5% for .20 cal.
Add 20% for .25 cal. in USA.
Add 10% for blue laminated stock in USA.
Add 15% for green laminated stock in USA.
Add 25% for HW Centennial model, marked "100 Jahre Weihrauch" (Germany) or "100 years Weihrauch" (UK version) in USA.

MODEL HW 98 - .177 cal., BBC, SP, 930 FPS, automatic safety, Field Target Competition model with adj. cheekpiece, buttplate.

MSR $625	$530	$450	$360	$295	$225	N/A	N/A

MODEL HW 100 - .22 cal., PCP, side lever action, fourteen-shot rotary mag., 16.25 in. BBL, no sights, blue finish, two stage adj. trigger, walnut thumbhole target stock with stippled grip, 38.6 in. OAL, 8.6 lbs. New 2004.

MSR $1,138	$950	$775	$695	$595	N/A	N/A	N/A

MODEL HWB CHAMP - .177 cal., BBC, SP, 590 FPS, adj. match target rear sight, hooded front sight, youth model.

MSR $545	$460	$395	$310	$250	$195	N/A	N/A

GRADING	100%	95%	90%	80%	60%	40%	20%

MODEL HW 95 - .177, .20, .22, and .25 cals., BBC, SP, SS, barrel length 19.7 in. (500 mm) (16.1 in., 410 mm for Carbine), 965-570 FPS, beech stock, checkered pistol grip, rubber buttplate. 7.8 lbs. New 2005.

	MSR	$365	$315	$265	$225	$195	$145	N/A	N/A

Add 5% for .20 cal.

Add 15% for .25 cal.

WELLS

Previous airgun designer located in Palo Alto, CA.

William Wells may be one of the greatest airgun innovators of the twentieth century. Born in 1872, he apparently started designing and producing experimental airguns in the 1930s. He became a design consultant to Daisy in 1947. He also produced many dozens of designs, mostly repeating pneumatic rifles, but his work also included air pistols and spring piston airguns. These designs are represented by actual working specimens. Identification may not be easy; the interested reader must refer to Hannusch's paper, cited below. Many are marked "Cde P" on the base of the grip. The base of the stock usually is marked with his favorite .180 caliber (true BB shot), but several other calibers are known, including .187. Many models were produced in the election year 1952 and are marked with a small elephant emblem engraved with the 52 date. Many of Wells' designs are incorporated into Daisy and other brand airguns. William Wells died in October 1968, still very alert at the age of 96. It is not possible to assign values to the wide variety of Wells' airguns at this time, but collectors should be on the lookout for his products. Ref: Larry Hannusch, 1999, *Airgun Revue 4*.

courtesy Beeman Collection

WESTERN AUTO

Catalog sales/retailer that has subcontracted various manufacturers to private label airguns.

To date, there has been very little interest in collecting Western Auto airguns, regardless of rarity. Rather than list Western Auto models, a general guideline is that values generally are under those of their "first generation relatives." As a result, prices are ascertained by the shooting value of the airgun, rather than its collector value. See "Store Brand Crossover List" located in the back of this text.

WESTINGER & ALTENBURGER

For information on Westinger & Altenburger, see Feinwerkbau in the "F" section.

WESTLEY RICHARDS & CO. LTD.

Current manufacturer located in Birmingham, England, and previously located in London, England.

Westley Richards previously manufactured the "Highest Possible" air pistols circa 1907 to late 1920s. Airgun production was quite limited; the highest known airgun serial number is 1052. For more information and current pricing on Westley Richards firearms, please refer to the *Blue Book of Gun Values* by S.P. Fjestad (also available online).

PISTOLS

TOP BARREL MODEL - .177 cal., BBC, SP, SS, rifled 9.7 in. barrel on top of compression tube/body tube, marked (WESTLEY RICHARDS "HIGHEST POSSIBLE" AIR PISTOL) on tube, piston moves rearward during firing, horn or bakelite grips, blue or nickel finished, 11.9 in. OAL, 3.1 lbs., patented 1907, marketed Jan. 1910 to late 1914.

✳ *First Variant* - some with heart-shaped opening in frame behind trigger, with smooth horn grip plates.

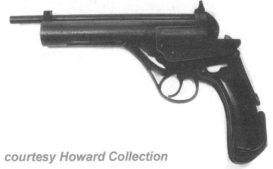

courtesy Howard Collection

	$1,500	$1,400	$1,300	$1,000	$750	$600	$500

Add 25% for nickel finish.

GRADING	100%	95%	90%	80%	60%	40%	20%

✳ *Second Variant* - vertically curved rear sight screwed to frame, frame behind trigger closed, checkered hard rubber grip plates.

courtesy Howard Collection

	$1,250	$1,150	$1,000	$750	$600	$450	$350

Add 10% for horn grips (transitional Model).
Add 25% nickel finish.

CONCENTRIC PISTON MODEL - .177 cal. BBC, SP, SS, piston concentric around central rifled 7.2 in. BBL, piston moves rearward during firing, 9.4 in.OAL, 2.3 lbs, patented 1921, marketed in 1924.

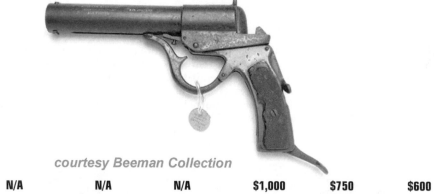

courtesy Beeman Collection

	N/A	N/A	N/A	$1,000	$750	$600	$500

Designed by Edwin Anson. Blued (two known in nickel). The length of the sleeve ("shoe") covering the rear of the body tube varies. Ref: AG:Dec.1998, May 1999, Dec. 2004.

WHISCOMBE

Current manufacturer of Whiscombe Opposed Piston Air Rifles. Situated at 'Runways,' Stoney Lane, Ashmore Green, Thatcham, Berkshire, RG18 9HG, England. Direct sales.

High-end, spring-piston rifles with twin pistons opposing each other rather than moving in opposite directions as in Giss patent airguns manufactured by Dianawerk where one piston is a dummy. The opposing action eliminates almost all recoil and intensifies power. Each piston has a pair of springs, the total of four springs gives up to 650 lbs. loading.

The authors and publisher wish to thank Tim Saunders for his valuable assistance with the following information in this edition of the *Blue Book of Airguns*.

RIFLES

MODELS JW50-JW80 - .177, .20, .22 or .25 cal., field target and hunting air rifles with high recoilless power without resorting to precharged gases or pumping. The model numbers, ranging from JW50 to JW80, indicate the piston stroke in millimeters. Smaller stroke guns usually are cocked by two stokes of an underlever. Larger stroke guns (70/80 mm) use three strokes. The large JW80 version, which requires a FAC license in Britain, produces up to 28 ft./lb. ME in .22 caliber and 30 ft/lb. ME in .25 caliber, blued or silverized steel finish, sporter or thumbhole stocks, action design, and standard or match trigger. 15 in. polygonal rifled barrel. About 450 rifles produced, most stocked for field target. Estimated about 2/3 sold into USA. Sporting stock versions about 9.8 lbs; thumbhole versions about 10.5 lbs. All guns hand built by John Whiscombe. Mfg. 1987 to present.

MSR	$2,200-$2,600	$2,000	$1,800	$1,600	$1,250	N/A	N/A	N/A

Add 10% for extra barrel.

Many upgrades and extras available. Please contact the company directly for more information and prices of their products (see Trademark Index listing).

WILKINS, JOE

Previous maker of the Predator PCP repeating air rifle located in England.

Sometimes incorrectly referred to as the Ripley Predator. However, Ripley Rifles, the small firm which produced the Ripley AR-5 rifle, is owned by Steve Wilkens, Joe's son. The Wilkens Predator was discontinued to a large degree because slide action guns are considered politically incorrect in Britain and the maker did not want to stimulate the Home Office into further control of airguns.

GRADING	100%	95%	90%	80%	60%	40%	20%

RIFLES

PREDATOR - .22 cal., PCP, Field Target rifle, fifteen- to sixteen-shot repeater, slide action loads and cocks with a single rapid stroke, power regulator, most set at 12 ft./lb., one at 18, and one at 26. 20 mfg. 1987-1999.

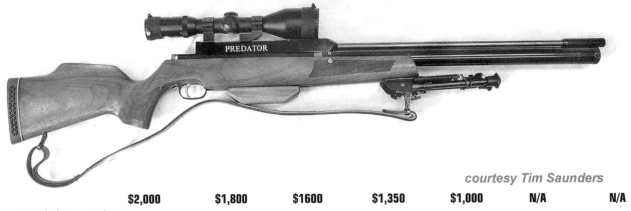

courtesy Tim Saunders

	$2,000	$1,800	$1600	$1,350	$1,000	N/A	N/A

One was made in .177 cal.

WILL

Previous tradename of Oskar Will of Zella-Mehlis, Thüringen, Germany, established in 1844.

His son, Oskar Will The Younger, was one of the most famous airgun makers in Germany before 1914. Circa 1923, the company was sold to Wilhelm Foss who operated it as Venuswaffenfabrik until 1945. Especially famous for air rifles, with large diameter central compression chambers, which used the extended trigger guard as a cocking lever ("Bügelspanners") . These guns carried on the tradition of the large receiver gallery airguns made in the USA in the mid-1800s. Such trigger guard lever guns (Bügelspanners) continued to be listed in European gun wholesaler catalogs into the 1950s. (See American Gallery Airguns section in the "A" section.) Actual old specimens of Will and Original Will airguns currently retail in the $500-$750 range, while newer copies, marked "Original", or without markings, retail in the $250-$350. Crank style air rifles and pistols (Kürbelspanners) from the Wills usually retail in the $750-$2,500 range

courtesy Beeman Collection

WINCHESTER

Current manufacturer located in New Haven, CT.

Beginning 2001, airguns under the Winchester label were imported again; this time from Spain. Sales and service are through Daisy Outdoor Products, located in Rogers, AR.

Between 1969 and 1975 Winchester imported eight rifle models and two pistol models into the United States from Meyer & Grammelspacher located in Germany. A total of 19,259 airguns were imported through 1973. See Dianawerk in the "D" section for a table of Winchester airguns made by M&G in Germany.

For more information and current pricing on both new and used Winchester firearms, please refer to the *Blue Book of Gun Vales* by S.P. Fjestad (also available online).

PISTOLS

MODEL 353 - .177 or .22 cal., BBC, SP, SS, 7 in. rifled steel barrel, 378 FPS, blue finish, composition plastic stock, hooded bead front and adj. rear sights, 2.75 lbs.

	N/A	$300	$250	$200	$150	N/A	N/A

1974 retail was $42.

MODEL 363 - .177 cal., BBC, SP, SS, 7 in. rifled steel barrel, 378 FPS, double piston recoilless design, micrometer rear and interchangeable front sights, fully adj. trigger, match grade composition plastic stock with thumb rest, 16 in. overall, 3 lbs.

	N/A	$450	$350	$300	$250	N/A	N/A

1974 RP was $64.

GRADING	100%	95%	90%	80%	60%	40%	20%

RIFLES

MODEL 333 - .177 cal., BBC, SP, SS, 576 FPS, diopter target sight, fully adj. trigger, double piston recoilless action, checkered and stippled walnut stock, 9.5 lbs.

	N/A	$700	$625	$500	$350	N/A	N/A

MODEL 416 - .177 cal., BBC, SP, SS, smooth bore barrel, blue finish, double pull-type trigger, wood stock, 363 FPS, fixed front and adj. rear sights, 33 in. overall, 2.75 lbs.

	$50	$40	$30	$20	$15	N/A	N/A

1974 RP was $21.

MODEL 422 - .177 cal., BBC, SP, SS, rifled barrel, blue finish, wood stock, double pull-type trigger, 480 FPS, fixed front and adj. rear sights, 36 in. overall, 3.75 lbs.

	$65	$50	$40	$30	$20	N/A	N/A

1974 retail price was $30.

MODEL 423 - .177 cal., similar to Model 422, except fixed ramp front and adj. rear sights, 36 in. overall, 4 lbs.

	$85	$65	$50	$40	$30	N/A	N/A

1974 retail price was $37.

MODEL 425 - .22 cal., similar to Model 423, except with 543 FPS, adj. double-pull type trigger, dovetail base for scope, non-slip composition buttplate, 38 in. overall, 5 lbs.

courtesy Beeman Collection

	$125	$85	$70	$55	$40	N/A	N/A

1974 retail price was $42.

MODEL 427 - .22 cal., similar to Model 425, except with 660 FPS, micrometer rear and hooded front sight, 42 in. OAL, 6 lbs.

	$195	$150	$125	$100	$75	N/A	N/A

1974 retail price was $48.

MODEL 435 - .177 cal. similar to Model 427, except with 693 FPS, micrometer rear and interchangeable front sight, checkered stock and adj. trigger, 44 in. OAL, 6.5 lbs.

	$225	$195	$150	$125	$100	N/A	N/A

1974 retail price was $70.

MODEL 450 - .177 cal., UL, SP, SS, rifled steel barrel, blue finish, 693 FPS, micrometer rear and interchangeable front sight, dovetail base for scope, checkered Schutzen style stock, rubber buttplate, 44.5 in. OAL, 7.75 lbs.

	$350	$300	$250	$200	$150	N/A	N/A

1974 retail price was $100.

MODEL 500X - .177 cal., BBC, SP, SS, 490 FPS, rifled steel barrel, micro-adj. rear sight, hooded front sight with blade and ramp, grooved receiver, sporter-style select walnut stock, 5.7 lbs. Mfg. in Turkey. New 2003.

MSR	$90	$85	$75	$60	$50	$40	N/A	N/A

Add 40% for Model 500XS with 4x32 Winchester scope new 2004.

MODEL 600X - .177 cal., BBC, SP, SS, 600 FPS, rifled steel barrel, micro-adj. rear sight, hooded front sight with blade and ramp, grooved receiver, sporter-style select walnut stock, 5.9 lbs. Mfg. in Turkey. New 2001.

MSR	$90	$85	$75	$60	$50	$40	N/A	N/A

Add 30% for Model 600XS with 4x32 Winchester scope new 2004.

MODEL 722X - .22 cal., BBC, SP, SS, 700 FPS, rifled steel barrel, micro-adj. rear sight, hooded front sight with blade and ramp, grooved receiver, rear safety button, sporter-style select walnut stock, 6.6 lbs. Mfg. in Turkey 2001-03.

	$115	$95	$75	$60	$50	N/A	N/A

Last MSR was $170.

MODEL 800X - .177 cal., BBC, SP, SS, 800 FPS, rifled steel barrel, micro-adj. rear sight, hooded front sight with blade and ramp, grooved receiver, rear safety button, sporter-style select walnut stock, 6.6 lbs. Mfg. in Turkey. New 2001.

MSR	$120	$115	$91	$70	$60	$50	N/A	N/A

Add 20% for Model 800XS with 4x32 Winchester scope new 2004.

MODEL 1000X - .177 cal., BBC, SP, SS, 1000 FPS, rifled steel barrel, micro-adj. rear sight, hooded front sight with blade and ramp, grooved receiver, rear safety button, sporter-style select walnut stock, 6.6 lbs. New 2001.

MSR	$140	$125	$105	$85	$75	$60	N/A	N/A

Add 15% for Model 1000XS with 3-9x32 Winchester scope new 2004.

GRADING	100%	95%	90%	80%	60%	40%	20%

MODEL 1000B - .177 cal., BBC, SP, SS, 1000 FPS, rifled steel barrel, micro-adj. rear sight, hooded front sight with blade and ramp, grooved receiver, rear safety button, black sporter-style composite, recoil pad, 44.5 in. OAL, 6.6 lbs. New 2004.

	MSR $135	$120	$105	$85	$75	$60	N/A	N/A

Add 15% for Model 1000SB with 3-9x32 Winchester scope (new 2004).

MODEL 1000C - .177 cal., BBC, SP, SS, 1000 FPS, rifled steel barrel, micro-adj. rear sight, hooded front sight with blade and ramp, grooved receiver, rear safety button, camo sporter-style composite stock, recoil pad, 44.5 in. OAL, 6.6 lbs. New 2004.

	MSR $150	$140	$125	$95	$85	$70	N/A	N/A

Add 15% for Model 1000SC with 3-9x32 Winchester scope (new 2004).

MODEL 1894 - BB/.174 cal., lever action, SP, 300 FPS, fifteen-shot mag., smooth bore steel barrel, micro-adj. rear sight, blade and ramp front sight, crossbolt trigger safety, western-style wood stock and forearm, 3.4 lbs. Imported from Turkey. New 2003.

	MSR $80	$75	$65	$50	$40	$30	N/A	N/A

WINSEL

Previously manufactured by Winsel Corporation of Rochester, NY.

PISTOLS

JET PISTOL - .22 cal., CO_2, SS, breech loading, brass barrel, button safety behind trigger, cocked and breech opened by pushing lever at bottom of grip, black plastic grips, aluminum frame, 12 in. overall, with cylinder attached, black crinkle paint finish on receiver and rear of barrel housing, glossy black elsewhere. Supplied with two CO_2 cylinders, one in a slim cardboard "mailing box" for returning cylinders to factory for refill, 2.3 lbs.

courtesy Beeman Collection

	N/A	$1,250	$1,100	$1,000	$900	$800	$700

Add 30% for original maroon factory box and papers.

Subtract 20% for each missing cylinder.

Most specimens are without one or both cylinders because the manufacturer went out of business while holding many customers' cylinders. They were destroyed.

WISCHO

For information on Wischo air guns, see B.S.F. in the "B" section.

WRIGHT MFG. CO.

Manufacturer located in Burbank, CA. Probably not in production at this time.

PISTOLS

WRIGHT TARGET SHOT JR. - .177 cal., SP, SS, rear plunger pulls out to cock, 2.5 in. smoothbore barrel unscrews for rear loading of pellet, shot, or dart. Diecast body includes checkered grip panels. 8.1 in. OAL, 1.0 lbs.

courtesy Beeman Collection

	N/A	N/A	$45	$40	$35	$30	$25

WYANDOTTE

Previous tradename of American Tool Works located in Chicago, IL.

For information on Wuandotte, see American Tool Works in the "A" section.

Y SECTION

YEWHA

Previous tradename of airguns manufactured in South Korea.

Yewha (Ye-Wha), reported to have been made by Tong-Il Industrial Co. Ltd. of Seoul, South Korea, but that may be only a trading company. Yewha may be the name of the maker. Distributed in United States by Beeman Precision Airguns in 1970s. These airguns apparently made only in 1970s. Due to anti-firearm laws in Korea, whole gun clubs may be equipped with these guns; club pictures show huge piles of ringneck pheasant taken with the B3 Dynamite airgun. Ref: AGNR - Oct. 1987, www.Beemans.net (see also the "A Shot of Humor" section in this book and on the www.Beemans.net website).

GRADING	100%	95%	90%	80%	60%	40%	20%

RIFLES/SHOTGUN

B-B OR B3 DYNAMITE - .25 cal., pump pneumatic (pump-rod-at-the-muzzle), SS, 28.7 in. smoothbore barrel, breech loaded with plastic cartridge loaded with birdshot or single lead balls, parkerized finish, hardwood stock, twenty or more pumps can produce up to 1000 FPS, 41.3 in. OAL, 5.75 lbs.

courtesy Beeman Collection

	100%	95%	90%	80%	60%	40%	20%
	$500	$450	$350	$300	$275	$250	$200

REVOLVING RIFLE - .177 cal., DA, similar to B3 Dynamite, except has six-shot revolving cylinder for pellets, exposed hammer, rifled barrel, parkerized finish.

courtesy Beeman Collection

	100%	95%	90%	80%	60%	40%	20%
	$1,000	$900	$850	$800	$700	$500	$350

TARGET RIFLE - PUMP ROD MODEL - similar to revolving rifle, except SS.

courtesy Beeman Collection

	100%	95%	90%	80%	60%	40%	20%
	$900	$800	$750	$700	$600	$400	$250

TARGET 200 - .177 cal., SL, SP, recoilless match target air rifle.

	100%	95%	90%	80%	60%	40%	20%
	$350	$300	$250	$225	$200	$150	$100

An unauthorized copy of the Feinwerkbau Model 300 of much lower quality and reliability.

NOTES

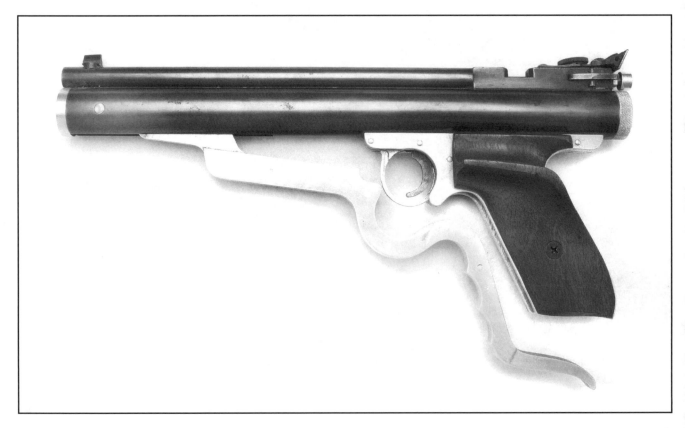

Mystery Pistol: A beautifully built, single-stroke, pneumatic air pistol bears no markings. Possibly built as an experimental gun or a prototype. Can you provide any information about this fine airgun? Beeman collection.

Z SECTION

ZENITH

Previous trademark manufactured by Nick Murphy of Sileby, Loughborough, England from about 2001 to 2003.

Nick Murphy developed and produced top level Field Target air rifles. All are .177 caliber Walther or Career barrels. All barrels are sleeved and free floating. Most stocks are made by custom stock maker Paul Wilson. All are built with special Zenith regulators. Ripley and Zenith air rifles were among the outstanding field target guns in German and English FT competition during 2003 and 2004. These were produced with a wide variety of features and finishes. Production stopped at a total of sixteen rifles. The most recent sale was for $3,100.

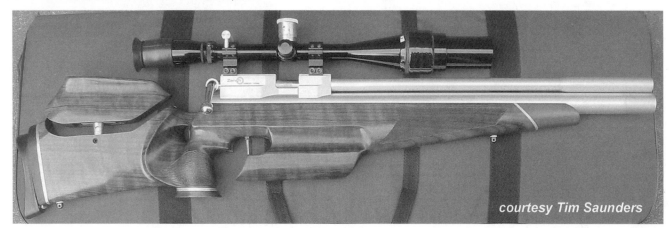

courtesy Tim Saunders

NOTES

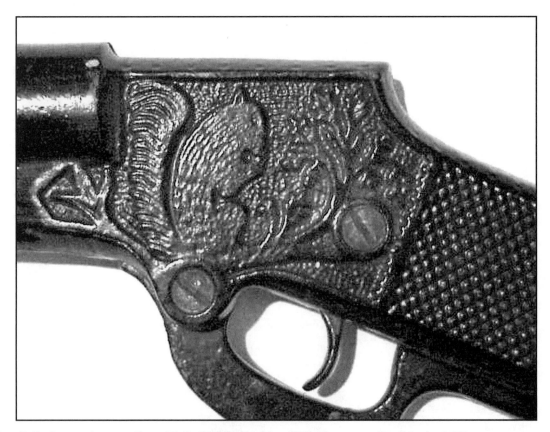

Columbian Heilprin receiver casting detail. The Columbian Heilprins were the heaviest BB guns ever made. Much prized by boys at the start of the 20th century for the gun's impressive heft and the elaborate figures of various animals on the cast iron receivers. Beeman Collection.

TRADEMARK INDEX

The listings below represent the most up-to-date information we have regarding airgun manufacturers (both domestic and international), trademarks, importers, and distributors (when applicable) to assist you in obtaining additional information from these sources. Even more so than last year, you will note the addition of website and email listings whenever possible—this may be your best way of obtaining up-to-date model and pricing information directly from the manufacturers, importers, and/or distributors. More and more companies are offering online information about their products and it pays to surf the net!

As this edition goes to press, we feel confident that the information listed below is the most up-to-date and accurate listing possible. Please note all the new email and website addresses. Remember, things change every day in this industry, and a phone/fax number that is current today could have a new area code or be gone tomorrow. International fax/phone numbers may require additional overseas and country/city coding. If you should require additional assistance in "tracking" any of the current airgun manufacturers, distributors, or importers listed in this publication, please contact us and we will try to help you regarding these specific requests.

-RING-SERVICE, INC.
227 West Lou Drive
acksonville, FL 32216
hone: 904-724-7419
ax: 904-724-7149

CURIGHT
737 Birdsong Rd.
homaston, GA 30286
hone: 706-647-5941

RON CZ s.r.o.
porter - see Top Gun Air Guns Inc.
porter - see Airguns of Arizona
porter - see Pyramyd Air, Inc.
ctory - Aeron CZ s.r.o.
setickova 23
02 00 Brno
zech Republic
hone/Fax: 420 (5) 4557-3080
Vebsite: www.aeron.cz
mail: info@aeron.cz

R ARMS
porter - see Pyramyd Air, Inc.
porter - see Pomona Air Guns
porter - see Top Gun Air Guns Inc.
ctory - Air Arms
ailsham Industrial Park
plocks Way, Hailsham
Sussex, BN27 3JF, ENGLAND
hone: 01323 845853
ax: 01323 440573
Vebsite: www.air-arms.co.uk
mail: sales@air-arms.co.uk

R GUN INC.
320 Harwin Dr. #201
ouston TX 77036
hone: 713-780-2415
ax: 713-780-4831
mail: agi2001a@hotmail.com

RFORCE AIRGUNS
O. Box 2478
t. Worth, TX 76113
hone: 817-451-8966
ax: 817-451-1613
Vebsite: www.airforceairguns.com
mail: staff@airforceairguns.com

RGUN EXPRESS, INC.
06 South Front Street
lontezuma, IA 50171
hone: 800-896-4867
ax: 641-623-5672
Vebsite: www.airgunexpress.com
mail: sales@airgunexpress.com

RGUNS OF ARIZONA
6 N Gilbert Rd.
lbert, AZ 85234
hone: 480-461-1113
ax: 480-461-3928
Vebsite: www.airgunsofarizona.com
mail: mail@airgunsofarizona.com

AIR RIFLE SPECIALISTS
P.O. Box 138
Pine City, NY 14871
Phone: 607-734-7340
Fax: 607-733-3261
Email: gusto@stny.rr.com

AIRROW
See Swivel Machine Works.

ANICS CORP.
Importer – see European American Armory Corp.
Importer - see Compasseco Inc.
Factory - Anics Corp.
7 Vorontsovo Pole St.
Moscow, 103062, RUSSIA
Phone: 7095-917-7405
Fax: 7095-917-1766
Website: www.anics.com
Email: anics@anics.com

ANSCHÜTZ
Importer - see Champions Shooter's Supply
Importer - see Gunsmithing Inc.
Warranty Repair/Gunsmithing Services - see 10-Ring-Service, Inc.
Factory - ANSCHÜTZ, J.G. GmbH & Co. KG
Daimlerstrasse 12
D-89079 Ulm, GERMANY
Fax: 011-49-731-401-2700
Website: www.anschuetz-sport.com
Email: JGA-Info@anschuetz-sport.com

ARMSCOR (ARMS CORPORATION OF THE PHILIPPINES)
Factory - Arms Corp. of the Philippines
Parang Marikina 1800
Metro Manila, PHILIPPINES
Phone: 632-942-5936
Fax: 632-942-0682
Website: www.armscor.com.ph
Email: armscor@info.com.ph

BSA GUNS (UK) LTD.
Importer - see Precision Airgun Distribution
Factory - BSA
Armoury Rd., Small Heath
Birmingham, W. Mids, B11 2PP, ENGLAND
Phone: 0121-772-8543
Fax: 0121-7730845

BAIKAL
Importer – see European American Armory Corp.
Importer - see Compasseco Inc.
Importer - see Pyramyd Air, Inc.
Factory - Baikal
Izhevsky Mekhanichesky Zavod
8, Promyshlennaya str.
Izhevsk, 426063 RUSSIA
Fax: 011-95-007-341-276-4590/765830
Website: www.baikalinc.ru
Email: market@baikalinc.ru

BAM (BEST AIRGUN MANUFACTURER IN CHINA)
Importer - see Xisico USA, Inc.
Factory - BAM
37 ZhongNan Road
WuXi, JiangSu Province, China 214024
Phone: 0510-5404803 or 5403117
Fax: 0510-5401258
Email: jsxsmm@pub.wx.jsinfo.net

BEC INC. (BEC EUROLUX AIRGUNS)
1227 West Valley Blvd.
Alhambra,CA 91802
Phone: 626-281-5751
Fax: 626-281-2960
Email: becline@yahoo.com

BEEMAN PRECISION AIRGUNS
Division of S/R Industries (Maryland Corp.)
5454 Argosy Dr.
Huntington Beach, CA 92649-1039
Phone: 714-890-4800
Phone: 800-227-2744 (orders only)
Fax: 714-890-4808
Website: www.beeman.com

BENJAMIN AIR RIFLE COMPANY
See Crosman Corp.

BENELLI
Importer - see Larry's Guns Inc.
Factory - Benelli Armi S.p.A
Via della Stazione, 50
61029 Urbino (PU) ITALY
Fax: 011-39-722-30-7207-307227
Website: www.benelli.it

BERETTA, PIETRO
Importer - Beretta U.S.A. Corp
17601 Beretta Drive
Accokeek, MD 20607
Fax: 301-283-0435
Website: www.berettausa.com
Factory - Fabbrica d'Armi Pietro Beretta S.p.A
Via Pietro Beretta 18
25063 Gardone Val Trompia
Brescia, ITALY
Phone: 011-39-30-8341-1
Fax: 011-39-30-8341-421
Website: www.beretta.it

BRENZOVICH FIREARMS & TRAINING CENTER
22301 Texas Hwy. 20
Ft. Hancock, TX 79839
Phone: 877-585-3775
Fax: 877-585-3775
Website: www.brenzovich.com

BROCOCK
Importer - see Airguns Of Arizona
Factory
River Street, Digbeth
Birmingham, England B5 5SA
Phone: 44-121-773-1200
Fax: 44-121-773-1211
Website: www.brocock.co.uk
Email: sales@brocock.co.uk

C Z (CESKA ZBROJOVKA)
Importer - CZ-USA
P.O. Box 171073
Kansas City, KS 66117-0073
Phone: 913-321-1811
Toll Free: 800-955-4486
Fax: 913-321-2251
Website: www.cz-usa.com
Email: info@cz-usa.com
Administration Offices - Ceska Zbrojovka
Svatopluka Cecha 1283
CZ-68827 Uhersky Brod
CZECH REPUBLIC
Fax: 011-420-63363-3811
Website: www.czub.cz
Email: info@czub.cz

CABELA'S INC.
One Cabela Dr.
Sidney, NE 69160
Phone: 800-237-4444
Fax: 800-496-6329
Website: www.cabelas.com

CHAMPIONS CHOICE, INC.
201 International Blvd.
LaVergne, TN 37086
Phone: (Orders Only) 800-345-7179
Phone: 615-793-4066
Fax: 615-793-4070
Website: www.champchoice.com
Email: champchoice@nashville.com

CHAMPIONS SHOOTER'S SUPPLY
P.O. Box 303
New Albany, OH 43054
Phone: 800-821-4867
Fax: 614-855-1209
Website: www.championshooters.com
Email: sales@ShootersCatalog.com

COLT'S MANUFACTURING CO., INC.
P.O. Box 1868
Hartford, CT 06144-1868
Phone: 800-962-COLT
Fax: 860-244-1449
Website: www.colt.com

COMPASSECO, INC.
151 Atkinson Hill
Bardstown, KY 40004
Phone: 800-726-1696
Fax: 502-349-9596
Website: www.compasseco.com
Email: staff@compasseco.com

CROSMAN CORP.
7629 Routes 5 & 20
East Bloomfield, NY 14443
Phone: 800-7-AIRGUN
Fax: 716-657-5405
Website: www.crosman.com
Email: info@crosman.com

DAISY OUTDOOR PRODUCTS
400 W. Stribling Dr.
P.O. Box 220
Rogers, AR 72757-0220
Phone: 479-636-3458
Fax: 479-636-1601
Website: www.daisy.com
Email: info@daisy.com
Daisy repair - Jim & Ann Coplen
P.O. Box 7297
Rochester, MN 55903
Phone: 507-281-2314

DAYSTATE LTD
Importer - see Daystate America/Precision Airgun Dist.
Factory
Birch House Lane
Cotes, NR. Stone
Staffordshire ST15 0QQ UNITED KINGDOM
Phone: 44-1782-791755
Fax: 44-1782-791617
Website: www.daystate.co.uk
Email: admin@daystate.co.uk

DIANAWERK, GmbH & Co. KG MAYER & GRAMMELSPACHER
Importer - see Dynamit Nobel - RWS
Repair/Gunsmithing Services - see 10-Ring-Service, Inc.
Factory Dianawerk, Gmbh & Co. KG Mayer & Grammelspacher
Postfach 1452
D-76404 Rastatt GERMANY
Phone: 49-7222-7620
Fax: 49-7222-762-78
Website: www.diana-airguns.de
Email: info@diana-airguns.de

DYNAMIT NOBEL-RWS INC.
A division of RUAG Ammotec USA Inc.
81 Ruckman Road
Closter, NJ 07624
Phone: 201-767-1995
Fax: 201-767-1589
Website: www.dnrws.com
Factory - Dynamit Nobel RWS
Postfach 12 61
Troisdorf D-53839 GERMANY
Email: RWS@dynamit-nobel.com

EURO IMPORTS
2221 Upland Ave. South
Phrump, NV 89048
Phone/Fax: 775-751-6671
Email: mrbrno@yahoo.com

EUROPEAN AMERICAN ARMORY CORP.
P.O. Box 1299
Sharpes, FL 32959
Phone: 321-639-4842
Fax: 321-639-7006
Website: www.eaacorp.com
Email: eaacorp@eaacorp.com

EXCELLENT AIRGUNS OF MINNESOTA
2979 Edgerton Street
St. Paul, MN 55117
Phone: 651-481-8631

FX AIRGUNS
Importer - see Airguns of Arizona

FALCON
Importer - see Falcon Airguns USA Inc.
Factory - Falcon Pneumatic Systems Limited
Unit 20, The Gateway Estate
Birmingham B26-3QD ENGLAND
Phone: 011-121-782-2808
Fax: 011-121-782-2886
Website: www.falcon-airguns.com
Email: sales@falcon-airguns.co.uk

FALCON AIRGUNS USA INC.
6825 Greenwich Lane
Dallas, TX 75230
Phone: 972-387-0311
or 877-357-3006
Website: www.falcon-usa.com
Email: sales@falcon-usa.com

FEINWERKBAU WESTINGER & ALTENBURGER GMBH
Importer - see Beeman Precision Airguns
Importer - see Brenzovich Firearms & Training C
Repair/Gunsmithing Services - see 10-Ring-Serv Inc.
Factory - Westinger & Altenburger GmbH
Neckarstrasse 43
D-78727 Oberndorf/Neckar GERMANY
Fax: 011-49-7423/814-223
Website: www.feinwerkbau.de
Email: info@feinwerkbau.de

GAMO USA CORP.
3911 S.W. 47th Avenue, Suite 914
Ft. Lauderdale, FL 33314
Phone: 954-581-5822
Fax: 954-581-3165
Website: www.gamousa.com
Email: info@gamousa.com

GUN POWER STEALTH
See Air Force Airgun.

GUN SOUTH, INC. (GSI)
P.O. Box 129
7661 Commerce Lane
Trussville, AL 35173
Phone: 205-655-8299
Fax: 205-655-7078
Website: www.GSIfirearms.com
Email: info@GSIfirearms.com

GUNSMITHING, INC.
30 West Buchanan Street
Colorado Springs, CO 80907
Phone: 800-284-8671
Fax: 719-632-3493
Website: www.nealjguns.com
Email: neal@nealjguns.com

HAENEL
Importer - see Gun South, Inc.
Importer - see Pilkington Competition Equipmer

HÄMMERLI AG
Importer - see Brenzovich Firarms & Training Ce
Importer – see Larry's Guns Inc.
Importer - see Wade Anderson
Warranty Repair/Gunsmithing Services - see 10 Ring-Service, Inc.
Warranty Repair/Gunsmithing Services - see Accuright
Factory - Hämmerli AG
Industrielplatz
CH-8212 Neuhausen, SWITZERLAND
Fax: 011-41-52-674-6418
Website: www.haemmerli.ch
Email: info@haemmerli.ch

HATSAN ARMS COMPANY.
Izmir - Ankara Karayolu 28. km. No.289
Kemalpasa 35170 Izmir - TURKEY
Phone: 90-232 878 9100
Fax: 90-232 878 9102 - 878 9723
Website: www.hatrsan.com.tr
Email: info@hatrsan.com.tr

IAR, INC.
33171 Camino Capistrano
San Juan Capistrano, CA 92675
Phone: 877-722-1873
Fax: 949-443-3647
Website: www.iar-arms.com
Email: sales@iar-arms.com

DUSTRY BRAND
Importer - see Compasseco
Importer - see Air Gun Inc.
Factory - Industry Brand
Shanghai Air Gun Factory
55 E. Shan Rd.
Pudong Shanghai CHINA 200127
Phone: 0086-021-58891260
Fax: 0086-021-58811381
Website: www.airrifle-china.com
Email: shairg@public.sta.net.cn

LARRY'S GUNS INC.
6 West Gray Rd.
Gray, ME 04039
Phone: 207-657-4559
Fax: 207-657-3429
Website: www.larrysguns.com
Email: info@larrysguns.com

LGUN
Importer - see Straight Shooters Precision Airguns
Importer - see Crosman Corp.
Factory
Universe House
Key Industrial Park
Willenhall, West Midlands UK WV13 3YA
Phone: 44 1902 722144
Fax: 44 1902 722880
Website: www.logun.com
Email: sales@airgunsport.com

MARKSMAN PRODUCTS
5482 Argosy Drive
Huntington Beach, CA 92649
Phone: 714-898-7535
Fax: 714-891-0782
Website: www.marksman.com
Email: sales@marksman.com

MATCHGUNS srl
Via Cartiera 6/d
43010 Vigatto
Parma, ITALY
Phone: 011-39-0521-632020
Fax: 011-39-0521-631973

MAUSER
No current U.S. importation.
Factory - Mauser Jagdwaffen GmbH
Zeigelstadel 1
D-88316 Isny, GERMANY
Fax: 011-4190-368-4750794
Website: www.mauserwaffen.de
Email: info@mauserwaffen.de

MENDOZA S.A. de C.V.
Importer - see Crosman Corp.
Importer - see Compasseco, Inc.
Factory - Mendoza S.A. de C.V.
Prolongacion Constitucion No. 57
Xochimilco, 16210, Mexico, D.F.
Phone: 5255 1084-1122
Fax: 5255 1084-1155
Website: www.pmendoza.com.mx
Email: pmendoza@mail.internet.com.mx

MORINI
Importer - see Champion's Choice
Importer - see Pilkington Competition Equipment LLC
Factory - Morini Competition Arm SA
Casella Postale 92
CH-6930 Bedano SWITZERLAND
Fax: 011-41-91-9-45-1502
Website: www.morini.ch
Email: morini@bluewin.ch

NORICA-FARMI S.L.A.
Avda. Otaola, 16
Eibar, Guipuzcoa, SPAIN 26000
Fax: 011-34-943-207-449
Website: www.norica.es
Email: farmi@norica.es

NYGORD PRECISION PRODUCTS, INC.
P.O. Box 12578
Prescott, AZ 86304
Phone: 928-717-2315
Fax: 928-717-2198
Website: www.nygord-precision.com
Email: nygords@northlink.com

PALMER CHEMICAL & EQUIPMENT CO., INC.
P.O. Box 867
Palmer Village
Douglasville, GA 30133
Phone: 928-717-2315
Fax: 928-717-2198

PARDINI, ARMI S.r.l.
Importer - see Larry's Guns Inc.
Factory - Armi Pardini S.r.l.
154/A Via Italica
I-55043 Lido di Camaiore, ITALY
Fax: 011-39-584-90122
Website: www.pardini.it
Email: info@pardini.it

PARK RIFLE COMPANY
Unit 68A, Dartford Trade Park
Powder Mill Lane
Dartford, Kent
ENGLAND DA1 1NX

PILKINGTON COMPETITION EQUIPMENT LLC
P.O. Box 97
#2 Little Tree's Ramble
Monteagle, TN 37356
Phone: 931-924-3400
Fax: 931-924-3489
Website: www.pilkguns.com
Email: info@pilkguns.com

PIPER PRECISION PRODUCTS
Box 95
Lamposa, TX 76550

PNEUDART, INC.
1 West 3rd St. Ste. 212
Williamsport, PA 17701
Website: www.pneudart.com

POMONA AIR GUNS
14962 Bear Valley Rd. Ste. G240
Victorville, CA 92395-9224
Phone: 760-244-9224
Website: www.pomona-airguns.com

PRECISION AIRGUN DISTRIBUTION
22 N. Gilbert Rd.
Gilbert, AZ 85234
Phone: 480-539-4750
Fax: 480-461-3928

PRECISION SALES INTERNATIONAL, INC.
14 Coleman Ave.
P.O. Box 1776
Westfield, MA 01086
Phone: 413-562-5055
Fax: 413-562-5056
Website: www.precision-sales.com
Email: info@precision-sales.com

PYRAMYD AIR, INC.
26800 Fargo Ave., Unit #A-1
Bedford Heights, OH 44146
Phone: 888-262-4867
Fax: 216-896-0896
Website: www.pyramydair.com
Email: sales@pyramydair.com

QUACKENBUSH AIR GUNS
2203 Hwy. AC
Urbana, MO 65767
Phone: 417-993-5262
Website: http://ns.connext.net/~daq/

RWS PRECISION PRODUCTS
See Dynamit Nobel-RWS

RÖHM GmbH
Importer - see Airguns of Arizona
Factory - Röhm GmbH
Heinrich Rohn Strabe 50
Sontheim/Benz GERMANY d-89567
Phone: 49-073-25-160
Fax: 49-073-25-16-492
Website: www.roehm.rg.de
Email: inforg@roehm.rg.de

RUTTEN HERSTAL
Importer – see Compasseco
Factory - Rutten Herstal
Parc Industriel des Hauts-Sarts
Premiere Avenue, 7-9
B-4040 Herstal, BELGIUM
Fax: 011-32-41/648589

SAVAGE ARMS, INC.
100 Springdale Road
Westfield, MA 01085
Phone: 413-568-7001
Fax: 413-562-7764
Website: www.savagearms.com

SIG ARMS, INC.
18 Industrial Park Drive
Exeter, NH 03833
Phone: 603-772-2302
Customer Service Fax: 603-772-4795
Website: www.sigarms.com
Factory - SIG - Schweizerische Industrie-Gesellschaft
Industrielplatz
CH-8212 Neuhausen am Rheinfall, Switzerland
Fax: 011-41-153-216-601

SMITH & WESSON
2100 Roosevelt Avenue
P.O. Box 2208
Springfield, MA 01102-2208
Phone: 413-781-8300
Fax: 413-781-8900
Website: www.smith-wesson.com

STEYR SPORTWAFFEN GmbH
Importer – see Pilkington Competition Equipment LLC
Factory - Steyr Mannlicher A.G. & Co. KG
Hauptstrasse 40
A-4432 Ernsthofen AUSTRIA
Fax: 01143-7435-20259-99
Website: www.steyr-mannlicher.com
Email: office@steyr-mannlicher.com

STRAIGHT SHOOTERS PRECISION AIRGUNS
2000 Prairie Hill Rd.
St. Cloud, MN 56301
Phone: 320-240-9062
Fax: 320-259-0759
Website: www.staightshooters.com
Email: shooters@staightshooters.com

SWIVEL MACHINE WORKS
11 Monitor Hill Rd.
Newtown, CT 06470
Phone: 203-270-6343
Website: www.swivelmachine.com
Email: swivelmachine@swivelmachine.com

TAU BRNO, spol. s r.o.
Importer – see Pilkington Competition Equipment, LLC
Importer – see Top Gun Air Guns Inc.
Stará 8, 602 00
Brno, Czech Republic
Phone: 420-5-4521-2323
Fax: 420-5-4521-1257
Website: www.taubrno.cz
Email: info@taubrno.cz

TOP GUN AIR GUNS INC.
8442 East Hackamore Dr.
Scottsdale, AZ 85255
Phone/Fax: 480-513-3778
Website: www.topgunairguns.com

THEOBEN ENGINEERING
Importer - see Theoben USA
Importer - see Beeman Precision Airguns
Importer - see Air Rifle Specialists

THEOBEN USA
Garden Grove, CA
Phone: 714-724-6169
Website: www.theobenusa.com

UMAREX SPORTWAFFEN GmbH & CO. KG
Postffach 27 20
D-59717 Arnsberg GERMANY
Fax: 011-49-2932-638222
Website: www.umarex.de

WADE M. ANDERSON
19296 Oak Grove Circle
Groveland, CA 95321
Phone: 209-962-5311
Fax: 209-962-5931
Email: hammerliusa@msn.com

WALTHER
Importer - see Smith & Wesson
Importer - see Champion's Choice Inc.
German Company Headquarters
Carl Walther Sportwaffen GmbH
Donnerfeld 2
D-59717 Arnsberg GERMANY
Fax: 011-49-29-32-638149
Factory - Carl Walther, GmbH
Sportwaffenfabrik
Postfach 4325
D-89033 Ulm/Donau, GERMANY
Fax: 011-49-731-1539170
Website: www.carl-walther.de
Email: sales@carl-walther.de

WEBLEY & SCOTT LTD.
Importer - see Airguns of Arizona
Importer – see Beeman Precision Airguns
Importer – see Pyramyd Air
Factory - Webley & Scott LTD.
Frankley Industrial Park
Tay Road, Birmingham
ENGLAND B45 OPA
Phone: 441-21-453-1864
Fax: 441-21-457-7846
Website: www.webley.co.uk
Email: guns@webley.co.uk

WEIHRAUCH SPORT GmbH & CO. KG
Airgun Importer - See Beeman Precision Airguns
Airgun Importer - See Pyramyd Air, Inc.
Firearms Importer - See European American Arm
Factory - H. Weihrauch, Sportwaffenfabrik
Postfach 25 Industriestrabe 11
D-97638 Mellrichstadt, GERMANY
Fax: 011-49-977-6812-281
Email: info@weihrauch-sport.de

WINCHESTER (U.S.REPEATING ARMS)
Administrative Offices
275 Winchester Avenue
Morgan, UT 84050-9333
Customer Service Phone: 800-945-1392
Fax: 801-876-3737
Website: www.winchester-guns.com

WISCHO JAGD-UND SPORTWAFFEN
Dresdener Strasse 30,
D-91058 Erlangen, GERMANY
Postfach 3680
D-91024 Erlangen, GERMANY
Fax: 011-91-31-300930
Website: www.wischo.com
Email: info@wischo.com

XISICO USA, INC.
16802 Barker Springs, Ste. 550
Houston, TX 77084
Phone: 281-647-9130
Fax: 208-979-2848
Website: www.xisicousa.com
Email: xisico_usa@yahoo.com

STORE BRAND CROSS-OVER LIST

Many companies sell airguns under their own name but which have been made by others. In many cases all of the models sold under a given brand may be made by another company and it may be impossible or difficult to know who is the actual maker. In other cases a known maker will produce "private label" or "store brand" models for various sellers based on models which they produce under their own name. Only rarely will the private label version be "just the same as" the original base model. The value of comparable models may differ, even hugely, from the base models. Rarely the private label will be a lesser grade version of the base model, but in many cases the private label gun will be an improved version and/or have different cosmetic features. In some cases the private label model will be almost an entirely different gun, only using many of the parts of the base model. Values may differ due to different features and variations, including power levels (higher or lower depending on regulations and demand in the selling area), stock designs, stock material and quality, calibers, sights, trigger mechanisms, etc. In some cases quality control will be higher on the private labels, simply because when the maker sells the guns under their own name returns will come back one by one, but when they make them in huge groups for another company, they may get returns of entire production runs, even thousands of guns, if there is a problem.

This table lists the actual manufacturer and the manufacturer's model that comes closest to the private label brand name and model numbers which will be found on the airgun. Once the name and model of the base model is determined, the reader should find the description of the base model to gather possible information on parts interchangeability, base specifications, and an idea of value range.

(NOTE: These tables are not complete; more information will be added in future editions. Readers are encouraged to submit information on known comparable models not yet listed.)

MONTGOMERY WARDS STORES, HAWTHORN BRAND

"Wards" number	Actual Manufacturer	Equivalent model	Notes
414A	Crosman	V350	
1180	Crosman	180	
415	Crosman	99	
412	Crosman	140	
447	Crosman	38C	
448	Crosman	38T	
435	Crosman	MK I	
445	Crosman	45	
434	Crosman	760	
438	Crosman	130	

J.C. PENNY'S STORES, PENNEY'S BRAND

Penny's number	Actual Manufacturer	Equivalent model	Notes
236	Daisy	1894	Wood stock and forearm

SEARS STORES, J. C. HIGGINS, SEARS, AND TED WILLIAMS BRANDS

Sears number	Actual Manufacturer	Equivalent model	Notes
126.10294	Crosman	V350	
126.1930	Crosman	140/1400	
126.1931	Crosman	180	
126.1932	Crosman	400	
126.1933	Crosman	166	
126.1934	Crosman	130	
126.1935	Crosman	150	
126.1936	Crosman	600	
126.1937	Crosman	45	
126.1938	Crosman	SA6	
126.1909	Crosman	150	
126.1910	Crosman	160	
126.294	Crosman	V350	
126.1923	Crosman	760	
126.2831	Crosman	180	
126.10349	Crosman	38C	
126.10350	Crosman	38T	
126.19041	Crosman	V350	
126.19131	Crosman	45	
126.19141	Crosman	166	
126.19151	Crosman	180	

Sears Stores, J. C. Higgins, Sears, and Ted Williams Brands, cont.

Sears number	Actual Manufacturer	Equivalent model	Notes
126.19161	Crosman	400	
126.19171	Crosman	160	
126.19181	Crosman	SA6	
126.19191	Crosman	150	
126.19201	Crosman	600	
123.19211	Crosman	130	
126.19241	Crosman	140	
126.19221	Crosman	38C	
126.19231	Crosman	38T	
126.19391	Crosman	M1	
126.19331	Crosman	760	
799.10276	Daisy	25	
799.19020	Daisy	111	
799.19025	Daisy	177	
799.19052	Daisy	1894	Octagon barrel "Crafted by Daisy"
799.19054	Daisy	1894	
799.19062	Daisy	300	
799.19072	Daisy	880	
799.1912	Daisy	1894	Black, round barrel, no scope rail
799.203	Daisy	94	
799.9009	Daisy	105	
799.9012	Daisy	111	
799.9045	Daisy	25	
799.9048	Daisy	1938	
799.9051	Daisy	1894	With scope bracket
799.9052	Daisy	1894	
799.9054	Daisy	1894	
799.9057	Daisy	1914	
799.9061	Daisy	572	
799.9062	Daisy	300	
799.9068	Daisy	840	
799.9072	Daisy	880	
799.9073	Daisy	1938	
799.9076	Daisy	822	
799.9078	Daisy	922	
799.9079	Daisy	922	
799.9082	Daisy	880	

Sears Stores, J. C. Higgins, Sears, and Ted Williams Brands, cont.

Sears number	Actual Manufacturer	Equivalent model	Notes
799.9083	Daisy	880	
799.9085	Daisy	850	
799.9093	Daisy	880	
799.9113	Daisy	900	
799.9115	Daisy	130	
799.9166	Daisy	95	
799.9215	Daisy	545	
799.9224	Daisy	7800	
799.924	Daisy	111	
799.9306	Daisy	557	
799.9313	Daisy	40	
799.9323	Daisy	562	
799.9355	Daisy	1880	
799.9382	Daisy	1880	
799.9393	Daisy	1880	
799.9478	Daisy	1922	
799.9498	Daisy	499	
799.9499	Daisy	499	
799.19083C	Daisy	880	Gold Receiver
799.19383C	Daisy	880	Gold Receiver and scope
799.19385C	Daisy	850	With scope
799.19478C	Daisy	922	
79919085C	Daisy	850	

WESTERN AUTO STORES, REVELATION BRAND

Revelation number	Actual Manufacturer	Equivalent model	Notes
GC3376	Crosman	760	First variation
GC3370	Crosman	73	
GC3375	Crosman	788	
GC3377	Crosman	766	
GC3360	Crosman	V350	
GC3367	Crosman	99	
GC3379	Crosman	140	
GC3416	Crosman	45	
GC3412	Crosman	38T	
GC3375	Crosman	166	

DIANAWERK COMPARABLE MODEL NUMBERS

Only airguns made by Dianawerk of Rastatt, Germany are considered here. The Diana name was taken to Scotland as war reparations after WWII. Scottish Dianas were m Milbro. Some were imported to the USA as economy airguns under the Daisy label. tant note: Comparable models often have different values due to different demand by tors, different levels of rarity, and, because distributors of private label guns often sp different power levels (for different markets, and not just mainspring differences), design, stock material and quality, calibers, sights, trigger mechanisms, etc. may diffe the basic manufacturer´s model. Beeman-marked and pre-1970 Winchester-marked generally sell for a premium. Early models of the same number may differ from more model.

Diana, RWS Original*	Geco, Peerless Beeman	Hy-Score	Winchester	Cros
1				
2		814		
5*		815T	353	
5G	700	825T		
6*		816M	363	
6G	800	826M		
6M	850	827M		
10	900	819SM		
15		808		
16		805	416	
22		806	422	
23 w/receiver rails		813 Mark1		
25 / 25D		801	425	
27*	100	807	427	
35*	200	809	435	
45	250	828		Chal 6100
50			450	
60		810M		
65		810SM	333	
66		811SM		
75	400,			
	400 Univ.	820SM		

* Also produced as Beeman´s "Original" series under the same model number.

AIRGUN LITERATURE
AN ANNOTATED PARTIAL REFERENCE LIST
By Dr. Robert D. Beeman

gely limited to separate publications such as books, periodicals, and booklets, rather than individual airgun articles. (For a large listing of airgun [ar]cles prior to 1990 see Groenewold [1990]). For more information and a detailed analysis of the references listed below, see the Literature Review [sec]tion of www.Beemans.net and a less up-to-date analysis in the Second Edition of the *Blue Book of Airguns*.

[PE]RIODICALS:

[Th]e latest contact and subscription information is available on www.Google.com. Older issues sometimes available at secondary book markets, eBay, [D]oug Law dlaw1940@yahoo.com (PO Box 42, Sidney, NE 69162), FSI at [9]06-482-1685, gunshows, etc.

[Air]gun Ads (Barry Abel, Box 1795, Hamilton, Montana 59840). Small monthly, [o]nly ads for airguns and accessories.

[Ad]dictive Airgunning. (www.airgunshow.net). January 2004 to date. Online format allows large articles and color pictures. Excellent for both collectors and [s]hooters.

[Air]gun Hobby (www.airgunhobby.com). October 2004 to date. Now America's [o]nly printed airgun periodical. Quarterly published by airgun enthusiasts [R]on Sauls and Jim Giles. Less glitzy than some previous airgun periodicals, [b]ut far superior in reporting airgun events and information on airgun collect[i]ng and use.

[Air]gun Illustrated. August 2002 to January 2004. The first five issues, with Tom Gaylord's input, were truly wonderful.

[Air]gun Journal (Beeman Precision Airguns). Small, only 1979 to 1984. Edited [b]y Robert Beeman. Many articles valuable to airgun shooters and collectors. [O]ne of the rarest of all airgun publications. Less than 500 copies of each of [t]he six issues were printed. Beautifully printed on heavy, textured deep tan [p]aper with green and brown masthead - extremely difficult to scan or photo[c]opy because of the dark paper. Back issues available at www.Beemans.net.

[Air]gun Letter. Monthly newsletter of 12-16 pages, plus *Airgun Revues* 1-6 of about [1]00 pages each, perhaps the world's best reference material on adult airguns. [C]losed August 2002 when editor Tom Gaylord moved to *Airgun Illustrated*.

[Air]gun News & Report (later as *American Airgunner*). Valuable articles, out of [p]rint.

[Air]gun World and Airgunner (both by Romsey Publishing Co., 4 The Court[y]ard, Denmark St., Workingham, Berkshire RG402AZ, England). British [m]onthlies. *Airgun World* articles of Roy Valentine (under pen name "Harvey" [i]n 1970s) and later, those of John Atkins in *Airgunner* and "Tim Saunders" in *Airgun World*, are especially valuable to collectors.

[Gu]ns Review. British gun magazine formerly carried excellent articles on airguns; [e]specially the pioneer research of John Walter and the late Dennis Commins [a]round 1970s.

[Ne]w Zealand Airgun Magazine. Pub. by Trevor Adams from February 1986 to [A]pril 1988.

[Ph]ilippine Airgun Shooter. Only four quarterly issues, plus an annual, in 1989.

[Sh]otgun News. Newspaper format, mainly firearm ads, but also airgun ads and [A]merica's only airgun column - by outstanding airgun writer Tom Gaylord.

[U.]S. Airgun (last issue as *Rimfire and Airgun*). Valuable articles for airgun shoot[e]rs and collectors, out of print.

[VI]SIER, Das Internationale Waffen-Magazin. Lavishly illustrated, prestigious [s]lick German language magazine. Basically a firearm publication, but con[t]ains some of the best written, best illustrated airgun articles ever. *VISIER* Specials, such as 1996 Special Number 4, may have only airgun articles.

[Ot]her gun periodicals sometimes have airgun articles: *Precision Shooting* and *The Accurate Rifle*, perhaps the best shooting magazines in the English lan[g]uage, frequently present excellent articles on airguns. *The Rifle* and *Guns* [p]reviously featured airgun columns. Most American gun magazines such as *American Rifleman, Arms and the Man, Guns and Ammo, Sports Afield*, etc. [h]ave only occasional airgun articles.

[RE]FERENCES:

[Ad]ler, Dennis. 2001. (Edited by Dr. Robert D. Beeman and S.P. Fjestad). *Blue Book of Airguns*, First Edition. 160 pp. Blue Book Publications, Inc., Minneapolis, Minnesota. Now a rare collectors' item (hardbounds sell for $100+).

Atkinson, R. Valentine 1992. *Air Looms. Gray's Sporting Journal*. Sept. 1992: 35-41. Beautifully illustrated report on some of the Beeman collection. Some garbled information.

Baker, Geoffery and Colin Currie. 2002, 2003. Vol 1: *The Construction and Operation of the Austrian Army Repeating Air Rifle*, 62 pp.; Vol. 2, *The Walking Stick Air Gun* 79 pp. From Bryan & Associates (864-261-6810 or BryanAndAc@aol.com) or directly from geoffrey.baker@virgin.net. Detailed photos, full-scale drawings, and measurements. Everyone even slightly interested in these amazing airguns and certainly anyone who contemplates opening one should have these guides. Wait for the 2005 revision of the Repeating Air Rifle guide. More guides in planning.

Beeman, Robert D., 1977. *Air Gun Digest*. 256 pp. DBI Books, Northfield, IL. Airgun collection, selection, use, ballistics, care, etc. When I did this volume way back in the 20th century when the field of adult airgunning hardly existed, I never dreamed that someday it would be called a classic collectible, but I'm not going to fight it.

Beeman, Robert D. 1977. *Four Centuries of Airguns*, pp. 14-26. *The Basics of Airgun Collecting*. Pp. 218-235 (Later reprinted together as *The Art of Airgun Collecting* by Beeman Precision Arms in 1986, 23 pp.). Considered as the first guide to airgun collecting. A key work. Should be teamed with the "Rare Air" airgun collecting article by R. Beeman in the First Edition of the *Blue Book of Airguns*.

Beeman, Robert and M.J. Banosky, John W. Ford, Randy Pitney, Joel Sexton. 1991. *Air Guns, A Guide to Air Pistols and Rifles*. National Rifle Association, Washington, D.C. Abbreviates and revises the original Beeman manuscript, but very useful introduction to airgun shooting and programs.

Beeman, Robert D. 1995. *The Odyssey of the Beeman R1*. Chapter in the Beeman R1 Supermagnum Air Rifle, pp. 1-9. GAPP. The real story of the gun that brought America into the adult airgun world - and gave rise to the HW 80.

Beeman, Robert D. and John Allen. 2002-2005. *Blue Book of Airguns*, Second through Fifth Editions. Blue Book Publications, Inc., Minneapolis, Minnesota. Price is not the primary purpose of these guides. Model ID and information are. From 19th century to latest guns. Valuable to all airgunners. Every volume has valuable articles; serious airgunners should have a complete set of all editions!

Bruce, Gordon. 2000. *Webley Air Pistols*. 224 pp. Robert Hale, London. The bible on Webley air pistols.

Brukner, Bruno, 2000. *Der Luftpistole*. Second edition, 230 pp. Journal Verland Schwend. Outstanding book on air pistols. All air pistol fans, not just those reading German, should have it. Just the diagrams are worth the price of admission.

Brychta, Frank S. 1994 a. *FSI Airgun Ballistic Tables*. 88 pp. 1994b. *FSI Advanced Airgun Ballistics*. 52 pp. Firearms & Supplies, 514 Quincy St., Hancock, MI 49930. Absolutely essential pair of books for all who are interested in airgun ballistics, field target shooting, and airgun hunting ballistics. Mainly very useful tables.

Cardew, G.V. & G.M. Cardew, E.R. Elsom. 1976. *The Air Gun from Trigger to Muzzle*. 96 pp. Martin Brothers, Birmingham, England. Highly technical. The best guide to internal airgun ballistics.

Cardew, G.V. & G.M. Cardew. 1995. *The Airgun from Trigger to Target*. 235 pp. Privately published. ISBN 0 9505108 2 3. Extension of Cardew's pioneer book to include external ballistics. Reveals how much and how little we know about airgun ballistics.

Chapman, Jim. 2003. *The American Airgun Hunter*. 234 pp. Chapman, Jim and Randy Mitchell, 2003. The Airgunners Guide to Squirrel Hunting. 128 pp. Jaeger Press, 67 Sentinel, Alviso Viejo, CA. www.geocites.com/echochap/airgun_hunter.html. The "American" book actually covers airgun hunting in several countries. Entertaining gab mixed into an essential guide - these fellows are most interested in results while I would lean more towards the quality of the gun. Great.

Churchill, Bob & Granville Davies. 1981. *Modern Airweapon Shooting*. 196 pp. David & Charles, Devon, England. Authors should be shot for using the word "weapon." Excellent introduction to formal airgun target shooting.

Darling, John. 1988. *Air Rifle Hunting*. 160 pp. Crowood Press. Classic view of hunting with an air rifle in England.

Dieter, Ernst 2002. *Luftgewehre und Luftpistolen nach 1945 aus Suhl und Zella-Mehlis*. 143 pp. WTS Waffentechnik in Suhl GmbH, Lauter 40, 98528 Suhl, Germany. Writing under a pseudonym, a former top engineer at Haenel presents invaluable information on almost 60 models - some not known to collectors before.

Dunathan, Arni T. 1971. *The American BB Gun: A Collector's Guide*. 154 pp. A.S. Barnes and Co., Cranbury, New Jersey. The pioneer work on BB gun collecting. Now badly out of date, but forever essential! The 1970 prices will bring tears to your eyes!

Elbe, Ronald E. 1992. *Know Your Sheridan Rifles & Pistols*. 79 pp. Blacksmith Corp. The best review of the Sheridan guns.

Fletcher, Dean. 1996a, 1996b, 1998a, 1998b, 1998c. *The Crosman Arms Handbooks*, 259 pp.; and *The Crosman Rifle* 1923-1950, 265 pp., *The Crosman Arms Model "160" Pellgun*, 144 pp., *75 Years of Crosman Airguns*, 223 pp., *Crosman Arms Library* (CD-ROM). Published by D.T. Fletcher, 6720 NE Rodney Ave, Portland, Oregon 97211. (For more Crosman info see also: Eichstädt, Von Ulrich and Dean T. Fletcher. 1999. *Eine Unbekannte Größe*. *Visier*, Feb. 99: 52-57 and Oakleaf, Jon B. 1979. *Vintage Crosmans. The Airgun Journal* 1(1): 1-3. Oakleaf, Jon B. 1980. *Vintage Crosmans II. The Airgun Journal* 1(2): 1-7.). The Fletcher works are simply the best, most essential guides to the Crosman and Benjamin airguns! Absolutely essential to anyone interested in these makes and the history of American airguns.

Fletcher, Dean. Undated. *The Crosman Arms Library*. CD with 888 full color scans of Crosman literature.

Fletcher, Dean. 1998c. *The Chronology of Daisy Air Guns 1900 - 1981* and *Daisy Toy and Metal Squirt Guns*. 18 pp. Published by D.T. Fletcher.

Fletcher, Dean. 1999. *The St. Louis and Benjamin Air Rifle Companies*, 305 pp. D.T. Fletcher - Publisher.

Friberg, Av Kenth. 2001. *Luftvapen*. 191 pp. Karlshamm\Göteborg, Sweden. (K. Friberg, Ekbacken 3, 37450 Asarum, Sweden). In Swedish; one of several guides to some airguns not generally known to Americans.

Galan, Jess I. 1988. *Airgun Digest*, 2nd Edition, 257 pp. DBI Books, Northbrook, IL.

Galan, Jess I. 1995. *Airgun Digest*. 3rd Edition. 288 pp. DBI Books, Northbrook, IL. Classic books, all aspects of airgunning. Outstanding author.

Gaylord, Tom. 1995. *The Beeman R1*. 174 pp. GAPP. One of the classic, best books on airguns. Highly recommended by many airgun writers. Includes a chapter by R. Beeman on the Beeman Rl as the precursor of the HW 80. The most useful book on the market for understanding the function and use of ANY spring piston airgun.

Groenewold, John. 1990. *Bibliography of Technical Periodical Airgun Literature*. 28 pp. Pub. by John Groenewold, Box 830, Mundelein, IL 60060. A great listing. John promises to go beyond 1990 "someday"!

Groenewold, John. 2000. *Quackenbush Guns*. 266 pages. Pub. by John Groenewold, Box 830, Mundelein, IL 60060-0830. Phone 847-566.2365. The definitive guide to the wonderful antique Quackenbush airguns.

Hannusch, Larry. 2001. *Pneumatic Reflections*. 280 pages. Self published by L. Hannusch, 5521-B, Mitchelldale, Houston, TX 77092 or lhannusch@netscape.net. Compilation of last twenty years of interesting and valuable articles on airgun collecting by one of the world's leading authorities.

Herridge, Les. 1987. *Airgun Shooting*. 96 pp. A & C Black, London.

Herridge, Les. 1994. *Airgun Shooting Handbook*., 80 pp. Andrew Publishing Co. Ltd.

Herridge, Les and Ian Law. 1989. *Airgun Field Target Shooting*. 100pp. Peter Andrew Publishing Co. Basic introductions to British field target airgun shooting.

Hiller, Dennis E. 1982. Th*e Collector's Guide to Air Pistols*, Revised Second tion. 187 pp. Published by Dennis Hiller. Rather dated, depressed values invaluable model info - mainly European models.

Hiller, Dennis E. 1985. *The Collectors' Guide to Air Rifles*, Enlarged Third tion. 276 pp. Published by Dennis Hiller. See above note. Again, lo invaluable information.

Hoff, Arne. 1972. *Air Guns and Other Pneumatic Arms*. 99 pp. Barrie and kins, London. A classic that everyone interested in the history of airguns ply must have!

Hoff, Arne, 1977. *Windbüchsen und andere Druckluftwaffen*. 105 pp. Parey, lin. Updated version of above; in German.

Holzel, Tom. 1991. *The Air Rifle Hunter's Guide*. 159 pp. Velocity Pres Lang St., Concord, MA 01742. Simply the best book on hunting with a rifle. Presents crow hunting as philosophically similar to fly fishing. "Killing as a Sport" chapter is one of the best ever presentations on the m ity and ethics of hunting. Includes outstanding, practical material on ballistics of airguns.

Hough, Cass S. 1976. *It's A Daisy!* 336 pp. Daisy Division, Victor Compto Corp., Rogers, Arkansas. Delightful history of the Daisy Company by o its longest term executives. Rare, a very desirable collectors' item - softbou

House, James E. 2002. *American Air Rifles*. 208 pp., 179 black and white 2003. CO2 Pistols & Rifles. Krause (www.krause.com). Both paperb books press the theme that pellet guns from Daisy, Crosman, etc. shou seriously considered by adults also. Some of the best ballistic info availab airguns of this level.

Hughes, D.R. 1973. *An original handbook for the model 35D, 27, 35 & 5 rifles*. 77 pp. and three fold-out plates. Pub. by D.R. Hughes, England. (I inal brand = Diana, RWS, Gecado, some Winchester, some Beeman, HyScore). Delightful guide to assembly, etc.

Hughes, D.R. 1981. HW 35. *A Handbook for Owners and Users of the H Series Air Rifles*. 65 pp. Optima Leisure Products, 75 Foxley Lane, Purley, rey, England. Another delightful Hughes tour through a famous airgun.

Janich, Michael D. 1993, *Blowguns, The Breath of Death*. 81 pp. Paladin Boulder, Colorado. Basic info on the most basic of airguns.

Johnson, Bill 2003. *Bailey and Columbian Air Rifles*. Book plus CD ava from Bill Johnson, PO Box 97B, Tehachapi, CA 93581. The definitive on some of America's most interesting and solid airguns (formerly knov Heilprin airguns). 1/4 and 1/2 scale detailed drawings. Values not given.

Kishi, Takenobu. 1999. *The Magnum*. Printed in Japan. ISBN 4-7733-65 C0075. In Japanese. Detailed info on airgun ballistics.

Kersten, Manfred. 2001. *Walther - A German Legend*. 400 pp. Safari 15621 Chemical Lane B, Huntington Beach, CA 92649-1506 USA. gorgeous masterpiece covers all Walther guns, including excellent covera the airguns. Also available in German.

Knibbs, John. 1986. *B.S.A. and Lincoln Jefferies Air Rifles*. 160 pp. Publishe John Knibbs Publications, Birmingham. Another classic British work o history and models of a leading airgun maker.

Kolyer, John M. 1969. *Compilation of Air Arm Articles and Data* by John K 130 pp. John Kolyer, 55 Chimney Ridge Drive, Convent, New Jersey 07 Primarily older airgun ballistic material. Pioneer work.

Kolyer, John M. & Ron Rushworth. 1988. *Airgun Performance*. 157 pp. S real Press, Newport Beach, California. Updated version of Kolyer's work. Even includes blowgun and slingshot data.

Law, Robert. 1969. *The Weihrauch Handbook*. 44 pp. Air Rifle Monthly, Gr ville, West Virginia. One of a series of how-to-do-it airgun maintenanc tuning booklets by one of America's early adult airgun hobbyists. Verbos very useful. Last supply available in Sale section of www.Beemans.net .

Lawrence, Andrew. 1969. *Development of the Hy-Score Air Pistol*. Engine Case Library No. 134. Department of Mechanical Engineering. Leland ford Jr. University. Extremely rare paper on the origin of the Ame HyScore concentric piston air pistols.

Marchington, James. 1988. *Field Airgun Shooting*. 200 pp. Pelham Books don (Penguin). Basic guide to British field target shooting.

oore, Warren, 1963. Guns, the Development of Firearms, Air Guns, and Cartridges. 104 pp., Grosset and Dunlap, New York, N.Y. Contains a wonderful, well-illustrated section on antique airguns.

unson, H. Lee. 1992. *The Mortimer Gunmakers*, 1753-1923. 320 pp. Andrew Mowbray, Lincoln, Rhode Island. Includes excellent material on the elegant large bore airguns made by the Mortimer family, 1700s to early 1900s.

onte, George C. 1970, *Complete Book of the Air Gun*. Stackpole, Harrisburg, PA. Somewhat lightweight and dated, but very useful.

car Will-Catalogue Venus Waffenwerk Reprint of 1902/03 catalog. 94 pp. Journal-Verlang in Schwäbish Hall.

rks, Michael R. 1992, 1994. *Pneumatic Arms & Oddities*, Vol. 1 and Vol. 2. 245 and 211 pp. Southwest Sports, 1710 Longhill Road, Benton, AR 72015. Fascinating collection of older American airgun patents.

nchard, Neal. 2002. *Daisy Air Rifles & BB Guns, The First 100 Years*. 156 pp., 300 color illustrations, MBI Publishing. Not really a guide, but a beautiful celebration of Daisy air guns!

no, Brett, (2004). *Airgun Index and Value Guide*. 13th edition, 150+ unnumbered pages in three-ring binder. Brett Reno, RR2 Box 63, Heyworth, IL 61745. No illustrations, descriptions, history, model details, etc. but invaluable for its literature references!

obinson, Ron, (1998) *The Manic Compressive* 125 pp.; (2001) Airgun Hunting and Sport, 138 pp.; (2003) *A Sporting Proposition*, 126 pp. Ron Robinson, 4225 E. Highway 290, Dripping Springs, Texas 78620. Three thoroughly Texan tomes on airgun hunting. Loves hunting with airguns, from favorite Beeman R1 to latest oriental big bore airguns. A real hunter, real character, real ego! Every airgun hunter should have all three.

anaker, Ragnar and Laslo Antal. 2001. *Sportliches Pistolen-schießen*. (Competitive Pistol Shooting). In German. 194 pp. Motorbuch Verlag, Postbox 103743, Stuttgart 70032, Germany. Includes a chapter on air pistol target shooting.

epherd, Arthur. 1987. *Guide to Airgun Hunting*. 123 pp. Argus Books, London. Very interesting, but severely British.

ith, W.H.G. 1957. *Smith's Standard Encyclopedia of Gas, Air, and Spring Guns of the World*. 279 pp. Arms and Armour Press, London and Melbourne. The initial bible of airguns, badly dated and with many errors, but absolutely indispensable.

öckel, Johan F., 1978-82. Revision edited by Eugene *Heer: Heer der Neue Støckel*. Internationales Lexikon der Büchsenmacher, Feuerwaffenfabrikanten und Armbrustmacher von 1400-1900. 2287 pp. Journal-Verlang, Schwend GmbH, Schwäbish Hall, Germany. Extremely expensive, extremely useful three volume guide to virtually all gun makers from 1400 to 1900. In German, but that is not much of a handicap for those speaking other tongues when looking up names and dates.

omas, James F., 2000. *The BB Gun Book - A Collectors Guide*. 75 pp. Self-published. (Basically a brief update of the classic 1971 Dunathan book).

ownshend, R.B. 1907. *The Complete Air-Gunner*. 88 pp. plus foldout figure. I. Upcott Gill, London and Chas. Scribner's Sons, New York. (reprinted). Delightful insight to airgunning at the beginning of the 20th century.

aister, Robert J. 1981. *All About Airguns*. 306 pp. Tab Books, Blue Ridge Summit, PA. Pot-boiler, largely derived from 1980 Beeman catalog.

ler, Jim. 1988. *Vermin Control with an Air Rifle*. Andrew Publishing Company, Ltd. Controlling what Americans call "varmints" or pests.

ade, Mike, 1984. The Weihrauch HW 80 and Beeman R1 Air Rifle, A User's Guide to Higher Performance. 19 pp. Techpress, Mike Wade Engineering, 87 Elgin Rd., Seven Kings, Ilford, Essex, England. Technical, excellent.

alter, John. 1981. *The Airgun Book*. 146 pp. Arms and Armour Press, London. British based register of then current airguns. Excellent.

alter, John. 1984. *The Airgun Book*, 3rd Edition. 176 pp. Arms and Armour Press, London. Contains best ever survey of airgun manufacturing history from 1900 to 1984.

alter, John. 1985, *Airgun Shooting, Performance Directory and Index of Suppliers from A to Z*. 96 pp. Lyon Press Ltd., West Hampstead, London. Tall, little guide to fit the vest pocket.

Walter, John. 1987. *The Airgun Book*, 4th Edition. Arms and Armour Press, London. Broadened the scope of this series. The last of an excellent series.

Walter, John. 2002, *Greenhill Dictionary of Guns and Gunmakers*. 576 pp. Greenhill Books, London and Stackpole Books, PA. Indispensable guide includes amazing amount of airgun information. Covers 1836 to 2000.

Wesley, L. and G.V. Cardew. 1979, *Air-Guns and Air-Pistols*. 208 pp. Cassell, London. Updated revision of a British classic on all aspects of airgunning and airguns.

Wolff, Eldon G. 1958. *Air Guns*. 198 pp., Milwaukee Public Museum Publications in History 1, Milwaukee, WI. A classic work on antique airguns. Try to find an original museum edition!

Wolff, Eldon G. 1963. *Air Gun Batteries*. 28 pp. Milwaukee Public Museum Publications in History 5, Milwaukee, Wisconsin. Concise guide to how airgun mechanisms, from early to modern, work. Rare, valuable. Reprints available in Sale section of www.Beemans.net.

Wolff, Eldon G. 1967. *The Scheiffel and Kunitomo Air Guns*. 54 pp. Milwaukee Public Museum Publications in History 8, Milwaukee, WI. A rare booklet on an unusual pair of antique airguns. Rare collectors' item.

OTHER LITERATURE:

In addition to following the current airgun periodicals and latest books, one cannot remain current, or develop understanding of older models, without consulting the latest and old catalogs from Beeman Precision Airguns, Dynamit-Nobel (RWS), Air Rifle Specialties, etc. There is a wealth of information in factory bulletins and ads. Beeman Precision Airguns was especially productive: look for pre-1993 *Beeman Technical Bulletins*, and the early *Beeman Precision Airgun Guide/Catalogs*, starting with Edition One (only 500 were printed!) in 1974, and *Beeman's Shooter's News*, basically a sales bulletin to its retail customers. Especially interesting to airgun collectors are the *Beeman Used Gun Lists* (the "UGL") published in the 1970s to 1990s. They hold a wealth of information on the large numbers of vintage and antique airguns sold by the company over that period. The former prices of the collectors' items will make today's collectors pale. Old Crosman manuals are also highly collectible.

Finding and Collecting Airgun Literature: Astute collectors, most notably Dean Fletcher and Doug Law, have realized that airgun literature itself has become a key field of collecting. Unlike the airguns themselves, the literature, especially the airgun company literature, generally is quickly lost. Thus the literature becomes both a challenge to collect and a vital link to the special history of the field, which, like so many histories, soon becomes very hazy. As every year passes, this literature becomes harder to find and more valuable in several ways. Many readers will find that many of the references mentioned here have been printed in only limited editions and can be purchased "not for love nor money." Try gunshows and the special order desks of Barnes and Noble and Brothers book stores, and the search services of their websites and those of www.Amazon.com, www.Alibris.com, and especially www.AddALL.com used and out of print books. Check the website of Ray Reiling of New York for the world's largest selection of out of print gun books; sometimes he has a few airgun books. Generally these books are not going to be easy to find, so act fast if you do find any. Some airgun literature is available in the "Sale and Wanted" section of www.Beemans.net. Doug Law dlaw1940@yahoo.com (PO Box 42, Sidney, NE 69162) specializes in the sale of airgun literature. (The *Blue Books of Airguns* themselves have become a very collectible series. Hardbound editions are the most sought and can sell for 100 dollars and up.)

INDEX

A

B

C

D

E

F

open ears

musical adventures for a new generation

Open Ears
Musical Adventures for a New Generation

Editor: Sara deBeer
Project and Talent Coordinator: Karen M. DiGesu
Design: Jodee Stringham/Hello Studio
Cover and Interior Design Illustrations: Chip Wass
Technical Diagrams: James Hurwit

ellipsis kids ...

To Emma, Ben and Jake - and all their cousins around the world

"It is wonderful that music can be the bridge to reach a child where words have failed."—Paul McCartney

The Nordoff-Robbins Music Therapy Foundation, founded in New York in 1988, contributes the sole support for a clinic at New York University which provides treatment for autistic and other severely disabled children. The clinic, under the personal direction of Drs. Clive and Carol Robbins, sees patients on a weekly basis in one-on-one sessions or in groups, depending on the individual needs of the child. The clinic also has a full-time research facility and training program leading to a graduate degree in the Nordoff-Robbins method of music therapy.

The Nordoff-Robbins method emphasizes the uniqueness of music as a means of communication for individuals with a wide range of handicapping conditions. This method of music therapy was developed by Dr. Paul Nordoff, an American composer and professor of music, and Dr. Clive Robbins, a special educator from England. Robbins says, "Music is the most basic way to reach handicapped children. It is the one thing that transcends all human emotion and feeling."

The therapy seeks to change the individual lives of handicapped children. Dr. Carol Robbins says, "There is much these children can't do. What we want to know is what they *can* do." It is a daunting task, but for those children struggling against crushing disabilities, music can sometimes make all the difference. Through music disabled children can begin to develop a greater understanding of themselves and the world outside, making it possible for them to reach out beyond the lonely world in which they are entrapped.

Because of the important role music plays in this therapy and with the positive results the program is achieving, the music industry is lending its support with performers such as Paul McCartney, Elton John, Pete Townshend, Phil Collins, Eric Clapton, John Mellencamp and Neil Young donating proceeds from concerts and record sales, and music industry executives hosting fund-raising dinners and auctions.

The Nordoff-Robbins Music Therapy method is now practiced internationally, with clinics in England, Germany, Australia and a recently opened clinic in New York. The Robbins' desire is to make music therapy available wherever it is needed. The Foundation's mission is to make it possible for them to open other facilities and outreach programs across the U.S. and to continue to practice their form of music therapy, bringing joy to the lives of the children and their families.

If you would like to contact Nordoff-Robbins, please call (212) 541-7948.

THE NORDOFF-ROBBINS MUSIC THERAPY FOUNDATION, INC.

contents

forward

Have you ever felt like you just couldn't wait to introduce two or three or five or ten amazing people to each other? Maybe you invited all of them to a party or a picnic, and it seems like you'll just explode if the day doesn't come soon. And finally, they're all together and everyone's talking at once and laughing and finishing each other's sentences and gesturing wildly as they try to explain things to each other and you think, "This is even better than I hoped!"

That's how I've been feeling as I've been putting this book together for you. Each chapter in here is written by somebody remarkable, someone who has spent a lifetime with open ears, a playful explorer of sounds and music. I can't wait for you to meet each one of them, to try out some of their ideas, and to let those ideas send you off on paths even *they* may not have traveled.

Well, I know that the sooner I finish this introduction, the sooner you'll start playing around with all the projects you'll find in these pages. Come on in, join the party, and let the sounds surround you!

Sara deBeer

everyday

Devi Mathieu

W. A. Mathieu

music

Every sound you make travels far and wide. When you feel good making music, that good feeling keeps going. Even a whisper goes on forever.

Music is made up of sounds, but can any sound be used to make music? Some people say that only certain sounds, like violins and flutes and drums, can be used for music. Other people say they hear music everywhere. Some people think two mosquitoes flying around are playing a musical duet with their wings. Others say, "No way!" Some people (older, mostly) say rap music is noise. What do you think? What about wind whistling around corners or rustling through leaves? Is that music or noise? Perhaps it depends on how you listen.

Symphony of Place

What are you hearing right now? If you pay close attention to all the sounds around you, you can hear a kind of symphony—a symphony with you in the center. Get a paper and a pencil, sit down and listen. Write down all the sounds you hear. If you were in the kitchen just before dinner, your list might look something like this:

chopping knife cutting carrots
water running in sink, then stopping
spoon clattering to the floor
beeping of microwave being set
horn honking from somewhere outside
refrigerator humming
pulsing noise of microwave
the chuk-chuk of a box of spaghetti being taken off the shelf
bubbling of a pot of hot water on the stove

You could call this "The Kitchen Symphony." You could also write a "Waiting for the Bus Symphony," a "Back Yard Symphony," a "Playground Symphony," a "Summer Day at the

by Allaudin & Devi Mathieu

Lake Symphony," or even a "Dentist's Office Symphony." Save the good ones. Later on, you can reread your notes and, using your mind's ear, hear your symphony all over again. Or you could go back to the same place, make new notes, and see how the symphony changes from one day to the next.

Slow-Turning Music
Cupping your hand behind your ear helps you hear because your hand helps catch more sound waves as they travel through the air. The more sound waves you catch, the more sound you hear. Go outdoors and stand in one place. Listen for a moment. Then cup your hands behind your ears and listen again. You can hear more, but not because the sound got louder. You hear more because your ears got bigger. Now keep your hands cupped behind both ears and slowly turn in a circle. You'll notice that turning like this helps you pinpoint the direction each sound is coming from.

What happens to your hearing when you close your eyes? Give it a try right now. First, keep your eyes open and listen to the sounds around you. Then close your eyes and listen again. When you don't have to pay attention to what you see, your mind seems to have more room in it for sound. Now try cupping both ears with both hands, turning slowly in a circle and closing your eyes. You've become one huge pair of revolving ears!

Blindfolded Sound Detective
You can tell a lot about an object by the sound it makes. Find a partner, a blindfold, and a pencil or pen. While one of you is

blindfolded, the other taps an object with the pencil. (If you promise not to peek, you can just close your eyes.) The person with the closed eyes has to guess what's being tapped. Can your ears tell the difference between a wooden table and a wooden floor? The wall and the door? A plastic cup and a glass bowl? Can sound tell you how big the object is as well as what it's made of? Try this game outdoors. Can you hear the difference between a building and a car? A tree and a post? A mailbox and a door knob?

Easy-to-Miss Music There are lots of beautiful sounds in the everyday world that most people never hear. Next time you tear some aluminum foil off the roll, hold it up to your ear and gently move it around. When you change a light bulb, hold the burnt-out bulb by its metal base and shake it gently, close to your ear. If you're at a fancy dinner, moisten a finger and run it around and around the edge of a stemmed glass. When you get it right, the glass will ring. Change the amount of liquid in the glass (take a sip) and the pitch of the ringing will change. This can turn into beautiful dinner music.

Listening to Quietness At night, when you're alone and it is quiet, open your ears wide. How quiet is quiet? Can you really hear silence, or are you just hearing fewer, softer sounds than you heard during the day? Try plugging up your ears with your fingers. What are you hearing? It might be the tiny motions of the air trapped in your ears, or the movement of fingers against skin. You might even hear your heart beating. Your body and your ears are like everything else—they have sounds of their own.

Life Drumming Almost any object likes to vibrate with sound. The strings of guitars and harps enjoy being plucked, flutes love to be breathed through, people love to sing. And you can hear how much cymbals like to crash together! Why shouldn't floors, walls, tables, hub caps, ladder rungs, and car roofs have a chance to vibrate, too?

Become a Life Drummer and give things like these the chance to vibrate. What's a Life Drummer? A Life Drummer is anyone who releases the sounds hidden inside objects like garbage cans, plastic buckets, empty jars and bottles, metal wires and stop signs. They like the sounds of toothbrushes brushing teeth and sticks being dragged across corrugated metal. They wake up fence posts, awnings, umbrellas, lamp shades, walls, floors, even air. Life Drummers use fingers, palms, knuckles, a stick, or a wooden spoon to release sounds trapped inside objects.

BUT: Life Drummers are always careful not to harm the very objects whose sounds they are setting free AND Life Drummers never stop thinking about the ears of others. It's fun to make lots of crashing noise, but it's not fun to be disturbed. If you suddenly get the urge to set some loud sounds free, check in with the folks around you. Better yet, invite them to join you for a group session of Life Drumming. Remember, the very best Life Drummers listen carefully to each other. They also know how to drum gently. Some of the best sounds in the world are gentle ones.

Angels in the Oven
Did you ever wonder what "choirs of angels" sound like? Here on Earth, right in your kitchen, is a sound that just might resemble heavenly singing. You will need a 2-foot length of string, a pencil, a removable grate from the kitchen oven, and a parent's permission to remove it. You want to be sure that the oven hasn't been hot recently!

Wind one end of the string several times around one of the rods on the edge of the oven grate and tie it. Wind the other end of the string around a finger, then put that finger at the opening of your ear, but don't stick it in-just leave it near the opening. Make sure you've picked a strong finger. The grate needs to be hanging free. If it's touching the floor, you'll stay earthbound. Ready? Strike the grate with the pencil. Presto, Choirs of Angels!

You can use the same string to extract similar sounds from forks, coat hangers, and other metal objects. Do some experimenting. There are all kinds of locked-up metal sounds just waiting for you to discover them!

The Laughing Piano
Find a piano. Sit on the bench. Depending on the piano, there will either be two or three pedals at your feet. Press down on the pedal to the right. Laugh out loud. Really loud. Stop laughing suddenly and listen. Keep the pedal down and sneeze, then listen. Bellow, then listen. Yodel, then listen.

What's happening? Your voice makes the piano strings vibrate. When they vibrate, they make their own sounds. (This is called resonating). What does holding down the pedal do? If you don't hold it down, pieces of felt prevent the piano strings from vibrating. Holding the pedal down moves the felt away from the strings so they are free to resonate with whatever sounds you send their way.

Sound Signals Make a sound that slowly fades away. Ring a bell or play one note on the piano with the pedal down, or pluck a guitar string. Listen to the sound fade away until you can't hear it anymore. Even now that you can't hear it, it hasn't stopped. As sound waves spread far and wide, they vibrate molecules of air, other people's eardrums, leaves, bird feathers. They move out into space and turn into forms of energy you can't hear. No one really knows what happens to them. Ring the bell or pluck the string again. This time, listen longer. Hitch a ride into space.

When you hear something, you can listen not only to the sound, but also to why the sound was made, the reason behind the sound. Is that a shout of anger or joy? Does the voice on the radio want to sing you a song about love or sell you a new car? When you make a sound, the reason behind your sound travels out into the world with your sound waves.

Whether you are famous for your music or someone busily making Everyday Music, the sound you make connects you to everyone and everything else in the world. When you feel good making music, that good feeling keeps traveling. Even a whisper goes on forever.

Adapted from *The Listening Book: Discovering Your Own Music* (1991) and *The Musical Life: Reflections on What It Is and How to Live It* (1994), both by W. Allaudin Mathieu, published by Shambhala Publications.

ALL god's creatures got a place in the choir

by Bernie Krause

When creatures want to be heard, they must learn to use their voices in a way that will blend with other animals...just like our musical chorus. When all these creatures sing together, they form a chorus of musical sounds so special that even people like us haven't been able to write music as breathtaking. No music is prettier to our ears.

Have you ever looked at a friend's face, someone you were talking to, and known you weren't getting through? The problem might have been the words you were using, but it also might have been that the place where you were standing was just too noisy. In order to be understood, we have to speak so that people can hear us. If the noise in the background is too loud, then our voice won't be heard.

Neighborhood Creature Choirs

What about the songbirds in our own backyards? Originally, before there were houses, cars and buses in our neighborhoods, many more creatures lived where we do. Can you imagine the streams that wound through the land, surrounded by all sorts of trees and wildflowers? Depending on where you live, there might have been buffalo, deer, elk, moose, foxes, wolves, bobcats, hundreds of kinds of birds and thousands of insects living where you now walk or ride your bike. When all these creatures sang together at sunrise, in the evening, or even during the day, they formed a breathtaking chorus of music.

The songbirds living around us today have had to adapt their songs to their new neighbors—us. What do I mean? Just open your door and tell me what you hear. Sometimes, on a summer evening when it's very quiet, you'll hear crickets. And sometimes, very early in the morning when everyone else is still asleep, birds will begin to sing. But mostly you'll have to listen very carefully to hear the complete songs of birds and the buzzing of insects because nearly everything we humans do makes noise. Our cars. Airplanes. Lawnmowers. Leaf blowers. Radios. Refrigerators. And television sets.

Fortunately, many birds, like robins, sparrows and wrens, have been able to change their voices so that they can be heard even when it's noisy nearby. They have had to learn to do this in order to communicate with others in their family. It's a little like having to scream to be heard when you're in a room with loud music or lots of other people talking at the same time. Although birds don't exactly scream, they do change their songs (or calls) so that their message won't be lost. Sometimes their voices will be higher. Sometimes lower. And sometimes a song will be longer or shorter than it would normally be in a forest.

Recording the Choir

This next spring or summer, get up just as it is getting light and open up your window. See if you can identify what birds and insects you hear. (If you do this for a number of days, you might find that you recognize certain calls, even if you don't know which creature is making which sound.) Maybe, if you have a small cassette tape recorder—you don't need anything fancy— you might want to record them so you can listen to them again.

Later in the same day, listen again. Have the human noises increased? Is it harder to pick out the bird and insect sounds? Again, try to record the sounds with your tape recorder. Listen to the difference in the bird/insect sounds when it's quiet outside and when it gets noisier. Do the same in the evening: first as folks are coming home from work and then after most humans have gone to bed.

This is one way to find out how we are affecting the natural world around us. If you really listen closely, you'll also hear how well the creatures who live near us are able to communicate with each other.

Creature Choirs Worldwide In the

forests of the world, all sorts of creatures—chimpanzees, frogs, birds, crocodiles, insects and more are part of a very large animal orchestra. These creature choruses have been the inspiration for many kinds of human music. It is only after recording animals and other natural sounds for the past twenty-five years that I finally figured this out, but people who live in the rainforests of the world have been creating music based on the forest sounds around them for hundreds and hundreds of years.

The music of the people of the South American rain forests has no doubt been influenced by the musician wren. This bird whistles a tune that sounds much like a flute playing the blues. Over time, he learned to sing these notes in a way that said many things to the other creatures living nearby. He was telling other male wrens that the tree he was singing in was HIS tree and no one else's, but this same song, if it was pretty enough, might attract a female to become his mate. "Stay away from my tree," said the message in his song. "But if you're a female musician wren, you can cross the line and we'll check things out." Most important, the wren created his song so it would fit with the sounds of all the other insects, birds, frogs and jaguars that lived in his forest home. On the one hand, his voice became part of a creature chorus where his song would blend in with all the others, while at the same time, no one else's sound would block his song from being heard.

On the other side of the world, in Borneo, the gibbons sing beautiful duets that echo through the rainforest at dawn. You can hear the singing of these tree-climbing apes for many miles. When you listen to the music created by the people of the Borneo rainforest, you can hear the influence of this animal music.

The people who live in the rainforests of the world make their instruments from the resources their homes provide. They use flutes made of bamboo, drums made of the buttresses of large fig trees or hides stretched over hollowed-out tree trunks. Then they create songs and rhythms based on the sounds of the forest. They use the forest as a virtual back-up band for their singing and music-making.

Composing for an Animal Back-up Band
Try to make up a song based on one of the backyard recordings you've made, or based on the sounds of the birds and insects you've been listening to. Use your tape as a back-up, weaving your song in and out of the natural sounds OR perform your song with the live orchestra nature provides, just as the people of the rain forests do. Choose the time when you heard the most interesting sounds.

Some Final Thoughts
No matter where people live, as long as they are closely connected to the land around them, the sound of whales, chimpanzees, American robins, frogs, insects, crocodiles and tiny insect larvae influence the creation of their music, just as the sounds of your backyard influenced your song. This is one of many bonds we have with the natural world, and one more reason that we need to work very hard to preserve what is left. We wouldn't want the great creature chorus to stop singing. If we listen carefully, no music is more inspiring.

page **21**

Title courtesy of Bill Staines' "A Place in the Choir", 1978, Mineral River Music (BMI)

the music of the stones,

The important thing is yourself: your heart; your soul; the light that shines within you and out through your eyes. When you meet a friend, you can see the light shining from them. When you're singing away quietly, nature can hear you. You are part of the incredible rhythms of nature, the music of the earth, the music under the earth.

the dance of the trees

I used to go off to the local woods or fields and there would be other children around playing football, climbing trees. A tree can beckon you, saying, "Climb me, climb me." (I was always good at climbing trees.) So I'd climb a tree and stay there, looking up into the branches, trying to see all the colors in the bark, reflecting on what was around me. A tree is more powerful than you can imagine. For every large field, there is one special tree. It is the conductor, organizing all other trees, the shrubs, the bushes, the insects, flowers and birds.

Next time you are in a field or wood, listen for the call, "Climb me, climb me." Settle down in the branches. Take long, deep breaths, slow down your vibrations, forget the worries of your day. Then stop thinking about breathing, stop thinking about thinking. For me, those were the times when the world would stop.

Then the wind might come. Trees love the wind because with wind they can stretch up and stretch down. Stay up in your quiet place. Take long, slow breaths, and watch the trees dance.

by Jon Anderson

Bird Duets

Once you're settled comfortably in a tree, start listening to the bees humming, the birds singing. The quieter you become, the more you'll hear. Pick out a particular bird song and when it pauses, imitate it. If you're a good mimic, the bird might pause a moment, as if it's thinking, "That doesn't sound QUITE like a real bird, but…" When it calls again, answer it. See how long you can keep this duet going.

Living in the north of England at the age of three or four, on a Friday night or a Saturday, I'd go to a place called Bluebell Wood. Yes, it was full of bluebells, and there was a little stream running through it. I would find two rocks and hold them in my hands, then strike them together: "ta-ca-ta; ta-ca-ta." I would play the rocks and hear the echoes all the way down the stream. The stream would be pounding over the rocks and I'd be splashing, playing the rocks, humming, singing, listening to the music around me.

If I sat on the forest floor and hit one stone against another, I'd release the vibrations in the stones. I could feel the earth underneath me resounding while I was banging stones and humming away. The branches which had fallen on the forest floor, I'd pick up and shake like rattles. There was always music in my hands, reflecting sound back to the earth mother.

Echo Ripples

As you explore hills and valleys, send your voice out ahead of you. You'll find that in certain spots, your voice will bounce back from three or four different directions. Stop there. Start to make rhythms. As the echoes join you, try for a ripple effect, weaving your sounds around the echoes.

Pebble Rattle

A Lakota-Sioux friend told me about a ceremonial rattle you might want to make. The Lakota-Sioux people find an anthill and select fifty-two stones from that anthill. The ants have selected those stones to be rattle stones. Pick up fifty-two small stones and place them in a closed container. Shake it with great reverence. How will you know which stones to choose? Trust your first instincts. Your hands will pick up the right ones for your rattle.

nigerian hand flutes

I want to emphasize that we all sing, everybody can dance, everybody can whistle, we all have imitative powers. These are all things that human beings have in common.

I grew up in Nigeria, in a very small fishing village forty miles from Lagos. My childhood was so interesting and so beautiful. Music was a daily occurance. I can remember very well waking up in the morning to hear the drums playing. I'd hear the drummers who had traveled to sing songs of praise to the chief of the village, or musicians who were welcoming a baby that had just been born, announcing the birth of the child. The drumming might be the preparation for the rite of passage for a young boy or young girl who is ready to take on the responsibilities of being an adult; it might be the announcement of the engagement of a young lady to a man. Or the drummers might be telling the village of a death, telling that someone, a chief or an elder, had become a spirit of the ancestors, reminding people that only the physical body was dead but the spirit never dies.

So no matter what I was doing, no matter where I went, I would hear the drums play, I would hear people singing. When the fishermen had a big catch, everybody in the village would celebrate with drumming and dancing because they knew that they would have plenty to eat and there would be plenty more to sell.

by Babatunde Olatunji

Even when I went to the marketplace, drummers would be playing in front of the stores of the market people, who would take time out to do a little movement, a little dance. People in my village always took time out to celebrate themselves, to celebrate life.

My morning would begin with the sound of drums; my day would end with the voices of the elders, telling stories to the children of the village. There were so many of us there. The moon would be shining, the stars would be so bright. This was the time the elders would tell all kinds of stories. These were the people who, through their experiences in life, could tell us stories that had morals, stories that would remind us of the consequences of our actions, or our inaction. With all these stories, there was always a song.

One story my great-grandfather would tell us was about the first upright flute that was ever made by man. And now I teach what my great-grandfather spoke of, the idea that all instruments had very basic, modest beginnings. Before making instruments, what did we do to amuse ourselves? Everywhere in the world people clap their hands and they always do it in rhythm. Stamping our feet in rhythm. Marching in rhythm. We started doing all of this before we started making instruments. And then, my great-grandfather showed us, people began to experiment with ways to bend their fingers and hands so they could play melodies, create songs. My great-grandfather taught us how to make these hand flutes as we sat at his feet beneath the moon.

Hand Flute 1

1. Take your left hand. Hold it in front of you so that you are looking at your palm, your fingers are pointing to the wall on your right, and your thumb is pointing to the ceiling. Stretch your left thumb back so that the membrane between your thumb and your index finger is stiff.

2. Put the first two fingers of your right hand up as if you are signaling "Peace" or "Victory." (Your right thumb is pressing the third and fourth fingers into your right palm.)

3. Keeping your hands in these positions, bring your hands together. You should be looking at the back of your right hand, and your two standing fingers should be between the thumb and first finger of your left hand.

4. Bend the two standing fingers of your right hand and wrap them around your left thumb. Their job is to help pull your left thumb back, so that the membrane of your left hand stays stiff.

5. Keeping your left index finger straight, wrap the other three fingers of your left hand around the back of your right hand.

6. The folded fingers of your right hand form a platform for your chin and your left index finger is resting on the side of your right cheek. You blow into the space between your right pinky and membrane of your left hand. If you pull on your thumb with your right fingers as you blow, you can play many different notes. I can play "Jingle Bells" and "The Star Spangled Banner."

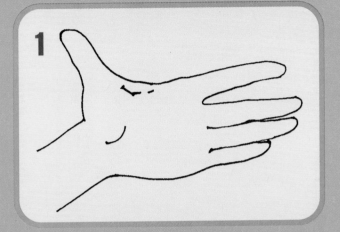

1

2

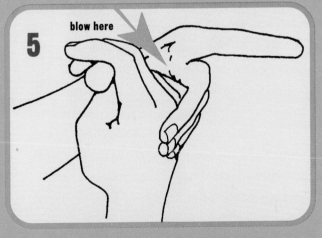

5

blow here

Hand Flute 2

1. Turn your hands so the palms are facing you.
2. Spread the fingers of your two hands apart.
3. Bring your fingers towards each other until they interlock, with the right index finger on top. Your fingers make a row of V's, with the tips pointing up.
4. Bring your wrists together and bend your fingers down. Now the tips of your fingers are resting on the knuckles of the opposite hand, and your two thumbs are resting on top of your right index finger.
5. Bend your thumbs. Press the top joints of your two thumbs together, so that your thumbnails are side by side.
6. You should see a small vertical opening between the lower joints of your two thumbs. Blow into that opening.

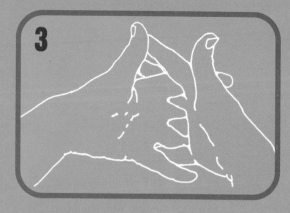

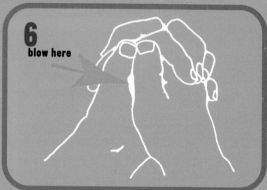

Hand Flute 3

1. Hold out your right hand as if you are about to shake hands with someone.
2. Bend the four fingers of your right hand so that they make a flat surface perpendicular to the palm of your right hand. Rest your thumb on your bent fingers.
3. Leaving your right hand in this position, slap your right hand into your left hand so that your thumbs are side by side, the first joints of the fingers of your right hand are resting on the membrane between your left thumb and index finger, and your left fingers are sticking out of the side of your curled up right hand.
4. Wrap your left fingers over the back of your right hand, covering the end of your "tunnel." Keep your left palm bent so that your hands make a cup, as if you are holding a small ball between your palms.
5. You should see a small vertical opening between the lower joints of your two thumbs. Blow into that opening. You can adjust the sound by lifting one or more of your left fingers.

Hand Flute 4

1. Bend the index finger of your left hand and rest its tip on the first knuckle of your tallest finger, so that your two fingers make the shape of a lower case "d."

2. Slide the palm of your right hand between the third finger and the longest finger, so that loop rests on the palm of your right hand.

3. Blow into the loop. You should get a very high pitched whistle.

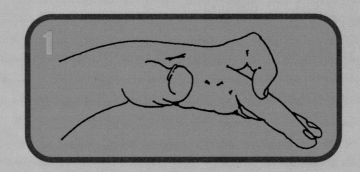

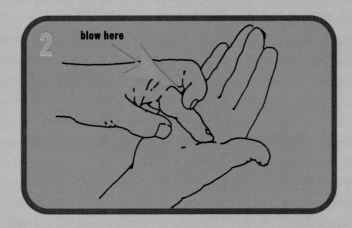

blow here

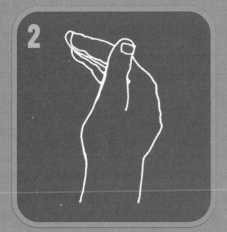

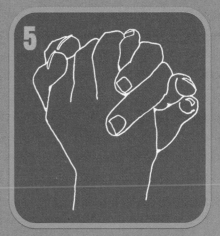

blow here

juba this and juba that, juba slapped the way to rap

Music can say things to me that nothing else can—it reaches a part of me where there aren't any words. Making music is even better than just listening—it's like being the heartbeat for this one big living thing we call life.

by Bill Harley

Music is part of everything we do. We can't help but be musical. And you don't even need an instrument. Long before people made drums or shakers or bought electronic drum machines, they hit themselves to make sounds. You can get wonderful sounds from the different parts of your body!

Bill Harley

1. Open your mouth and make a tall "o" with your lips. Rap the top of your head with your knuckles. You sound like a coconut.

2. With your mouth still open, slap your cheek with your open hand. Open your mouth wider, and the sound is higher. You can play songs with your mouth and your hands.

3. See how many different sounds you can get out of your hands. Clap your hands with your hands very flat and straight. Then cup them slightly and clap them. Go back and forth between the two sounds.

Experiment with the different sounds you can get from different parts of your body. Listen closely to each one. Can you combine them? Don't hurt yourself. Once, I kept hitting my cheeks trying to get different sounds and woke up the next morning with bruised cheeks. "What happened to you?" a friend asked. "I was practicing music," I answered.

Hitting yourself one time makes a sound. But when you do it a second time and a third, you have rhythm. And when you have rhythm, you have music, since music is just organized sound. Almost all music uses rhythm, or sound made at regular intervals, using it as the backbone to hang all the other sounds on. Most of our rhythms are very closely related to the beat of our hearts.

These days, rap is some of the most popular (and rhythmic) music around. When we listen to it, we think we're hearing something brand new. While the instruments or words might belong to today, rap grew out of rhythms and patterns that have been around for hundreds, even thousands, of years. One of these old rhythms that's still going strong today is called "Juba."

I learned "Juba" from a musician named Bill Vanaver. Bill Vanaver learned it from a woman named Bessie Jones, who had a musical group called the Sea Island Singers. Bessie Jones founded her group to teach people the music she'd grown up with, music her ancestors had passed down from the time they were brought as slaves to the Sea Islands, islands off the coast of the state of Georgia.

"Juba" is both a song and a clapping pattern—the rhythms were brought from Africa almost three hundred years ago. Once you learn how to do it, you can beat a fancy rhythm to your favorite song or make up your own rap piece. You'll be part of something that's thousands of years old.

What you need: Not much. Sit in a chair so your feet are flat on the floor. You can do this in your shorts, but your thighs will get red after a while. Wearing long pants is a good idea.

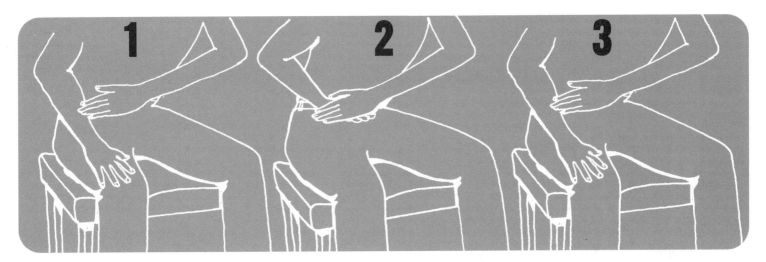

The basic pattern:

1. Hit your right thigh with your right hand.

2. Move your left hand so it is directly over your right thigh, the spot which your right hand just hit. Bring up your right hand so the back of your right hand hits the palm of your left hand.

3. Hit your right thigh with your right hand again.

4. Repeat the process, only on your left side. Your left hand hits your thigh. Bring your right hand over your left thigh and raise your left hand to hit your right hand. Then hit your left thigh again with your left hand.

5. Repeat the pattern.

One tip worth remembering: Your right hand always hits your right thigh, and your left hand always hits your left thigh. If you start crossing hands and thighs, you'll end up all tied up worse than a sneaker lace or pretzel or something worse.

You will notice that what you are doing is broken up into two groups of three—one on your right side, and one on your left. Work on the pattern very slowly at first. Veeeeerrrry slowly! Continue working on it so that you can keep up the pattern at a smooth, steady pace without stopping. A steady beat is much more important than speed. In order to be able to get to the next step, you need to be able to slap without thinking about it. Don't try to go too fast! (Should I say that again?)

Once you can do the pattern without thinking, it's time to create a cross-rhythm. What's a cross-rhythm? Try counting like this every time there is a slap: "One, two, three, four, one, two, three, four, one, two, three, four." At first, counting in four seems to go against the rhythm of the slapping in three. But as you continue, you will find something interesting happening. The rhythm keeps changing as you count. That's a cross-rhythm. Cross rhythms are very common in African drumming.

Keep in mind, it's like walking and chewing gum at the same time, or learning to ride a bike. Once you get the hang of it, it's easy, but if you think too much about it, steam comes out of your ears. It's what drummers love about being drummers. If you really like this, maybe you're supposed to be a drummer!

Once you can count in four on every slap, then try counting in four on every other slap. Take your time. It will sound like this

One!	two!	three!	four!
slap slap	slap slap	slap slap	slap slap
One!	two!	three!	four!
slap slap	slap slap	slap slap	slap slap

When you're counting on every other slap, you will really begin to hear the weird cross rhythms. As you get good at it and can speed up your clapping while

keeping the rhythm steady (very important!) you will want to cut back even more and just count on every fourth slap.

Show your parents what you've done. They'll be so impressed they will buy you a new bike. Or at least say "That's nice, dear," which is almost as good. Almost.

When you can keep up the beat and count every fourth slap, you're ready to sing, or chant, or rap. At first, choose a song or a poem that you know very well, so you don't have to think about it. Thinking causes problems. Try singing "Row, row, row your boat" or "Mary had a little lamb" at first, even if you don't like them.

Row	**Row**	**Row**
slap slap slap slap	**slap slap slap slap**	**slap slap**
your	**boat**	**gent- ly**
slap slap	**slap slap slap slap**	**slap slap slap slap**
down	**the**	**stream...**
slap slap	**slap slap**	**slap slap slap slap**

If you know some jump rope rhymes, like "Teddy Bear, Teddy Bear" or "Miss Mary Mack," try them. Or you might want to try the original "Juba," the one passed down through Bessie Jones' family. It's a chant about slavery and refers to the hard times the slaves had. The word "juba" means "a little bit," and the "Juba" chant goes like this:

It's juba this and juba that and juba killed a yellow cat
Get over double trouble, juba
You sift the meal, you give me the husk
You bake the bread, you give me the crust
You cook the meat, you give me the skin
And that's where my momma's trouble begins
Juba....Juba....Juba....Juba....

Do you see why people say "Juba" reminds them of rap? Maybe it's that mixture of rhythm and words, words with a little bite to them. Once you learn the rhythm, you can create your own variations on the basic pattern. By experimenting very slowly, you'll be able to do fancier things with your slapping, like sneaking in little slaps to your feet, or just going up and down on one thigh an extra time.

The same goes for words. Once you're good at other people's rhymes, you can make up some of your own. Here's a piece I wrote to chant while I was slapping around. I wrote it a while ago but it's still a favorite of mine and my audiences. Even my mom likes it!

50 Ways to Fool Your Mother By Bill Harley ©Round River Music. All Rights Reserved

Early in the morning when you open up your eyes
You can hear the coffee perking and the egg your
mother fries
Lyin' in your bed you start to feel blue
When you think of all the things that you really
want to do

You want to play baseball, you want to ride your bike
You want to read a comic book, you want to
take a hike
But no you don't, there's something else to do
Dress yourself and have breakfast, you've got to go
to school
If just this once you didn't have to go
But if you ask they'll just say no
If only you think a moment, there's something
you can do
There must be 50 ways to fool your mother

It's really rather simple if you only stop and think
You could tell her you got sick last night and threw
up in the sink
Say you got the measles, say you got the mumps
Tell her that you're too depressed and way down in
the dumps
Say that you're not you, there's a martian in
your place
You're really on a rocketship somewhere in
outer space
Oh, you've got to use your head, but I'm sure you'll
find a way
There must be 50 ways to fool your mother.

You could tell her that your teacher said you've
done so well
You don't have to go to school today, you can rest
a spell
Tell her that a tidal wave is comin' to your town
If you try to get to school you just might drown!
Say a herd of elephants is roamin' through the streets

That your shoes have shrunk, they won't fit on
your feet
Say your school was zapped into hyperspace
There must be 50 ways to fool your mother.

You could tell her that your turtle's sick, you've got
to stay at home
You're waiting for the President to call you on
the phone
Say you're sore and achey: there's a poundin'
in your head
That your legs won't move, you can't get out of bed
Tell her that you won't get up, you know it's just
a dream
You know your real mother would never act
so mean
Put some powder on your face until it's really white
Heat up the thermometer over the light
Take some iodine and put some spots upon
your face
There must be 50 ways to fool your mother.

So your mother finally buys it and says "OK
But if you're so sick, you can't go out to play.
You've got to stay at home, you've got to get
some rest
I can help you with your homework, you can study
for your test
Maybe by tomorrow you'll feel OK
I'm really very sorry that you're sick on Saturday"
SATURDAY! I didn't know it was Saturday!

Your mother smiles sweetly as she gets up to leave
You should have known that mothers got something
up their sleeves
There must be some way out of this, something
you can do
Are there 50 more ways to fool your mother?
50 ways to fool your mother? 50 ways to fool
your mother?

Remember the sounds we made at the very beginning, when you hit your head?

That's a good way to end your piece.

Ouch!

Good luck. Make music. And don't hit yourself too hard!

39

For a further discussion of
"Juba" and other songs and
games, see *STEP IT DOWN*,
by Bessie Jones and Bess
Lomax Hawes, University of
Georgia Press, 1972, 1987

♡ ✌☺ & ℬ
Forever yours,

rhythm as a heartbeat, music as a language, and spoons as an instrument

Music is harmony. Harmony is unity in diversity. We practice and demonstrate alone. We develop and play together. PLAY ON!

OK, check this out. Clap your hands. Go ahead. Set the book down and clap your hands, just once, easy. Now clap twice. Now four times. Clap at the same speed as you read these words: one, two, three, four. Do it again, if you like. That's your rhythm. The speed at which you read, walk, chew food, talk, exercise any action: that's your own personal rhythm. Don't let anyone ever convince you that you have no rhythm. You got a heartbeat? You've got rhythm! You may or may not relate to another person's rhythm, but that doesn't mean you don't have any.

Hi there. My name is Artis. I'm the "Spoonman," or so some people call me. I have become famous because I play spoons as a virtuoso. Spoons are a *primary* instrument to me, like a guitar to a guitarist or a piano to a pianist. Consequently, many people ask me, "How'd you do dat?"

Well, when I was ten years old, a man named Howard, who played spoons told me I could use any two spoons and that they didn't have to be attached. I believed him, but I never tried it that way till I was in my twenties. Instead, I played "musical-spoons" made and manufactured by Walt Haines in collaboration with Lawrence Welk. Here are some ideas for making your own set of attached spoons, like those "musical-spoons" I first used, *and* some hints about using unattached spoons.

Don't let these instructions stop you from doing much more research and development on your own. I mean, nobody ever showed me how to hold the spoons, or gave me any real lessons, yet I've been making a living at this for more than twenty years. The key? Eccentric involvement.

So go get two spoons and let's make some sounds.

Getting Started

Let's begin with two teaspoons. Even if you have fully grown hands, let's use standard sized teaspoons for now. In fact, if you're really serious, get

by Artis

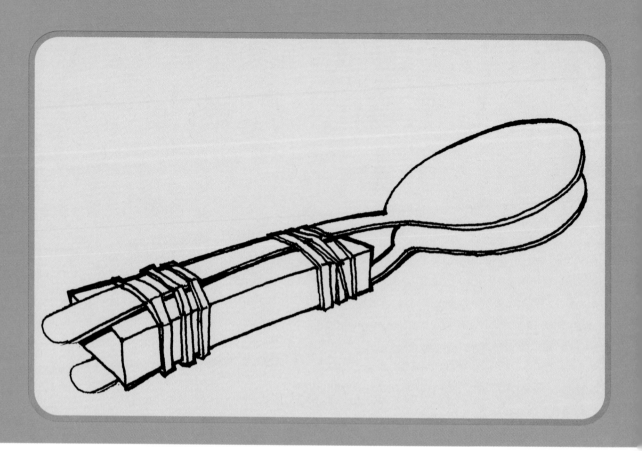

four teaspoons, some heavy tape or rubber bands, and a small block of wood about 1" wide, 1/2" thick, and 3" long. Go ahead, I'll wait.

Got it all?

OK, cool!

Place the block of wood between the handles of two spoons so that the outside bottoms of the spoons are facing each other. The spoons should not quite touch when you grip your hand around the spoon handles and the wood. Now wrap the handles and wood tight with the tape or rubber bands. This pair of "musical-spoons" can be used with much more ease while you develop a grip for just holding two separate spoons.

The Grip

It's all in the grip and the grip is all in you. There are, of course, several ways to hold spoons in order to play them. I hold them two fingers apart, the top one between my thumb and forefinger, the bottom one between my third and fourth fingers. You may want to hold them only one finger apart. Another way is to put them on either side of your thumb and fold your other fingers around your thumb and spoons like a fist. The main thing is that they work comfortably for you.

How to Make Music with Spoons

Once you've got hold of them *firmly* (either the attached or the unattached set), hit your leg with the cup of the bottom spoon and your hand with the cup of the top spoon. The idea is, they don't make a sound until you hit something with them. Try hitting your leg above your knee on a down stroke and, with your other hand over your leg, strike the palm of that hand on the up stroke. Do it several ways, one beat down and one up, two down and one up, one down and two up, etc. Use your wrist. Be imaginative.

Another stroke is to run the spoons down the outstretched fingers of the opposite hand. Run from the top forefinger to the bottom little finger in one smooth stroke.

Extend your opposite arm and bend the elbow so your hand is directly above your bicep. Hit your palm, bicep, and both legs in one fell stroke. Gently. Deliberately.

You may also hit your lips where they meet your cheeks. Hit half over your mouth and half over your cheek. Gently.

Now you can incorporate all these strokes in one move. Check it out. Start with a gentle hit to your mouth, then run down your fingers on your opposite hand, move directly to the palm of that hand, then on to your bicep and each thigh. Slowly. This first time is practice, not music. You'll play music later today or tomorrow, but this is practice. Don't be discouraged. Practice is always a challenge.

You can play off the bottom of your feet, your tummy, the backs of your thighs, "ham-bone" style. Whatever comes to mind that is not damaging anything, you can say, "Artis said it was OK!"

Keep in mind that as some aspects get easier, others get more challenging. For instance, the more you play, the more likely it is that you'll get blisters. Blisters will eventually become calluses, which are protective, but blisters hurt a bit before they become calluses. When this happens, use band-aids and disinfectant on the blisters. You may also want to wrap the spoon handles with tape to soften them.

How to Get Different Tones from Your Spoons

When I hit my mouth, I change the tone by changing the shape of my lips and the placement of my tongue. You can also use the palm of your hand as a sound chamber to vary the tone of the spoons. This works especially well with wooden spoons or muted spoons. Muted spoons are cool.

When someone around the house or hood says, "Enough with the spoons already!" use muted spoons. Take two spoons that you like but aren't your favorite sound. The more round the bowl of the spoon, the better. Put tape on the outside surface of the bottom of the bowl of the spoons. Now play them. Quiet, huh? They also have a more wood-like sound, a lower frequency vibration.

Remember, always respect other people's requests or demands for quiet. No matter what music you're playing, if it's not welcome, then it's trespassing; that's when it becomes noise. The difference between music and noise is not the rhythm or the volume; it's the listeners' appreciation. If it's appreciated, it's music. If it's not appreciated, it's noise. So be considerate.

I'm proud to be part of your life. I encourage you to play, play, play. For the rest of your life, play anything, everything, delightfully, seriously, enchantingly.

journey to the big one

Have you ever tried to make up music with some friends and lost your place? This finger counting game could help you and your friends get better at keeping a group rhythm going. The only danger is you might burst out laughing while you're doing it. But if you do, just start over. We call it a Hindu Finger-Counting Game because it's based on the way musicians in India are taught to use one of their hands to keep track of long phrases of music.

Keep in mind that you're preparing to set off on a sixteen-beat journey, and what we call the "Big One" is where you're headed. When you get there, give that beat a huge accent, like fireworks exploding or a rocket ship firing. Then take off on the next sixteen-beat journey, once again heading toward the "Big One."

Why sixteen beats? Hindu music is set up in cycles of sixteen beats. A sixteen-beat cycle is also a common phrase length in popular and classical American and European music (four measures of what musicians call 4/4 meter). And, for the purposes of this game, our hands have sixteen convenient spots, four on each finger multiplied by four fingers.

by David Darling

Here's what you do

Begin by sitting in a circle, facing the other people in your group. Four people is a good amount to start with. It's important to form a circle so

a hindu finger counting game

Music is one of the greatest activities to participate in that I know of. It can, of course, be totally consuming when each of us finds the right kind of music to participate with. I have always thought that participating in music is a birthright. I hope you enjoy this rhythmic game for all ages.

David Darling

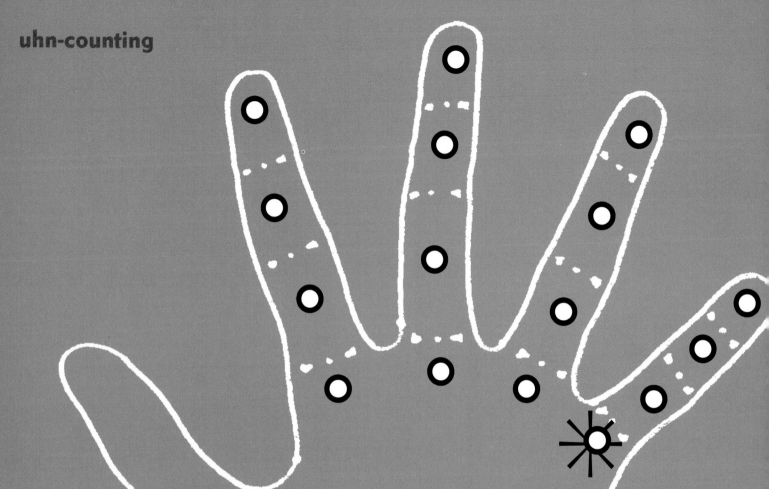

if you are right-handed, just reverse this diagram!

page **48**

you can see the other people involved in the game. One of the game's powers is seeing everybody's hand doing the same motion. It helps you create energy together, like everybody in a band playing the same note. Watching all the hands doing the same motion also keeps the game's momentum visible, not to mention the way watching each other makes it easier to stay together. And of course, you get to see the funny faces each person is making as you're all struggling to get the hang of this.

Each of you extends one hand (the hand you'll use for counting) into the center of the circle. Which hand? Use your "strong" hand, the one you write with, throw with, etc. Keeping your palm up, have your thumb start at the bottom of each finger, and work its way up, as shown in the diagram. First touch the four spots on the pinky, then the ring finger, then the middle finger, and finally the index finger.

At first, give **each** spot on **each** finger a strong sense of weight and importance. You can do this by saying the same vowel sound, such as "Uhn," on each spot. Make sure to give the "Big One," which is always at the bottom of the pinky (the starred place in the hand shown) the strongest accent.

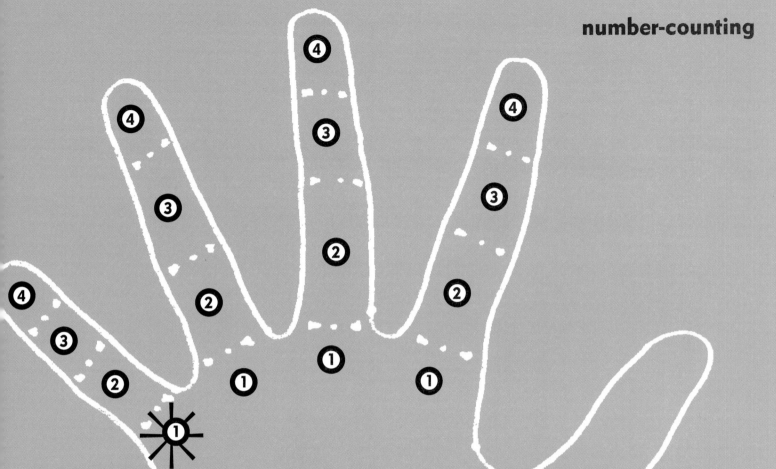

if you are
left-handed,
just reverse this
diagram!

Now count out loud from one to four on each finger as the thumb touches the four indicated spots. As before, start with the pinky, then move to the ring finger, the middle finger, and finish with the index finger. While emphasizing the count of "1" on each finger, remember to put an **especially loud** accent on the "Big One." Every return to the "Big One" on the bottom of the pinky is the beginning of another sixteen-beat statement.

You may have been experimenting with this much of the game on your own, trying to get the feeling for using your thumb to count the beats. If so, you've probably discovered that this is a wonderful game to play by yourself. It's a great thing to keep in mind when you find yourself with a little time on your hands. Just start dividing that time into beats and the wait will fly by.

But back to your group. While sitting in your circle, start counting together by gesturing with your hands, bringing your hand up and then down to show the beat. As your thumb reaches the top of each finger, you lift your hand up to indicate the beat is going back to one. Bring it down as you start the next set of four beats.

Now It's Time To Introduce Solo Parts

In the centuries-old tradition of Hindu music, certain syllables, rather than numbers, are spoken to keep track of the count on the hand. In your group, each person will have a turn to create a wild-sounding improvised rap or chant that follows the steady beat of your finger-counting. Make up as many different kinds of rhythmic and dramatic vocal soundings as you can think of. Using short syllables that start with percussive consonants (ka ka ka guh tuh guh tuh ka deh deh poo) is very successful for rhythmic vocal soloing. Making up and singing your own Indian-sounding vocabulary ("Din-dah ta-ka ta-ka getty-gedah" and so forth) while counting on your hand can also be really fun. You could throw in whatever words (favorite foods, names) come to mind: "Pizza pizza pizza pie, David dug a hole and he started to fly." Play with all kinds of sounds and have a good time with it.

When should you pass the solo on to the next person? Your group will need to choose the number of fingers each solo will last. Then, simply pass the solo after the designated number of fingers, while keeping your finger-counting together. Easy choices for passing the solo are at every finger (four beats), every two fingers (eight beats), or at every four fingers (sixteen beats).

By visually showing each other (in silence, without counting aloud) the count on the hand, your group can also experiment with using silence as part of your musical composition. This can also enable you to re-enter together after a silence — something that otherwise can be hard to accomplish. If your group wants a dramatic ending, agree to the number of sixteen-count phrases your improvisation will last, or designate a leader to indicate the approach of the ending. This way, you'll all end at precisely the same time.

If you stand rather than sit when you play this game, **you can add body movements to your music.** You should continue to face each other, doing your finger-counting, keeping your group in a circle. As you feel the beat, begin to step from foot to foot, staying in place. Left foot, right foot, left foot, right foot, so that your whole body is doing a dance. Try moving forward and backward. Come close together at the "Big One," lifting your hands high and shouting that great loud accented beat, then move apart until the "Big One" approaches once more. The group can also keep the beat with a repeated sound, similar to the sounds used to accompany the first diagram. This can provide a background rhythm which the soloists can play off of.

When you start the solos, encourage each vocal soloist to move into the middle of the circle while the rest of the group stays back. The soloist can fill the circle with his or her own free movements, creating a dance which goes along with the improvised vocal piece. Have the soloist rejoin the circle at the return to the "Big One." If you like, each soloist returning to the circle can select the next soloist by tapping a shoulder or using another agreed-upon signal.

Another option for this game is to **create a duet** (two people or two equal groups), with the two parts counting in different meters. In the third diagram shown, one part of this duet counts in threes while the other part is counting in fours. (A musician would say that one part is in a meter of 3/4 while the other part is in a meter of 4/4). The standard musical term for this kind of "duet" is polyrhythm. In a polyrhythmic duet such as this, both partners must continually listen and look at each other, making sure they stay together in a common pulse while keeping track of where they are in the sixteen-count cycle.

a right hander counting in 4s
a right hander counting in 3s

create a duet

Notice that in this example, the group counting in three's will be saying two "1s" in a row at the place where their sixteen-count cycle begins again:

1-2-3, 1-2-3, 1-2-3, 1-2-3, 1-2-3, 1, 1-2-3, etc.

Stay with it until the group is comfortable with the cross-accented rhythms. Both sides should try to hear their rhythm working **in conjunction** with that of the other, and avoid blocking out the opposing rhythm from their hearing. Become aware of the moment when both sides say "One" simultaneously. If you stay with this long enough, the polyrhythm will transform itself from two opposing rhythms to one overall pattern that works together, sounding rather like a complicated and fascinating piece of machinery.

The Hindu Finger-Counting Game has the potential to be used in many ways. Once you have learned the basic counting sequence, be open to many other ways to play this game. If you do this for a long enough period of time, the sixteen beat cycle becomes second nature to you, internalized in your body. Remember to try it as a solo adventure, practicing your own natural musicianship. Whether on your own or with a group, you'll find the game can refine your sense of time in an improvisation and can help you keep track of pulse. It can be a musical exploration where your wildest creative energies can take you off into the realms of dreamland. It's also a lot of fun.

sing your

Phoebe Snow

heart out

Nothing is more healthy and beautiful than the sound of your voice singing real loud.

What do I want to say to you? Simply this: You should feel free to sing anywhere and anytime. I know you may prefer to go into a room by yourself and sing in private. That's great! Keep enjoying the sound of your own voice in your own ears, but don't ONLY sing when you're by yourself, when you're sure no one else is listening. Fill your world with song! On the school bus, walking down the street, in the shopping mall, between bites of a hamburger. Make singing part of the natural rhythm of your daily movements.

Yes, I know, what I'm suggesting sounds kind of embarrassing. Still, just remind yourself that singing should be as natural as shouting or whispering. It shouldn't be something that you think about doing but something you just do, to express how you're feeling at that particular moment.

But how do you take that first step, that step beyond "I can't sing now; somebody might hear me?" That really depends on you, on what you feel comfortable with. Ask yourself, am I a hummer, a chanter, or a singer?

First Steps For Hummers
Are you the kind of person who softly accompanies yourself with sound while you work on a project or walk to a friend's? There may be no words to your humming; you may not even be aware of them unless somebody tells you you're disturbing them. Even while you're apologizing for bothering them you should give yourself a pat on the back for bringing music into another place. Take pride in your humming!

page
53

by Phoebe
Snow

First Steps For Chanters

Maybe you're not a hummer. Maybe you're most comfortable with rhythm. There's plenty of fun words to march to while you're moving along. How about:

Left, left, left, right, left.
I left my wife and forty four kids
In the middle of the kitchen with nothing but gingerbread
Left, left, left, right, left.
Do you think that I did right,
Right, right, left, right.

Well, okay, some of these chants are a little old-fashioned. So play around with the words "left" and "right" as you step along and create your own.

First Steps For Singers

Maybe you're ready to belt out a tune from day one. That's fantastic! But if you start feeling embarrassed when you're about to burst into song, and yet you want to sing, not hum or chant, remember, there's power in numbers. Seek out a fellow song-lover and take your show on the road. How to get past opening jitters? Well, one way is to challenge each other to a musical memory contest. Pick a topic: rain, dancing, traveling—let whatever's going on for you both that day inspire you. And then take turns singing whatever songs you can think of that reflect that theme. You might surprise yourself with how many songs you can come up with. Of course, once one of you has begun a song, the other should feel free to join in.

For example, what songs can I think of about singing? There's "Singing in the Rain," "Doe, a Deer, a Female Deer," (and for that matter, the title song from *The Sound of Music*), and "Sing, Sing a Song" (from *Sesame Street*). And there's a beautiful song, "His Eye is On the Sparrow," which I just recorded for a gospel album that goes, "I sing because I'm happy, I sing because I'm free, His eye is on the sparrow, and I know He watches me." I'm sure if you and I were walking together, you could come up with many more songs that have words like "sing" or "singing" in them, and your songs would probably help me remember a lot more, too.

Second Step For One And All

Okay, all you hummers, chanters, and challenge singers. Now that you've taken the first step, jump in with both feet and sing! If you can't remember all the words to your favorite song, hum parts and sing the rest, or make up new words. You might come up with even better lyrics than the original ones! And keep inviting friends to join you. Sometimes funny songs are good ones to start with. Pick some you remember from when you were little, like "Michael Finnegan":

There was an old man named Michael Finnegan,
He had whiskers on his chin-ne-gan,
Along came the wind and blew them in again,
Poor old Michael Finnegan. Begin again.

There was an old man named Michael Finnegan,
He kicked up an awful din-ne-gan,
Because they said he must not sing again,
Poor old Michael Finnegan. Begin again.

There was an old man named Michael Finnegan,
He went fishing with a pin-ne-gan,
Caught a fish and dropped it in again,
Poor old Michael Finnegan. Begin again.

There was an old man named Michael Finnegan,
He grew fat and then grew thin-ne-gan,
Then he died and had to begin again,
Poor old Michael Finnegan. Begin again.

Or try an echo song like "The Littlest Worm"

Singer one   **Singer Two (echo)**

1

The littlest worm	(the littlest worm)
I ever saw	(I ever saw)
Was stuck inside	(was stuck inside)
My soda straw	(my soda straw)

3

I took a sip	(I took a sip)
And he went down	(and he went down)
Right through my pipes	(right through my pipes)
He must have drowned	(he must have drowned)

Together

The littlest worm I ever saw
Was stuck inside my soda straw.

I took a sip and he went down
Right through my pipes; he must have drowned.

2

He says to me	(he says to me)
Don't take a sip	(don't take a sip)
For if you do	(for if you do)
I'll really flip	(I'll really flip)

4

He was my friend	(he was my friend)
He was my pal	(he was my pal)
And now he's gone	(and now he's gone)
For evermore	(for evermore)

He says to me don't take a sip
For if you do I'll really flip.

He was my friend, he was my pal
And now he's gone for evermore (sob, sob!)

Feel free to invent your own verses. While you're at it, if you've never heard these songs sung, play with the sound of the words and create your own way to sing it. And, of course, don't imagine I'm saying you should only sing silly songs. Sing all the songs you like best, from the ones you just heard yesterday to the ones you've been listening to all your life.

Maybe you've read this far and then all of a sudden, your mind starts coming up with excuses. "If Phoebe could hear what I sound like, she'd understand why I keep my mouth closed. She's talking about those other kids, the ones who can really sing, the ones everybody thinks should take private voice lessons."

You're wrong. I'm talking about you! And there's no human out there who can't sing! How do I know? My daughter taught me. Just knowing my daughter Valerie has given me the confidence to say to you, you *can* sing! Let me explain.

Valerie has a number of physical disabilities, but she's a fighter, a fighter who loves music. When she was born, I was told she wouldn't live more than a year. I was also told that she was deaf. Neither statement was right. Now she's nineteen years old and is constantly inspiring me. She loves to sing even though her singing doesn't sound like singing. It's more like little screams and yells, because even though she can hear and she can make a lot of sounds, she can't say words. When she was little, she'd sing around the house a lot, but I wasn't sure she'd ever sing in public, and I don't think she was either. Let me tell you about her debut.

When Valerie was fourteen years old, her school's music teacher let Valerie and the other disabled boys and girls from her class sit in for choral class, but no one from Valerie's class ever sang. They just sat and listened to the other children singing. Then one day, the class had to take a test and the room was quiet. After about 10 minutes of this, Valerie made a face as if she were disgusted and let loose. "La, la, la, la!" She knew it was time to sing and since no one else was doing it, she figured it was up to her. Her teacher and classmates were so amazed that Valerie was actually singing that they decided to let her stay in the room and sing while they worked on the test. So, for the next half hour, Valerie sang and they wrote. And Valerie's been comfortable singing in front of other people ever since.

Once you get started singing around the clock, you may be surprised at how natural it feels to be singing, and how unnatural it feels to stop. Don't hold back. If you're ready to sing and no song comes to mind, make one up on the spot—words, tune, and all. Again, let your situation inspire you. If you're feeling angry, sing a loud let-me-tell-you-how-I-feel song. If you're proud or disappointed or eager to see what's around the next bend, let those feelings swell out in song. You may find that certain songs become important rituals for you. You may have a song you always turn to to keep your courage up or one that lets everyone know you're on top of the world.

My younger sister had a song she sang over and over to herself at night to put herself to sleep. The tune would vary, but her words were:

The puppy next door is round and fat
And he likes to chase my cat
But she ran out on a limb
Up in a tree away from him.

For my sister, this was a comfort song, a way to gradually feel safe and secure and relaxed enough to sleep. It was a comfort to me as well, although I'm not sure if my sister (or even I) realized it. My sister was singing her heart out, and she touched mine as well. So don't hold back. Start singing—who knows whose hearts you'll touch? I know you'll strengthen your own.

anyone can be

Pete Seeger

The important thing is not, "Is it good music?"

What is the music good for? That's the important question.

My parents were both dedicated professional musicians, teaching at Juilliard Institute, New York City. My mother left musical instruments all around the house. I can remember banging on a piano, squeezing on a push-pull accordion, tapping on a marimba, blowing on a harmonica. Whatever was around, I'd just make a racket on it. Age eight I was given a ukelele. Started picking out chords, learning their names. Plunk, plunk. All by ear. I resisted learning to read music; I started out as an ear musician.

a songwriter

My father was researching some of the few collections of folk music available in those days. I learned from him that there were often different versions of the same song. People change words, melody, make up new verses. This was an important lesson: you can choose the version of the song you want to sing.

It was Woody Guthrie who helped me see how one can make up a new song by changing around an old song. Who cares if it's not completely original? The aim in this world is to do a good job, not to try and prove how original one can be. So I've often tried putting new words to old tunes. When my family moved up to the country from New York City, I used the tune of "The John B. Sails."

So load up the moving van,
Here comes the moving man,
Leave New York City far behind.
Goodbye, goodbye,
Goodbye, goodbye,
Leave Greenwich Village a long way behind.

© 1951 & 1993 Folkways Music

by Pete Seeger

Making Up Song Lyrics

Learn from songs that seem to stick in people's minds the longest. One thing you'll notice is that there is no one rule you have to follow. Is it necessary that song lyrics rhyme? Sometimes yes, often no. Look at the great old spirituals which sing so well. "Steal Away." "Kumbaya." "Didn't My Lord Deliver Daniel." Look at the children's song "Where is Thumbkin?" So if rhyming comes easily to you, good. But if you can't find good rhymes, . . .well, remember there's lots of good songs without a single rhyme in them.

You'll notice that many which stick in our memory have repeated lines. Some songs repeat the first line of a verse, others repeat the last line. Experiment with both choices. What does repetition do? Perhaps it gives one time to savor different meanings in the words. Or time to think: "What the heck is the next verse?" Maybe it reinforces an idea. Often it encourages a listener to join in.

Using Nonsense Sounds

Singers in many parts of the world like to give out sounds that have no strict meaning. Some Native American songs are mostly "vocables." (Vocable is a fancy way of saying "sounds with no strict meaning.") Irish and some English and Scottish songs are full of "nonsense words." "Hey diddle diddle, Too-ri-oo-ri-ay." The Hasidim use "Hi-di-di." I think it's a little like repeating the last line of a song. In a narrative song with compact words, they slow down the action so you can savor it. Again, experiment with your own lyrics. See if you like alternating recognizable words with some vocable or other.

Dialogue Songs

Many old songs were built around a dialogue. Instead of just giving one point of view, a dialogue song can give two or more points of view. It could be a funny song like "There's a Hole in the Bucket, Dear Liza" or mournful like some of the old ballads. Your listeners get drawn into the story and start identifying with some of the people in there. Be wary of trying to write editorials in rhyme. Better: tell a story, paint a picture.

Zipper Songs

What's a zipper song? My friend Lee Hays came up with that name to describe any song that could get a new verse by zipping in one new word or phrase. Some familiar examples are: "If You're Happy and You Know It" (zip in "clap your hands"; "stamp your feet"; "slap your knee," etc.) or "Old McDonald Had a Farm." A zipper song is a good starting place for beginning songwriters. Lee used this technique when he wrote the following words:

"If I Had a Hammer" (as sung by Peter, Paul and Mary)

If I Had A Hammer

1
If I had a hammer
I'd hammer in the mornin'
I'd hammer in the evenin'
All over this land.
I'd hammer out danger,
I'd hammer out a warning,
I'd hammer out love between
My brothers and my sisters,
All over this land.

2
If I had a bell
I'd ring it in the mornin'
I'd ring in the evenin'
All over this land.
I'd ring out danger,
I'd ring out a warning,
I'd ring out love between
My brothers and my sisters,
All over this land.

3
If I had a song
I'd sing it in the mornin'
I'd sing in the evenin'
All over this land.
I'd sing out danger,
I'd sing out a warning,
I'd sing out love between
My brothers and my sisters,
All over this land.

Making Up Melodies

No tune fits your new words? Dissatisfied with old tunes? Well, it's not impossible to make up new melodies. But it's easiest to start by changing an old melody just a little. As in any other field of endeavor, whether cooking or carpentry, it's normal to start by imitating. Using recipes. As you keep experimenting with different tunes, you'll find yourself beginning to make small changes according to your own personal likes and dislikes. Then with luck comes the wonderful discovery that there is no great crime in making bigger changes.

Quake survivors want to leave island

'Leper priest' to move closer to sainthood

**Kitchen & Bath
Yard Sale.
One Day Only.
Sat. June 3rd. 8am-4pm**

Direct from the Distributor

Whirlpool baths by
Jacuzzi. American
Standard products.
Kitchen & Bath sinks
and faucets plus a
large selection of
designer plumbing
products. Don't miss it!

If you don't read music or you don't play an instrument, believe me, playing guitar or piano doesn't necessarily help. It can hinder. Some of the greatest melodies have come from parts of the world where melodies are sung unaccompanied. They have to be good enough to stand up by themselves, without a sea of harmony supporting them.

Melody Games to Get You Started

1) Try improvising variations on any tune you know, or are listening to. This is no more than any jazz musician does. Think of three very different people you know. Try changing "Yankee Doodle" as it would be sung by each of those three people. If you know something about different kinds of music, try imagining that you are a musician from a different tradition or a different part of the world. How would they change that tune?

2) Try slowing a tune down, or speeding it up. Put it in a different "mode," major or minor. Start by changing one or two notes in the beginning, middle, or end. Then change whole phrases. Think about the slight differences between "Baa, Baa, Black Sheep" and "Twinkle, Twinkle, Little Star."

3) Here's a game I've often played while driving a car: put tunes to highway billboards. Pretend it's a singing commercial you hear on the air. You can play the same game leafing through magazines or newspapers. Sing the headlines. What you'll learn is what the world's best composers have long known: it's easy to make up a half-good melody. But to make up an unforgettable one takes luck, and for all anyone knows, help from the Great Unknown. Nevertheless, I agree with Thomas Edison. ("Genius is five percent inspiration and ninety five percent perspiration.") Practice may not make perfect, but it sure as hell makes for improvement.

What to Write About
That's up to you. But if you learn to have a sense of how much fun it is to make music, and how much fun it is to let music participate in every aspect of your life, you'll be making up songs of many kinds.

I'd like to see everybody find musical ways to combine work with fun, to make a dance out of sweeping floors, making beds. Here's a song my daughter Mika and I came up with in the middle of a big house cleaning.

1

Sweepy, sweepy, sweepy (**3X**)

Sweepin' up the floor

Sweepy, sweepy, sweepy (**3X**)

'Til there ain't no more!

2

Dusty, dusty, dusty (**3X**)

Dustin' up the shelf

Dusty, dusty, dusty (**3X**)

Doin' it myself!

3

Putty, putty, putty (3X)
Puttin' things away
Putty, putty, putty (3X)
Then go out and play!

4

Moppy, moppy, moppy (3X)
Moppin' up the room
Moppy, moppy, moppy (3X)
Foom! Foom! Foom!

5

Cleany, cleany, cleany (3X)
Clean the window panes
Cleany, cleany, cleany (3X)
'Til you see through again!

6

Throwy, throwy, throwy (3X)
Throwin' things away
Throwy, throwy, throwy (3X)
Far away!

7

Makey, makey, makey (3X)
Makin' up the bed
Makey, makey, makey (3X)
That's what I said!

8

Shakey, shakey, shakey (3X)
Shakin' out the sheet
Shakey, shakey, shakey (3X)
'Til the two ends meet!

9

Washy, washy, washy (3X)
Washin' up the dishes
Washy, washy, washy (3X)
And the soap suds squishes!

© 1957, Ludlow Music

We have songs for putting a baby to sleep, songs to sing to ourselves when we're lonely, songs for singing at church, at a rally, a meeting, a party. Why not songs to sing while waiting for a bus, while waiting for a game to start, when pushing a car out of a mudhole, for picking up litter, for calling a meeting together? I'd like to see people through the world making up new songs for each other all the time, for birthdays, for weddings, for any special occasion, as well as remembering other songs that may be centuries old.

I'll end with one more song inspired by my children, this time by my daughter, Tinya, when she was age 3. Many songs ask questions."The Star Spangled Banner"; "Somewhere Over the Rainbow"; "Brother, Can You Spare a Dime?" "Where have All the Flowers Gone?" Perhaps this is a place for you to start. If you're wondering where to begin, try experimenting with the repetitions in this song. Insert some things you find yourself wondering about these days, and sing your creation to someone you know. You could be filling the air with wonder.

So if you're wondering where to begin, try experimenting with the repetitions in this song. Insert some things you find yourself wondering about these days, and sing your creation to someone you know. You could fill the air with wonder.

I Wonder, I Wonder, I Wonder

1

I wonder, I wonder, I wonder
What Tinya can possibly do?
I wonder, I wonder, I wonder
What Tinya can possibly do?

2

She can play with her blocks,
Or go throw some rocks,
Or climb a tree and look at the view.
I wonder, I wonder, I wonder
What Tinya can possibly do?

3

I see someone's hand,
I see someone's hair,
I hear someone go peek-a-boo.
I wonder, I wonder, I wonder
What Tinya can possibly do?

4

She crawls on the floors,
She looks 'round the door.
She's trying to wear my shoe.
I wonder, I wonder, I wonder
What Tinya can possibly do?

5

I see someone's hair,
I see someone's toe,
But I can't guess possibly who.
I wonder, I wonder, I wonder
What Tinya can possibly do?

© 1970 Stormking Music

A note about the fine print above. In a sense, a good song should be "the precious possession of the people." A poor song is hardly worth the paper it's printed on. I used to be contemptuous of copyrighting anything. But right now in this dangerously unbalanced world, if something is not "owned," it is also fair game to be mistreated or misused. I now urge folks, if they do a lot of songwriting, to at least keep dated notebooks or tapes of all their song attempts. They can copyright a batch of them at one time: "Song Attempts, 1996" and so on. In any case, don't be afraid of working with other musicians and songwriters. You can learn how to get in touch with them through magazines like Sing Out!, Box 5253, Bethlehem, PA, 18015. But you can get your own songwriting started anywhere, anytime.

Based on selections from the autobiography: *WHERE HAVE ALL THE FLOWERS GONE: A SINGER'S STORIES, SONGS, SEEDS, ROBBERIES* (SING OUT! Pub. 610-865-5366) also, quotations from PBS Bill Moyers interview with Pete Seeger; and also a talk on songwriting, Connecticut Songwriter's Association, 3/13/95

music as a Lifeline

Music is like magic. It's a powerful force for good. If you're feeling down, listen to a great piece of music and the power of music can lift you up.

When I was a kid, whenever I was a bit depressed, I'd always reach out for a guitar. I still do. I've always believed that making music is the best way, sometimes the only way, of expressing what you really feel. People who sometimes have difficulty with language can often express themselves in music. A few years back, I visited a center for music therapy in Britain where I just took along my guitar and played for some kids. Just like my own kids when they were little, these kids couldn't resist touching and strumming my guitar. Music was the bridge. Watching the music therapists at work, and seeing how the kids responded to my session with them, I was reminded again of how music can heal. It can do more than just ease the pain. It can throw a lifeline to people who can't be reached in any other way.

If you spend any time around young kids, maybe your younger brothers or sisters, or maybe if you're babysitting someone else's kids, think about letting music be your bridge. What could you do? Any parent knows that you can make instruments out of most

by Paul McCartney

things—banging an overturned washing-up bowl, taping a few toilet rolls together to make a trumpet, filling a bag with sand and shaking it. The idea is to capture kids' imaginations; the more imaginative *you* can be in doing that, the more they will get into it.

Or you could start out by just listening to some music with them. Pick out some of your favorite songs or ask them to pick out some of theirs, then let them see you respond to the music. If you feel like dancing, dance—get them to join you. If you usually sit while you listen, let them curl up with you. Don't worry about the right way to get them to connect to the music; music itself can be the teacher.

Music can also be a bridge for building friendships with kids your own age. If you're someone who likes to write songs, you might want to approach someone else you know who likes making music and see if they'd want to try working together. One possible starting place could be, rather than just jump off the deep end, share a couple of songs you've been having trouble finishing and say, "Tell me what's wrong with these." If your friend has some that aren't quite working, you could try to fix up each other's songs, and you'll be off and running. The next step would be to try to write a song from scratch, now that you've got a feeling for each other's strengths.

What I've found when I work with other musicians is that the minute you get into a formula, you're in deep trouble. I try to keep each song different, because it's so easy to fall into ruts. You think you've got the hang of something and you say to yourself, "Ah, we write upbeat numbers." So then I say, "Okay, on the *next* one, let's try to write a soully ballad, or a rocker." I've always thought of a songwriter being someone who could turn his hand to this or that as a craftsman, rather than be stuck in one rock 'n 'roll mode or ballad mode.

The same goes for where you rehearse and perform. If you practice or perform in the same place all the time, music can become work, and you want it always to be play. I think you get the best results when you keep taking risks.

Building bridges, taking risks. All part of making music. And music is a gift that belongs to all of us, a universal language that can give a voice to people who would otherwise never be heard.

Based on: The BBC program "The Power of Music," an exploration of music therapy narrated by Paul McCartney, courtesy of Nordoff-Robbins Music Therapy Foundation; "Farewell to the First Solo Era," interview in *Musician*, February, 1988 and correspondence with Ellipsis Kids..., 1995.

rubber band banjo

Kids love music — any kind of music, as long as it's lively.

Most children have very talented ears because they are so willing

to enjoy the process of experimenting with sounds.

The banjo has been celebrated by all sorts of songs, from "Oh, Susanna," to "I've Been Working on the Railroad." (You know, "strumming on the old banjo.") Why not make your own banjo?

What You'll Need:
a shoebox (the bottom, not the top)
10-20 rubber bands of different sizes and widths

How to Make It:
Slide lots of rubber bands around the width of the box. Use small rubber bands for a small shoebox, big rubber bands if you have a big shoebox.

How to Play It:
Hold your rubber band banjo with the open part facing up. Lift each rubber band and stretch it a little with one hand. Pluck the rubber band with your other hand. You'll notice that you can change the notes you're playing by pulling more or less as you lift the rubber band. Try plucking out melodies like "Mary had a Little Lamb," "Three Blind

by Shari Lewis

Mice," or "Twinkle, Twinkle, Little Star." Here's a banjo song that I like to sing, written by Rob Battan and Stormy Sacks.

Rubber Band Banjo

1

I know banjo players come and go,
But there's one thing that I've come to know
That an audience applauds and stands
For a banjo made of rubber bands.

Chorus:

See the people smilin'
Oh, the joy that it brings,
When I start to pickin'
On my rubber band strings.
While the music's playin'
It's a holiday
My rubber band banjo,
Puttin' on a good show
How I loved to play.

2

Though it may not sound like much at all
I still dreamt I'd play a concert hall.
So I practiced ev'ry night and day
'Til at center stage I got to play.

Chorus:

See the people smilin'
Oh, the joy that it brings,
When I start to pickin'
On my rubber band strings.
While the music's playin'
It's a holiday
My rubber band banjo,
Puttin' on a good show
How I loved to play.

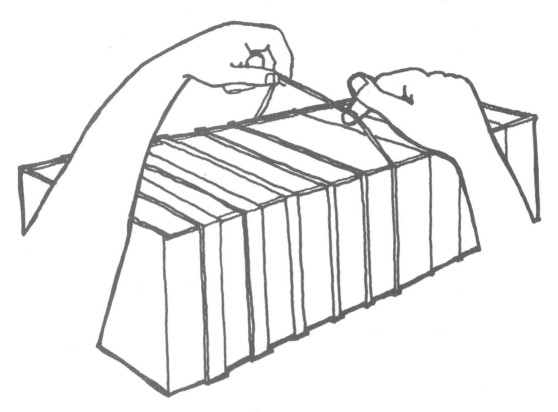

3   Yes, my act stayed pretty much the same,
But still ev'rybody knew my name.
So they called me from a studio,
Gave me my own television show.

Chorus: See the people smilin'
Oh, the joy that it brings,
When I start to pickin'
On my rubber band strings.
While the music's playin'
It's a holiday
My rubber band banjo,
Puttin' on a good show
How I loved to play.

You can use Rob's words and come up with your own tune. Or make up song lyrics of your own. Have fun, and don't worry about making music to please anyone but yourself! As my mother always used to say, "Wouldn't the woods be silent if only the best birds sang?"

how to make a den-den

a japanese fan drum

One day, while shopping at an import store, I picked up a small Oriental-looking drum on a stick. I twisted the stick back and forth, making the two wooden beads on strings connected to the side of the drum bang against the skin drum heads. Even though I was an experienced percussionist and a jazz drummer, at first I had trouble controlling the bouncing beads.

I don't distinguish between "real" instruments and "toys". Anything that makes sound can be used to create music.

When I turned the drum handle slowly, the wooden beads hit the drum skins, but then dropped very quickly on top of my hand. I tried spinning the handle faster and the motion of the beads became easier to control. Now I was smiling and chuckling to myself as the beads went plink, plank, plink, plank, hammering out a steady beat. This little drum was different from all the other drums in my large collection of percussion instruments from many lands.

I walked up to the cashier, playing my new discovery: plink, plank, click, clack. People looked on in amusement, perhaps wondering why a grown man would buy such a strange little toy. I asked the cashier if she knew what this drum was called, but she wasn't able to tell me anything. So I began trying to find out all I could about this tiny rattle.

I learned that my new drum was from Japan and that it was called a den-den. Some people call them fan drums, since you play it by moving it back and forth instead

by Yohuru
Ralph
Williams

of hitting it with a stick. There is a very special den-den called the Furi-tsuzumi. Picture a long staff with a small den-den on top and a larger one lower down. It uses tiny bells instead of beads, and makes a pleasant jingling sound as you twirl that long staff.

Since that Saturday afternoon back in 1971, I have collected seven fan drums. I've bought four Japanese versions similar to that first one I fell in love with. They have big handles and are painted black. The drum heads are covered with thin white animal skin. Going around the handle is a pattern of tiny carved grooves. There are also tiny grooves all around the wood body of the drum.

I found a fan drum from West Africa which uses two short pieces of wood about 1/4 inch long instead of wooden beads. The skins used for the drum heads are similar to the skins on my other African drums: furry dark brown skin with white streaks. I also have a Northeastern American Indian version. It is painted bright red and is much smaller than the Japanese ones. It has very small black wooden beads and makes a much higher sound. I am fascinated by the history of these fan or rattle drums. As a drummer, I'm especially impressed by the important role they played in Japanese and Egyptian culture. If you watch the movie *The Karate Kid II* closely, you'll see one traditional use of the den-den; they have been used for hundreds of years at wrestling matches or karate fights. If you were watching a karate match, you'd sound your den-den to encourage the contestants you were supporting, and to celebrate if they won. But the den-den is not just used for fights. It is also an important prayer object for Buddhist priests, carried in processions for special ceremonial events.

The sistrum of ancient Egypt, an instrument related to the fan drum, was also important for religious ceremonies. "Sistrum" means "something shaken"; the Egyptian sistrum was a metal pole topped with a curved bar hung with bells on each end. Also called an Isis clapper in honor of the goddess Hathor-Isis, sistrums were believed to have power over evil spirits. Women (usually priestesses) carried these rattling staffs to show their high rank. If you carried one without the queen's approval, you might be punished severely.

So, if you want to show the world how important you are, or you're planning a karate match, or you need to chase away evil spirits, or you'd just like to add another instrument to your collection, read on and I'll describe some den-den variations I've created using everyday household containers.

What You'll Need:

cardboard cylindrical container
(for example, oatmeal, grits, or raisin container)
wooden dowel, about 10-12 inches long
two wooden beads
string
tape or glue
pencil or marker
something sharp and pointed to poke a hole with
(you may need help with that part)
decorations: construction paper, glitter, whatever you like

How to Make It:

1. Tape or glue the cover on the end of your cardboard cylinder so that both ends are closed.

2. Use the pencil or marker to mark a spot **not** on the ends you just closed, but in the middle of the long part of your cylinder. Imagine that's your top hole. Now mark a spot matching it on the bottom of the cylinder. These marks are where you'll push the wooden dowel through your container. (see drawing)

3. Use your sharp object to poke holes through your two marks. The holes must be just large enough so that the wooden dowel can slide through them.

4. Push your dowel through the holes. Leave at least 1/4 inch sticking up on the top.

5. Tape or glue the dowel to the container at both holes. Make sure it's fastened strongly enough so that the container does not move when you roll the dowel back and forth between your hands.

6. Cut two pieces of string. Each piece should be a little bit longer than your container. Tie a wooden bead to the end of each string.

7. Take one bead and hold it in the center of your container's end (the drum face). Pull the other end of the string tightly along the length of the container. Tape it right in the middle of the side of the container. (The spot should be halfway between the places where the dowel connects to the container.) Do the same thing on the other side of your container with the other wooden bead.

8. Decorate!

More Ideas: Try using bells or bottle caps instead of wooden beads. If you use bottle caps (plastic or metal), you'll need to tape them to the ends of the string unless you have a drill and permission to use it. If you do have a drill, or there's someone around who can drill some holes for you, you might also try using metal or plastic cans. You need to drill, not just punch, the holes for the handle when you use metal or plastic cans. Experiment with different combinations of sounds: plastic on metal; metal on cardboard; plastic on plastic; wood on metal, and so on. You could try to make a Furi-tsuzumi, with two den-dens on the same handle.

How to Play Your Den-Den I hope you've enjoyed making the rattle drums as much as I do, but I have to tell you that the real fun begins with playing them. You can hold the dowel in one hand and twist it back and forth, or hold the dowel

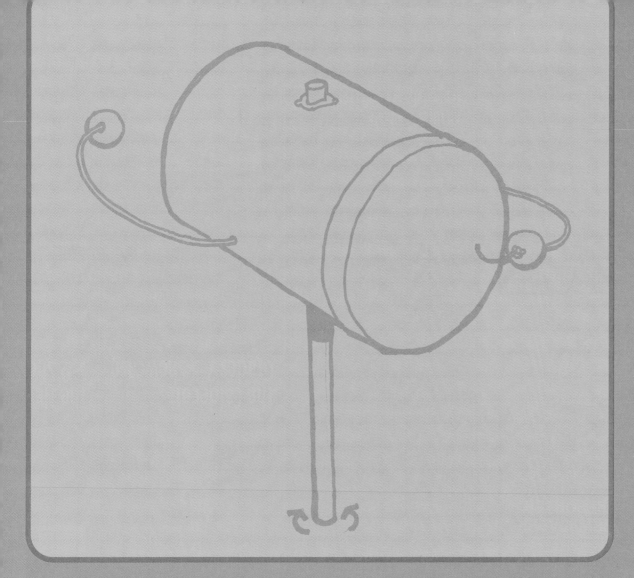

between your hands and roll it. Try it both ways and see which works for you. No matter how you hold it, keep in mind that you want to twist it, not shake it.

You remember how I started out in the import store, right? I found I had to twist the den-den fast enough so that the beads (or bottle caps) would fly back and forth, hitting the drum heads. See if you can get yours to beat out a fast rhythm. You might like to use a repeated word to help you keep your rhythm. Try, "Al-li-ga-tor, al-li-ga-tor, al-li-ga-tor, al-li-ga-tor." Now try a slow beat. How about "Den-den-den-den." If you want to try something in the middle, you could repeat, "Sis-trum, sis-trum, sis-trum, sis-trum."

These patterns can help you to build up the ability to control the bouncing beads. I now use den-dens in all my concerts, and the audiences are fascinated, surprised and tickled by them. They're wonderful to watch and listen to at the same time!

...listen to me, listen well my friend.

All good things are coming to an end.

Only you and I will be left to face it.

The jungles are going, going.

Who knows what will remain.

Listen to me well my friend.

When I feel a little sadness

The berimbau brightens up my day.

I was nine or ten years old and living in Venezuela when I first started paying attention to the musical instruments around me. As in most Latin American countries, music in Venezuela is an important part of most holidays or celebrations; people play music for Carnival (like Mardi Gras) and Christmas, weddings and birthdays. They even play music for funerals. And, of course, they play music just for the fun of it. Many of my friends played musical instruments. By the time I was twelve, we were performing for ourselves and our families. In the month of December, we would form *aguinaldos*, groups with guitars, drums, maracas, and *guiros* (a grooved gourd which is played with a stick.) We would go around our

rainsticks and

neighborhood singing Spanish Christmas songs with African rhythms and Guarani sounds, a mixture typical of Latin American music. (The Guarani are the native people of Bolivia, Paraguay, and southern Brazil.) The complicated interplay of rhythms created by the drums and maracas gave the songs a contagious, happy feeling I wanted to be part of, but when I tried playing these rhythms, I felt clumsy and uncoordinated. Instead, I studied the accordion and the guitar, which seemed to come pretty easily for me at the time. It never occurred to me back then that I would ever be able to play percussion, let alone become skilled at making my own percussion instruments.

It wasn't until 1977, the same year my first daughter, Naya, was born, that I got my first conga drum. That was the year a group of friends and I decided to form a theatre troupe called "The Illuminated Elephants" which would take shows to all the most remote places of the world. We hoped to live with and learn from the native people we visited. Our own group included people from Mexico, Denmark, Argentina, Sweden and the U.S.A. For four years, we toured through the western United States, and Mexico. We came into contact with the music and culture of some of the oldest native tribes of North and Central America.

by Giovanni Ciarlo

berimbaus

Giovanni Cibó

During this time, I heard an amazing variety of different musical styles and musical instruments. I still have instruments given to me by the people we visited. One of the most beautiful and interesting instruments I encountered during this time was the "rainstick." Strangely enough, I first saw someone playing the rainstick during a concert of jazz music. I went to hear a musician named Antonio Zepeda, an avant-garde jazz musician who uses traditional and pre-Hispanic percussion instruments, and I saw someone making enchanting rhythm and water sounds by tilting a tightly woven basket in the shape of a tube. It seemed to have seeds inside which made the unusual sounds. I was told it was a Brazilian instrument called a *palo de lluvia*.

Later on our tour, in the small town of Tepoztlán in the state of Morelos in Mexico, I saw a group of traditional musicians who played a palo de lluvia they had made themselves from a bamboo pole. I became good friends with these musicians and asked them how to make the rainstick. I knew I couldn't weave a tube-like basket, but I thought I could manage to fill a tube of bamboo with seeds. It was a little more complicated than that, but I succeeded. Perhaps I should have held off until I knew a little more, though. After I made my first rainstick, it rained so hard in Mexico City that it completely flooded my basement video studio. I now know that the palo de lluvia is used during rituals to the rain gods. Using the rainstick, the shaman of the tribe could talk to the clouds (rain gods) and ask them to send more rain if the rains have been too scarce or less if the rain has been too plentiful.

In Africa, on the other hand, the rainstick has a very different use. A tribal chief would use it as a talking stick to measure the amount of time available to a person who wished to state a complaint. If the speaker was interesting or the topic was important, the rain would fall slowly. If the person talking was too boring or long-winded, the chief could cut the time short by letting the rain fall faster.

Learning to make the rainstick completely changed my life. (It wasn't just that it flooded my studio, which happened to be my only source of income at the time.) I became interested in learning to make other kinds of instruments, like those used for centuries by the traditional cultures of the Americas. I've probably made more than five thousand instruments since that day in 1982 when I made my first rainstick. My wife, Kathleen, and I continue to seek out people who can teach us more about how to make various musical instruments. We sell most of the instruments we make, but we also use them when we perform with our group, Sirius Coyote.

So, here are the instructions for making a rainstick. If you find that making it has changed your life, don't say I didn't warn you!

the rainstick

What You'll Need:

twenty-four-inch heavy cardboard tube, 1–1/2 inches in diameter
(one place to look for a tube like this is in a fabric store)
2 heavy cardboard circles, 1–1/2 inches in diameter,
to cover the ends of the tube. (If you're lucky, you might find plastic caps that fit. Some mailing tubes for posters are just the right size.)
1 pound of one inch roofing nails (nails with large heads)
1 cup of small, loose, hard filling
(Use unpopped popcorn, lentils, rice, or #3 size fish tank gravel)
roll of clear wrapping tape, 2 inches wide
six foot long piece of string (optional)

How to Make It:

1. Use a pencil to draw a spiral along the whole length of the tube. Make your line go in the opposite direction from the glue line of the tube; you don't want the nails to split the tube along the glue line. One way to draw the line is to tape one end of the six foot length of string to one end of the tube, and then wind the string around the outside to create a spiral (like a candy cane stripe). The lines of your spiral should be about two inches apart. When you reach the bottom of the tube, tape down the other end of the string. (You will probably have some string hanging off the end of your tube; that's nothing to worry about.) Now trace the spiral formed by the string, then take the string off the tube.
2. Mark the spot on your spiral which is one inch down from the tube's edge. Then mark a second spot on your spiral which is one inch from the other end of the tube.
3. Take a hammer and drive the roofing nails into the tube along your spiral lines. Put the first nail through your mark. The rest of the nails should be very close together, with only a space the size of the width of your pointing finger between them, until you reach your second mark. You should have created a nail spiral which starts and stops one full inch from either end of the tube.
4. Cover one end of the tube with a plastic cap or tape a cardboard circle to the end. Make sure the tube is securely sealed.
5. Pour in the cup of seeds or gravel.

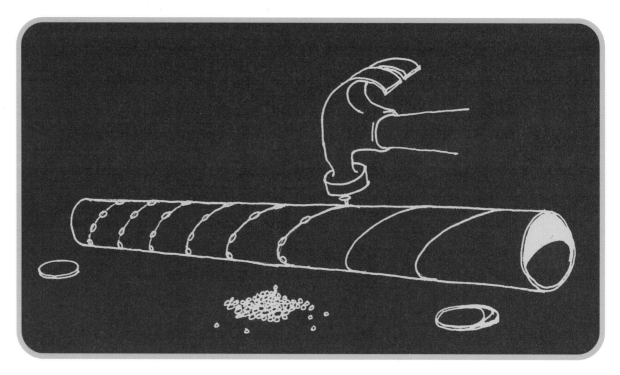

6. Seal up the other end of the tube.

7. Decorate by drawing color patterns, or a picture story. You might want to use traditional African or Indian designs. If you used paint, let it dry.

8. Cover the whole tube with clear wrapping tape.

How to Play It: You play the "rainstick" by tipping it on end and then turning
it back again. You can also hold it horizontally and shake it to make rhythms.

More Ideas: Now that you've made your first one, you might want to try a piece of bamboo for a different sound. Make sure the ends are cut straight. You'll need to use a metal bar to clear out the thin membranes inside the tube which separate the sections of the bamboo. You'll also need to cover the ends with round pieces of wood, drill holes along your spiral lines, and insert 1/8-inch wooden dowels cut one inch long in place of roofing nails. Dab each dowel piece into a little glue first so that it will stick and sand the rough ends once the glue dries. A third material to consider using is a PVC tube (PVC tubes are plastic tubes for plumbing which you'll find at a hardware store.) Again, you'll need to drill holes along your spiral. Then you'll follow the directions for the cardboard model. For both the bamboo and the PVC tube, you should use a drill with a 1/8-inch drill bit.

the berimbau

I make stringed instruments in addition to a wide assortment of percussion instruments. One of my favorite string instruments is the *berimbau*, with its exotic sound and rhythmic possibilities.

It also has a fascinating history. It was developed from an African bow and arrow and brought to Brazil by the slave trade in the 1700s. Because the plantation slaves were forbidden to train as warriors, they developed a martial art that looked a little like a dance so they could work out without getting into trouble. A berimbau player would be the lookout. If the plantation owners were spotted coming near, the berimbau player would give a signal and the warrior training session would turn into a spectacular dance.

Today, the berimbau is used to accompany a form of martial arts game called *capoeira*. Two players do jumps, kicks, and spins in mid-air to the driving rhythm of the berimbau and drums accompanied by singing and clapping. Some people believe that break dancing is a modern form of capoeira done to hip-hop music. Students tell me they've seen a movie called *Only the Strong* which featured capoeira players and berimbau music. So if you're curious, you could try to see that movie. Or you could try to see some live capoeira players. Capoeira competitions are held regularly throughout the world.

These days, in addition to accompanying the capoeira competitions, the berimbau is used as a musical instrument in its own right. Once you've made your own, you might try to search out some berimbau recordings so you'll get an idea of the great variety of sounds and rhythms you could play on your new instrument.

What You'll Need:

a green four-foot-long straight hardwood stick, one inch in diameter Cut the stick from maple, oak, or other hard woods. To get green wood, you need to cut it from a living tree. Don't use wood you find on the ground.

one pound coffee can
one foot long nylon shoelace
a flat rock the size of an Oreo cookie
a 1/4-inch dowel 15 inches long

a five-foot-long, 20-gauge steel wire use thin piano wire (get it from a piano tuner) or wire from the hardware store.

hand saw
pliers
knife
drill with 1/8 inch bit

How to Make It:

1. Peel all the bark off the hardwood stick with your knife. You should have a four-foot length with minimum bend in it.

2. At a point about 1/2 inch down from each end of the stick, carve a notch or an indentation into both sides of your stick. (See picture) Both ends of the stick should now look

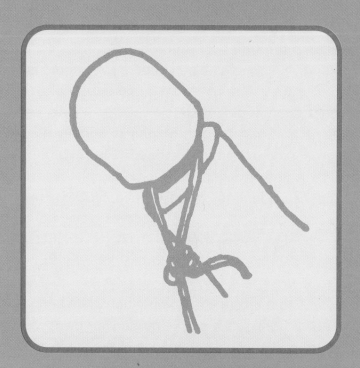

like a wood person, with a 1/2-inch tall head, a narrow neck, and shoulders. When, in step 5, you slip the loops of wire on each end of the stick, the notches will prevent the loops from sliding down the stick.

3. Let the stick dry a few days.

4. Make a loop on one end of the wire, wrapping the wire's end around the loop a few times so that the loop will hold under pressure.

5. Attach the wire securely to one end of the stick by slipping it over the stick's end and sliding it into place on the "neck."

6. Bend the stick so that it looks like a bow for shooting arrows. You will probably need to clamp it or get a strong friend to help you to bend it.

Then attach the other end of the wire. You may need to use the pliers. The wire has to be tight and well stretched so that when you pluck it, it rings.

7. Drill two holes in the middle of the bottom of the coffee can. Your holes should be 1/2 inch apart.

8. Thread both ends of the shoelace through the holes of the coffee can so that the two ends are on the inside. Cross the laces about 1 inch up from the coffee can's bottom and tie a strong knot. Turn the can over and pull on the lace. You should have made a 2- inch loop which sticks up from the can's bottom.

9. Slip your bow through the shoelace loop. Push the loop up the bow until it is about one foot up from the end of the bow. The can should press against the stick and the loop should make a tight pull on the wire. (See picture)

How to Play It:

1. Hold the bow vertically in your left hand, balancing the shoelace on your little finger. Curl your middle two fingers around the stick.

2. Place the flat stone between the thumb and pointing finger of your left hand. Your pointing finger is bent, with the stone resting on top of it. Your thumb holds the stone in place.

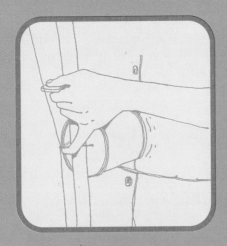

3. Now, hold the 15-inch dowel in your right hand like a pencil and use it to hit the string just above the can.

4. You can use the stone to make three sounds:

    a. Pull the stone away from the wire and play. (This is called an open string).

    b. Press the stone firmly against the wire and the sound should get higher.

    c. Press the stone lightly on the wire and make a buzz.

5. Use the open mouth of the can against your stomach to "dampen" the sound; pull it away from your stomach for a louder sound. Try to switch back and forth so that the can adds a "Wa-Wa-Wa-Wa" sound to your music.

6. It will take some time to get used to it, so keep practicing!

    More Ideas: If you want your berimbau to be more like the ones in Brazil, you could use a dried gourd the size of a large grapefruit. You'll need to cut it so that you have a rounded container with a three inch opening on one side. In Brazil, instead of going to a piano tuner or hardware store for wire, you'd probably cut a wire from an old bicycle tire. You'd have to cut the rubber off in the inside hole of the tire until you exposed the steel wire. Then you'd pull the wire with your pliers and sand off all the rubber.

good luck and happy music making!

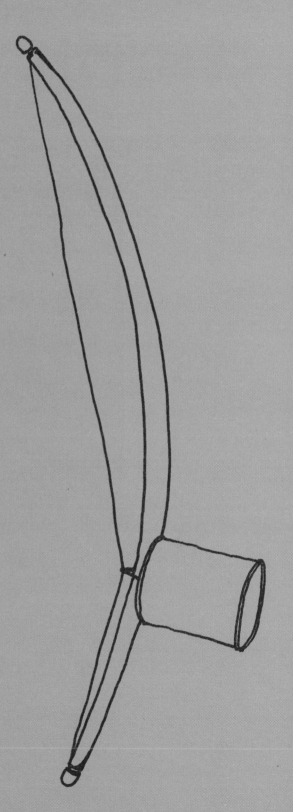

hums, drums and chickens-in-a-cup

I firmly believe that we humans are ALL born musicians (and artists, and poets, and creators...) There is a proverb from southern Africa that says, "If you can walk, you can dance; if you can talk, you can sing." We should stop thinking of music as a spectator sport and reclaim it as our birthright. In this way we'll discover our inner power as well as a great source of joy.

Have you ever heard that question about the tree falling in the forest? You know, does the tree make any sound if there's no one there to hear it? You could think about that one for a long time. My husband is a philosopher and this is the kind of question he spends his time trying to answer. But, frankly, I'd rather **make** sounds…loud sounds, soft sounds, noises and music.

For example, when I was your age, my friends and I would sit outside and blow lightly over the rims of empty Coke bottles. Because we lived close to Lake Michigan, we were trying to imitate the sound of the fog horn we heard warning the freighters to look out for fog banks and shoals. These days, I travel around the world sharing music with people of all ages. And when I'm home with my husband and two daughters, we're always singing. We sing when we wash dishes, while we're driving in the car, and when we're getting ready to go to bed. So music is a big part of my life.

If you're reading this book, you must also be someone who likes to make all different kinds of sounds. That's why I thought I'd tell you some of my ideas of how to

by Sally
Rogers

Sally Rogers

Photo: Susan Wilson

make musical instruments (some people might call them noisemakers) using stuff you probably have around your house.

To help you make these instruments work well, there's a little bit you need to know about the science of instrument building. Do you know what you need to make a sound? Think of different instruments you've heard. What do they all have in common? A scientist would tell you that some part of them vibrates.

If you were a scientist studying an orchestra, you'd notice strings vibrating when they were bowed or plucked, reeds vibrating when someone played the oboe or clarinet and a column of air vibrating when the flute played. You'd see the lips of the trumpet players vibrating in their mouthpieces, and all the percussion instruments themselves would be trembling, not from fear, but from being struck by drumsticks and mallets.

As you play the Chicken-in-a-Cup, the Jelly Donut Drums, the Straw Horns, and the Glass Harmonica, see if you can figure out what part of the instrument makes the sound. If you're not getting any sound, ask yourself, "Which part should be vibrating to make the sound?" Then you can make tiny changes to that part until you get it to work. Kind of like a scientific experiment.

chicken-in-a-cup

When I was thirteen, I lived in Brazil for a year. I especially loved the Samba parades at Carnival time. (Like Mardi Gras, it's a celebration right before Lent.) In those Samba bands, people play an instrument called a *guica* (GWEE-kah). Chicken-in-a-Cup is my version of a homemade guica.

What You'll Need:
a plastic 4 to 8 oz. disposable cup
2 feet of waxed dental floss
a toothpick
something sharp and pointed to poke a small hole with

How to Make It:
1. Poke a small hole through the center of the cup's bottom. The hole should be just barely big enough so you can thread two strings of dental floss through it. (**Note**—You may need help with this step)

2. Lay a toothpick at the center of the length of floss and tie the floss around it securely. (A square knot works well.)

3. Turn the cup so that the open end is down. Poke both ends of the floss down through the hole. Reach inside the cup and pull the floss until the toothpick lies flat across the cup's bottom. The toothpick should be on the outside of the cup.

How to Play It:

Hold the cup in one hand, the open end toward the floor. Pinch the floss tightly between your thumb and first finger, starting just inside the cup. Jerk the string, letting it slide through your thumb and forefinger. You can pull pretty hard. You need to hold the floss quite tightly to get the "clucking" sound. (You might want to wrap the excess string once around your pinky as well. Try it both ways.)

If you practice, you will be able to play the "chicken" fairly rhythmically and soon you could start your own Samba band!

Troubleshooting: If you don't get a sound, you probably are not holding the floss tightly enough as you pull. Or you might be holding it so loosely that it slides too easily through your fingers. It is the friction of the string against your fingers that gets the string to vibrate, which is what makes the noise.

More Ideas: Try using different kinds of floss or other kinds of string for this instrument. Each different kind will change the sound. Try pulling on the dental floss in the open air without the cup. Although it still vibrates, you can hardly hear it. It is the cup which amplifies the sound of the vibration. (That means it makes the sound louder.) Try making the instrument using cups of different sizes, shapes, and materials.

jelly donut drums

A few years back when I took a trip to Washington, D.C., I was walking down the sidewalk when a group of teenaged boys came tearing down the other side of the street, carrying broom handles and sticks. Startled by their sudden appearance, my first thought was that they were getting ready to begin a huge street fight. Boy, was I wrong! Within thirty seconds, I was listening to some of the best street music I've ever heard. I couldn't help dancing, and I wasn't the only one. Lots of people stopped to listen and, before long, everyone was dancing.

These young drummers were using those broomhandles and broken sticks as drumsticks. Some of their drums were metal garbage cans turned upside down, but the

best sounds came from white plastic pails. They beat on the sides and bottoms of those pails and created an amazing assortment of sounds. They performed for us for about half an hour. Then, as quickly as they'd started, they stopped playing, gathered up the tips we'd given them, and took off for another street corner. The only thing they left behind were our memories of their beat.

In me, they also left a longing for one of those large white plastic pails. When I got home, I asked around. I found out that when donut shops buy jelly filling, it comes in plastic pails like the ones those street musicians used. The fillings come in different size pails (one to five gallons). If you ask for a pail once the jelly's all gone, the donut shop might give it to you or might ask you to pay fifty cents or a dollar. Very cheap drums! When I play them, I like to call them my Jelly Donut Drums. I still can't match the rhythms I heard that day in Washington, D.C., but at least I have the drum to practice on. And now you know where to go to get your own set of Jelly Donut Drums.

straw horn band

Have you ever tried to make a loud noise with a piece of grass in the summertime? You just place the flat blade (as wide as you can find) between your two thumbs and blow hard until you get it to vibrate. I still do this every summer! Well, this straw horn sounds a lot like a piece of grass. But, unlike the grass blade, you can change this horn's note. That's why you can get a group of friends together and make a straw horn band.

What You'll Need:
soft plastic drinking straws, like the ones at fast-food restaurants
a pair of scissors
a permanent marker

How to Make It:
1. Mark a dot on the edge of one end of the straw. (**Note**-If you're good at imagining spots on straws, you can do both this step and step two without actually marking your straw. Just imagine those three points, and go to step three, where you'll cut from one imaginary point to the next.)

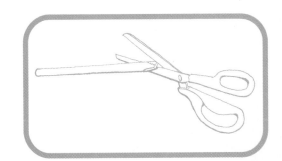

2. Keeping your first mark so it is halfway across the top of the straw end, make a mark one inch down on each side of the straw, keeping your first dot in the center.

3. Cut a small wedge from each side of the straw, connecting each side mark with the center one. You will have made two pointed flaps. The flaps are actually a double reed, like those on an oboe.

How to Play It:

1. Place the "reeds" between your lips and blow, keeping your lips tightly puckered around the straw. **Do not bite the straw!**

2. Once you get a sound, keep it going. As you blow, cut off small pieces of the straw and listen to the pitch change. When you hear a note you especially like, stop cutting!

3. Have each person in your group make a different length straw horn. Take turns playing notes. You're like a human pipe organ!

Troubleshooting: If you're not getting a sound, your reed is not vibrating. Try tightening your lips. You could also try moving the straw in and out of your mouth as you blow. Just move it a little at a time until you get a sound. You may need to trim your reed, making it narrower or evening off the two sides so that they are the same length. Cut it very carefully and only a little at a time.

If a lot of spit is dripping out of your straw, try to stop the saliva river. It doesn't help the sound and it's gross!

If worse comes to worst, you can always cut off the end you've been working on and start over! But don't give up!

More Ideas: If you really want to be like a human pipe organ, have your group of straw horns stand in order from lowest to highest. Try to play some simple songs, one note at a time. You may need to pick a conductor to point at each person when it's time for that horn's note. Remember, it's hard to play the straw horn and laugh at the same time!

glass harmonica

This is inspired by a haunting musical instrument popular in the late 1700s. If you'd like to see an elaborate version, look for a picture of the "Glass Armonica" designed by that American wonderman, Ben Franklin.

What You'll Need:

4-8 matching glasses or goblets (the thinner the glass, the better)
pitcher of water

How to Make It:

1. Line your glasses up on a counter.
2. Pour different amounts of water into each glass. The one on the left should have the least amount of water and the one on the right should have the most.
3. Test the note each glass plays by tapping it **lightly** with the side of a spoon. You can "tune" the glasses by adding or pouring out a little bit of water at a time.
4. Wet the rim of each glass. Now wet your finger. Rub your wet finger gently around the rim until it begins to make a sound. Try making up a tune by using all the glasses.

If you're lucky enough to have eight of the same glasses or goblets, you can adjust the water in each glass until you have a "Do-re-mi" scale. Then you can try to play some familiar simple tunes. You might want to ask each member of your straw horn band to choose a glass, and create a glass harmonica band. Again, a conductor might help all of you keep the tune going!

I should warn you that not every set of glasses will give you a complete 8-note scale. I bought some wine glasses and could only get five notes out of the eight glasses. The goblets weren't big enough to make the whole scale.

Parting Words
Have you been thinking about that tree in the forest? Did it make noise when it fell? I wasn't there and neither were you, so how will we ever find out? If you figure it out, let me know. I'll tell my husband.

Troubleshooting: If you're having trouble getting a sound, maybe your finger is too wet, or too dry. You also might be pressing too hard on the glass rim, or not hard enough.

It's possible that the glasses you picked are very hard to use this way. Try making music with a different kind of glass to help discover if it's the glass or your technique that is the problem.

It's also possible that your fingertips are too oily. Wash your hands with soap and water, and try again.

More Ideas: You could try this experiment: Take glasses of different sizes and thicknesses (but not plastic ones). Put 1/2 cup of water (or at least the same measured amount) in each glass. Now tap each one lightly with a spoon. You'll discover that even though they all have the same amount of water, they don't all play the same note. Now try to get them to hum using your wet finger on the rim of each glass. You'll find that some make sounds and others don't, no matter how good your technique is.

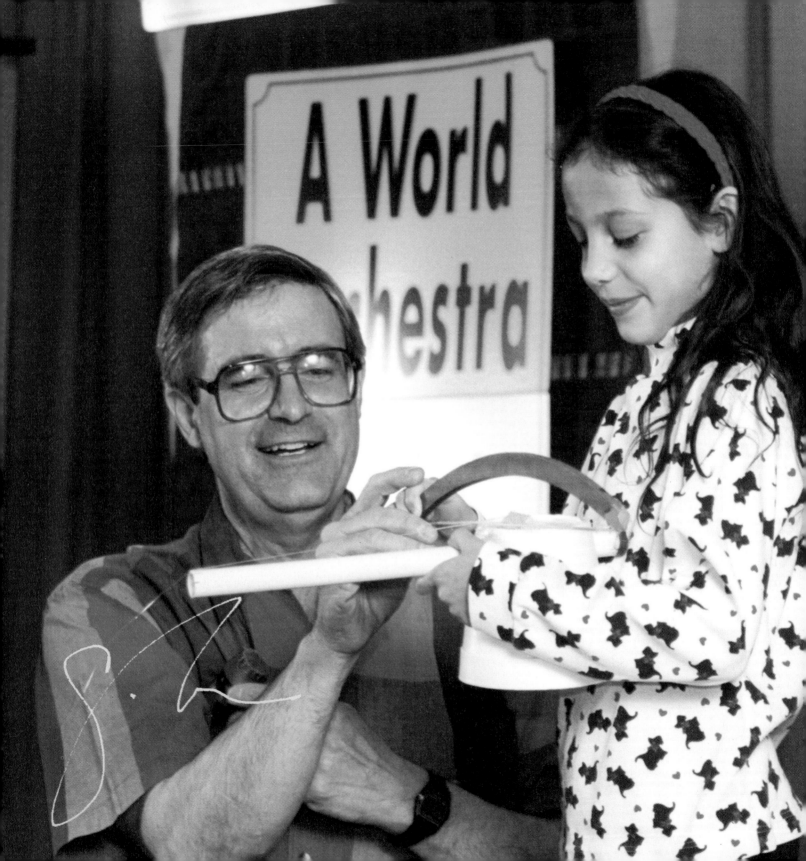

build your own world orchestra

My interest in music and building things began when I was a young child. My mother was a musician and my father was an engineer. It seems like I combined their interests and wound up building music. I would like every child in the world to have an opportunity to make and play a simple musical instrument, then enjoy their own musical performance.

What on earth is a World Orchestra? Is it a group that plays instruments from around the world? Or is it musicians who use instruments made from recycled materials, in an attempt to help protect our planet? Yes and yes! The instruments I describe can help you know more about music from other countries. At the same time, you'll be using materials which are usually thrown away.

And what kind of a doctor am I? I studied music and instrument-building in college and I have a doctorate, or Ph.D., in music. I didn't just stay in one place while I was studying music. I traveled to different countries and saw young people in each country making their own simple instruments. I came back to the U.S. and made a few of my own designs using tools and materials we have around us. Gradually, I developed new designs and now I make over 130 different instruments. I built these instruments the way children around the world might, using common materials and simple designs.

by Dr. Craig Woodson

I am both a musician and a teacher. I travel around America showing students of all ages how to make and play simple musical instruments. Sometimes I work with performance groups like The National Symphony Orchestra, The Cleveland Orchestra or The Kronos String Quartet. In these programs, I help young people in the audience make their own instruments. Then they play along with the professional musicians as an audience orchestra.

As you look over the instruments in this chapter, you'll notice that each instrument represents a different way of making music and each comes from a different part of the world. You shake the *ganzá* from Brazil, you pull the *buhai* from Romania, you pluck the *ānandalaharī* from Bengal and you blow the *ghayta* from Morocco. I'm having you start with the instrument which is the simplest to make, and finish up with the one which is the most challenging. Don't be afraid to ask for help as you work on these projects. Another word for an orchestra is an ensemble, and "ensemble" comes from the French word for "together." Friends who want to be part of a World Orchestra don't just *play music* together. They also help each other every step of the way.

What's the first step? Get your materials together. To make all four instruments, you'll need four 8-ounce styrofoam cups, one 12-ounce styrofoam cup, two teaspoons of dried split peas, a roll of 3/4-inch-wide masking tape, one plastic straw (a spoonstraw, if possible), and dental floss (waxed is best). You'll also need a ruler, scissors, a pencil (newly sharpened), crayons, a toothpick (rounded with pointed ends), and your hands. Yes, your hands are important tools: pinchers, grabbers, scrapers, holders, measuring units, and more!

Instruments of the World Orchestra

Ganzá - rattle from Brazil, South America
Buhai - friction drum from Romania, Europe
Ānandalaharī - string plucker from Bengal, Asia
Ghayta - double reed from Morocco, North Africa

ganzá

If you traveled to Brazil or other parts of South America, you would see popular bands using the ganzá, a rattle filled with beans. During festival times, you would see a lot of ganzás!

What You'll Need:

2 empty, dry styrofoam cups, 8 ounce size

2 teaspoons of dried split peas

3/4 inch wide masking tape

crayons

How to Make It:

1. Put two teaspoons of split peas in one of the cups.

2. Tear off three short pieces of masking tape (as long as your little finger) and stick them to the side of the other cup's opening.

3. Place the cup with the tape on top of the cup with the peas in it with the openings facing each other. Press the tape on the bottom cup to hold the two cups together.

4. Place a piece of tape around the center to join the cups together more securely.

5. Decorate your ganzá with crayons. Be careful not to break the styrofoam cups.

How to Play It:

1. Hold the ganzá by grasping the middle area, that you just taped, between your thumb and first two fingers of your hand.

2. Shake the instrument with a back and forth motion as if you are waving hello to yourself.

> **Troubleshooting:** The sound comes from the sides of the cup. If you touch those areas, the sound will not be as loud.

> **More Ideas:** The rattle makes different sounds depending on how you shake it. Use the back and forth motion to explore different rhythms.

buhai

In Romania, this instrument would be made from a small barrel with a goat skin tacked on one end. A bunch of horsehair is pulled through a hole in the center of the goatskin drumhead. When the horsehair is pulled with a sliding motion, it makes the drumhead roar. The buhai is used for sound effects: to create ghost sounds and animal sounds.

What You'll Need:

one styrofoam cup, 12-ounce size

3/4-inch-wide masking tape

ruler

crayons

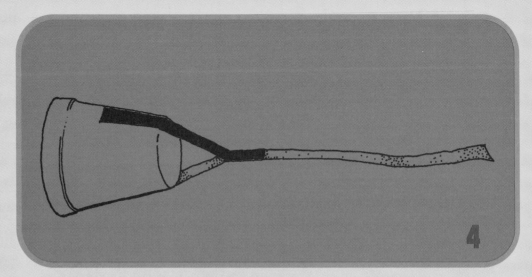

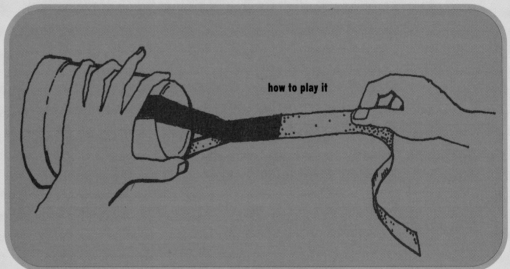

how to play it

How to Make It:

1. Use the ruler to measure out two pieces of tape: tear off one three-inch-long piece of tape and one nine inch long piece.

2. Stick one piece of tape on the edge of the bottom of the cup so the tape hangs down from the cup.

3. Place the other piece of tape so that it hangs down from the opposite side of the cup's bottom edge.

4. Pinch the short piece to the long piece. When you stick them together, the two pieces of tape under the cup will make a capital letter "Y."

5. Decorate your cup with crayons.

How to Play It:

1. Hold the cup around the bottom with your thumb and index finger.

2. Place your thumb on the sticky side of the tape. Gently pinch the tape between your thumbprint and the fingerprint of your index finger.

3. Slide your gentle "pinch" down the tape and the friction sound will begin. Remember—don't pinch too hard.

> **More Ideas:** To get a low-pitched sound, pull slowly and loosely all of the way down the tape. To get a high-pitched sound, pull with a tighter pinch and a faster motion, and just slide a short distance (1-2 inches).

ānandalaharī

This instrument is based on a string instrument used by folk musicians in Bengal (east India). The traditional instrument could have one or two strings. We will make a one-string version. First, you'll prepare the cup as an amplifier, then you'll prepare the string. You'll also use tape to make a pick for plucking your ānandalaharī.

What You'll Need:

> **one styrofoam cup, 8-ounce size**
> **waxed dental floss**
> **3/4-inch masking tape**
> **round, pointed toothpick**
> **ruler**

How to Make It:

1. Tear off a one-inch piece of masking tape and stick it to the center of the outside bottom of the cup.

2. With the point of your toothpick, push a hole through the center of the tape, piercing the cup's bottom.

3. Place a second piece of masking tape one inch long on the inside of the cup, covering the hole you just made.

4. Use the toothpick point exactly as you did in step 2 to punch the hole again; this time you will also poke through the new piece of tape on the cup's inside bottom. You now have a cup with a piece of tape on both the inside and outside of its bottom, and a hole through the middle of its bottom about the same size of a toothpick. This is the amplifier for your ānandalaharī. (That means the cup will "amplify" the sound, making the sound louder.)

5. Measure out a 24-inch piece of dental floss. Fold it in half and join the ends together.

6. Tear off a 4-inch piece of masking tape and press the joined ends of the dental floss onto one end of the tape. The floss and tape should look like a flag (the tape) on a pole (the floss.)

7. Fold a small section of the tape over the floss. You should have a square of tape containing the floss and still have a sticky tape "flag" extending from the non-sticky square. (The square is not sticky because that part of the tape is stuck together with the floss inside it.)

8. Wrap the floss twice around the non-sticky square of tape.

9. Finish wrapping the tape around the floss. You have created a square of masking tape which will make a sturdy end for your string.

10. Pull the floss to a point at the other end. Push that point through the hole in your cup amplifier.

11. Tear off a 4-inch piece of masking tape and press it to the untaped end of the floss. The floss and tape should again look like a flag on a pole.

12. Now repeat steps 7 to 9 to finish off the other end of the floss. You now have a cup pierced by a doubled length of dental floss; squares of masking tape are on each end of the floss.

13. To make a pick to pluck the string, tear off a six inch piece of tape. Fold the tape over itself one inch at a time, so that you end up with a one inch by 3/4-inch piece of thick tape.

How to Play It:

1. Hold the cup's bottom with one hand.

2. Bite the taped end with your teeth and pull the string tightly.

3. Hold the pick in your other hand and pluck up and down on the string.

> **More Ideas:** If you don't have a toothpick, you could use a sharpened pencil to make the hole in the bottom of the cup. You could also try using kite string instead of dental floss.
>
> When you're playing, try plucking near the middle of the string. Then try plucking near one end of the floss.
>
> Another possible position to use when playing your anandalahari is to hold the cup under your armpit, pinch the taped end of the floss between the fingers of the same hand, pull the string tightly, and use your other hand to hold the pick and pluck.

ghayta

Traditionally, the tube of this instrument would be made out of apricot wood and the double reed mouthpiece would be made from a river reed wrapped into a "V" shape. Musicians in Morocco play the ghayta to entertain those who come to the marketplace.

What You'll Need:

plastic straw
one styrofoam cup, 8-ounce size
3/4-inch masking tape
medium-sized scissors
ruler
newly-sharpened pencil

How to Make It:

1. Choose one end of the straw to be your reed. Pinch that end to slightly flatten it, then cut triangular pieces off each side it so that it is flat at the top with slanted sides as shown. It should resemble the shape of a steeple. This trimmed end is called a double reed.

2. To make a finger hole, pinch the straw around one inch up from the other end. Use the scissors to cut across the raised section created by your pinch. You should have made an oval-shaped hole.

3. Pinch another spot one inch higher up the straw (towards the reed) and use the same method to cut a second hole.

4. Take the cup and turn it upside down, so that you are looking at the cup's bottom. Press your pencil point into the center of the bottom of the cup.

5. Slide the flat end of the straw into this hole until there is about 1/4 inch of the straw inside the cup. The rest of the straw is above the cup, with the reed at the top.

6. Tape several pieces of masking tape from the straw to the cup so that the cup is securely attached to the straw.

How to Play It:

1. Place the reed into your mouth (about one inch inside your lips) and pinch down with your lips (like women do when putting lipstick on). Be sure not to bite or press down on the reed itself since that is the area that has to move around to get sound.

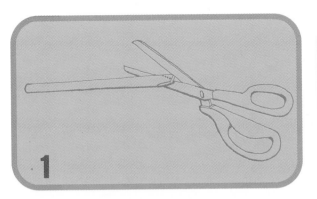

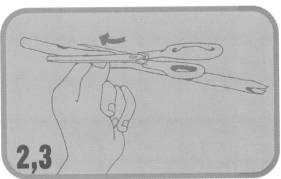

1

2,3

2. Blow with a lot of pressure (like blowing bubbles in water with a straw).

3. Keep the straw supported by your thumb, and use the pads or fingerprints of your index fingers to cover and uncover the fingerholes. Cover both holes for the lowest sound, leave both holes open for the highest sound, and cover just the hole nearest the reed for a sound in the middle.

> **More Ideas:** If you can find a spoonstraw, use that instead of a regular plastic straw. It makes a better instrument. First, cut off the spoon. Then follow the directions for making the ghayta.
>
> If you want to change the sound of your ghayta's three note scale, you can vary the distance between the holes or between the lowest hole and the cup. Slight changes can make big differences.

Garry Kvistad

garry's garbage band

Making an instrument is one of music's greatest joys...Almost no pleasure is to be compared with the first tones, tests and perfections of an instrument one has just made. Nor are all instruments invented and over with...The world is rich with models —but innumerable forms, tones, and powers await their summons from the mind and hand. Make an instrument—you will learn more in this way than you can imagine. Lou Harrison - American composer (b. 1917)

I'm going to show you how to make a garbage band. If you're like me, you've got all sorts of forgotten stuff collecting in drawers and heaped in piles in your garage because you just knew it would come in handy someday. You were right! Now's the time to pull it out and use it to make instruments.

As Lou Harrison points out, there are all kinds of instruments waiting for you to summon them. I've got a few suggestions to get you going. The Colaphone, for example.

by Garry Kvistad

colaphone

What You'll Need:

8 glass bottles with screw caps (16 oz. works well)
water
wooden spoon
masking tape
permanent marker

How to Make It:

1. Use the tape and marker to label the bottles from 1 to 8.

2. Fill each bottle with water. Start on the left and fill bottle 1 until it is almost full. Put less water in each bottle until you reach bottle 8, which should have the least amount of water.

3. Tune your Colaphone. When you tap them with the spoon, the bottles should play the notes of a "do re mi" scale. Bottle 8 should play the same note as bottle 1, but one octave higher. Use a piano, a toy xylophone, or your voice as a guide. Add or pour out water from each bottle until your Colaphone sounds right. Adding water makes the sound lower; pouring water out makes the sound higher. Replace the caps.

How to Play It:

1. Tap the sides of the bottles with the wooden spoon.

2. If you remove bottles 4 and 7, you'll have a 5-note pentatonic scale. This scale is more common in the music of countries like Asia and Africa, sometimes called "non-western" music. A song you might know that uses the pentatonic scale is "I'd like to Teach the World to Sing." Try to play it by following this musical "score." (a "score" tells musicians what notes to play.)

21242124   256565   65686568   645424

3. Write down your own musical scores, using the numbers on the bottles to record the songs you make up on your own.

4. Try a "trill." Jiggle the stick back and forth between two bottles.

5. Rearrange the bottles so that when you tap from left to right, the notes play a melody. Here's an example: **6451**. What does that sound like? (Big Ben clock chime)

Troubleshooting: If you can't get a complete scale with 16 oz. bottles, try using some other size bottles to play the missing notes.

More Ideas: Hear what happens when you tilt a bottle on its side as you tap it — the sound changes.

Now compare blowing into a bottle to tapping the bottle. Almost everyone has created sounds by blowing into a partially empty glass bottle. If you add liquid to that bottle and blow again, the sound gets higher. Why? Because you're making the column of air smaller, and it's the air that's vibrating when you blow into a bottle.

The opposite is true of your Colaphone. When you tap a bottle, then add water to it, the sound gets lower. Why? Because this time, it's the glass that's vibrating. When you add water, you're making what vibrates heavier, there are fewer vibrations per minute, and that leads to a lower sound.

juice jug sekere (Say "shake-er-ay")

This instrument is styled after a Nigerian rhythm instrument, made of beads or shells strung around a gourd; similar instruments are found in many other parts of Africa. I like thinking of the sekere as an inside-out maraca, since the beads are strung around the outside of the resonating chamber (a gourd, or in this case, a plastic jug) instead of being contained inside. The result is a much louder sound with a sharper rhythm.

What You'll Need:

Empty 42 oz. plastic juice jug (those with ribbed sides, like Juicy Juice, give off the best sound)

ziti and elbow macaroni (uncooked)

8 pieces of thin but strong string (each 38 inches long)

3 pieces of thin but strong string (each 24 inches long)

How to Make It:

1. As you're making this sekere, keep in mind that it's important to tie all knots very tightly! Double knot each knot and then trim the excess string only when you are all finished. Do not trim too close to the knot — leave ends of at least one inch. All excess string can be hidden in the ziti.

2. Begin by stringing 8 ziti (the larger macaroni) onto one of the 24-inch pieces of string. Make a "belt" by tying this firmly around the middle of your jug.

3. Make a second horizontal band around the bottom of your jug. Use the second 24-inch length of string and 8 more ziti. Tie firmly.

4. Your third horizontal band will be a "necklace" at the top of the jug. Use the third piece of 24-inch string and 4 ziti. Tie it firmly around the mouth of your jug.

5. Once you have three horizontal bands, use the remaining string and the elbow macaroni to make 8 vertical bands. Tie one end of each of the 38-inch pieces of string to the "necklace." (You'll be tying two pieces of string in between each piece of ziti.)

6. One by one, thread elbow macaroni onto each piece of string. When you reach the "belt", wind the vertical string once around the "belt" string, then resume threading macaroni down the side of the jug. When you reach the bottom band, again wind the string once. Wait to tie the final knot.

Try to keep the same number of macaronis in the "necklace" to "belt" section, and in the "belt" to bottom section.

At the middle and bottom of your jug, each vertical string should be separated by a ziti.

All of the vertical bands should be strung a little looser than the horizontal bands.

7. Thread more elbow macaroni onto each of the strings hanging from the bottom ziti band. Tie all eight of the elbow macaroni strings together at the place where they meet on the jug's bottom. This whole procedure may sound a little tricky, but with patience, you'll be able to get it to work!

How to Play It:

Grasp the mouth of the bottle and shake to a steady rhythm. You can also create rhythms by holding the macaroni and twisting the bottle—this will rotate the jug and the macaroni will rub against the ribbed surface. Or, hit the sekere alternately between your thigh and the palm of your hand (similar to the technique used when playing the spoons).

More Ideas: Use beads, buttons, or shells instead of the dried macaroni to make a more colorful instrument. Or you could color the macaroni before you use it.

garden hose horn

Horns shaped like this were first played as hunting signals and later became part of the orchestra. Valves were added to create the modern French horn.

Before making your horn, try using the hose as a telephone between you and a friend—all you need to do is whisper into one end and the other person will hear you loud and clear! Why? Tubes channel sound. The hose gives your voice a clear and protected path for traveling from you to your friend.

What You'll Need:

old garden hose (at least 2 feet long)
2 empty plastic bottles (2-liter bottles work best)
duct or masking tape
permanent marker

How to Make It:

1. Cut the metal connectors (the parts that attach to a faucet or sprinkler) from the ends of the hose.

2. Check the hose for holes. Seal any holes you find with tape.

3. Make a mark on one of your bottles about 4-5 inches down from the top. Starting at your mark, draw a line around the bottle until you have divided the bottle into two parts. The top part should resemble the shape of a funnel.

4. Cut along your line. Your plastic "funnel" should be about 4-5 inches long and 4-5 inches in diameter.

5. Tape this "funnel" to one end of the hose. This is the bell of your horn. (Like the bell of a trumpet.)

6. On the top of your second bottle, cut right below the rim which held the cap on. You should have a piece which is about 1-1/2 inches long. This is your mouth piece.

7. Place your mouthpiece over the other end of the hose, with the end you cut touching the hose. You will be blowing into the "top" of the bottle. You may need to use several layers of tape to keep the mouthpiece in place.

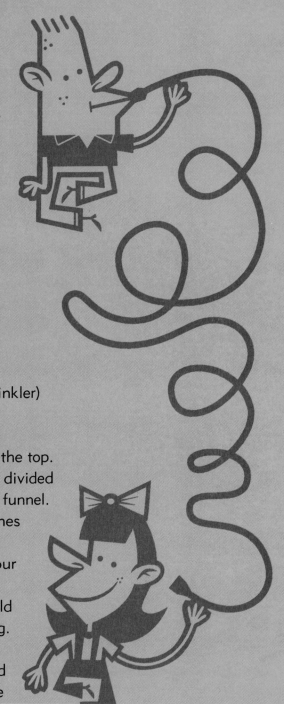

How to Play It:

1. With tight, pursed lips, blow into the mouthpiece with a buzzing sound.
2. You can change the pitch (make the sound higher or lower) by tightening or loosening your lips.
3. By covering and uncovering the funnel with your hand while you're blowing, you can create a "wah-wah" effect like a trumpet player.

junkyard jinglestick

Sticks with bells like these are played throughout the world. Some names for them are the Jingling Johnny, Njuka Jingle Stick and the Turkish Crescent.

What You'll Need:

An old wooden broom handle or straight stick (about 4 feet long)
a wooden spoon
2 aluminum pie plates
2 aluminum cans, one large and one small
dried beans or seeds
metal bottle tops (the kind used on beer bottles)
screws with washers or double stick foam tape
duct tape or stapler
nails
hammer

How to Make It:

1. Lay the stick flat on the ground.
2. Attach one pie plate to the stick with several screws and washers or with the double-stick foam tape.
3. Fill the pie plate with dried beans or seeds and cover with the second pie plate. Seal edges of the two pie plates with tape or staples.
4. Flatten the bottle caps with a hammer.
5. Use one nail to attach two flattened bottle caps loosely to the stick. Add more sets of bottle cap jinglers.
6. Put the two cans together side by side. Wrap tape around them until they are firmly joined together. Then use tape to attach them to your jinglestick so that the cans do not move.

How to Play It:

1. Stamp the Junkyard Jinglestick on the ground and you'll have a great rhythm instrument.

2. Hold the Jinglestick in one hand while you tap the two cans with the wooden spoon, beating out different rhythms. Now try to tap all the noisemakers while you're stamping out a steady Jinglestick beat.

3. Play along with a record. Use your Jinglestick to make a racket at the end of every sentence or phrase of the song.

4. You can also use this instrument as a type of rainstick by holding it horizontally in the air and rotating it gently.

More Ideas: Find a rubber crutch tip or little kid's sneaker and put it on the bottom of the stick to cushion the impact. If you want a sturdier rhythm instrument, one to withstand a hurricane of music, use the screws to attach an old metal pie plate to the stick; you could still use an aluminum pie plate for the cover. Similarly, you could nail or screw the aluminum cans in place.

Don't stop with pie plates, 2 aluminum cans and bottle caps. Look around for anything that can be shaken or hit, anything that will make a sound you like. Use more cans of all sizes, bike bells, containers filled with dried macaroni or rice. Attach the noisemakers to the stick in whatever way is most practical: string, tape, screws, staples.

Add long rubber bands or old springs; stretch them out as you're playing, and let them snap back, making all sorts of surprising sounds. Before you know it, you'll have changed your Jinglestick into a One Man-Band!

Here's a challenge! Try tapping the different noisemakers twice as fast as you're stamping. (Tap, tap/stamp, tap, tap/stamp, tap, tap/stamp)

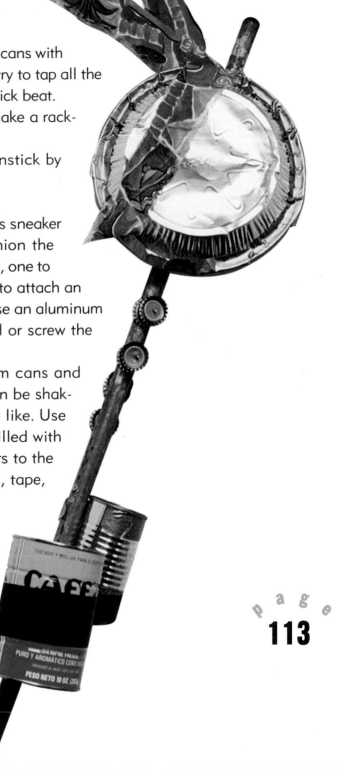

1. Invite friends to join your band. Have everyone spend some time exploring each individual instrument. Each person will discover something new that others did not see. Share your ideas!

2. Find a steady beat and have everyone play it together. Have one person play a little louder and skip one or two beats. Then have that person return to the group beat. After a few beats, have another person play louder and change the rhythm slightly. In this way, each player can create their own solo.

3. Have one person start playing a simple tune on the Cola-Phone, like "Twinkle, Twinkle, Little Star." Here is the musical score:

11 55 66 5 (rest)	**44 33 22 1** (rest)
55 44 33 2 (rest)	**55 44 33 2** (rest)
11 55 66 5 (rest)	**44 33 22 1** (rest)

"Rest" means pause (don't play).

Add rhythm by having the other musicians (sekere, garden hose horn, and jinglestick) come in one at a time. As the song builds and all the instruments are added, remember to listen to the other players. If you hear someone else playing a rhythm you like, try it on your instrument. It's fun to hear how musicians respond to each other. This is the beauty of playing music together!

4. You can rehearse by yourself by using a tape recorder to record the music you make. Then you can play it back and accompany yourself!

Final Thoughts
In the 1940s, a performer named Spike Jones and his band, The City Slickers, made music with instruments made from junk-tin cans, old car horns, hammers and plungers. These days, audiences have been flocking to see a show called *Stomp*, a production which features musicians who use brooms, paper bags and newspapers to play amazing rhythms.

Now that you've assembled your own band, remember that music can happen anytime you have a bunch of people together—with or without "real" instruments. And don't forget to check the garbage on a regular basis. The possibilities of what you might find are endless…as endless as the possibilities for instruments you can create from what other people call garbage.

homemade instrument

Ruth Pelham

neighborhood band

"In these challenging times when so many of us feel a yearning for roots and a sense of belonging, we can feel deeply connected to each other by sharing something as seemingly simple as the experience of playing instruments and singing together.

When I was growing up, my family and I loved to make music together. We sang a lot of songs and played along to the beat by tapping a spoon against a pot like a drum, shaking a half empty cereal box like a rattle, or clanking two pot lids together like cymbals. Friends and neighbors who dropped by for a visit would clap their hands, tap their feet, snap their fingers or jingle keys, and they'd become part of the band, too.

I'm grown up now, and I still enjoy making music with things I find around my house that clang, bang, scrape, pluck, and boing. I also love helping people learn more about using their voices and homemade instruments to make music together. So, back in 1977, I dreamed up a way to make this happen by starting an organization called **Music Mobile** which is still going strong today.

I got a van, covered the sides with big bulletin boards, and tacked on beautiful, colorful drawings made by children in the city of Albany, NY, where I live. Then I bolted a big outdoor speaker on the front of the van and wrote a catchy theme song to play as I drove through different neighborhoods. When children heard the music, they'd come running out of their houses. One by one, dozens of them would find the Music Mobile parked in an empty lot or a neighborhood park. We'd sing songs, build and play musical instruments, and make new friends as we all joined together to become a Homemade Instrument Neighborhood Band.

You, too, can start your own Homemade Instrument Neighborhood Band. **First, you'll need other people to be part of your band**. You can have as few as two or three people, or as many as you want. Ask your family, your friends and the kids in your class to join. Ask the people who live on your block, on your road, in your building or in your housing development. Ask people of all different ages. Being in a band is a great way

With every voice, with every song

We will move this world along

And our lives will feel the echo

Of our singing"
from "Turning Of The World" by Ruth Pelham

page
117

by Ruth
Pelham

for people to get to know each other, and you just may be surprised by how many people will want to be part of it!

Next, you'll need to get together with the people in your band to plan what you're going to do. You can start out by inviting the band to a special meeting. You may want to meet at your house, at your school, in the library, or whatever place is easy for all the band members to get to. You'll want to talk about what instruments you're going to play, what songs you're going to sing, where you'll perform, who will be in your audience and how you're going to let people in your neighborhood know about the performance.

You may also want to talk about ways that the people in the band will treat each other. Being considerate of each person is part of any band's success, and is as important as any of the songs or instruments. When you hold meetings, you may want to decide that each person will have a chance to share an opinion before any decision is made. People may want to take turns leading the meeting, just as they may want to take turns conducting the band. The goal is for everyone to feel like a valued member of the group.

You'll need to decide what instruments you want to make and play. Musicians make many different sounds by tapping, scraping, plucking, blowing or shaking their instruments. Think about what kind of instrument each band member likes to play. And remember, you can invent new instruments by experimenting with the sounds made from everyday things like coat hangers, cardboard tubes, cans, bottlecaps and rubber bands. Let me tell you about two of the many instruments that I teach people how to make. I call one a Balloon Drum Rattle and the other a Scraper-Can-Chime.

balloon drum rattle

The Balloon Drum Rattle is a fun musical instrument that takes less than 15 minutes to make!

What You'll Need:

an empty tuna fish or cat food can

tape

a large balloon (a 12-inch round balloon works best)

20-30 pieces of dry macaroni

a pair of scissors

a piece of construction paper (optional)

crayons or markers (optional)

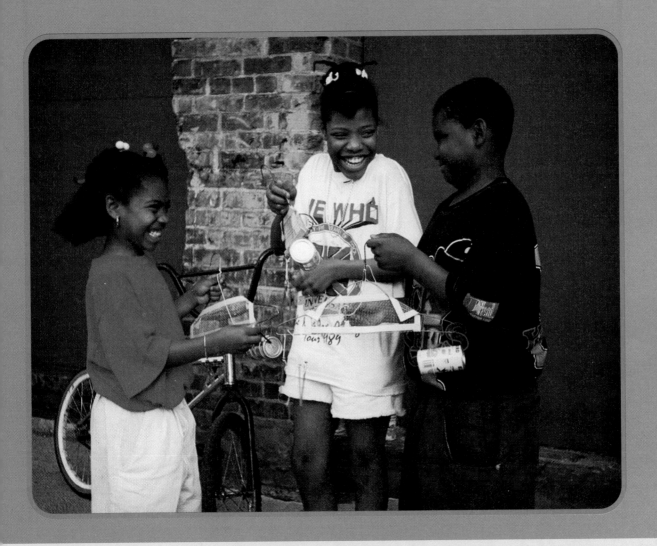

fun **making** music to stop and think, "I'm singing off key — I'd better not sing!" or "I don't know how to play these spoons — I'd better not play!" Instead, we were making music that was ours, music that came from the rhythms and feelings inside us, and from being together with each other in a spirit of friendship and community.

How about putting this book down now so you can make some music that is **yours?** Call up some friends and neighbors, round up the people you live with, and have fun! Go into the kitchen and play the pots and pans. Look around the house for things you can put together to make some new and different sounds. Sing the songs you love. Make up some new songs. Once you've done all that, give yourselves a big, big round of applause for becoming your own special Homeade Instrument Neighborhood Band!

make-at-home sound effects

I know that when I make sound effects I sometimes look and sound goofy, but I also know that when I do my sound effects just right, the story being told comes to life and it's fun, too!

Hello, my name is Tom Keith and I like to make noises—lots of noises. I work on a radio show where they tell stories, and I make sounds (or sound effects) that help the story seem more real. For example, if the storyteller mentions that a horse pulling a carriage passed by, I somehow have to make the sound of a horse pulling a carriage. I suppose I could get a real horse and carriage, but there usually isn't enough room. Instead, I get two coconut shell halves and hit them together for the sound of the horse's hooves trotting on the pavement, and at the same time jingle a ring of keys for the sound of the carriage. Other times I make sounds using my voice, like when a cat meows or a dog barks or an ocean wave crashes on a seashore. So, as you can see, there are lots of ways to make sound effects.

by Tom Keith

To give you an idea of how all this works, let me suggest some things you could use to make sound effects that would help to tell a story called "Flash in the Dark." Here's a list of the things you'll need:

A pair of shoes

A small paper bag like what you would get when you buy something from the drug store.

A door that's easy to open and shut

A newspaper

A piece of waxed paper

A cover to a cooking pot and a spoon

A comb and more waxed paper

A tape recorder and blank cassette (if you want to record your efforts)

You'll know what to do with most of these objects when the time comes, but you may want to practice using the comb and waxed paper. Take the comb and with the teeth of the comb facing down, fold the waxed paper over the teeth. Hold the waxed paper tightly against the comb and place the comb so that your lips are just touching the waxed paper. Gently hum into it so your lips buzz. It might take some practice and it might tickle. (As well as using this for the sound effects in this story, you can also use it like a kazoo.) Here are some of the sounds you'll need to make with your voice:

An owl: say "whoo-whoo whoo-whoo" using a medium-high voice .

A dog howl: "ow-ooo."

A horse whinny: say "neeee" in a high voice and laugh at the same time.

The sound of wind: pucker your lips like you are going to whistle but instead of blowing real hard you blow just hard enough to get a soft whistle; sometimes it takes a lot of breath.

I think that is all you'll need. So now it's time to get started. I find that it's easier when one person tells the story and another person does the sound effects. Whoever reads the story should know that any words surrounded by ( ) should not be read. Those words let the sound effects person know what sound to make at that point in the story.

Here's the story: The morning after Halloween I woke up and discovered I had no electricity in my house. None of my clocks worked and I had no idea what time it was, but then I heard the bell at City Hall strike five o'clock **(hold the cooking pot cover by the handle and gently strike the edge with a spoon five times)**. Since the electric furnace wasn't working, the house was cold so I thought I should start a fire in the fireplace. I lit a candle, got up, and started walking to the living room. **(hold a shoe in each hand by the top and hit**

the bottom of the heels together and then the toes to create the sound of walking, but don't go too fast). Luckily I had the logs and paper ready to go, so I used the candle to set my paper on fire which soon had the logs burning with a glow that warmed the house (take a piece of waxed paper and gently roll it around in your hands for the sound of a fire).

Now that I was awake I decided to go to the mailbox and see if the morning paper had arrived. I walked to the door and opened it (use the shoes for the same walking sound as before, then open the door). It was very dark outside and my mailbox was at the end of my long driveway. I could hear the wind (wind sound) rustling the leaves in the trees (gently rustle the paper bag). High up in one of the trees I heard an owl ("whoo-whoo whoo-whoo"). I stepped outside (close door) and mounted my trusty horse, Flash (sound of horse whinnying), and started down my driveway toward the mailbox (cup your hands and gently hit your chest with the rhythm of a horse slowly galloping).

Suddenly, the moon came out from behind the clouds and lit up my driveway, so I could see the mailbox waaay at the end of the lane. Then, in the distance, I could hear dogs howling at the moon (dogs howling) and decided maybe I should hurry up (faster galloping sound). I finally reached the mailbox, and when I opened it and pulled out the paper, out flew a bee that started buzzing all around me (comb and waxed paper — use a high pitched hum like the sound a bee would make). I took the paper and swung at the bee several times trying to scare it off, but it just kept flying all around me. Finally I took one big swing and the bee disappeared (stop buzzing). I had no idea where the bee went, but I didn't want to stick around to find out.

I turned Flash toward the house (whinny) and raced back up the driveway (fast gallop). As soon as we got back to the house, (say, "Whoa, boy!"), I jumped off of Flash and ran into the house (open door and then close door). I stood leaning against my door until I could catch my breath. Finally I walked (sound of walking with shoes) to the chair near the fire (sound of fire) and sat down. When I opened the paper, out flew the bee (buzzing sound), and it started flying all around me. All I could do was sit very still until it landed on my shoulder. I then realized that the bee didn't want to hurt me. It just wanted to sit by the fire and get warm just like me.

You sure got busy near the end of the story with all of those sound effects, didn't you? Now it's your turn to make up a story. Can you think of a completely different story using the same sound effects? Here are a couple more things you can use:

Macaroni from a box of macaroni and cheese for the sound of eating bugs.

An old piece of cloth for a tearing cloth sound.

A styrofoam picnic plate for the sound of wood breaking.

Kitty litter in a box for the sound of walking on a gravel path.

Be sure that you get permission to use these items for your sound effects. Now use your imagination and have fun!

it's

Fred Penner

showtime!

There are so many wonderful things to do in this world, so much to learn, and so much to share with others. Be PROUD of who you are, and keep the music in your heart

Now that you've made some instruments and explored making musical sounds, are you thinking about sharing your talents with an audience? If you are, read on. There are many different kinds of performances. You can start by putting on an informal show with your friends and family. My four children are constantly calling my wife and me into the living room for their latest production. Sometimes we see an instant show, something they just dreamed up that afternoon. Other times, we enter a space that has been changed into a theater, and it's clear that a lot of time and thought was put into the performance.

What kind of things do performers need to think about when they're planning their show? You'll need to ask yourself:

Who's going to be in the show?
What kind of show do we want to do?
Where will we perform?
How can we make sure the audience can see and hear?

Who's Performing What?

Talk about the show with your friends until you find some who wants to join in. (If you're like my kids, you might include brothers and sisters. The advantage of using family members is that you're all under one roof, which makes rehearsing easier.) Then decide what kind of show you want to do. Will you play music, sing songs, dance, tell stories, act out a story together? Do you want to

by Fred
Penner

have a variety show, where you have a little of everything? It is important that each performer knows what he or she is going to do. Once you have a clear idea of your performance and your cast is excited and raring to go, the fun (and the work) begins!

planning for your audience

Step 1: Choosing a Performing Area
Remember, if your audience is human, they have eyes and ears. So you need to think about what you want them to see and hear. Start by deciding where you're going to hold your show. A performance can happen anywhere, inside or outside, as long as there's enough space for both the performers and the people who will see it. So ask yourself, "Where is this show going to happen?"

Will it be in someone's basement or playroom?
Will it be outside in a backyard?
Can you use the school playground or a real stage?
How about a living room or somebody's grandfather's barn?

Make sure you get permission to use the space before you start getting it ready for your show. (And be aware, if you're performing outside, that your show may get rained out. Schedule a raindate!)

Step 2: Designing the Stage
When the audience looks at your performing area, what do you want them to think and feel? Many performances use sets and props to build the atmosphere of a show. In Canada, where I live, I do a television show called "Fred Penner's Place." I want the people who watch my show to think about

how nice it is to be outside. So my set has lots of trees and rocks and tunnels and a hollow log. Pay attention to the sets used on some of the movies or television programs you like. Notice how different sets make you feel. What can you do in your performing area to create a similar mood? You may not be able to set up next to the ocean, but you could put out a beach towel and a lot of seashells and drape some blue filmy cloth over some chairs to suggest water. Think about the details: costumes, hats, particular tables and chairs, plants and flowers, posters, draped sheets and tablecloths. These are all things that can give your stage a special feeling.

Step 3: Lights

If you're not going to be setting up particular lights, make sure you've picked a well lit space. Your show will be much more fun for the audience if they can see the performers. In a traditional theater, the stage is brighter than the audience, and you might want to try to set up special lights to give that effect. Lighting is a job that should only be done by older members of your cast, since lights equals electricity, and those who don't know what they're doing could get bad shocks or start fires.

A simple spotlight that can be controlled by even the youngest members of your cast is a flashlight. You could create a colored spotlight by shining the flashlight through a thin colored cloth. The idea behind spotlights, plain or colored, is to give your stage a feeling of excitement, so that your audience has the sense that this is a place where something wonderful is going to happen.

Step 4: Sound

So far, we've been planning for the audience's eyes. Now it's time to think about ears. Before your show has started, while your audience is coming in, think about playing some music for them. Whether they're hearing live performers or taped music, the audience starts to feel that they are part of the excitement.

You might also use some sound effects, like the ones you read about in Tom Keith's chapter. (A fast way to write sound effects is "sound fx.") Sometimes sound fx are perfect to surprise the audience and get them ready for the next part of the show, or to announce that the show is about to begin!

Try playing some of your new instruments with some recorded music. It might help the sound of your performance. But you also want to be sure that the tape player doesn't drown you out!

If you're using a big performing area, you may need microphones and a sound system. These can be very tricky. Most performers have professionals who set up both the lighting and sound systems. You might want to do the same. Maybe somebody's parent knows a lot about mikes and wires. Ask for their help!

Practice, Practice, Practice

You want your show to be as good as possible, right? Play your instrument, sing your song, dance your dance. You are getting ready to share a little bit of yourself with others. Rehearsals are important. You can each rehearse your own part, and you should try to have some rehearsals with the whole cast.

When you are in front of an audience, big or small, they deserve the best show you can give them. As well as practicing your part of the show, you need to do general exercises to strengthen your body and your voice. Here are some exercises that I do to get ready for performances.

Body warm-up:

Stretch one arm to the sky, then the other arm.
Left, right, left, right, etc.

Slowly reach down and touch your knees, then your toes.
(You can do an action song like, "Head, Shoulders, Knees, and Toes.")

Shake your hands quickly, so they're loose and wobbly.
Now do the same with your arms, your hips, your legs, your feet.

Voice warm-up

Take a deep breath, let it out with a sound: "Ah-ah-ah-ah-ah"
Do it with each of these:
"Ee-ee-ee-ee-ee"; "i-i-i-i-i"; "oh-oh-oh-oh-oh"; "uu-uu-uu-uu-uu"
Now one more deep breath, and let it out with a mixture of sounds:
"Ah-ee-i-oh-uu"
Say some tongue twisters to relax your mouth:
1) Peter Piper picked a peck of pickled peppers.
2) She sells sea shells by the sea shore.
3) The tip of the tongue, the teeth, the lips.
4) Copper kettles carry comfort killing cough and cold.
5) How much wood would a woodchuck chuck, if a woodchuck could chuck wood?
Try saying each of these ten times. . . . .GOOD LUCK!

This is just a sampling of some of the warm-ups I find helpful. Keep in mind that every performer has a different way of warming up. Now that you have a sense of what kinds of exercises I use, you might want to make up some of your own. Ask other performers you meet for their suggestions. Keep searching until you find just the right warm-ups for you, the ones which help you relax and help your voice and body get prepared to put on a show.

Plan the Flow of the Show

Think carefully about what act you are going to start with. The first piece you present to your audience establishes the mood for the rest of the show. I usually start with a bright up-beat tune that gets the audience's feet tapping. I also like to begin with songs that they know already or songs that have parts they can join in with.

Once you've chosen your opening act, you need to think about the show as a whole. Try to organize the parts of your show so that one act leads into another. That doesn't mean you have to put all the most similar acts together. Sometimes it's good to change the moods, to go from a fast song into a slow one, or from a very happy song into something more thoughtful.

Experiment by putting your acts in different orders and see which seems to make the most sense. You might want to have someone (a Master of Ceremonies) come out and talk to the audience in between each number. The important thing is to make sure that your audience stays interested and enjoys the whole show.

it's showtime!

You have spent a lot of time getting ready for the show, and now all you have to do is DO IT! You've thought carefully about what you want to do. Don't be nervous. Be strong and proud of your talents.

If things aren't going exactly the way you planned, don't let it bother you. Performers have to be ready to adapt to change. Remember, "The show must go on!"

There is nothing like a live performance. The people in the audience are enjoying the people on the stage. Energy is flowing from one human being to another. There are moments when you feel like crying and moments when you laugh out loud and the whole room fills with laughter. Most of all, there's the excitement of creating sounds and pictures for others. If you're like me, you'll discover that as soon as you've finished one show, you can't wait to start planning the next!

Mickey Hart

When the rhythm is right you feel it with all your senses. The head of the drum vibrates as the stick strikes it. The physical feedback is almost instantaneous, rushing along your arms, filling your ears. Your mind is turned off, your judgment wholly emotional. Your emotions seem to stream down your arms and legs and out the mouth of the drum; you feel light, gravityless, your arms feel like feathers. You fly like a bird.

coming full circle

For almost as long as I can remember, playing the drum has stimulated certain changes in my consciousness — my body awareness starts to fade, time disappears. If the rhythm is right, then I know it instantly. *Ahhhh*, I say, this goes with my body tempo, this relates to how I feel today, how fast my heart is beating, what my thoughts are, what my hands feel like. A feeling not unlike trust settles over me as I give myself to the rhythm.

When a group of people pick up drums and rattles and begin to share rhythm, getting in tune with each other and themselves, they start to play with the deeper mysteries of rhythm. As they continue drumming together, a new voice, a collective voice, emerges from the group. This is what I call entraining. Maybe if I tell you about a few times some kids and I experienced this, you'll have a better idea of what I'm talking about.

My old friend Wavy Gravy, was running Camp Winnarainbow in Mendocino County, California, a summer camp for children, and he asked me to come and spend three weeks teaching the kids about drums.

I borrowed one of the Grateful Dead's trucks, and Ram Rod (my equipment manager) packed it with instruments from my collection. I never set out to be a collector of drums; it just happened. Some people like to have lots of cats and dogs around, or art on the walls, or shelves full of mementos. I like drums; they calm me.

Many *bullroarers* went into the truck. One of the most ancient instruments on the planet, the bullroarer is basically a strip of wood with a rope attached that is swung around the head in an arc, emitting a sound that ranges from a slow *whooo* to a piercing shriek. Swing one over your head for ten or fifteen minutes and a globe of sound will form with you at the center.

We also put in *berimbaus*, musical bows from Brazil. The berimbau doesn't make a loud sound, but it's a remarkably penetrating one. You can hear it a long way off, like

by Mickey
Hart

a snake hissing in the jungle. Most instruments that work on your inner core have to be loud. Not the berimbau.

There were also slit gongs, thirty hoop drums, enough instruments for every kid in camp who wanted to really experience rhythm and noise.

What was I up to? I was thinking back to the time I had worked with some kids as part of a pilot program to build self-esteem in children with mental retardation. The people who invited me thought that even the most disabled would be able to play concussion sticks and rattles, that virtually anyone could master noise. But I had also wanted to show these kids that they could create rhythm. I planned to record what happened and then play it back to them at maximum volume—overwhelm them with themselves.

I'd filled several tables with different instruments, rattles on one table, concussion sticks on the other, then demonstrated the sound of each and let the kids choose the one that most appealed to them. At first they were tentative, almost fearful. But the sight of me, acting crazier than any of them, beating on my hoop drum and making animal yells and obviously having a good time, overcame their resistance. Within five minutes we were a percussion orchestra; within fifteen minutes we'd entrained. Just a brief linking up, but they all felt it, because they all stopped and looked around bewildered. It was amazing to watch. They went from noisy ecstasy back to their old condition in seconds. They no longer trusted the instruments.

The only thing that rescued me was the tape. "Listen to yourselves," I'd told them. "You're a percussion orchestra—you're making music!" And then I cranked up the volume and let them hear themselves. They went mad and started laughing in amazement. One young boy, I'd been told was autistic grabbed a *dumbek*, a Middle Eastern drum, and shut himself in a closet where he drummed and chanted for hours.

Now, at Camp Winnarainbow, I hoped to give the kids a similar sense of power, a taste of the spirit side of drumming. The first thing I did after I arrived at camp was to search for a perfect spot, a place that contained magic, power, a place of such presence that all your senses start tingling, as if the volume has been turned up inside you, outside you, everywhere. I hunted around but no place seized me like that, so I asked Wavy for help. He pointed past the lake, toward the crest of a distant, steep hill, upon which sat an immense old redwood hay barn.

It was the most isolated spot in the camp. It felt good to be in this abandoned cathedral-sized building, particularly in the late afternoon when the sun fell at just the right angle revealing all the dust motes and hay chaff dancing in the warm afternoon air. I drove the truck up to the barn, carefully unpacked the instruments, and placed them around the barn. I wanted to create a garden of percussion.

Then I invited kids to hike up to the barn and meet me there. About twenty-five of the one hundred campers showed up. I demonstrated some simple rhythms and then told the kids to relax, just play, forget being nervous, let the instruments take them where they wanted to go.

It's amazing how quickly people can entrain. These kids locked up after about twenty minutes. They found the groove, and they all knew it. You could see it in their faces as they began playing louder and harder, the groove drawing them in and hardening. It lasted about an hour. These things have life cycles — they begin, build in intensity, maintain, and then dissipate and dissolve. When it was all over everyone started laughing and clapping. They were celebrating themselves and they were also celebrating the groove. Although they had no words for it, they knew that they had created something that was alive, that had a force of its own, out of nothing but their own shared energy.

Percussion Orchestra
Now it's your turn. If you'd like to create some of this energy yourself, find a group of friends who would like to do some drumming, and gather up some instruments. Use whatever drums or rattles you own. If you need more, thumb through the pages of this book for ideas.

Some of you may be thinking that you need a trained leader to do the initial demonstration; the kids I worked with had me to start things off. That started us in a particular direction, but it's not the only direction. If you've found a group interested in exploring rhythms and ready to have fun, you've got all you need.

When you get together, bring plenty of instruments so each person can experiment with several sounds before choosing their favorite. You might decide to set up a tape player so you can record yourselves, the way I did with the first group I told you about. Once everyone's settled on an instrument, you'll be ready to play together, searching for a beat you like. If you're a person who remembers words better than rhythm, you might want to think of a phrase to help you keep the beat. Give your group enough time for the rhythms to join together, and celebrate yourselves when you're through.

Note If you want to know more about that summer camp group and how I got them to work with me to make a community drum, you can read the whole story in **Drumming at the Edge of Magic** (© 1990 by Mickey Hart. Reprinted by permission of Harper Collins Publishers, Inc.) This chapter was adapted from that book and from a Senate speech I gave in 1991 called "Forever Young: Music and Aging."

biographical information

ARTIS THE SPOONMAN Artis the Spoonman began his career in 1972 in a small cafe where he worked as a dishwasher, delighting customers by playing the spoons to tunes on the juke box. Since then, Artis the Spoonman has traveled throughout the U.S. and Canada playing sidewalks, festivals, television, radio, hospitals and schools. Using common kitchenware, Artis can provide the beat for any tune. He is a faster-than-the-eye-can-see perpetual-motion machine whose avant-garde solo spoons arrangements need no accompaniment. Artis has performed with a wide variety of well-known artists and has won the admiration of thousands wherever he's traveled. His fans include the popular rock band Soundgarden, who immortalized him in the hit song and video **Spoonman.** His spellbinding spoons are a remarkable rhythm source, and coupled with his contagious spirit he will change your life—or at least your ideas on cutlery.

TOM KEITH In 1973 Tom Keith began working as a studio engineer at Minnesota Public Radio, where he met Garrison Keillor, who was hosting a morning drive-time show. He appeared on Keillor's morning program doing various character voices. In 1975, at the request of Keillor, Keith began performing voices on the fledgling program, **A Prairie Home Companion.** His imaginative blend of voice work and sound-effects wizardry keep him there today.

BERNIE KRAUSE For over twenty years Bernie Krause has been a bio-acoustics researcher who has orchestrated the sounds of the jungle, the sea and the stream into aural compositions that you can actually dance to. He has been immersed in the field of electronic music for longer than that and appeared on the first commercial synthesizer album (**The Zodiac,** 1967). Since then he has wandered remote regions of the world, lugging his thirty five-pound Nagra recorder and listening to the many-voiced call of the wild. He has recorded gurgling streams and booming thunderstorms, as well as the sounds of iguanas, tadpoles and killer whales.

GARRY KVISTAD Garry Kvistad is the musician and instrument builder responsible for the development of Woodstock Chimes and the creation of Anyone Can Whistle. A graduate of the Interlochen Arts Academy, he earned his B.Mus. from the Oberlin Conservatory of Music, and his M.Mus. from Northern Illinois University, which recently honored him with its Distinguished Alumni Award. He has been president of Woodstock Percussion, Inc. since 1979 and a member of Steve Reich and Musicians since 1980, recording with them for Nonesuch Records. He has also been appointed a New York State delegate to the 1995 White House Conference on Small Business.

FRED PENNER Recognized internationally for his contributions to family life, Fred Penner is an exceptional recording artist and live performer. Born and raised in Winnipeg, Fred began performing early, in grade school productions and choirs, while teaching himself to play guitar. After earning a degree in Economics and Psychology, Fred worked in a treatment center for emotionally and physically challenged children where he used his musical talents to entertain and comfort the young patients. In 1987, Fred and a partner formed Oak Street Music, a record company specializing in children's and family-oriented music. Through the label Fred has released **Fred Penner's Place,** and **Happy Feet** as well as dozens of other popularly received aural and visual treats.

YOHURU RALPH WILLIAMS Yohuru Ralph Williams is a professional musician, visual artist and community educator. Since 1974, he has taught percussion to students from elementary school to college level. Besides his work as a percussion instructor in the Connecticut school system, he has also provided private instruction for specially selected high school students. Yohuru studied jazz percussion at Berklee College of Music and has performed with such jazz luminaries as Benny Goodman, Gerry Mulligan and Don Elliot. He also composed and recorded soundtracks for children's films, including the National Library Award Winner **Brother To The Wind.**

DAVID DARLING David Darling is a classically trained cellist who began his career as an elementary and secondary school teacher of band and orchestra. He later taught music and served as orchestra conductor and faculty cellist at Western Kentucky University. He joined the Paul Winter Consort in 1969 and experimented with the blending of different musical genres and styles, including jazz combined with Brazilian, African, Indian and other world musics. In addition to David's solo and composing career, he is the co-founder of Music For People, a non-profit educational network for people interested in fostering music and improvisation for self-expression.

SALLY ROGERS Sally Rogers is a family entertainer who can squeeze music out of a stick and song out of an eighth grader. For years, she has been delighting audiences of all ages on three continents through her singing and songwriting. The music education major from Michigan State University is noted for her accomplishments in the recording field. She has thirteen albums to her credit and a hit song, **Circle of the Sun** that has been performed by such notable children's performers as Fred Penner, Sharon, Lois & Bram, Eric Nagler and Rick Avery. Her guitar and dulcimer accompaniments have been called "sterling" and her voice has been described as "a brilliant instrument…captivating, beautiful, and pure."

RUTH PELHAM Ruth Pelham is a performer, songwriter and educator who is acclaimed by Pete Seeger as "one of America's greatest songwriters." For nearly three decades, she's been performing for people of all ages and captivating audiences with her unique blend of warmth, spontaneity, and a passionate vision for peace and social justice. Dozens of musicians have recorded and performed her songs, and her own recordings include **Look to the People Under One Sky** and **Collage.** Ruth is the founder and director of Music Mobile, Inc. which presents performances, workshops, residencies, community events and professional development programs for schools, festivals and community-based organizations.

BABATUNDE OLATUNJI Known as "the master of the drum," Babatunde Olatunji is perhaps the best known symbol of traditional African culture in America today. The Nigerian-born musician offers a rich immersion in the songs, folklore, dances and drumming of Africa. Baba teaches the basics of African hand drumming, advanced percussion, and the roots of rhythms in the Yoruba language, which are reproduced on drums through chants, body percussion, and dance. Baba's **Drums of Passion** album (over 5 million sold since it was released in 1959) is considered the premier introduction of African rhythms into the American music scene. Baba was a partner in forming the Grammy-winning drum and percussion ensemble album **Planet Drum** with Mickey Hart of The Grateful Dead.

JON ANDERSON One of art rock's most aggressive conceptualizers, Jon Anderson was the co-founder of the British rock band Yes. His cherubic tenor voice is one of the band's most distinctive elements. As a lyricist, he has been mystically obscure and always prolific. Aside from Yes, Anderson has engaged in numerous side projects, including several successful outings with synthesizer wizard Vangelis and *Deseo*, a collection of Brazilian-influenced tunes, reflecting his growing interest in world music.

GIOVANNI CIARLO Giovanni Ciarlo is an artist, craftsperson, educator, and folklorist with extensive Latin-American musical experience. He has lived and worked in Venezuela, Mexico and the U.S. performing and teaching about global culture. His group Sirius Coyote, combines Afro-Latin rhythms, ancient Meso-American melodies, and contemporary World Beat in an exciting performance of traditional and original music.

BILL HARLEY Familiar to many adults as a regular commentator on NPR's **All Things Considered,** Bill has also been described as "the Mark Twain of kids' music". He does all sorts of music on his ten albums, from string band and rock and roll to Cajun and traditional ballads. Bill's tapes include **Come Out and Play, Big Big World Monsters in the Bathroom** and **Tales From the Sixth Grade.** All of Bill's recordings have won awards, including five gold awards from the Parent's Choice Foundation. Bill brings humor and insight to his observations about growing up and parenting like no other performer can.

MICKEY HART Mickey Hart has been a percussionist with The Grateful Dead for over twenty-five years. In addition, he is the executive producer of The World (Rykodisc), a series of unique recordings of music from around the world. His most recent work in the series, **At the Edge,** is a companion piece to his book, **Drumming at the Edge of Magic** (© 1990 by Mickey Hart. Reprinted by permission of Harper Collins Publishers, Inc.). Hart has also composed music for several television and film projects and he serves on the board of the Smithsonian Institution's Folkway Records. He is also the author of **Planet Drum**, a visual encyclopedia of percussion.

SHARI LEWIS Three generations of children and parents alike have marveled at the energy and grace of Shari Lewis. She is an award-winning entertainer, ventriloquist, author, symphony conductor, and mother. Winner of Emmy and Peabody Awards as the sidekick to Lambchop, the wise-cracking, cute-as-a-button hand puppet, Shari Lewis has written twenty two books and a syndicated newspaper column and has made dozens of audio and video recordings. Her latest sidekicks include the lovable Charlie Horse and Hush Puppy.

ALLAUDIN AND DEVI MATHIEU Allaudin and Devi Mathieu live by a creek in Northern California, where they are happily married to each other. Allaudin plays the piano, makes recordings, composes and teaches music. Devi sings soprano, grows vegetables and writes about science for kids and grown up scientists. Together they give concerts and write books. Every day they take a long walk along the road in front of their house, even if it's raining. Allaudin loves to listen to the ringing of far away bells but he doesn't like the sound of cracking knuckles. Devi would rather not listen to rush hour traffic, but she does love the soft hoot of owls at dusk.

PETE SEEGER For more than fifty years, Pete Seeger has been singing true, funny, sad, gentle and incisive songs for audiences ranging from toddlers to nonagenarians. And in all those years his concern for issues and his audiences has remained undiminished. An expert guitarist, Pete also popularized the 5-string banjo. He is also a great champion of communal singing. Among his biggest hits are, **If I Had a Hammer** (with Lee Hays), **Where Have All the Flowers Gone,** and

Turn, Turn, Turn. Pete's public career—as activist, artist, spokesperson and sailor—has paralleled his personal commitment to working for a better world for all.

PHOEBE SNOW Phoebe Snow has been a singer of extraordinary quality and deep conviction for the last twenty years. In 1975, she was nominated for a Grammy award for her hit single **Poetry Man.** Later that year she scored again with the duet with Paul Simon, **Gone at Last.** In the last few years, Phoebe has performed several times at The White House for the President. She has lent her voice to many charitable organizations for fundraising efforts. Her's has also become a household voice with her many national television commercial campaigns ranging from Stouffer's foods to the "Celebrate the moments of your life" jingle for General Foods.

PAUL McCARTNEY In addition to changing and enhancing the face of popular music in the 20th century, (anyone remember the Beatles?) Paul McCartney has invested time and talent ensuring that a new generation of performers and musicians have a shot. In 1995, he launched The Liverpool Institute for the Performing Arts. McCartney and his new musical chum Elvis Costello will lecture on the art of songwriting. The same year, to benefit another musical school, McCartney played an intimate show at St. James Palace for the Royal College of Music—a nice step up from his days at the Cavern Club.

CRAIG WOODSON Craig Woodson makes simple musical instruments with children and adults all across the U.S. He earned his Ph.D. in music (instrument technology) at U.C.L.A. He is a musician who plays mostly percussion instruments and is also a teacher of music and musical instrument making. His interest in music and building things began in his childhood home when he was very young. His mother was a musician and his father an engineer, a combination Craig credits with influencing him to "build music." After a three-year instrument-building project in Ghana, Craig began presenting children's instrument-building programs in 1991, with performance groups such as The National Symphony Orchestra, The Cleveland Orchestra and The Kronos Quartet.

ABOUT THE EDITOR A professional storyteller since 1978, Sara deBeer took her first folklore courses while an undergraduate at Yale University. As part of her studies, she received a Robert C. Bates Fellowship to study storytelling traditions in Ireland. Sara then explored the connection between storytelling and learning while earning her Master's degree from Bank Street College of Education. Sara's been a featured artist at the Connecticut Storytelling Festival in New London, CT and the Three Apples Festival in Harvard, MA and is listed with CONNTOURS, Connecticut's directory of outstanding performing artists. Her tape, Seven Stories, offers listeners 90 minutes of tales selected from her wide repertoire of international folktales. As well as performing for listeners of all ages, Sara is also an experienced classroom teacher known for her workshops guiding teachers to integrate the arts into on-going classroom studies. She lives in Connecticut with her husband and son.

139

For additional information on any of the *Open Ears* authors, please contact:

> **ELLIPSIS KIDS**
> **20 LUMBER ROAD**
> **ROSLYN, NY 11576**
> **1•800•788•6670**

What Instruments Does This Book Show You How to Make? Check Out This Instrument Index:

Aerophones (Instruments you blow into, making the sound by vibrating air)

Membranophones (Instruments with a stretched membrane/drumskin which you tap, strike or blow into)

Idiophones (Instruments you shake, stamp, rub or hit; these have no stretched membrane)

Chordophones (Instruments with strings which you pluck, strum or bow; the sound is made by vibrating the strings)

Photo Credits

Page 10 John C. Leissring
Page 12 Larry Bercow
Page 15 Larry Bercow
Page 17 Fred Mertz
Page 20 Fred Mertz
Page 22 Glen Wexler
Page 25 Larry Bercow
Page 26 Courtesy of Olatunji Music
Page 28 Larry Bercow
Page 33 Susan Wilson
Page 37 Larry Bercow
Page 38 Larry Bercow
Page 40 R.F. Russell
Page 43 Larry Bercow
Page 45 Gina White
Page 47 Robert Houser
Page 52 Courtesy of Nordoff-Robbins
Page 58 Courtesy of Sing Out!
Page 62 Larry Bercow
Page 67 Kevin Winter
Page 68 Larry Bercow
Page 69 Larry Bercow
Page 70 Ron Batzdorf
Page 74 Courtesy of Wide World of Percussion
Page 76 Larry Bercow
Page 82 Kathleen Sartor
Page 84 Larry Bercow
Page 89 Susan Wilson
Page 92 Larry Bercow
Page 96 Joseph W. Darwal
Page 106 Courtesy of Woodstock Percussion
Page 115 Larry Bercow
Page 116 Stanley Rowin
Page 119 Ruth Pelham
Page 123 Ruth Pelham
Page 124 Alan L. Mayor
Page 128 Albert Cheung Photography
Page 130 Larry Bercow
Page 135 Bill Scott

Acknowledgments

SARA DEBEER WOULD LIKE TO THANK: Joel deBeer Zeiger for sharing his skills in building and troubleshooting; Talasi (12) and Jasmine (10) Brooks for their close readings and honest assesments; Synia and Jeff McQuillan, and the staff and students of Edgewood School for their help with the photoshoot; Cindy Sedlmeyer and Elsa G. deBeer for their support, encouragement, and thoughtful feedback; and all the *Open Ears* authors for taking me places I've never been before!

ELLIPSIS ARTS WOULD LIKE TO THANK THE FOLLOWING FOR THEIR HELP IN THE CREATION OF THIS BOOK: Salvatore Affinito, Geoff Baker, Jamel Bellamy, Jane BenDavid, Linda Benjamin, Debbie Block, Jasmine Brooks, Ilene Brown, Jenny Charno, Steve Ciabattoni, Tim Cleary, Howard Cohen (360° Productions), Katherine David, Karen Davidson, Nicole and Sandra Davis, Joe Dera, Peter DiCecco, Kimberly and Whitney Douglas, Mike Frank, Zachary Fisher, Tony Ganem, Maureen Gleissner, Mary Hilts, Ogom Ifejiks, Robert Kernen, Andrew Klein, Kat Krause, Michelle Kreps, Diana Lewis, Ron Luft, Synia and Jeff McQuillan, Michele Midler, Mark Moss (Sing Out!), Jay Mulford, Eric Nemeyer (Sing Out!), Gilles Paquin, Tricia Pesce, Matt Petosa, David Pittman, Karen Poglinco, Ian and Sunny Ralfini, Katie Rechdahl, Angel Romero, Chris Roslan, Stormy Sachs, Kathleen Sartor, Toshi Seeger, Michele Schoenberg, Jonah Simon, Paul Skiff, Danielle Sweder, Judy Tipograph, Shari Umansky, Cathy Wawrykow, Lana Wraith, Don Yates (KCMU Seattle), Doug York.

Headline font "Kaartoon Uncial" designed by Josh Korda